THE CORPORATION

Since Alexander Litvinenko, my co-author of *Blowing Up Russia*, was killed in November 2006 in London, it was painful to find out that in June 2007 the Moscow apartment of Vladimir Pribylovsky, a journalist and historian and friend, was searched by agents from the Federal Security Service (the KGB's successor). They were looking for sources for this book and confiscated his computers and notes.

—Yuri Felshtinsky
February 13, 2008

the

CORPORATION

RUSSIA AND THE KGB IN THE

AGE OF PRESIDENT PUTIN

YURI FELSHTINSKY
VLADIMIR PRIBYLOVSKY

ENCOUNTER BOOKS ⟨e⟩ NEW YORK • LONDON

This Work of *The Corporation* is published by arrangement with Gibson Square.

First edition published in 2008 by Encounter Books, an activity of Encounter for Culture and Education, Inc., a nonprofit, tax exempt corporation. Encounter Books website address: www.encounterbooks.com

Manufactured in the United States and printed on acid-free paper. The paper used in this publication meets the minimum requirements of ANSI/NISO Z39.48–1992 (R 1997) (*Permanence of Paper*).

FIRST AMERICAN EDITION

LIBRARY OF CONGRESS CATALOGING-IN-PUBLICATION DATA

Felshtinsky, Yuri, 1956–
The corporation : Russia and the KGB in the age of President Putin / Yuri Felshtinsky, Vladimir Pribylovsky.
p.   cm.
Includes bibliographical references and index.
ISBN-13: 978-1-59403-246-2 (hardcover : alk. paper)
ISBN-10: 1-59403-246-7 (hardcover : alk. paper)
1. Russia (Federation)—Politics and government—1991
2. Putin, Vladimir Vladimirovich, 1952-
3. Federal'naia sluzhba bezopasnosti Rossii. I. Pribylovskii, Vladimir. II. Title.
DK510.763.F47   2008
947.086092—dc22
2008042258

10 9 8 7 6 5 4 3 2 1

CONTENTS

v

INTRODUCTION

A Gift for the President

In October 2006, Anna Politkovskaya was murdered in her apartment building. A well-known Russian journalist who had published numerous books in many languages, Politkovskaya was also an uncompromising critic of the Russian government, of Russian policies in Chechnya, of the Russian army in Chechnya, and of President Putin as the head of a government that allowed crimes to be committed in Chechnya. It was natural to suppose that Politkovskaya's murder had been carried out on instructions from some pro-Kremlin Chechen leader, such as Ramzan Kadyrov, who was then negotiating with Putin about the possibility of becoming president of Chechnya in circumvention of the constitution of the Chechen Republic. (Kadyrov, born in 1976, was officially too young for this post.) Offering Putin a gift, doing something nice for him, would be appropriate. On October 7, Putin's birthday—in keeping with the best traditions of the East—this gift was presented to him: the head of an enemy. Anna Politkovskaya was murdered as a birthday present for Vladimir Putin.

Those who killed Politkovskaya could have done the job on October 6 or October 8. But they knew that Putin would be pleased by a gift from them on his birthday. Apparently the gift did please the recipient. On March 2, 2007, Ramzan Kadyrov became the president of the Chechen Republic.

We began writing this book in 2003, but had no plans to complete it in the next few years. We wanted to wait until Putin left office and the period of his rule could be assessed. But in June 2007, the Federal Security Service of Russia raided the apartment of Vladimir Pribylovsky and took his computers and research materials. If our book is being read by the FSB without our consent, do we have any right to deny ordinary readers the possibility of becoming acquainted with its contents?

The twentieth century has entered the history books as an age of tyrants—Stalin, Hitler, Mussolini, Mao Zedong, to name just a few. Great or small, communist or nationalist, these tyrants brought unspeakable evil to their victims and left behind rich material for historians to ponder. Against this background, we ask: Is Putin another despot of similar kind? Will he re-create something that resembles the old Soviet Union? Will the world, as a result, see a new cold war?

In any case, we are dealing with another of Russia's experiments. This one is being conducted not by the Communist Party, but by the FSB. The goal of the experiment is to obtain control over Russia—to gain unlimited power, which gives access to unlimited money, which in turn creates the possibility of absolute power.

Under Soviet rule, everyone was poor, even the members of the ruling nomenklatura. Stalin and Brezhnev had power, but no money. Their apartments, cars, and dachas belonged to the state. They had no yachts or airplanes; they could not go carousing abroad. They did not put their children on the boards of Russia's largest corporations. The members of the new ruling corporation, the FSB, want both power and money, for themselves and for their close relatives. Examples are not hard to find. The son of Mikhail Fradkov, former prime minister, heads the board of directors of the state-run Bank for Development and Foreign Economic Affairs (Vnesheconombank). The son of Nikolai Patrushev, former FSB director, is an advisor to the head of Rosneft. The youngest son of Sergei Ivanov, deputy prime minister, is the vice president of Gazprombank.

Putin himself also represents a completely new phenomenon. All the dictators previously known to us have been self-motivated and self-appointed. All of them seized power by risking their lives and held on to it with great difficulty. Usually, they came to a violent end, like Trotsky, Hitler, Mussolini, Ceausescu. Less often, they died in peace like Franco, Mao, Tito, and Pinochet. In some cases (Lenin and Stalin), we do not know for certain whether a dictator died a natural death or was killed by rivals.

Putin did not fight his way to the president's seat. He was selected by the Federal Security Service of Russia. It was this system—which FSB agents themselves often call the "*kontora*," the "organization"—that got President Yeltsin and the Russian oligarchs to appoint him as Yeltsin's successor.

Putin comes across as a dull little man, not a colorful or charismatic one. He has no ego. He does not thirst for power and does not enjoy wielding it. He looks more like a plaything in someone else's hands. The oligarchs who helped Putin become president believed that these hands were theirs. It turned out, however, that the hands steering Putin belonged to a completely different group—the *kontora*. These hands installed Putin as president precisely because they were not looking for a colorful, charismatic, independent person, who might come to like power and decide to become a dictator. And dictators always kill, as is well known, always beginning with those who are close to them, those who brought them to power, their comrades, colleagues, and companions. The Stalin experience turned out to be very edifying in this regard. A new Stalin is not wanted either by the new businessmen or by the old state security agents. Dull, uninteresting Putin suits everybody.

Under the Soviet regime, the country was ruled by a single political party, armed with a communist ideology. Under Putin, the numerous political parties that form the Russian parliament (the State Duma) are weak. This is no accident. The FSB has no need of a strong political party, since a powerful party will inevitably become a rival for power and thus pose a threat to the FSB. The Duma itself is weak, divided, controlled by the president. The FSB also has no interest in ideology, since any ideology sooner or later leads to the creation of a political party, and such a party is called "political" because it strives for power—which, in the case of Russia, will have to be wrested from the FSB.

One of the FSB's distinctive characteristics is its perpetual desire to monitor and control everything and everyone. Control on the individual level is difficult, not to say impossible. It is easier to control groups. The active part of the country's adult population is already organized into groups one way or another, and all these groups (businesses, nongovernmental organizations, political parties, and such) have FSB personnel embedded in them. These individuals inform their organization about everything that happens around them. Things are more difficult with young people. They are harder to organize into groups, harder to control, and extremely difficult to infiltrate, since the FSB's employees, agents, and informers are usually mature individuals. The old Soviet experience can be useful in this respect, of course, and new creativity also helps; so the FSB has been able to monitor the grassroots successes of various youth organizations. If they become successful, like the "Nashi" movement, they are taken over and used to enforce the FSB's power, eliminating the possibility that they might become rivals.

In its modern incarnation, the FSB has adopted the mantra of capitalism—so hated in the Soviet ideology—and thinks like a corporation. It prefers to buy or to subjugate rather than to kill. Nonetheless, the FSB is an organization of killers. And if it believes that it has to protect itself from an imminent danger, a danger that can no longer be controlled, it kills. It is for this reason that Anna Politkovskaya and Alexander Litvinenko were murdered. Each of them represented a serious danger to the FSB corporation and could not be taken under control or bought.

To be fair, it must be acknowledged that the system of corporate rule was conceived and created not by the FSB, but by the oligarchs. In June 1996, Yeltsin, who seemed to have no chance of getting re-elected democratically, was leaning toward declaring a state of emergency in the country; canceling the election, thereby preventing the victory of the Communist Party candidate Gennady Zyuganov; and remaining a hostage of those who favored a solution by force—Alexander Korzhakov, head of the Presidential Security Service; Mikhail Barsukov, director of state security; and their loyal collaborator and partner in power, Oleg Soskovets, deputy prime minister. This was the security services' second, awkward attempt (after the failed August Putsch in 1991) to take over the government of Russia. But this attempt failed.

In the final hours, when the president's decree canceling the election and declaring a state of emergency in the country had already been signed, one of Russia's ruling corporations—the corporation of the oligarchs—offered Yeltsin money, newspapers and TV channels, and a multitude of campaign managers who were prepared to organize his presidential campaign, but on the condition that he forgo the option of solving the problem by force, that he rescind the decree canceling the election and declaring a state of emergency, that he fire Korzhakov-Barsukov-Soskovets, and that he conduct a democratic election. Yeltsin heard the members of the oligarch corporation, accepted their help, entered into a formally fair fight with Zyuganov, and won. Naturally, the critics asserted that Yeltsin's victory had not been fair, that the newspapers and TV channels bought by the oligarchs had all taken Yeltsin's side. But no one had any particular sympathy for the Communists either. The events of August 1991 and October 1993, which were widely seen as the Communists' attempts at revenge, were still too fresh in people's memories.

In July 1996, Yeltsin was re-elected president. But this victory came at a price. The corporation of the oligarchs became a shareholder in the government. For the next four years, this corporation governed the country. The president of this corporation was Yeltsin. Surrounded by the security services on all sides, clashing and contending with one another, inexperienced in politics (along with everyone else in democratic Russia), despising the people, and not believing in democracy generally or Russian democracy in particular, the corporation of the oligarchs reached the conclusion that a top official from the security services must be elected president in 2000. For some reason, it was believed that this top official could be easily bought and controlled by the oligarchs.

By 1999–2000, every oligarch had his own high-ranking, tried-and-tested man in the security services. And every one of these state security men had his own tried-and-tested oligarch. Roman Abramovich, Boris Berezovsky, and Anatoly Chubais had Colonel Vladimir Putin, director of the FSB. Vladimir

Gusinsky had Army General Filipp Bobkov, deputy director of the KGB of the USSR. Yuri Luzhkov had Yevgeny Primakov, deputy director of the KGB of the USSR, director of the Central Intelligence Service of the USSR, and director of Russia's Foreign Intelligence Service. Mikhail Khodorkovsky had KGB General Alexei Kondaurov. And so on.

The oligarchs and the state security men who were close to Yeltsin explained to the president that only a former head of the FSB would be able to guarantee his and his family's immunity after he left office. It did not matter which former head it was—here Yeltsin was given a choice; but it had to be a former head of the FSB. Because if the Communists came to power, they would put Yeltsin in jail for using tanks to dissolve the parliament in 1993; if the democrats came to power, they would put him in jail for starting the first and second wars in Chechnya and for genocide against the Chechen people; and whoever came to power would certainly try to put Yeltsin and his family in jail for his privatization of the Russian economy and the large-scale corruption that followed.

Yeltsin believed them, and with his own hands—the same hands that in August 1991 took the government of the country away from the Communists—he gave the government of Russia to a top official from the FSB by appointing him as his own successor. In one year, he tried out three different people for the role. The first candidate for the position of Russia's future president was Yevgeny Primakov. He was appointed prime minister in August 1998, but dismissed in May 1999: he did not suit the oligarchs because he openly promised to release ninety thousand criminals from prison and fill their cells with ninety thousand businessmen if he became president. The next candidate was Sergei Stepashin, director of the FSB in 1994–1995. He did not suit Yeltsin's "family"—or more precisely, he did not suit some of its members: the oligarch Roman Abramovich, the president's advisor and future son-in-law Valentin Yumashev, and the president's chief of staff, Alexander Voloshin. It seemed to them that Stepashin was shifting to the side of Yeltsin's rival for power in the country—the mayor of Moscow, Yuri Luzhkov. In August 1999, Stepashin was dismissed. In his place came Putin, up to that time the director of the FSB. Yeltsin liked Putin, and the oligarchs liked him. And on December 31, 1999, he was chosen to be Yeltsin's successor as the next president of Russia.

The oligarchs—with the exception of Vladimir Gusinsky, who had bet on the wrong horse—believed that their corporation was still in power. It was they, after all, who had jointly supported Putin; it was they who, during the election campaign, had assisted him using all of the same mechanisms and managers that had secured victory for Yeltsin in 1996. But there was another corporation that, unbeknownst to the populace, was supporting Putin and working to secure his victory using its own resources and its own methods: the corporation of the FSB. And Putin's first steps as president were marked by a conspicuous loyalty toward members of both corporations.

Little by little, however, the balance of power shifted in favor of the FSB. First, the empires of Gusinsky and Berezovsky—who had begun to oppose Putin—were destroyed, and Gusinsky and Berezovsky ended up in exile abroad. Then Mikhail Khodorkovsky's empire was dismantled, while Khodorkovsky himself was arrested and convicted. At the same time, a number of regional elected offices were replaced with positions appointed by the president. In the context of Russia's pervasive corruption—which blossomed particularly in local elections—the elimination of regional elections and the establishment of president-appointed positions appeared in many respects to be something good. But Putin began to appoint KGB-FSB officers to all vacant positions, as well as to all government and political positions of any importance.

Not everyone understood what was going on, or not all at once. And when they did understand, it was too late. Between 70 and 80 percent of all top positions in the government had been captured by the security services and the military. For the first time in history, the country's government had been taken over by the KGB-FSB—by people who had spent their whole adult lives working in the KGB-FSB system, who hated America and Western Europe, who had no positive program and no experience in building anything. They knew only how to control, to subjugate, to destroy. As with smoking and cancer, as with the Gestapo in Nazi Germany, not a single good word can be said in defense of this organization, which was not destroyed in August 1991 only because of a historical misunderstanding.

It is ironic how political leaders are sometimes remembered by history for what they themselves would certainly have considered to be minor and unmemorable events. What we already know is that President Putin will be remembered in Britain as the person who used a dirty nuclear bomb to poison his political opponent in the center of London.

In Chechnya, Putin will be remembered as the man who "whacked" Chechens "in the outhouse." But the legacy of Putin-the-president is rapidly being extended by the track record of Putin-the-prime-minister in the government of President Dmitry Medvedev.

Georgia has always occupied a special place in Russian history. This border region of the Russian Empire was able to preserve its identity and spiritual independence. Georgia's brief period of political independence between 1918 and 1921 ended with its forced annexation to the Soviet Union, where much was determined by the fact that until 1953 the country was ruled by the Georgian Joseph Stalin, and that his loyal assistant and executioner—the head of the Soviet secret police, the future KGB—was the Georgian Lavrenti Beria.

Making generalizations about entire national groups is always risky. Nonetheless, it is fair to claim that, on the whole, the attitude of Russians toward Georgians during the Soviet period was positive. Georgia became the main producer of fruit and wine for all of Russia and managed to preserve many features of a market economy. During the hungry Soviet years, Georgia prospered by comparison with other Soviet republics. Of all the republics in the USSR, little Georgia had the highest money flow (followed by Armenia and Azerbaijan, with Russia in fourth place despite its enormous size). Georgians were respected for their tangerines, their wine and cuisine, their contributions to Russian culture, but mainly because they— by contrast with Russians—managed to make their country prosper.

In 1991, Georgia became independent. From the dissolved Soviet Union it inherited two autonomous republics: South Ossetia and Abkhazia. According to long-forgotten maps pulled out of dusty archives, it turned out that these territories belonged to the newly formed Georgian state. But the Ossetians and the Abkhazians thought otherwise, and they were supported by Russia. This support cost Russia its good relations with Georgia, and it cost Georgia its good relations with Russia. During the Russian-Chechen wars, Georgia welcomed Chechen refugees and closed its eyes when Chechen separatists penetrated into Georgian territory to recuperate, regroup, and rearm. Relations between Russia and Georgia grew openly hostile.

When Putin came to power, Russia's security services and army were just waiting for an excuse to punish Georgia for its refractoriness. Following the completion of the main military actions in Chechnya and the formation of Kadyrov's puppet government, the invasion of Georgia became only a matter of time. How exactly the Russian-Georgian war was planned and begun is something that we are unlikely to discover any time soon. But it is obvious that the Russian side was remarkably well prepared for it and that in August 2008 the Fifty-Eighth Army, with the support of the Russian navy and air force, made an accelerated advance and rapidly destroyed or occupied all the strategically significant points of its tiny neighbor. For the first time since 1991, Russian troops carried out military operations outside the borders of their territory, setting a dangerous precedent, and the world merely watched to see how events would play out.

Today, it is too early to predict the eventual consequences of the invasion of Georgia. An immediate outcome of the brief war will be Russia's recognition of South Ossetia's and Abkhazia's independence; but without international recognition, this independence will mean little. At the same time, the fact that Russia has recognized the sovereignty of two former autonomous republics of the USSR sets another precedent, one that is dangerous for Russia itself: sooner or later, other former Soviet autonomous republics that are now part of Russia—Chechnya, Dagestan, Ingushetia, and Tatarstan—will demand independence as well. And if this happens, the party responsible for yet another breakup of the Russian Federation will turn out to have been its former president and current prime minister, Vladimir Putin.

Yuri Felshtinsky
Vladimir Pribylovsky
September 8, 2008

LIST OF ABBREVIATIONS

AFB	Federal Security Agency
APR	Agrarian Party of Russia
ASSR	Autonomous Soviet Socialist Republic
BKA	German Federal Criminal Police Office (Bundeskriminalamt)
BND	German Federal Intelligence Service (Bundesnachrichtendienst)
CEC	Central Election Commission
CEER	Committee for External Economic Relations
CIS	Commonwealth of Independent States
CPRF	Communist Party of the Russian Federation
CPSU	Communist Party of the Soviet Union
DVR	Democratic Choice of Russia (party)
ESA	European Space Agency
FAPSI	Federal Agency for Government Communication and Information
FESCO	Far Eastern Shipping Company
FOM	Public Opinion Foundation

FSB	Federal Security Service
FSFO	Federal Service for Financial Health and Bankruptcy
FSK	Federal Counterintelligence Service
FSO	Federal Protection Service
FSU	Former Soviet Union
GIU	Main Engineering Directorate
GKU	Main Control Directorate
GNI	State Tax Inspectorate
GNS	State Tax Service
GPU	State Political Directorate
GRU	Main Intelligence Directorate
GUVD	Municipal Directorate of Internal Affairs
IOC	International Olympic Committee
IRC	International Relations Committee
KGB	Committee for State Security
KSTU	Krasnoyarsk State Technical University
LDPR	Liberal Democratic Party of Russia
LSI	Leningrad Shipbuilding Institute
LSU	Leningrad State University
MB	Ministry of Security
MBVD	Ministry of Security and Internal Affairs
MGB	Ministry of State Security
MGSU	Moscow City Social University
MNVK	Moscow Independent Broadcasting Corporation
MSB	Interrepublican Security Service
MSGU	Moscow State Social University
MSTU	Bauman Moscow State Technical University
MVD	Ministry of Internal Affairs
NBP	National Bolshevik Party
NDR	Our Home Is Russia (party)
NKGB	People's Commissariat of State Security

NKVD	People's Commissariat of Internal Affairs
NPRF	People's Party of the Russian Federation
NPSR	Popular-Patriotic Union of Russia
NTS	National Alliance of Russian Solidarists
NTV	Independent Television
OGPU	Joint State Political Directorate
OMON	Special Forces Police Squad
ORChD	Society of Russian-Chechen Friendship
ORT	Public Russian Television
OSCE	Organization for Security and Cooperation in Europe
OVR	Fatherland–All Russia bloc
PACE	Parliamentary Assembly of the Council of Europe
PGU	First Main Directorate
PST	Free Labor Party
PTK	St. Petersburg Fuel Company
RBRT	Russian Business Round Table
ROIPP	Russian Public Institute of Electoral Law
ROPP	Russian United Industrial Party
RSF	Reporters Without Borders
RSFSR	Russian Soviet Federative Socialist Republic
RUBOP	Regional Directorate for Combating Organized Crime
SBP	Presidential Security Service
SBR	Security Service of Russia
SED	Socialist Unity Party of Germany
SPS	Union of Right Forces
SSR	Soviet Socialist Republic
SVR	Foreign Intelligence Service
TOTs	Tatar Public Center
TsEZh	Center for Journalism in Extreme Situations
TsOS	Center for Public Relations (KGB)
TsSN	Center for Special Operations

UBEP	Directorate for Fighting Economic Crime
UPS	Directorate for Government Communications
USB	Directorate of Departmental Security
VChK	All-Russian Extraordinary Commission
VTsIK	All-Russian Central Executive Committee
VTsSPS	All-Union Central Council of Trade Unions
ZGV	Western Group of the Soviet Army

"We are in power again, this time forever."

—Vladimir Putin, Prime Minister,
speaking before an audience of FSB agents, Moscow, 1999

"We did not reject our past. We said honestly:
'The history of the Lubyanka in the twentieth century is our history. . . .'"

—Nikolai Patrushev, Director of the FSB,
from an interview in Komsomolskaya Pravda,
December 20, 2000, the Day of the FSB

FIRST PROLOGUE

The History of a Name

In December 1917, the Bolshevik government created an organization from which no good ever came to anyone. And because this organization was useful and necessary in theory, while being absolutely destructive in practice, it was continually reformed and renamed, in the hopes that this would bring about a change in its nature. But its nature remained unaltered. Today this organization is called the FSB—the Federal Security Service of the Russian Federation. This book will become easier to read if one keeps in mind the following brief history of the FSB's many names.

On December 20, 1917, the Council of People's Commissars of the Russian Republic passed a resolution, signed by Lenin, establishing the All-Russian Extraordinary Commission for Combating Counter-Revolution and Sabotage (VChK). In August 1918, the VChK changed its name to the All-Russian Extraordinary Commission for Combating Counter-Revolution, Speculation, and Corruption. The VChK's first head was Felix Dzerzhinsky.

On February 6, 1922, the All-Russian Central Executive Committee (VTsIK) of the Russian Soviet Federative Socialist Republic (RSFSR) passed a resolution abolishing the VChK and establishing the State Political Directorate (GPU) as part of the RSFSR's People's Commissariat of Internal Affairs (NKVD).

On November 2, 1923, after the formation of the Union of Soviet Socialist Republics (USSR) in December 1922, the Presidium of the USSR's Central Executive Committee established the Joint State Political Directorate (OGPU) as part of the USSR's Council of People's Commissars.

On July 10, 1934, the Central Executive Committee passed a resolution making the OGPU part of the NKVD.

On February 3, 1941, the NKVD was split up into two independent organs: the NKVD and the People's Commissariat of State Security (NKGB). But already in July of the same year, the NKGB and the NKVD merged once again into a single People's Commissariat, the NKVD. In April 1943, the NKGB was created anew.

On March 15, 1946, the NGKB was transformed into the Ministry of State Security (MGB) of the USSR. Also at that time, all People's Commissariats started being referred to as ministries.

On March 7, 1953, two days after Stalin's death, the Ministry of Internal Affairs (MVD) of the USSR and the MGB were merged into a single MVD of the USSR.

On March 13, 1954, the Committee for State Security (KGB) was established as part of the Council of Ministers of the USSR. In 1978, the reference to the Council of Ministers was eliminated from the name of the agency. From then on, it was known simply as the KGB of the USSR.

On May 6, 1991, the head of the Supreme Soviet of the RSFSR, Boris Yeltsin, and the head of the KGB of the USSR, Vladimir Kryuchkov, approved the formation of a Committee for State Security of the RSFSR (the KGB of the RSFSR), with the status of a national republican state committee.

On November 26, 1991, the president of the USSR, Mikhail Gorbachev, signed a decree "On the establishment of temporary provisions for the Interrepublican Security Service (MSB) of the USSR."

On December 3, 1991, the president of the USSR, Mikhail Gorbachev, signed a law "On the reorganization of the organs of state security." This law abolished the KGB of the USSR and replaced it with two new agencies: the Interrepublican Security Service (MSB) and the Central Foreign Intelligence Service of the USSR.

On December 19, 1991, the president of the RSFSR, Boris Yeltsin, signed a decree "On the establishment of a Ministry of Security and Internal Affairs of the RSFSR" (MBVD). With the creation of this agency, the MSB was effectively abolished. However, on January 14, 1992, the Constitutional Court of the Russian Federation ruled that Yeltsin's decree went against the constitution of the RSFSR and repealed it.

During the period 1992–1993, the Russian Federation's state security organs were part of the Ministry of Security (MB) of the Russian Federation. On December 21, 1993, Yeltsin signed a decree abolishing the MB and establishing the Federal Counterintelligence Service (FSK) of the Russian Federation.

On April 3, 1995, Yeltsin signed a law "On the organs of the Federal Security Service in the Russian Federation," on the basis of which the FSB became the legal successor to the FSK.

All these years, the VChK-FSB was located in the same building—at the very heart of Moscow, on Lubyanka Street. That is how the building was called: Lubyanka.

SECOND PROLOGUE

In school, Russia's future president Vladimir Putin was called "Uti-Puti," either for his duck-like walk (from *utka*, "duck") or because of the following story.

On the suggestion of their older friends, and with help from their favorite teacher, young Volodya Putin and his classmates once spent their summer vacation raising ducks—in order to eat them at the end of the summer. The time to kill one of the ducks arrived. Everyone refused to chop off the poor bird's head. In order to make things less sad, the children decided to play a game. They put the duck on trial and convicted it of breaking the rules of life: eating more than the others, swimming farther than it was allowed to, going to sleep later than all the rest. They put a rope around the duck's neck and dragged it to the executioner's block, a simple log. Some of the boys refused to be executioners. Volodya Putin did not refuse. He threw a red blanket over himself, which was supposed to represent an executioner's mantle, covered his head—because the executioner's face is supposed to be hidden—and said: "Lead in the unfortunate victim. Place its head so that I can cut it off with one blow without seeing it."

—From the memoirs of Vladimir Putin's teacher, Vera Gurevich,
Vladimir Putin: Parents, Friends, Teachers, second edition
(St. Petersburg: St. Petersburg Law Institute, 2004).

1

Korzhakov's Conspiracy

COMPONENT NO. 1: THE PRESIDENTIAL SECURITY SERVICE (SBP)

After the government coup by the State Emergency Committee in August 1991 failed and the Soviet Union collapsed, the KGB was formally dismantled and split up into various independent agencies. One of the first of these new agencies was the Presidential Security Service (SBP), formed on the basis of the former Ninth and Fifteenth Directorates of the KGB, which had been responsible for the security of top government officials, members of the party nomenklatura and their families, and important government sites. The SBP was created by Alexander Korzhakov, the former bodyguard of Yuri Andropov (head of the KGB and later head of the Soviet government) and subsequently the bodyguard of Boris Yeltsin.

Despite the importance of providing security for top government officials, the nature of the Ninth Directorate's functions had relegated it to the status of a subordinate department. Its staff and directors were inferior in skill and knowledge to foreign intelligence and counterintelligence officers. Ninth Directorate staff member Korzhakov—a man believed to be loyal to Yeltsin—knew perfectly well that any agency responsible for the security of even the president, and even such a willful president as Yeltsin, must under ordinary circumstances be of secondary importance within the newly formed successor organization to the KGB. But in 1991–1992, the situation in Russia was not ordinary, and Korzhakov did everything he could to make the Presidential Security Service essentially a mini KGB. At the head of the new agency that replaced the dismantled KGB—the Security Service of Russia (SBR)—Korzhakov placed his own man, the former Kremlin commandant Mikhail Barsukov, who silently assented to Korzhakov's superiority over him. After successfully implementing the idea of creating an independent security service for the president and filling all key positions with people personally loyal to himself, Korzhakov effectively became—without this being noticed by anyone, least of all by his boss, Yeltsin—the second man in Russia.

It's a bad soldier, however, who doesn't dream of becoming a general. And in Russia, it's a bad security chief who doesn't dream of taking the place of the person he keeps secure. In Korzhakov's case, that place was occupied by Yeltsin. Ever since the historic days of August 1991—when Korzhakov, a man full of vigor and still unknown to the great Russian nation, was seen on the news around the world standing behind Yeltsin like a devoted dog, ready to tear any enemy to shreds or to protect Yeltsin from a bullet with his own body—Yeltsin's security chief wanted to replace Yeltsin at his post. In order for this wish to be fulfilled, several components had to fall into place.

Korzhakov built up his own security service, the SBP, with its own special forces—called the Center for Special Operations (TsSN)—quickly and without much difficulty. What proved more difficult was shaping public opinion in the country. Korzhakov needed his own television outlets and his own newspapers, especially since he wasn't the only one who dreamed of occupying Yeltsin's seat. And Korzhakov's main rival, Filipp Bobkov, did have his own television and newspapers. But who was this now almost forgotten man?

THE RIVAL: FILIPP BOBKOV

Television, a powerful instrument of propaganda and a means for shaping public opinion, had been under constant control by the KGB in Soviet times. The Fifth Directorate of the KGB, with its various divisions across the Soviet Union, was responsible for fighting against "ideological diversions by the enemy." Here, "the enemy" meant countries with a different ideology and morality—a bourgeois ideology and morality, based on free enterprise and civil liberties. All the capitalist countries and their allies were considered enemies.

The term "ideological diversions" could easily be given a broad interpretation and used in an expansive fashion. It encompassed such concepts as "harmful ideological orientation," which could be applied to any activity that did not fit within the country's political framework or ideological canon. The KGB, unswervingly following the political course determined by the Central Committee of the CPSU—specifically, by its Department of Agitation and Propaganda—carried out a wide-ranging fight against all expressions of dissent in Russia. In order to achieve total control over the political situation in the country and the mindset of its people, the security organs recruited agents among Soviet and foreign citizens alike, serving important strategic and tactical aims in the process. A vital strategic aim was to consolidate the CPSU's ideological influence within the Soviet Union, in the other countries of the socialist bloc, and around the world. An associated tactical aim was to install the agents of the security services at all positions in society, in order to counteract "harmful ideological influences" on the population and to conduct counterpropaganda exercises against enemy countries.

For many years, practically since its inception, the KGB's Fifth Directorate had been headed by Filipp Bobkov. He retired from the KGB at the beginning of 1991, having attained the position of deputy director of the KGB and the rank of army general. Soon he became quite well known as a consultant to the oligarch Vladimir Gusinsky, the owner of the Most Corporation, which included Most Bank and Media-Most, along with other enterprises. In reality, Bobkov was the head of the corporation's security service. Gusinsky had been within Bobkov's field of vision for many years, having already become familiar to the Fifth Directorate during the preparations for the 1980 Olympics in Moscow.

Bobkov's deputy in the Fifth Directorate was Major General Ivan Pavlovich Abramov. Later, when Bobkov became deputy director of the KGB—replacing Viktor Mikhailovich Chebrikov, who was appointed head of the KGB after Andropov became general secretary of the CPSU—Abramov became the head of the Fifth Directorate and a lieutenant general. The officers who served under Abramov called him Vanya Palkin (from *palka*, "stick") for his tendency to petty tyranny and his rigid, often unfair attitude toward his subordinates. At the end of the 1980s, Abramov, who dreamed of becoming deputy director of the KGB and had a real chance of seeing this dream come true, was transferred—unexpectedly for everyone, most of all himself—to the General Prosecutor's Office and appointed deputy general prosecutor.

Abramov's deputy was Vitaly Andreyevich Ponomarev. A veterinarian by training, and subsequently a party operative, Ponomarev was sent to work at the KGB in the beginning of the 1980s. He soon became the head of the KGB's regional office in the Chechen-Ingush ASSR, and shortly after that he was transferred to Moscow and appointed deputy head of the KGB's Fifth Directorate. In this way, he became Abramov's deputy. This occurred on the eve of the 1985 international youth and student festival in Moscow, a politically significant event that Ponomarev was ordered to supervise through the divisions of the Fifth Directorate. During the preparations and while the festival was going on, Ponomarev became acquainted with the main director of the opening celebration, Vladimir Gusinsky— the very same person who, several years later, would become one of the richest and most influential people in Russia and Bobkov's "boss."

Thus, while Korzhakov was creating his mini KGB through the Presidential Security Service of President Yeltsin, Bobkov was building his own mini KGB through the empire of his old acquaintance Vladimir Gusinsky.

The Most Corporation's security service, which was headed by Bobkov, consisted predominantly of Bobkov's former subordinates from the Fifth Directorate and was the largest and most powerful security service in the country. Its staff and its projects were substantially larger than those of Korzhakov's SBP. The Most Corporation's security service collected information about a wide range of topics in contemporary Russian life. It assessed the landscape of competing political forces within the government and assembled files on prominent politicians, businessmen, bankers, and various state and commercial entities. Korzhakov's analysts were no match for their former colleagues from the KGB, who now toiled at the Most Corporation's security service not for the sake of an idea but for high wages, in dollars rather than rubles, receiving a salary that was many times greater than General Korzhakov's own nominal income. Bobkov's smart and experienced procurers of information and analysts could not but notice the steps that Korzhakov was taking toward increasing his sway and creating an influential group of supporters. In addition, Bobkov's employees maintained good professional relationships with their former colleagues who had stayed behind at the FSB, the Federal Security Service.

THE CONFLICT OF 1994

At the end of 1994—with a presidential election scheduled for 1996—Korzhakov and Bobkov decided to see which of them was stronger. Gusinsky had declared that he could make whomever he wanted president. Korzhakov had replied that "it's not our place to choose the president," and he entered into open war with Bobkov. On December 2, 1994, a detachment from the SBP's Center of Special Operations (TsSN) attacked the cortege of Vladimir Gusinsky. The TsSN officer Viktor Portov later recalled, "Our task was to provoke Gusinsky into action and to find out whose support he had secured in the government before making such declarations."

On the morning of December 2, an armored Mercedes and a jeep transporting Gusinsky's bodyguards were traveling from Gusinsky's dacha to Moscow on the Rublyovsko–Uspenskoye highway. At a turn in the road, a Volvo carrying TsSN operatives wedged itself between the jeep and the Mercedes. Traveling neck-and-neck at 60–70 miles per hour, the two cars reached Kutuzovsky Prospect in Moscow and came to a stop between City Hall, where Gusinsky's office was located, and the White House.

Meanwhile, Gusinsky had called Yevgeny Savostyanov—the head of the FSB office for Moscow and the Moscow region—and the Moscow Directorate of Internal Affairs (GUVD), and told them that he was being attacked by criminals. (It was not yet clear who the people pursuing him were.) Savostyanov sent a unit from the Antiterrorism Department; the head of the GUVD dispatched a rapid response team. A shootout ensued, during which no one was hurt, since it turned out that the attackers were agents from Korzhakov's SBP, and Gusinsky's men had to give in. The TsSN agents dragged the passengers out of Gusinsky's jeep and laid them face down in the snow. This marked the end of Korzhakov's operation, which entered history as "Operation Face Down in the Snow."

This brilliant maneuver revealed General Savostyanov to be one of Bobkov's political allies. On the same day, at Korzhakov's request, General Savostyanov was dismissed from his post by Yeltsin. He was replaced by Korzhakov's protégé Anatoly Trofimov, whose job in Soviet times had been monitoring "dissidents."

COMPONENT NO. 2: CHANNEL ONE

Korzhakov's victory proved illusory, as the Gusinsky-controlled media proceeded to destroy him. From that day on Korzhakov was doomed, although he realized as much only in 1996, when it was already too late. Nonetheless, in December 1994 he learned a key lesson from what had just happened: In contemporary Russia, control over one's own mini KGB is not enough; one also needs a media empire—one's own private media outlets. To Korzhakov, the most natural and tantalizing object to devour seemed to be Russian TV's Channel One, which reached up to 180 million viewers. Here too, however, Korzhakov's position turned out to be not particularly strong.

Under the KGB, the Ninth Directorate—on the basis of which the SBP was created—was traditionally separated from the others. Most of its subdivisions were situated on the territory of the Kremlin, where the people and sites that had to be protected were located. The employees and directors of the Ninth Directorate rarely came in contact with members of other operative subdivisions of the KGB's central apparatus. Consequently, the Ninth Directorate had no agents in the mass media, among prominent politicians, or in academic circles.

In an economic sense, the perestroika movement that began in the USSR constituted first and foremost an unprecedented restructuring of government property. Among the first to catch the smell of big money were the functionaries of Soviet television. Growing businesses needed advertising, and the possibilities of television for this purpose were unlimited. Many television stations, competing with one another, rushed to offer their services to businesses seeking to advertise on Russian central TV. The advertisements were paid for largely in U.S. dollars, and a substantial part of these payments ended up in the pockets of producers and their subordinates, who worked directly with clients. Fourteen newly formed advertising agencies were operating on Russian central TV during the period described here. They bought airtime from the producers of various television programs, divided it up as they saw fit, and sold it to clients interested in placing commercials on TV. The airtime was purchased at wholesale prices, in chunks ranging from tens of minutes to several hours per day and for periods ranging from several days to several months per year, and then resold in chunks of seconds or minutes, at considerably higher rates. The profits from such transactions were enormous. The revenue obtained in this way was not credited to the accounts of state television; instead, it was distributed among a group of people who had managed to circumvent the government and to divide the vast TV advertising market among them.

All this activity—which took place at the Ostankino television center, located in the Ostankino TV tower, the tallest building in Moscow—was monitored by at least thirty KGB agents, who carefully reported everything about this off-the-books business to their superiors, since all serious correspondence with agencies and organizations was conducted exclusively through the KGB office (the First Department) of the television center. And all these people had ties with Bobkov. So how did they end up at the television center, and who were they—these people who knew one another, helped one another, and promoted one another, both in Soviet times and afterward?

OFFICERS OF THE ACTIVE RESERVE

In addition to the official KGB agents who oversaw Soviet television, its various departments employed many members of the state security apparatus who worked in secret—residents and agents recruited from the television staff or retired KGB officers embedded among television employees. In FSB terminology, these people were "officers of the active reserve." Their positions, and the very concept of the "active reserve," appeared during Yuri Andropov's tenure as head of the KGB from 1967 to 1982.

There were active reserve officers in many ministries, departments, and government agencies. (Prior to 1991, everything in the USSR belonged to the government.) These officers would be established at specific workplaces through a routine bureaucratic procedure: the KGB would submit a report to the CPSU Central Committee justifying the need for such a position in one of the USSR's state structures; this would be followed by a resolution from the Central Committee's Secretariat either in favor of or against the KGB's proposal; after which, if the proposal was approved, the Politburo would ratify the new position and send appropriate instructions to the government. On Bobkov's initiative, an active reserve position was even created in the Central Committee. In fact, what Bobkov was trying to do was establish KGB control over so-called "party money." At the height of perestroika, these funds were transferred abroad and never discovered. Clearly, they were transferred by the active reserve officers whom the KGB had planted in the Central Committee. At the time, Bobkov was the first deputy head of the active reserve—that is, second in command.

Gradually, the active reserve officers of the KGB-FSB were given positions in all organizations of any importance—enterprises, agencies, institutes, and businesses, including television—while remaining on the staffs of their KGB divisions. They fulfilled their official functions at their new jobs in civilian or military settings, but their primary task was to promote state security interests. FSB officers who had formally retired, but in fact had been transferred from the KGB-FSB mainly to civilian positions, would function in their new jobs as secret agents of the KGB-FSB. This was truly a revolutionary innovation by the KGB, which was protecting its rear, as it were, in the event of unforeseen developments. At this time, people started to say that there was no such thing as a *former* state security agent; instead, there were officers of the KGB-FSB's active reserve in civilian or military jobs.

When Bobkov became deputy director of the KGB, he was replaced as head of the Fifth Directorate by Major General Yevgeny Fyodorovich Ivanov (who later, after the dismantling of the KGB, headed the analytic department at Gusinsky's Most Corporation). As an active reserve officer at the Central Committee of the CPSU, Ivanov was sent to work in the administrative department, which oversaw the Soviet Union's entire law enforcement system: the General Prosecutor's Office, the Supreme Court, the KGB, and the Ministry of Internal Affairs. After about two years, now with the rank of lieutenant general, Ivanov returned to the KGB in the position of deputy director, a position with a great deal of power. In the absence of the KGB director, he oversaw foreign intelligence and the activities of Group A ("Alfa")—elite commando units subordinated directly to the head of the KGB.

During the perestroika years, Ivanov transformed the KGB's Fifth Directorate into the Directorate for the Defense of the Constitutional Order, or "Directorate K." The active reserve officer position vacated by Ivanov after he left the CPSU Central Committee was filled by another member of the Fifth Directorate, Alexander Nikolayevich Karbainov, former secretary of the Komsomol committee for the Krasnoyarsk region. It was he who actually reorganized the Fifth Directorate into Directorate K. Karbainov soon became the head of the KGB's press office, which was transformed under his supervision into the KGB's Center for Public Relations (TsOS)—the new propaganda outlet of Russia's restructured state security apparatus. Karbainov's next appointment could have been predicted: he was sent to work as an active reserve officer under another former Komsomol leader, the Russian oligarch Mikhail Khodorkovsky. Later, Karbainov's deputy at the TsOS, KGB General Kondaurov, also went over to Khodorkovsky as an officer of the active reserve; Kondaurov became the head of Yukos's analytic department.

ALEXANDER KOMELKOV

The deputy director of the Fifth Directorate department that oversaw Russian television was Major Alexander Petrovich Komelkov, a graduate of the Moscow Institute of Culture. He had been nicknamed "Eggplant" by his drinking buddies and colleagues at the directorate because of the purplish color of his face. Komelkov came to the television department from the department that oversaw Moscow State University and the Lumumba Peoples' Friendship University. His father had served in the First Main Directorate of the KGB (foreign intelligence) and this had determined the development of Komelkov's career.

After coming to the television department, Komelkov brought over his old acquaintance from the Fifth Directorate, Valentin Vasilievich Malygin, who became the head of the television center's KGB office (the First Department). Malygin's candidacy for this position was supported by the head of the Fifth Directorate, General I. P. Abramov, and the appointment was quickly and easily approved by the KGB.

Major Vladimir Stepanovich Tsibizov, senior member of the Fifth Directorate's First Department, was appointed as the Fifth Directorate's active reserve officer at the television center. He was reponsible directly to the head of the television center's KGB office. Tsibizov had come to the KGB—where his uncle had been employed for many years—after graduating from the State Institute of Theater Arts. At the Fifth Directorate's First Department he oversaw the Goskontsert agency, which supervised the tours of Russian artists abroad and organized tours for foreign artists in the territory of the USSR.

The Ostankino television center was a so-called "regime site." Special passes were required to enter the building (permanent passes for employees, one-time passes for visitors). As head of the "regime department," KGB officer Tsibizov was well acquainted with the list of people who visited Ostankino. If necessary, any visitor could be denied a pass on Tsibizov's orders, and any employee could have his belongings searched when entering or leaving the building.

During the perestroika years, Komelkov and Malygin made skillful use of their "administrative resource"—the Ostankino television center—by selling airtime on television and radio stations and renting out facilities to commercial television enterprises. For Komelkov, this had a disastrous outcome: he was given a dishonorable discharge for failing to fulfill his professional duties.

Shortly after leaving the television center, Komelkov opened a restaurant on Kutuzovsky Prospect in Moscow, across from the Triumphal Arch. During the 1992 summer Olympics in Barcelona, he set up a successful business renting out Russian ships near the Spanish coast to serve as hotels for tourists. But more than anything else in the world, Komelkov—who had served for fifteen years in the KGB's Fifth Directorate—wanted to work in the Ninth Directorate, specifically in the capacity of an "attached" officer (responsible for the personal security of a top official in the government or the Communist Party). However, he failed to meet certain criteria that were used to select candidates for such positions. Most of these criteria had to do with the candidate's physical profile. First of all, he had to be at least five feet nine inches tall and in excellent physical shape. Most of the "attached" officers in the Ninth Directorate were former Soviet athletes who had been highly successful in various sports. Komelkov, who was only five feet six inches and carried some extra weight, was objectively unsuited for this kind of work. But his dream lived on, and in the end it came true.

When the USSR had collapsed and a new presidential security service was created, Korzhakov needed people. Komelkov was recommended to him—despite having been fired from the KGB—by Gennady Zotov, his old school friend from the Institute of Culture and later his colleague at the Fifth Directorate. Zotov was a former agent in the Fifth Directorate's Fourth Department, which oversaw religion in the USSR and monitored religious activists; later he became the head of the FSB's departmental security service, a lieutenant general, and a representative of Russia's security services in Bulgaria.

Korzhakov spoke with Komelkov in person, asking him to gather information about everything that happened at the television center. Above all, Korzhakov was interested in people and groups that had negative attitudes toward the president and the SBP. Komelkov was also expected to influence editorial policies in a manner that was favorable to Korzhakov. Finally, Korzhakov warned Komelkov that there must be no leaks of information from him to his former Fifth Directorate colleagues, who were now working under Bobkov for Gusinsky, and that, on the contrary, he should try to use his old connections as much as

possible in order to gather information about everything that
went on at the Most Corporation.

Prior to being fired from the KGB, Komelkov had been one
of the heads of the department that oversaw the Ostankino
television center. As someone who still retained a great deal of
valuable information about TV workers and who could renew
his old contacts with them, Komelkov was the SBP's ideal man
for working among television employees. Korzhakov also took
into account the fact that Komelkov had been found guilty of
corruption and fired from the KGB, and was upset at his former
colleagues—especially his old boss, Bobkov. Korzhakov thus
had reasons to expect that Komelkov would be able and willing
to work against his former Fifth Directorate colleagues, who
made up the core of Bobkov's Most Bank staff.

In addition, after being fired from the KGB, Komelkov had
had time to work in the private sector and to establish contacts
with Moscow's business and criminal circles. The heads of
Moscow's organized crime groups—particularly the Solntsevo
bandits—had been frequent visitors at his restaurant on Kutuzovsky Prospect, which happened to be one of the government
routes monitored by the Ninth Directorate and later by Korzhakov's SBP. Consequently, Korzhakov knew everything about
Komelkov's restaurant, just as he did about the Russian ships
that had been sent to the Olympics in Spain (and about the offshore accounts where Komelkov had deposited the money that
he had earned there). In other words, Korzhakov knew enough
about Komelkov both to make him a loyal subordinate and to
destroy him if necessary.

Komelkov went to work. For many years he had been
acquainted with Yuri Balev, who had retired from the KGB
as head of the Second Department in the Directorate for the
Defense of the Constitutional Order, the successor organization to the KGB's Fifth Directorate. Despite the change of
name, everything at the directorate had remained the same. The
department that Balev had headed in the Fifth Directorate had
dealt with ethnic problems in the USSR. When the name of the
directorate changed, the number of this department remained
unaltered, and its directors and staff stayed on at their old
posts. The Second Department was one of the directorate's
most important in terms of the problems it had to address, par-

ticularly during the perestroika years. Everywhere in the country, decentralizing tendencies were on the rise: many republics, from the Baltics to the Caucasus to Central Asia, had started thinking about independence and the possibility of leaving the USSR. It was these nationalist movements that Balev's department had been delegated to fight against.

After the collapse of the Soviet Union, Bobkov, who had gone over to Gusinsky's Most Corporation, invited his former subordinate Balev to join him. Balev became one of Gusinsky's leading analysts at Most Bank's security service. He remained on friendly terms with Komelkov, possibly with a view to obtaining information about Korzhakov's agency. Komelkov, in turn, was hoping to obtain information about Bobkov's agency from Balev, and at one point he openly made Balev an offer to spy for Korzhakov. Balev did not simply refuse Komelkov's offer, but declared that he was cutting all ties with him. Several days later, Balev was cruelly beaten near his home by unidentified individuals.

Komelkov had a much easier time obtaining information about the goings-on at the television center. His old contacts and connections had remained intact. With Korzhakov's powerful backing, he quickly managed to become a sufficiently influential person at Ostankino. His opinions mattered. Few were willing to go against him. Most staff appointments were now coordinated with Komelkov.

During this whole period, the commercialization of state television went on unabated. Those who had had time to privatize individual TV channels made enormous profits. Komelkov carefully monitored these processes and possessed reliable information about who had received how much and from whom. Upon returning to the television center he noted, not without regret, that he had already missed out on many opportunities. The financial groups that had taken shape at the television center were in no hurry to admit any newcomer to the established, behind-closed-doors procedures for distributing airtime and divvying up the vast monetary proceeds, in the millions of dollars.

At the end of the 1980s, Sergei Lisovsky, a former Komsomol functionary, appeared at the television center. Prior to his arrival, he had become rather well known in Moscow for organizing huge discotheques at the Olimpiysky sports complex. In 1991, he organized two television advertising agencies: LIS'S and Premier SV. Until 1998, Premier SV controlled 65 percent of the TV advertising market. It was through Lisovsky that Korzhakov decided to step into the TV advertising business. In 1995, acting through Komelkov, who knew precisely what kinds of profits Lisovsky was making from his advertising business, Korzhakov sent one of his men to see Lisovsky. This man, who presented himself as an SBP colonel, arrived at Lisovsky's office in a Mercedes, drove Lisovsky to his own office in the Kremlin, and demanded a monthly payment of $100,000. Lisovsky refused. On the following day, his business was wrecked by people from the Presidential Security Service.

VLADISLAV LISTYEV

At the end of 1987, a reporter by the name of Vladislav Listyev came to work in television. Within a few years he became the most prominent reporter on TV—everyone's favorite. Listyev had grown up in a simple family and lost his father early on. He attended the best educational institution in the country, Moscow State University, where he studied journalism.

There were many foreign students at Moscow State University, coming from all over the world. All were closely monitored by the KGB. Moscow State University and the Lumumba Peoples' Friendship University were under the operational control of the Fifth Directorate's Third Department. The KGB recruited faculty and students en masse—both Soviet citizens and foreigners—in order to achieve a more comprehensive surveillance over foreign students and gain a more thorough understanding of their political views and orientations, their personalities and psychology. Agents recruited among foreign students received considerable attention, since they were destined to become what the KGB referred to as "subsidence agents." In the West, such agents are known as "sleeper agents." Their principal mission was to establish a presence for the KGB in any country that was of interest to the KGB, and to occupy a place in society that gave them access to information of interest to the Soviet Union's security organs.

Many of the foreigners who graduated from Moscow State University and the Lumumba Peoples' Friendship University attained high professional positions and social status after returning to their own countries. They included members of ministers' cabinets, prominent political and social activists, diplomats, and famous journalists. In addition to their high levels of education, what facilitated their successes was the fact that most of them had influential relatives in their own countries. Those foreign students who had no influential relatives, and who came to study in the USSR on the recommendation of foreign Communist parties, were destined to become illegal agents: they would go on to work in various parts of the world under assumed names and with fabricated identities.

The recruitment of foreign undergraduate and graduate students into the KGB's agent network required the involvement of Soviet citizens. This was how, at the beginning of the 1980s, the future TV reporter Vladislav Listyev crossed the path of KGB Senior Lieutenant Alexander Komelkov, staff member of the Fifth Directorate's Third Department.

Moscow's prestigious colleges were attended by the children of the Soviet and Communist Party elite and the children of the artistic community. To the small number of students who came from simple Soviet families, it was obvious that their opportunities after graduation would be severely limited in comparison with those of their well-connected classmates. The children of the elite received the most interesting and promising internships during the course of their schooling and after graduation. Consequently, their careers unfolded with ease and success. On the other hand, those who lacked this kind of support had to rely on their own strengths and abilities, or else try to obtain support by marrying someone from the elite. There was one other way, too: they could obtain support from the KGB by joining the ranks of the numerous agents and members of this organization.

The process by which candidates were picked for recruitment into the KGB constituted a kind of social selection. According to the KGB's instructions, members of the top levels of the Communist Party nomenklatura and members of their families could not be recruited into the KGB's agent network. The same constraints applied to the relatives of currently employed KGB officers. As for members of the Soviet artistic elite, there were no constraints on their involvement in secret activities in behalf of the state's security interests.

As a result, the agents who were recruited among college students came for the most part from the middle and lower classes of Soviet society. A considerable number of them were children of simple working families who thought that by helping the KGB they were demonstrating their loyalty to the Soviet regime and could count on assistance subsequently. And indeed, the KGB actively promoted its agents, thus creating "agents of influence" who occupied a prominent place in the political and social life of the country while furthering the interests of state security.

Vladislav Listyev, a sociable and athletic student at Moscow State University's journalism school, could not but attract the attention of supervisors from the Third Department of the Fifth Directorate. With the assistance of the school's KGB supervisor, he joined a group of students who were engaged in the intensive study of foreign languages. A couple of years later, he was able to transfer to the newly created school of international journalism—a school that a great many students wished to attend, including those with highly influential relatives. The phone calls made in Listyev's behalf went as high as the rector of the university and the dean of the school. It was obvious to everyone that the new school's future graduates would have excellent prospects for working abroad—the greatest dream of many Soviet people. But in the selection of students, the KGB had the last word.

Shortly after he was admitted to the school of international journalism, Listyev was included in a group of students selected for pregraduation internships abroad. The documents required to leave the country had to be filed with the state security organs. Candidates for trips abroad were subjected to thorough investigations by the various subdivisions of the KGB. These investigations included a so-called "home assessment," which involved the collection of information about the candidate's way of life and his relatives. Such "assessment" projects were implemented by the Seventh Department of the KGB office for Moscow and the Moscow region. This department was in charge of organizing surveillance over "objects of operational interest," as well as "home assessments" for all operational and staff departments of the KGB's central apparatus and its Moscow branch. "Assessments" were also conducted at the request of departments that were responsible for doing background checks on Soviet citizens filing documents for travel abroad—on work assignments, for personal reasons, or as tourists. These were called "special background checks," and the divisions responsible for them were consequently known as "special background check divisions."

Listyev's "home assessment" resulted in a negative characterization of him and his close relatives. His special background check file (all Soviet citizens who submitted documents for traveling outside the country had such files) contained the following note: "Known to the Third Department of the Fifth Directorate of the KGB." This meant that the subject was either part of the KGB's agent network or that he was being examined as a potential candidate for recruitment. Due to the negative information collected about him and his family, Listyev was denied the right to leave the country, even with the endorsement of the Fifth Directorate. He was also excluded from the group of students selected for pregraduation internships abroad.

When candidates were selected for work in the Soviet media—especially radio and television—their candidacies were invariably coordinated with the KGB. Promotions to higher positions, as well as transfers to other forms of media, were likewise controlled by state security. The Fifth Directorate's supervisors did not forget about Vladislav Listyev. With their help, despite a far from impeccable biography, he was hired to work in the foreign broadcasting department at Soviet national radio. Shortly afterward, he encountered a KGB officer whom he had already met as a university student—Alexander Komelkov, the former KGB overseer of a number of university faculties, who had been transferred in the mid-1980s to the Fourteenth Department of the Fifth Directorate and appointed as the department's deputy director. With the support of Komelkov (and the KGB), Listyev was able in 1987 to join an elite group of young reporters who had been invited to work on television for the new youth program called *Vzglyad*. And although Listyev repeatedly came to work drunk or failed to come to work at all, even missing his own broadcasts, the principle of all-forgiveness remained in effect toward him. No one touched Vladislav Listyev.

Over the years, *Vzglyad* became one of the most popular shows on television and its hosts were national favorites. Listyev himself grew more and more popular every year. His professional skills developed, as did his authority among his colleagues. In 1990, he became the artistic director of the extremely popular show *Pole Chudes*, as well as *Tema* and *Chas Pik*. After the failed coup of August 1991, he was appointed the general producer of the television company.

COMPONENT NO. 3: OLEG SOSKOVETS

During those years, Alexander Korzhakov was playing a complicated and farsighted political game. Having come to power at a relatively young age and—as it seemed to him—destined to remain in power for a long time, he did not even consider the possibility that he might lose his power. He was ready to fight for it with any means necessary, and he deliberately encouraged President Yeltsin's drinking habit in order to incapacitate him. For the role of Yeltsin's successor, Korzhakov had settled on the deputy prime minister of the Russian government, Oleg Soskovets, former director of the Karaganda Metallurgical Combine. True to his principle of promoting and employing only people with incriminating records, Korzhakov chose Soskovets because he knew that criminal proceedings had been initiated against him for large-scale theft at the Karaganda Metallurgical Combine. In other words, Korzhakov already had the incriminating evidence he needed against Soskovets.

Korzhakov's plan was relatively simple: All government power would effectively be concentrated in the hands of Korzhakov, as the head of the SBP; Mikhail Barsukov, as the director of state security; and Soskovets, as the deputy prime minister (somewhat analogous to vice president). They would retain control over all law enforcement agencies in the country, the military-industrial complex, and the arms trade within Russia and beyond its borders. The Russian Duma had to be transformed into a manageable instrument at any price. Yeltsin had to be kept drunk and perpetually incapacitated, or else die of alcohol poisoning. By that point, it would be desirable to have a state of emergency declared in the country, under one or another pretext, which would eliminate the need to hold a scheduled or early presidential election. Such a state of emergency would make it possible to appoint Soskovets as Yeltsin's successor or acting president. At some point, control would be acquired over Channel One, Russia's main television channel. This would make it possible to conduct the right kind of election campaign, to hold a "democratic" election at a moment advantageous to Soskovets, and to make Soskovets the formal president.

The deadline for Korzhakov's planned operation, which could more accurately be described as a government coup, was already known: it had to take place no later than the legally scheduled presidential election on June 16, 1996.

COMPONENT NO. 4: MONEY

Among his familiars, Korzhakov would sometimes slip up and say something along the lines of: "What do you think? Wouldn't I be able to govern a country like Russia?" For Korzhakov, Soskovets was merely a temporary political instrument to be used to achieve a final goal: absolute power. But he needed money— very big money that he could use to buy up the leading politicians, the Duma, and the voters. The question was where to get this money.

Using the SBP to extort money from businesses, businessmen, and government officials, Korzhakov disposed of considerable financial resources, including hard foreign currency. These resources were spent with the aim of preparing a creeping government takeover. The SBP spent over $50 million to acquire sophisticated eavesdropping equipment from abroad, a large part of which was installed inside the Kremlin. The monitoring was all-pervasive. The Kremlin's offices were crammed with complex German bugging devices, and although the high-ranking officials who occupied these offices generally suspected that their premises had been bugged, they could do nothing to oppose Korzhakov's and Barsukov's system of total surveillance. Sergei Filatov, President Yeltsin's chief of staff at the time, constantly complained to reporters that he was forced to communicate with visitors in his own office by writing notes, and that the most important negotiations had to be conducted in the hallway outside. By 1995, according to the estimates of various analytic organizations, Korzhakov's security service numbered over 40,000 people. (Under Andropov, the KGB and the Foreign Intelligence Service together had about 37,000 employees.)

When he appointed Komelkov to "look after" Ostankino, Korzhakov had no idea what sums of money circulated at the television center. Later, when he at last appreciated the approximate level of profits that were coming in from advertising, he set himself the task of bringing these financial streams—which escaped the notice of the tax agencies and the state budget— under his own control. This money would undoubtedly have been enough for any government coup. What Korzhakov needed, however, was a man who was completely unaware of the ultimate aims of his planned operation to take over the government, who had no experience in the world of big politics, who had no contacts in the Kremlin, and who at the same time was widely respected in the world of television. This man had to be convinced that everything he did was for the good of the country, since everything had to appear on the outside as if financial order were being brought to television in the interests of the state. On Komelkov's firm recommendation, Vladislav Listyev was chosen for the job.

Korzhakov, who was on close terms with President Yeltsin's family, started to sell Yeltsin on the idea that Listyev was the man who represented the future of Russian television. In September 1994, Korzhakov got Listyev appointed vice president of the Academy of Russian Television. And in January 1995, Listyev became the general manager of ORT, the television channel that had been created on November 30, 1994, following the privatization of the state-run Channel One in accordance with a decree issued by President Yeltsin on Korzhakov's initiative.

For Korzhakov, Listyev was an ideally naive figure. He wanted to be the producer of entertaining shows on ORT and did not see himself in any larger capacity. What Korzhakov and Komelkov demanded of Listyev, however, was something altogether different: his task was to facilitate the takeover of ORT's entire advertising market and to redirect all proceeds from the sales of airtime to accounts controlled by Korzhakov's SBP.

A few days after his appointment in January 1995, Listyev made a public announcement: from now on, all advertising on ORT would be consigned to a limited number of companies under his personal control. Television workers panicked. The newspaper *Vecherny Klub* commented:

> This is understandable. Advertising means money. It is the income of television companies and the income of private individuals. Both legal and illegal. Television workers even have a special word—dzhinsa—for shows, clips, and information programs that are produced off the books. Payment for such programming goes directly to its producers, bypassing official accounts. Now, Ostankino will no longer have this kind of trough to feed at (according to estimates, the monthly fall in revenue will be 30 million rubles). Such a change is bound to have major consequences.

About half of Russia's TV advertising business was controlled by Lisovsky's company, Premier SV.

One of the people who came up with the idea of reforming and privatizing Channel One was Boris Berezovsky. He proposed creating a joint-stock company: the government would retain control over 51 percent of the shares, and 49 percent would go to private investors loyal to President Yeltsin. This would give the president effective control over ORT, and most importantly, it would allow him to use it as a resource in the 1996 presidential campaign. This plan satisfied Yeltsin, and it satisfied Korzhakov, who stood behind Yeltsin and whom Berezovsky at that time considered an obvious ally. Thanks to the fact that he had such an ally, Berezovsky's political influence in the Kremlin undoubtedly increased, and his company LogoVAZ obtained access to Channel One's advertising market and signed the corresponding agreement with the advertising magnate Sergei Lisovsky. In addition, 49 percent of ORT's shares were retained by a group of individuals chosen by Berezovsky, and first and foremost by Berezovsky himself.

After the privatization of Channel One, and on the instructions of Korzhakov and Komelkov, Listyev decided to focus his attention on the sale of airtime. The off-the-books sale of airtime for advertising reduced the channel's profits by millions of dollars. Listyev's supervisor, SBP officer Komelkov, was sufficiently familiar with the business plans of the principal advertisers. Thanks to his colleagues—the head of Ostankino's "regime department," FSB Lieutenant Colonel Tsibizov, and the head of ORT's First Department, FSB resident V. V. Malygin—Komelkov possessed information about all of the advertisers' connections and the organizations that provided for their financial support and security. The names of individuals who frequented the various television offices were known to him through the department that issued passes to the Ostankino tower. And records from the FSB and the Ministry of Internal Affairs could be used to identify those among them who had links to various organized crime groups in Moscow.

Korzhakov and Komelkov knew everything about ORT's advertising business. Listyev first opened negotiations with Lisovsky, who was prepared to offer ORT compensation in return for the right to supervise the channel's advertising and thus to retain his control. At the same time, Listyev began negotiations with another entrepreneur in the advertising business, Gleb Bokiy, who represented the BSG Industrial Trade Group. The negotiations dragged on, while Listyev in the meantime started his own advertising agency, Intervid. On February 20, 1994, Listyev announced a temporary moratorium on all forms of advertising until ORT worked out new ethics standards. It was clear that this was Korzhakov's attempt to deal a blow to Lisovsky and Bokiy, perhaps even to drive them out of the advertising business altogether, by switching all clients over to Intervid.

Listyev, Lisovsky, and Bokiy met on March 30, 1994, in a little restaurant on Kropotkinskaya Street in Moscow. Lisovsky and Bokiy demanded that Listyev share advertising airtime with them, and the inexperienced Listyev gave in. This was obviously a mistake. On the following day, this mistake was corrected: on Spartanskaya Street, Bokiy's Cadillac was riddled with six bullets from a TT-model pistol. Just to make sure, a grenade was tossed inside the vehicle as well. Bokiy died on the spot.

On April 9, the head of Vargus-Video, G. Topadze, who owned 6.5 percent of ORT's advertising business, was shot. An assassination attempt against Berezovsky followed in June, injuring Berezovsky and killing his driver. In order to forestall another assassination attempt, Vladimir Gusinsky immediately flew Berezovsky out of Russia on his private plane. Such an open intervention by Gusinsky-Bobkov had to demonstrate to anyone interested that the recent murders and assassination attempts had been carried out by the Most Corporation's clearest rival.

Lisovsky's turn came next. It was believed that he was under the protection of Sergei Timofeyev ("Silvestr"), the leader of the Orekhovo crime gang. In September 1994, "Silvestr" was blown up in his Mercedes along with his driver. Someone was methodically and cold-bloodedly eliminating Listyev's rivals. This "someone" was General Korzhakov, who was all-powerful in those years. He was fighting for total control over ORT in anticipation of the summer 1996 presidential election.

Korzhakov pressured Listyev. He needed money to prepare public opinion for the replacement of Yeltsin—whose drinking he continued to encourage—with the young and energetic deputy prime minister, Oleg Soskovets. He needed total control over ORT. Time was running out: the Russian presidential election was approaching, and Korzhakov and his team had little confidence that the current president, whose popularity rating was extremely low, could win. Korzhakov determined that necessary expenditures would amount to approximately $50–$60 million. Listyev was not able to procure this money for Korzhakov. Consequently, Korzhakov had to get rid of Listyev at once and take control over ORT into his own hands.

It is difficult to determine the exact point at which the plan to murder Listyev took shape, but it is evident that this operation was intended to fulfill many different goals. First, Listyev would be eliminated. Second, the blame for the arrangement of Listyev's murder would be cast on Berezovsky—who was an influential presence in Russia and on ORT, and who at that time exercised an influence over Yeltsin as well—and on Listyev's main competitor in the advertising market, Lisovsky. Third, Berezovsky would be arrested, and Yeltsin—disappointed in Berezovsky, Lisovsky, and Anatoly Chubais, an influential reform-oriented politician with ties to both of them—would hand control over ORT to a new person named by Korzhakov, while Korzhakov and his people would get the 49 percent of ORT's nongovernment shares. Lisovsky, now a suspect, would also be unable to continue his business dealings with ORT.

At that time, Listyev was anticipating a visit from the Solntsevo crime group. He had nixed a project that they were interested in, and he expected them to come to him and demand compensation in the amount of several million dollars. Listyev had asked Komelkov to intervene and shield him from their extortionate demands. The simplest form of protection, as Listyev supposed, would be to deny them admission passes to the Ostankino building. The fact that the members of the Solntsevo gang had been allowed to enter the building indicated to Listyev that Komelkov and his SBP supervisors had abandoned him. It may have been the Solntsevo gangsters who received the order from Komelkov to eliminate Listyev. In any case, on March 1, 1995, Listyev was no more. He was killed inside his apartment building. It is inconceivable that Komelkov should have carried out this operation without Korzhakov's express instructions.

Just as Korzhakov had planned, suspicion fell first and foremost on Berezovsky and Lisovsky. However, the SBP's attempt to arrest Berezovsky at the LogoVAZ office on Novokuznetskaya Street in Moscow failed. Berezovsky had time to get in touch with Prime Minister Viktor Chernomyrdin, who prevented the arrest. Through the Gusinsky-controlled media, materials that incriminated Korzhakov and Barsukov were leaked. Chubais, who was respected by Yeltsin, spoke out in support of Berezovsky and Gusinsky. ORT remained in Berezovsky's hands, and Korzhakov ended up not getting the advertising money and the $50–$60 million that he needed to reshape public opinion. That was when he decided to opt for the cheapest strategy of all, which did not require a public relations campaign on television.

COMPONENT NO. 5: A SMALL—BUT BY NO MEANS VICTORIOUS—WAR

Chechnya had become the weakest link in Russia's multinational mosaic, but the KGB raised no objections when Dzhokhar

Dudayev came to power there because they regarded him as one of their own. General Dudayev, a member of the CPSU since 1968, was transferred from Estonia to his hometown of Grozny as if deliberately in order to oppose the local Communists, to be elected president of the Chechen Republic, and to proclaim the independence of Chechnya (Ichkeria) in November 1991—as if to show the Russian political elite what kind of disintegration was in store for Russia under Yeltsin's liberal regime. It was probably no accident that another Chechen who was close to Yeltsin, Ruslan Khasbulatov, would also be responsible for inflicting fatal damage on his regime. A former functionary of the Komsomol's Central Committee and a Communist Party member since 1966, Khasbulatov had become speaker of the Russian parliament in September 1991. It was precisely this Khasbulatov-led parliament that Yeltsin would forcibly dissolve—using tanks—in October 1993.

By 1994, the political leadership of Russia was already aware that it could not afford to grant independence to Chechnya. Allowing sovereign status for Chechnya would make the disintegration of Russia a genuine possibility. But could they afford to start a civil war in the North Caucasus? The "party of war," which relied on the military and law enforcement ministries, believed they could afford it as long as the public was prepared for it, and it would be easy enough to influence public opinion if the Chechens were seen to resort to terror tactics in their struggle for independence. All that was needed was to arrange terrorist attacks in Moscow and leave a trail leading back to Chechnya.

On November 18, 1994, the FSB made its first recorded attempt to stir up anti-Chechen feeling by committing an act of terrorism and laying the blame on Chechen separatists. An explosion took place on a railroad track crossing the Yauza River in Moscow. According to experts, it was caused by two powerful charges of approximately 1.5 kilograms of TNT. About twenty meters of the railroad bed was ripped up, and the bridge almost collapsed. It was quite clear, however, that the explosion had occurred prematurely, before the next train was due to cross the bridge. The shattered fragments of the bomber's body were discovered about one hundred meters from the site of the explosion. He was Captain Andrei Schelenkov, an employee of the Lanako oil company. His own bomb had blown him up as he was planting it on the bridge.

It was only thanks to this blunder that the immediate organizers of the terrorist attack became known. Lanako's boss—who had given his firm a name beginning with the first two letters of his own last name—was thirty-five-year-old Maksim Lazovsky, a highly valued agent of the FSB office for Moscow and the Moscow region, also known simply as "Max." It would later become known that every single one of Lanako's employees was a full-time or freelance agent of the Russian security services, and that all subsequent terrorist attacks in Moscow during 1994–1995 were also organized by Lazovsky's group. In 1996, the terrorists from the FSB were arrested and convicted by a Moscow court. But by that time, the first Chechen war had become a *fait accompli*. Lazovsky had done his job.

War in Chechnya offered a very easy way to finish off Yeltsin politically, a fact understood only too well by those who provoked the war and organized the terrorist attacks in Russia.

COMPONENT NO. 6: ARMS SALES

In Soviet times, arms exports were controlled by the Main Engineering Directorate (GIU) of the Ministry of Foreign Economic Relations. Most of the GIU's employees were staff officers of the Main Intelligence Directorate (GRU). After the revolution of August 1991, however, the head of the Presidential Security Service, Korzhakov, decided to take control of the stream of revenue that came from the arms trade. On November 18, 1993, in order to regulate and systematize the complicated business of selling armaments, Yeltsin signed secret decree No. 1932-s, establishing a state-owned company, Rosvooruzhenie, to represent the interests of Russia's military-industrial complex in dealing with foreign companies involved in the arms trade. The same decree conferred control over Rosvooruzhenie's activities onto the SBP.

To this end, Department V (from *vooruzhenie*, "armaments") was established in the SBP. Its main function was to control the activities of Rosvooruzhenie, as well as Goskhran and Gosdragmet. General Samoilov became the head of Rosvooruzhenie. At the head of Department V, Korzhakov placed his loyal subordinate Alexander Kotelkin. Born in 1954, Kotelkin graduated from Kiev's Higher Military Engineering School and served in the air force for a number of years. Then he was hired by the GRU and sent to study at the Diplomatic Academy of the Ministry of Foreign Affairs. At the end of the 1980s, he served as a military intelligence officer under diplomatic cover at the USSR's permanent mission to the United Nations.

While living in the United States, Kotelkin was noticed by the FBI due to his many romantic liaisons with the wives of Soviet diplomats working at the UN, and also due to his non-traditional sexual relations with colleagues from the GRU. He maintained close relations with Sergei Glazyev, a deputy minister in the government of Yegor Gaidar, and later minister of foreign economic relations. With Glazyev's assistance, Kotelkin was appointed head of the Main Directorate of the Military-Engineering Association (the successor organization to the GIU) at the Ministry of Foreign Economic Relations. At this post, he abused his official position, receiving bonuses in the tens of thousands of dollars from the enterprises under his control.

When Rosvooruzhenie was created in 1993, Korzhakov made sure that it was precisely Kotelkin who was appointed head of Department V, which controlled the newly formed government entity. Korzhakov had sufficient incriminating evidence against Kotelkin to guarantee that he would do whatever he was told. In November 1994, Kotelkin became the head of Rosvooruzhenie. As a result, from that point until the summer of 1996, when Korzhakov was dismissed from government service, Korzhakov and his people among Rosvooruzhenie's employees were able to appropriate several hundred million dollars.

COMPONENT NO. 7: STATE OF EMERGENCY

Right before the 1996 election, Korzhakov, Barsukov, and Soskovets persuaded President Yeltsin that he had no chance of beating his main rival, CPSU candidate Gennady Zyuganov, and that the only way to hold on to power in the country was to declare a state of emergency—using the ongoing war with the Chechen Republic as a pretext. There was some logic to this suggestion.

If Zyuganov came to power, he would undoubtedly put Yeltsin in jail for dissolving the parliament in 1993. The forced dissolution of Russia's legislative body could easily be portrayed as an unconstitutional act, with all the attendant consequences. If the democrats came to power, they could easily prosecute Yeltsin for starting the first Chechen war, for war crimes committed by the Russian army in Chechnya, and for the genocide of the Chechen people. And any new president could question the legality of Yeltsin's privatization of the Russian economy. So Yeltsin signed a decree canceling the presidential election and declaring a state of emergency.

Before this decree was made public, however, its contents became known to all those whom Korzhakov had not had time to eliminate: Berezovsky, Chubais, Gusinsky, Lisovsky, and all those who would later be known as the Russian oligarchs. In a single concerted effort, the likes of which has not been seen since in Russian history, they gained admittance to Yeltsin's office—with help from his daughter Tatyana Dyachenko—and offered him the use of money, newspapers, and television instead of tanks and decrees declaring a state of emergency. And Yeltsin rescinded the decree that he had already signed; fired Korzhakov, Barsukov, and Soskovets; and appointed Chubais as his chief of staff. Berezovsky vouched for Yeltsin's support on ORT, Gusinsky on NTV; Lisovsky was in charge of advertising; the almost unknown Roman Abramovich handled the extra-budgetary financing. Starting out with a popularity rating of 2 to 3 percent, Yeltsin managed to get the highest percentage of votes in the first round in June. He entered the second round in July and beat his main rival, Zyuganov. Shortly afterward, on August 31, 1996, Yeltsin signed a peace agreement with the Chechen Republic. The first Chechen war came to an end. Russia returned to the path of democracy. Komelkov left the SPB, returning to the FSB as deputy head of the Directorate for the Defense of the Constitutional Order.

2

Who Is Mr. Putin?

AN ALTERNATIVE BIOGRAPHY

On March 9, 2000, a Yak-40 jet crashed seconds after taking off from Sheremetyevo Airport in Moscow. Nine people were on board: Artyom Borovik, president of the Sovershenno Sekretno publishing enterprise; Ziya Bazhayev, head of the Alliance Group Holding Company and a Chechen by nationality; his two bodyguards; and five crew members.

The Yak-40, which Bazhayev had leased about a year earlier from the Vologda Air Company through Aerotex, a Moscow airline, was supposed to fly to Kiev. The report of the committee investigating air travel incidents indicated that the Vologda air technicians had failed to treat the airplane with a special antifreeze fluid prior to takeoff and that its wing flaps had been opened to only 10° instead of 20° as required for takeoff. However, the temperature at Sheremetyevo on the morning of March 9 had been no lower than –4°C, with no precipitation, and there was no need to treat the airplane with Arktika antifreeze. In addition, the Yak-40 could easily have taken off with the wing flaps open to only 10°; this would simply have meant a longer acceleration and a "lazy" takeoff. Judging by the fact that the airplane crashed close to the middle of the runway, which in

Sheremetyevo is 3.6 kilometers long, its takeoff distance had been adequate—approximately 800 meters.

Immediately after the deaths of Borovik and Bazhayev, the media suggested that the catastrophe had not been an accident and that the airplane had been sabotaged by the Russian security services. In the preceding days and weeks, Borovik (through Bazhayev) had been collecting materials about Putin's childhood, and these materials were supposed to be published on March 12, 2000, right before the presidential election. What was it, then, that Borovik was preparing to publish? What was it that had so alarmed Putin and those who were behind him?

Borovik possessed evidence of the fact that Putin's biological mother was not Maria Ivanovna Putina, born in 1911, but a completely different woman: Vera Nikolayevna Putina, born in 1926 in the town of Ocher (Perm region) and residing to this day in the village of Metekhi in Georgia (Kaspi district), about an hour's drive from Tbilisi. The current president of the Russian Federation, Vladimir Vladimirovich Putin, had himself lived in the village of Metekhi between the ages of three and nine.

This information was considered a state secret for the following reasons: The KGB had been particularly interested in recruiting orphans or foster children. It was believed that such young people—who were deprived of the warmth and protection of their biological parents; who in many cases had been abandoned and betrayed by their parents; who were hurt, humiliated, beaten down—would enter the KGB as if they were entering a new family, seeking genuine protection from all the evil people they had encountered during their childhood in an all-powerful state structure that was feared by the whole country. The young Putin took up judo for self-defense. He joined the KGB because he believed it was the only way to develop into a powerful and respected person. Over time, the KGB really did become his family. And if everything that Vera Putina has said is true, then one may see Putin's work in the KGB and his advancement through the government in a new light. Hurt, betrayed, and deprived of parental warmth during his childhood, Putin turned to the KGB first and foremost to find a new family there and to settle scores with the world that had injured him. And when the KGB-FSB—or the *kontora*, as they call themselves—started promoting Putin through the ranks of the government in the 1990s, they were certain of at least one thing: no candidate for president would be more devoted to the FSB than Putin.

Vera Nikolayevna, who claimed that she was Putin's real mother, related the following in a video interview:

> Originally, I'm from the Urals. I went to a technical college there, too. In college, I met a young man. He was Vova's father. Vova was born in 1950. I don't even want to remember his father. He lied to me. I was already pregnant when I found out that he had a family. I left him immediately. Vova was raised for a whole year by my parents. Then, when I was sent to do my postgraduate service in Tashkent, I met my [current] husband, Georgy Osepashvili. He was in the army then. When I married him, we moved to Metekhi and after a while my mother brought Vova here too. He was three years old at the time.
>
> But soon, when we started having our own children, my husband didn't want Vova to live with us anymore. He didn't beat him—he just didn't want Vova to be here. Who wants someone else's child? Once, my husband's sister even gave Vova away to some childless army major, keeping it a secret from me. I barely managed to find him and took him back. I had to take Vova back to my parents. They wanted me to keep my new family intact. Basically, I exchanged Vova for my girls. After that, I never saw Vova again, although I constantly looked for him and asked my parents where he was. Nobody wanted to tell me anything. Later, I found out that Vova was already in the KGB and had forbidden everyone to tell me where he was. . . .
>
> Of course, I'd heard that Vova was working for the KGB, and then in the Russian government. Sometimes my daughters talked about him. The people in my village talk about him constantly. But now his childhood is classified information and he doesn't want to recognize me as his mother. . . . People from the KGB came to my house, took all my family photographs, and told me not to tell anyone about Vova.[1]

The photographs were taken away in January 2000, when either FSB agents (according to one account by local residents) or Georgian law enforcement (according to another account) came to Metekhi and asked all about Volodya Putin. The agents confiscated Vera Nikolayevna's photographs of her son and warned her not to tell anyone about him.

Beset by reporters, Georgian president Eduard Shevard-nadze felt compelled to make a statement about Putin's relatives. He suggested that it be left to "Putin himself to get to the bottom of this issue."[2]

Volodya Putin from Metekhi received his education at the local high school. Some of his old classmates have been interviewed. Gabriel Datashvili, head of the Kaspi district planning organization, said that he had been friends with Volodya and that they were the best students in their class:

> In school, we both got the best grades and were close friends. He basically had no other friends besides me. . . . He was a very quiet, secretive child. After school, he often went fishing or came to my house and we played together: war games, sword-fighting, lakhti, and wrestling. I had one photograph of him. He gave it to me when he left. He wrote on it: "To Gabriel from Vova, in memory." . . . If Putin remembers the period of his life that he spent in Metekhi, he has to remember me. . . . He was a small, weak boy, with light hair and blue eyes. . . . Then his mother, Vera Putina, took him back to Russia to her parents. . . . As far as I know, this was caused by family problems. Also, Vera had new children then. When Vova was taken to Russia, she already had two girls, Sofia and Lyuba. Then, in 1961, she had another boy, and after him, two more girls.

One resident of Metekhi, Uncle Gogi, described how Putin had seriously injured his finger while fishing:

> Vova was standing next to his school and bawling. There was a fishing hook stuck in the tip of his left-hand index finger. It couldn't be removed without pulling out a piece of flesh. The blood was gushing. "Don't be afraid, sonny, it will heal," I told him. . . . He cried a lot. I hugged him, calmed him down, and tore out the hook. He must have a small scar left.

Other distinctive marks were two conspicuous bumps at the corners of his forehead (hidden by hair). People said that schoolchildren in Metekhi even teased Volodya and called him the devil because of these bumps.

Dali Gzirishvili was the same age as Putin and went to the same school:

> He was a small, weak child with brusque movements like his mother's. I didn't even know that his name was Vladimir. I called him simply Vova. That's what everyone called him. His mother called him Vovka. . . . I'm certain that the acting president of Russia is our Vovka. It can't be anyone else. He looks so much like his mother. . . . He was so fair-haired, with spiky hair. I knew that he wasn't Georgy's son. I felt very sorry for him. I helped him. They were very poor. I brought him apples, pears, grapes, anything I could get. He always took everything. We played lakhti and burti together by the river. He was so sad. He went fishing all the time. Uncle Gogi pulled out a fish hook that got stuck in his hand. There must be a mark. He got very angry and cried when people called him names. The people here knew that it made him angry, and they called him names, and he got angry and cried.

Nora Gogolashvili, an elementary school teacher, recalled her student Putin as follows:

> A quiet, sad, introverted child. His favorite activity was wrestling. He was almost always unhappy about something. Didn't do any physical work, but was a very good student. Had a very difficult family life. . . . Vova came to school in patched-up clothes. They called him my stepson. Whenever anyone hurt him, I defended him. I pitied him so much. . . . I felt so sorry for him. He stuck to me like a cat.

Oleg Iyadze, a wrestler from Metekhi and about ten years younger than Putin, met with the future president at wrestling meets. As Iyadze recalls:

> From the very beginning, he was grim and reserved. Only said hello if someone else said hello to him. He had the same attitude toward Russians, if you can believe it. A cold personality. To walk up to someone and start a conversation—that wasn't in his nature. . . . He was a very reserved person. He was working in the KGB at the time and was as silent as the tomb. I saw him only at wrestling meets. . . . By the way, there was a time when his half-sister called his uncle and his uncle

told her that Vova had become a big man in the Russian government. But whether this is the same Vova Putin who is now the acting president of Russia, it's hard to say. But he and Vera Putina from Metekhi look like two peas in a pod. That much I can say.

According to some publications, however, Putin himself walked up to Iyadze, greeted him, and said, "I also have some connection to Metekhi."[3]

Vera Putina was visited by reporters once again on March 11, 2000, the day of Artyom Borovik's funeral. Vera Nikolayevna had apparently started to realize that people whom she did not know were dying because of her. "I'm afraid that Volodya won't become president because of me," she said. There were about twenty reporters in all, including correspondents from Russia's NTV. They inspected Vera Putina's passport and birth certificate, checked the last names of her parents, and verified the name of Putin's father: Platon Privalov. Everything that she said was recorded by several cameras, including NTV's. (The NTV interview was never aired.)

The reporters also paid a visit to Putin's sister (on his mother's side), Sofia (Sofio) Georgievna Osepashvili, born in 1954, currently a nurse at a TB hospital in Tbilisi. After looking at a photograph of the fourteen-year-old Putin, which had by then been published in the book *First Person: Conversations with Vladimir Putin* (this was the earliest known photograph of the future president), Sofia said:

Look at him and look at me—if this is not my brother, then show me my brother. . . . I sent him telegrams to Ocher, to his commissariat. At first they told me that they didn't have any such Putin there. Then they told me that I shouldn't look for him anymore. It turns out that he was already working for the KGB by that time.

Without a doubt, they resembled one another. Sofia had another photograph in which Volodya was seven years old. This photograph had been preserved only because Sofia lives in Tbilisi, not in Metekhi.

And so, Vera Putina brought her son to her parents, Anna Ilyinichna and Mikhail Illarionovich. They, in turn, almost immediately handed him over to a childless relative, Vladimir

Spiridonovich Putin, who became the official biological father of Russia's future president. Vladimir Spiridonovich took Volodya away to Leningrad, and Vera Nikolayevna was told that her son had been sent to a boarding school. "After I gave him to my parents," Vera Nikolayevna recalls, "my father became ill and the child was sent to a boarding school."[4]

In terms of education, the years of study at the Georgian school turned out to have been a complete waste. In Leningrad, instead of going into the fourth grade, Volodya entered the first grade on September 1, 1960, a month before his tenth birthday. It was then that the year of his birth had to be altered on his birth certificate, from 1950 to 1952, apparently so that the child would not be emotionally traumatized. Putin's official biography begins on this date: September 1, 1960.

PUTIN'S BIOGRAPHY ACCORDING TO OFFICIAL SOURCES

Vladimir Vladimirovich Putin, a Russian by nationality, was born in Leningrad on October 7, 1952. He was the third child in his family, though his parents' first two sons had died in infancy (the first before the war, the second of diphtheria during the siege of Leningrad).

His father, Vladimir Spiridonovich Putin, was born in 1911 in St. Petersburg. At the beginning of the First World War, his entire family left St. Petersburg for the town of Pominovo in the Tver region. Putin's mother, Maria Ivanovna Putina (née Shelomova), was born in the neighboring town of Zarechye, also in 1911. His father served in the Red Army as a submariner. In his youth, before the war, he was a village Komsomol activist. Putin's parents were married in 1928. They moved from the Tver region to Peterhof before the war. When the war began, his father left for the front as a volunteer and went on to serve in an NKVD fighter battalion. At the beginning of the siege of Leningrad, Putin's mother, with the help of her brother Ivan Ivanovich Shelomov, a naval officer (died in 1973), made her way from Peterhof to Leningrad.

Putin's grandfather on his father's side, Spiridon Ivanovich Putin, worked his whole life as a cook—at first in Gorki near Moscow, "where Lenin and the whole Ulyanov family lived. When Lenin died, the grandfather was transferred to one of

Stalin's dachas. . . . He outlived Stalin as well, and at the end of his life, already retired, he lived and cooked at a sanatorium for the party's Moscow city committee in Ilyinskoye."[5] The grandfather died in 1979; the grandmother, Olga Ivanovna, in 1976. Both of them are buried in the Ilyinskoye cemetery in the Krasnogorsk district of the Moscow region.[6] Putin's ancestors on his father's side had been living in the Tver region since the beginning of the seventeenth century, in the villages of Turginovo and Pominovo. Putin's first known ancestor, a landless peasant by the name of Yakim Nikitin, lived in the village of Borodino, in the Turginovo parish, and was a serf of the boyar Ivan Nikitich Romanov, the uncle of Czar Mikhail Fyodorovich.[7] Putin's grandmother on his mother's side, Elizaveta Alekseyevna Shelomova, was fatally wounded by a stray bullet during the German attack on the Tver region in October 1941.

In the 1950s, Putin's father served in the militarized guard of the Yegorov Railroad Car Factory in Leningrad. Later he worked as a technician at the same factory and was the secretary of his section's party bureau. Putin's mother worked after the war as a hospital attendant, a food inspector at a bakery, a security guard, and a janitor in a medical laboratory. Both parents died of cancer, the mother at the beginning of 1999, the father on August 2, 1999. They are buried in the Serafimovskoye cemetery in St. Petersburg.

PUTIN'S EDUCATION

From 1960 to 1968, Putin attended School No. 193 on the Griboyedov Canal in Leningrad. He was the head of his Young Pioneer troop. After finishing eighth grade, he entered high school No. 281 in Sovietsky Pereulok—a magnet school specializing in chemistry, affiliated with a technological institute. After graduating in 1970, he entered the international law department of Leningrad State University's law school. He graduated in 1975, submitting a thesis on "The Principle of the Most Favored Nation in International Law." He went on to get a Ph.D. in economics. The topic of his dissertation, defended at the St. Petersburg Mining Institute on June 27, 1997, was "Strategic Planning for the Renewal of the Mineral–Raw Materials Base of a Region under Conditions of Developing Market Relations,

St. Petersburg and the Leningrad Region." (His dissertation defense committee included Sergei Glazyev.) While studying at the university, Putin met Anatoly Sobchak, who for a time taught him economic law as an associate professor.

At Leningrad State University, Putin entered the CPSU and remained a member until it was banned in August 1991. In 1985, he completed the Higher School of the KGB in Moscow— "School No. 101," also known as the Andropov Red Banner Institute, now called the School of Foreign Intelligence.

LOST YEARS

According to his official biography, Putin was born on October 7, 1952, when his mother, Maria Ivanovna Putina, was forty-one years old. This would have been a rare occurrence; in the Soviet Union, women as a rule did not give birth at such an age. Volodya entered the first grade in Leningrad on September 1, 1960, when he was almost eight years old. His school friend Vyacheslav Yakovlev has provided one of the few pieces of evidence that Putin grew up in Leningrad.

> The president could not have had a Georgian period in his life, because we went to school together from first grade through tenth. Volodya and I entered the first grade together, at School No. 193, in 1959. I remember that he came with his mother, carrying an enormous bouquet of roses. We lived in the same building at the time, walked to school together, and came back home together. By the way, before entering school, I also saw Volodya in the yard with his parents.[8]

This is the only statement that exists about the preschool period of Putin's life, and it is not particularly convincing. For one thing, Yakovlev was off by a year, evidently adding the standard seven years to 1952, the year of Putin's birth.

A statement by Putin's neighbor Vyacheslav Chentsov sounds more credible: "Putin and I are four years apart. I was probably about twelve when I first noticed him in the yard."[9] In other words, Chentsov did not remember seeing Putin before the latter was already eight years old and in the first grade.

According to Putin's unofficial biography, he was born on October 7, 1950, when his mother, Vera Nikolayevna, was twenty-four years old. Volodya attended school in Metekhi between the ages of six and nine, completing three grades. And it was precisely for this reason that three years of Putin's life had to be "lost." They disappeared in the following way. Volodya entered school in Metekhi on September 1, 1957, when he was almost seven. When he finished the third grade in the summer of 1960, he was nine. He was then sent to Vera Niko-layevna's parents and shortly after that to his new parents. By September 1, 1960, Volodya was already living in Leningrad, and on October 7, 1960, he turned ten. At this point, the year of his birth was changed on his birth certificate from 1950 to 1952. When Volodya entered school in Leningrad, he was once again seven years old (turning eight on October 7, 1960, according to his birth certificate).

PUTIN IN THE KGB

After completing Leningrad State University in 1975, Putin received an assignment to work at the KGB. For about five months, he worked at the secretariat of the KGB's Leningrad office, "pushing some papers around."[10] From February to June 1976, he attended retraining courses for operational personnel. Then he served for half a year at the Leningrad KGB office— according to him, in a "counterintelligence unit . . . dealing with foreign elements,"[11] and according to the testimony of his co-workers, in "The Five," the Fifth Department of the Leningrad KGB, part of the Fifth Directorate, which oversaw the "struggle against ideological diversions by the enemy" and the surveil-lance of dissidents. While working at the "counterintelligence unit," Putin attracted the "attention of foreign intelligence offi-cers," after which he received an offer to transfer from "The Five" to the First Main Directorate (PGU, foreign intelligence) and was sent to attend a year-long retraining program in Mos-cow. After returning to Leningrad, he served "four and a half years" (1979–1983) in the First Department of the Leningrad KGB.

In 1984, after being promoted to the rank of major, Putin was sent to the Andropov Red Banner Institute, which he attended under the assumed name "Platov." Here, Putin was the head of his section and specialized in German-speaking countries (Austria, Switzerland, West Germany, East Germany—the PGU's Fourth Department). Upon completing his courses in 1985, Putin was sent to the KGB office in East Germany, where he served as director of the House of Soviet-German Friendship in Dresden.[12] As a KGB representative, he oversaw the conduct of Soviet students in East Germany. His duties at one time included surveillance over Hans Modrow, who was then the secretary of the Dresden office of the Socialist Unity Party of Germany (SED) and would later become East Germany's last Communist premier. He also investigated anti-Communist acts of protest in East Germany.[13]

Volodya Putin who lived in the town of Metekhi was a wrestler, having taken up wrestling to defend himself against teasing and name-calling. KGB agent Vladimir Putin excelled at sambo and judo. Volodya Putin who lived in the town of Metekhi spent whole days by the river alone with a fishing rod. Foreign intelligence major Vladimir Putin belonged to the Dresden society of amateur fishermen while stationed in East Germany. Vera Nikolayevna Putina has a distinctive "duck-like" gait. The elected president Vladimir Putin jokes about his own "duck-like" walk.[14]

In 1986, the head of the KGB, Vladimir Kryuchkov, traveled to East Germany to meet with Hans Modrow. Subsequently, Kryuchkov could not recall PGU officer Putin and concluded that Putin had most likely not been an active intelligence officer, but merely a staff member of some other division of the KGB who had received a work assignment in East Germany for the standard span of five years. This is also how Kryuchkov explained the fact that Putin, after returning to the USSR at the beginning of 1990, began working with the staff of the KGB's Leningrad office.[15]

In 2004, the memoirs of Vladimir Usoltsev (real name: Vladimir Gortanov, also known as Vladimir Artamonov), a retired KGB lieutenant colonel who had emigrated to the Czech Republic, were published in Moscow. Usoltsev had worked with Putin in Dresden and he writes about the Dresden period in Putin's life. He jokes that the Soviet Union's Berlin agents spent most of their time collecting free fashion catalogues in department stores in West Berlin and then selling them to fashion designers and seamstresses back home. He and Putin had no such opportunities in Dresden, so they talked their Berlin colleagues into giving them some catalogues. Putin was much more successful at this than Usoltsev because many of the agents stationed in Berlin came from Putin's hometown of Leningrad.

Usoltsev lists his Dresden colleagues without giving their last names: Sergei, Boris, Sasha, Nikolai, Viktor, Volodya-with-a-mustache, little Volodya. However, he immediately specifies that it was Putin whom everyone called "little Volodya," while Usoltsev himself was known as "big Volodya." Moreover, Usoltsev does not disguise the name of the head of the Dresden foreign intelligence group, the elderly Colonel Lazar Lazarevich Matveyev, who was especially fond of Captain Putin.

The business-savvy Sergei, little Volodya's best friend when it came to drinking Radeberger beer, is undoubtedly Sergei Viktorovich Chemezov, currently the general manager of the Rosoboronexport Federal State Unitary Enterprise. Putin's fellow Leningrader Boris, on whose recommendation Colonel Matveyev took Putin under his wing, is Boris Alexanderovich Mylnikov, who until November 2006 was the head of the CIS Antiterrorism Center. Sasha from the Penza region is Alexander Ivanovich Biriukov, currently the head of the tax collection service in the Penza region. The Dresden agents Viktor, Nikolai, and Volodya-with-a-mustache are Viktor Adianov, businessman; Nikolai Tokarev, since 2000 the general manager of the Zarubezhneft Company; and Vladimir Bragin, currently retired and living in Sochi. Putin's Berlin supervisor, who is unnamed in Usoltsev's account, may be identified as Yuri Sergeyevich Leschev, his former boss at the KGB's Leningrad directorate, currently a retired and emeritus state security agent. Another of the unnamed Berlin agents is Andrei Yurievich Belyaninov, who during Putin's Dresden tenure was the head of the Federal Service for Defense Contracts, and since 2006 has been the director of the Federal Customs Service.

Putin also had German acquaintances in Dresden—Stasi officers, intelligence agents, and simply friends. Some of them now work at Dresdner Bank and Deutsche Bank, Putin's favorite financial institutions during his time as deputy mayor of St. Petersburg. Today, these banks are helping Putin break Mikhail Khodorkovsky's Yukos into pieces. The German memoirist Irene Pietsch could have shed light on all these connections, but she carefully avoids mentioning names in her book *Piquant Friendship*: "These were East Germans whom Putin had met in Dresden and who were now living in Moscow, where the husband occupied a managing position in one of the large German banks—the same one whose chairman had organized Lyudmila's trip . . ."; "the husband was a Stasi colleague of Volodya's . . ."; "in Hamburg . . . Lyudmila's hotel room had been reserved by the same German bank whose name was more and more often mentioned in connection with Lyudmila and Volodya."

Usoltsev's memoirs are considerably more informative. Explaining how Putin managed to receive two promotions within the KGB and two promotions within the CPSU during his stay in Dresden—and how he was later able to charm first Sobchak and then Yeltsin—Usoltsev writes: "Volodya knew how to be polite, friendly, obliging, and unobtrusive. He was capable of making anyone like him, but he was particularly successful with people who were old enough to be his father."

In addition, Usoltsev notes that Putin's attitude toward the Soviet government in conversation with his friends was unusually critical for a KGB agent:

> Gradually, it became clear to me that Volodya had already absorbed all of this dissident wisdom back in Leningrad, while working at the Fifth Directorate, which was aimed at combating "ideological subversion." It appeared that, in the part of the battlefield that Volodya had been responsible for, the "ideological subversives" had won. In our conversations, he mentioned many dissidents with esteem. He was especially respectful of Solzhenitsyn. I had never encountered anything even resembling such attitudes among the agents of the Fifth Directorate's Krasnoyarsk and Minsk offices.

Conversing with outsiders, Putin knew how to be ironically hypocritical. "In the presence of others, Volodya without embarrassment engaged in conversations about 'Zionist influences' on Sakharov," Usoltsev recalls."However, his tone of voice had a dose of irony that was always clear to me. This summed him up completely: why make things difficult for yourself by spitting against the wind?"[16]

3

Putin in St. Petersburg

BACK IN THE USSR

In the first half of 1990, Vladimir Putin—officer of the KGB's active reserve, former secretary of the party organization of the KGB's office in Dresden, senior assistant to his department head, and member of the party committee of the KGB's East German office—returned to his hometown of Leningrad. Accounts differ as to the exact date of his return. According to the long interview given by Putin to three *Kommersant* reporters at the beginning of 2000, which formed the basis of his pre-election book *First Person*, he stayed in Dresden until January 1990: "When in January 1990 we came back from Germany, I was still working for the state security organs, but was quietly starting to think about a backup landing strip for myself."[1]

The president's wife, Lyudmila, remembers almost the same date: "We came back to the Soviet Union at the beginning of 1990, on February 3, I think."[2] However, Putin's old co-worker from East Germany, the former KGB Lieutenant Colonel Vladimir Gortanov (whose memoirs were published under the pen name Vladimir Usoltsev) insists on a different date. First, Usoltsev was in Leipzig on business in the spring of 1990, and he visited Putin in Dresden. Second, Usoltsev saw Putin for the last time when he and his boss, Yevgeny Beliavsky, visited his former co-worker in Dresden in the summer of 1990.[3]

It is unlikely that any of these old KGB hands are trying to "confuse their trail." Possibly, one of them is misremembering the events. Or perhaps Putin did not immediately give up all his business in East Germany and from February to July 1990 lived (and worked) in two places at once, making periodic trips from Leningrad to East Germany and to Dresden in particular, where Usoltsev encountered him on two occasions. There is some indirect evidence in support of this hypothesis. One of the former KGB agents stationed in Berlin remembers arranging hotel accommodations for Putin in the spring of 1990 when Putin visited Berlin on a short work assignment. This co-worker of Putin's—an old friend and classmate from the Andropov Red Banner Institute—recalls that Putin "wanted to write a doctoral dissertation," but he had no "impression that Putin was preparing to leave foreign intelligence."[4]

Lyudmila Putina recalls this period of their life with some bitterness: "As soon as we came back to Leningrad, my husband immediately threw himself into work. I think that he had become so tired of having a stable and regular routine in Dresden for four and a half years that in St. Petersburg he simply was never at home. It looked as if my husband had disappeared, as if he had run away from home." Nor did Putin bring his salary home to his wife. Lyudmila says: "For three months, he was not paid his salary. I remember that by the end of the third month I started getting seriously alarmed because we simply had no money. But then, everything was paid to him all at once."[5]

Whether Putin continued visiting Germany after February 1990 in connection with his old "foreign intelligence" work thus remains unknown. No later than the beginning of spring 1990, however, his main official place of work became Leningrad State University (LSU). There, according to the president's official biographer, Oleg Blotsky, Putin became "assistant to the rector for international issues—a position that was traditionally held by foreign intelligence officers."[6] But former KGB General Oleg Kalugin characterized Putin's official duties at the university somewhat more broadly: according to him, Putin was not merely a "foreign intelligence agent," but the KGB's resident at LSU.

In addition to the assistant to the rector on international issues, LSU had a position with a higher status that was also given to "KGB officers in plainclothes": the pro-rector on international issues. This position was occupied in 1990 by Yuri Molchanov. In effect, Molchanov and Putin worked together, and according to a number of sources—including reporter Boris Vishnevsky, a columnist for *Novaya Gazeta* and a member of the Yabloko party's leadership, who was personally well acquainted with most of St. Petersburg's politicians—Putin's official title was not "assistant to the rector," but "assistant to the pro-rector."[7] His duties in this position included monitoring and supervising foreign students at LSU.

Thus it was Molchanov, the pro-rector on international issues (and not the LSU rector Stanislav Merkuriev), who was Putin's immediate superior, on paper as well as in practice. It is quite possible that Molchanov was also Putin's immediate superior in the active reserve of the KGB. (Jumping ahead, let us point out that in the fall of 2003, Molchanov became St. Petersburg's deputy governor in charge of investments, overseeing most of the city's major projects, while Sergei Mironov, a close friend and former business partner of Molchanov's stepson, Andrei Molchanov, became the head of the upper house of the Russian parliament.)

At LSU, Putin began to display his managerial abilities. Universities at this time had no right simply to rent out their facilities to foreign persons, physical or legal. This prohibition could be circumvented, however: the lessor and the lessee could set up a joint venture and legally use the lessor's property "jointly." The Soviet (government) side's share of such a joint venture's capital could be minimal. Molchanov and Putin established a joint venture of this kind between LSU and Procter & Gamble, in which LSU's ownership was only 1 percent. Procter & Gamble thereby acquired the right to occupy one of the mansions on Universitetskaya Embankment and for a whole year provided professors with hard-to-find American soap and laundry detergent.[8] One might suppose, of course, that in return for renting out the building, Putin and Molchanov received not just soap and laundry detergent from Procter & Gamble, but money as well.

THE SECOND IN COMMAND AT THE ST. PETERSBURG MAYOR'S OFFICE

Soon, without resigning from the KGB or the university, Putin was given a third place of work, under Anatoly Sobchak. In his last interview, Sobchak said that he had remembered Putin as "a good student" and therefore had invited Putin to work with him after an encounter at the university.[9] It is obvious, however, that Sobchak was not telling the truth. Putin was sent to work with him by the KGB, which foresaw Sobchak's prospects.[10]

Putin himself tells a somewhat different story, but even from his own recollections it unequivocally follows that his transfer had been coordinated by his immediate superiors at the KGB:

Stanislav Petrovich Merkuriev was LSU's rector at the time. . . . At the university, I reestablished contact with my old friends from the law school. Some of them had stayed on at the law school, defended dissertations, and were now teachers, professors. It was one of them that asked me to help Anatoly Sobchak, who had by then become the head of the Lensovet [Leningrad city council]. He simply told me that Sobchak had no one on his team, that he was surrounded by crooks, and he asked me if I could help Sobchak.

"How?" I asked.

"Leave the university and go to work for him."

"You know, I have to think about it. After all, I'm a KGB agent. And he doesn't know it. I might compromise him."

"Go talk to him," my friend advised me.

It should be said that Sobchak by this time was already a well-known and popular figure. I myself followed what he said and what he did with great interest. I didn't like everything he did, that's true, but I respected him. It was also nice to know that he was a teacher from our university, a teacher with whom I had studied—although when I was a student, I had no personal contact with him. Later on, people often wrote that I had been almost his favorite student. That wasn't true. He was simply one of the professors whose lectures I attended for one or two semesters.

I met Anatoly Alexandrovich at the Lensovet, in his office. I remember our meeting well. I came in, introduced myself, and told him everything. He was an impulsive person and immediately said to me: "I'll talk to Stanislav Petrovich Merkuriev. Come to work for me. You can start on Monday. That's all. We'll work it out right now. You'll be transferred."

I had to tell him: "Anatoly Alexandrovich, it would be a pleasure for me to do so. This work interests me. I even want to transfer. But there's one thing that will probably make this transfer difficult."

He asked me: "What is that?"

I said: "I must tell you that I'm not simply an assistant to the rector. I'm a staff officer of the KGB."

He started thinking. This really was a surprise for him. He thought about it for a while. Finally he said: "So, who gives a . . . ?"

Of course, I didn't expect such a response, although I'd gotten used to many things over the years. We were seeing each other for the first time, after all. He was a professor, a doctor of law, the head of the Lensovet—and this was how he answered me. Without mincing words, so to speak.

Then he said to me: "I need an assistant. To be honest, I'm afraid to enter my reception office. I don't know who those people are in there."

. . . The boys who were sitting in Sobchak's reception office at this time and who formed his inner circle, as it were, conducted themselves in a gruff, crude manner, in the finest traditions of the Soviet Komsomol school. This naturally aroused great irritation among the deputies. . . . Since I understood this, I told Anatoly Alexandrovich directly that I would work for him with pleasure, but that I would then have to tell my superiors at the KGB that I was leaving the university.[11]

Sobchak was not a naive politician. He understood that the KGB was a very powerful force in Leningrad and that it was trying to plant its people in his entourage. But Sobchak was a naive human being. He believed that he would be able to outmaneuver the KGB. Oleg Kalugin writes that he personally informed Sobchak that there was a KGB officer named Scherbakov on his team. Sobchak replied: "Dear Oleg, I feel lonely. I need a person who can maintain contacts with the KGB, which controls the city." Sobchak asked Kalugin if he could recommend anyone. Kalugin, laughing, replied that no such person existed. This is when Putin showed up.

At the KGB, Putin's announcement that Sobchak was offering him a job was greeted with wild enthusiasm. No one expected that a KGB agent could be attached with such ease to the second highest ranking democrat in Russia, after Yeltsin. Putin recalls how he came "to inform his superiors" that he had an opportunity to work for Sobchak:

> I came to my superiors and said: "Anatoly Alexandrovich has made me an offer to leave the university and to go work for him. If this is impossible, I am ready to resign."
> To "resign" from the university, naturally, not from the KGB.
> They told me: "No, why resign? Go and work for him, no problem."[12]

Putin's university classmate Leonid Polokhov, who went on to become a Lensovet deputy, recalls that he first ran into Putin in the Mariinsky Palace (the city council building) in May 1990, when the council was holding a session to "ratify a deputy mandate for Sobchak." Polokhov says: "I came out of the meeting room and suddenly saw Putin. He told me that he was working for Sobchak as an assistant on international issues."[13]

Sobchak was indeed elected to the Lensovet on May 13, 1990—to a seat that had been left vacant after the March elections—so that he could be made its chairman. The leaders of the Lensovet's democratic majority (Pyotr Filippov and Marina Salye) had been unable to settle on which of them should occupy the top office, so they decided to invite one of the democratic members of the national parliament to become the head of the Lensovet. People's deputy Yuri Boldyrev rejected this offer, but people's deputy Anatoly Sobchak accepted it. One of their fellow deputies from the national parliament and the democratic Inter-Regional Deputy Group, Gavriil Popov, had already become the head of Moscow's city council (the Mossovet), while another, Sergei Stankevich, was his deputy. On May 23, ten days after being elected as a deputy, Sobchak was chosen as speaker of the Lensovet.[14]

It was exactly at this time, between May 13 and May 23, that Putin became Sobchak's assistant. It seems improbable that the operation to "attach" Putin to Sobchak was conducted precisely then by sheer coincidence. More likely, the KGB already knew from its own sources that Leningrad's democrats were about to elect Sobchak speaker of the Lensovet and was anxious to finalize Putin's transfer to Sobchak's office beforehand. Thus, Putin does not tell the whole truth in his memoirs and rearranges the actual order of events somewhat.

The identity of the "university classmate" and "friend from the law school" who had advised Putin to go work for Sobchak remains a mystery. For some reason, Putin does not tell us his name. This unnamed friend may have been Anatoly Shesteryuk, Putin's university classmate and a docent at LSU's law school; or it may have been the lawyer Nikolai Yegorov, also Putin's university classmate and a teacher at the university. Putin may have discussed this topic with Yuri Molchanov, the LSU pro-rector, who would certainly have provided backing for him in this matter both at LSU and within the KGB. But Molchanov was not a friend of Putin's from the law school, since he was not a lawyer but a physicist by training. Finally, Putin may also have consulted other "lawyers," including ones who did not work at the university, such as his KGB colleague Viktor Cherkesov, an LSU law school alumnus from the class of 1973 and one of Putin's closest friends and collaborators.

Right from the start, the prevailing opinion in Leningrad was that Putin had been "attached" to Sobchak by the KGB.[15] Even more radical opinions were voiced in the press: it was alleged that Putin had gotten hold of some compromising materials against Sobchak at the university, enabling him to manipulate the mayor in the future.[16] This was the opinion, for example, of the well-known Leningrad democrat Boris Vishnevsky:

My explanation (you can quote me) is simple: as assistant to the pro-rector on international issues, Putin had to read all the denunciations that LSU professors wrote against one another. I do not rule out the possibility that Putin came across some document signed by Sobchak. And what would have become of Sobchak's unblemished image as the father of Russian democracy if this document had been published?

Actually, the story of Putin's "attachment" to Sobchak was no different from numerous other such stories involving the embedding of KGB agents in other political and business organizations, beginning with Alexander Korzhakov's "attachment" to Yeltsin and Filipp Bobkov's "attachment" to Vladimir Gusinsky. Moreover, this pattern was characteristic not only of Russia, but also of the other republics of what was then still the USSR. Thus, the already quoted Vladimir Usoltsev (also known as KGB Lieutenant Colonel Gortanov), who had returned to the USSR before Putin, was dispatched by his KGB supervisors to Belorussia to serve as the deputy chief engineer at the Electronic Technology Research and Manufacturing Combine in Minsk. There, Gortanov joined the team of Alexander Dobrovolsky, the leading Belorussian democrat at the time, and became the manager of his election campaign for the Congress of People's Deputies of the USSR.[17] In Moscow, attempts were made to embed KGB Colonel Yevgeny Saushkin in the inner circle of Mayor Gavriil Popov, with Popov's own consent. Saushkin was an investigator who had once handled the case of the famous Soviet dissident Alexander Ginzburg. With Popov's support, Saushkin became a Mossovet deputy from the Democratic Russia movement. This was the end of his career as a democrat, however. After the Soviet Union collapsed in August 1991, he abandoned politics and went into business. But Popov acquired a new assistant and advisor in the non-staff KGB agent Konstantin Zatulin, who made two unsuccessful attempts to get elected to the Mossovet as a deputy from the Democratic Russia movement. (Today, Zatulin is an advisor to Mayor Yuri Luzhkov in Moscow and a United Russia deputy in the State Duma, the lower house of the Russian parliament.)

In Moldavia, Mircea Druk, who presumably was an agent of the KGB, became the head of the People's Front government. In Abkhazia, Tamaz Nadareishvili, also presumably a KGB agent, was elected as a deputy to Abkhazia's Supreme Council. Thus, neither Putin nor Gortanov nor Saushkin was an exception to the rule. All were examples of the KGB's general policy of embedding agents in democratic political organizations and private businesses. In this way, the KGB's active reserve officers became scouts in the enemy camp of the democrats, just as they had earlier been scouts abroad.

A SPECIALIST IN DEALING WITH PEOPLE

Sobchak was a politician who tended to get into conflicts and was not an easy person to deal with: he was arrogant, hot-tempered, and irritable. He was a brilliant orator, but had absolutely no talent for reaching agreements, making compromises, or coordinating his interests even with his allies and likeminded thinkers, not to mention his opponents or personal adversaries, who always surrounded him in large numbers. The politicians of Leningrad (which soon became St. Petersburg) acknowledged Sobchak's popularity and were initially prepared to treat the speaker of the Lensovet as first among equals. Sobchak, for his part, viewed them as nonentities or worthless demagogues. He recognized Leningrad's famous writers and academicians as being more or less on his own level, but he never regarded the city's democratic leaders or ordinary Lensovet deputies as his equals.

During his first months as Lensovet speaker, Sobchak lost the respect and support of St. Petersburg's deputies and of his own executive committee (the Lensovet's governing organ). At the same time, however, he retained the sympathy of the city's residents, which enabled him, after he resigned from the Lensovet, to become triumphantly elected as mayor in June 1991. Sobchak felt at ease in front of the awestruck "people" when he was elevated above them on a speaker's podium, and when he was surrounded by respectful students, and when he was giving orders to obedient functionaries. But he had absolutely no interest in routine organizational-administrative work, and he constantly needed people who could free him of his daily administrative duties. Therefore, Sobchak's throne was surrounded primarily by individuals who came out of the Komsomol or from managerial-administrative positions, and who knew how to read their boss's moods and how to please him—faceless executive managers without a sense of personal dignity, but with certain administrative talents. As is well known, one such manager was Vladimir Anatolyevich Yakovlev, who first served as Sobchak's deputy and then successfully squeezed his boss out of his job and became mayor of St. Petersburg.

Two individuals who differed to some extent from the other members of Sobchak's entourage were Anatoly Chubais and

Alexei Kudrin. But Chubais, too—despite his pragmatic flair for remaining on good terms with his superiors and for finding a use for all people, even the inconvenient ones—had partly fallen out of favor with Sobchak by the end of the summer of 1991. If Yegor Gaidar had not taken Chubais to work for him in Moscow after he became deputy prime minister in the new government in the fall of 1991, it is unlikely that Chubais's relations with Sobchak would have remained good.

As one of Putin's classmates from the Andropov Red Banner Institute recalled, at the institute they were taught "the correct way to establish relations with people . . . to form interpersonal relations, to influence people."[18] And Putin himself liked to say, "I am a specialist in dealing with people."[19]

The milestones of Putin's career as a "specialist in dealing with people" are: Putin's immediate superior in Dresden, KGB Colonel Lazar Matveyev; Mayor Anatoly Sobchak; Sobchak's wife, Lyudmila Narusova; Sobchak's and Narusova's daughter, Ksenia; President Yeltsin's property manager, Pavel Borodin; Yeltsin himself; Yeltsin's daughter Tatyana; the oligarch Boris Berezovsky; the German chancellor Gerhard Schröder; the U.S. president George W. Bush; the Italian prime minister Silvio Berlusconi.

Practically all of Putin's friends and close acquaintances from the KGB's "Big House" on Liteiny Prospect, the Andropov Red Banner Institute, the KGB's Dresden office, as well as his colleagues from the mayor's office and those who collaborated with him to build a criminal form of capitalism in St. Petersburg, are now part of the Russian government. Putin established excellent relations with all of them.

Boris Berezovsky recalls how Putin, as director of the FSB, came to his house with flowers to wish Berezovsky's wife, Yelena, a happy birthday—right at the time when Prime Minister Yevgeny Primakov's anti-Berezovsky campaign was at its height.

"You're crazy," said the astonished Berezovsky. "Primakov will find out. . . ."

"He can go to hell," Putin replied. "I'm not afraid of him."

Berezovsky saw that this was a person he could trust, a person he could rely on.

Meanwhile, Putin went to wish Yevgeny Primakov a happy birthday as well, with another bouquet of flowers.

Putin was indeed not afraid of anything, because all his steps were discussed and approved in advance by the leadership of the KGB or the *kontora*. With the *kontora*'s approval, he could support Sobchak in August 1991 and wish Berezovsky's wife a happy birthday during the height of the harassment campaign against him. And continue climbing up the career ladder, higher and higher.

"VICE SOBCHAK"

Initially, Putin worked for Sobchak on a voluntary basis, continuing to toil away at the university at the same time; it was only after two months that he transferred to a permanent position under Sobchak as an officer of the active reserve.[20] Putin served as official advisor to the speaker of the Lensovet from July 1990 to June 1991. The Lensovet's staffing structure was ratified at the beginning of July 1990, and from then on, all of deputy Sobchak's assistants, including Putin, became officially known as his "advisors."

On June 12, 1991, Sobchak was elected mayor of Leningrad. In accordance with a referendum held at the same time, the city was renamed St. Petersburg in September 1991. Putin later recalled:

> I played a certain role in helping Sobchak to become the city's first popularly elected mayor. I persuaded many deputies to establish the position of mayor in St. Petersburg, following Moscow's example. As head of the Lensovet, Sobchak could have been removed by the other deputies at any moment. . . . In the end, I managed to convince some of them that a mayoral position would be beneficial for the city. In addition, we managed to mobilize the district heads who felt the same way. They could not vote, but they could influence their deputies. As a result, the decision to establish a mayor's office in St. Petersburg was passed by the Lensovet by a margin of one vote.[21]

Putin clearly exaggerates his role in establishing a mayor's office in St. Petersburg and in getting Sobchak elected. In

1991, Putin was unknown to most of the deputies and had no authority. The idea of establishing a mayor's office came from the Lensovet's committee on government organization, headed by Mikhail Gorny, with the aim of forcing Sobchak to take responsibility for at least something in the city and not shift all accountability onto the Lensovet's executive committee.

One of the first things that Sobchak did after becoming mayor was establish the St. Petersburg International Relations Committee (IRC), appointing Putin as its head. This happened on June 28, 1991. From then on, Putin's status indeed began to grow. He turned out to be in charge of a very important bureaucratic agency.

In August 1991, Putin played a certain role in the complicated negotiations that Sobchak was conducting with the Leningrad KGB in order to ensure that the KGB would remain neutral in the conflict between the city's democratic government and the State Emergency Committee. During the course of these negotiations, provisions were made to secure guarantees for KGB agents in the event of a victory by the democrats. Anatoly Kurkov, a member of the State Emergency Committee and Leningrad's top "chekist"—described by Putin as "a very decent man"[22]—not only went unpunished but remained at his post as head of the KGB's St. Petersburg and Leningrad region office until the end of November, when he transferred to the KGB's active reserve and went into the banking business. In his place, and over the protests of former dissidents, Sobchak appointed Putin's friend Viktor Cherkesov, about whom Sobchak himself had said: "Cherkesov works for those who are in control. These are people for whom the terms 'rule of law' and 'democracy' simply have no meaning. They only understand orders. For them, laws and rights are nothing but obstacles." But since Sobchak believed that the KGB controlled the city, he concluded that it would be impossible to govern without the KGB.

From June 1991 on, whenever the St. Petersburg city government was reorganized, Putin's role and influence increased. After the liquidation of the State Emergency Committee, Putin resigned from the KGB, left the Communist Party, and was transferred to the KGB's active reserve with the rank of lieutenant colonel. He was appointed deputy mayor of St. Petersburg at the end of 1991, while remaining at the helm of the IRC.

From 1992 on, it was Putin that Sobchak started leaving in charge during his private trips abroad (although Putin, too, spent a great deal of time in other countries). It was Putin who kept the seal with Sobchak's signature. In the mayor's absence he always made independent decisions.[23] Putin has even described how Sobchak, before leaving, would give him blank sheets of paper with his signature already in place.[24] At the same time, Putin tried to remain in the shadows as much as possible, leaving all public functions to Sobchak; he avoided advertising himself and rarely made appearances on television or in the press. Possibly, this was because speaking in public was always difficult for him. On the rare occasions when he had to appear before the Lensovet, his speeches sounded short and stiff. Putin was simply afraid of speaking at length, and he employed stiffness to cover up his lack of oratorical skill. Sobchak once said: "Putin came back from the meeting. I'd never seen him in such a state. He was all blue for some reason, and it looked like he had lost a few kilograms!"

Gradually, Putin acquired control not only over foreign economic relations, but also over many other important areas of the city's political and economic life. Specifically, he coordinated the work of St. Petersburg's law enforcement agencies, including the Internal Affairs Directorate (GUVD) for St. Petersburg and the Leningrad region, the Administrative Directorate, the Hotel Directorate, the Justice Department (headed by Alexei Kudrin), the Registration Chamber, and the Public Relations Directorate (headed by Alexander Bespalov). As a result, an unwritten rule developed at the mayor's office: all key decisions had to pass through Putin. Sobchak, too, considered it important that the drafts of his decisions and resolutions be stamped with his deputy's approval. Putin was also put in charge of the Committee on Operational Issues at the mayor's office. Deputies noted that Putin, by contrast with Sobchak, always conducted city government sessions "in a business-like and effective manner."

On March 16, 1994, Sobchak once again reorganized St. Petersburg's city government, forming a new government and becoming its head. Putin was appointed first deputy head of the government, deputy mayor in charge of international and foreign economic relations, and head of the International Relations Committee. Several first deputy mayor and deputy mayor positions were created. In addition to Putin, the two individuals who became first deputy mayors were St. Petersburg's future mayor Vladimir Yakovlev (head of the Committee on the Municipal Economy at the mayor's office) and Alexei Kudrin (head of the Committee on Economics and Finance), who would become a minister in President Putin's government. Valery Malyshev (Sobchak's chief of staff), Vitaly Mutko (head of the Committee on Social Issues), Mikhail Manevich (head of the Committee on City Property Management), and Oleg Kharchenko (head of the Committee on City Planning and Architecture) became deputy mayors.

Later in the year, Putin's official title was changed again, to first deputy mayor of St. Petersburg and head of the International Relations Committee. Yakovlev, Kudrin, and Malyshev were also first deputy mayors and heads of city government committees.

Sobchak hardly interfered at all in the everyday activities of his deputies and was only interested in his public duties. Although he occasionally displayed a tendency to petty tyranny when it came to minor details, Sobchak generally reigned rather than governed, and sometimes spent months at a time traveling abroad.

In effect, St. Petersburg under Sobchak was governed by two deputy mayors, Putin and Yakovlev. (The third de facto co-ruler of St. Petersburg, somewhat less important than the other two, was Kudrin, the city's minister of finance.) One might say that Putin and Yakovlev divided the city's economy between themselves like brothers: Yakovlev inherited the old Soviet city economy, construction, the housing and residential complex, and transportation, while Putin was given control over the new capitalist economy, privatization, foreign investments, and joint ventures. Putin did not aspire to visible power, preferring instead the role of an éminence grise. By contrast, Yakovlev cautiously (given Sobchak's jealous personality) but methodically promoted his image in the city, coming across as a businesslike executive manager; and this is what enabled him, in the spring of 1996, to surprise Sobchak by entering the mayoral race and to defeat Sobchak in the election.

In March 1994, Putin was appointed head of a task force to prepare plans for the reconstruction and expansion of the Pulkovo airport. In April, he joined the supervisory council of the St. Petersburg Bank for Reconstruction and Development. (Sobchak and Yakovlev also joined the supervisory council.) At the same time, Putin was delegated to oversee the election campaign for the new St. Petersburg Legislative Assembly on behalf of the city government, and to create a political coalition—All of St. Petersburg, led by Sergei Beliayev, former chairman of the Committee on City Property Management—that would be supportive of the mayor's office. All of St. Petersburg had little success in the political arena, and more than half the city's districts did not participate in the spring 1994 election.

In the fall of 1994, Putin oversaw an election for the legislative assembly in which about half the seats went to businessmen who were loyal to the mayor's office and to politicians of a centrist and moderate-democratic orientation (the so-called "United Democratic List," which included candidates from All of St. Petersburg, the St. Petersburg Democratic Union, and some independents). Second place in the election was taken by the Leningrad Communists (four seats), and third by the Favorite City coalition (three seats). One the independents elected to the assembly was Sergei Mironov, a protégé of the Molchanov family.

With support from a group of independent deputies in the legislative assembly, Putin managed to get the Favorite City faction to withdraw the nomination of Rear Admiral Vyacheslav Scherbakov—which was unacceptable to the mayor's office—and to have the neutral Yuri Kravtsov (a Favorite City member) elected speaker of the assembly. He also succeeded in getting the independent deputies Sergei Mironov and Viktor Novoselov elected deputy speakers.

At the end of April 1995, Prime Minister Viktor Chernomyrdin instructed Sobchak to establish a St. Petersburg office for Our Home Is Russia (NDR), a pro-government party that was being created on Yeltsin's orders. It was evident that the party's political objective would be to support Yeltsin's candidacy in the 1996 presidential election.

Sobchak assigned the organization of the St. Petersburg NDR office to Putin, who became head of the party's organizational committee. The twenty-one members of the committee included deputy Vladimir Kolovay, president of the joint venture Lenvest; Anatoly Turchak, president of the Leninets company; deputy Sergei Nikeshin, president of the Dvatsaty Trest finance and construction company; Boris Petrov, general manager of the St. Petersburg office of the ITAR-TASS news agency; Lyudmila Verbitskaya, rector of St. Petersburg State University; and Dmitry Rozhdestvensky, president of the Russkoye Video television company.

At the time, the St. Petersburg branch of former prime minister Yegor Gaidar's party, the Democratic Choice of Russia (DVR), had two wings: a "pragmatic wing" (mainly businessmen) and a "human rights wing" (mainly old dissidents). Putin persuaded the DVR's pragmatic wing to help in the creation of NDR. A ceremonial assembly was held on May 5, 1995, to establish an NDR office in St. Petersburg. At this assembly, Putin was elected head of the regional office's advisory board. In Moscow on May 12, at a congress that established NDR as an official party, Putin joined NDR's 126-member political council. He remained head of the party's St. Petersburg office until the summer of 1997.

On June 21 of that year, the third assembly of NDR's regional branch in St. Petersburg granted Putin's request to be relieved of his duties in view of the fact that he was moving to Moscow after being appointed head of the Main Control Directorate. Anatoly Turchak became the new head of NDR's St. Petersburg office. He was replaced in 1999 by Andrei Stepanov, president of the Petersburg Fuel Company. The chairmanship of NDR's St. Petersburg office was taken over by Vladimir Litvinenko in 2000. All three of these individuals were appointed by Putin, who remained a member of NDR's political council until he was elected president in 2000, although he did not take part in the party's congresses starting with the seventh congress in 1999.

In summer through fall of 1995, Putin supervised NDR's election campaign for the second convocation of the State Duma. The campaign was costly and elaborate. Putin managed to raise 1.1 billion nondenominated rubles for NDR (while NDR's central campaign headquarters raised no more than 15 million rubles). This money came mainly from St. Petersburg banks. The residents of St. Petersburg were overwhelmed by a multitude of color posters with Chernomyrdin's picture on expensive advertising stands—up to five identical posters on a single stand, and ten to fifteen posters on a single building wall. (The same thing could be observed in Moscow.) Putin himself explained this excess by saying that NDR's national leadership had given him a large number of posters and he saw no reason to let them go to waste.

Nonetheless, NDR lost the election. The "ruling party" managed to nominate a candidate (Alexei Alexandrov) only in the Northwestern District—one of eight city districts—and Putin's man lost the election to the Yabloko party's candidate, Anatoly Golov. In the party-list vote, NDR's list received the third-highest number of votes in the city (12.78 percent of the vote), coming in behind Yabloko (16.03 percent) and the Communist Party of the Russian Federation (13.21 percent), and slightly ahead of the DVR–United Democrats bloc (12.37 percent). NDR won only two seats in St. Petersburg, which went to Alexei Alexandrov and the mayor's wife, Lyudmila Narusova. Another member of St. Petersburg's NDR, Sergei Beliayev, also became a deputy; his votes came from the federal part of NDR's party list.

In March 1996, Putin joined the St. Petersburg branch of a movement for the public support of the president, a coalition of organizations that were in favor of a second term for President Yeltsin. This move provoked a response from Igor Artemyev, the head of Yabloko's St. Petersburg office and the authorized representative of candidate Grigory Yavlinsky (and currently the antimonopoly minister in President Putin's government). Artemyev submitted a complaint to the city prosecutor's office, claiming that Putin's participation in the movement violated the law "On the fundamental guarantees of citizens' voting rights," and specifically the restriction against "using specific official positions in order to create advantages for specific candidates." The prosecutor's office did not pursue this complaint, choosing to accept Putin's official explanation that he had joined the movement not as first deputy mayor, but as head of the NDR regional office.

In the spring of 1996, while serving as leader of this movement's and of NDR's regional headquarters and working toward

Yeltsin's re-election, Putin was also occupied with the campaign to get Sobchak re-elected as mayor of St. Petersburg. It was to Putin that Sobchak had assigned the task of persuading the deputies of the city's legislative assembly to shift the date of the election from June 16 to May 19 in order to cut short the campaigns of his opponents, the most dangerous of whom appeared to be Yuri Boldyrev. As Vishnevsky tells it, Putin arrived at the legislative assembly on the early morning of March 13 with a presidential decree that permitted the date of the election to be changed to May 19, and the draft of a resolution by Sobchak to reschedule the election. For a whole week, Putin "twisted the arms" of the deputies—coaxing some, promising top positions in the mayor's office to others, and asking yet others to come to terms with the inevitable.[25] As a result of Putin's exertions, on March 20—the last day when the election could still be legally rescheduled—a majority of the deputies voted in favor of the change. First deputy speaker Sergei Mironov, who presided over the hearing, proceeded as if a quorum had been reached, even though there was no quorum.

This bit of foul play, however, did not help Sobchak—or his campaign managers, Putin and Kudrin. Sobchak lost the election to Yakovlev.

The fact that Sobchak had little chance of being re-elected became clear at the very beginning of the campaign. NDR's fund had allocated a modest amount of resources to print the posters that so appealed to Putin, but this was clearly not enough to secure victory for Sobchak. Putin understood this now. More money was needed. At the beginning of April, at the White Nights Resort in Sestroretsk, Putin met with a group of heads of firms and joint-stock companies that had been co-founded by members of the city government. He proposed that they all chip in to Sobchak's campaign fund. Contrary to his expectations, the conversation turned out to be difficult. For all intents and purposes, the entrepreneurs denied Putin's request, letting him know that he could count only on the dividends received by the mayor's office on the city's share of the capital. They did not wish to invest their own resources in Sobchak's campaign: they saw that Sobchak would not get re-elected with Korzhakov working against him.

As Sobchak's campaign manager, Putin also pinned great hopes on material support from the Congress of Small and Mid-Level Businesses. But Sobchak failed to appear at the congress's key session; he simply forgot. Naturally, the congress refused to help the mayor. Putin's old friends Mikhail Mirilashvili and Dmitry Rozhdestvensky—the heads of Russkoye Video—promised to provide advertising for Sobchak on St. Petersburg's Channel Eleven and on federal television channels. In return, Sobchak promised to provide them with $300 million of subsidy credits. On Korzhakov's instigation, however, the Federal Tax Police began examining Russkoye Video's finances at this time, and Sobchak's public relations campaign on television never got off the ground.

Consequently, on the eve of the election, Sobchak and Putin were left without any resources. Putin was blamed for the defeat, accused of "completely failing to grasp the specifics of electoral techniques" and of "creating a political vacuum around Mayor Sobchak." But what could Putin do for such a lame duck without money?

Putin has said that after his and Sobchak's defeat, he declined the new mayor's offer to stay on as his deputy.[26] In this case, however, Putin was not telling the truth. Yakovlev could not have wanted to keep Putin as his deputy. This is what Vishnevsky has to say on the matter:

> There's a myth that when Sobchak lost the election, Yakovlev asked Putin to stay on, and Putin indignantly refused. All of that is nonsense. Two days after Yakovlev became mayor, I was in Smolny on some kind of business. I ran into Yakovlev. We were standing and talking. Some bureaucrat came up to us and said: "Vladimir Anatolievich, Putin is here. He's sitting and waiting to see how you will decide about him." I will always remember Yakovlev's reply. He turned red and said: "I don't want to hear anything more about that asshole."[27]

PUTIN'S IRC AS A MULTI-INDUSTRY CONCERN

As head of one of the most important committees at the mayor's office, Putin took an active part in the region's economic activities. His International Relations Committee co-founded several dozen and registered several thousand commercial enterprises in St. Petersburg. No uniform system for registering businesses existed at that time, and such registrations were handled by several different departments of the city government, including the IRC, which mainly registered joint ventures and other companies with foreign involvement or export-import interests. Companies that received "Putin's" registrations can usually be easily recognized in the mayor's office database by the prefix "AOL" in their license numbers—for example, AOL-165, AOL-244, and so on.

According to Putin himself, his position at the mayor's office "allowed him to solve a large number of problems that were of interest to various business organizations."[28] For example, he was co-founder of the city's most elite clubs, which allowed him to become personally acquainted with or have access to all the country's prominent businessmen, since they all frequented these clubs, which they themselves had created for their own use. In 1992, as head of the IRC, Putin personally facilitated a contract between the mayor's office and KPMG, a major international audit firm, and oversaw an investment project to organize Coca-Cola production facilities in St. Petersburg. He also helped a number of German companies get established in the city. He was instrumental in helping BNP-Dresdner Bank open a branch in St. Petersburg, making it one of the first foreign banks on Russian territory. Until December 2006, this bank's Russian subsidiary was headed by Putin's old German acquaintance Matthias Warnig, a former Stasi officer who had fled to Russia after the unification of Germany in order to avoid possible prosecution by the German government. In addition to serving as chairman of the Russian office of BNP-Dresdner Bank, Warnig subsequently became a Rossiya Bank shareholder.

Putin also secretly controlled the border department at the mayor's office. This department had monopoly rights to trade in goods confiscated by customs. Since it set its own prices, its own trusted wholesale dealers were given privileged access to tons of confiscated metals, shipments of alcohol, and all other goods that, due to inexperience or malicious intent, had not been outfitted with proper documentation and certification for import or export from the region.

"THE LIST OF PUTIN'S CRIMES"

Russia is a corrupt country ruled by corrupt officials, and everyone knows it. Many economic crimes were committed during the Yeltsin years (1991–1999), but they were not committed by Yeltsin personally out of self-seeking motives. This is something that Yeltsin's friends and enemies would probably agree on. With Putin's arrival, the situation changed. The head of the government was now a man who personally participated in operations that are most often known in everyday parlance as crimes. Of course, the formal right to define a crime in all civilized countries belongs to the courts. Therefore, we should emphasize that when we use the word "crime" in this chapter, we are not using it in a formal, legal sense—especially because not all of the accusations that have been brought against Putin in recent years have been verified. Some of them may be based on rumors. Others have been collected and publicized by his opponents or ill-wishers.

One such list of Putin's crimes appears to have been put together at the beginning of 1999. The document's style and appearance—the layout and typography—suggest that it was composed at one of the lower tiers of either the St. Petersburg prosecutor's office or one of the city's police precincts. It is possible that the report was prepared for a member of Mayor Yakovlev's entourage, or even for the mayor himself, in order to discredit Putin, whose career was flourishing. (He was already director of the FSB by this time.) Some of the facts laid out in this report are corroborated by other sources; others sound hollow. Nonetheless, the people who wrote it probably knew what they were writing about. But the typist who typed up the body of the text did not know whom the report was about and left the name of its protagonist blank. Putin's name was typed in later on an electric typewriter, along with the name of the organization for which he worked, the KGB.

Usually, the FSB left names blank not in reports about top government officials—to whose number Putin undoubtedly belonged at the time—but in reports about "objects of operational interest" and in analytic documents and reports dealing with the KGB's own agents, so as to prevent the technical staff (secretaries and typists) from knowing who was the subject of a particular document. But since Putin headed the FSB during those months, it is unlikely that this report about him was put together at the organization that he managed.

Here are some excerpts from this document concerning Putin's activities:

In the opinion of many people who knew Putin well, his desire for personal enrichment and absence of moral limits came to light at the very beginning of his career. . . .

He participated in privatization. Specifically, he facilitated the privatization of the following entities:

- Baltic Sea Steamship Company. Control over the company allowed him to arrange for the sale of Russian ships at reduced prices. All transactions were handled by crime boss I. I. Traber.
- The Samtrest Liquor Factory (through crime boss M. M. Mirilashvili, "Misha Kutaissky").
- Astoria Hotel.

In the fall of 1998, 40% of the shares of the Astoria Hotel were offered up for sale in St. Petersburg. Putin tried to increase his stake in the company that owns the hotel by buying the shares. However, he failed to do so: the shares were bought by A. V. Sabadazh, the director of the AFB-2 alcoholic beverage production facility. Putin threatened Sabadazh and told him that he would destroy the production facility and its owner. At the end of 1998, the two sides arrived at a compromise: Sabadazh paid Putin off (about $800,000).

When St. Petersburg's Channel Eleven was privatized (with Putin's help) and sold to the Russkoye Video channel, privatization regulations were violated. In connection with this case, criminal charges have been brought against Russkoye Video. They are currently under review by Yu. M. Vanyushin, senior investigator for cases of special importance at the Directory for the Investigation of Cases of Special Importance in the General Prosecutor's Office. D. Rozhdestvensky, the general manager of Russkoye Video, who paid for Putin's wife's trips abroad, has been arrested based on the evidence in the case.

The Russkoye Video Company illegally produced pornographic movies. The work was handled by D. Rozhdestvensky. . . . The materials of the case are in the possession of V. A. Lyseiko, deputy head of the Directorate for the Investigation of Cases of Special Importance at the

General Prosecutor's Office and the head of the investigative team. Deputy General Prosecutor Katyshev is acquainted with the facts of the Russkoye Video case. Putin is trying . . . to influence the outcome of the investigation.

As deputy mayor of St. Petersburg, Putin was responsible for licensing a number of casinos. He received $100,000–$300,000 in exchange for each license.

Putin's closest business collaborator is R. I. Tsepov, head of the Baltik-Eskort security agency. (The agency was founded by a certain Zolotov, who had formerly served as head of Sobchak's private security and is currently the head of Putin's private security.) In 1994, Tsepov was charged in accordance with Article 222 of the Russian Criminal Code of 1996 (illegally possessing and carrying firearms).

Despite this charge, Tsepov remains a staff officer at the Seventh Department of the St. Petersburg Regional Directorate for Combating Organized Crime. It was Tsepov who collected the money when licenses for the city's gambling businesses were handed out. The Conti casino may serve as an example. Its head, Mirilashvili, pays a monthly fee to Putin through Tsepov. The Farmavit Company pays Putin $20,000 every month.

In 1995, Tsepov gave Putin's wife an emerald that he had won in a card game from the crime boss "Botsman." "Botsman" had stolen the emerald in South Korea in 1994. Interpol has a search warrant out for the emerald (1995–1996 catalogues). Tsepov works for Putin on the condition that Putin will cover up his activities. Through Putin, Tsepov has obtained five different cover documents, including identity papers from the FSB, the SVR, and the Ministry of Internal Affairs.

In March 1998, Deputy General Prosecutor Katyshev revived criminal charges against Tsepov (the case is under review by the aforementioned investigator Yu. M. Vanyushin). At the present time, Tsepov is hiding from criminal prosecution in the Czech Republic, having left Russia using false identity papers (an international passport and driver's license made out under a false name by the FSB's St. Petersburg office).

The investigative team of the prosecutor's office (Yu. M. Vanyushin) possesses evidence that Makutov, the former head of a specialized bureau of ritual services, paid Putin $30,000 every month.

With the help of St. Petersburg's deputy governor Grishanov (former commander of the Baltic Fleet), Putin was involved in selling navy ships through the port of Lomonosov.

This port, which is located on the territory of a former military-naval base and was created by Sobchak, Putin, and Cherkesov, is a major crossing point for contraband exports of natural resources from Russia and for the import of foreign goods into our country. Russkoye Video's sea office was one of the organizations that handled such import-export transactions.

In the spring of 1996, approximately $30 million was transferred from Tsarskoselsky Bank to a Swiss bank account for Sobchak's election campaign. The transfer was overseen by Putin, Cherkesov, and Grigoriev. (The relevant materials are in the possession of B. O. Desyatnikov, head of the regional FSB's counterintelligence service.)

V. Golubev, administrative head of the Vasileostrovsky district, has been acquainted with Putin since both of them worked together at the Leningrad office of the KGB of the USSR. The former colleagues organized a number of companies for siphoning and appropriating budget resources.

Putin created a system for "selling" children abroad through the Tsentralny district orphanage in St. Petersburg. (The relevant materials are in the possession of V. A. Lyseiko, head of the investigative team, and Deputy General Prosecutor Katyshev.)

As deputy mayor, Putin organized the sale of submarines to other countries through the Leningrad Admiralty Association. In 1994, the association's deputy general manager was killed (according to one account, for refusing to authorize the illegal sale of military property to other countries).

The Baltic Financial Group (Kapysh, general manager) pays monthly fees to Putin and Cherkesov. In 1994–1995, Kapysh entered into conflict over an oil terminal at the Morskoy port with one of the terminal's managers. Kapysh ordered a contract killing of this manager. For $50,000, Putin persuaded the manager to resolve the conflict . . . after which, the manager emigrated to Israel.

According to existing evidence, Kapysh gave Putin $6,000,000, allegedly as a contribution for the 1996 presidential campaign. The money passed through one of the region's banks, which was shut down shortly afterward. [Pavel Kapysh was killed in the summer of 1999—the authors.]

The Dvadtsaty Trest Corporation, which was created by Putin and Legislative Assembly deputies Nikeshin and Goldman, transferred budget resources allocated for the construction of the Peter the Great business center to Spain. This money was used to buy a hotel in the city of Torrevieja. A part of the stolen resources went toward the purchase of a villa for Putin in the Spanish city of Benidor. (The relevant materials are in the possession of the Ministry of Finance's Audit Department for St. Petersburg and the Leningrad region.)

In 1997, Putin and Cherkesov illegally sold a building belonging to the newspaper *Chas Pik.* (The case is currently in court.) They have caused losses in the amount of several hundred thousand dollars to the newspaper *Moskovsky Komsomolets.*

Because Putin spent several years as second in command in Russia's crime capital, the "List of Putin's Crimes" may be considered endless. To it should probably be added a charge that is most clearly formulated in Vladimir Ivanidze's article, "Shady Connections in the Northern Capital: A Ton of Cocaine Has Been Discovered inside a Container for Canned Meat," published in the newspaper *Sovershenno Sekretno* in August 2000. As Ivanidze wrote, major channels for delivering cocaine to Europe passed through Russia. The narcotics trade was conducting operations on a very large scale: the shipments apprehended in Europe were hundreds of kilograms in size. But there was no evidence for the existence of a Russian delivery channel until a container of Colombian canned meat was seized near Vyborg in February 1993 and found to hold 1,092 kilograms of cocaine packed in jars. The participants on the bottom rung of the operation—Russian, Colombian, and Israeli citizens—were arrested, but the organizers of the sale escaped scot-free.

The cocaine obviously was not meant for Russia; the "canned meat" was supposed to be delivered to Germany. The shipment was being monitored, as European security services were conducting an operation with the aim of uncovering the entire narcotics network that stretched from Colombia to Germany. The cocaine was supposed to have been apprehended and destroyed in Germany, and all the participants in the crime were supposed to have been arrested. But everything turned out quite differently. The cocaine was apprehended by the Russian security services and stored for over two years at a warehouse in St. Petersburg, although by international rules it was supposed to be destroyed; and in 1996 it was shipped to Moscow "for further work"—right when Putin himself moved to Moscow. No one heard anything about this cocaine ever again.

After the ton of cocaine was impounded, the heads of the drug trade created a whole network of companies in St. Petersburg and Moscow, including a joint venture involving Putin's IRC. Foremost among these was the Belgian company DTI, created by Oskar Donat—who was arrested in Israel as a suspect in the Vyborg cocaine case, but soon released for lack of evidence. DTI was supposed to deliver the Colombian "meat products" from St. Petersburg to Holland. Yuval Shemesh, a partner of Donat's family in this business, was one of the people arrested and subsequently convicted on charges of organizing the delivery of the cocaine to Europe. Donat's and Shemesh's joint company, JT Communications Services, created one of the largest paging enterprises in St. Petersburg and Moscow. This, however, was merely a front for their real business activity, which was selling narcotics. It was to provide for this clandestine activity that DTI opened one of the largest customs terminals in St. Petersburg. DTI's principal partners in this connection were the Security Association of the Internal Affairs Directorate for St. Petersburg and the Leningrad region and the Special Department of the St. Petersburg military-naval base.

DIGRESSION ON THE MEANING OF THE WORD "CRIME"

Normally, the actions that are liable to criminal prosecution are those constituting violations of existing laws that are not subsequently repealed. In this respect, the situation in Russia during the 1990s was unique. After the collapse of the Soviet Union in August 1991, the old Soviet laws were not formally repealed, but they became virtually impossible to enforce—apart from those governing criminal offenses against individuals (murder, infliction of bodily injury, simple larceny, and robbery).

Soviet laws were largely aimed at ensuring the absence of private enterprise and private property. They included prohibitions against the use and possession of foreign currency; operations involving foreign currency were classified among the most serious crimes and in certain cases were punishable by death. There was a system of residence permits, essentially prohibiting people from moving to another place of residence and from changing jobs, which had not been formally repealed.

After August 1991, Russia was left in a state of lawlessness. But considering the atmosphere of global anarchy at that time, the level of self-regulation attained in Russia should be recognized as extremely high rather than extremely low, as might appear at first glance. The population developed its own rules of conduct relatively quickly, replacing the defunct Soviet laws with "understandings." And this was what the due process of law in Russia was based on, at all levels—on understandings.

Naturally, this system was defective. Many officials in Moscow and the provinces invented and altered laws, decisions, resolutions, and regulations in accordance with their own political and economic interests and those of their economic dependents and collaborators. Sometimes a law could be tailored to a specific operation (such as the "deposit auctions" for the privatization of government property in exchange for symbolic money), and then radically altered to suit another analogous operation. Under such conditions, with legislation and enforcement being what they were, even the most innocent administrative-economic action by an official or businessman was bound to violate something. At the same time, the most flagrant and unscrupulous economic and financial schemes often did not qualify as direct violations of the law and were not subject to prosecution.

All financial transactions were handled in cash—so-called "black money," which did not show up on the books—in rubles and foreign currency. Given the government's total lack of ability to monitor financial transactions, all attempts to collect taxes by relying on old tax regulations were meaningless. And it was simply impossible to create a new tax code for the country that Russia had become, with its wild, dynamic, rapidly developing capitalism. As a consequence, Russia's entire population paid no taxes on its off-the-books income, received in cash.

In 2000, when Putin came to power, the situation changed. No new laws were created, but the system of understandings was abolished. Judicial and law enforcement officials, appointed by the president, now began to investigate and prosecute the economic activities of the Russian population during the period of 1991–2000. These officials, however, had themselves contributed to the economic "crimes" of the previous decade. The government's main weapon became its power to select targets for persecution, investigation, and punishment from among the general population at its own discretion. Since everyone was vulnerable to such attacks, Putin and the government that he headed acquired the ability to destroy any opponent by investigating the victim's economic activities during the 1990s. The case of Mikhail Khodorkovsky—the arrested and convicted head of the Yukos Oil Company—became a classic example of this strategy. While Khodorkovsky had become an oligarch and a billionaire over the years, he had nonetheless remained a private entrepreneur, not a government official. There were hardly legitimate grounds for taking him to court for using loopholes in the existing legislation in the interests of his business. And although the president's political motives for putting Khodorkovsky in prison were obvious to everyone, the Russian court (which is neither free nor independent) took a formal approach to the case and convicted him of numerous violations committed by him and his company during the tumultuous preceding decade.

By contrast, there was no prosecution of Vasiliy Shakhnovsky, a top official in the Moscow mayor's office, although after leaving government service he became the owner of 7 percent of Menatep, the Gibraltar-based offshore bank that owned Yukos. It was none other than Shakhnovsky—as an employee of Moscow city government—who had overseen the transfer of Yukos's Moscow holdings to Menatep. In other words, it was obvious that Shakhnovsky had received 7 percent of the shares as a bribe.

The children of Prime Minister Viktor Chernomyrdin and those of Rem Vyakhirev, longtime head of Gazprom's board of directors, had become major shareholders in Gazprom by the end of Chernomyrdin's tenure as prime minister. But no one prosecuted them for their patently illegal dealings.

The case of Army General Alexander Starovoitov, head of the Federal Agency for Government Communication and Information (FAPSI), dragged on for several years. He was suspected of receiving a 20 percent commission fee on all purchases that his agency made from the German company Siemens, which paid the fee officially, in accordance with its contract with FAPSI. Starovoitov, on the other hand, naturally did not deposit these payments into the government budget. Attempts were made to put him on trial for bribe-taking, but they came to nothing. There are thousands of similar examples.

By any logic, after the economic lawlessness of 1991–2000, the whole population should have been given amnesty for the economic crimes of that decade, and any efforts to investigate and punish economic corruption should have been aimed only at government officials who took bribes and were guilty of extortion. Putin did exactly the opposite: he pardoned the crimes of the government officials, but reserved the right to investigate possible violations by businessmen.

This was accomplished in a rather clever fashion. In May–June 2000, the president-controlled State Duma passed a resolution to pardon all Russian citizens who had been decorated with government awards—essentially all government officials, including the members of the Duma, since every official who had spent any length of time in central or local government had received at least one government award, either during Soviet times or during the Yeltsin years. Essentially, the government had declared a limited amnesty for its own members. True, by making this move it incurred unexpected additional expenses. Vladimir Gusinsky, who was arrested at exactly this time, turned out to have been decorated with an Order of Friendship by Yeltsin, so he could not be charged with economic crimes that he had committed prior to 2000. Consequently, he was simply asked to hand over his property and to leave the country.

When the Russian parliament passed the amnesty law in June 2000, President Putin was also the recipient of a government award, having been decorated with the Order of Honor. Therefore, Putin's activities in St. Petersburg—which are described in this chapter and which often resemble activities that are classified as "economic crimes"—cannot serve as grounds for criminal prosecution against him.

THE LICENSING SCANDAL

The first and best-known scandal connected with Vladimir Putin's activities at the St. Petersburg mayor's office is the "raw materials in exchange for food" operation. At the end of 1991, as head of the St. Petersburg IRC, Putin initiated a program to provide food for St. Petersburg from abroad in exchange for

Russian raw materials. Putin himself described the situation as follows:

> In 1992, when the country was basically going through a food crisis, St. Petersburg was experiencing major problems. Our businessmen then proposed the following plan: they would be allowed to sell products abroad, mainly raw materials, and in return they would commit themselves to delivering food products [to St. Petersburg]. We had no other options. Therefore, the International Relations Committee, of which I was the head, agreed to this proposal. We obtained permission from the head of the government and handed out the necessary authorizations. The plan started working. The firms exported raw materials.... Unfortunately, some of the firms failed to fulfill the main part of the agreement: they did not deliver food products from abroad or they did not deliver as much as they were supposed to. They did not fulfill their obligations to the city.[29]

Putin dates the beginning of these events to 1992, but the first known document signed by Putin is dated December 4, 1991. On that day, Putin sent a letter to the Committee for External Economic Relations (CEER) of Russia's Ministry of the Economy. CEER was headed by Pyotr Aven—who currently is the president of Alfa Bank, a billionaire, an oligarch, and an eternal companion of Putin's. In this letter, Putin wrote:

> From January to February 1992, the region will be able to obtain food products only by importing them in exchange for exports.... For the period of January-February 1992, the region needs: 83,000 tons of frozen meat, 11,000 tons of butter, 3 tons of evaporated milk, 0.4 tons of baby food, 4.5 tons of vegetable oil, 56 tons of sugar, 2 tons of garlic, 3.5 tons of citrus products, 8 tons of cocoa. The total cost is $122 million.
>
> In view of the urgency of the situation and the need to begin exchange transactions, I am requesting that quotas be set for the export of the following types of raw materials: 750,000 cubic meters of wood, 150,000 tons of petroleum products, 30,000 tons of nonferrous scrap metal, 14 tons of rare-earth metals (tantalum, niobium, gadolinium, cerium, zirconium, yttrium, scandium, ytterbium), 1,000 tons of aluminum, 1 ton of copper, 20 tons of cement, and 1 ton of ammonium, at a total cost of $124 million.

In order to ensure the safety of the exchange transactions, I am also requesting permission to import 120,000 tons of cotton. Finally, I am requesting that the committee headed by myself be given the right to assign quotas and to issue licenses.[30]

On February 1, 1992, Pyotr Aven initialed Putin's request to grant the St. Petersburg IRC "the right to assign quotas and to issue licenses," and on March 25, Russia's Ministry of the Economy issued order No. 172, granting the St. Petersburg IRC the right to issue export licenses. Putin's committee, however, began issuing licenses even before it received official permission to do so.

The deputies of the St. Petersburg Legislative Assembly, who were in conflict with Sobchak and were assiduously trying to undermine the mayor's office, soon found out about this. Already on January 10, 1992, the thirteenth session of the city council established a special commission to investigate the activities of the IRC. The commission was led by Marina Salye, who headed the assembly's committee on food supply, and Yuri Gladkov, a member of the committee on trade and community services. (During the period 2003–2007, Gladkov was the deputy speaker of the assembly and a member of the Union of Right Forces faction.) The findings of the investigation surpassed the deputies' boldest expectations.[31]

RAW MATERIALS IN EXCHANGE FOR FOOD

Putin himself claimed that neither he nor his committee issued any export licenses: "We had no right to issue licenses. That's the whole point. The licenses were issued by various offices at the Ministry of the Economy. This is a federal organization that had no relation to the city's administration."[32]

But as the materials of Salye's investigation show, licenses were issued by the IRC and Putin acknowledged the fact that they had been issued. In a report "On the state of affairs concerning the issuing of licenses for supplying the city with food products," dated January 14, 1992, which the IRC head was obliged to submit to the St. Petersburg Legislative Assembly investigating commission, Putin wrote: "As of January 13, 1992, the International Relations Committee of St. Petersburg has issued licenses to the companies and in the amounts indicated in the [accompanying] table." This was followed by a list of the licenses that had been issued.

In 1991–1992, Putin used the pretext of providing food for the residents of St. Petersburg to make contracts with intermediary firms for the export of oil and gas products, lumber, metal, cotton, and other raw materials, costing over $92 million. In doing so, he failed to coordinate the IRC-issued export quotas with the Ministry of the Economy; that is, he went against the government's orders of January 9, 1992. Nor did he publicly announce a competitive bidding process to grant the licenses; that is, he went around the government's resolution No. 90, dated December 31, 1992, "On issuing licenses and quotas for the export and import of goods (products, services) on the territory of the Russian Federation in 1992." The firms that received licenses were handpicked by Putin himself.[33] They were not raw materials exporters; they did not specialize in raw materials; and they did not present contracts with foreign firms for the import of food products. Some of the firms were foreign; in other words, they were not subject to monitoring and review by the Russian government.

From a legal point of view, all the contracts made by the IRC were defective: some had not been signed or stamped by both parties, and some had accompanying supplements that were missing stamps or signatures; some were not dated; two were missing supplements that were mentioned in the contracts; some contained mathematical errors, corrections, changes. Some of the contracts were in Finnish without a Russian translation. In four of the contracts made by the IRC, "represented by Putin," Putin's printed name had the signature of his deputy, Alexander Gavriilovich Anikin, next to it. The total amount of money for which such defective contracts had been made added up to over $11.5 million.[34]

Putin himself signed at least four documents, including two licenses. One of them was issued to the Nevsky Dom company on December 20, 1991, granting it the right to export 150,000 tons of oil products (fuel oil, diesel oil, gasoline), costing over $32 million. The other was issued to the joint-stock company Fivekor, on December 26, authorizing it to export 50,000 cubic meters of wood, costing approximately $3 million (in exchange for evaporated milk). In addition, Putin signed two contracts. The first, signed on December 25, was a contract to grant a license to Georgy Miroshnik, the president of the International Trade Center Concern (Intercommerce–Formula 7), for the export of 150,000 tons of oil products (in exchange for frozen meat, potatoes, and sugar). The second, signed on January 3, 1992, was a contract with the LOKK (Leningrad Red Cross Society) municipal enterprise, authorizing it to receive a license for the export of rare-earth metals and three tons of A5N aluminum in exchange for 1,750 tons of meat.[35] Later that month, however, the license for the export of 150,000 tons of oil products passed from Miroshnik to Vladimir Smirnov's Nevsky Dom.

The LOKK municipal enterprise, which was interested in exporting aluminum, was nothing but a "commercial *publishing* enterprise" of the Red Cross Society's regional public organization. The head of the firm was Sergei Borisovich Platonov, who later became a business partner of Roman Tsepov, the head of the private security agency employed by Sobchak's wife and daughter, as well as Putin. Intercommerce–Formula 7, Miroshnik's Moscow-based company, was connected with the former Stasi officer Matthias Warnig. At least Lyudmila Putina's German friend Irene Pietsch claims that in 1996 she would receive faxes from Lyudmila on Intercommerce stationery when Lyudmila was staying in Moscow with the Putins' friends: "These were East Germans whom Putin had met in Dresden and who were now living in Moscow, where the husband occupied a managing position in one of the large German banks."[36] The "East Germans" were Warnig and his wife, and the "large German bank" was Dresdner Bank.

The four known documents that Putin signed personally were dated earlier than February 2, 1992, when Putin's letter was initialed by Aven, and earlier than March 25, 1992, when the Ministry of the Economy granted Putin's committee the right to issue export licenses. As for the two licenses referred to above, they were issued even before the corresponding contracts with the participating businesses had been made: the contract with Nevsky Dom was signed in January 1992 (the exact date is not indicated) and the contract with Fivekor was signed on November 1, 1992. The contract was for more than $32 million. It was made by A. G. Anikin and Nevsky Dom's deputy director

V. M. Vitenberg, but signed by two completely different people, whom the St. Petersburg city council's special commission was unable to identify. The licenses bore the signatures of Putin and the general manager of a completely different company, registered at a different address, but with the same name—Nevsky Dom.

This was not the only license signed for Putin by his immediate subordinate Alexander Anikin, the deputy head of the IRC and head of the directorate of external economic relations. Anikin signed at least thirteen licenses and contracts dated before the IRC received its official permission to issue licenses from CEER. All these contracts involved barter agreements: the committee issued companies "licenses to export" specific types and amounts of raw materials, while the companies undertook to exchange the raw materials for food. In violation of resolution No. 90, made by the federal government on December 31, 1991, which granted the right to issue licenses for the import and export of goods exclusively to CEER and its local representatives, the St. Petersburg IRC issued licenses for transactions amounting to more than $95 million.

The true objective of the "contracting parties" was not to deliver food to St. Petersburg. The whole point of the operation was to make a formal contract with a person whom one could trust, to issue him a license, to use this license to force customs to open the border, to send a shipment abroad, to sell it, and to pocket the proceeds. This is why there was no public bidding process for the licenses. Naturally, in order to bring this grandiose venture to fruition, one needed one's own "partners" from the underground economy, criminal and mafia groups, and all kinds of front organizations. Subsequently, Putin did not forget any of the people involved in this operation. For example, the former head of a division of the St. Petersburg Internal Affairs Directorate, Vladimir Mikhailovich Vitenberg, who participated in this venture, is now the general manager of the Krechet Security Enterprise, a private agency, and co-owner of several trading companies.

The profit-seeking motives of the IRC's members are confirmed by the colossal commission fees that were stipulated by the contracts, ranging from 25 percent to 50 percent. Meanwhile, the penalties for failing to deliver the food supplies were negligible. This, too, went against government regulations, which required all hard-currency proceeds from the barter operations to be used for the purchase of food for the city's population. Thus, the IRC's contract with LOKK, which Putin signed personally on January 3, 1992, stipulated a commission fee of $540,000 (25 percent). The contract between the IRC, "represented by committee chairman V. V. Putin," and the International Wood Market (Interlesbirzha), "represented by vice president V. N. Krylov," which was signed on January 10, 1992, stipulated a commission fee of $5,983,900 (50 percent). The IRC's contract with the Svyatoslav company, signed by the IRC and Vasily Khovanov, stipulated a commission fee of $12 million for the sale of 20,000 tons of cotton. The total commission fees for twelve contracts exceeded $34 million; on average, each commission fee constituted 37 percent of the sale.[37]

It is possible that the Moscow-based Svyatoslav was controlled by Dzhaldasbek Aitzhatanov, general manager of the Moscow Textile Production Enterprise, and Yuri Lvov, president of St. Petersburg Bank. These two individuals were also on the board of directors of Unikombank, which shared Svyatoslav's Moscow address. Several firms that received licenses from Putin opened accounts at Lvov's St. Petersburg Bank, and one of these firms was registered at this bank's address. It was precisely in order to carry out further hard-currency operations that Lvov, V. Smirnov, and Putin established the St. Petersburg currency market in 1992.

In addition to the unusually high commission fees, the contracts stipulated unusually low prices for the raw materials being exported. In the IRC's contract with the Dzhikop Corporation, to which the IRC had granted a license for the export of 13,997 kilograms of rare-earth metals, the prices of most were as low as one-seventh, one-tenth, one-twentieth, or even one two-thousandth of their market rates. For example, the contract stipulated a price of 72.6 DM for one kilogram of scandium, while the market price was higher than 150,000 DM. Through this contract alone, with its dumping-level prices, the city lost and somebody else made over 14 million DM, or over $9 million.[38]

Sometimes, licenses were issued for transactions that were smaller than those agreed upon in the contracts that preceded them. The IRC's contract with the Interwood Corporation, for instance, stipulated that the corporation would be issued a license to export 25,500 cubic meters of pine lumber, costing $2,805,000. What the corporation actually received, however, was a license to export only 500 cubic meters. The IRC made an identical contract with the Sansud company. The customs office did not accept the company's documents.[39] On January 15, 1992, the ship *Kosmonavt Vladimir Komarov*, which was taking raw materials out of the country, was stopped. Only on February 23, when Putin took personal responsibility for the matter, was the ship permitted to leave the country.[40]

The IRC's licensing agreements exhibited other price irregularities. For example, the same industrial wood cost $110 per ton in contract No. 4 and $140 per ton in contract No. 9. Ferrous scrap metal was assessed at $50 per ton in contract No. 6, while its real price in Czechoslovakia, where it was being exported, was at least $410 per ton. In contracts Nos. 3, 5, 7, and 8, sugar was assessed at $280 per ton, while its actual price at the time was less than $200.[41]

In 1992, Putin's IRC also granted the right to export aluminum and nonferrous metals to the Strim Corporation (also known as the Kvark Corporation in 1992).[42] Strim was led by Vladimir Yakunin, a KGB active reserve officer, and Yuri Kovalchuk, a businessman. Its members included Andrei Fursenko, future minister of education and science, and Vladimir Kolovay, the founder of one of St. Petersburg's first joint ventures and general manager of the Proletarskaya Pobeda shoe factory. All four were Putin's colleagues and collaborators in the KGB's invisible incursions into the private sector. The Strim Corporation sold its metal to obscure intermediaries at dumping-level prices; it then bought food products at prices that were artificially inflated. This clearly indicated the existence of an agreement on the side—a parallel contract that gave the difference between the artificially low prices of the sales and the artificially high costs of the purchases to an intermediary company.

Through Yakunin, who was on the board of directors of the Baltic Sea Steamship Company, Putin also controlled several other foreign trade organizations, which were given most-favorable-treatment status: Lenimpex, Lenfintorg, Lenexpo, and Veliky Gorod (the last of which mainly handled the contraband export of nonferrous metals).

As a result, Putin and the businessmen who stood behind him deprived the citizens of St. Petersburg of the only possibility to obtain food through trade that existed at the time. He also deprived the city of approximately $100 million. These are the losses that can be accounted for. But the government of Russia issued export quotas on raw materials in the amount of about $1 billion during those years; what happened to the remaining $900 million is not known. What is known is that 997 tons of highly refined A5N aluminum, costing over $717 million, disappeared—as did 20,000 tons of cement and 100,000 tons of cotton, costing $120 million.[43] Of the food imports received in exchange for what was exported but disappeared, only 128 tons of vegetable oil can be traced.[44]

The city "did not do everything that it might have done," as Putin himself acknowledged.

> We should have worked more closely with law enforcement and we should have used coercive tactics to make these companies deliver what they had promised. But it was useless to take them to court: they dissolved immediately, ceased to operate, and exported their goods. In essence, we had nothing to charge them with. Think back on those years: all kinds of organizations and pyramid schemes appeared all over the place. . . . We simply were not expecting it.[45]

But Putin, naturally, was the last person interested in pursuing and prosecuting these "organizations" and investigating their shady transactions. As Marina Salye's special commission concluded, "the analysis of the situation surrounding the export-import operations to provide food for the population of St. Petersburg was significantly hampered by the mayor's office officials responsible for the operations, V. V. Putin and A. G. Anikin," who failed to submit information and documents detailing the licensing deals.

> The discrepancies in the documents analyzed [by the commission] cannot be accounted for merely by the unprecedented carelessness and irresponsibility with which A. A. Sobchak, V. V. Putin, and A. G.

Anikin treated requests to provide answers to the deputies' questions.
. . . These discrepancies stem from attempts to conceal the true state
of affairs, to delay and confuse the investigation by making it necessary to verify an infinite number of facts. . . . From the legal point of
view, most of the contracts signed by the IRC allow the intermediary
firms to renege on their commitments. . . . The actions of IRC head V. V.
Putin and his deputy A. G. Anikin reveal a special interest in forming
contracts with and issuing licenses to specific individuals and firms.
. . . The head of the IRC, V. V. Putin, and his deputy, A. G. Anikin, have
displayed a degree of incompetence that borders on bad faith.

As a result, the special commission recommended that Putin
and Anikin be dismissed from their positions.

The special commission's materials were sent to the Main
Control Directorate of the presidential administration (which
was then headed by Yuri Boldyrev) and to the St. Petersburg
prosecutor's office (to city prosecutor Vladimir Yeremenko).
Minister Pyotr Aven, the former head of CEER, was officially
notified of the commission's findings.

For a while, the city council succeeded in prohibiting Putin
from issuing licenses; but on March 25, 1992, Aven once again
granted Putin's committee the right to issue licenses (order
No. 172). At the time, the St. Petersburg affairs of Aven's ministry were supervised by the newly appointed deputy minister
Mikhail Yefimovich Fradkov—who in the spring of 2004 would
become the prime minister of Russia.

On March 31, 1992, Yuri Boldyrev made a resolution concerning the special commission's report: "The Main Control
Directorate has received documents from St. Petersburg city
council representatives attesting to the necessity of removing
the head of the city's International Relations Committee Vladimir Vladimirovich Putin from his post. I request that the question of appointing him to any other post not be raised before
the Main Control Directorate reaches its final decision regarding this issue."[46]

The findings of the special commission's investigation
were heard by the city council on May 8. The council decided
to request that Mayor Sobchak dismiss Putin and Anikin from
their posts. But the St. Petersburg prosecutor's office found

nothing illegal in Putin's actions, although the city prosecutor sent Sobchak a statement about "the International Relations Committee's improperly written contracts and the incorrect format of certain licenses."

Ultimately, the scandals surrounding the IRC forced Anikin to resign (he became the general manager of Lenfintorg), and some of the contracts made under Putin were dissolved. Anikin's position passed to his deputy Alexei Borisovich Miller, who since May 2001 has been the head of Gazprom's board of directors.

As for Putin's assertion that the firms had "dissolved," the president was not telling the truth. Almost all of the physical and legal persons involved in the 1992 licensing controversy continued to participate in the economic life of the city and the country. Many of them followed Putin when he moved to Moscow, gaining in status as they did. Georgy Miroshnik's Moscow-based Intercommerce–Formula 7 was virtually the only exception to this rule.

Georgy Mikhailovich Miroshnik—who is also known as Nikolaides, and who according to some accounts is a descendant of the Nikolaides family, a clan of Tbilisi Greeks—was adopted by Mikhail Miroshnik, a Moldavian NKVD officer. In Soviet times, he was convicted three times and served a total of four years in prison. During perestroika, he opened a cooperative and founded the Formula 7 concern. In 1991, he became an advisor to Russia's vice president, Alexander Rutskoy. Miroshnik served as head of the Moscow Agroindustrial Market, purchasing goods from the Western Group of the Soviet Army (ZGV). He accused the ZGV's commander, General Matvei Burlakov, of theft when he himself was charged with appropriating $18 million. When Miroshnik was in Spain with Rutskoi as part of a government delegation to the Olympics in July 1992, his dacha outside Moscow was raided and searched. He did not come back to Russia and was put on the wanted list. In 1997, he was arrested in the United States while carrying a Greek passport made out to Nikolaides and sentenced to a year in prison for the possession of an unregistered weapon. After serving his sentence, he was deported to Greece—despite a request from the Russian General Prosecutor's Office to extradite him to Russia—and was handed another prison sentence there. Upon his release, he returned to Moscow with two passports (Greek and Russian) under the name Konstantin Atmansidis. On December 9, 2001, Miroshnik was arrested in Moscow, and the following November he was given a two-year sentence, of which he had already served almost a year. He was released in January 2003, before his term was over, on account of good behavior and poor health.

THE ST. PETERSBURG CASINO AFFAIR

At the end of 1991, St. Petersburg's law enforcement agencies, steered by Putin's IRC, entered into partnerships with the city's organized crime groups. This period saw the first divisions of property between two groups of people who controlled St. Petersburg, which was not for nothing known as the "crime capital of Russia": the chekists (KGB officers) and the criminals. The formal agreement between "the city" (the KGB) and "the businessmen" (the gangsters) concerning the joint organization of and control over the gambling business became a classic example of this kind of partnership.

In accordance with an order signed by Sobchak, the gambling business was supervised by Putin personally. The text of Sobchak's resolution read as follows:

Mayor of St. Petersburg
Order No. 753-r of December 24, 1991
ON THE REGULATION OF THE ACTIVITIES OF ENTERPRISES THAT DERIVE AN INCOME FROM THE GAMBLING BUSINESS IN THE ST. PETERSBURG FREE ENTERPRISE ZONE

In order to regulate the activities of all forms of enterprises that derive an income from the gambling business:

1. A permanent supervisory council will be established at the mayor's office for monitoring casinos and the gambling business. The supervisory council will include:
V. V. Putin, head of the International Relations Committee
G. S. Khizha, head of the Economic Development Committee
S. F. Medvedev, head of the Main Financial Directorate
D. N. Filippov, head of the Tax Inspections Office

N. M. Gorbachevsky, deputy head of the St. Petersburg Internal Affairs Directorate

A. I. Karmatsky, deputy head of the Federal Security Agency (AFB)

V. V. Putin will serve as the head of the supervisory council.

2. By January 15, 1992, in accordance with city council resolution No. 38, passed on October 15, 1991, the supervisory council will develop rules for operating gambling machines, proposals for fees, and procedures for levying municipal taxes on enterprises that have the right to operate gambling machines, card tables, roulette tables, and other gambling operations, on the territory of the city and the districts within the administrative jurisdiction of the St. Petersburg city council. The proposal packet will be submitted for review to the city council in January 1992.

3. A task force will be created in order to develop standard documentation for the regulation of activities associated with the gambling business. The task force will include:

K. A. Boldovsky, O. A. Safonov, V. V. Polomarchuk (International Relations Committee); N. N. Prikhozhdenko (Main Financial Directorate); V. I. Bakhvalova (Tax Inspections Office); M. I. Mikhailov, A. N. Gudz (City Internal Affairs Directorate); G. A. Korniyenko (Federal Security Agency); N. K. Lasovskaya (Mayor's Office Justice Committee).

By January 20, 1992, the task force will prepare a resolution on licensing the activities of businesses that derive an income from gambling operations.

4. By January 30, 1992, the heads of the district offices, the St. Petersburg Internal Affairs Directorate, the Main Financial Directorate, and the Tax Inspections Office will review the rights of all forms of enterprises involved in the gambling business to engage in the said form of business.

5. By January 30, 1992, the task force will prepare plans for a competition to find the best approach to organizing casinos in St. Petersburg. The task force will organize an open competition in accordance with this project once the project is approved.

6. By April 1, 1992, the city property committee, in coordination with the supervisory council, will allocate the necessary facilities for housing casinos.

7. The taxes collected on the casinos' profits will be used to finance top-priority social programs.

8. Oversight over the execution of this order is assigned to the head of the International Relations Committee, V. V. Putin.

Mayor of St. Petersburg, A. A. Sobchak

The Federal Security Agency (AFB) mentioned in the document was the former KGB and the future FSB of Russia. St. Petersburg's *siloviki* (the politicians who came from the security services) owned 51 percent of the shares in the gambling business. Organized crime groups owned 49 percent. On paper, only losses were indicated.

In his book *First Person* (2000)—without suspecting that Sobchak's order to appoint him as head of the city's gambling business would ever be made public—Putin himself described what happened to the proceeds from this business:

This was not my first visit to Hamburg. I was studying their gambling houses in the line of duty, if you can believe it. At that time, we were trying to bring some order to St. Petersburg's gambling business. I believed—I don't know whether I was right or not—that the gambling business is a form of enterprise that should be controlled by a state monopoly. But my position went against the antimonopoly law, which had already been passed. Nonetheless, I tried to do things so that the government, represented by the city, might establish firm control over the gambling industry.

To this end, we created a municipal enterprise that did not own any casinos, but controlled 51 percent of the shares of the city's gambling establishments. This enterprise included representatives from the main regulatory organizations: the FSB, the tax police, the tax inspections office. The expectation was that the government, as a shareholder, would receive dividends from 51 percent of the shares. In reality, this was a mistake, because you can own as many shares as you like and still not be able to control anything: all the money left the gambling tables without leaving a trace. The casinos' owners showed us nothing but losses. In other words, while we were calculating the profits and deciding how they could be used—toward the city's economic development, toward social subsidies—they were laughing at us and showing us losses. This was a typical mistake made by people who are encountering a market for the first time.

Later on, especially during Anatoly Sobchak's election campaign in 1996, our political opponents tried to find some kind of incriminating evidence in our activities, to accuse us of corruption. They claimed that the mayor's office had been involved in the gambling business. These claims were ridiculous. Everything that we did was absolutely transparent. The only thing that one can argue about is whether it was the right thing to do from an economic point of view.

Since the arrangement turned out to be ineffective and since it failed to achieve the desired results, it must be acknowledged that it had not been properly thought through. But if I had continued working in St. Petersburg, I would have finished off these casinos in any case. I would have forced them all to work for the needs of society and to share their profits with the city. This money would have gone to retired people, teachers, and doctors.[47]

It is hard to imagine that the casino-owning partners continued laughing and stealing for a period of four years (1992–1996) while the officials and agents of the FSB, the tax agencies, and the mayor's office either didn't notice or didn't do anything about it. More logical is to suppose that the officials were getting their share—just as they were everywhere else in the country, and not just in the gambling business. So where did the money go?

The "municipal enterprise" mentioned by Putin was the Neva Chance company. Putin's account, however, is imprecise. In March 1992, two subdivisions of the mayor's office—Putin's IRC and the Committee on City Property Management, which was then headed by Sergei Beliayev—created not a municipal enterprise, but a joint-stock company, named simply Casino. Putin's friend Valery Polomarchuk, an FSB active reserve officer, was appointed head of the company.

Initially, it was planned that this joint-stock company owned by the mayor's office—or rather, by two of its committees— would become directly involved in the gambling business itself, and that its sizable proceeds would be channeled into the budgets of various departments of the mayor's office by its head, who was trusted by its founders and above all by Putin. Such an organization, however, was vulnerable from a legal point of view. Therefore, the Casino company dissolved within a month, and in its place the mayor's office itself established a municipal enterprise called Neva Chance. But the address indicated on Neva Chance's official registration documents was the address of Putin's IRC—6 Antonenko Lane. This new enterprise was also headed by Valery Polomarchuk. Effective control over Neva Chance thus became consolidated in Putin's hands, while the other committees, including Sergei Beliayev's Committee on City Property Management, were squeezed out of a controlling stake in the operation and a share in its profits.

By contrast with the Casino joint-stock company, the Neva Chance municipal enterprise did not need to become directly involved in the gambling business. Along with other physical and legal persons, it was registered as the co-founder of both newly created and already existing gambling establishments, becoming the co-owner of these enterprises. Neva Chance's share of the authorized capital of these firms was usually 51 percent. It contributed this share not in cash (which the mayor's office did not have), but by relinquishing the right to collect rent for the facilities that the casinos occupied. The mayor's office and its committees contributed to the authorized capital of other commercial organizations—outside the gambling sphere—in exactly the same manner. This arrangement had been invented by the IRC's legal expert, Dmitry Medvedev. He was one of the first people in St. Petersburg, and in Russia as a whole, to figure out how the government could "join" a joint-stock company without breaking existing laws: not by contributing land or real estate, but by contributing rents on land and real estate. Today, Dmitry Medvedev is the president of Russia.

In July 1992, a closed joint-stock company named Neva Chance was founded to supplement the Neva Chance municipal enterprise. The new company was registered at the same IRC address, 6 Antonenko Lane, and had the same Polomarchuk at the helm. In February 1993, yet another organization was created, the Neva Chance open joint-stock corporation, again led by Polomarchuk but registered at 53 Sadovaya Street. This corporation had two new co-founders (replacing the mayor's office): the Committee on City Property Management and the Telekazino closed joint-stock company (founded earlier by the

Neva Chance municipal enterprise), together with Russkoye Video, headed by Dmitry Rozhdestvensky and Vladimir Grunin, colonel and former head of the "T" ("terrorism") service of the Leningrad KGB.

If by this point the reader has become completely confused, then the arrangement has done what it was supposed to do. This was precisely the reason for the constant creation of new organizations with the same name, registered at different or identical addresses, owned by different or identical co-founders, who often appeared as the co-owners of other organizations with the same names, but with other co-owners. With several different companies named Neva Chance to keep track of, neither the inquisitive deputies in the city council nor the investigators in the prosecutor's office could ever determine who owned or co-owned what, who controlled what, and who received which profits.

At the beginning of 1994, Polomarchuk was replaced as general manager by Igor Gorbenko, the founder and co-owner of the Conti casino, St. Petersburg's very first gambling establishment. Gorbenko's partner and principal owner of Conti was the mafia boss Mikhail Mirilashvili (now serving an eight-year prison term for organizing a revenge killing of two smalltime career criminals). At the same time, the firm acquired a third and altogether strange co-founder: St. Petersburg's International Rescue Fund. Just how the fund contributed to the city's rescue by getting involved in the gambling business, no one knew.

All together, between 1992 and 1995, the Neva Chance company founded about twenty-five different commercial enterprises, predominantly in the gambling industry or serving the gambling industry (for example, the Polli Plyus Company, the St. Petersburg Lotteries Company, several casinos—Telekazino, Fortuna Casino St. Petersburg, Panda, Sirius, Venetsiya, Kleo, Arkada). At least one of them (Fortuna Casino St. Petersburg) was headed by Polomarchuk. The Arkada Casino Company was co-founded by Neva Chance and Mirilashvili, Boris Spektor, and Dmitry Rozhdestvensky. Neva Chance entered into partnerships with analogous organizations in Moscow—for example, with the Olbi Group, owned by the Moscow-based financial magnate Oleg Boiko. The Planeta St. Petersburg gambling establishment was founded by Neva Chance and Planeta Olbi, a Moscow-based company (along with Boris Spektor). One of the co-founders of the St. Petersburg Lotteries Company was the Olbi Group. In December 1993, Polomarchuk became the head of the Olbi Group's St. Petersburg branch, Olbi St. Petersburg (after resigning from his post as general manager of Neva Chance and being replaced by Gorbenko).

In May 1993, the St. Petersburg municipal prosecutor's office—under city prosecutor Vladimir Yeremenko, who had already come up against Putin in the case of the illegal export licenses—reviewed the activities of an organization connected with Putin's gambling business, the joint venture Melodiya. The investigators determined that the firm had illegally acquired a $16 million profit from the gambling business. This prompted a general investigation by the prosecutor's office, which revealed that there were 180 gambling houses and 1,600 gambling machines operating in the city, and that in addition to the 26 registered casinos, the charters of over 100 other commercial enterprises made provisions for gambling activities. Meanwhile, a resolution passed on June 26, 1991, by Russia's Council of Ministers specified that businesses operating gambling establishments were required to obtain licenses from the Ministry of Finance. In St. Petersburg, there was only one casino—the Admiral municipal casino—that had such a license, which had been given to it by Yegor Gaidar, former deputy prime minister and minister of economics and finance. From the standpoint of federal law, every other gambling establishment in the city was illegal.

On February 12 and April 2, 1992, Mayor Anatoly Sobchak issued orders No. 134-R and No. 170-R instructing the administrators of the city's districts to shut down unlicensed gambling establishments.[48] These orders from the mayor were ignored by the gambling establishments, which had permits from their local district governments and from officials at the mayor's office. In their defense, they cited the fact that Russia had no formal federal law governing the gambling business. (Naturally, permits to operate gambling businesses in the city were granted, usually at the local level, in exchange for a bribe.)

The St. Petersburg prosecutor's office sent Sobchak an official report on September 3, 1993, notifying him that *all* gambling establishments in the city, with the exception of the Admiral casino, were operating without federal licenses and thus violating the law. The prosecutor's office also noted that the Lenatraksion company, which operated gambling machines, had been illegally given a special license to run a gambling business—license No. 274, dated May 27, 1992, signed by Putin.[49] This gambit by the prosecutor's office produced no visible results.

In October 1993, the country was shaken by a general political crisis. Tanks were used to lay siege to the White House in Moscow, where the rebellious parliament was in session with Ruslan Khasbulatov presiding. Sobchak and Putin ended up on the winning side of this contest, and, as is well known, no one judges the winners. In 1993–1994, there were three election campaigns in a row: for the new Russian parliament at the end of 1993, for the St. Petersburg Legislative Assembly in the spring of 1994, and the special election for the Legislative Assembly. No one had any time to discuss the legality of the city's casinos, and thus the issue resurfaced only during the St. Petersburg mayoral race in the spring of 1996.

Sobchak's opponents—and the opponents of his campaign manager, Putin—posed legitimate questions about the proceeds of the gambling business, in which the municipal organizations controlled by Putin owned a share of 51 percent. Four years later, Putin responded to these questions: "The casinos' owners showed us nothing but losses. . . . But had I continued working in St. Petersburg, I would have finished off these casinos in any case."

It should be noted that Putin "finished off" casinos in a highly selective fashion. The former overseer of the entire network of St. Petersburg's casinos, Valery Polomarchuk, left the Olbi Group to become Lukoil's representative in St. Petersburg. Today, the business of his brother Vladimir, his son Oleg, and his nephew Kirill is thriving in the city. At least once after being elected president, in 2002, Putin celebrated New Year's Eve at Polomarchuk's St. Petersburg apartment; and under Polomarchuk's protection, Lukoil's president, Vagit Alekperov, he was admitted into the tightly knit group of men and took part in the celebration.

Igor Gorbenko is today the president of the Conti Group and a leader of the gambling industry in Moscow and the country at large. Gorbenko created the Jackpot Unified Gambling System along with Boris Spektor. Like many of Putin's friends from St. Petersburg, Spektor followed Putin to Moscow, where he became the deputy general manager of the Jackpot Moscow Gambling System.

The one deviation from this pattern is Rozhdestvensky, Putin's former accomplice in the gambling business (and a close collaborator in establishing a St. Petersburg office for NDR in 1995). If Putin did not "finish him off" personally, then he allowed others to do so. Rozhdestvensky was arrested by the General Prosecutor's Office in September 1998, when Putin was director of the FSB. In the charges against him, no mention was made of the gambling business. The case began with tax claims against the St. Petersburg TV channel Russkoye Video, which had been privatized by Rozhdestvensky, followed by claims against the privatization itself. The real reason for the investigation, however, was the fact that Rozhdestvensky had sold his channel to Vladimir Gusinsky, who at that time was Putin's main political enemy. In the big political game, Gusinsky was betting on other horses: Yuri Luzhkov, Yevgeny Primakov, and Grigory Yavlinsky.

Rozhdestvensky was sent to the St. Petersburg FSB's pretrial detention facility. He was released, on the condition that he not leave the country, in August 2000—after the presidential election, which Putin had won, and after coming down with multiple diseases in prison, including a serious form of diabetes. In January 2002, he was sentenced to three years in prison but immediately pardoned. He died half a year later. According to the official account, the cause of death was a heart attack. There were speculations that Rozhdestvensky had been poisoned, however, and that he had been released from prison only so he could be poisoned while at liberty and the prison administration would not be held responsible for his death.[50]

THE SPAG COMPANY AFFAIR

On May 13, 2003, forty employees of Germany's Federal Criminal Police Office (BKA) raided the offices of the St. Petersburg Real Estate Holding Company (St. Petersburg Immobilien und

Beteiligungen Aktiengesellschaft or SPAG) in the little town of Mörfelden-Walldorf, in the south of Hessen. At the same time, the apartments of the company's managers were searched. Gerhard Schröder was informed about the police operation. Russia's Ministry of Internal Affairs was also notified. The unusual openness of the police stemmed from apprehensions that actions affecting a firm that once had ties to Putin might lead to complications on the diplomatic front.

On the same day, searches were conducted in a total of twenty-eight business and residential locations in the Rhein-Main region, Hamburg, and Munich. One of the companies searched was the Bavarian bank Baader Wertpapierhandels-bank AG, which had acquired 30 percent of SPAG's shares and had put them up for sale on the stock exchange. In the spring of 2003, SPAG's shares were still traded on the German stock market—in Berlin, Bremen, Stuttgart, Munich, and electronically. The shares cost 0.64 euros, having declined by approximately 98 percent from the record-high level (35.28 euros) reached in the summer of 1999.

SPAG had its own history. In 1992, Putin led a delegation from St. Petersburg on a visit to Frankfurt, where he and another member of the delegation, Vladimir Smirnov, persuaded a group of Frankfurt investors to create the SPAG company. This was Putin's and Smirnov's second trip to Frankfurt. In 2001, Smirnov described how he met Putin: "I met Vladimir Vladimirovich Putin in 1991 in Frankfurt-am-Main, where the question of attracting the first private Western investments to our city was being decided. . . . I have known Volodya for ten years now, and in all this time he has never once disappointed me, as an entrepreneur, as a professional, or as a human being."

On August 4, 1992, SPAG was established and registered with the Chamber of Commerce and Industry in Frankfurt. With Russian-German daughter companies as intermediaries, SPAG was supposed to use the money of foreign investors to purchase, renovate, and build real estate in St. Petersburg. The company's founders included Rudolf Ritter (the brother of Liechtenstein's national economy minister, Michael Ritter), a lawyer who was officially the deputy chairman of the company's advisory board and effectively the company's head;

the St. Petersburg Committee on City Property Management; St. Petersburg Bank; and the German-Russian joint venture Inform-Future.

In August 1992, the Committee on City Property Management was headed by Sergei Beliayev. St. Petersburg Bank was headed by Yuri Lvov (Russia's deputy minister of finance in 2000–2001, and subsequently the head of Gazprombank). Inform-Future was headed by Vladimir Smirnov, who had been employed as an advisor on Sobchak's staff since 1992. In February 2000, Smirnov became chairman of the board of the St. Petersburg Futures Exchange, a noncommercial partnership. From May to December 2001, he worked in Putin's Presidential Property Management Directorate as the general manager of the Product Deliveries Office. On January 3, 2002, he became the deputy general manager, on January 4 the temporary acting director, and in March the general manager of Tekhsnabexport, a state-owned company that exports uranium to other countries.

In addition to entrepreneurs, four government officials from the St. Petersburg mayor's office, including Putin, joined SPAG's advisory board in 1992. The mayor's office received two hundred shares of the company, but Putin transferred these shares to Smirnov in December 1994.

SPAG enjoyed Sobchak's patronage. "You have our political and administrative support," Sobchak wrote to SPAG in a letter of salutation. Apart from Putin, various individuals joined the constantly changing membership of SPAG's board of consultants. They included German Gref, future minister of economic development and trade; Oleg Kharchenko, head of the Committee on City Planning and Architecture; and Mikhail Manevich, who occupied various posts in the city's administration (until he was killed in August 1997). Putin himself, according to the company's documentation from 1992, was the "deputy head" of the company. According to other sources, he was merely a "consultant." Officially, he received no salary from SPAG. On May 23, 2000, SPAG's website announced that Putin was relieving himself of his duties before taking the presidential oath of office. By the following day, this announcement had disappeared. The current SPAG director, Markus Rese, explained that Putin had worked for the company as a consultant together with German Gref prior to March 2000.

On July 13, 1994, Putin's IRC registered the Znamenskaya company, headed by Vladimir Smirnov. The owner of 2,520 shares or 50.4 percent of Znamenskaya's authorized capital was SPAG. Through VS Real Estate Investments Ltd., a company registered on the island of Jersey, Smirnov's own offshore company came to own another 43.6 percent (beginning on October 20, 1995). The remaining shares belong to approximately ten other physical and legal persons, some of whom changed in 1995.

The structure of the joint venture Inform-Future, 51 percent of whose shares were owned by SPAG, was no less complex. Its eight co-owners included Smirnov himself and his two offshore firms, VS Real Estate Investments Ltd. from Jersey and E. C. Experts Ltd. from the Isle of Man. Until October 27, 1995, the territorial production complex of the housing division at the St. Petersburg mayor's office—a city government agency—was listed as one of the company's co-founders. From May 1991 on, the head of Inform-Future was Smirnov.

In other words, from 1994 on, Smirnov served as the head of two St. Petersburg firms—Znamenskaya and Inform-Future—that were wholly controlled by SPAG and connected with each other as well.

Less than a month after Inform-Future was registered, with lightning speed by Russian standards, it obtained a right to the indefinite use of 1,287 square meters of land in the center of St. Petersburg. The authorization was granted on instructions from Mayor Sobchak and signed on October 21, 1992. Article 2 of these instructions stated: "The joint Russian-German enterprise Inform-Future is to be given a plot of land, 1.2 hectares in area, on Konstitutsiya Square, in block 15, to the west of Varshavskaya Street, for building a hotel and a commercial center, for a period of 50 years." Inform-Future's partner in this joint venture was the territorial production complex of the housing division of the St. Petersburg mayor's office. In the city's tax inspection office, however, Inform-Future was registered under a different address, and its Russian partner—the city of St. Petersburg—had somehow evaporated, leaving the company with only three co-founders: E. C. Experts Ltd., VS Real

Estate Investments Ltd., and SPAG. Smirnov remained the general manager of the company.

The history of the Znamenskaya company followed a similar course. Less than a month after the company was registered, the city government gave it a whole block in the center of the city for the creation of a "business center." The city was to be compensated 1.5 billion rubles for relocating the displaced residents of buildings that were demolished or rebuilt. A year and a half later, another resolution on the same question included a request by Sobchak that Znamenskaya pay up the money it owed to the city. St. Petersburg's new mayor, Vladimir Yakovlev, also signed an order demanding that Znamenskaya's management pay its debt of 1.5 billion rubles. This meant that Smirnov had never paid the city the money it was owed for relocating the displaced residents.

In August 1994, Putin, representing the mayor's office, signed another important order, which had no direct relation to SPAG but did have a direct relation to Smirnov: Putin's order established the Petersburg Fuel Company (PTK). In 1997–1998, Smirnov was PTK's general manager; from January to May 2000, he was its president and the head of its board of directors. PTK's vice president from July 1998 until the beginning of 2000 was Vladimir Kumarin (also known as Barsukov). The company was given monopoly rights to the retail gasoline trade, including delivering gasoline to all city agencies. On top of this, Putin also signed an ordinance establishing a network of Petersburg Fuel Company gas stations.

Russia's law enforcement organs considered Kumarin (nicknamed "Kum") to be the founder, leader, and brain of the Tambov crime organization. In 1990–1993, Kumarin served a prison sentence for extortion. After being released in early 1993, he went into business in St. Petersburg, including the restaurant and casino business. According to some accounts, his crime organization was the biggest in St. Petersburg; according to other accounts, it was the second most important in terms of power and size. It included three to four hundred men who specialized in extortion, kidnapping, robbery, and criminal attacks. The organized crime group disposed of a surveillance service and a radio telephone monitoring service, had agents on the staff of the St. Petersburg Internal Affairs Directorate, maintained contacts with the Tornado and Komkon private security agencies, and was considered the most disciplined of the city's criminal organizations. There was an assassination attempt against Kumarin in 1994, killing his driver and bodyguard. Kumarin himself survived, but lost an arm. After a month in a coma, he went to Germany and Switzerland for medical treatment. Kumarin returned to St. Petersburg in 1996, changing his name to Barsukov.

PTK's shareholders included various legal and physical persons. The Committee on City Property Management owned the largest number of shares, 14.5 percent. A number of administrative organizations for the St. Petersburg and Leningrad regions also owned shares. Five percent of the shares were owned by Vita-X, a firm belonging to Viktor Khmarin, the honorary consul to the Seychelles Islands. Khmarin was Putin's friend and classmate at the university; his sister Lyudmila Khmarina was Putin's ex-bride, abandoned by Putin on the eve of their wedding.

At the beginning of 1996, SPAG officially notified the German Commercial Register that it possessed "major real estate holdings in St. Petersburg." The representative of the Chamber of Commerce and Industry in Frankfurt added, in the official documents, that "the rights to the St. Petersburg property remain unclear." Smirnov, however, repeatedly told interviewers that the construction and renovation projects in St. Petersburg were being funded exclusively through the sale of shares in the holding company's St. Petersburg affiliates on the Frankfurt stock exchange. Some publications even mentioned a price of 140 DM per share. But this was a serious exaggeration, and the actual price of SPAG's shares on the German stock exchange dropped almost without interruption after they were first offered for sale in 1997.

Between 1994 and 1998, Smirnov, Ritter, and Putin met repeatedly to discuss SPAG's problems. Klaus-Peter Sauer, a German accountant who participated in the creation of the company and remains one of its directors to this day, met with Putin six times, both in Russia and in Frankfurt. Sauer has also attested to at least one meeting between Putin and Ritter in

1994–1995. It is known for certain that Ritter met with Smirnov in August 1998.

The partners had a lot to talk about. The construction of a hotel and business center was supposed to be completed by 2001, as indicated in an official city notice. The project required $80–$100 million in foreign investments. On its website, SPAG announced that it was the only foreign organization that had acquired the right to invest in major construction projects in St. Petersburg. The company had in fact invested approximately 140 million DM in construction projects. But on the whole, SPAG's dealings increasingly resembled a simple scam.

It was at this time that the partnership between SPAG and Kumarin-Barsukov began. In the spring of 2004, German police questioned Kumarin-Barsukov (with the Russian General Prosecutor's Office acting as an intermediary). He spoke about it in an interview:

> What could I tell them? I myself found out about this project only in 1996, when I was receiving medical treatment in Germany after an assassination attempt. At that time, I was introduced to Rudi [Rudolf Ritter] and other people through mutual acquaintances, and they invited me to take part in the Znamenskaya project—we had to relocate the residents of three hundred communal apartments and build a business center. I joined its board of directors as vice president of the Petersburg Fuel Company in order to see if we should become involved in this project. We even relocated people from about seven communal apartments. But then we decided that we could make more money building gas stations, and I left the project.[51]

In reality, Kumarin-Barsukov joined Znamenskaya's board of directors only in 1999. He was elected to the board by four shareholders who remained unnamed in the company's prospectus. One of them was Smirnov.

In April 1999, in a report on Liechtenstein's role as a European center for money-laundering, the German intelligence agency (BND) named Rudolf Ritter, SPAG's founder and director, as an agent of the Ochoa brothers' Colombian drug cartel and Russian crime organizations. The BND reported that Ritter had created a whole network of front companies for the purpose of laundering money. The money was transferred through the Romanian IRB Bank (International Bank of Religions) to acquire real estate in Russia, which brought profits to Ritter, a major shareholder in SPAG.

The BND and other intelligence agencies, including Liechtenstein's, first took note of SPAG because the Austrian prosecutor Spitze—who had been appointed by Hans-Adam II, Prince of Liechtenstein, to investigate money-laundering operations— had come to the conclusion that Ritter was helping to transfer substantial amounts of money from SPAG's St. Petersburg headquarters to Vaduz, Liechtenstein's capital. On May 13, 1999, Rudolf Ritter was arrested in Vaduz in an operation carried out jointly by the Liechtenstein police and the Austrian finance team. Four other lawyers and businessmen were arrested along with him, including his partner Eugen von Hoffen-Heeb. Ritter was charged with illegal transactions amounting to $6–$8 million, which he had carried out in 1995.

On December 17, 1999, after the arrest of Ritter and von Hoffen-Heeb, the SPAG shareholders who had not yet been arrested held an "emergency meeting" to negotiate a merger between the company and its St. Petersburg daughter companies, Znamenskaya and Inform-Future, in whose authorized capital SPAG owned 51 percent of the shares. By signing a pledge agreement with Znamenskaya (on top of its 1997 investment contract), SPAG became Znamenskaya's owner, acquiring all its real estate in the historic center of St. Petersburg. This property included a business center on Tambovskaya Street (owned by Inform-Future) and the Nevsky International Center, a commercial and recreational complex (owned by Znamenskaya). In return for this "pledge," Smirnov received money. During the first half of 2000, SPAG transferred to Znamenskaya a sum amounting to millions of German marks.[52]

In 2000, the Ukrainian government, headed by Leonid Kuchma, suddenly became involved in the intrigues surrounding the SPAG affair. By this time, Russia's security services had spent a large amount of money in Germany to buy up documents that could compromise President Putin. One set of files concerning Putin turned out to be in the possession of Ukrainian intelligence (having been transferred to the head of the Ukrainian Security Service, Leonid Derkach). All this might never have come to light, had not a group of Kuchma's security officers directed by General Yevgeny Marchuk, the former head of the Ukrainian KGB, started illegally eavesdropping on and recording conversations in Kuchma's office in 2000. Among the hundreds of hours of recorded conversation, there were some that concerned the German intelligence file on Putin. These unauthorized recordings, known as the "Kuchma Tapes," were carried out of the country and, through the efforts of a whole group of people, were made public.

The Kuchma Tapes unequivocally prove one decisive fact: German intelligence did have a file on Putin's involvement in illegal operations, and in the opinion of the Ukrainian government it was undoubtedly compromising to President Putin. Here are some excerpts from these recorded conversations, from June 2000:

First Conversation

DERKACH: Leonid Danilovich, we have acquired interesting information from the Germans here. All right. This person has been arrested. He has not yet been transferred. Here.

KUCHMA (reading): Ritter, Rudolf Ritter.

DERKACH: Yes. In the case against these. For drug trafficking ... Here they are, the documents. Here, they have taken out the documents. And here is Vova Putin.

KUCHMA: This is about Putin?

DERKACH: So the Russians have bought up all of this. All of these documents here. We have the only ones left. And I think that Patrushev will be [in Kiev] on the fifteenth-sixteenth-seventeenth [of June]. This is for him to work on. . . .

KUCHMA: Hm.

DERKACH: But we'll keep them ourselves. They want to shut down everything here.

Second Conversation

KUCHMA: Give them out to Patrushev only if he signs for them! Are these truly valuable materials or not?

DERKACH: About . . .

KUCHMA: About Putin.

DERKACH: Yes. There's a lot that's very valuable. This is really a company that . . .

KUCHMA: No, you tell me, should we give this to Putin or tell him that we have these materials? . . .

DERKACH: Well, we could. But he will still know where we got these materials. . . .

KUCHMA: I'll say that our security service has interesting materials. I won't even send them to him.

DERKACH: And say that we got them from Germany, and that everything they had is in our possession. . . . No one has anything else. . . . Now, I've prepared all the documents about Putin and I've given them to you.

KUCHMA: All right, if it comes down to that. I'm not saying that I'll hand them over personally. Maybe you should give them to Patrushev?

DERKACH: No, I just . . . No matter how we decide, we'll have to hand them over in any case. Because they have bought up all these documents from all over Europe. Because ours are the only ones left. This security service in Germany . . . Therefore, he is very interested.

KUCHMA: What if I say that we have documents, authentic documents in Germany. Without going into details.

DERKACH: Aha.

KUCHMA: I'll say: "Give your people an order. Let them get in touch with our security service." And when they get in touch with you, you'll tell them: "I gave them to the president. Shit, I can't take them back from him."

DERKACH: Good.

KUCHMA: We have to play a little too.

Third Conversation

DERKACH: And another question, about Putin . . .

KUCHMA: I said: "Our security service got some materials from the Germans. They might be of interest to your country. So if you don't object, we will hand them over to Patrushev. The head of my security service will hand them over to Patrushev." I said: "I don't know whether the documents are valuable or not." So I was very proper about everything.

DERKACH: That's what you said, yes?

KUCHMA: Yes, yes. Did you meet with Patrushev?

DERKACH: I met with him, but I can't go ahead without you.

Fourth Conversation

KUCHMA: . . . From here on, our security services will continue working with the Russian security services. We have normal cooperation, and the process is in motion. . . . They have also begun looking into Putin. . . . I've been shown materials from Germany, absolutely reliable ones, about the creation of a company in St. Petersburg, in which Putin was involved. . . . The materials are authentic. . . . We have one stolen set, so to speak. The Russians have bought up everything else, down to the smallest details.

The international investigation of the activities of Ritter, von Hoffen-Heeb, and SPAG lasted for several years. On July 13, 2001, the prosecutor's office of Liechtenstein presented the arrested parties with charges of money-laundering and abuse of trust. Eugen von Hoffen-Heeb had already been sentenced to eight years in prison for fraud one month earlier, but he had filed an appeal. Liechtenstein's chief prosecutor, Gottfried Klotz, explained in an interview with *Kommersant* that "these gentlemen received proceeds from drug deals that were carried out by Colombian cartels and they laundered them on the stock market by buying SPAG's shares. On top of this, they bought the shares at inflated prices—in other words, while laundering money, they also defrauded their clients. In this way, they appropriated about 226,000 Swiss francs ($133,000)."[53] It was expected that the case would go to trial in October 2001. But this did not happen.

If Liechtenstein's prosecutor's office and the German government presented no claims against Putin, in the United States this matter was approached with greater caution. At the insistence of U.S. government officials, Russia was put on the Financial Action Task Force blacklist of states involved in money-laundering. According to a former top U.S. government official, one of the main reasons for putting Russia on the blacklist consisted in a large file of intelligence reports in which Putin's name appeared in connection with SPAG's illegal operations—even though the secretary of the Financial Action Task Force, Alison Benney, claimed that Russia was being put on the blacklist for ten different reasons, and not because of Putin and SPAG.[54]

Ritter's lawyers did not remain idle either, however. According to Hermann Bockel, who represented his interests, Ritter—the head of twenty-four trust funds in Liechtenstein—had been cleared of all but two charges. One of them was indeed connected with SPAG's shares, since the investigators believed that German investors had been defrauded of 300,000 DM by Ritter's actions. The other charge had no relation to SPAG; the investigators accused Ritter of accepting $1.5 million from a certain Juan Carlos Saavedra, who was suspected of working for Colombia's Cali drug cartel. Prior to being deposited into Ritter's trust funds, the Colombian's money was sent in bags from Milan and Madrid across Liechtenstein's borders.

After decisive steps were taken by the Germans, the Ritter and von Hoffen-Heeb case finally went to court in Liechtenstein in October 2003 (although the prosecutor's office had filed its indictment on December 9, 2002, presented it before the court on December 12, and registered it on December 23). The defendants argued that they had not laundered criminal money but had merely used legal methods for minimizing their taxable income. Von Hoffen-Heeb was given another year in prison (in addition to his eight-year sentence, of which he had already served three years). Ritter was given a suspended sentence of eighteen months for selling thirty SPAG shares to German investors at inflated prices outside the stock market.

Germany's law enforcement remained unsatisfied with the Liechtenstein court's verdict, and the Darmstadt prosecutor's office started another investigation into SPAG's money-laundering operations.[55] As of today, however, Ritter has not been put on trial in Germany. Perhaps German law enforcement agencies are waiting for the day when Putin is no longer in power and they will be able to question him for the missing answers to certain questions.

As for Liechtenstein, both Ritter and von Hoffen-Heeb were finally acquitted by a decision of the Liechtenstein Supreme Court, which went into effect in February 2005. In the court's opinion, Ritter had been unaware of the fact that his Colombian client Juan Carlos Saavedra was a criminal; neither of the defendants was guilty of money-laundering; and neither had any connections with drug cartels or other criminal organizations.[56]

THE "KUCHMA TAPES" AS A SOURCE FOR STUDYING CORRUPTION IN RUSSIA

The German intelligence file on Putin was not the only thing discussed in Kuchma's office when unauthorized recordings were being made there in 2000. Other matters pertaining to Putin and Russia came up as well. Among them:

1. In 2000, in violation of both Ukrainian and Russian law, the Russian company Sibaluminum was involved in the illegal and secret purchase of the Ukrainian company Ukrainian Aluminum for $100 million. This money was transferred to the offshore accounts of White Orient World Invest Ltd., based in Limassol, Cyprus. The Russian company avoided paying $20 million in Russian taxes, while Ukrainian Aluminum avoided the corresponding Ukrainian taxes.

2. With the knowledge and on the instructions of the Ukrainian president Leonid Kuchma, between $50 and $60 million in cash was illegally dispensed by Ukraina Bank for Putin's presidential campaign in Russia. In exchange for this money, $268,500,000 of Ukraine's government debt to Russia was written off after Putin's electoral victory. In other words, Putin used Russia's government budget to finance his own campaign, paying Ukraine $200 million from Russia's budget to do so. This money did not go to the Ukrainian treasury, however, but was transferred to offshore accounts on the instructions of the Ukrainian government. The transfer was handled by the Ukrainian company Itera.

These facts are drawn from the following transcripts of two conversations between President Leonid Kuchma and Mykola

Azarov, the head of Ukraine's tax administration. The vagueness and confusion of the text do not reflect errors in transcription or translation; this is exactly how Ukraine's government officials talk.

First Conversation: April 17, 2000

AZAROV: So you will now meet with Putin tomorrow, yes?

KUCHMA: Yes.

AZAROV: All right. Maybe you can give him the materials? For us, who we're dealing with is very important. If we're dealing with offshore companies, then not only does our money vanish, nor only does Russia's money vanish into offshore accounts, as is happening now, but there is real documentation of actual contracts. If an agreement for the delivery of oil products, gas, has been made with an offshore company, then we have no idea about anything and no control over anything. We don't know where everything is going. Therefore, I think that Putin must become interested in the question of where his money is going. Why shouldn't we work without intermediaries? Here, we can give him a report. The transactions go through eight or nine offshore companies. If we made agreements directly between our countries—our organizations and their organization, the Russian organization, directly, what objections could there be? We don't receive a kopek for any of this. . . . Practically everything is delivered through the offshore companies. I prepared this file for you. In general, of course, it would be good to work something out, so that we might be given information about all of these issues. But for now, Russia is a dark forest for us. It is sometimes easier for us to obtain information somewhere in Latvia than in Russia. I understand why, of course. Because all of them are implicated.

KUCHMA: Implicated. You said it.

AZAROV: All of them are implicated, involved. . . . Now about Ukrainian Aluminum. In general, are you aware of how all of that was privatized?

KUCHMA: Well, basically, Russian Aluminum was behind it.

Azarov: Sibaluminum.

Kuchma: Sibaluminum.

Azarov: But in principle, it was privatized—you can laugh if you want to—by the Cyprus offshore company, White Orient World Invest Ltd. Cyprus, Limassol.

Kuchma: This is where the money will come from?

Azarov: Yes. Where the money will come from.

Kuchma: This is Russian money. . . . Now, they are effectively under Putin's protection. . . . But these are enormous sums.

Azarov: Yes. But Cyprus, Limassol.

Kuchma: They don't pay anything from Cyprus.

Azarov: Well, now let's think about where this money will go. After all, we're also looking at this whole business in a strange way. We're building a budget. Our budget and Russia's budget. If all of this was done not through Cyprus, but directly, the way it was supposed to be done, then the Russian budget would have gotten its 20 percent, and we would have gotten ours.

Kuchma: Yes.

Azarov: But now we are going through all of these clients, and so on and so forth. . . . I'm just telling you so you know.

Kuchma: Well, I know that already. The most important thing is that it was sold for $100 million.

Second Conversation: July 15, 2000

Kuchma: Where did all the money go? Figure it out. Before the election in Russia, at Putin's request, we paid, I don't know, something like fifty or sixty million dollars. In cash. An export-import bank gave one loan and someone else also gave.

Azarov: Ukraina. Ukraina Bank.

Kuchma: Yes? Ukraina Bank?

Azarov: Yes.

Kuchma: The export-import bank settled its accounts with Ukraina Bank. It made an additional two million. . . . They told me that it gave about twenty million dollars out of thirty. So, go and make sure. This first thing I can go and make sure myself, if they won't give you the information. You must know how much Russia wrote off. I'm certain, and when they asked me, they told me, so to speak, that they wrote off not 53.7 million, but that they wrote off five times that amount.

AZAROV: The opposite.

KUCHMA: The opposite! In other words, they wrote off much more than that.

AZAROV: Much more.

KUCHMA: So then, did he show this "more much" or not? And this difference—

AZAROV (interrupting): In our mutual accounts.

KUCHMA: In our mutual accounts. And this difference, where did it go? It went through Itera, so as not to go through Gazprom. It would have been too noticeable there, so to speak. It was taken out directly through the offshore zones. Right? So just go and make sure.

THE OZERO COOPERATIVE

Every Soviet citizen wanted to have a good apartment and a dacha. Few people had a good apartment. Almost no one had a dacha. The future president, Vladimir Putin, wanted a good apartment and a dacha as soon as circumstances allowed. And circumstances allowed him to acquire them as early as 1993, just over a year after he became deputy mayor.

One of the most fashionable neighborhoods in St. Petersburg is Vasilievsky Island. It was to this neighborhood that Putin moved while working in St. Petersburg city government. He acquired an apartment in building No. 17 on Vasilievsky Island's second metro line in a very strange way. This building was put under major renovation, at city expense. The remodeled apartments in the elite building were intended to go to people on a waiting list to receive apartments from the city; but instead they went to completely different individuals. One was Putin, who explains his move to building No. 17 by saying that he exchanged apartments with somebody else. Indeed, on February 23, 1993, Putin received "exchange authorization" No.

205553/22. However, the column that was supposed to contain information about the person with whom Putin was exchanging apartments was left blank.

One is forced to draw the sad conclusion that a government official could not afford to buy an apartment and a dacha on his government salary, and needed some form of illegal income as well. Putin, of course, had this kind of income.

At the end of 1992, Putin bought two adjacent plots of land, 3,302 and 3,492 square meters in area, to build a dacha in the town of Solovyevka, in the Priozerny district of the Leningrad region. By the summer of 1996, a two-story dacha "resembling a palace" (152.9 square meters) had been built. Putin's summer house—registered in the name of his wife, Lyudmila—was worth about $500,000. "The house was made of brick, but the interior had wood paneling," Putin recalled, and there was a sauna on the first floor.

On August 12, 1996, Putin and his friends, including the husband of his secretary Marina Yentaltseva, celebrated a "wake for his old job"—the one he had lost because of Sobchak's defeat in the election. After spending some time in the sauna, they took a dip in a nearby lake and then returned, going into the recreation room without noticing that the sauna had caught fire in their absence. Putin's younger daughter, Katya, was in the kitchen on the first floor and ran outside immediately, while his older daughter, Masha, and Marina Yentaltseva were getting ready for bed on the second floor.

Wrapping himself in a sheet, Putin ran up to the second floor. He led his daughter and secretary out to the balcony, tied several sheets to the railing, and lowered Masha and Marina Yentaltseva to the ground, while Yentaltseva's husband caught them below.

All of the Putins' cash went up in flames along with their dacha—since like all true Russians, they did not keep their money (dollars, of course) in a bank; they kept it all in a briefcase. After evacuating his daughter and secretary from the second floor, Putin tried to locate the briefcase with his savings, but he couldn't find it in the dark (as the electricity had gone out as soon as the fire started):

And then I remember that the briefcase with the money is still in the room—all our savings. I think: how can I leave without the money? I come back, look around, stick my hand in one place, then another. . . . And I realize that another couple of seconds and everything will be over—there won't be any need to hurry. . . . Naturally, I give up looking for my treasure. I jump out on the balcony. The flames are roaring. I climb over the railing, grab the sheets, and begin to climb down. Suddenly, I realize: I'm naked. I only had time to wrap a sheet around myself. So picture the scene: the house is blazing, a naked man with a sheet wrapped around him is climbing down, the wind is spreading the sails, and people are standing around on the ground and watching in silence and with great interest. . . .

The house burned to the ground. The firemen arrived. But they ran out of water. But the lake is literally right there. I tell them: "How could you run out of water? There's a whole lake here!" They agree: "There's a lake. But there's no hose." The firemen came and left three times before everything burned to the ground. . . .

When the firemen made their report, they concluded that the builders were to blame: the heater hadn't been properly assembled. And if they're to blame, then they must pay for the damages. . . .

The first option was for them to pay in money. But it wasn't clear what money. . . . Basically, it wasn't clear how to assess the damage. So I liked the second option better: to force them to reconstruct everything on the same scale as it was before. This is what they did. They built exactly the same frame and hired a Polish company that finished everything. The builders did all of this in a year and a half. Everything became as it was before the fire and even a little better. Only we asked them to take away the sauna.[57]

The construction company could not refuse a request from a prominent official to "reconstruct everything on the same scale as it was before," free of charge.

While the builders were reconstructing the dacha, Putin, in order not to lose any time, created a dacha cooperative. On November 10, 1996, eight individuals signed an agreement establishing the Ozero dacha cooperative on the shore of the Komsomolskoye lake. In addition to Putin, who was then the deputy head of the Presidential Property Management Directorate, the co-founders of the cooperative included: the owners of the Strim Corporation and Rossiya Bank shareholders Yuri Valentinovich Kovalchuk and active reserve officer Vladimir Ivanovich Yakunin (a former KGB officer under diplomatic cover, currently chief vice president of the Russian Railways Company, created on the basis of the Ministry of Transportation); Andrei and Sergei Fursenko (brothers); Nikolai Shamalov, a Rossiya Bank shareholder and businessman who delivered equipment manufactured by the Siemens Corporation to St. Petersburg's dental clinics, and whose son Yuri has for some reason been appointed the head of Gazfond, Russia's largest pension fund; Viktor Myachin, the head of Rossiya Bank; and Vladimir Smirnov, who became the head of the cooperative.

The Ozero cooperative was protected by the Rif private security agency, owned by Barsukov-Kumarin. There was a lot to protect: three-story dachas built in the middle of the forest, a radio tower, a meteorological station, a landing for helicopters used by President Putin, FSB director Nikolai Patrushev, the president's plenipotentiary representative for the Northwestern District, Viktor Cherkesov. . . .

It was probably here on the banks of Komsomolskoye lake that Putin—perhaps because he was so traumatized by the incident of his dacha and the briefcase with his money burning up right in front of his eyes—developed a passion for constructing residences for himself. This passion truly took off once he became president.

From Yeltsin, Putin inherited twelve presidential residences and mansions: Novo-Ogarevo (Moscow region), Vatutinki (Moscow region), Rus' (Zavidovo, Tver region), Gorki-9 (Moscow region), Valday (Novgorod region), Bocharov Ruchey (Sochi, Krasnodarsk region), ABTs (Moscow), Shuyskaya Chupa (Karelia), Volzhskiy Utyos (Samara region), Sosny (Krasnoyarsk region), Angarskie Khutora (Irkutsk region), and Tantal (Saratov region). In March 2001, the Presidential Property Management Directorate sent the economic ministries a request to approve a project to rebuild the Vatutinki presidential mansion. The project included plans to purchase several Jacuzzis at a cost of $2.7 million.

Also in 2001, the historic Konstantinovsky Palace in Strelna near St. Petersburg was added to the list of presidential residences. The palace had to be renovated for this purpose, at an estimated cost of $50–$150 million.

At the beginning of 2003, Putin issued an order for the Vavilov Horticultural Research Institute to vacate its premises on St. Isaac's Square in St. Petersburg. The building was to be transferred to the Presidential Property Management Directorate, with a view to making it another presidential residence, since Strelna was located too far from the city center.

On April 29, 2003, the Moscow Shipbuilding and Repair Factory launched the newly manufactured yacht *Pallada*, costing approximately $4 million and intended for the president's use during sea trips. Previously, Putin had used the motor ship *Rossiya*, listed on the accounts of the Moscow River Fleet (and modernized in 1994 for Yeltsin in Finland), as well as the motor ship *Kavkaz*, which belonged to Federal Border Security.

But all this happened later. For the time being, left without a job after Sobchak's defeat, Putin decided to transfer as an officer of the active reserve to the Lenfintorg company. He became the company's general manager, a position reserved for him as a "backup landing strip." But then he suddenly received a summons to Moscow.

4

Putin in Moscow

DEPUTY HEAD OF THE PRESIDENTIAL PROPERTY MANAGEMENT DIRECTORATE

After Anatoly Sobchak was defeated in the St. Petersburg election and clouds began to gather around Putin as a result of the investigation into the IRC's activities, the question of transferring him to Moscow, preferably with a promotion in rank, became urgent. Anatoly Chubais, who in the summer of 1996 became Yeltsin's chief of staff, rendered Putin an invaluable service at this time: he obtained a transfer for Putin from St. Petersburg to Moscow and an appointment to the position of deputy head of the Presidential Property Management Directorate. For the St. Petersburg investigators and deputies who were looking into corruption in the city, Putin was now out of reach.

The new position promised work on a large scale. As deputy head of the Presidential Property Management Directorate from June 1996, Putin oversaw the real estate owned by the directorate, valued at approximately $600 billion. After the collapse of the Soviet Union, by order of President Yeltsin, Russia's foreign possessions were also put under the management of this directorate. They consisted of 715 properties in 78 different countries, adding up to over 550,000 square meters.

Putin was followed to the Presidential Property Management Directorate by his old Dresden acquaintance, KGB officer Sergei Chemezov. Here is what Chemezov himself said about this transfer: "I was recommended for the position of head of the Department of Foreign Economic Relations by Vladimir Vladimirovich. My work consisted of trying to bring some order into the use of Russia's foreign possessions, and of returning to the government what it had once owned but had lost due to poor management. Sometimes things came to light that made your hair stand up on end."

A part of Russia's foreign property was located in the territory of former Soviet republics and the countries of the Eastern Bloc. When the Soviet forces stationed in East Germany and the Western Group of the Soviet Army stationed in the territory of Poland, Czechoslovakia, and Hungary—comprising three million and almost one and a half million men, respectively (not counting their families)—were sent back to Russia, they left behind them a considerable amount of various kinds of property: kindergartens, schools, cultural centers, friendship society buildings, as well as buildings that housed foreign trade agencies, press offices, and so on. A certain part of the Soviet Union's foreign property was handed over to Eastern European countries. By agreement, the real estate could be transferred for sums approved by both sides or even for nothing. For enterprising people, this opened up broad opportunities. Real estate could be transferred for one price on paper and for a different price in reality—the difference ending up in the pockets of the various interested parties who were responsible for carrying out these transactions, which amounted to many millions of dollars.

Filipp Turover, a former Soviet citizen residing in Switzerland and serving as a consultant to a major Swiss bank, has made interesting observations about corruption in the upper echelons of the Russian government:

> Volodya Putin—that is a special story and a long story. I had a chance to encounter him. . . . During his eight months in the Presidential Property Management Directorate in 1996–1997, Putin was respon-

sible for Soviet property abroad. Let me explain. In addition to the former Soviet Union's debts, Russia inherited its foreign property, worth many billions of dollars, including property that belonged to the CPSU. In 1995–1996, various organizations made claims to this property: the Ministry of Internal Affairs, Minmorflot, and many others. But at the end of 1996, Yeltsin issued a decree that all of the USSR's and the CPSU's foreign property was to be transferred not to the Ministry of State Property, but for some reason to the Presidential Property Management Directorate. And it was at this point that Mr. Putin got his paws on it. Naturally, on orders from above. When he undertook the so-called classification of the foreign property of the former USSR and the CPSU in 1997, all kinds of corporations, proxy firms, and joint-stock companies were immediately formed. A large part of the most expensive real estate and other foreign holdings was transferred to these organizations. Thus, its foreign possessions reached the government in a highly pilfered form. And it had been pilfered by the current prime minister.

At the time, Putin was the prime minister.

The head of the Presidential Property Management Directorate was Pavel Borodin. Until 1993, he had been the head of the city council in Yakutsk. At this post, he had had an opportunity to win over Boris Yeltsin, who visited Yakutia in 1990. Yeltsin remembered the warm reception he had been given in the middle of the frozen Yakutian winter: traditional Yakutian tents set up for the important guest right on the airfield, a magnificent traditional fur costume handed to him as he came out of his airplane, a big banquet held in his honor.

Borodin was appointed acting head of the Main Social-Manufacturing Directorate of the presidential administration on April 1, 1993. In November, he became the head of the newly created Presidental Property Management Directorate. In 1996, he acquired a new deputy, Vladimir Putin, who brought with him a tried and tested officer of the FSB's active reserve, Sergei Chemezov. On August 23 that year, the Presidential Property Management Directorate signed a contract with Mercata, a Swiss company, for the renovation of the Grand Palace in the Kremlin. This lucrative contract was awarded without a competitive bidding process. Shortly afterward, Mercata won a bid to renovate the building of the Accounts Chamber. The total cost of the contracts amounted to approximately $492 million. As Swiss investigators subsequently established, in exchange for these contracts Mercata had paid $62 million in commission fees, 41 percent of which (equal to $25,607,978) was transferred to Swiss bank accounts controlled by Borodin and his relatives.

Borodin and Putin were unable to establish good relations with one another, however. It is possible that Borodin, as a representative of the old-school bureaucrats, perceived the young, energetic, and aggressive Putin as a threat to his own position (and rightly so). On the other hand, it is obvious that Putin, as an officer of the FSB's active reserve in Borodin's agency, both from Borodin's point of view and in actual fact was a spy who had been sent to him and who acquired access to all the secrets of the Presidential Property Management Directorate, which probably was comparable in size only to Gazprom.

Putin's job at the directorate was to oversee foreign economic relations and all the directorate's contractual and legal affairs. He was also responsible for creating companies to manage the Kremlin's property in other countries. Putin's first order of business at the directorate was to find apartments in Moscow for himself and the colleagues he had brought with him from St. Petersburg, since an apartment in Moscow is a very important step in building a government official's career and financial well-being.

People at the directorate suspected that Putin was loyal to other people and organizations, and that he had designs to take Borodin's place. Borodin did not intend to repeat Sobchak's mistake. Putin was not even admitted to the directorate's main office on Nikitsky Lane; his office was located on Varvarka Street. True, Putin did end up occupying Borodin's seat for three days when Yeltsin, on his daughter's advice, fired Borodin. But Yeltsin was quickly persuaded to reinstate Borodin. No one except Borodin took any note of this temporary dismissal. Borodin remembered it, and shortly after resuming his post he requested that Putin be taken away from him. The vengeful Putin paid Borodin back: as soon as Putin became acting president, he removed Borodin from his post and appointed him secretary of the Union of Russia and Belarus—the most meaningless of all government organizations.

HEAD OF THE MAIN CONTROL DIRECTORATE

As is the rule in Russia's bureaucratic machine, Putin was transferred and given a promotion at the same time. Chubais became first deputy prime minister in March 1997, being replaced as the president's chief of staff by Yeltsin's future son-in-law Valentin Yumashev. Chubais and Yumashev, who supported Putin, soon managed to obtain a new appointment for him from the president. Putin became deputy chief of staff and head of the Main Control Directorate (GKU) on March 25, 1997. He replaced another member of "Chubais's St. Petersburg team" at this post—Sobchak's former deputy and Putin's old acquaintance Alexei Kudrin, who now became deputy minister of finance. In fact, it was precisely Kudrin who had recommended Putin as a replacement for himself, and since Putin was also backed by Chubais and Yumashev, the appointment to the high post went through. Among the reasons cited for Yumashev's support of Putin's candidacy was the loyalty that Putin exhibited toward his former boss, Sobchak, and his lack of excessive interest in politics.

From his cramped quarters on Varvarka Street, Putin moved to a magnificent office on Staraya Square that had once belonged to Arvid Pelshe, a member of the Soviet Politburo and head of the Party Control Committee of the CPSU Central Committee. Discussing his new job, Putin stated that he planned to inspect various government organizations, natural monopolies, the armed forces, and the military-industrial complex. He intended to identify abuses within these organizations and thus to improve the state of the government budget. Putin emphasized that the GKU is an organization that acts in an advisory capacity: its findings about legal violations would be sent to the General Prosecutor's Office, while the inspections themselves would be carried out jointly by the GKU, the General Prosecutor's Office, and other law enforcement agencies. The main thrust of the GKU's work under Putin's leadership was aimed against the inappropriate use of budget resources in the various regions of the country and in Moscow itself. The first document that Putin signed as head of the GKU was an order to begin inspections precisely along these lines.

At his new post, Putin started actively gathering information about the eighty-nine constituent subjects of the Russian Federation and, above all, about their governors. Sensible reports about the state of affairs in the regions began to arrive at the Kremlin from the depths of the GKU. Regional inspections, organized by the GKU and carried out by the federal government, became more frequent and strict. Some governors correctly assumed that this was Putin's way of gathering incriminating evidence against them, which was not difficult to do. A great deal of unfinished business concerning the corruption of local governments and inappropriate use of budget resources had piled up in the regional prosecutor's offices during the Yeltsin years. Perhaps this incriminating evidence against the governors was the golden key that opened up their hearts: during his one-year tenure at the GKU, Putin did not quarrel with a single governor and found a common language with all of them, even with the intractable governor of the Krasnoyarsk region, Alexander Lebed.

In May 1998, major personnel changes occurred in the Yeltsin administration. On May 25, Putin was appointed deputy chief of staff with responsibility for regional policy. By contrast with his predecessor, Yeltsin's old colleague Viktoria Mitina, Putin was given the title of first deputy chief of staff. On June 1, he was replaced as director of the GKU by FSB Lieutenant General Nikolai Patrushev, also a product of St. Petersburg. It was Putin who had brought Patrushev to Moscow and it was Putin who recommended him as his replacement.

Mitina's resignation and Putin's appointment to her post were seen as a move by the administration to establish firm control over the regional governments (in preparation for the 2000 election, among other things). Mitina, in the opinion of observers, had been unable to handle this task. It was expected that Putin—thanks to the contacts he had established with the regional heads and the leverage he had acquired over them as director of the GKU—would be more effective.

At the first press conference he gave in his new capacity, on June 4, Putin said that the country's leadership was going to devote more attention to regional politics, and that the carrying out of presidential orders, decrees, and resolutions at the local level would be subjected to closer scrutiny, but there would be no "tightening of the screws." Putin also talked about his achievements as head of the GKU: the abuses that had been discovered (involving the inappropriate use of budgetary resources) and the criminal proceedings that had been initiated.

For example, Putin pointed to violations that had come to light in the financial dealings of Rosvooruzhenie and the ongoing inspection of this company. The inspection had been triggered primarily by the fact that Rosvooruzhenie was headed by a Korzhakov appointee, Yevgeny Ananiev. Putin's plan was to install an acquaintance of his, an officer of the FSB's active reserve, at the top of this juicy piece of the Russian economy, third in importance after oil and gas. Putin won this chess match brilliantly. He managed to get Ananiev dismissed, restructured Rosvooruzhenie, and placed an old colleague from foreign intelligence, Andrei Belyaninov, at the helm. (Chemezov became Belyaninov's first deputy.)

On July 15, 1998, Putin replaced Sergei Shakhrai as head of the presidential commission to prepare agreements on dividing authority between the federal government and the regions of the Russian Federation. Since that time, not one such agreement has been signed.

DIRECTOR OF THE FSB

By order of the president, Putin was appointed director of Russia's Federal Security Service (FSB) on July 25, 1998. His activities in this capacity, directly responsible to the president, were coordinated in part by the prime minister. At the time, the prime minister was Sergei Kiriyenko. In presenting the new director to the FSB staff, Kiriyenko characterized Putin as a man who had experience in working for the security services and fighting economic crime. Putin remarked in his speech that he was "coming home" to the FSB and that he was set to embark on major constructive work. Nonetheless, in his book *First Person* he recalled taking on his new appointment without much enthusiasm. Whether he was being honest in this regard, however, is another matter.

Many FSB staff employees greeted Putin's appointment without much enthusiasm as well. Shortly after the appointment, Kiriyenko's government—the youngest in Russian history, considered pro-Western and reform-oriented—was dismissed. Replacing Kiriyenko was Yevgeny Primakov, former deputy head of the KGB, director of the Foreign Intelligence Service (SVR), and an obvious opponent of Yeltsin and his entire entourage. For the high brass of the FSB, Primakov's appointment as prime minister meant, if not an already accomplished government coup, then at least the beginning of one. Putin, who had been inherited from the Kiriyenko era, was not taken seriously. On top of that, he was merely a lieutenant colonel. In a military organization, where people took such things seriously, Putin's military rank could not be mentioned without either amusement or resentment.

The nature of Putin's former work at the KGB was also cause for derision. Putin had worked in East Germany, where foreign intelligence employed its flunkies. The top tier of agents was sent, of course, to capitalist countries, especially to the United States and Western Europe. Had the KGB taken Putin seriously as an expert, he would have worked in West Germany, not in East Germany.

But it was precisely because the central leadership of the FSB did not regard Putin as one of its own that Chubais and Yumashev had astutely placed him at the head of the FSB. Putin's predecessor, FSB General Nikolai Kovalev, had been too much at home in the organization. And he had a clear political objective: to seize power in Russia, just as Korzhakov had once attempted to do. Except that his aim was to seize power not for himself, but for Yeltsin's ideological opponents. Because obtaining power in Russia is in many ways connected with possessing money, Kovalev tried to bring the country's main economic organizations under his control by using the FSB's two largest economic departments, the Department of Economic Counterintelligence and the Department of Counterintelligence for Strategic Objects. This is what led to Kovalev's dismissal and the beginning of the FSB reform that Putin was deputized to implement. People in Yeltsin's entourage reasoned that Putin, who had attained only the rank of lieutenant colonel in the provincial East German city of Dresden, must hold a grudge against the system and would remain loyal to the Kremlin, not to the Lubyanka.

One of Putin's objectives at his new job was to counteract the growing tendency for the mayor of Moscow, Yuri Luzhkov, and the mayor of St. Petersburg, Vladimir Yakovlev, to exert more and more influence on the regional heads of the FSB. In other words, the FSB's Moscow and St. Petersburg directorates were essentially under the command not of the FSB director, but of the city government leaders. This state of affairs had been brought about by economic factors. It had been a long time since any FSB officer lived exclusively on his official government salary; all of them received bags of cash in addition. This money had to come from somewhere, and the FSB's regional offices constantly entered into direct commercial relations with city government officials, offering them various services in return for money: private security, business protection, and so on. The larger the city, the more influential were the heads of its FSB office. Prior to Putin's appointment as FSB director, the head of the FSB office for Moscow and the Moscow region could compete with the director of the FSB in terms of political influence in the government, and far outstripped the director of the FSB in terms of economic capabilities.

Putin must be given his due: he handled the task of reforming the FSB brilliantly. First of all, he showed the FSB's senior officer tier who was boss, and he did so in a rather jesuitical manner. He removed from the staff roster—that is, fired—about two thousand FSB officers, including all the employees of the two economic departments and the senior generals in the FSB Collegium. He then appointed his old KGB colleagues to the vacated positions in the Collegium. All were from St. Petersburg: General Viktor Cherkesov, General Sergei Ivanov, and General Alexander Grigoriev. In October 1998, Putin appointed Nikolai Patrushev, another old acquaintance from St. Petersburg, as his own deputy. Two other colleagues of Putin's from the Leningrad KGB were also transferred to Moscow: Vladimir Pronichev (who became the head of the Department for Combating Terrorism) and Viktor Ivanov (the head of the FSB's Departmental Security Service—internal counterintelligence).

Captain Igor Sechin became Putin's assistant and representative in the FSB. In less than half a year, he rose to the rank of colonel. (FSB director Putin was promoted to the rank of colonel as well.)

In place of the eliminated Department of Economic Counterintelligence and the Department of Counterintelligence for Strategic Objects, six new departments were established, with new chairmen. Here Putin gathered up the old employees from the FSB's discontinued economic departments who had been removed from the staff roster, thus completing the agency's reorganization, which had taken about a month. None of the employees who had been removed from the staff roster was left without a job. Putin did not reduce the FSB's total number of employees.

Putin also made working at the FSB attractive from a financial point of view. He obtained regular financing for the FSB, and—going directly to Yeltsin and thus avoiding the bureaucratic ladder—he also obtained salary increases for FSB agents, bringing them up to the levels of SVR (Foreign Intelligence Service) and FAPSI (Federal Agency for Government Communication and Information) agents. On March 29, 1999, Putin was appointed secretary of the Security Council of the Russian Federation, while retaining his post as director of the FSB. In terms of his career, then, Putin's work at the FSB must be considered a success.

In terms of fighting crime, however, it was less impressive. During Putin's tenure as director of the FSB, the following major crimes occurred in Russia (almost all of them unsolved):

- Murder of Alexander Shkadov, president of the Association of Russian Diamond Manufacturers, at his dacha near Smolensk (August 1, 1998).
- Assassination attempt against Said Amirov, mayor of Makhachkala (August 8, 1998).
- Explosion outside the FSB's Lubyanka headquarters (August 13, 1998). Alexander Biriukov, from the left-wing group New Revolutionary Alternative, was charged with organizing this explosion and arrested in 1999; he was subsequently diagnosed as a paranoid schizophrenic.

- Murder of Anatoly Levin-Utkin, editor-in-chief of the magazine *Yuridichesky Peterburg Segodnya*, "Legal St. Petersburg Today" (August 20, 1998).
- Murder of Said-Muhammad Abubakarov, mufti of Dagestan, and his brother in the courtyard of the Central Mosque of Makhachkala (August 21, 1998).
- Murder of Alexei Vukolov, president of the Russian Public Fund for Disabled Army Veterans, outside Moscow (September 3, 1998).
- Another assassination attempt against Said Amirov in Makhachkala (September 4, 1998).
- Murder in St. Petersburg of Yevgeny Agarev, deputy head of the City Committee on the Consumers' Market (September 28, 1998).
- Kidnapping in Grozny (September 29, 1998) and murder (October 3, 1998) of Akmal Saidov, deputy representative of the government of the Russian Federation in Chechnya.
- Murder by radio-controlled mine of Dmitry Filippov, president of the Petersburg Fuel Company, former candidate for governor of St. Petersburg, and a close associate of Gennady Seleznev, speaker of the State Duma (died on October 13, 1998, from injuries sustained on October 10).
- Wounding in St. Petersburg of Seleznev's advisor and sponsor Mikhail Osherov in an assassination attempt (October 16, 1998).
- Murder in Moscow of Alexander Berlyand, general manager of the Toms-Neft-Vostok company (October 20, 1998).
- Murder in the Moscow region of Yuri Keres, investigator in the special prosecutor's office (October 20, 1998).
- Assassination attempt in Grozny against Akhmad-hadji Kadyrov, mufti of Chechnya (October 26, 1998).
- Murder of Nikolai Shapin, deputy general manager of the Chelyabenergo company (November 1, 1998).

- Murder of Yevgeny Fedoryakin, chief of the Novorossiysk Transportation Police (November 5, 1998).
- Murder in Moscow of Alexander Gontov, advisor to the governor of the Kemerovo region (November 18, 1998).
- Murder in St. Petersburg of the democratic activist Galina Starovoitova (November 28, 1998).
- Assassination attempt against Pyotr Biryukov, first deputy prefect of Moscow's Central District (November 28, 1998).
- Murder in Chechnya of three British citizens and one citizen of New Zealand (the foreign experts were kidnapped on October 3, 1998; their decapitated bodies were found on December 10).
- Assassination attempt against Pyotr Kucheren, a lawyer (December 16, 1998).
- Car explosion next to the U.S. embassy in Moscow (January 17, 1999).
- Arson of Ministry of Internal Affairs building in Samara (February 10, 1999); fifty-seven employees died in the fire.
- Murder in Moscow of A. Polyakov, editor of the magazine *Rossiysky Advokat*, "Russian Lawyer" (March 4, 1999).
- Kidnapping in Grozny of Gennady Shpigun, the Russian Ministry of Internal Affairs' special representative in Chechnya (March 5, 1999).
- Pogrom in a synagogue in Novosibirsk (on the night of March 8, 1999).
- Explosion in a market in Vladikavkaz; over sixty people killed, over one hundred wounded (March 19, 1999).
- Assassination attempt against Andrey Golushko, first deputy head of the Omsk region's administration; Golushko was seriously wounded (March 22, 1999).
- Attempted grenade-launcher attack on the U.S. embassy in Moscow (March 28, 1999). One of the terrorists subsequently gave an interview describ-

ing his participation in the attack; he was arrested and convicted.

- Murder of Kurban Bulatov, deputy general prosecutor of Dagestan, in Makhachkala (March 31, 1999).
- Another explosion next to the wall of the FSB's Lubyanka headquarters (April 4, 1999). Three young women from the underground group New Revolutionary Alternative were subsequently convicted of planning this explosion.
- Murder in St. Petersburg of Gennady Tumanov, the Liberal Democratic Party of Russia's coordinator for St. Petersburg and the Leningrad region (April 9, 1999).
- Assassination attempt against Islam Burlakov, head of the Republican Court of the Karachay-Cherkess Republic (April 13, 1999).
- Attempt to blow up Iosif Kobzon's office at the Intourist Hotel, injuring sixteen people (April 26, 1999).
- Mines planted in the Sholom Jewish theater in Moscow (May 10, 1999).
- Assassination attempt against Colonel Nikolai Aulov, deputy head of the Northwestern RUBOP office (Regional Directorate for Combating Organized Crime) in St. Petersburg, and his wife; both were seriously wounded by shots from a sniper's rifle (May 26, 1999).
- Second assassination attempt against Akhmad-hadji Kadyrov, mufti of Chechnya (end of May 1999).
- Murder of Gennady Nedvigin, hetman of the Grand Army of the Don Cossacks (June 6, 1999).
- Murder of Valentin Kudinov, mayor of the city of Dedovsk, Moscow region (June 22, 1999).
- Murder of Genrikh Epp, mayor of the city of Kyzyl, leader of the Tuva branch of the Democratic Choice of Russia (DVR) party (July 21, 1999).
- Grenade-launcher attack on the LogoVAZ Reception House (August 8, 1999).

There was only one operation that Putin carried out successfully: removing Russia's corrupt general prosecutor, Yuri Skuratov, from his official post. Why Skuratov had decided to fight corruption in the Presidential Property Management Directorate and Yeltsin himself is hard to say. It may have been out of loyalty to Korzhakov; or it may have been out of political sympathy with the Communists; or it may have been under pressure from Yevgeny Primakov, who was prime minister at the time and had an extremely negative attitude toward Yeltsin and his inner circle (the so-called "family"), including Pavel Borodin, head of the Presidential Property Management Directorate. The one thing that Skuratov, or any of the general prosecutors of Russia who came after him, could definitely *not* be suspected of was a sincere desire to fight corruption in the upper tiers of the Russian government.

In any case, Skuratov initiated criminal proceedings on charges of corruption against the Presidential Property Management Directorate on October 8, 1998. In collaboration with their Swiss colleagues, Russian investigators had uncovered a series of abuses perpetrated in the making of contracts to renovate the Kremlin and to refurbish the president's airplane, including many millions of dollars deposited to the bank accounts of Borodin, his daughter, and his son-in-law. Skuratov's findings shook Yeltsin's throne. The word "impeachment" began to be heard in the State Duma more and more.

Six months after the investigation began, however, criminal charges were brought against Skuratov himself. He was accused of conducting himself in a manner inconsistent with his position and title. In March 1999, the FSB obtained a videotape in which a naked person "resembling" Skuratov was shown having sex with two equally naked call girls. Moscow's deputy prosecutor launched criminal proceedings against Skuratov on the night of April 1. The rush to prosecute was easy to explain: the Swiss prosecutors were swiftly forging ahead in their investigation of the illegal dealings of the Swiss companies that had been engaged to renovate the Kremlin, and it was necessary to put an end to this investigation as quickly as possible. This could be done only by replacing the general prosecutor, whose dismissal, according to law, had to be approved by the upper house of the Russian parliament, the Federation Council. The procedure was long and complicated.

By contrast with their Russian colleagues, the Swiss prosecutors saw their investigation through to the end. Their findings resulted in Pavel Borodin's highly publicized arrest in the United States, where he was attending the inauguration of President George W. Bush, followed by his extradition to Switzerland. Borodin's trial brought to light the corrupt arrangement that he and his Swiss accomplices had agreed upon. The Swiss court fined Borodin about $375,000, but Borodin refused to acknowledge his guilt and refused to pay the fine. Russia refused to pay Borodin's fine as well. The bail money to secure Borodin's release from the Swiss jail was put up by one of his Swiss partners. The case ultimately ended up as a farce.

The attacks on Skuratov virtually coincided with attacks on Filipp Turover, a witness for the Swiss prosecutor's office whose testimony was used by the Swiss and Russian investigators. After Skuratov resigned, the Moscow prosecutor's office brought criminal charges against Turover, a Swiss citizen. Here is what Skuratov wrote about Turover in his book *A Version of the Dragon*: "Turover helped us more than the FSB, the Ministry of Internal Affairs, and the SVR put together. All of his statements, alas, were confirmed. Not one instance of false testimony on his part was established. Our security services, in order to defend the Kremlin, started working on Turover and discrediting him." Accused of lying, incitement to crime, bribery, and theft, Turover was put on the Russian wanted list and subsequently on the Interpol wanted list as well. Russia's accusations against Turover were not borne out, however, and after some time the case was closed.

The most important role in the operation to discredit and remove Skuratov was reserved for Putin. It was his agents who had rented and paid for the apartment where Skuratov had his meeting with the call girls. It was his agents who had videotaped the general prosecutor having sex. It was Putin who ended up in possession of the videotape that showed "a person resembling the general prosecutor," as Russian newspapers put it, since they had no right to assert that the man shown on the tape was Skuratov himself. And it was Putin who publicly voiced President Yeltsin's demand that Skuratov resign so as to avoid a scandal. After Skuratov refused, the video of the sexual escapades was shown on the state-run Rossiya TV channel (RTR). It had been delivered to the RTR head Mikhail Shvydkov personally, as reporters joked, by "a person resembling the director of the FSB." Somewhat later, the same video was also shown on Sergei Dorenko's program on Russia's main television channel, ORT (Channel One).

On April 7, 1999, FSB director Putin reported in a televised speech that experts in the FSB and the Ministry of Internal Affairs had made a preliminary assessment and had reached the conclusion that the video of the general prosecutor's sexual escapades was genuine. Putin then once again voiced the opinion that Skuratov should resign voluntarily. He also announced that the "activities" recorded on the video had been paid for by "individuals involved in criminal cases" that were being investigated by the General Prosecutor's Office, and demanded that the materials of the two criminal cases be "merged" into one: the case against Skuratov, based on Article 285 of the Criminal Code of the Russian Federation ("Abuse of Official Position"), and the case against the individuals who had illegally videotaped him, based on Article 137 ("Interference into Private Life"). In the end, the individuals who had made the scandalous video remained officially unknown, and it was never legally established whether or not the "person resembling the general prosecutor" was in fact the general prosecutor. Nonetheless, Skuratov was forced to resign. He was replaced by Vladimir Ustinov.

Meanwhile, a scandal connected with the names of Boris Berezovsky and Alexander Litvinenko had erupted in the press. On November 17, 1998, a group of FSB officers led by FSB Lieutenant Colonel Litvinenko—although formally the senior member of this group was not Litvinenko, but Colonel Alexander Gusak—gave a press conference at Interfax, Russia's biggest news agency, which was broadcast by all of Russia's television channels across the entire country. The officers claimed that the leadership of the FSB had given them orders to kill the executive secretary of the CIS, Boris Berezovsky. Several days earlier, on November 13, the newspaper *Kommersant* had published an open letter from Berezovsky to Putin in which Berezovsky informed Putin of the existence of a Communist nomenkla-tura conspiracy within the security services aimed at protect-ing criminals within the FSB. Although the criminal orders to assassinate Berezovsky had been issued under Putin's prede-cessor, Nikolai Kovalev, the new director of the FSB reacted to Berezovsky's statements in an extremely harsh fashion. He announced that his agency did not participate in political games but served to protect the constitutional order and the safety of the individual, society, and the government within the bounds of the law. Putin condemned any interference by political forces (alluding to Berezovsky) in the work of the FSB, which, in his words, must receive guidance from the president alone. The director of the FSB considered any attempts at such interfer-ence to be destabilizing to the country as a whole.

This scandal put Putin's and his agency's reputation in dan-ger. At a meeting with Putin, the president expressed concern about the situation and recommended that Putin look into the essence of the allegations advanced by Litvinenko's group against the leadership of the FSB. In response, Putin declared that "in the event of a confirmation of any of the statements about the criminal activities of our employees, we will get rid of them mercilessly, regardless of their rank or position, and hand over their materials to the prosecutor's office."

However, public opinion and the press—which were inclined to ascribe control over top government officials to the Russian oligarch Berezovsky—began to suspect that all the ongoing events represented a conspiracy between Putin and Berezovsky whose ultimate objective was to hand con-trol over the FSB to Berezovsky and his people, one of whom was believed to be Litvinenko. Such a public mindset repre-sented a threat to Putin. People knew about the open conflict between Berezovsky and Prime Minister Primakov, in whose cabinet Putin was a member; the General Prosecutor's Office was trying to bring charges against Berezovsky for committing economic crimes; and an association between Putin and Ber-ezovsky would clearly be detrimental to Putin. This was espe-cially so because Berezovsky had started losing his influence within Yeltsin's entourage, and Putin—who was part of this entourage and closely acquainted with everyone in it—could not but know this.

Putin realized that the best way to defend himself against suspicions of having ties to Berezovsky was to attack him in public. He took at least a neutral position with regard to the actions of Prime Minister Primakov and the General Prosecutor's Office against Berezovsky and his organizations; he insisted that the FSB fire Litvinenko and the other officers who had participated in the Interfax press conference on November 17, 1998, including Colonel Gusak, the senior officer in Litvinenko's group, who had not taken part in the press conference but had given testimony corroborating Litvinenko's charges. He then insisted that Litvinenko and Gusak be arrested, and allowed Berezovsky to be essentially expelled from the country. And he did all this in order to distance himself from Berezovsky and to escape the link that Berezovsky was trying to foist upon him.

According to many reporters and government officials, Berezovsky, for his part, was also waging war against Primakov. Putin could have become the first victim of this war, while its last victim could have been Primakov himself. Former FSB director Kovalev, for example, claimed that Berezovsky tried to use the scandal that erupted after the Litvinenko press conference to undermine the influence of the FSB, and that this was connected to Berezovsky's longstanding plan—originally conceived when he became deputy secretary of Russia's Security Council in October 1996—to create a security service under the control of the Security Council and to place Litvinenko at its head. Such a plan, if it ever really existed, was based more on fantasy than on reality. Nonetheless, Putin could not but see a threat to himself in the projects of the energetic Berezovsky. And he had no intention of risking his career. Arresting Litvinenko and Gusak, and squeezing Berezovsky out of Russia, were deliberate preventive strikes.

IN RUSSIA'S SECURITY COUNCIL

Putin became a permanent member of the Security Council of the Russian Federation in October 1998 and served as its secretary from March to August 1999. The aspirants to this position—which had earlier been occupied by Nikolai Bordyuzha (who had previously been fired from the post of Yeltsin's chief of staff)—included Sergei Kiriyenko and Viktor Chernomyrdin.

After it proved impossible to reach an agreement with either of them that would also be acceptable to the Kremlin, the circle of possible candidates narrowed down to the heads of the law enforcement agencies. The selection among them was based on which had the least loyalty to Prime Minister Primakov. Thus, the candidacy of Vyacheslav Trubnikov, director of the SVR (Foreign Intelligence Service), was rejected on account of his close ties to Primakov. Putin, on the other hand, although he did not quarrel with Primakov and maintained steady formal relations with him, oriented himself toward a subordination not to Primakov, who was trying to control the work of the FSB, but to the Kremlin—to Yeltsin and his inner circle.

It is also possible that by nominating Putin for the Security Council, Yeltsin was trying to balance out his appointment of Alexander Voloshin as chief of staff. Voloshin was seen as Berezovsky's man. He had worked in Berezovsky's organizations before being launched into politics and was considered Berezovsky's protégé. Voloshin's appointment as the president's chief of staff could not but be interpreted by absolutely everyone in the country as a sign of Berezovsky's growing influence on the Kremlin.

As both director of the FSB and secretary of the Security Council at the same time, Putin got his hands on serious levers of influence and a degree of power that was probably comparable only to that of Prime Minister Primakov. It was during this period that an open standoff between Primakov and the Kremlin began. Exploiting the support of a parliamentary majority and the general prosecutor's scandalous revelations, Primakov tugged at the mantle of power, pulling more and more of it around himself. The country witnessed something resembling a creeping coup. In the State Duma, the Communists tried to turn against Yeltsin the wave of anti-American sentiment that arose as a result of the Yugoslavian crisis and began hatching plans to impeach the president. Left-leaning ministers received key positions in Primakov's cabinet. Gradually, all power in the government ended up in the hands of the old Communist forces. The only stronghold that President Yeltsin had left was the Kremlin, and the Kremlin was powerless and thus practically inactive. And Primakov, who stood at the head of this coup, skillfully created the impression that he was a bulwark against the Communist tide, the last barrier standing in the way of Yeltsin's overthrow.

At this moment—a moment critical for the country and for his rule—Yeltsin took a step that might have seemed like one he would never bring himself to take. On May 19, he signed a decree to dismiss Primakov, who was then at the height of his power and popularity, from the position of prime minister. The virtual dominance of Communists collapsed like a house of cards. The opposition in the Duma fell silent. All talk of impeachment ended. Skuratov resigned. Yet after getting rid of a prime minister who had been the head of the SVR, Yeltsin picked a new prime minister who had been the head of the FSK (the former KGB and the future FSB), Sergei Stepashin. This was a net that Yeltsin could not escape. He could now pick prime ministers only from among the officers of the FSB. This was the price he had to pay for remaining in power himself and for transferring power to a successor who could guarantee him and his family immunity from criminal prosecution by the Duma and the General Prosecutor's Office.

During Putin's tenure as secretary of the Security Council, a number of topics were discussed at the council's meetings. First, there was the situation in the North Caucasus, particularly in Chechnya; in May 1999, after Stepashin was confirmed as prime minister, Putin obtained a presidential decree that increased the role of the FSB's divisions in the North Caucasus. Second, the Security Council deliberated over the development of Russia's nuclear potential in the face of what the Kremlin saw as the global hegemony of the United States, which had been demonstrated during the Yugoslavian crisis.

The Security Council met on May 12, 1999, to discuss the situation in the Balkans. Putin's remarks at the meeting were brusque:

> Russia will not be satisfied with the role of a technical courier in the Yugoslavian crisis, the role of a country that merely carries proposals from one country to another. . . . We are seeing a one-sided attempt to destroy the world order that was created under the aegis of the United Nations after the Second World War. We must react to this challenge by changing our conception of our own national security.

Putin repeatedly discussed the situation in the Balkans and various security-related aspects of Russian-American relations by telephone with Sandy Berger, national security advisor to the president of the United States. After one of the Security Council's meetings, Putin declared that Russia deserved a great deal of credit for the fact that a political settlement had been reached in the Balkan crisis, alluding to his own role in the process. He also worked on the issue of Russia's role in peacekeeping activities in Kosovo. And by June 1999, when the possibility of Stepashin's resignation became a subject of discussion, Putin was already being viewed as a possible successor.

PRIME MINISTER

A third deputy prime minister position was created by order of the president on August 9, 1999. By the same order, Putin was appointed to the new position. On the same day, Yeltsin issued another order dismissing Sergei Stepashin's cabinet and appointing Putin temporary acting prime minister. This sequence of events was explained by the fact that, by law, only the deputy prime minister could be appointed to the position of acting prime minister.

In a televised speech on August 9, Yeltsin named Putin as his successor for the presidency of the Russian Federation:

> I have now decided to name a person who, in my opinion, can bring society together. Relying on the broadest political powers, he will ensure the continuation of reforms in Russia. He will be able to surround himself with those who will have to bring renewal to the great nation of Russia in the twenty-first century. This is the secretary of Russia's Security Council, the director of the FSB, Vladimir Vladimirovich Putin. . . . I have confidence in him. But I want everyone who will vote in July 2000 to have confidence in him as well. I think that he has enough time to show his worth.

In a televised interview on the same day, Putin stated that he accepted Yeltsin's offer and would run for president in 2000.

On August 16, the State Duma confirmed Putin's nomination for the position of prime minister (223 votes in favor, 84 against, 17 abstaining). Of the Communist Party deputies, 32 (including Duma speaker Gennady Seleznev) voted in favor of Putin; 52 CPRF deputies (including Anatoly Lukyanov and Albert Makashov) voted against him; the rest abstained or did not vote (Gennady Zyuganov did not vote). A number of deputies from the left-wing Narodovlastie party also voted against Putin. Eighteen deputies from the Yabloko party (including Grigory Yavlinsky) voted in favor; eight Yabloko deputies voted against; the rest abstained or did not vote. The other parties voted in favor of the confirmation virtually unanimously.

Summing up Putin's first months in office as prime minister, the newspaper *Novaya Gazeta* wrote: "Once upon a time, in a very democratic country, an elderly president appointed a young and energetic successor to the position of chancellor. Then the Reichstag went up in flames. . . . Historians still haven't established who it was that set it on fire, but history has shown who stood to benefit." In Russia, however, "the elderly chief handed the position of prime minister to a successor who had yet to be democratically elected. Then residential buildings started exploding and a new war in Chechnya began—a war that is now being praised to the skies by arch-liars." These events which shook the nation were clearly connected to the advancement of yet another person: on August 16, 1999, Nikolai Patrushev was appointed director of the FSB. And then things really started to happen.

5

The Second Chechen War

PLANNING THE SECOND CHECHEN WAR

Russian voters faced a spectacular list of candidates in the 2000 election: the old chekist Primakov, who self-assuredly proclaimed that if elected he would arrest ninety thousand businessmen—essentially the entire Russian business elite; the young chekist Putin, who before coming to power stressed the necessity of continuing Yeltsin's policies; and the Communist Zyuganov, whose chances of winning were nil. In order to put ninety thousand businessmen in jail, Primakov would have to arrest sixty people per day, including weekends and holidays, for the duration of his four-year term as president. The young chekist Putin promised to be less bloodthirsty. Might the drama of the election campaign have been scripted by someone along the lines of good cop/bad cop?

It is evident that—whoever eventually became Yeltsin's successor—both the Duma election in December 1999 and the presidential election in March 2000 were meant to take place to the cannonade of the second Chechen war. In January 2000, the former director of the FSK and former prime minister Sergei Stepashin shed a certain amount of light on the issue of when precisely the decision to begin military operations had been made. "The decision to invade Chechnya was made already in

March 1999," he remarked in an interview. The invasion had been "planned" for "August–September," and "this would have happened even if there hadn't been any explosions in Moscow" (the September 1999 apartment-house bombings). "I was preparing for an active intervention. We were planning to be on the north side of the Terek River by August–September," Stepashin said, adding that Putin, "who was the head of the FSB at the time, possessed this information."

During this period—a tragic time for the country—Putin appointed Nikolai Patrushev as head of the FSB. The sensational crimes committed under Putin as director of the FSB begin to look like the pranks of petty hoodlums when they are compared with the crimes committed under his successor. It appears, however, that it was precisely such a man that Putin needed as director of the FSB.

BUYNAKSK, SEPTEMBER 4, 1999

On September 4, 1999, in the city of Buynaksk, Dagestan, a car packed with explosives was blown up next to a residential building in a military complex. Sixty-four residents—servicemen and members of their families—lost their lives. On the same day in Buynaksk, a ZIL-130 automobile holding 2,706 kilograms of explosive substances was discovered in a parking lot surrounded by residential buildings and an army hospital. In this case, the explosion was prevented only by the vigilance of local citizens.

The terrorist attack in Buynaksk was prepared and carried out by the Main Intelligence Directorate of the Russian Federation (GRU), headed by Colonel General Korabelnikov. The operation was supervised by the head of the GRU's Fourteenth Directorate, Lieutenant General Kostechko. The terrorist attack was carried out by a team of twelve GRU officers, who had been sent to Dagestan specifically for this purpose. All this came out in the testimony of GRU Senior Lieutenant Alexei Galkin, who was captured as prisoner of war by the Chechens in November 1999. It is clear that Galkin's testimony was given under torture; but this testimony should be considered accurate. At least, after escaping from captivity and giving a second (voluntary) interview to *Novaya Gazeta*, Galkin did not claim that he had lied about the GRU and the other members of his group while he was a prisoner of war.

THE TERRORIST ATTACKS IN MOSCOW, VOLGODONSK, AND RYAZAN (SEPTEMBER 1999)

Soon after the bombing in Buynaksk came a series of apartment-house bombings in Moscow, Volgodonsk, and Ryazan—all mentioned by Galkin as well. Early in the morning on September 9, a residential building on Guryanov Street in Moscow was blown up. On the early morning of September 13, another apartment house in the capital was bombed, this one on Kashirskoye highway. On September 16, a residential building on Volgodonsk exploded. On the evening of September 22, local residents and police averted the explosion of an apartment house in Ryazan. These terrorist attacks, which were the largest in Russia's history and claimed the lives of approximately three hundred people, became the cause of a full-scale war with the Chechen Republic, which has claimed the lives of many thousands and crippled the existence of many millions of people.

Today, we know a great deal about the apartment-house bombings. Preparations for them began when the Russian government made a political decision to begin the second Chechen war: in March–April 1999. The practical implementation of the terrorist attacks was left to the FSB and the GRU. In Buynaksk, the residential building that housed members of the armed forces was blown up by the GRU, since the FSB's involvement in this operation could have led to an interagency conflict between the FSB and the Ministry of Defense. In Moscow, Volgodonsk, and Ryazan, the terrorist attacks were organized by the FSB.

This was the chain of command in charge of the operation: Putin (former director of the FSB, future president)—Patrushev (Putin's successor as director of the FSB)—FSB General German Ugryumov (director of the counterterrorism department)—Abdulgafur ("Max" Lazovsky) and Abu-Bakar (Abubakar), the two FSB operatives directly responsible for the practical organization of the bombings. Tatyana Korolyova, Achemez Gochiyaev, and Alexander Karmishin were the founders of the company whose warehouses received shipments of hexogen disguised as bags of sugar. (These people were possibly used without their own knowledge; they may have had no idea that explosives were being delivered to their storage facilities.) Adam Dekkushev, Yusup Krymshamkhalov, and Timur Batchayev were the individuals recruited by "Chechen separatists" (FSB agents) to deliver explosives disguised as bags of sugar to the basements of buildings destined for liquidation in Volgodonsk, and possibly also in Moscow; but they were under the impression that the locations to which they were delivering the explosives were merely temporary storage spaces, and that the explosives would ultimately be used to blow up "federal targets." Finally, the participants included FSB operatives Vladimir Romanovich and Ramazan Dyshekov, who carried out the apartment-house bombings in Moscow, and also the FSB agents who were apprehended and videotaped—but whose last names were not disclosed—after attempting to blow up a residential building in Ryazan on the night of September 23, 1999.

KASPIYSK, MAY 2002

It should be noted that the bombing attempt that failed in Ryazan was repeated successfully by the FSB in the Dagestani city of Kaspiysk in May 2002. This operation took place in two stages. From the FSB point of view, the first stage must be considered a success. At 9:50 A.M. on May 9, during a military parade commemorating the anniversary of the Soviet victory in World War II, on Lenin Street, not far from Kaspiysk's central square, unknown terrorists detonated an MON-50 directional landmine, enhanced for greater destructive capability, containing the equivalent of three to five kilograms of TNT. The explosive device had been placed on a stand by the edge of a road that was on the parade route. There were 177 casualties from the explosion, including 63 members of the armed forces and 72 children; 44 people, including 12 children, lost their lives.

President Putin, speaking on the same day in connection with the terrorist attack in Kaspiysk, demanded that "the criminals be identified, exposed, and punished as soon as possible." "Crimes of such cruelty inevitably give rise to strong emotions," Putin declared. "These emotions must not get in the way of a rigorous investigation of this crime. . . . These crimes were perpetrated by scum, for whom nothing is sacred, and we are entirely entitled to treat them the same way we treat Nazis, whose only aim is to bring death, to sow fear, to kill."

Putin ordered that an interagency group be established to investigate the terrorist attack, under the direction of Patrushev. He had Patrushev fly out to the Dagestani capital of Makhachkala immediately to oversee the investigation in person. The Russian government received condolences for the Kaspiysk attack from the Bush administration, the British and French foreign ministries, the Council of Europe, and so forth.

At a press conference in Makhachkala shortly afterward, Patrushev announced that the terrorist attack had been organized by Chechen separatists, that a "group of individuals has been identified, consisting of over ten people . . . who were taking orders directly from field commander Rappani Khalilov." On the night of May 10, five persons suspected of organizing the attack in Kaspiysk were arrested—in St. Petersburg, which is located at a considerable distance from Kaspiysk. The arrested parties denied any involvement in the attack. At least three of them had irrefutable alibis. The public did not believe that the arrested parties had anything to do with the attack.

The terrorist attack in Kaspiysk would have remained no different from any other Chechen terrorist attack were it not for events that followed several days later. On the evening of May 16, Kaspiysk's law enforcement organs announced that they had prevented another attack. Three terrorists had been caught attempting to set up an MON-100 landmine, similar to the one that had been detonated on May 9, on one of Kaspiysk's main thoroughfares. The terrorists had been apprehended in possession of the explosives. In addition to the landmine, the police discovered an electric detonator and a remote control device in their car.

At first, everything developed according to the Ryazan 1999 scenario. The city's government triumphantly announced to the whole world that the terrorists had been caught and an attack had been averted. Then came an unexpected hitch, similar to the one in Ryazan. When they were arrested, the terrorists did not offer any resistance but said the police had no right to arrest them. At least one of the arrested parties, Rashid Dzhabrailov, presented a "cover document"—identity papers from Dagestan's Ministry of Internal Affairs. Even so, all three were arrested so that their identities could be established.

What happened then is not known, since the FSB immediately blocked all further information about the planned and averted attack "in the interests of the investigation." At the same time, Patrushev appeared on ORT television and announced, just as he had in September 1999 in connection with the arrests in Ryazan, that "the arrested parties had no connection with terrorists and that no terrorist attack had been planned in Kaspiysk."

True, the Dagestani leadership was surprised and shocked, just as the local government of Ryazan had been surprised and shocked. "What nonsense he's saying!" the Dagestani authorities declared in response to Patrushev's announcement. ". . . The republic's security services believe that a terrorist attack had been planned. And they are not making any declarations only because they are afraid of hindering the investigation."

Nonetheless, on Moscow's orders, the investigation of the terrorist attacks in Kaspiysk on May 9 and May 16 was called to an end. Patrushev's incautious statement was forgotten. No one was interested in the identities of the three arrested parties. And President Putin no longer mentioned the Nazi-like "scum, for whom nothing is sacred."

Patrushev himself received nothing but encouragement. He had already been promoted to the rank of army general on July 11, 2001, his fiftieth birthday. At the beginning of 2003, by secret order of President Putin, he was decorated with the title "Hero of Russia," bestowed on him "for successes in the war in Chechnya." It is true that, by order of the president, command of the Operating Headquarters for the Direction of the Antiterrorist Operation in Chechnya was transferred from the FSB (i.e. Patrushev) to the Ministry of Internal Affairs (i.e. Boris Gryzlov). But this obvious acknowledgment of the failure of his policies in Chechnya became the only punishment that Patrushev has incurred.

THE ETERNAL CHECHEN CONFLICT

The second Chechen war did not receive the kind of coverage from the Russian media that the first one did, when the press and television enjoyed absolute freedom. Reporters' accounts of military operations in Chechnya became subject to stricter ideological control every time the government shut down or appropriated another newspaper, every time the editorial staff of another independent television station was fired, every time the authorities promulgated another set of secret or public instructions concerning the coverage of events in Chechnya. In essence, the Russian population received information only when extraordinary events occurred, about which it was impossible to keep silent.

Even so, in October 2001, Sergei Yastrzhembsky reported the number of Russian casualties in Chechnya over the two years of the second Chechen war: 3,438 killed and 11,661 wounded. According to the Committee of Soldiers' Mothers, the total number of casualties as of January 2002 was at least double the official figure, and the number of soldiers and officers killed was about 6,000. In February 2003, new official figures were released for the total number of casualties sustained by Russia's armed forces as a whole between October 1, 1999, and December 23, 2002: 4,572 killed and 15,549 wounded.

Here are the most serious losses suffered by federal troops and the civilian population in Chechnya due to terrorist attacks organized by the Chechen separatists:

- Federal troops in Chechnya lost four helicopters over a peirod of two weeks at the end of January and the beginning of February 2002. Several top military officials, including two generals, were killed when their helicopter was shot down on January 27.
- Chechen separatist missiles killed 119 Russian servicemen on their way to Grozny aboard an Mi-26 helicopter on August 19, 2002. Putin declared a day of mourning on August 22. On September 1,

separatists shot down an Mi-24 helicopter, killing its crew.

- On the evening of October 23, 2002, a troop of Chechen fighters (approximately fifty men) headed by Movsar Barayev penetrated into Moscow and took about eight hundred people hostage during a performance of the musical *Nord-Ost* at the Dubrovka theater complex, demanding the withdrawal of Russian troops from Chechen territory. Putin held a meeting at the Kremlin on October 25, after which FSB director Patrushev announced that the government was willing to spare the terrorists' lives if all the hostages were released. On the evening of October 25, the terrorists pledged to execute the hostages if their demands were not satisfied. Fearing that the insurgents might blow up the building if an attempt were made to take it by force, the authorities pumped sleeping gas into the theater on the night of October 26. Then, special forces units burst into the building and shot the sleeping terrorists. Although the terrorists were successfully prevented from blowing up the building, twenty-nine hostages died from the effects of the gas and the incompetence of the rescue workers. Forty more hostages died from the effects of the gas over the next six months.

Apologizing before the victims' relatives, Putin did not mention the problem of Chechen separatism, but attributed the events to international terrorism. He decorated General Vladimir Pronichev—first deputy director of the FSB, who had supervised the operation to destroy the terrorists—with the Hero of Russia award; and he gave the same award to the unnamed chemist who had pumped the gas into the building. No law enforcement official was punished for allowing the terrorists to penetrate into Moscow; the government's main grievances were directed against television reporters for errors committed during the coverage of the events, which may have aided the terrorists.

- A few months after the theater attack, Anna Politkovskaya, a *Novaya Gazeta* reporter, tracked
down one of the Chechen terrorists who had participated in the hostage-taking and who was also
an agent of the FSB. Khanpash Terkibayev gave
Politkovskaya an extensive interview, which was
subsequently published in *Novaya Gazeta* and on
the Internet, and then he left for Chechnya. Shortly
thereafter, on December 9, 2003, he was killed in
a car accident—much like Vladimir Romanovich,
the FSB agent who had participated in organizing
the terrorist attacks in Moscow in September 1999.
The contents of Terkibayev's interview were of no
interest to Russia's law enforcement agencies.

  Soon after the Dubrovka tragedy, on December 15, 2002, Putin signed an order to appoint new
personnel to the Federal Antiterrorist Commission.
Putin himself became the chairman of the commission. His deputies were Boris Gryzlov, the minister
of internal affairs, and FSB director Patrushev.

- On December 27, suicide bombers blew up the
republican government complex in Grozny, killing
over 72 people, mainly technical personnel and
policemen. Over 200 people were injured.

- During religious festivities in the village of
Iliskhan-Yurt on May 14, 2003, three female suicide
bombers blew themselves up, killing 26 people and
injuring 150.

- On June 5, 2003, a female suicide bomber blew herself up in a bus in Mozdok (North Ossetia), killing
19 and injuring 12.

- On July 5, two female suicide bombers blew
themselves up in Tushino in Moscow, killing 16 and
injuring 40.

- On July 10, there was a failed attempt to blow up
a cafe on Tverskaya Street in Moscow. The female
suicide bomber was arrested, but an FSB specialist
died while deactivating the explosives.

- On August 1, a suicide bomber blew up a military
hospital. According to official records, 50 people

were killed and 80 were injured. (There are reasons to believe that the actual numbers were higher.)

- On September 3, terrorists blew up a Mineralnye Vody–Kislovodsk commuter train, killing five and injuring over 30 others.
- On December 5, the eve of Russia's parliamentary elections, the Mineralnye Vody–Kislovodsk commuter train was blown up once again, leaving 44 dead and dozens injured.
- On December 8, a female suicide bomber on her way to the State Duma blew herself up near the National Hotel, killing six and injuring others.
- On February 6, 2004, about 40 people were killed in an explosion in the Moscow metro between the Paveletskaya and Avtozavodskaya stations. An investigation revealed that a suicide bomber had blown himself up inside a metro car along with the passengers.
- A bomb exploded in the bleechers of Grozny's Dinamo stadium on May 9, 2004, killing Akhmad Kadyrov, president of Chechnya; Hussein Isayev, head of Chechnya's State Council; and five others.
- In June, Chechen fighters attacked the settlements of Nazran and Karabulak in Ingushetia. Several dozen people were killed.
- In August, two airplanes—a Tu-154 and a Tu-134—exploded after taking off from Moscow's Domodedovo airport.
- Also in August, there was a terrorist attack near the Rizhskaya metro station in Moscow.
- A major terrorist attack occurred September 1–3, 2004, in a school in the North Ossetian city of Beslan, where over 1,000 students and teachers were taken hostage. When Russian forces stormed the building without adequate planning, 330 people died, including over 100 children. Shortly after the Beslan crisis, Putin was accused of displaying indifference to the event; one of the reasons for

this charge was a speech he made on September 4, which was mostly devoted not to the murdered children but to the problems of nation-building and external threats.

After eliminating the top Chechen commander, Shamil Basayev, murdering two presidents of the unrecognized Chechen Republic, and creating a pro-Moscow puppet government headed by the Chechen president Ramzan Kadyrov, Putin was able on the whole to localize the Chechen conflict, to disunite the Chechens, and to reduce the role of the Russian army in military operations in Chechnya to policing and punitive functions.

Still, the Chechen question remains the most troublesome problem for Putin and Russia. The Russian government has repeatedly made unsuccessful attempts to have Akhmed Zakayev, the representative of the Chechen government in exile, extradited from London, where he has been granted political asylum. On October 28, 2002, Russia's Ministry of Internal Affairs announced that Putin was canceling a scheduled visit to Denmark, where he was expected to participate in a meeting between Russia and the European Union in November, because the World Chechen Congress was being held in Denmark.

Another "minor" event connected with Putin's pronouncements occurred in Brussels on November 11, 2002. What Putin said in this instance is likely to enter the annals of history in much the same way as Nikita Khrushchev's famous outburst at the United Nations, when he removed one of his shoes and started banging it on the desk. In response to a question from a French reporter about human rights violations in Chechnya, Putin remarked: "If you want to become a complete Islamic radical and are even prepared to get circumcised, then I invite you to Moscow. Our country has many religions and we have specialists in this problem too. I would recommend that the operation be performed in such a way that nothing can grow back after it."

After Putin's answer, the hall fell silent. The interpreter was unsure how to translate his words.

6

"Operation Successor"

IN SEARCH OF THE RUSSIAN PINOCHET

At the first session of his cabinet, Putin announced that Sergei Stepashin's resignation had been brought about "not by a negative assessment of the actions of the prime minister and his cabinet, but by the president's desire to change the internal political configuration in the country in the run-up to the State Duma election, the presidential election, and in connection with the increasing hostilities in the Caucasus." By "increasing hostilities in the Caucasus," Putin meant, above all, incursions into Chechnya by guerilla troops from Dagestan under the command of Shamil Basayev, with whom Russian troops were engaged in prolonged battles in Dagestan.

The need to change the "internal political configuration" stemmed from the ongoing conflict within the government between Stepashin and Nikolai Aksenenko, the first deputy prime minister, who was supported by Berezovsky. Under Putin, the influence of Aksenenko, who was the main representative of "the family" in the prime minister's cabinet, was expected to decline, especially because Putin's nomination had been supported by Alexander Voloshin, the Russian oligarch Roman Abramovich, Anatoly Chubais, Valentin Yumashev, and Yeltsin's daughter Tatyana Dyachenko, who occupied an official position as Yeltsin's advisor. But most importantly, Putin had been supported by Yeltsin.

The new government was not only supposed to secure the outcome of the presidential election, but also to provide for a smooth parliamentary election in December 1999. Stepashin did not want to oppose the union of the Duma's two central parties—Fatherland, formed by Yuri Luzhkov in January, and All Russia, formed by Mintimer Shaimiev in April. This union represented a serious threat to the Kremlin. Stepashin refused to become involved in the creation of a force that could compete with them, and the Kremlin came to the conclusion that Stepashin had reached a tacit agreement with Luzhkov and Primakov (who was considered the favorite in the presidential race and an obvious candidate for Yeltsin's seat) to surrender everything to Primakov. This is what determined the decision to dismiss Stepashin and appoint a new prime minister.

Another change in the government was a risky move for Yeltsin, above all because no one in the country knew who Putin was. His ascent had been too rapid for his face to become familiar. On the day of his appointment, Putin announced his intention to stay the course set by the old government, both in economic policy and in domestic issues, especially concerning Chechnya and Dagestan. Yet when Putin came to power, reporters and members of the public alike expressed apprehensions of a severe clampdown in the federal government's policies in the North Caucasus and in domestic politics generally, including a possibility that the government might declare a state of emergency and call off the presidential election—especially if the Kremlin was uncertain of the victory of Yeltsin's successor, Putin.

In any event, Putin was seen as the "firm hand" that was supposed to conquer the sympathies of Russia's voters. The same role had already been augured for Stepashin, who had been deliberately compared to Augusto Pinochet. But Stepashin had turned out to be too "weak," in the Kremlin's opinion. Among other things, as one of the initiators of the first Chechen war, and having already been burned in Chechnya once, Stepashin was not enthusiastic about the idea of starting a second Chechen war, although a decision to do so had essentially been made already in March 1999, when Putin was head of the FSB.

Stepashin was also not ready to declare a state of emergency in the country. In other words, he did not want to enter history as a Russian Pinochet—by contrast with Putin.

THE SECOND CHECHEN WAR AND PUTIN'S PUBLIC RELATIONS CAMPAIGN

On September 14, 1999, shortly after the explosion of the second apartment building in Moscow, Putin addressed a session of the State Duma on the issue of fighting terrorism. The main points of his speech were as follows: (1) reestablishing the subordination of local law enforcement agencies to federal agencies; (2) repression based on ethnic background is unacceptable; (3) Chechnya as a terrorist camp; (4) a critical reassessment of the Khasavyurt accords, which ended the first Chechen war; (5) temporarily closing Chechnya's borders; (6) Chechnya remains a subject of the Russian Federation; (7) demanding that the Chechen government hand over criminals; (8) merciless elimination of bandits who crossed the border; (9) a special economic regime with respect to Chechnya; (10) forming a (pro-Russian) Chechen government in exile; (11) the need for antiterrorism laws; (12) politicians who exploit the current situation for election purposes are no better than terrorists.[1]

The real beginning of the second Chechen war, however, was predetermined by the events of September 22–23 in Ryazan. After that fiasco, the FSB refused to make any further attempts to blow up residential buildings in Russia. The terrorist atrocity in Ryazan was the last one in the September series. Military operations had to be initiated at once, before Russian public opinion—which was still based on independent media sources—could find out about the Ryazan "learning trials," put the facts together, and reach the conclusion that the terrorist atrocities in Russia were being organized by the security services in order to start another Chechen war.

On September 23, the head of the Moscow FSB, Alexander Tsarenko, announced that the Moscow explosions had been organized by Chechens and that the perpetrators had already been apprehended. (Subsequently, both of the Moscow-based Ingushes whom Tsarenko had in mind when he referred to

"Chechens" were released in view of the fact that neither had any connection to the explosions.) On the same day, the Russian air force bombed the Grozny airport, an oil refinery, and residential neighborhoods on the northern outskirts of the Chechen capital.

On September 24, speaking in Astana, the capital of Kazakhstan, Putin announced that the air strikes had been directed "exclusively against combatants' bases and this will continue wherever terrorists are found. . . . We will whack them in the outhouses if that's where we find them." On the same day, Patrushev reported that there had been no attempt to blow up an apartment building in Ryazan, but rather a "learning trial." The war was already in motion, however. On October 1, Russian tanks crossed Chechnya's administrative border and advanced five kilometers.

Two months into the second Chechen war, it became clear that the military operations had been initiated by the Russian government in order to begin implementing a strategic decision: the transition of the country from a path of reform (Yeltsin's policy) to a military-chekist-bureaucratic path (Putin's policy). Putin's anti-Chechen, pro-chekist decrees, written in the language of a military commander, looked bizarre for the Russia of 1999, not just in content but also in form. Thus, on December 6, the residents of Grozny were presented with "Putin's ultimatum"—a demand by Russian military command in Chechnya for the residents of Grozny to leave the city via "safety corridors" before December 11. "Persons remaining in the city," the ultimatum stated, "will be considered terrorists and bandits. They will be eliminated by the artillery and the air force. . . . All those who have not left the city will be eliminated."[2]

Subsequently, it was specified that the ultimatum was addressed only to combatants, not to all residents of Grozny. On January 13, Putin approved a ban on entering and leaving Chechnya for men between the ages of ten and sixty. The ban was signed by General Viktor Kazantsev, but already on January 15 it was repealed after public protest. When the leadership of the Ministry of Internal Affairs met on January 21, Putin warned about the growing danger of a new wave of terrorist atrocities by Chechen separatists in Russian cities.

On the "Day of the Chekist," December 20, Putin had reinstated a memorial plaque in honor of Yuri Andropov, the former head of the KGB, on the wall of the FSB building in Moscow. Speaking at a banquet for FSB employees that evening, he remarked: "I wish to report that a group of FSB employees assigned to work undercover in the government has successfully completed the first phase of its mission."[3] A widely read Moscow newspaper also quoted Putin as saying: "The criminal organization has been successfully infiltrated. Just a joke."[4]

All the same, the military-chekist thrust of Putin's policies became more and more apparent. On December 31, Putin signed a government decree reinstating military preparation in the schools. In February 2000, he signed an order to call up reserves for active duty, and then an order reinstating "special departments" (military counterintelligence) in the army. These were political agencies whose aim was to monitor the ideological reliability of military personnel, including not just the officers but the soldiers as well. The special departments had been dissolved after the collapse of the Soviet Union, being seen as anachronistic. Now this secret police of the armed forces—a kind of military KGB—was brought back to life.

These were alarming signs. They indicated that Yeltsin might be replaced by a man with the mindset of a Soviet-era KGB officer, a militarist who saw his principal enemies in the United States and a unified Europe. But during those months, many were inclined to see the new prime minister's actions as populist moves intended to placate the nationalism of certain groups of voters.

On February 6, after completing the assault on Grozny, which had lasted many days, Putin announced that "the terrorists' last remaining haven—Grozny's Zavodskoy district—has been taken and a Russian flag has been raised above one of the administrative buildings. So we can say that the operation to liberate Grozny has ended." Evidently, Putin was in a hurry to complete his "small victorious war" before the March presidential election. The Russian army had occupied about 80 percent of Chechnya's territory over a relatively short period of time, September–October 1999. Its military operations were accompanied by serious losses and a great deal of rhetoric about the necessity of preventing the further disintegration of the Russian Federation and about bringing Chechnya back under the federal government's control. On the whole, Russian public opinion, frightened by the September terrorist attacks, supported Putin's policies in Chechnya; even his crude remarks about "whacking the terrorists in the outhouses" worked to his advantage. After the military campaign began in Chechnya, Putin's popularity—thanks to the unswerving support of the Berezovsky-controlled Channel One of Russian television (ORT)—started growing steadily. By the beginning of the election campaign, he was no longer an unknown, but a candidate with a popularity rating as high as 50 percent.

PUTIN AS ACTING PRESIDENT

In the national election for the third convocation of the State Duma, on December 19, 1999, the Unity bloc won 23.32 percent of the vote, coming in second after the Communists (24.29 percent). Yevgeny Primakov's and Yuri Luzhkov's Fatherland–All Russia bloc (OVR) won 13.33 percent; the Union of Right Forces (SPS) won 8.52 percent; Vladimir Zhirinovsky's Liberal Democratic Party of Russia won 5.98 percent; and Yabloko won 5.93 percent. On the same day, Putin's principal opponent in the upcoming presidential election, Yevgeny Primakov, announced that he would not run. Those who had been planning to solidify Putin's position as a claimant to the throne resolved to make him a formal heir.

Thus, the parliamentary election was a success for Putin. The Interregional Unity Movement (abbreviated as "Medved")— formed shortly before the election on the initiative and through the efforts of Boris Berezovsky, who had developed both the ideology and the symbolism of the new party—unexpectedly for everyone fell less than one percent short of the Communists in the party-list vote. When the parliament's single-constituency votes were added to its total, Medved became the largest party faction in the Duma. Even more important was the fact that Medved's votes had been taken away from Primakov and from Luzhkov. Their Fatherland–All Russia bloc had won only slightly more than 13 percent of the vote, instead of the 30 to 40 percent that they had expected. The voters had also given considerable support to the Union of Right Forces, led by Sergei Kiriyenko and running on the slogan: "Putin for President! Kiriyenko for the State Duma! We need young people!" By contrast, the Communist opposition had lost its absolute majority in the Duma. Berezovsky's Channel One had supported Unity and Putin in any way it could, forgetting all about honesty and objectivity.

In his New Year's address on December 31, 1999, President Yeltsin announced that he was resigning from the presidency and appointing Putin as acting president until the election on March 26—earlier than previously scheduled. In return, and in accordance with a pre-existing agreement with Yeltsin, Putin issued a decree at the beginning of January 2000 granting the first president of Russia and his family immunity from all legal or administrative prosecution.

In January, two factions backing the acting president were formed in the new Duma: Unity (headed by Boris Gryzlov and Frants Klintsevich) and People's Deputy (Gennady Raykov). Two other centrist, establishment-oligarchic factions—Regions of Russia (Oleg Morozov) and Fatherland–All Russia (Yevgeny Primakov, Vyacheslav Volodin)—also declared their loyalty to Putin. These four pro-Putin factions contained over half the Duma's deputies. During the Duma's third convocation, from 230 to 235 deputies formed a hard presidential majority, almost always voting in accordance with the orders of the president's deputy chief of staff, Vladislav Surkov. In addition to the Duma's center, which backed the acting president, Zhirinovsky's LDPR became almost as loyal, as did a large part of the SPS (headed by Sergei Kiriyenko, as well as Boris Nemtsov and Irina Khakamada).

With the solid backing of the center, the presidential administration pushed whatever legislation it needed through the Duma without encountering any obstacles, relying on an absolute majority of 226 votes. When it was necessary to enact constitutional reforms requiring a supermajority (300 votes), the administration relied either on the liberal-centrist, "right-wing, pro-Putin" constitutional majority (the center, LDPR, SPS, Yabloko) or on the nationalist, "left-wing, pro-Putin" majority (the center, LDPR, CPRF, and the pro-Communist Agrarian Party).

Independence from the presidential administration and a relatively oppositional stance was exhibited by the CPRF. Occasionally, opposition from the right ("systemic opposition") would come from Yabloko, certain independents (Vladimir Ryzhkov), and several SPS deputies (Sergei Kovalev, Yuli Rybakov, Sergei Yushenkov, Viktor Pokhmelkin, Vladimir Golovlev). Boris Nemtsov sometimes wavered between loyalty and opposition—although this opposition was reflected more in his rhetoric than in his votes. During the second convocation of the Federation Council, the upper house of the legislature, Putin was opposed to some extent only by the president of the Chuvash Republic, Nikolai Fyodorov. But Fyodorov soon thought better of it and his opposition also dwindled.

THE PRESIDENTIAL ELECTION

On January 13, 2000, during a trip to St. Petersburg, Putin officially confirmed his intention to run for president of Russia and announced his support for Vladimir Yakovlev—Sobchak's assistant and subsequent rival—in the St. Petersburg gubernatorial race. On February 15, Putin registered with the Central Election Commission as a candidate for the presidency.

While campaigning in Irkutsk on February 18, Putin came out in support of the SPS-proposed idea for a referendum on four issues: increasing guarantees for the protection of private property; limiting deputies' immunity; sending only contractual military personnel to areas of armed conflict; and limiting the president's right to dismiss his cabinet without demonstrable cause. On the same day, he approved of the idea of "prohibiting sex, violence, and terrorism" on television.

Putin had never before stood for elected office. Observers recalled an interview two years earlier in which he had talked about his unwillingness to participate in an election campaign, citing the fact that the candidate must make promises that he cannot keep, and consequently has to be unaware of the meaning of his own words or must deliberately lie. Putin's career also received some attention. His supporters pointed to his work in the Sobchak administration as proof of his commitment to reform. His opponents, particularly Grigory Yavlinsky, stressed his work for the KGB and the FSB, portraying him as a devotee of the old political order and the practices of the KGB.

"An Open Letter from Vladimir Putin to Russian Voters" was published in the press on February 25. At a Moscow meeting with his supporters three days later, Putin declared that "it is vitally important to create equal conditions for all participants in the political and economic life of Russia. We must make it impossible for individuals to latch on to power and use it for their own purposes. No clan, no oligarch must be involved in regional or federal government. All of them must be equally distanced from political power and all of them must rely on equal means." However, the idealistic principles laid out by Putin were not observed even for a single day, least of all by Putin himself.

First Person: Conversations with Vladimir Putin, a book compiled of three interviews with *Kommersant* reporters, was published during Putin's election campaign. This little volume, hastily assembled on Boris Berezovsky's initiative, was the only serious publication devoted to Putin that existed at the time. Today, many of the pronouncements in this book can at best draw a smile. For instance, as a possible way of solving the problems facing Russia, Putin mentioned the monetarization of subsidies, that is, replacing the numerous government benefits received by various groups of people—a system inherited from Soviet times—with monetary compensation. When an attempt to implement this undoubtedly progressive idea was eventually made, it turned out to be the most unpopular of Putin's economic policies and was never brought to fruition.

On the whole, however, Putin—as a staff employee of state security who had spent his whole adult life working for the KGB under the ideological control of the Communist Party—had no ideology or political program of his own. He confined himself to general populist phrases. Back in 1999, at the beginning of his tenure as prime minister, he had given the following response to a question about his potential platform in the presidential race: "My main objective is to improve people's lives. We will work out a political platform later." Then, in 2001, in response to a question about how he envisioned the Russia of 2010, he said: "We will be happy." If by "we" Putin meant the people who would be in power in Russia, then he was telling the truth.

During the period before the election, the Kremlin tried to foist upon voters the idea that there was no alternative to Putin, pointing out that his main rival was the Communist Party candidate, Zyuganov, undoubtedly a worse choice for Russia. Indeed, according to surveys it was not only the adherents of Unity and the SPS that were intending to vote for Putin, but also certain supporters of Zyuganov's CPRF and Yavlinsky's Yabloko—although the heads of these parties were also taking part in the election. Putin's victory in the upcoming election was supposed to give legitimacy to the already established "Putin regime."

In the presidential election, Putin was officially supported by Boris Gryzlov's and Sergei Shoygu's Unity bloc, Viktor Chernomyrdin's NDR, Yuri Luzhkov's Fatherland, Vladimir Yakovlev's and Mintimer Shaimiev's All Russia bloc, Gennady Raykov's People's Deputy bloc, the SPS, Mikhail Lapshin's Agrarian Party of Russia (APR), and a number of other organizations. Special and invaluable support for Putin came from Berezovsky's ORT television (Channel One).

Somewhat disoriented by the campaign, Putin promised everything to everyone. At a meeting with voters in Zvezdny Gorodok on March 2, he promised to support the Mir Space Station, assuring his audience that "the issue is merely one of financing and it will be resolved." (A year later, Putin as president approved the liquidation of the space station; it was sunk on March 6, 2001.) In a BBC interview on March 5, Putin told viewers in the West that he did not rule out the possibility of Russia entering NATO—a statement that greatly perplexed many Russian politicians and government officials. (Russia did not join NATO, but rather intensified its anti-NATO rhetoric, backing it up with declarations about withdrawing from various agreements, opposing ballistic missile defense, and resuming the practice of sending strategic bombers on regular flights, which had been discontinued in 1992.)

During a "working trip to the Chechen Republic" on March 20, Putin made a widely publicized flight on a Su-27 fighter aircraft as a second pilot-navigator. This circus performance was obviously calculated to increase his popularity among simple voters. But the people who were making a president out of Putin had not explained to him why they had put him inside a military plane, so Putin, in response to questions from the American TV interviewer Ted Koppel, became confused and muttered that he had flown on the Su-27 in order to reduce costs.

All the same, Putin's airplane had not landed in vain. He was elected president on March 26 with 39,740,434 votes (52.94 percent) according to official records.

HOW ELECTION OUTCOMES ARE FALSIFIED

Putin's victory in the first round of voting gives rise to well-founded suspicions, since voter fraud in his favor was discovered in a number of regions, including Dagestan, Bashkortostan, the Saratov region, Tatarstan, and others. Putin was given tens of thousands of votes that had been cast for other candidates. In the three months between the parliamentary and the presidential elections, the Central Election Commission's official lists of registered voters grew by 1,300,000 people (from 108,072,000 in the parliamentary election to 109,372,000 in the presidential election), despite a decline in Russia's population by 800,000 annually. Most likely, the actual proportion of votes received by Putin on March 26 was 48 or 49 percent.

The techniques for falsifying election outcomes for the State Duma and the gubernatorial and presidential races are more or less identical. Looking at the facts for all elections and referendums between 1993 and 2003, one can identify two broad approaches. The first involves "correcting" the vote count; the second involves the introduction of additional ballots. Each of these general approaches encompasses several different tactics.

Under the first approach, for example, any number of extra votes may be added to a candidate's tallies by the precinct election commissions. More often, however, the "correction" is made when the precinct tallies are summed up by the district and territorial election commissions. Nothing is altered in the records of the ballots handed out. Sometimes, the tallies are "corrected" (at both the regional and the district level) on the pretext of alleged mistakes.

The main advantages of this method (from the falsifiers' perspective) are its simplicity and ease, and, in the event of a "correction" at the regional level, the negligible number of persons who are involved in and have knowledge of the operation. Its principal disadvantage is that a simple comparison between the number of ballots handed out according to the ballot book records and the number of votes cast according to the precinct records will clearly reveal that the latter exceeds the former. If the fabricated votes were added at the regional level, the inconsistency is discovered by comparing copies of the precinct records with records compiled at the territorial commission and/or with the territorial commission's official tables of composite vote tallies.

It is also possible to increase the number of votes cast for a candidate by adding extra ballots that were never actually cast but were recorded as having been handed out in the ballot book records. The recipients of the extra ballots may be listed as voters who traditionally do not participate in elections (lists of such voters can be purchased from image-maker firms, and election commission officials frequently have such lists at their disposal); or individuals who are deceased or who have moved, or "fabricated persons" with fictional addresses (such as extra apartments in a large apartment building). This is done at the precinct level. Such falsifications can be discovered either by comparing the number of ballots actually cast with the records in the ballot books, or by interviewing individuals who are listed in the ballot book records as having received ballots, with a view to identifying those among them who did not actually vote, who have moved, who are deceased, or who never existed.

In addition, votes cast for opposition candidates or for "none of the above" can be transferred to the government-backed candidate in the vote tallies. The falsified numbers can be entered into precinct records while votes are being counted and then transcribed by the territorial election commissions. This method is labor-intensive, since it involves a considerable amount of arithmetical computation. The advantage of this approach, however, consists in the fact that falsifications at the precinct level cannot be detected by an examination of ballot book records: in order to identify falsifications, the actual ballots cast for each candidate must be recounted. But a similar kind of forgery at the regional level can be detected by a comparison of precinct records (or their copies) with the territorial commission's tables of composite vote tallies.

Finally, the number of ballots cast for an "undesirable" candidate can simply be reduced. The ballots may be uncounted and discarded (as happened, for example, with the ballots cast for Skokov-Lebed's Congress of Russian Communities in Makhachkala in 1995, when bags of "leftover" ballots ended up in the town dump). Ballots cast for "undesirable" candidates can also be defaced while they are being counted with the addition of an extra check mark, making it appear as if a voter had voted for two candidates at once, thereby invalidating the ballot. The advantage of both these methods is simplicity. The disadvantage is that simplicity implies ease of detection. If the "unneeded" ballots are discarded, the total number of ballots will decrease. If the ballots are defaced, the fabrication becomes more conspicuous: for example, if 10 percent of the ballots in one election district are defaced, while in neighboring districts the defaced ballots constitute less than 2 percent of the total, this immediately gives rise to well-founded suspicions. But if all ballots are destroyed soon after the elections (as was the case in 1993, 1995, 1996, 1999, 2000), it is impossible to prove that ballots were defaced deliberately.

A candidate's total vote count may be increased with extra ballots added to the total at the voting precincts before, during, or after the election, with no indications made in the ballot book records. Mobile ballot boxes and early voting create an almost legal reserve of extra votes for the "right" candidates. Sometimes extra ballots are even printed deliberately. (Such cases have been recorded in Bashkortostan under President Murtaza Rakhimov, for example.) Extra ballots are added both at the precinct level, where they are thrown into ballot boxes, and at the regional level, where they are dumped into bags that are unsealed, which is contrary to law, or have their seals broken.

The disadvantage of this method of falsification is that the total of all the votes according to the records can still be compared with the number of ballots handed out (according to the ballot book records); similarly, the number of ballots in the ballot boxes can be compared with the number of ballots handed out. In order to avoid this detection, the extra ballots added to the total can also be recorded in the ballot book records. In this case, voters who do not traditionally participate in elections and "dead souls" of every variety are listed as the recipients of the ballots. The votes of deceased individuals are usually cast in advance of the general election, and the votes of living ones at the end of the day.

This is the most labor-intensive and "high-quality" method of falsification, detectable only by interviewing a large number of voters or purely by accident, if a person who has never before voted shows up and discovers that someone has already voted for him, or if a relative of a deceased voter discovers the signature of the deceased in the ballot book records. It is evident that low voter turnout makes the falsifiers' work easier, while active voter participation—including voting for "none of the above," which remained an option until the summer of 2006, or simply walking away with the ballot—makes their work more difficult.

OBSERVERS AND COPIES OF RECORDS

Naturally, it is easier to falsify election outcomes if observers from parties or international organizations are not present at the voting precincts. The presence of observers, however, provides no guarantee against falsification. Sometimes they are so dependent on the government that they are not prepared to make a public statement about voter fraud. Alternatively, the observer may be independent but neither well qualified nor attentive. Finally, the observer may personally monitor everything that takes place at the voting precinct but have no way of seeing what happens at the district and territorial election commission offices. He can only compare the numbers on his copy of the precinct records with the composite vote tallies published by the territorial election commission. But in order to prove that an election commission is guilty of fraud, the observer needs notarized copies of the precinct records. Precinct election commissions are required to provide observers with such copies as soon as they are requested, but usually it is only the most persistent observers who are able to obtain good copies of properly filled-out records. Unfortunately, observers as a rule are not persistent, nor are they always sufficiently educated in election regulations. As a result, the copies of the records that are given out to observers according to the law are very often filled out hastily, with obvious mistakes and omissions. Such records can be used to evaluate whether fraud has taken place, but they are unsuitable for subsequent use in a legal context.

Igor Borisov, the deputy head of the Coordinating Council of the Russian Public Institute of Electoral Law (ROIPP). pointed out in November 2001 that an overwhelming majority of the observers' copies of records that were offered to the institute for analysis "do not meet the requirements of electoral law and do not constitute legal documents." Borisov explained: "Most of the records have empty columns—they can be filled in with any numbers whatsoever, and then it can be claimed that the records do not adequately correspond to the originals. Practically none of the observers' copies meet the notarization requirements as stipulated in Article 21 of the law 'On the election of the President of the Russian Federation.'"[5]

It is precisely on the pretext that copies of records have been improperly notarized or are missing various columns that the General Prosecutor's Office has up to now rejected most claims of voter fraud as having no legal weight; when cases have been taken up, they have been brought to trial extremely infrequently; and when they have been brought to trial, they have fallen apart in court. In 2000, after the prosecutor's office received allegations of fraud in the presidential election at the voting precincts of the Saratov region, the regional prosecutor was forced to check twenty precincts, and the results of the recount confirmed a discrepancy between the records and the officially notarized copies. But the plaintiffs were denied their request to initiate criminal proceedings because, as the heads of the territorial election commissions subjected to the recount told the prosecutor's office, when the copies of the records were given out "the numbers contained in the copies were not verified against the numbers contained in the originals by members of the committee."[6] In essence, the prosecutor's office declared that it was not the election commissions that had falsified the election results, but rather the observers in all the precincts where votes had been recounted who had forged their own copies.

THE ELECTION OUTCOME OF MARCH 26, 2000

According to the records of the Central Election Commission (CEC), Vladimir Putin received 52.94 percent of the vote on March 26. But when voting ended at 8 P.M., Putin had received only 44.5 percent of the vote—although his percentage increased as voting moved from east to west. (The opposite phenomenon had been observed in the Duma election of December 19, 1999: as voting moved westward, the numbers for the Communist Party consistently improved, while those for the pro-Putin Unity party consistently declined.)

As the counting continued through the night of March 26–27, the number of votes cast for Putin did not reach 50 percent before 2 A.M. At that point, the head of the CEC, Alexander Veshnyakov, triumphantly announced: "Vladimir Vladimirovich Putin, fifty and one hundredth of a percent." At 10 A.M., Putin had 52 percent; and in the final vote count on April 7, he had 52.94 percent (39,740,434 votes).

The outcome of the election resembled the last pre-election polls by the most respected polling organizations. On the other hand, the 2.94 percent of the vote that secured Putin's victory in the first round of voting is within the error range deemed acceptable by current polling techniques—usually around 3 or 3.5 percent. So there is little point in citing pre-election polls to back up Putin's victory.

The Dagestan Case

Independent investigations to uncover fraud in the presidential election of March 26, 2000, took place in only two regions— Dagestan and the Saratov region. The infractions in Dagestan were investigated (following a complaint by Zyuganov's campaign headquarters) by the Duma's "Committee on Studying the Practice of Applying the Russian Federation's Electoral Law in Preparing and Conducting Elections and Referendums in the Russian Federation," headed by Alexander Saliy (CPRF).

According to official records, Putin had received 877,853 votes (over 75 percent) in Dagestan.

Saliy's committee did not recount the actual ballots and did not compare them with the official results.

Incidentally, fearing that the committee would attempt to recount the ballots in at least some of the precincts, the Dagestan government had taken the necessary precautions. Abdulla Magomedov, a Makhachkala police officer stationed at the entrance of the republic's government headquarters building, saw officials (who showed him their passes) carrying large bags with papers out of the building and burning them right on the street. The policeman, citing his official duty as security guard, insisted on inspecting the contents of the bags and determined that they were filled with ballots that had been cast for Zyuganov. "I know what they look like—I was an observer during the voting," the policeman said.[7]

Saliy's committee focused its attention on comparing copies of the precinct records that had been given to observers with the official figures for the same precincts as recorded at a higher level, by territorial election commissions. Saliy's committee disposed of 453 copies of precinct records. (Dagestan has 1,550 voting precincts in all; observers from Zyuganov's headquarters were unable to obtain copies of records from the other precincts.) Fourteen district election commissions and two municipal commissions came under investigation. All together, 174 different precinct records were examined.

Subsequently, the findings of Saliy's committee were published in the newspaper *Sovietskaya Rossiya*, with comparative tables of records and official figures for three territorial election commissions—the Suleyman-Stal, the Magaramkent, and the Kizilyurt—along with a composite table of forgeries at sixteen territorial election commissions. For example, precinct No. 1036 of the Suleyman-Stal election commission: the observers' copy of the precinct records indicated 801 votes for Zyuganov, while the territorial commission's official records showed 150 (651 votes stolen); the copy indicated 452 votes for Putin, while the official records showed 2,038 (1,568 added). Precinct No. 1044 of the same territorial commission: 862 of 863 votes stolen from Zyuganov, 1,572 votes added to Putin's

227. All together, in 34 of the 40 examined precincts of this territorial election commission, 8,462 votes had been stolen from Zyuganov and 13,805 votes had been added for Putin.

In precinct No. 0580 of the Kizilyurt territorial election commission, 295 of 495 votes were stolen from Zyuganov and 1,151 votes were added to Putin's 315. In precinct No. 0586, 279 of 399 votes were stolen from Zyuganov and 1,203 were added to Putin's 84. All together, in 20 of the 26 precincts of the Kizilyurt territorial election commission, Zyuganov's total vote count was reduced by 6,161, and Putin's was increased by 14,105.

Saliy's committee discovered that when the signature of the precinct chairman on the copy of the records was identical with the signature on the original, no changes had been made in the copy, and that all such precincts had been carried by Zyuganov. In cases where the signatures were not identical, Putin had won by a landslide, and the signatures that appeared in the observers' copies were identical to the genuine signatures of the precinct chairmen, while the signatures in the official records were not. From this it followed that the copies were genuine, while the official precinct records had been "corrected" by the territorial election commissions.

Saliy's committee tallied the "corrections" in all of the sixteen territorial election commission records that it examined. All together, according to the composite table of falsifications published by Saliy, over 187,000 extra votes had been added to Putin's total vote count in Dagestan.[8]

Saliy's committee sent these findings along with copies of the precinct records to the General Prosecutor's Office as early as the summer of 2000. The prosecutor's office did not bring charges against the officials suspected of forgery, nor did it bring charges against *Sovietskaya Rossiya* for libel. Veshnyakov, head of the CEC, also did not file suit to protect his honor and professional reputation.

Extra ballots were also added in Dagestan. *Sovietskaya Rossiya* received fifteen such ballots for Putin from the city of Izberbash, all bearing the stamp of precinct No. 0832. Photocopies of these ballots were reproduced in the newspaper.[9]

Forty percent of the precincts in Dagestan had no cancelled, unused ballots. This would appear to mean that in each of these precincts, exactly the same number of people had voted as there were ballots. Of course, this is highly unlikely. Evidently the ballots that were unused, instead of being cancelled, had simply been added to the rest.

Yevgenia Borisova, a *Moscow Times* reporter, conducted her own investigation of voter fraud in a number of regions, including Dagestan. Borisova checked the figures of Saliy's committee and reached the conclusion that 57,162 votes should undoubtedly be considered as having been stolen in Putin's favor. The other tens of thousands of votes—out of the more than 187,000 "corrections" in Saliy's table—she assessed as uncertain, disagreeing with the committee's counting procedure. Borisova also compared the territorial election commission tables with the copies of records from another 71 precincts that Saliy's committee had not examined. The picture in these precincts was the same. Thus, according to the copy of the records of precinct No. 0876, Putin received 1,070 votes, while the records of the territorial commission gave him 3,535; according to the records of precinct No. 0903, Putin had won 480 votes, while the territorial commission's records said he had won 1,830; and so on.

Of the 71 records inspected by Borisova and her assistants, 63 contained evidence of falsification. They added up to 31,101 more votes stolen for Putin. That makes 88,263 votes in all, based on records that constituted only 16 percent of all Dagestan records.[10]

Saratov Region

A similar situation was discovered in the Saratov region. According to the testimony of A. Bidonko, a territorial election commission member, when figures from the precincts began to arrive at three o'clock in the morning of March 27, it became clear that neither Putin nor Governor Dmitry Ayatskov (there was a simultaneous gubernatorial election in the region) would get 50 percent of the vote. All night long, the records were rewritten, and the unused ballots were cancelled only in the morning.[11] The Communists brought charges on this account, but the court refused to hear the case, instead sending it for a recount to the same territorial election commission—which established, by taking a vote, that everything had been done according to the rules.

Observers from Zyuganov's campaign headquarters were able to obtain 700 notarized copies of precinct records from the Saratov region, which had 1,815 voting precincts in all. *Sovietskaya Rossiya* reporter Zhanna Kasyanenko compared the records of 28 precincts and found that 3,769 votes had been added to Putin's total in these precincts (with 1,540 votes being stolen from Yavlinsky and 827 from Zyuganov).

Other candidates too were not neglected by the territorial election commissions of the Saratov region. Here are the most blatant cases:

Precinct election commission No. 1576: Govorukhin had 12 votes and was left with none. Pamfilova had 16 and was left with 6. Podberezkin had 3 and was left with none. Skuratov had 9 and was left with zero. Out of 30 votes cast for "none of the above," 10 remained. In all, 50 extra votes had been added to Putin's total.

Precinct election commission No. 1617: Here, 200 of Zyuganov's 445 votes, 100 of Yavlinsky's 138 votes, 40 of Tuleev's 41 votes, 30 of Pamfilova's 32 votes, 20 of Zhirinovsky's 28 votes, and 10 of Titov's 18 votes had been stolen. Out of 28 votes cast for "none of the above," 8 remained. In all, 420 extra votes had been added to Putin's total.

Zhanna Kasyanenko inspected 28 records, including materials from ROIPP (Russian Public Institute of Electoral Law). ROIPP itself analyzed 829 copies of records from precincts in the Saratov region (constituting 45.47 percent of all precincts), comparing them with the composite tables of the territorial commissions—not just the records of the CPRF observers (700 copies), but also the records of observers from Yabloko and other parties. Out of these 829, ROIPP found approximately 100 precinct records whose figures had been changed in the composite tables of higher-level committees, and reached the conclusion that "a large part of them deviates in favor of V. Putin."[12] ROIPP did also discover "a number of precincts" in which extra votes had been given to Zyuganov. In precinct No. 107, Zyuganov had been given an extra 6 votes; and in precinct No. 452, Putin had been given an extra 31 votes, Zyuganov an extra 10, and Zhirinovsky a single extra vote.

After the General Prosecutor's Office received complaints about fraud in the presidential election at voting precincts in the Saratov region, the regional prosecutor's office was forced to recount the records of twenty precincts. The results of the recount corroborated the discrepancy between the figures in the records and the officially notarized copies. The plaintiffs were given a response—signed by A. Makasheva, chief prosecutor of the Administrative Department Overseeing the Execution of Laws and the Legality of Juridical Acts—with a refusal to initiate criminal proceedings due to the fact that, as the heads of the territorial election commissions subjected to vote recounts told the General Prosecutor's Office, when copies of records had been released, "the figures contained in them had not been verified against the figures in the original records by the members of the committee."[13]

Mordovia

In precinct No. 207 of the city of Yoshkar-Ola, an advisory precinct commission member, L. Korostelev, was forcibly removed by the police from the building where the votes were being counted, on orders from the precinct commission chairman, N. Bolshakov. When Korostelev was permitted to return to the building, he discovered "a great number of defaced ballots for Zyuganov. I am convinced that they had been defaced on purpose, and deliberately during my absence—covered with additional dashes and signs." Naturally, the head of the precinct election commission, his deputy, and his secretary refused to sign the copy of the precinct records assembled by Korostelev.

Bashkortostan

Here, the results were falsified directly in the precinct records. In precinct No. 2921 of Bashkortostan, the votes cast for Putin and Zyuganov were simply switched: immediately after the count, Zyuganov had 252 and Putin had 110, but the official record shows the reverse.

In the Bashkirian village of Priyutovo, in precinct No. 514, a former teacher named Klavdiya Grigoryeva was present as an observer while votes were counted, and she wrote down for her own records: 862 votes for Putin, 356 for Zyuganov, 24 for Zhirinovsky, 21 for Titov, 12 for Yavlinsky. By contrast, the totals in the precinct's official records showed 1,092 votes for Putin, 177 for Zyuganov, and zero for the others.

Unfortunately, neither the figures in these records nor those of other records in Bashkortostan were compared by any investigative committee with the ballots in the ballot boxes. (The year-long period during which ballots must be preserved by law ended on March 26, 2001, and they were destroyed.) And no prosecutor's office will accept an observer's personal notes as grounds for initiating criminal proceedings based on Article 142 of the Russian Criminal Code.

No direct orders "from above" were observed during the March 2000 presidential election in Bashkortostan. However, the results of an exit poll conducted by Gleb Pavlovsky's Foundation for Effective Politics were distributed to all the precinct election commissions in Bashkortostan while voting was still in progress. In this way, the precinct commissions were made to understand—without any explicit orders or instructions—that the final outcome in Bashkortostan must be "not worse" than the nationwide exit poll.

Tatarstan

Mintimer Shaimiev, president of Tatarstan, once said: "We orient the voter, and he votes accordingly. This is a pragmatic approach, and this is how we work with voters."[14] It was not the voters alone that were oriented, however, but the election commissions as well. Precinct No. 2729 followed the government's recommendations with such enthusiasm that all but two of 286 ballots turned out to have been for Putin. Most likely, this was done at the precinct level.

At another precinct in Tatarstan, Yabloko's observer Olga Tarasova noted that extra ballots for Putin were added and ballots for other candidates were removed while votes were being counted.

Alkhat Zaripov, a sixty-five-year-old resident of a large apartment building in Kazan (107 Yu. Fyuchik Street), noticed that the voting precinct had 209 apartments listed for his building, while he knows for certain that there are only 180. The records for the neighboring building likewise showed 108 extra apartments. Zaripov demanded an explanation, but the election commission member simply collected the lists and left.

The *Moscow Times* published a photograph of Pyotr Filippov, a retired seventy-one-year-old resident of the town of Tatrsky Satlyk in Tatarstan, who arrived at the voting precinct late in the day on March 26 intending to vote for Zhirinovsky, but discovered that someone had already signed for him as having received a ballot. In precinct No. 263 in Kazan, CPRF observers stopped a man with twelve ballots for Putin; in precinct No. 265, they stopped a woman with similar, unaccounted ballots.

Kaliningrad Region

Kaliningrad had no fewer than forty-four recorded instances of discrepancies between the figures on the records and the figures on the copies given to observers. The total number of ballots stolen for Putin was 42,500. The chairman of the Kaliningrad regional election commission explained that due to the lack of copy machines, the copies of the records were filled out by hand and then signed by members of the precinct election commissions without being verified. In other words, according to the election commission, it was not the territorial election commissions (or precinct election commissions) that had siphoned off an additional 42,500 for Putin, but the observers who had conspired and for some reason falsified the figures in their copies.

Kursk Region

In Kursk, the Communist Party succeeded in proving in court that voter fraud had taken place at precinct No. 426, showing that 104 out of 610 ballots had been falsified in Putin's favor. But the heads of two election commissions in the Kursk region were fired by the governor after Zyuganov had won in their districts.

Kabardino-Balkaria

According to the records given to observers, Putin received an extra 2,864 votes in all. In precinct No. 179, the observers discovered that only 640 people had come to vote, while 972 ballots had been removed from the ballot box.

Primorye

After voting ended, local residents found several torn-up ballots for Zyuganov at precinct No. 1047. The court declined to hear the case.

Chechnya and Ingushetia

Naturally, the outcome of the March 26, 2000, election in Chechnya has no relation to reality. No one there checked any records. Even so, it is clear that all the figures are complete fabrications: 191,000 votes for Putin, about 86,000 for Zyuganov, 35,000 for Yavlinsky, 22,000 for Dzhabrailov. If the totals ascribed to the "pacifist" Yavlinsky and the Chechen Dzhabrailov may be seen as resembling the truth, then Vladimir "whack them in the outhouses" Putin and the imperialist Zyuganov could hardly have received more than 100,000–120,000 votes between them (since according to various estimates this was the number of Russian troops in Chechnya in March). Everything else is a patent falsification. A simple mathematical calculation reveals that every member of the Russian army in Chechnya voted twice.

In exactly the same way, the military administration's imagination had given 48.03 percent of the vote in the Chechen Republic to Chernomyrdin's NDR in 1995. This percentage was a nationwide record for the NDR. In 1996, Yeltsin got 65.11 percent in the Chechen Republic in the first round of voting and 73.38 percent in the second.

The outcome for Ingushetia looks almost as incredible: in this republic, suffering under the yoke of "counterterrorist operations," the official records show a grand total of 85 percent (94,000 voters) as having cast their ballots for Putin!

Indirect Evidence

In addition to the direct evidence that extra ballots (for people who had not voted) were added after voting ended, there are two pieces of indirect evidence.

The first piece of indirect evidence: according to the official records of the CEC, the total number of voters eligible to vote in the State Duma election on December 19, 1999, was slightly above 108,072,000. Only three months later, the number of eligible voters had risen by 1,300,000!

The second piece of indirect evidence is the spike in official voter turnout during the final hours of voting. Along with a constantly rising percentage of votes cast for Putin, turnout increased dramatically during the final two or three hours of voting. At 7 P.M. Moscow time, turnout was 54 percent, but two hours later it had risen to 67 percent. Apparently, instead of watching the country's two most popular TV shows, which were airing that night, vast crowds of people suddenly flooded the voting precincts.

WHAT WAS THE TOTAL NUMBER OF VOTES ADDED TO PUTIN'S VOTE COUNT?

Saliy tried to estimate how many votes had been stolen for Putin in Dagestan, and he arrived at the figure of approximately 700,000—based, evidently, on the figure of 180,000 for sixteen territorial election commissions. The *Moscow Times* reporter Yevgenia Borisova carried out her own calculations, based on the figure of 88,263 for 16 percent of the records, and came up with approximately 550,000 votes. According to official records, Putin received a total of 877,853 votes in Dagestan.

Thus, the winner in the first round of the presidential election in Dagestan was in reality not Putin, but Zyuganov.

Can the scale of the falsification in Dagestan be extrapolated to the country as a whole? Probably not: Dagestan is both a "red" and a Muslim region, and thus it always votes differently from the rest of the country. In addition, documents there are falsified more boldly than in other parts of Russia.

By contrast, the Saratov region is much more indicative of Russia as a whole. Therefore, it is useful to estimate first of all how much was stolen in Putin's favor in this region. According to the previously quoted interview with Igor Borisov, who cited ROIPP's findings for about a hundred precincts in the Saratov region, "if these figures are extrapolated for the region as a whole, taking the figures in the observers' copies of the records for the absolute truth, Putin will lose about 4 percent of the vote in a region in which he won 58 percent, and these 4 percent will be divided among the other candidates. In other words, the final outcome will not change: Putin will have about 54 percent left in the Saratov region." In this region, 4 percent of the vote is almost 61,000.

In Bashkiria, where according to official records Putin received 1,387,179 votes (over 60 percent), the exact scale of the falsification is known, unfortunately, for only one precinct—the village of Priyutovo. If the falsifications in Bashkiria as a whole took place on the same scale as in Priyutovo, then Putin had an extra 291,000 votes added to his total.

The situation apparently begins to resemble Dagestan only in the relatively sparsely populated Republic of Kalmykia (with 77,714 votes—over 70 percent—supposedly cast for Putin) and Ingushetia. Selective samples in the Kaliningrad and Nizhny Novgorod regions reveal that the outcomes there were "corrected" in approximately the same way as in Saratov, while in Primorye, Tatarstan, and Kabardino-Balkaria the falsification took place on approximately the same scale as in Bashkiria.

Thus, Putin received the following stolen votes: 800,000 votes from people who, as the so-called "ministry of elections" (CEC) admitted, "may have voted twice"; 550,000 votes in Dagestan; 291,000 in Bashkiria; 131,000 in the Saratov region; at least 42,500 in the Kaliningrad region; tens of thousands of completely fabricated votes in Chechnya and Ingushetia; and further—Kalmykia, Kabardino-Balkaria, Primorye, the Nizhny Novgorod region, the Kursk region, and the remaining regions. If we begin to add up these figures, and then consider that the 2.94 percent of the vote that made Putin president in the first round of voting constituted only 2,200,000 votes, we can justifiably conclude that he did not actually win the first round of the election. Most likely, he received 48–49 percent of the vote in Russia as a whole (approximately the same as in the Saratov region). By the way, this is the figure on which most experts agree when speaking "off the record."

Today, probably no one doubts that Putin would have won the election in the second round in any case. But at the beginning of 2000, his victory did not seem as certain—at least not to the president's staff or to the "ministry of elections." Therefore, there was no second round of voting on May 7. Instead, there was an inauguration.

7

The FSB, the Oligarchs, and the Clans

The FSB corporation has always considered those who are not its members to be enemies. It is therefore not surprising that after coming to power, the corporation's members in Moscow and in local governments, from President Putin on down, have dedicated themselves to intensifying control over the population ("the vertical of power"), confiscating property (doing away with inconvenient oligarchs), planting FSB agents (officers of the active reserve) in the enemy's ranks, hunting down countless spies employed by an imaginary enemy (most often for the crime of "divulging government secrets"), and finally, waging a war that was instigated by the FSB corporation itself (in Chechnya). All these corporate battles might have looked like games if they didn't involve the destruction of an actual country (Russia) and the deaths of actual people (mostly Russians and Chechens).

CREATION OF THE FEDERAL DISTRICTS AND DISMISSAL OF THE FEDERATION COUNCIL

In his inaugural speech on May 7, 2000, Putin focused on the importance of preserving Russia's unity and consolidating the government. This was precisely the objective of one of Putin's most significant steps during his first term of office: reforming the structure of the federal government. Putin signed a decree on May 13 creating seven federal districts, with a plenipotentiary representative of the president in each. On May 17, he addressed the nation on television to announce the beginning of a reform in the federal structure.

On May 18, plenipotentiary representatives of the president were appointed in the seven newly created federal districts. FSB General Viktor Cherkesov became the president's plenipotentiary representative in the Central Federal District, which included Moscow. FSB General Georgy Poltavchenko became the president's plenipotentiary representative in the Northwestern Federal District, which included St. Petersburg. Three of the five remaining plenipotentiary representatives were KGB-FSB officers as well.

Putin's aim was to "consolidate government power." During the Yeltsin years, the fundamental laws of Russia did indeed have an objective weakness in that they had been created under specific historical circumstances and fitted to a specific president—Boris Yeltsin. What Putin was trying to do was rewrite the fundamental laws of Russia in order to make them suit the demands of the corporation that had put him in power—the FSB.

Yeltsin had endeavored to bring about the greatest possible decentralization in Russia. He understood that the Soviet Union had fallen apart in August 1991 because of its excessive centralization, which had created an untenable multinational empire that could not compete in the modern world. By contrast, Putin started moving back toward a centralized system of governance.

The decree that established seven federal districts became a classic example of the usurpation of government power by an elected official. In terms of the established laws of the Russian government, the decree's provisions were unconstitutional and would not have stood up in court in any juridically literate country. The very fact that such a decree could be issued clearly indicated that Russia was under arbitrary rule, not limited by the Constitutional Court, by the laws, or by common sense. It also showed that the elected president of the country had no intention of serving as a "Guarantor of the Constitution."

Putin's second most important innovation was the law "On the formation of the Federation Council of the Russian Federation." This law replaced an elected Federation Council with one appointed by the president. Instead of being an elected governing body with independent authority, the council was remade into a banal bureaucratic agency. The popularly elected regional governors who had formed the Federation Council in accordance with the Russian constitution would now delegate their representatives to the new Federation Council, after coordinating their nominees with the Kremlin—and this right did not even extend to all of those regional executives.

The reform of the Federation Council and the creation of plenipotentiary representative offices in the federal districts effectively deprived elected governors of their influence in the capital and their power at home. In bureaucratic Russia, where all local projects required the Kremlin's approval, governors and their representatives could no longer solve the problems they encountered since government officials at the federal level no longer saw them as legitimate partners elected by the people. The federal leadership also found it harder to resolve local issues through the governors' representatives who made up the Federation Council, since these representatives had no authority at the local level. No one had elected them. Consequently, no one supported them.

Putin's reforms obviously went against Russia's constitution and could have been legitimated only through a formal change in the constitution—by a two-thirds vote in the State Duma. But the proposal to create seven federal districts and to change the status of the Federation Council was not put before the Duma, since Putin did not have two-thirds of the votes at that time.

ALEXANDER VOLOSHIN, THE RUSSIAN BONAPARTE

The decree that created seven federal districts was the brainchild of the president's chief of staff, Alexander Voloshin. This decree put all government power in the country into his hands. Stalin never even dreamed of the powers that Voloshin allocated to himself. Between the elected president and the eighty-nine elected heads of the federal subjects, a buffer of seven bureaucrats was created, and all seven were, by law, directly subordinated to Voloshin.

The "Resolution Concerning the Plenipotentiary Representative of the President of the Russian Federation in the Federal District" stipulates that "the plenipotentiary representative is an official of the federal government and part of the president's staff" (in effect, subordinate to Voloshin). Federal district representatives are appointed and dismissed from their positions by the president only "at the discretion of the president's chief of staff" (that is, Voloshin). The "deputies of the plenipotentiary representative" are also "part of the president's staff" and consequently subordinated not to the "plenipotentiary representative," their immediate superior, but to Voloshin. The formulation of this resolution was almost cynical in its transparency: "Appointments of the plenipotentiary representative's deputies, their dismissals from their positions, as well as promotions and disciplinary measures carried out with respect to such officials, are to be carried out by the president's chief of staff" (Voloshin).

The plenipotentiary representative's regional office was also subordinated not to the plenipotentiary representative and his deputies, but to Voloshin: "Managerial supervision of the activities of the plenipotentiary representative will be performed by the president's chief of staff." "The duties of the plenipotentiary representative will be performed directly by the office of the plenipotentiary representative, which is an independent subdivision of the presidential administration." "The president's chief of staff . . . will approve the structure and size of the staff of the plenipotentiary representative's office, and determine the number of the plenipotentiary representative's deputies." In other words, the budgets of the plenipotentiary representatives were also determined by Voloshin.

Voloshin did not explicitly list the rights that he reserved for himself in the new Federation Council, because he was more interested in dismissing the old council than in creating a new one. In fact, he held a grudge against the Federation Council for a terrible humiliation that it had once inflicted on him. It was Voloshin who had been deputized by Yeltsin to persuade the Federation Council to remove Yuri Skuratov from his post as general prosecutor. His speech before the Federation Council, which was broadcast over the whole country, turned into a catastrophic defeat for the Kremlin. Voloshin, a bureaucrat through and through, turned out to be worthless as a public speaker. His speech was so unconvincing that the Federation Council voted against Skuratov's dismissal, and Skuratov, who was attempting to undermine Yeltsin's regime, remained at his post despite the existence of a compromising videotape of him with two call girls. It was then that the vindictive Voloshin decided to dissolve the Federation Council at the first opportunity. That opportunity presented itself immediately after Putin came to power.

THE VERTICAL OF POWER

The legislative packet submitted for review and confirmation to the Duma—proposing revisions in the federal structure and in local self-governance—formed the basis for the construction of the so-called "vertical of power," which was supposed to restore to Russia the rigid centralization of the Soviet era. The third and final piece of proposed legislation in the packet concerned the rights of the governors and the federal government to dissolve local legislative assemblies in the event that Moscow found their decisions to be at variance with federal law. This bill was proposed primarily in order to safeguard the federal government against situations such as Chechnya, in which the local parliament of a constituent subject of the Russian Federation made a decision effectively to secede from Russia.

Putin reserved the right to dismiss elected officials, including governors, when advised to do so by the prosecutor's office, both on the local and on the federal level. In a country where the prosecutor's office had never been independent and was one of the most corrupt parts of the government, the new law meant that Putin would always be able to get prosecutors to agree to remove any elected official that he found inconvenient.

Finally, the federal government could now regulate laws and control local governments "in cities of federal significance, capitals and administrative centers of the constituent subjects of the Russian Federation, cities with a population over 50,000, border territories, closed administrative-territorial formations, closed military settlements." In other words, the federal government acquired direct control over almost all of Russia.

Putin's proposed legislation was confirmed by the Duma and became a subject of discussion during Putin's first visit to the writer and Nobel Prize winner Alexander Solzhenitsyn. Putin had a long conversation with Solzhenitsyn at his home on September 20, 2000. Looking at the famous portrait of Pyotr Stolypin that hung in the writer's office, Putin asked: "Is that your grandfather?" Solzhenitsyn gently corrected him and told him that the man in the portrait was Stolypin, a prime minister in pre-revolutionary Russia.

Putin made a good impression on Solzhenitsyn. "His arguments are weighed with extreme care"; "his mind is quick and alert"; "no personal thirst for power, intoxication with power or with being in power"; "self-regulation is the foundation of our existence. . . . He really understands and knows this. On this point, we were in remarkable agreement."

Somewhat later, Solzhenitsyn understood that, precisely in the matter of self-regulation, he had been the victim of a cheap public relations stunt. In an interview with *Moskovskiye Novosti*, June 19–25, 2001, Solzhenitsyn reflected on Putin's widely publicized visit:

> I did indeed give him a few pieces of advice. But I have not seen him follow any of them. Of course, he agreed about self-regulation. But who would disagree about self-regulation? No one. Everyone praises it. And no one wants to promote it. On the contrary, they restrain it and choke it. I emphatically asked Putin not to destroy the state ecological committee, the independence of the forest management office. I saw no need whatsoever to wreck the Federation Council. It is completely unclear to me what they created in its place—some kind of intermediary, amoeba-like formation. Yes, I really did tell him what I could. And after that, we had no further contact.

Putin visited Solzhenitsyn again only in 2007. This time, Solzhenitsyn had no critical remarks to make about Putin.

Back in May–June 2000, Putin had begun to repeal various pieces of regional legislation as being at variance with the Russian constitution. On May 11, he repealed statutes in Ingushetia and the Amur region. On May 16, he asked the governor of the Smolensk region to repeal resolutions made by the local executive government. On June 8, he stopped a series of decrees by the president of Adygea, Aslan Dzharimov, from going into effect. On June 30, he blocked certain resolutions made by the Voronezh regional government under Governor Ivan Shabanov.

Putin made skillful use of stick-and-carrot policies toward regional rulers; and he made no less skillful use of the opposition between Yeltsin's entourage and the oligarchs, on the one hand, and the "chekists" (FSB-KGB officers whom Putin was bringing into the government), on the other. He signed a decree on September 1 establishing the State Council, a new advisory organ consisting of the heads of the executive governments of all the constituent subjects of the Russian Federation. On December 5, he withdrew Russia from the Bishkek agreement on visa-free travel by citizens of CIS member states within the territory of those states. Foreign passports and foreign visas now became necessary for traveling between certain CIS member states.

In December 2000, Putin insisted on having the Duma approve a hybrid form of state symbolism. The three-color flag chosen under Yeltsin remained Russia's flag. The two-headed eagle of pre-revolutionary Russia remained on Russia's coat of arms. But the red banner of Soviet times became the official banner of the Russian army, and the old anthem of the Soviet Union became the new national anthem—with the words changed to reflect the fact that the USSR had disappeared from the map of the world.

After taking unconstitutional steps to secure his position in office (or perhaps laying the groundwork for a third presidential term, which would require a formal change in the Russian constitution), Putin sought to set many regional heads who did not wish to relinquish their positions on the same course. In November 2000, the president's representative in the Duma, General Alexander Kotenkov, helped the governors' lobby push through a legislative amendment that allowed sixteen governors and regional presidents (including, retroactively, the president of Tatarstan, Mintimer Shaimiev) to run for a third term. In January 2001, Kotenkov facilitated the passage of the so-called "Boos amendment" (named after Georgy Boos) in the lower house of parliament, which enabled sixty-nine heads of regional executive governments (including Yuri Luzhkov and Murtaza Rakhimov) to run for a third term, and seventeen of them (including Shaimiev) to run for a fourth term. In return for this favor, Luzhkov effectively gave the president control over Fatherland, his organization in the Duma. On April 12, 2001, Fatherland merged with Unity into a single pro-Putin party.

Putin's critics have repeatedly characterized various pieces of legislation that he signed into law as anti-Russian, directed against Russia's national interests. For example, on July 10, Putin put his signature on amendments to the law "On the protection of the environment" (which were passed by the Duma on July 6). These amendments repealed the ban on importing spent nuclear fuel into Russia. He also signed a decree setting up a special task force on issues related to the import of spent nuclear fuel. As a consequence, it became possible to import nuclear waste into Russia.

On May 31, 2001, Putin signed a new citizenship law (passed by the Duma on April 19 and approved by the Federation Council on May 15). This law put former citizens of the USSR, including Russian emigrants (over twenty million Russians), on the same footing as all other foreigners if they wished to obtain Russian citizenship. As a result, tens of thousands of Russian army personnel—who prior to entering the military had had permanent resident permits in former Soviet republics that had separated from Russia—lost their Russian citizenship.

During a visit to Moscow by the president of Turkmenistan, Saparmurat Niyazov, on April 10, 2003, Putin agreed to dissolve the Russian-Turkmen agreement on dual citizenship. On April 22, Niyazov signed a decree that gave holders of two passports two months to decide which of the two countries they wanted to be citizens of. After the end of this period, Russian citizens who lived in Turkmenistan and had Turkmen citizenship automatically forfeited their Russian citizenship. About one hundred thousand people lost their Russian citizenship as a result of this law. After a series of articles in Russian newspapers claimed that Russia was betraying its own citizens ("the sale of citizens in exchange for gas"), Russia's minister of foreign affairs, Igor Ivanov, had a telephone conversation with his Turkmen counterpart, Rashid Meredov, on April 26, 2003. In the course of the conversation, Ivanov expressed "serious concern about the one-sided and hasty actions of the Turkmen side to end the dual citizenship agreement between our countries." But no further steps were taken either by the Ministry of Foreign Affairs or by the president.

At the same time, Putin also put his signature on laws that could be characterized as "pro-Russian." Thus, an amendment to the law on languages, signed on December 11, 2001, made it illegal to use any alphabet except the Cyrillic for the official languages of the Russian Federation. The aim was to prevent the Latinization of the Tatar language, which was initiated by President Shaimiev in Tatarstan.

Putin also made repeated attempts to bring Belarus closer to Russia and even merge it with the Russian Federation. During talks in Moscow with Alexander Lukashenko, president of Belarus, on August 14, 2002, Putin proposed two basic options for the "further progress of Russian-Belarusian unification": either "complete integration into a single state," with Belarus's seven districts becoming constituent subjects of the Russian Federation, or a "supranational formation on the model of the European Union." Putin proposed to hold a referendum in Russia and Belarus in May 2003 "on the question of final unification." Both options received a negative response from the Belarusian side. No referendum was held. On September 4, 2003, in a letter to Lukashenko that addressed various theoretical issues related to the construction of a unified state, Putin once again stated that, "concretely speaking, the following basic options exist for the further progress of Russian-Belarusian unification: full integration into a single state, a supranational union on the model of the European Union, or work toward unification on the basis of the existing Agreement about the Creation of a Unified State." Lukashenko ignored the letter.

The decree to create seven federal districts became a signal—a signal to steal the vestiges of state power that had not yet been privatized by the president and his chief of staff. The battle over this remaining power was fought not by those who had a right to do so according to the Russian constitution, but by those who had the necessary strength and resources—by coercive government agencies and clans.

OLIGARCHIC CLANS AROUND THE THRONE

One of the first to identify the post-Soviet regime as an oligarchy was Alexander Solzhenitsyn. At the end of 1996, he explained that in Russia,

> Skillful members of the former upper and middle echelons of the old Communist government, together with parvenus who have suddenly acquired wealth by devious means, have formed a stable and closed oligarchy of about 150–200 individuals, which decides the fate of the nation. This is the appropriate label for the current regime of the Russian government. . . . The members of this oligarchy are driven by a shared lust for power and money—they display no higher motives to serve the Fatherland and the people.[1]

Solzhenitsyn's characterization of Yeltsin's Russia as an oligarchy was based on the classic dictionary definition of this term: "A form of government in which all power is concentrated in the hands of a small number of courtiers, nobles, oligarchs."[2] In Greek, "oligarchy" means "rule by the few" (*oligoi*, "few"; *arche*, "rule, government"), and "oligarchs" are "the ruling few, the ruling minority."

Oligarchy was first described as a form of government by Plato in Book XIII of *The Republic*, where Socrates discusses oligarchy with Adeimantus. Plato himself may have coined the word, although an earlier origin cannot be ruled out. According to Plato, oligarchy is a form of government based on possession of wealth: only the wealthy have the right to govern. And rule by the rich must necessarily be rule by "the few." Plato characterizes oligarchy as an unjust form of government, in which the rulers' goal is not the general welfare, but their personal interests.

Aristotle developed and elaborated on Plato's ideas in his *Politics, Athenian Politeia,* and *Rhetoric.* According to Aristotle, the three basic features of oligarchy are: rulers are recruited from among the rich or the rich select rulers from among their friends; rulers do not depend on citizens (this is the difference between oligarchy and democracy, rule by the citizens); rulers pursue their own interests rather than the general welfare (this is the difference between oligarchy and Aristotelian aristocracy). Drawing on the various political regimes that existed in Greece during his time, Aristotle classified oligarchies into four types, distinguished by the ways in which the government is formed (whether government offices are bought, co-opted, inherited, or taken by force); the degree of economic disparity (from moderate to extreme); and the degree of lawlessness in the state (from an unjust legislature that favors only the few, to completely arbitrary rule).

Apart from a few details—such as government officials being appointed by lot—Aristotle's description turned out to be universal. Oligarchic forms of government later emerged in republican and late imperial Rome, in medieval Venice, in nineteenth- and twentieth-century Latin America, in contemporary Southeast Asia, in postcolonial Africa, and in the post-Soviet states.

Under Yeltsin, Russia did not yet have a fully formed oligarchic regime. Oligarchy coexisted quite well with certain features of classical tyranny (arbitrary rule by a single individual), as well as anarchy, as well as the frail beginnings of democracy. The "tyranny" of "Czar Boris," it must be said, was quite good-natured on the whole, manifesting itself more in petty tyranny and willfulness than in the systematic repression of citizens' rights and liberties. Far more conspicuous under Yeltsin were signs of anarchy, including the semifeudal anarchy of the regional rulers. Under Putin, the willfulness and anarchy decreased, but all traces of geniality vanished as well. As Viktor Shenderovich remarked, "the old boss was big, bibulous, and blissful; the new one is small, sober, and mean."[3]

If the structure of Putin's government is viewed through the lens of the classical conceptions of oligarchy, it will be seen to correspond to Aristotle's second type: only the rich have access to political power; economic disparity is great but not extreme; the government selects itself—essentially through cooptation; laws exist, but they are written by the government, for the government. But it displays leanings toward the first, moderate type of oligarchy (the citizens have some say in selecting the government), and also toward the third and fourth, "dynastic" types (economic disparity is moving toward an extreme, and elements of the hereditary transfer of power are beginning to appear).

More or less the same type of oligarchy can be found in most Third World countries, particularly in Africa. This is not surprising; by most developmental parameters, Russia is now somewhere between Latin America and Africa. While President Putin's advisor Andrei Illarionov would have Russia aspire to catch up to Portugal, instead it is lagging behind Colombia and drifting in the direction of Nigeria in terms of economic growth, democracy, and general welfare.

Like other Third World countries today, Russia has no formal property qualification for holding high government office; but in reality, there is a property qualification. Russia's oligarchy can also be described as possessing a bureaucratic-administrative character, rather than, say, a financial one (as in Singapore). The oligarchs are the nomenklatura elite: the president at the top, the president's staff, the ministers, the Kremlin's plenipotentiary representatives in the federal districts, the governors, the directors of the FSB, the Ministry of Internal Affairs, the prosecutor's offices, and the army. Some big-business figures also belong to the ruling oligarchy—they are the ones who hold important offices in the government. Roman Abramovich and Alexander Khloponin are oligarchs because they have purchased high government offices for themselves with their own money. Vladimir Potanin and Boris Berezovsky are oligarchs because they occupied such offices in the past. Mikhail Fridman and Oleg Deripaska are oligarchs because they have unofficial high-ranking government connections, which are even more powerful than some political offices. Vladimir Gusinsky is an oligarch because he controls an influential TV channel.

Mikhail Khodorkovsky, although he is rich and until recently was influential, never held political office or controlled a media outlet; but he has been called an oligarch because of his political ambitions. In English, there is a term of Japanese origin for such individuals: tycoon. The American version of the famous Russian movie *Oligarkh* was called *Tycoon*. (In France, the title was *Un nouveau russe*, "A New Russian.") Those who jailed Khodorkovsky—Vladimir Putin, Viktor Ivanov, Boris Gryzlov, and Vladimir Ustinov—are all classic oligarchs: they occupy high government offices, they are not poor, and they govern in their own interests rather than for the general welfare. Thus, the objection that Khodorkovsky and Berezovsky are much richer than their persecutors carries no weight—particularly when Khodorkovsky is in prison and Berezovsky has only by a miracle managed to avoid it.

Not all the Thirty Tyrants, the classical prototypes of oligarchic rule as described by Aristotle in *Athenian Politeia* (404 B.C.), were the richest men in Athens; some were simply friends or servants of the richest men. It nowhere says that Critias (the first among the Thirty) was the richest. But Critias confiscated property from the richest men around him—as did some oligarchs of later times. It is not wealth that makes a tycoon into an oligarch, but a combination of wealth, public political power acquired through wealth, and the use of this power for self-seeking motives. The main reason behind the secret-police oligarchy's harsh persecution of Berezovsky and Khodorkovsky was the fact that both had openly announced their intentions to seek political power: Berezovsky from 1996 onward, and Khodorkovsky when he said in an interview that by 2008 he intended to stop taking an active part in business and devote himself to politics.

OLIGARCHIC CLANS UNDER YELTSIN

An oligarchy typically has a clan structure and is divided into competing groups and cliques. This was the case with the Thirty Tyrants, the Roman Senate, the Venetian Council of Ten, the Latin American juntas of the nineteenth and twentieth centuries, and the regimes of postcolonial Africa. It is also the case with today's Russia.

The oligarchic order of post-Soviet Russia was more or less fully formed by about 1996. Due to the country's deeply rooted, centralized bureaucratic system, and to the resulting quasi-monarchical nature of the Russian constitution, the oligarchy took shape around the head of the government and developed a "court-like" character. The most prominent oligarchic clan under Yeltsin was the oil-and-gas clan of Chernomyrdin-Vyakhirev. Its rival was the Korzhakov-Barsukov-Soskovets group (who were the *siloviki* at the time). A tight Moscow clan headed by Yuri Luzhkov also developed under Yeltsin. Finally, the ideological group of "Petersburg liberals" headed by Anatoly Chubais began its transformation into the independent oligarchic clan of the "Petersburg economists."

By the end of Yeltsin's rule, the clan called "the family" had taken shape, leaving the other groups with much less room to maneuver. This clan consisted of Roman Abramovich, Boris Berezovsky, Alexander Voloshin, Valentin Yumashev, and Tatyana Dyachenko. Powerful regional clans became established in the provinces: the clan of Murtaza Rakhimov in Bashkortostan, Mintimer Shaimiev in Tatarstan, Kirsan Ilyumzhinov in Kalmykia, Eduard Rossel in the Urals, Vladimir Yakovlev in St. Petersburg.

These oligarchic administrative-economic clans became the main players in the political process, while political parties, movements, blocs, and parliamentary factions became their instruments. Official political entities are not independent; they come out of clans and cliques, blocs and coalitions. Our Home Is Russia (NDR), the official "ruling party" of the late Yeltsin period, was the political instrument of a coalition of several clans (Chernomyrdin's, Korzhakov's, Luzhkov's, certain regional clans, and an early stage of "the family"). This coalition fell apart in 1998–1999, and by the time of the 1999 election, several new parties had emerged from it: Fatherland (the instrument of Luzhkov's mayoral office), All Russia and Voice of Russia (two regional groups), Unity ("the family's" instrument). After Putin's victory in the presidential election, NDR essentially reconstituted itself under a new name, United Russia. This was a result of the fact that the main clans and groups had coalesced around the person of Putin—although this did not mean that all interests were harmonized or that the new president's collaborators were monolithic in character.

OLIGARCHIC CLANS DURING PUTIN'S FIRST TERM AS PRESIDENT

When Vladimir Putin came to power, he did not become a sovereign ruler who made all decisions independently without taking the opinions of his entourage into account. Moreover, he did not enjoy—and continues not to enjoy—his principal form of activity: the day-to-day governing of the country. It is enough to notice how the traffic jams that paralyze one-third of Moscow appear and disappear when the president drives to work and when he drives back home. The morning traffic jam usually occurs not before eleven o'clock in the morning: the president is driving to the Kremlin. Often, another traffic jam occurs at five or six in the evening: the president is coming home. Putin is not fanatical about political power. Much more than political power, he enjoys sports and a healthy lifestyle. What he wants from political power are mainly the pleasures that are inaccessible to an ordinary athlete: a flight on a fighter plane, a ride in a submarine, the chance to fire a Topol-M missile, being able to wear a Patek Philippe Calatrava watch.

That is why Putin has always been surrounded by workaholic collaborators—such people as Alexander Voloshin, Dmitry Medvedev (who replaced Voloshin), Vladislav Surkov, or Dmitry Kozak. Entrusting his day-to-day work obligations to his collaborators, Putin is forced to come to terms with the fact that, by doing so, he is in effect ceding a substantial part of his power. This, however, is a typical situation in oligarchies, even when the top oligarch is himself a workaholic.

The oligarchy of Putin's first term as president consisted of four administrative-economic clans: the "old Kremlin" or "family" clan (inherited from Yeltsin and his "family"); the "old Petersburg" group (also known as the "RAO UES of Russia," the "Petersburg economists," or the "Chubais clan"); the "new Petersburg" or "secret police" clan (also known as the "Petersburg chekists" or the "*siloviki*," or the "junta," as *Novaya Gazeta* recently proposed); and the "mayor's office" (Luzhkov's clan in the capital). In recent days, in connection with the beginning of a reshuffling of the president's entourage, there have been signs that yet another influential clan is emerging—the clan of the "Petersburg lawyers." Each of these clans has commercial interests that it controls, and each has its own political instruments in the form of parties, Duma factions, and deputy coalitions. They are distinguished by their practical policies, their preferred strategies, and their ideologies.

OUT-OF-FAVOR OLIGARCHS

After winning the presidential election in 2000, Putin began to take a much tougher stance toward the oligarchs. On June 19, addressing the Chamber of Commerce and Industry, he called on entrepreneurs who had taken their capital out of Russia to bring it back, promising that they would not be penalized: "The government must not pester people and ask where they got their funds if it itself was unable to ensure normal conditions for investment." But Putin threatened sanctions if the entrepreneurs refused to bring their money back: "I'm not going to say that your assets will be frozen tomorrow, but if decisions of this sort start being made . . . you will choke on all the dust you'll swallow running around from court to court to have your assets unblocked."

This speech was delivered against the background of the recently begun attack on Vladimir Gusinsky's media empire. Gusinsky, who had supported Primakov and Luzhkov in the election, became a personal enemy of both Putin and Voloshin, who even before the election swore to have Gusinsky put in prison if Putin won. At the same time, Putin entered into conflict with another Russian oligarch, Boris Berezovsky, who had publicly criticized Putin on a series of fundamental political issues, including the creation of the seven federal districts, the dismissal of the Federation Council, and the president's tactless conduct following the *Kursk* submarine disaster in August 2000.

On August 12, 2000, Putin went on vacation at the Bocharov Ruchey presidential residence in Sochi, and he did not interrupt his vacation after being informed that an explosion had hit the *Kursk* in the Barents Sea, killing 118 people. He remained in Sochi while the Russian navy pretended to carry out rescue operations (which, as it turned out, were a complete sham). Putin met with relatives of the submarine crew members in Vidyayevo on August 22 and promised to recover the bodies of the dead sailors for burial within a few weeks. Several bodies were indeed recovered in October, but the recovery of the remaining bodies and the submarine itself was postponed until the summer of 2001 and then dragged out until October.

When asked what happened to the submarine in a television interview with Larry King on September 8, Putin replied with a smile: "It sank." His response threw King and all of America into confusion. Confusion was observed in Russia as well. Berezovsky, who still retained control over ORT at the time, probably could have swayed the management of the television channel to soften the reporters' natural reaction. Instead, he took the stance of a silent observer, and when his silence was correctly interpreted by ORT's reporters, they criticized Putin with a vehemence unmatched either before or since.

The Kremlin remembered how brilliantly Berezovsky had conducted Putin's public relations campaign through ORT in 1999–2000; and it remembered the difficulties that had arisen because Putin's political opponents, Primakov and Luzhkov, used Gusinsky's NTV channel against Putin. Watching the anti-Kremlin campaign unleashed by indignant TV reporters on ORT and NTV because of the Kremlin's ineffective response to the *Kursk* submarine disaster, the Kremlin immediately began taking steps to pull Russia's main television channels away from their owners.

This project was enthusiastically overseen by the neurotic and power-loving Voloshin, who was taking revenge first on Gusinsky, for supporting Luzhkov and Primakov; and second on Berezovsky, his former partner, friend, and boss, for refusing to submit to Putin's orders, which were conveyed to him most often by Voloshin himself. It is not surprising that relations between Berezovsky and Voloshin during these days became openly hostile.

The third in the series of out-of-favor oligarchs was Mikhail Khodorkovsky, the head of Yukos. He started to compete with the Kremlin politically by giving financial support to the biggest oppositional forces in the Duma, from Yabloko to the CPRF. Moreover, at a meeting between Russian entrepreneurs and the president, Khodorkovsky openly challenged Putin by raising the issue of government corruption in the oil and gas industry.

But the story of Khodorkovsky's arrest had an economic side as well. Some time before the unexpected arrest, an agreement had been reached regarding the sale of 20 percent of Sibneft's shares to Yukos for $3 billion. These shares were owned by Roman Abramovich. Khodorkovsky had already transferred money to accounts controlled by Abramovich and was waiting for the transfer of the Sibneft shares. It was at this moment that, very conveniently for Abramovich, the government intervened: on October 25, 2003, Khodorkovsky was arrested on charges of tax evasion and fraud.

Shortly after his arrest, the government cancelled the sale of Sibneft shares to Yukos. Those shares remained in Abramovich's possession, but he did not return to Yukos the money that he had been paid for them. At the same time, Abramovich used blackmail and extortion to buy up about 50 percent of the Sibneft shares that were controlled by Berezovsky and his partnet Badri Patarkatsishvili, paying $1.35 billion for them. Then Abramovich sold 70 percent of Sibneft's shares to Gazprom for about $13 billion. Khodorkovsky learned about all these mind-boggling developments from newspapers that were delivered to him in his jail cell.

It merits pointing out that Voloshin's seemingly unstoppable rise was cut short precisely because of Yukos. The confident Voloshin had agreed to underwrite the deal between Abramovich and Khodorkovsky (for a price, of course) without knowing that it was not intended to unify Sibneft and Yukos, as Abramovich had officially declared, but was a complicated maneuver concocted by Abramovich and Putin that would end up with Khodorkovsky losing Yukos and Abramovich selling Sibneft not to Yukos (which would be destroyed by the government), but to Gazprom. Once he realized that he had been unwittingly used by Putin and Abramovich in a multibillion-dollar swindle, Voloshin resigned on October 30.

The case of Khodorkovsky and Yukos remained one of the biggest news stories during Putin's second term as well. The Khodorkovsky trial ended on May 31, 2005, and the former oligarch—over the unceasing protests of the opposition and foreign critics—was sentenced to nine years in prison. On September 22, the sentence was reduced by one year. It is not likely, however, that Khodorkovsky will ever be released.

The destruction of Yukos and the arrest of Khodorkovsky were softened by the silent reaction of the majority of Russia's business elite and by positive economic developments in the country as a whole. True, the main cause of these positive developments was the high price of oil and gas during Putin's time in office (as opposed to the exceptionally low oil and gas prices during the Yeltsin years). But the fact remains that Russia's GDP grew at an average annual rate of 6.5 percent under

Putin; there was a budget surplus and a trade surplus; and the country's gold reserves increased, while its foreign debt fell from 50 percent to 30 percent of GDP. Putin undoubtedly deserves credit for introducing a new tax code with significant reductions in so-called "circulation taxes" for businesses and a flat personal income tax of 13 percent.

THE PETERSBURG CHEKISTS

The foundation of the president's ideological program was the consolidation of government control over all organizations, associations, and parties. This was achieved through legislative activity and changes in personnel.

When Putin came to power, a great number of FSB officers, active reserve officers, and other law enforcement personnel—from the prosecutor's office, the police, and the army—flooded into government at the local and federal levels. It is difficult to trace all the new promotions and appointments given to the *siloviki* because not all former or currently active state security agents are out in the open about their departmental affiliation. It stands to reason, therefore, that the known appointments are merely the tip of the iceberg.

The objectives of Russia's security services were explicitly formulated in a brief obtained by *Moskovskiye Novosti* and published on October 8, 2002. In this brief, unnamed top officials recommended that former employees of Russia's security services "directly embed themselves . . . in economic, commercial, entrepreneurial, and banking organizations, regulatory agencies, and organs of the executive government." The document explained: "Creating cover organizations and firms will make it possible to increase contacts with entrepreneurs and businessmen through such organizations, to establish a broad agent network, and to obtain information of operational interest through direct access to relevant documents."

This brief did not add anything fundamentally new to the long-established institution of the FSB's active reserve, except that it came to light and was published without becoming an object of active public discussion and without coming under the scrutiny of parliamentary committees. The fact that the FSB was secretly penetrating the everyday civilian life of Russia was no longer a surprise to anyone.

The secret-police clan, or the clan of the "Petersburg chekists," consists of Viktor Ivanov, deputy chief of staff; Igor Sechin, aide to the president; Nikolai Patrushev, director of the FSB; Boris Gryzlov, former minister of internal affairs and speaker of the newly elected State Duma; Sergei Ivanov, minister of foreign affairs; Yuri Zaostrovtsev, former deputy director of the FSB; Yevgeny Murov, director of the Federal Protection Service (FSO). The nucleus of this group took shape while its principal members were still based in St. Petersburg. At the time, they represented something like a regional business consortium that had its roots partly in the KGB and partly in the police force. Many of this clan's members (such as Ivanov, Gryzlov, Patrushev) were closely linked by their overlapping positions as co-founders of a series of commercial entities (Blok, Borg, Teleplus, and other companies) under the aegis of the St. Petersburg International Relations Committee, i.e. Putin.

Other collaborators with Putin during his tenure as Sobchak's deputy who did not come out of the KGB—such as Vladimir Kozhin, presidential property manager, and Alexei Miller, head of Gazprom—also belong to the "new Petersburg" group. Vladimir Ustinov, the general prosecutor and a former "family" protégé, went over to the chekist side in summer–fall 2000. Now he is connected to the chekists by a dynastic union as well, since his son married Igor Sechin's daughter.

The chekist clan holds administrative control over the state system of arms production and trade. In particular, Viktor Ivanov heads the board of directors of the Almaz-Antey Air Defense Concern, formed after the Antey Corporation merged with Almaz, producers of air defense technologies.

The clan has close ties with the following major entrepreneurs: bankers Sergei Pugachev and Sergei Veremeyenko (Mezhprombank); oil magnates Vagit Alekperov (Lukoil), Sergei Bogdanichikov (the state-owned company Rosneft), Vladimir Bogdanov (Surgutneftegaz), Gennady Timchenko (Kirishineftekhimexport).

Archimandrite Tikhon Shevkunov of the Sretensky Monastery is considered to be the shadow ideologist of the chekist clan. He is the spiritual father of the "Orthodox banker" Sergei Pugachev, and there are persistent rumors that he is also the spiritual father of Lyudmila Putina.

The chekist clan had initially chosen Gennady Raikov's and Gennady Gudkov's People's Party of the Russian Federation (NPRF) as its central political tool. (The party had actually been created under Vladislav Surkov's patronage, but he had no use for it and abandoned it.) However, the NPRF failed to pass the 5 percent threshold, although it did manage to get two dozen of its single-member constituency candidates elected to the Duma. Because there was no possibility of creating even a separate deputy group out of the NPRF deputies, most of them were herded into the United Russia faction.

While cultivating the NPRF, the *siloviki* did not neglect to work on United Russia as well. Initially, Vladimir Bespalov, an old colleague of Putin's from the St. Petersburg NDR office, was delegated to take over the party. The task proved too much for him and he was transferred to Gazprom, while Viktor Ivanov's protégé Valery Bogomolov became the secretary of United Russia's general council. Boris Gryzlov was brought back to party work, becoming the head of the party's supreme council, initially while remaining head of the Ministry of Internal Affairs.

The chekists also focused their attention on the Homeland bloc—now a Duma faction—headed by Sergei Glazyev and Dmitry Rogozin. Actually, the ubiquitous Surkov had also participated in the creation of Homeland, in order to reduce the number of votes cast for the CPRF. But Surkov had cut off his support for this organization once he saw that it was exceeding the limits of the task for which it had been created. The *siloviki*, by contrast, offered their patronage to Homeland—or at least to its loyal Rogozin wing, since Rogozin was pretty close to them ideologically and had been sending the right signals for quite some time.

In the regions, the chekists prefer to bulldoze over all obstacles without being particular about their means; they replace governors freely, as long as they have people available. It was the chekists who overthrew Alexander Rutskoy in Kursk (on orders from the vengeful Putin, who never forgave Rutskoy for his harsh criticism of the handling of the *Kursk* submarine disaster), forced the Ingushes to accept Murat Zyazikov, schemed against Mikhail Nikolayev in Yakutia, and attempted to unseat Kirsan Ilyumzhinov in Kalmykia and Murtaza Rakhimov in Bashkortostan. They have enjoyed relatively peaceful successes as well: the gubernatorial victories of FSB agents Viktor Maslov in the Smolensk region and Vladimir Kulakov in the Voronezh region, as well as the election of General Vladimir Shamanov as governor of the Ulyanov region.

The chekists are considered, not without reason, to be the source of President Putin's "new course" initiative: the policy of reorganizing the "protection" arrangements of various economic entities on the pretext of restoring rule of law. First, the chekists destroyed Gusinsky's media business, instigated a rupture between Putin and Berezovsky—welcomed, of course, by Putin himself—and pushed Berezovsky out of Russia. Then they attacked Vladimir Potanin's Interros, a business that had expanded under Chubais's patronage, and evidently subordinated Potanin to their own agenda. (In return for his understanding, they supported the candidacy of Potanin's partner Alexander Khloponin in the gubernatorial election in the Krasnoyarsk region.) The partly state-owned Gazprom was swept clean of private commercial hangers-on associated with Chernomyrdin-Vyakhirev (Itera) and then connected with other commercial hangers-on (Eural TG).

One of the branches of the chekist clan (Yuri Zaostrovtsev and his allies in the General Prosecutor's Office) played an excessively obvious and active role in the rivalry to offer "protection" to the furniture import business, coming into conflict with the interests of "the family's" Customs Committee. The scandal surrounding the companies Tri Kita and Grand became an example of the open rivalry between government law enforcement agencies over the right to offer protection to businesses. If in other matters the chekists allegedly sought to defend state interests and to convict lawbreakers, in this instance they were unable to masquerade as protectors of the public good, since the Customs Committee was trying to convict the lawbreaking businessmen, while the FSB and the General Prosecutor's Office were defending them and trying to convict the prosecutors who were trying to convict the businessmen.

The chekists likely do not question the right to private property as such; they have been property owners themselves since their days in St. Petersburg. But they seem to have rather bizarre notions of the economics of private business and a sincere belief that the administrative regulation of the economy is a general good, particularly when it concerns the so-called "strategic" areas of the economy. Finally, the chekists have no experience in running businesses, especially large-scale enterprises. All this foretokens great economic upheaval—for the chekist corporation has acquired a solid and enduring influence over the president, who is himself a chekist, and it has no intention of relinquishing its power.

Sergei Ivanov has always been seen as the chekists' main candidate for the post of prime minister: he is the minister of defense "in plainclothes," whose airplanes and helicopters keep falling, whose submarines keep sinking, whose missiles don't get off the ground, whose soldiers desert in whole companies and battalions, and whose conscripts die of cold on the way to their units. Rumors of Ivanov's appointment as prime minister—in place of Mikhail Kasyanov—surfaced as early as October 2000. In response to these rumors, those who opposed such an appointment carried out a special operation in the press. The newspaper *Stringer* published a "top secret" file titled "The Tactical-Technical Foundation for a Transfer of Power from the President of the Russian Federation to His Successor with an Accompanying Intensification of the Government's Role in Society." This text was sent to the newspaper's officers by an unknown source. It described the steps that had to be taken for Putin to appoint a certain "Andropov-2" first as prime minister and then as his successor. Ivanov was easily recognizable as "Andropov-2," the "successor."[4]

In November 2000, Alexander Prokhanov's newspaper, *Zavtra*, accused the media—which had been spreading rumors of Ivanov's impending promotion—of conducting a deliberate campaign against him with the objective of forestalling his advancement: "These forces, which once spent a considerable amount of time discrediting the 'Petersburg chekists,' are today devoting most of their attention to the topic of Ivanov's impending 'premiership.' . . . They are trying to portray a kind of 'virtual false start' for Ivanov, aiming in this way to diminish the weight and significance of this figure."[5]

It is not known whether Putin came to believe in the existence of an "Andropov-2" plan or in Ivanov's ambitions to become prime minister. But Sergei Ivanov did not become prime minister at the time. Nor did he become prime minister when Kasyanov actually was replaced. Besides Ivanov, the most discussed chekist candidate for the post of prime minister was Boris Gryzlov, who became the speaker of the Duma in December 2003. (His post of minister of internal affairs went to another protégé of Ivanov's, Rashid Nurgaliyev.) Rather unexpectedly for everyone, however, the position of prime minister was given to Mikhail Fradkov—Russia's representative in the European Union, "honorary counterintelligence agent of Russia," and former director of the Federal Tax Police. Despite his departmental ties with the KGB-FSB, Fradkov had not previously been a core member of the "Petersburg chekist" group. For the chekists and for Putin personally, he was sufficiently "one of their own" to be entrusted with the post of "technical prime minister," which had now been taken away from "the family"; at the same time, he was not so much "one of their own" as to be too precious to dispense with should the need arise.

THE MAYOR'S OFFICE

The mayor of Moscow heads the fourth most important federal oligarchic group, which is somewhat removed from the president's "court." The administrative wing of this clan is represented by the leadership of the Moscow mayor's office: Yuri Luzhkov, Vladimir Resin, Valery Shantsev, Iosif Ordzhonikidze, Oleg Tolkachev. Its economic wing consists of Vladimir Yevtushenkov and Yevgeny Novitsky (Sistema), Yelena Luzhkova-Baturina (Inteko).

In the past, the "protection" of the mayor's office facilitated the rise of Vladimir Gusinsky (Most Group) and Mikhail Khodorkovsky (Menatep Group). But Gusinsky lost his mayor's office patronage as early as 1995, when Luzhkov became afraid of entering into conflict with Korzhakov following Korzhakov's anti-Gusinsky raid on the Most Bank headquarters in December 1994. Khodorkovsky, after buying Yukos, relinquished his mayor's office patronage on the eve of the Russian financial crisis in August 1998. The political tools of the mayor's office include the Boos-Volodin group within the United Russia party and its Duma faction.

Luzhkov has such control over United Russia's Moscow deputies in the Duma that they occasionally rebel against their overseers from the president's staff when the mayor's office needs them. Thus, United Russia's Fatherland–All Russia group in the Duma—in which most of Luzhkov's supporters were concentrated in the Duma's third convocation—and the Moscow deputies from the Regions of Russia group attempted to block the sales tax cut planned by the Kremlin in late 2002 and early 2003. (Sales taxes are extremely profitable for the capital's treasury.) Surkov's admonitions were ineffectual, and it took a personal chat between Putin and Luzhkov to get Boos and Volodin to order their deputies to surrender.

After a change in the president's cabinet, Alexander Zhukov—one of the most influential and capable lobbyists for the mayor's office in the Duma (elected from the United Russia party, a member of the Regions of Russia group in the former Duma, first deputy speaker in the newly elected Duma)—was appointed to the post of first (and only) deputy prime minister. Despite his generally liberal views, in cases of conflict between liberal theory and the practical interests of "Moscow" (i.e. the mayor's office), Zhukov usually sided with the mayor's office in the Duma. This, however, did not guarantee that Zhukov would remain loyal to Luzhkov as deputy prime minister. Zhukov has decent relations with some of Chubais's friends and a "family connection" with the chekists: his father, Dmitry Zhukov, a writer and once a well-known fighter against the Zionist-Masonic plot, had an earlier career as a foreign intelligence officer.

The mayor's office has groups of influence in all major political parties, from Yabloko to the CPRF. There used to be a powerful pro-Luzhkov group within the SPS (Union of Right Forces). The mayor essentially controlled the Moscow office of this party, which remained rather hostile to him on the federal level. And although the Luzhkov lobby in the SPS has lost much of its influence (once Vladimir Platonov, head of the Moscow City

Duma, went over to United Russia), the mayor's office retains some control over the Moscow regional office of the SPS.

The main propaganda outlet of the Luzhkov clan is the TVTs television channel, which is expanding its broadcasting facilities to reach the entire country. Media outlets that are controlled by commercial entities with links to the mayor's office include the Sistema Mass Media holding company (the newspapers *Sovietskaya Rossiya* and *Literaturnaya Gazeta*, the Rosbalt news agency, and the Govorit Moskva and Obschestvennoye Rossiyskoye radio stations). Luzhkov is also supported by the popular newspaper *Moskovsky Komsomolets* and the Sovershenno Sekretno holding company (the newspapers *Versiya* and *Sovershenno Sekretno*).

The political views of Luzhkov and his circle are in many respects close to those of the *siloviki*: anti-Western, economically antiliberal, demanding a more "active" foreign policy toward the countries of the former Soviet Union and the Balkans, and supporting a full reinstatement of the institution of residence permits (at least in the capital). The economic views of the Luzhkov and chekist clans are also similar in some respects. Indeed, the secret-police wing of the oligarchy is aiming to establish on the scale of the country as a whole the kind of regulated capitalism that already exists in Moscow. However, the "hungry" *siloviki* from St. Petersburg envy the "overfed" bureaucrats from Moscow and are not opposed to giving them a good shake, just as they are already "shaking" the Khodorkovsky empire.

THE PETERSBURG LAWYERS

During Putin's years in St. Petersburg, his entourage was not limited to his former colleagues from the KGB. In particular, the St. Petersburg IRC extended its patronage to another group of government officials and businessmen who, like the chekists, were linked by their overlapping positions as co-founders of various commercial entities (but without similar "horizontal" links to the chekists). This group included Dmitry Medvedev, co-owner of the Ilim Pulp Enterprise; Dmitry Kozak, head of the legal committee of the St. Petersburg mayor's office; Yuri Kravtsov, speaker of the St. Petersburg Legislative Assembly; Sergei Mironov, currently chairman of the Federation Council; and Yuri Molchanov, head of the Vozrozhdenie Peterburga Corporation (currently the deputy governor of St. Petersburg, formerly the pro-rector of Leningrad State University who recommended Vladimir Putin to Anatoly Sobchak in 1990). Most of them once attended the law school at Leningrad State University. Viktor Zolotov, head of Putin's personal security service, is also close to this group. Once he became president, Putin brought Medvedev and Kozak to Moscow. In January 2004, Valery Nazarov, former head of the St. Petersburg Committee on City Property Management, who is also considered to be close to Kozak and Medvedev, was transferred to Moscow as well.

When Putin decided in the summer of 2001 to appoint his old partner and St. Petersburg acquaintance Sergei Mironov to lead the Federation Council, it became necessary for the St. Petersburg Legislative Assembly first to agree to send Mironov as its representative to the council. This request was conveyed from Putin to St. Petersburg through Igor Sechin. The assembly was forced to comply. In December of the same year, Mironov became the chairman of the Federation Council.

Beginning in November 2003, Dmitry Medvedev occupied a key post as the president's chief of staff (successor to Voloshin). Dmitry Kozak, after serving as deputy chief of staff to the president, became head of the government staff. In terms of his authority, Kozak's role in the government was at least as great as that of the deputy prime minister, Alexander Zhukov. While the "Petersburg lawyers" group is still relatively compact, it has every chance of growing into a full clan, comparable in influence to all the others.

After becoming chief of staff, Medvedev began playing his own game in regional politics. His approach is more in keeping with the traditions of the cautious Alexander Voloshin than of the decisive Viktor Ivanov. The chekists were ready to devour Murtaza Rakhimov as he schemed to hold on to the presidency of Bashkortostan: they didn't allow him to deny his opponents the right to register; they caught him printing additional voting ballots that were to be used to falsify election results; and they brought the Bashkortostan elections to a seemingly impossible second round. It was only a short step to the "liberation of the Bashkir nation from the criminal regime of Rakhimov," but at the last moment Medvedev embraced Surkov's viewpoint and helped him convince Putin that the old and reliable Rakhimov was preferable to a pig in Sergei Veremeyenko's chekist poke. As befits a loyal Putinist, Veremeyenko called off his opposition, leaving no one to catch Rakhimov's forgeries and falsifications, and the Bashkir president easily won the second round. As was to be expected, Rakhimov thanked the Kremlin with a record-high percentage of Bashkir votes for Putin in the Russian presidential election.

DMITRY MEDVEDEV AND ILIM PULP ENTERPRISE

Dmitry Medvedev was a lawyer by training. As a graduate student, he studied with Sobchak and was the informal head of Sobchak's election campaign for the Congress of People's Deputies of the USSR in 1989. He also served as the legal expert for Putin's International Relations Committee. Medvedev is considered to have invented a widely used method by which government could "join" a joint-stock company without breaking existing laws: not by contributing land or real estate, but by contributing rents on land and real estate.

From November 2003 to November 2005, Medvedev was the president's chief of staff. He replaced Alexander Voloshin in supporting the popular political operative Gleb Pavlovsky, who was working out a procedure by which Medvedev could inherit the presidential seat. In November 2005, Medvedev became the first prime minister of the Russian government.

Ilim Pulp Enterprise (IPE), a Russian-Swiss joint venture, was registered with the International Relations Committee on April 30, 1992 (registration number AOL-1546), with a statutory fund of one million rubles. The enterprise was founded jointly by Technofirm, a limited liability partnership, which supplied 50 percent of the statutory fund; Intersez Switzerland (a company registered on July 1, 1991, registration number 5601/1991, with a statutory capital of 50,000 francs), which supplied 40 percent of the statutory fund; and the Ust-Ilimsky cellulose plant, which provided 10 percent of the statutory fund. The general manager of IPE was Zakhar Smushkin. The manager in charge of legal issues was Dmitry Medvedev.

IPE became one of the co-founders of the previously registered Rus' Insurance Company, which had been founded in 1990 by A. Krutikhin, a CPSU regional committee director, together with V. Reznik and A. Alexandrov. Some time later, the limited liability partnership Ilim Pulp Enterprise was re-registered as a closed joint-stock company, no longer with the International Relations Committee, but now with the participation of the closed joint-stock company Fincell, 50 percent of whose shares were owned by Dmitry Medvedev.

"DIRECT EMBEDDING"—ACCORDING TO THE INSTRUCTIONS

Russia's sociological institutions have conducted numerous studies to determine the level of the FSB's involvement in the country's civilian life. According to Moscow's Center for Postindustrial Studies, 15 percent of men working in Russia are employed in various state enforcement agencies. In the top tiers of the government, 43 percent come from the security services, the police, the prosecutor's office, or the army. Other researchers believe that the FSB's share in ruling the political and economic life of the country is even greater: from 70 to 80 percent.

The takeover of the government at the federal and regional levels is being done through appointments of new top officials in place of old ones. This policy was initiated by FSB General Viktor Ivanov, who was in charge of personnel in President Putin's cabinet. It was he who promoted FSB officers—naturally, with the president's knowledge—to all vacant positions. The personal right to appoint and to dismiss, which Voloshin had acquired for himself, ended up in Ivanov's hands.

Here are several examples of the way in which midlevel government personnel has changed in the last few years.

- On May 27, 2000, FSB General Sergei Ivanov was appointed secretary of Russia's Security Council.
- In July 2000, Vyacheslav Trubnikov, who had been head of the SVR (Foreign Intelligence Service) since 1996, was appointed deputy minister of foreign affairs of the Russian Federation with the rank of a federal minister. Trubnikov had worked in the KGB's First Main Directorate (foreign intelligence) since 1967.

- In August 2000, Yuri Demin, former head military prosecutor, was appointed first deputy minister of justice of the Russian Federation. He had been appointed to the Main Military Prosecutor's Office after serving as head of the FSB's legal-contractual directorate. At the same time, the first deputy head of the FSB, Alexander Medyanik, was appointed first deputy minister of federation affairs and national and migration policies.
- On March 28, 2001, Putin began to make the first major changes in his cabinet. The two main law enforcement agencies were brought into the FSB's sphere of influence. Sergei Ivanov became minister of defense, replacing Marshal Igor Sergeyev. Boris Gryzlov became minister of internal affairs, replacing Vladimir Rushailo, who in turn replaced Sergei Ivanov as secretary of Russia's Security Council. Mikhail Fradkov was appointed head of the Federal Tax Police, while Alexander Rumyantsev became the new minister of nuclear energy.
- In April 2001, Nikolai Negodov was appointed personnel director of the Baltika Breweries company. Born in 1949, Negodov attended the Leningrad Shipbuilding Institute, together with future FSB director Patrushev, and graduated in 1973. (Patrushev graduated one year later.) From 1977 until being appointed to Baltika, he worked for the FSB. For his last three years there, he was the first deputy head of the FSB office for St. Petersburg and the Leningrad region.
- In July 2001, shareholders elected Vadim Glazkov as president of the Petersburg Fuel Company. Glazkov was born in 1955. He worked in state security from 1984 to 1992 and then, like Putin, joined the St. Petersburg mayor's office.
- In August 2001, Sergei Verevkin-Rakhalsky was appointed first deputy director of the Federal Tax Police. He was born in 1948 and graduated from the Leningrad Electronics and Optics Institute. In 1986, he became head of the KGB office for

the Sakhalin region; in March 1999, he became head of the FSB office for Primorye. In April 2000, Verevkin-Rakhalsky was appointed deputy minister of taxes and receipts and was transferred to Moscow. At the same time, Anatoly Tsybulevsky (born 1950), head of an FSB directorate, was appointed deputy director of the Federal Tax Police.

- On June 3, 2002, FSB General Alexander Zdanovich—head of the FSB's public relations office, who had worked in state security since 1972—was appointed deputy head in charge of security issues on Channel Two (Rossiya) of Russian television. (No such position had existed on Channel Two before this time.) This was an open challenge to the public and the media. Putin was testing the level of criticism and disgruntlement that the appointment would elicit. Disgruntlement was not slow in coming. Alexander Abramenko, the editor-in-chief of the TV show *Vesti*, resigned in protest against this highly charged appointment. When on June 4 an interviewer asked Zdanovich whether he was still a member of the FSB's active reserve, the general replied with as much impudence as time would allow: "As is well known, there is no such thing as a former chekist. But I would not want to go into details. In the problems that I will have to deal with, I will of course be helped by my colleagues. Out of feelings of solidarity."

- In September 2002, after the death of academician Vyacheslav Shakhov, FSB active reserve officer Sergei Dyakov became head of the Military Insurance Company's board of directors.

- In October 2002, FSB officer Vladimir Ostrovsky was appointed head of the FSFO's (Federal Service for Financial Health and Bankruptcy) interregional territorial agency for the Volga Federal District. Born in 1956, Ostrovsky received an undergraduate education and then completed the KGB's Higher School. Until 2001, he had worked at the FSB office for the Sverdlovsk region. His last position there was senior representative in charge of cases of special importance.

- In February 2003, Valery Golubev was appointed general manager of the Gazkomplektimpex company (a daughter company of Gazprom). Golubev was born in 1952 and, like Patrushev, graduated from the Leningrad Shipbuilding Institute. He then completed the KGB's Higher School in Minsk and the Andropov Red Banner Institute in Moscow. Until 1991, Golubev worked at the KGB; then he went over to the secretariat of the St. Petersburg mayor's office. In 1993, he became the administrative head of the Vasilieostrovsky district. In 2002, he became the representative of the Leningrad Region Legislative Assembly in the Federation Council.

- In April 2003, Nikolai Spasichenko was appointed vice president in charge of security and relations with the government at the SIBUR company. Spasichenko was born in 1946. From 1972 until 1995, he worked at the KGB-FSB and "resigned" (was transferred to the federal reserve) with the rank of colonel. After his resignation, Spasichenko became the head of security at Petersburg City Bank and then at the Petersburg Fuel Company. In 1997–1999, he served as deputy general manager at the Petersburg Oil Terminal. In 1999–2000, he was head of security at the St. Petersburg Seaport company; then he returned to Petersburg Oil Terminal, becoming the company's deputy general manager in charge of regulations and personnel.

"SPYMANIA"

As one newspaper commented, "spies don't walk around in herds, but chekists don't know this." The spy scare that has gripped the country on a scale unseen since Soviet times is a direct consequence of the FSB's takeover of the government.

Addressing the State Duma in April 2000, Putin made a statement that could only have evoked bemusement at the time:

> If the minister of foreign affairs is observed maintaining contacts with the representatives of foreign governments beyond the bounds of his official duties, then he, just like all other members of the government, State Duma deputies, leaders of Duma factions, just like all other citizens of the Russian Federation, will be subjected to specific procedures as prescribed by criminal law. And I must say that the latest operations being conducted within the Federal Security Service tell us that this is entirely possible.

Neither Russian law nor the Criminal Code of the Russian Federation, however, contained any formal prohibition against contacts with foreigners.

On September 9, 2000, Putin laid down the "Doctrine of Informational Security," which envisioned the revival of elements of state censorship—"in order to make more effective the body of legal limits on access to confidential information." The doctrine did not so much establish censorship as indicate the direction in which civil liberties and freedom of speech were heading. Relying on this document, the FSB began actively hunting after spies, while government officials started zealously protecting government secrets. The FSB was so convinced that most of Russia's citizens were spying on their own country that it published the following announcement on its official website, fsb.ru:

> Citizens who collaborate with foreign intelligence services may get in touch with the FSB of Russia through a telephone hotline to become double agents. In such cases, the monetary compensation received by such agents from foreign security services will remain unaffected, and they will work with top level FSB employees. Anonymity and confidentiality are guaranteed.

This announcement was accompanied by an excerpt from Article 275 (high treason) of the Russian Criminal Code:

> A person who commits the crime described in this article, as well as those in Articles 276 (espionage) and 278 (forcible seizure of power or

forcible retention of power), will be absolved of criminal responsibility if his actions, by being communicated to the security organs in a voluntary and timely fashion, help to prevent further harm to the interests of the Russian Federation and if his actions do not constitute other crimes.

On May 24, 2001, Ekho Moskvy radio received a document signed by Ilya Zakharov, deputy director of the Institute of General Genetics of the Russian Academy of Sciences. The document was part of a program developed by the Presidium of the academy "to prevent the infliction of harm to the Russian Federation." It read as follows:

To the attention of laboratory heads and group supervisors.

Dear Colleagues:

In keeping with a program developed by the Presidium of the Russian Academy of Sciences "to prevent the infliction of harm to the Russian Federation," please urgently (before June 1) submit information about any international agreements (contracts) that your laboratory (group) is currently participating in. Also, please comply with the following requests:

1. Inform the management office in a timely manner about foreign grant applications that are being prepared and submit copies of applications to the academic secretary.

2. Inform the Institute of General Genetics' international department about all visits to your laboratory (group) by foreigners.

3. Submit reports about the results of work trips abroad to the international department in a timely manner.

4. Submit copies of all articles sent out for publication in other countries to the institute's academic secretary.

One can assume that similar documents were sent to all of the country's scientific institutes. In 2001, to demand that Russian scientists disclose their contacts with foreigners and their applications for international grants, submit copies of articles being sent to other countries for publication, and report on foreign travel, was tantamount to establishing an inquisition.

The wave of criminal cases against scientists, military personnel, and government officials began in the 1990s with two chemists who were working on problems associated with developing and destroying chemical weapons, Vil Mirzayanov and Lev Fyodorov. Even though their guilt could not be proved, Mirzayanov and Fyodorov were held for several months in pretrial detention. They had been arrested for publishing an article in which they described the production of modern forms of chemical weapons in Russia.

In 1994, Vadim Sintsov—director of foreign economic relations at a military metallurgical firm (Special Machine Building and Metallurgy) and former head of the Main Directorate of the USSR's Ministry of Defense Technology—was arrested for treason in the form of espionage (Article 275 of the Russian Criminal Code). Sintsov had passed classified information about Russian armaments to British foreign intelligence. He was sentenced to ten years in prison.

At the end of 1995, charges were brought against the environmentalist Alexander Nikitin. In February 1996, he was arrested and charged with treason in the form of espionage. The charge was brought by Vladimir Putin's friend Viktor Cherkesov, who headed the St. Petersburg FSB office at that time. Nikitin had contributed to a Bellona report about nuclear safety in the Northern Fleet. This was regarded as an act of treason.

Nikitin spent ten months in the FSB's pretrial detention facility in St. Petersburg until the deputy general prosecutor Mikhail Katyshev signed an order for his release in December 1996. Nevertheless, the charges against him were not withdrawn. And the environmentalist continued being dragged from court to court for several more years.

FSB director Vladimir Putin became involved in the trial. "Our department acts on state interests," Putin remarked.

Let me make a comment about Nikitin. What was it that really happened in his case? He penetrated into the library and obtained information that was classified. By the way, in return for this "public service" he received monetary compensation. Of course, there is another question that one might ask: how relevant is this information today? And from the point of view of tact, including international-ecological tact, one can probably consider reducing his punishment. But this is something that the court must decide. Unfortunately, in addition to using diplomatic cover, foreign security services very actively employ various environmental and public organizations, commercial enterprises, and philanthropic foundations. That is why such organizations will always be closely watched by us, no matter how much we are pressured by the media and by public opinion.[6]

But in 1999, Putin was not yet president, and the information that the FSB and Putin personally considered *really classified* had not been found to be such by the court. On September 13, 2000, the Presidium of Russia's Supreme Court acquitted Nikitin of all charges.

The case of Grigory Pasko—correspondent for *Boyevaya Vakhta*, the newspaper of the Pacific Fleet—began in 1997. The FSB claimed that Pasko had divulged information about the ways in which the military harmed the environment. Specifically, he was accused of passing classified information to the Japanese about a Russian submarine accident, which was a government secret. As a result, he was arrested on ten counts of treason in the form of espionage. The materials collected against Pasko, however, contained no direct evidence that he had intended to pass his writings to the Japanese media, even though the materials were voluminous: all of his correspondence was read, his phone was tapped, his apartment was bugged, and he himself was under close surveillance.

On July 20, 1999, Pasko was convicted, although he was charged with violating a completely different law: Article 285, par. 1 of the Russian Criminal Code (abuse of official position). But he was immediately pardoned and taken out of custody in the courtroom. Neither Pasko nor the FSB was satisfied with this outcome: the pardoned Pasko sent an appeal to the Supreme Court's military board—and also brought a suit to protect his honor and dignity against the head of the Pacific Fleet's regional FSB office, Rear Admiral Nikolai Sotskov—while the Pacific Fleet's regional FSB office sent the military board a protest against an "unjustifiably lenient" sentence.

In a new Pacific Military Court trial on December 25, 2001, Pasko was found guilty of espionage and sentenced to four years at a maximum security prison. At a press conference in Paris on January 15, 2002, President Putin said that he did not consider it feasible to interfere with the actions of the judicial system, but he would be willing to consider Pasko's appeal for clemency if the latter were to submit such an appeal to him. Putin emphasized—as he had done in the case of Nikitin—that Pasko had been charged with passing documents marked "classified" to foreign citizens for monetary compensation. The implication was that this fact had been conclusively established and was not contested by anyone, not even Pasko's lawyers.

But on February 13, 2002, the Russian Supreme Court responded to complaints from Pasko's lawyers by ruling that the Ministry of Defense had had no legal right to classify the information that Pasko had divulged. This ruling had no effect on the president's opinion about the "classified" nature of the information, however, or on Pasko's position. Pasko, who never did submit an appeal for clemency to Putin, was finally released—nominally before the end of his term—by the Ussuriysk Municipal Court on January 23, 2003. He had spent a total of two and a half years in prison.

In 1996, Platon Obukhov, an employee of the Ministry of Internal Affairs, was arrested on charges of treason in the form of espionage for passing classified information to British foreign intelligence. Obukhov was found mentally ill and made to undergo compulsory medical treatment.

Also in 1996, Vladimir Makarov, a career diplomat, was arrested on charges of treason in the form of espionage for giving the CIA information about the T-82 tank and about the staff of the Soviet Union's foreign representative offices. He was sentenced to seven years in prison by the Moscow Municipal Court and then pardoned by the president.

In 1997, Moisey Finkel, senior scientist at the Fourteenth Naval Scientific Research Institute, was arrested on charges of treason in the form of espionage for passing classified information about hydroacoustic complexes to the CIA. He was sentenced to twelve years in prison.

Also in 1997, the police arrested Igor Dudnik, a major in the Strategic Missile Forces. He was charged with treason in the form of espionage and divulging government secrets. Allegedly, he had tried to pass a compact disk containing classified information about Russia's Strategic Missile Forces to the CIA. Dudnik was sentenced to twelve years in prison.

Valentin Moiseyev, deputy head of the First Asian Department at the Ministry of Foreign Affairs, was arrested in July 1998. He was charged with spying for South Korea, whose representatives had allegedly recruited the diplomat in Seoul while he was stationed there from 1992 to 1994. According to the prosecutor's office, Valentin Moiseyev had worked for the South Korean security services from 1994 until 1998. Allegedly, he had met with a South Korean foreign intelligence officer about sixty times and had given him copies of twenty-three documents describing collaborations between Russia and North Korea, including collaborations of a military nature. In return for this, he had been paid $500 per month. The total amount of money that he had received amounted to $14,000. Moiseyev himself claimed that he had maintained friendly relations with members of the Korean embassy, and that the materials he had passed on to them were not classified but had been previously published and formed the basis of his scientific lecture on "Russia's Policies in the Korean Peninsula." On December 16, 1999, the Moscow Municipal Court found the diplomat guilty and sentenced him to twelve years in prison, ruling that the quoted scholarly articles and official publications contained classified information.

After the conviction, Moiseyev's lawyers filed an appeal with Russia's Supreme Court, which overturned the conviction and sent the case back to the lower court. In August 2001, the Moscow Municipal Court again found Moiseyev guilty of espionage and sentenced him to four and a half years in prison, after taking into account his health and positive work references. His lawyer Anatoly Yablokov remarked that the reduced sentence stemmed not from the court's humane attitude toward spies, but from the absence of any proof of guilt. On March 14, 2002, following a decision by the Ministry of Justice, Moiseyev, who suffered from a chronic stomach ailment, was transferred to a hospital in Torzhok. After being released on December 31, he announced his intention to fight for acquittal and appealed to the European Court for Human Rights in Strasbourg.

In February 1999, criminal charges were filed against Professor Vladimir Soifer, head of the nuclear oceanology laboratory at the Pacific Oceanological Institute in the Far Eastern Department of the Russian Academy of Sciences, and a member of the Kurchatov Institute Federal Scientific Center. Soifer was studying the aftereffects of the explosion of a nuclear reactor in a submarine stationed in Chazhma Bay, near Vladivostok, in 1985. All the facts that Soifer was analyzing had been published both in Russian and in foreign scientific journals.

The FSB's Primorye office conducted an inspection of Soifer's laboratory at the end of February. According to the FSB, its agents found copies of documents issued by the radiological, chemical, and biological defense service and hydrographic documents produced by the Pacific Fleet, all marked "classified" and made in violation of the regulations governing classified records. Specifically, copies had been made of two classified reports, hydrological descriptions and a top secret map of Strelok Strait, Razboynik Bay, and Chazhma Bay in the Sea of Japan, where the Pacific Fleet keeps its nuclear submarines. Such maps usually indicate depths, underwater currents, and temperatures; but these maps also indicated the locations of Russia's submarines. Soifer admitted that he had violated the regulations governing the copying of documents, but he justified his actions by arguing that these documents had been marked classified without adequate cause.

In June, the FSB's Primorye office determined that Soifer's activities "threatened the state and military security of the country" and raided Soifer's apartment in order to "inspect the use of classified documents." The FSB seized various documents and materials, including copies and photographic negatives of maps marked "classified." Soifer's research was interrupted and his laboratory was sealed. At the professor's request, the Presidium of the Russian Academy of Sciences' Far Eastern Department appointed a six-person expert committee to look into the matter. The committee analyzed the materials that Soifer was using and reached the conclusion that none of the materials that he kept at home contained government secrets. The members of the regional FSB office disagreed. They did not bring charges against Soifer, however, but confined themselves to issuing a warning. The head of the FSB's Primorye office at the time was Major General Sergei Verevkin-Rakhalsky.

After this, Soifer himself brought charges against the local FSB office, and on February 11, 2000, the Sovietsky District Court in Vladivostok ruled that the search conducted in the scientist's home had been illegal. The court also found that FSB employees, during the search, had illegally confiscated analyses of scientific data on tapes and computer disks, as well as Soifer's passport, and ruled that the confiscated items must be returned to their owner.

The local FSB office appealed this decision before the regional court, but in April 2000 the Primorye Regional Court declined to hear the appeal. Soifer himself believed that criminal proceedings had been initiated against him in order to stop him from taking part in radiological and ecological studies of Chazhma Bay. According to him, the former administration of Primorye had plans to create a joint venture in Chazhma Bay, funded by American, Russian, and Japanese capital, for refining Middle Eastern oil and shipping it to Asian and Pacific countries, and Soifer's research could interfere with this project.

In 1999, the police arrested Vladimir Shchurov, a professor at the Pacific Oceanological Institute who ran a laboratory that studied ocean acoustics. Shchurov was accused of divulging government secrets: allegedly, he had passed classified information about Russian military technology to the Chinese.

Shchurov was detained at the Russian-Chinese border in August 1999 while attempting to travel to Harbin. Customs officials seized acoustic modules for telemetric equipment that had been produced by Shchurov's laboratory. Shchurov was taking these modules to China in order to conduct joint experiments with colleagues at Harbin Engineering University. Agents of the FSB's Primorye office decided that "the system created by the laboratory of ocean acoustics could be used for military as well as peaceful purposes." The FSB's experts determined that the technology created at the Pacific Oceanological Institute had no analogues in the world and consequently classified it as a government secret. All the laboratories involved in the creation of the system were sealed, the system's documentation was confiscated, and joint research projects related to the system were cut short. Yet the laboratory did not have a military-industrial orientation or any contracts with the military, no secret was made of the studies being carried out jointly with the Chinese, and all the necessary documents for these projects had been approved by the appropriate government offices, including the FSB.

The FSB's Primorye office in turn declared that the scientists had presented customs officials with unreliable information about the instruments' technical specifications, and that some time before this, classified technical blueprints had been confiscated from another member of Shchurov's laboratory, Yuri Khvorostov, as he was leaving for China. These classified blueprints had been concealed among scientific-technical documentation; in addition, they had been photographed, and the film had then been left inside a camera to give the impression that it had not been exposed. This was the basis on which the FSB accused Shchurov and Khvorostov of illegally exporting technology, trafficking in contraband, and divulging government secrets.

In August 2000, Shchurov's twenty-eight-year-old son, Alexander, was found dead in his apartment. He had been hanged. The police contended that he had committed suicide, while the parents insisted that he had been murdered. Vladimir Shchurov and his wife also reported that they had later discovered that laser disks containing documentation of all the father's and son's work—expeditions, records, sketches, and blueprints— were missing.

After his son's death, Vladimir Shchurov announced that he wished to leave Russia. "Our science is being killed," he said. "The FSB's iron burns everything. And the situation in the country makes living here impossible. We are being killed. . . . The country is being killed." Shchurov was not permitted to leave the country, however, and after a year-long investigation he was accused in accordance with Article 188 (smuggling), Article 189 (illegal export of technology, scientific and technical information, and rendering services that may be used to create weapons of mass destruction, armaments, and military technology), and Article 289, par. 2 (divulging government secrets with heavy consequences).

In the end, the Primorye prosecutor's office withdrew all charges against Khvorostov due to lack of evidence, while Shchurov, in August 2003, was found guilty of divulging government secrets, sentenced to two years in prison, and immediately pardoned. Neither the charge nor the sentence specified what it was that Shchurov was supposed to have divulged. During the hearings, the judge accepted the findings of experts from the Ministry of Defense as conclusive and refused to hear the opinion of civilian specialists.

Shchurov did not admit guilt, but he did not appeal his conviction either: "I am an old, sick man. I lack the strength, the resources, and the health to do this. I was prepared for any sentence. It's hard to believe in the law when it is being ignored. It's good that the prosecutor's office exhibited some humanity and withdrew a large part of the charges."

Igor Sutyagin, head of the military-technological and military-economic policy studies sector at the Institute of the United States and Canada, was arrested at his home in Obninsk on October 27, 1999. (The warrant for his arrest was issued on October 29.) Sutyagin was charged with spying for the United States (Article 275). Specifically, he was accused of selling classified information to Nadya Locke and Sean Kidd, U.S. military intelligence officers working under cover at Alternative Futures, a British consulting firm.

The FSB accused Sutyagin of criminal activity on five different counts: he was charged with having had five meetings with members of foreign security services, and with having passed on to them information about five different topics. This information concerned the RVV-AE air-to-air missile and the MiG-29 SMT airplane. In addition, according to the prosecution, Sutyagin had conveyed information about the plans for Russia's strategic nuclear forces until 2007, about the Defense Ministry's work to develop permanent readiness units, and about the structure and current state of Russia's early warning system. The prosecution also alleged that Sutyagin, while employed as a teacher at the Russian navy's Obninsk Educational Center, had pried the professional servicemen who attended classes there for information in order to pass it on to foreign intelligence. Sutyagin had worked at the center as a volunteer since 1994, without being compensated for his labor. The case was initially investigated by the Kaluga region's FSB office.

On December 27, 2001, the Kaluga Regional Court acknowledged that the agency that had carried out the preliminary investigation had violated criminal and procedural laws in appointing experts and obtaining expert opinions about the facts of the case, and that it had thus violated the rights of the defendant. The court therefore sent the case back for further investigation, and Sutyagin was transferred to the Lefortovo pretrial detention facility in Moscow.

Igor Sutyagin's trial in the Moscow Municipal Court began on March 15, 2004. Sutyagin was found guilty of spying for the United States—of collecting, storing, and conveying to American military intelligence information that constituted a government secret. The jury decided that he deserved no leniency and the government prosecutor requested a seventeen-year sentence. On April 7, the court sentenced Sutyagin to fifteen years in a maximum security prison. The beginning of his sentence dates from the day of his formal arrest (October 29, 1999).

Meanwhile, Sutyagin himself did not admit guilt. He claimed that he had no access to government secrets and had used only open sources in his studies. Sutyagin's lawyers had incontrovertible proof that all the information contained in his papers was drawn from open sources and available to anyone who wished to read them, and also that he had never had access to government secrets.

Sutyagin's lawyers brought an appeal before the Supreme Court on April 14, 2005, requesting that the lower court's conviction be overturned because "significant legal and procedural violations had taken place" in the course of the trial. Specifically, the jury had been changed without cause during the trial and the court had examined evidence that was inadmissible in the opinion of the defense. In addition, "the questions put before the jury by the court went beyond the bounds of the charges against Sutyagin: specifically, the jury was asked whether Sutyagin had acted on assignment from foreign intelligence, although this was not one of the charges against him."

The judge formulated her questions to the jury in such a way as to suggest "right" answers. For example, she omitted the word "classified" when she asked them to decide whether Sutyagin had handed over materials in return for money.

On April 23, 2004, the Public Committee for the Defense of Scholars sent an open letter to the Parliamentary Assembly of the Council of Europe. The committee had been created on October 2, 2002, by a group of scholars and human rights activists out of concern for talented scholars who were wrongfully accused of serious crimes by the FSB. The open letter read, in part:

> Even trial by jury turns out to be merely a clever imitation of fairness and justice if the case in question has been initiated by the FSB. Such, at any rate, was the trial of Igor Sutyagin. There was not even a hint of putting the two sides on an equal footing: all of the prosecution's wishes were satisfied, while the legitimate demands of the defense were ignored. The jury's unanimous votes on questions that distorted the meaning of the charges cast doubt on its independence. Even in theory, a group of twelve people could not have unanimously voted in favor of the prosecution's dubious evidence.

The letter was signed by Vitaly Ginzburg (Nobel laureate, member of the Russian Academy of Sciences), Lev Ponomarev (National Movement for Human Rights), Sergei Kovalev (human rights activist, prisoner of conscience), Grigory Pasko (reporter, prisoner of conscience), Yuri Ryzhkov (member of the Russian Academy of Sciences), Alexei Simonov (Glasnost Defense Foundation), Ernst Cherny (human rights activist), and Father Gleb Yakunin (human rights activist, prisoner of conscience, priest).

In 1999, the police again arrested Alexander Nikitin, a navy captain. He was charged with espionage and divulging government secrets while preparing a report on "The Northern Fleet as a potential risk for the radioactive pollution of the region" for the Norwegian organization Bellona. Nikitin was acquitted by the St. Petersburg Municipal Court.

Also in 1999, the police arrested Sergei Velichko, a navy major and deputy ship commander. He was charged with espionage and collaborating with Swedish intelligence. The Baltic Fleet's Military Court sentenced Velichko to five years in prison.

In the same year, Russian police arrested a U.S. citizen, Edmond Pope, who was a retired officer of U.S. naval intelligence. He was charged with espionage. In December 2000, the Moscow Municipal Court sentenced Pope to twenty years in prison. By order of President Putin, he was pardoned in February 2001 and sent home to the United States.

In April 2000, in connection with the Pope case, the police arrested Anatoly Babkin, a professor at the Bauman Moscow State Technical University and chairman of MSTU's rocket engineering department. Babkin was charged with espionage, accused of passing classified information about Russia's Shkval torpedo to Edmond Pope. Initially, he had been the principal witness in Pope's trial, providing evidence that confirmed the American citizen's guilt; but subsequently he had revoked his statements, claiming that he had given them under pressure and while suffering from a heart ailment.

In February 2003, Babkin was convicted of high treason and given a suspended sentence of eight years in prison (in light of his advanced age and reputation). The court found him guilty of passing technical reports about the Shkval rocket-propelled torpedo to Edmond Pope, identified as an American spy. Babkin was put on probation for five years, stripped of his "Honored Science Worker" status, forbidden to engage in professional and scientific activity for three years, and prohibited from being the chairman of MSTU's rocket engineering department for another three years. Babkin himself claimed that he had given documents to Pope in a completely official capacity, as part of the collaboration between MSTU and Penn State University. (The collaboration agreement had been signed in 1996.) The Russian navy's representatives estimated that the MSTU professor, by revealing the secrets of the Shkval torpedo, had inflicted damages in the amount of 26,800,000 rubles (less than $1 million): this was the sum that figured in the civil case that the navy brought against Babkin.

On February 16, 2001, the police arrested Valentin Danilov, a physicist and director of the thermophysics center at Krasnoyarsk State Technical University (KSTU). Representing KSTU, Danilov had signed a contract with the Lanzhou Physics Institute of the China Aerospace Corporation in 1999. The contract was made through the China Precision Machinery Import-Export Corporation. Under this contract, Danilov was to manufacture a research stand to model the electrization of the surface of solid bodies in a vacuum under the impact of medium-energy electrons and ultraviolet radiation. This phenomenon is observed when satellites are impacted by plasma in space. On May 24, 2000, the Krasnoyarsk region's FSB office filed charges against the physicist, accusing him of divulging a government secret. Almost a year later, on February 16, 2001, Danilov was further accused of treason in the form of divulging government secrets and also of fraud. The first charge—espionage (Article 275 of the Russian Criminal Code), which carries a prison sentence of twelve to twenty years—was brought by the FSB. The charge of fraud—or more precisely, of wasteful spending of resources—was brought by KSTU. The sum that figured in the case was 446,000 rubles (less than $15,000). The scientist was arrested and put in Krasnoyarsk's pretrial detention facility.

According to the FSB, Danilov had given Russia's classified technological plans to the Chinese. Danilov's lawyers possessed expert testimony to the effect that Danilov's inventions had been declassified eight years earlier. The defendant's lawyers were confident of their success.

After a year and a half in prison, Danilov was released from custody by a decision of Krasnoyarsk's Central District Court on the condition that he not leave the country. During this whole time, the FSB had been unable to present any conclusive evidence of the physicist's guilt. Danilov himself believed that "a physicist can never be a traitor to his country. Scientists are given Nobel Prizes for discoveries made in physics, even though these discoveries can be used to create weapons. A physicist discovers nature's secrets, not the government's secrets."

After Danilov was released from pretrial detention, he ran for the State Duma as a deputy from Yenisey electoral district

No. 48. He lost the election, however, winning only 6.42 percent of the vote. In December 2003, he was acquitted by a jury. Eight of the twelve jurors found the evidence presented by the prosecutor's office unconvincing and cleared the physicist of all charges. After the hearing, Danilov announced that he had been completely confident that he would be acquitted, but also said that his arrest had set Russian science back in terms of openness to international collaboration. Specifically, a satellite that had been created jointly by China and the European Space Agency (ESA) could have been created by China and Russia, since the Russian scientists' plans were better than those of the ESA.

In January 2004, the Krasnoyarsk prosecutor's office turned to Russia's Supreme Court to appeal Danilov's acquittal. A delegation of Krasnoyarsk state security representatives—"a whole team from the Krasnoyarsk FSB office"—arrived in Moscow. "What their relation to the case is at the moment is not clear," one of Danilov's supporters commented, "since their role ended when they submitted their materials to the prosecutor's office."

As a result, the Russian Supreme Court repealed Danilov's acquittal on June 9, 2004, and sent his case back to the lower court. His lawyers believed that the Supreme Court's decision had been dictated from above. In November, Danilov was convicted of spying for China and sentenced to fourteen years in a maximum security prison.

In 2001, the police arrested Viktor Kalyadin, the general manager of Elers-Electron Ltd. Kalyadin was charged with treason in the form of espionage. He was accused of passing classified information to the CIA and sentenced to five years in prison.

Also in 2001, the police arrested Alexander Zaporozhsky, former deputy head of the First Department of the SVR's Foreign Counterintelligence Directorate. Zaporozhsky was charged with treason in the form of espionage. He was accused of passing classified information about the activities and personnel of Russian foreign intelligence to the American security services. The Moscow District Military Court sentenced him to eighteen years in prison.

Again in 2001, the police arrested Mikhail Trepashkin, a lawyer and FSB colonel who had taken part in Alexander Litvinenko's press conference in 1998. The Moscow District Military Court sentenced him to several years in prison.

On December 15, 2002, FSB director Patrushev announced that the government was refusing to extend the visas of thirty Peace Corps volunteers (the Peace Corps had been working in Russia without any obstacles since 1992) because they had been "collecting information about the sociopolitical and economic situation in Russia's regions, about government employees and administrators, and about the course of the elections." Patrushev portrayed this refusal as a victory for the FSB in its battle against foreign spies in Russia.

Meanwhile, the war on homegrown spies continued apace. From May to December 2004, eleven people were convicted of espionage in Primorye.

On March 17, 2006, the Novosibirsk region's FSB office initiated criminal proceedings on charges of divulging a government secret against Oleg Korobeinichev, a well-known chemist. Korobeinichev managed to prove his innocence, however, and forced the FSB's investigators to apologize. In 2007, the same FSB office initiated criminal proceedings against Igor and Oleg Manin, two employees of Novosibirsk State Technical University, again on charges of divulging government secrets. The FSB's investigators had found the classified materials in a book that the scientists had published in an edition of fifty for the fiftieth anniversary of the Siberian branch of the Russian Academy of Sciences. All fifty copies of the book were confiscated.

The absurdity of all these accusations and espionage cases is made even deeper by the fact that it is almost always left up to the FSB to determine what constitutes a government secret and what constitutes divulging a government secret, while every year the courts become less and less independent. As a consequence, dozens of scientists have ended up in prison and hundreds have been prevented from working. The Russian and the international public are not unaware of these incidents. Everyone is aware of them. Everyone writes about them. But as President Putin has said, "Comrade wolf knows whom to eat. He eats and doesn't pay attention to anyone."

8

The President's Friends
or "Agents and Objects"

During the 1999–2000 presidential election campaign, it was difficult to describe and explain what exactly was wrong with Putin as a candidate. He was unknown outside of St. Petersburg, which made it hard to say anything either good or bad about him. Only one thing was already clear in 1999: Putin came from the KGB, where he had spent his whole adult life.

Special people selected the individuals who worked in this organization, and the people they selected were very special as well. Most of those who lived in the enormous country did not often come into contact with these classified persons, and if they did, then they often did not know that their colleagues, friends, and even relatives were working for state security. By contrast, those who worked for state security knew each other and knew about each other exceedingly well. And by the will of the mighty organization that employed them, they helped one another, promoted one another, appointed one another to higher and higher positions, and spread out over boundless territories like a malignant tumor. The uninitiated population could never understand what it was that explained the career successes of this or that person, who often had no distinguishing professional abilities or was distinguished precisely by his lack of professionalism. Obtuse colleagues became managers, and people were forced to conclude that the Soviet system (or Russia as a country) was flawed. But "the system" was not as mindless as all that. It was simply a completely different system from the one that people imagined. The system of the KGB-FSB pursued a simple goal: to use any means necessary to appoint its own active reserve officers or recruited agents to all managerial positions.

In this chapter, we will tell about a few of Putin's friends and acquaintances and about one of his enemies; and we will try to explain what is wrong with a president from the KGB. What is wrong with such a president is that he drags up behind him thousands of little Putins who are no more distinguished than he is, but all of whom are state security employees or agents. These are his friends; or more accurately, they are not his friends at all, but his colleagues from the KGB-FSB. If the KGB-FSB orders him to do so, Putin will betray them, sell them, and "finish them off" if necessary—just as today he is "finishing off" the active reserve officers who were sent to work under Mikhail Khodorkovsky and who have been sacrificed to the multibillion-dollar economic project of pillaging Yukos. They have simply become expendable—victims of circumstance.

A state security employee has no friends. People whom he encounters fall into two categories: agents and objects. An agent is someone you recruit, who provides you with information, who is your source. An object is someone you "work on" or "develop"—in other words, you start keeping a file on him, formally or informally. Sometimes an agent becomes an object or an object becomes an agent. Probably, Putin has consciously classified every person whom he has ever met in his life as an agent or an object. But nothing could be more naive than to think that Putin has or ever had friends, although the word "friend" is one of the most frequently used in any language. We, too, cannot avoid using the word "friend" in this chapter with reference to many people whose paths have crossed President Putin's. But every time the reader sees this word, he should understand that this "friend" is no friend, but a colleague from the KGB-FSB or an agent, often in the formal sense of the word. Or even an object. And so, here are some of the president's "friends."

SERGEI CHEMEZOV

A rather charismatic man appeared in Moscow at the end of the 1980s. His name was Sergei Chemezov. Today, his name is quite widely known in Russia; among other things, he is a friend of President Putin's. Chemezov's occupation is selling Russian arms, and he does this quite successfully as head of the Rosoboronexport company. Russia is the second-biggest arms dealer in the world, surpassed only by the United States. The volume of the Russian arms trade exceeds $5 billion per year.

When he settled down in Moscow in 1989, Chemezov was unknown. He had grown up in Irkutsk. After graduating from the local polytechnic institute, he worked for a short time at the Irkutsk Scientific Research Institute for Rare and Nonferrous Metals. He got married, was hired by the KGB, and served in the KGB's second counterintelligence department for the Irkutsk region. Then he was sent to East Germany to work for Soviet foreign intelligence—the KGB's First Main Directorate.

The official (public) side of Chemezov's job was working for the Luch Scientific Production Association in Dresden, which was involved in developing nuclear energy. His main task, however, was to obtain Western countries' technical and technological secrets for Department T in the First Main Directorate of the KGB. In an October 2005 interview, responding to a question about his joint work with Putin, Chemezov remarked: "Why deny what happened? It's true, we worked in East Germany at the same time. From 1983 to 1988, I was the head of the Luch association in Dresden, and Vladimir Vladimirovich came there in 1985. We lived in the same house and spent time with each other both as colleagues and as neighbors." Neither of them, however, managed to make a career in foreign intelligence; both had to return to the Soviet Union.

Major General Yevgeny Kubyshkin was a longtime employee of the KGB's Fifth Directorate (the future Directorate for the Defense of the Constitutional Order). He had climbed up the ranks in the state security organs, having even been the second secretary of the KGB's party committee. This was quite a prestigious position, one that guaranteed further promotions. Kubyshkin had been selected for the KGB's party committee while working as head of the Fifth Directorate's Eighth Department, which dealt with the so-called Jewish extremists: Anatoly Sharansky and other famous refuseniks. Kubyshkin's appointment to the highest party organ of the KGB, employing over 32,000 party members, was facilitated by the head of the Fifth Directorate, Lieutenant General Filipp Bobkov, who was diligently installing people loyal to him in various high posts within the KGB system.

After serving as second secretary of the KGB's party committee for a time, Kubyshkin was appointed first deputy of the KGB's Inspections Directorate. Shortly thereafter he was promoted to the rank of major general. In terms of its power, the Inspections Directorate was second only to the Personnel Directorate. It was in the offices of these two directorates that the fates of the KGB's top officials were decided. Bobkov was able to promote his people thanks first and foremost to Kubyshkin. And so, the head of the Fifth Directorate's Second Department (which handled nationalist extremists), Nikolai Golushko, became the head of the KGB's secretariat, then the head of the KGB's Ukraine directorate, and finally the head of the KGB itself. The head of the Fifth Directorate's Seventh Department (prevention of illegal arms trade and the activities of anonymous persons harboring terrorist or other socially harmful intentions), Alexander Golovin, became the head of the KGB's Uzbekistan directorate. Several other department heads from the Fifth Directorate became the heads of KGB regional directorates. Probably no other part of the KGB produced as many top-tier officials as Bobkov's Fifth Directorate, while Bobkov himself became the deputy head and then the first deputy head of the KGB.

Kubyshkin himself, however, did not bolt up the career ladder. In about two years, he returned to the Fifth Directorate as deputy head, with no prospect of future promotions. As deputy head of the Inspections Directorate, the extremely direct and rigid Kubyshkin managed to make powerful enemies among the top rank of the KGB. These were experienced schemers who knew how to take advantage of Kubyshkin's excessive taste for women and liquor; they were able quickly to remove him from a position of responsibility and effectively put an end to his career. After coming back to the Fifth Directorate, Kubyshkin was ordered to oversee a number of departments, including the Eleventh Department, which had been created in 1977 in order to provide for counterintelligence oversight of the channels of international sports exchange. The most pressing concern at the time had been to provide security for the upcoming 1980 Olympics, which took place in Moscow and Tallin.

The staff of the Eleventh Department consisted mainly of longtime employees of the Fifth Directorate. The appearance of Chemezov—a new employee, and moreover a new employee who came from the provincial city of Irkutsk—was frowned upon in the department, since Chemezov had been appointed by the generally disliked General Kubyshkin. Moreover, the new employee's arrival was accompanied by a series of "irregularities," violating the usual procedures through which employees of the KGB's peripheral organs were normally transferred to its central apparatus. As a rule, an employee who was transferred to the central apparatus would be appointed to a position several notches below the one he had occupied at his provincial place of work. Chemezov, however, was appointed to the same position that he had previously held—senior operative—evidently because he had come to Moscow from Dresden. In addition, as an officer of the active reserve, Chemezov was appointed deputy general manager of Soyuzsportobespechenie and assigned to an agency that oversaw the purchase of sports equipment and clothing from abroad for Soviet athletes. Chemezov was also given an apartment in Moscow, which was a significant bonus in Soviet times. (Many Moscow KGB employees spent years on a waiting list in order to move to better living quarters.)

At Soyuzsportobespechenie, Chemezov became close with the general manager, Viktor Galayev, a former Komsomol worker, head of one of the sports directorates of the USSR's State Sports Committee, and secretary of this agency's party committee. Soyuzsportobespechenie's monopoly over the purchase of athletic equipment allowed Galayev and Chemezov to enter into agreements with foreign firms in such a way that a part of the money from the contracts would end up in their own pockets, and by the standards of the time, the money was not trivial—tens of thousands of dollars.

In the early 1990s, Galayev and Chemezov began selling chicken legs in St. Petersburg, a popular business at the time.

They invested about $100,000 in their enterprise. The business operated unofficially, through proxies, since as government employees Galayev and Chemezov (who was also a KGB officer) had no right to engage in private commercial activities. But dishonest business in Russia obeyed dishonest rules, and Galayev and Chemezov got cheated out of their proceeds. They were thus confronted with the problem of getting their money back from their double-dealing partners in St. Petersburg. Going to the law was out of the question since the business was illegal. Only one option remained: to seek help from criminals.

One of Chemezov's chekist colleagues was a young officer who had briefly served in the Fifth Directorate's Third Department, Senior Lieutenant Yuri Zaitsev. For several years, Zaitsev had worked as a civilian specialist (without military rank) in one of the divisions of the KGB's Directorate for Government Communications (UPS); at the same time, he was enrolled at the National Legal Correspondence Institute (VYuZI). After he graduated, Zaitsev was ordered to oversee Soyuzsportobespechenie, where he met and became close with Chemezov. Soon, Zaitsev left to go into business as an officer of the active reserve.

By chance, Zaitsev came in contact with the Soviet marshal Anatoly Konstantinov and his son Arkady, who had worked at the General Prosecutor's Office of the USSR as an investigator on cases of special importance and held the rank of senior counselor of justice. Using his father's connections in the defense industry, Arkady was trying to set up a business selling aviation technology. Russia's defense industry in those years was in a desperate situation. Left without government contracts, defense enterprises did what they could to survive, selling expensive products for close to nothing. Arkady had no problems with offers to buy aviation technology—from MI-8 helicopters to the gigantic Antey military transport planes. What was difficult was finding buyers. On his father's advice, Arkady Konstantinov took on Yuri Zaitsev as an assistant, assuming that his FSB connections might be useful. He was not mistaken. Zaitsev soon received information from colleagues in the FSB that a Chinese firm was interested in eight MI-8 helicopters. In a short time, Arkady Konstantinov was able to find the right number of helicopters and the Russian side quickly purchased them at a good price: $875,000 each. The factories that produced the helicopters were glad to receive this money, since they were in dire straits financially. Over $800,000 was deposited to Arkady Konstantinov's account in one of the German banks as a commission fee for him and Zaitsev. In return for their services, Zaitsev's colleagues in the FSB received a fax machine and a photocopy machine, which were hard to obtain in Russia.

A few months later, Konstantinov and Zaitsev each bought a nice apartment in Moscow and a Volvo. This was the end of their good luck, however. There were no more offers to purchase aviation technology. The Russian company that had bought the helicopters for China was unable to see the deal through and received no money from the Chinese side. The helicopters were warehoused somewhere, and the interest on the company's bank loan kept growing. True, this had no relation to Konstantinov and Zaitsev; nonetheless, the partners split up. Moreover, Zaitsev believed that Konstantinov had not paid him his full share of the $800,000. For this reason, Zaitsev organized a "fighters' brigade," headed by the ex-boxer Pechenochkin, and used it to threaten Konstantinov and his friend who lived in Germany and controlled his German bank account—the account holding the money that Konstantinov had received as a commission fee. This is how Zaitsev entered the loan collection business in Russia and Europe.

Shortly afterward, the head of the company that had purchased the helicopters—who owed a large debt to one of the banks—was killed under unclear circumstances. The FSB was obviously well informed about Zaitsev's new business. And when it came Chemezov's turn to collect $100,000 for chicken legs that had never been delivered, he turned for assistance to his old acquaintance Zaitsev.

It turned out, however, that Chemezov's $100,000 had been stolen by an organization that was protected by the Kazan crime group, all-powerful in St. Petersburg. Zaitsev's "fighters" were unable to get his money back and, after a shootout with the Kazan gangsters, barely escaped from St. Petersburg with their lives. That was when Chemezov turned to Alexander Petrovich Yevdokimov, an officer in the KGB's Fifth Directorate and former Ministry of Internal Affairs supervisor over the KGB's

3V Directorate. Yevdokimov was closely acquainted with the heads of the Chechen mafia, which was active in Moscow in the early 1990s, since he was either the head of one of the Chechen crime groups himself or its consultant. For the Chechens, however, $100,000 was a small sum, and Yevdokimov decided not to get involved in a conflict with St. Petersburg over this money. Chemezov had one last hope left: his old acquaintance from Dresden.

ROMAN TSEPOV

Roman Tsepov (real last name: Belinson) was born in 1962 in the town of Kolpino near Leningrad. After graduating from high school, he was employed as a metal worker at the Izhorsky factory. Then he was drafted into the army. Roman's mother was the chief dental surgeon in the correctional system for Leningrad and the Leningrad region. This was what allowed a young man with the Jewish last name "Belinson" to enroll in the Ministry of Internal Affairs' Higher Political School after leaving the army. It was here that he changed his name to "Tsepov," when he joined the ranks of the CPSU. Roman Tsepov served in the internal security troops and resigned (or, according to other sources, was fired) at the beginning of the 1990s with the rank of captain.

In 1992, Tsepov opened one of the first private security agencies in St. Petersburg, the Baltik-Eskort company (license No. 020004), and became its general manager. The idea to create a private security agency had come from Viktor Zolotov, a former officer in the Ninth Directorate of the KGB and subsequently of the Federal Protection Service (FSO). As an officer of the FSB's active reserve, Zolotov formally oversaw the private security agency for the FSB, while at the same time, as an official employee of Baltik-Eskort, he managed security for the mayor of St. Petersburg, Anatoly Sobchak. The private security agency's second FSB supervisor was Igor Koreshkov, a colleague of Putin's from the Leningrad KGB office.

Thus, Sobchak, who because of his position had a right to federal security protection, was protected by the FSO, while Sobchak's family (his wife, Lyudmila Narusova, and his daughter, Ksenia) and the city's deputy mayor, Vladimir Putin, none of whom had a right to federal security protection, were protected by Tsepov's private security agency, where Zolotov was listed as an employee—although he was simultaneously an officer in the FSO and head of security for Sobchak. It was not easy to unravel these complicated arrangements, but their upshot was that Sobchak, his family, and Putin were all protected by the same people from the Zolotov-Tsepov team.

In a 1999 interview with the newspaper *Versiya*, Tsepov recalled those years:

> I provided security for Sobchak's daughter and sometimes his wife. No more than that. . . . In St. Petersburg city government, steamship navigation was supervised by Putin. And the government contacted our agency. We made a contract and worked with Putin. Our work consisted in watching: he went into the house, he came out of the house, he got into his car, he got out of his car. . . .
>
> At that time, Putin's status didn't entitle him to security protection from the FSO. Today, all of St. Petersburg's deputy governors have security protection and all of them employ private security agencies. Naturally, the question comes up: who pays for all this? It costs money, after all. But at that time, in 1996, I took only a few kopeks from Putin, because he was useful to me—the fact that the agency provided security for the deputy mayor increased its prestige. Putin paid only for the salaries of his two bodyguards, $400–$500 per month. And he could afford it. He was a useful client.[1]

Tsepov did not reveal everything about his relations with Putin, however. It was precisely Tsepov who collected money from businessmen for St. Petersburg's International Relations Committee. It was to Tsepov that Putin sent his old friend Chemezov when the latter turned to Putin for help; and by contrast with everyone else, Tsepov was able to return to Chemezov the $100,000 that had been stolen from him. Thanks to Putin, Tsepov could take part in major commercial transactions, such as the privatization of the Baltic Sea Steamship Company.

Baltik-Eskort became the main private security agency for St. Petersburg's city hall. It was among the first in St. Petersburg to receive a license granting its employees the right to carry firearms. Tsepov himself became a staff officer in the Seventh Department of St. Petersburg's Regional Directorate for Combating Organized Crime (RUBOP) and had documents from St. Petersburg's Directorate of Internal Affairs and the regional FSB office. (When necessary, Tsepov could present papers from a panoply of state enforcement organizations.) Many of Baltik-Eskort's cars were equipped with sirens and flashing lights, while Tsepov himself had a "free pass"—a special document that guaranteed that his car would not be stopped or searched.

Baltik-Eskort immediately obtained contracts to provide security for prestigious buildings in the center of the city, cruise ships, and visiting pop stars. By putting many employees of St. Petersburg's government and law enforcement agencies on their payroll, including Zolotov himself, Tsepov and Zolotov created a system that allowed businessmen to use Baltik-Eskort to resolve conflicts with partners and gangsters. Baltik-Eskort could also protect the traffic of off-the-books cash that was used by the city's government and businessmen when they wanted to make deals with one another, by gangsters and businessmen when they wanted to make deals with the mayor's office, and by businessmen when they wanted to make deals with gangsters. Alexander Tkachenko—also known as "Tkach," and considered to be the head of the Perm organized crime group—worked for some time at Baltik-Eskort. Tsepov had dealings with Alexander Malyshev (head of the Malyshev organized crime group), who was later killed; with the Shevchenko brothers, one of whom was killed and the other of whom was given a suspended seven-year sentence for extortion. It should be noted that the 1990s in St. Petersburg, and in Russia as a whole, were the bloodiest years in terms of shootouts and contract killings. But not one person who received protection from Tsepov's security agency was killed. For the most part, Tsepov was on the attacking side rather than the defensive side.

ANATOLY SOBCHAK'S ESCAPE TO FRANCE

In 1995, as part of their general plan to take over power in Russia, Alexander Korzhakov and his collaborators decided to unseat Yeltsin's supporter Anatoly Sobchak from his post as mayor of St. Petersburg. The Second Department of the Directorate for Fighting Economic Crime (UBEP) in St. Petersburg began "working on" Sobchak's family and entourage in May 1995. An interagency operational-investigative group was established in December to look into evidence of corruption in Sobchak's mayor's office. The group was officially created by an unprecedented joint order from Anatoly Kulikov, minister of internal affairs; Mikhail Barsukov, head of the Security Service of Russia (SBR, the former KGB and the future FSB—the KGB was being constantly renamed and restructured at that time); and the general prosecutor, Yuri Skuratov. The political motives behind Sobchak's harassment were obvious. Everyone knew that the order to have Sobchak removed from his post had come from the all-powerful Korzhakov. But the fact that in St. Petersburg—"Russia's crime capital"—corruption flourished and government officials took exceedingly large bribes was also known to everyone. The fight was not conducted in a gentlemanly fashion.

The St. Petersburg investigative group was headed by Leonid Proshkin, the deputy head of the Investigative Committee of Russia's General Prosecutor's Office and one of Russia's most famous investigative officials, who was in charge of many important government corruption cases. Over the course of a year, the investigative group collected several dozen volumes of documents in support of criminal case No. 18/238287-95. According to the investigators, the St. Petersburg construction company Renaissance had been given ownership of several apartment buildings in the city on the condition that it would renovate them, and it had paid for this major contract by selling renovated apartments to mayor's office employees and their relatives at reduced prices. The investigation discovered documents signed by Sobchak that had secured most-favorable-treatment status for Renaissance, while the company's head, Anna Yevglevskaya, confirmed that she had paid $54,000 to relocate the residents of city-owned apartment No. 17 in building No. 31 on Moika Embankment. This apartment shared a wall with apartment No. 8, which was occupied by Anatoly Sobchak, his wife, and their daughter. After the residents of apartment No. 17 were relocated, the apartment became Sobchak's; to cover up this fact, however, it was officially transferred to Sergeyev, the private chauffer of a close friend of Sobchak's wife. The mayor's niece Marina Kutina (née Sobchak) also obtained better living quarters, as did the head of Sobchak's staff, V. Kruchinin.

Evidence of corruption at the St. Petersburg prosecutor's office also came to light. The office's property manager, Nazir Khapsirokov, had signed a contract with a Turkish firm, Ata Insaat Saanyi Ticaret Ltd., to have the prosecutor's office building repaired and renovated for a sum of $5,855,435. The Turkish firm received $3 million less than the agreed amount. The cost of the repairs was inflated by 100 percent. The city prosecutor's daughter somehow obtained an apartment.

Sobchak tried to defend himself. On May 20, 1996, the St. Petersburg branch of the party Our Home Is Russia sent letters to the president, the general prosecutor, and the prime minister, expressing "strong objections to the harassment and libel [to which Sobchak was being subjected by] the General Prosecutor's Office." The letter further stated:

> On the pretext of "fighting corruption," the General Prosecutor's Office is using its work for political purposes and discrediting the government. L. G. Proshkin's investigative group is giving interviews and, against all procedural norms, publishing unsubstantiated materials in the Communist press—*Sovietskaya Rossiya, Pravda, Narodnaya Pravda*—which are being used as promotional flyers in the election campaign. In view of these facts, the St. Petersburg organization Our Home Is Russia demands that decisive measures be taken to put an end to the use of law enforcement agencies for political purposes.

All of this was absolutely true—but so was the evidence of corruption collected by the criminal investigation. Among those who signed the letter was the head of the board of Our Home Is Russia's St. Petersburg office, Vladimir Putin.

From a political point of view, Sobchak lost this battle: on June 2, 1996, Sobchak's deputy Vladimir Yakovlev was elected as the new mayor. The "apartment affair," however, did not die down after Sobchak's defeat in the election. In December, a new General Prosecutor's Office investigator, Nikolai Mikheyev, became head of the investigative group. In the summer of 1997, the investigation led to the arrests of the head of the planning and economic department (Glavsnab) of the St. Petersburg mayor's office, V. Lyubina; Mayor Sobchak's former assistant on housing issues, L. Kharchenko; and the head of the mayor's staff, V. Kruchinin. By the fall, relying on the testimony of the arrested individuals and other collected materials, the investigative group was already prepared to bring charges against Sobchak himself and members of his inner circle. Plans were in the works for the arrest of a large group of people, including the former mayor.

At this time, Putin was already in Moscow at a height that the St. Petersburg investigators could not reach; but he covered up for Sobchak, knowing that he was thus indirectly protecting himself as well, since the investigation was also looking into his own financial activities. The investigation's note "On certain aspects of the work of the operational-investigative group of the St. Petersburg Directorate of Internal Affairs" stated:

> We have obtained evidence of crimes—the use of an official position for private purposes—committed by Putin, one of the high-ranking officials in the president's administration, a member of the Chubais team. The official position that Putin currently occupies considerably hinders the work of the operational-investigative group and allows A. Sobchak to feel relatively safe.

Putin, who at that time was deputy chief of staff and head of the Main Control Directorate (GKU), did as much as he could to thwart the "apartment affair." The St. Petersburg prosecutor's office brought a number of charges against St. Petersburg police officers who had been involved in the investigation of the Sobchak case. Some of them, including the supervising officers, were arrested. Sobchak's wife, Lyudmila Narusova, began paying regular visits to Putin in Moscow. They always met alone, so the details of their conversations are not known. It was precisely Narusova who informed Putin that Russia's General Prosecutor's Office, after long debate, had made the decision to arrest Sobchak. And Sobchak's arrest would imperil his whole entourage—first and foremost, Putin himself.

On October 3, 1997, the now ex-mayor Sobchak was called in for questioning by the prosecutor's office. It was expected that he would be presented with charges and then arrested. Neither the democrats nor Putin could allow this to happen: the democrats, because Sobchak was their symbol; and Putin, because after Sobchak's arrest the threads of the investigation would lead to him. On Putin's instructions, an emergency response team from the Regional Directorate for Combating Organized Crime (RUBOP) removed Sobchak from the prosecutor's office and took him to a hospital, where the director of the Military Medical Academy, Yuri Shevchenko—a person close to Sobchak's family and a close acquaintance of Putin's—at once gave Sobchak a highly dubious diagnosis: heart attack.

Realizing that Sobchak was being freed from arrest, investigator Mikheyev met with the heads of Russia's Ministry of Health and arranged for an independent examination of Sobchak's health by Moscow doctors. But this examination—which the General Prosecutor's Office had no right to conceal from officials in the Kremlin, who did not want Sobchak to be arrested—never took place. On November 7, 1997, three days before the Moscow cardiologists were scheduled to arrive in St. Petersburg, RUBOP officers Shakhanov and Milin, led by the first deputy head of the FSB's St. Petersburg directorate, Alexander Grigoriev, removed Sobchak from the hospital and took him to France on a private plane, which had been chartered from the Finnish airline Jetflite by the famous cellist and conductor Mstislav Rostropovich. The operation to remove Sobchak was organized by Vladimir Putin. An ambulance drove out directly onto the runway at Pulkovo airport; Anatoly Sobchak and Lyudmila Narusova emerged from it, boarded the plane, and flew away.

When he became president, Putin did not forget the people who had helped him carry out this operation. Yuri Shevchenko became Russia's minister of health. Alexander Grigoriev became head of the Federal Agency for State Reserves. Rostropovich became a close friend of Putin's.

As minister of health, Shevchenko acquired the nickname "Dr. Death," since mortality among Russians rose sharply during his tenure, and 129 people lost their lives due to inadequate medical treatment after gas poisoning in the freeing of the *Nord-Ost* hostages at the Dubrovka theater in Moscow on October 23, 2002. After five years of failure, Shevchenko was dismissed from his post.

NAZIR KHAPSIROKOV AND ASHOT YEGHIAZARIAN

Nazir Khapsirokov, the property manager of the General Prosecutor's Office, was born in 1952, in the Karachay-Cherkessian village of Khabez. His father, Khazir Khapsirokov, was a professor at the Karachay Pedagogical Institute. After graduating from high school, Nazir entered the institute where his father taught. During vacations, along with other students, he made money by working as an instructor at the Dombai ski resort, and here already he displayed an enterprising spirit: he would tell each of the groups he worked with that it was his birthday, and money would then be collected for a gift, making a decent supplement to his salary.

After graduating from the institute, Nazir became the secretary of his district Komsomol committee, and then an instructor at his district party committee. He continued to drink heavily, however, and his habit got so out of hand that the question arose of expelling him from the party committee. He was saved when his father, a respected man in the Karachay-Cherkess Republic, intervened on his behalf. But his career as a party functionary was over. Nazir left his native city and became the director of a household services factory, organizing underground production of knitted goods at his place of work. In the Soviet Union, such people were called "shop organizers" (*tsekhoviki*). They produced goods at government expense in government-owned enterprises, but these goods were not mentioned in any documents, as if they did not exist. And all the money from their sale went to the organizers of these complicated and risky private businesses, which were prohibited by Soviet law. Sooner or later, "shop organizers" were arrested. This is what happened to Nazir. Criminal charges were brought against him and he was put in a pretrial detention facility.

Criminal cases involving "shop organizers" were handled by the KGB, since large-scale economic ventures were regarded as a form of economic sabotage and a threat to the foundations of the state. The RSFSR's Criminal Code even prescribed the death penalty for illegal operations that involved over one million rubles. At the very least, Khapsirokov was facing a long term in prison. But he was offered freedom and the dropping of criminal charges against him in exchange for collaboration with the KGB.

When Khapsirokov started building dachas outside Moscow for federal and Moscow city government officials in the early 1990s, criminal charges were once more brought against him for overspending his resources by an amount exceeding half a million dollars. In other words, he was accused of stealing over $500,000. He blamed everything on his deputy, who disappeared. Khapsirokov himself switched to a different job, becoming an executive manager in Russia's General Prosecutor's Office. The general prosecutor at the time was the former head of the president's Main Audit Directorate, Alexei Ilyushenko. When Khapsirokov was appointed to his new post, reports appeared in the press that the budget resources allocated to the General Prosecutor's Office for the maintenance of all the prosecutor's offices in the country were kept on accounts at Moscow National Bank and Unikombank, which were headed by Khapsirokov's friend Ashot Yeghiazarian.

Ashot Yeghiazarian was born in Moscow on July 2, 1965. In the late 1970s, he emigrated with his family to Los Angeles. In the 1970s, the USSR opened a general consulate in San Francisco, which provided diplomatic cover for Soviet foreign intelligence activities and handed out visas to Americans wishing to visit the Soviet Union. All copies of forms for obtaining entrance visas were sent to the Consular Directorate of the USSR's Ministry of Foreign Affairs and to the KGB—to the Central Unit of Operational Communications. This made it possible for various divisions of state security to take an active part in the process of handing out (or refusing) entrance visas to foreign citizens. The employees of the consular departments of the USSR's— and later Russia's—embassies were usually foreign intelligence officers, working under diplomatic cover. Consequently, the KGB and the FSB were always informed well in advance when any foreign citizen made plans to visit the country.

In Yeghiazarian's biography, everything looked peculiar. In 1991, at the age of twenty-five, Yeghiazarian became the head of the Foundation for the Social-Economic Development of the Moscow Region. In 1993, he created and became the head of Moscow National Bank (whose name does not sound at all Russian). In 1995, the bank became one of the largest in Russia (after which it went bankrupt). The bank held the accounts of the Moscow regional government, the Ministry of Defense, Rosvooruzhenie (the state-owned arms export company), the Russian Space Agency, and the General Prosecutor's Office. In 1996, Yeghiazarian left the bank and became deputy chairman of the board of directors at Unikombank. The son of the new general prosecutor, Yuri Skuratov, became one of the managers of this bank; the obliging banker Yeghiazarian repaired and renovated Skuratov's apartment, in return for which he was appointed advisor to Russia's general prosecutor, a post he continued to occupy until 1998. The clue to Yeghiazarian's success lay in the fact that he had been recruited as an agent of Russia's Foreign Intelligence Service (SVR).

It was precisely these two agent-friends, FSB agent Khapsirokov and SVR agent Yeghiazarian, who were used by Putin to work on the case of Yuri Skuratov, who as general prosecutor was investigating economic crimes committed by members of Yeltsin's entourage. In 1998, Unikombank—where Yeghiazarian was employed—provided the funds to rent the apartment in which certain unknown individuals, subordinates of FSB director Putin, made a videotape of "a person resembling the general prosecutor" of Russia, Yuri Skuratov, amusing himself with two call girls. This videotape ultimately forced Skuratov to resign.

Unikombank soon collapsed. When it declared bankruptcy, the Moscow region hard-currency domestic loan bonds that it was holding disappeared, as did $230 million that had been allocated to the MAPO MiG corporation for the production of fighter planes for India. This money was never found. Several lawsuits followed the bank's collapse, but none of them affected Yeghiazarian. And when the amount of incriminating evidence against Khapsirokov and Yeghiazarian attained critical mass and started to pose the threat of an investigation and an arrest, Khapsirokov took shelter in the president's staff, while Yeghiazarian found safety in the Russian parliament, becoming a Duma deputy from the Liberal Democratic Party of Russia (LDPR) and thus obtaining immunity.

CHEMEZOV UNDER THE PRESIDENT

Yevgeny Ananiev—former KGB officer, head of MAPO Bank's board of directors, and editor-in-chief of the *Megapolis-Express* newspaper—became the head of Rosvooruzhenie in 1997. Ananiev had been supported by Alexander Korzhakov, head of the Presidential Security Service, and Oleg Soskovets, deputy prime minister, prior to their resignations.

Shortly thereafter, by order of President Yeltsin, additional organizations were created to facilitate the sale of Russian arms abroad: Promexport and Russian Technologies. The appearance of new arms dealers gave rise to competition among them and a sharp decline in sales. This led in 1998 to a wholesale review of the activities of Rosvooruzhenie by the Main Control Directorate of the presidential administration, headed by Putin's appointee Nikolai Patrushev. What the review discovered remained a secret, although in June 2004 the Italian media reported that Ananiev, the former head of Rosvooruzhenie, was being charged by the Italian authorities with laundering $18 million that had been received by him and a group of Russian parties from the government of Peru as a bribe for giving Peru a discount on MiG-29 fighter planes.

After becoming the head of the government, Putin immediately united Russia's arms dealers into a single organization, Rosoboronexport, in order to make it easier to monitor their monetary flows. At the head of the new organization, he installed his old foreign intelligence colleague Andrei Belyaninov, and as Belyaninov's first deputy he appointed Sergei Chemezov. The Government Commission for Military-Technological Cooperation with Foreign Countries was headed by Putin personally.

In 2004, Chemezov replaced Belyaninov and became the head of Rosoboronexport. In December 2006, President Putin signed a decree "On certain issues of military-technological cooperation between the Russian Federation and foreign countries," which gave Rosoboronexport monopoly rights over Russian arms sales. Prior to the signing of the decree, eighteen other defense enterprises had the right to deliver spare parts and maintenance services for previously sold arms to foreign countries. In addition, a number of major producers of military technology—such as the manufacturers of MiG fighter planes, the KBP Instrument Design Bureau, and the NPO Mashinostroyenia Military-Industrial Corporation—also had independent access to the foreign market. After the decree, all Russian arms sales were concentrated in the hands of one of the people closest to Putin, Sergei Chemezov.

In terms of volume and profitability, the sale of arms is the third-largest business in Russia, after oil and gas. Andrei Belyaninov, who headed Rosoboronexport before Chemezov, acknowledged in one of his interviews that the money remaining abroad with agents and middlemen was not subject to monitoring and control. In addition, in the spring of 2007, the Duma Committee for Defense prepared a bill allowing Rosoboronexport, which has forty-four offices in foreign countries, to use the accounts of Russian embassies and other delegations in foreign countries—not to deliver the proceeds from arms sales back to Russia, but to keep them on the diplomatic bank accounts of embassies, consulates, and other representative delegations.

The new law also allowed Rosoboronexport to form barter arrangements for arms sales. In principle, there was nothing new about this. The Soviet Union made extensive use of similar arrangements in selling arms to developing nations that were unable to make scheduled payments in hard currency. Some paid in bananas, others paid in oranges. Such contracts were handled by various divisions of the Ministry of Foreign Economic Relations. The same agency also handled the sales of the natural products that it received, disposing of them on the territory of the USSR. The new law entrusted all these functions to Rosoboronexport. The law was accompanied by an explanatory note:

> The attraction of payments in the form of natural products stems from the fact that developing nations, particularly those of the African region, are not always able to meet payments, as well as from the fact that it is economically expedient for importers of Russian military production to pay for the products they receive with goods that they produce (textiles, palm tree oil, etc.).

Thus, the note went on to report, $150 million worth of munitions were delivered to Indonesia in 2003–2004; payment was made in palm oil products. Currently, plans are being made for the sale of $400 million worth of arms to Thailand; payment will come in various food products, which will not be delivered to Russian territory (meaning that Rosoboronexport will not have to pay value-added tax).

This approach to selling Russian arms and paying for them opened up broad possibilities for manipulating prices, receiving off-the-books commission fees, and appropriating substantial sums of money, since complicated barter arrangements made monitoring and control over sales and payments virtually impossible.

In 2007, Rosoboronexport and all its daughter enterprises were unified in the newly created Russian Technologies Ltd. Chemezov now became the head of the whole corporation. In addition, Rosoboronexport received Oboronprom's packet of shares; the Perm-based Motovilinskiye Zavody munitions plant; two-thirds of the shares of Russia's largest titanium corporation, VSMPO-Avisim, which produces 20 percent of the world's titanium; the Russpetsslal steel company; and the AvtoVAZ automobile factory. The new corporation was exempted from the government's direct control. Its head was appointed by the president personally. In other words, Putin had created a monopolistic military superstructure in Russia for the production and sale of arms, on the model of Gazprom, which deals in natural gas.

Not surprisingly, people who were involved in investigating Russian arms sales to foreign partners, as well as the partners themselves, found themselves in a high-risk area. In March 2007, the *Kommersant* correspondent Ivan Safronov "fell out" of the window in the stairwell of his apartment building. A former serviceman, Safronov had been investigating Russian arms sales to Syria and Iran. In June, the Egyptian billionaire Ashraf Marwan, who had made his fortune selling Soviet and Russian arms, fell from the balcony of his apartment in London.

On July 5, 2007, Oleg Orlov, a Russian citizen, was strangled to death in pretrial detention facility No. 13 in Kiev. Ukraine suspected Orlov of involvement in two crimes: illegally selling a P-14F radar station to Eritrea, which was at war with Ethiopia, in the fall of 1999 (false papers stated that the radar station was being sold to Romania); and illegally selling Kh-55SM air-launched cruise missiles to China and Iran. In both cases, the arms had been delivered through the Ukrainsky Spetsexport company. Until 2004, Orlov had lived in Karlovy Vary, Czech Republic; he had asked the Czech government for political asylum, but his request was denied. While attempting to leave for the United Arab Emirates, Orlov was arrested in the Prague airport and then deported to Ukraine, where the Ukrainian Security Service (SBU) had brought criminal charges against him. The same charges had also been brought against Vladimir Yevdokimov, general manager of the Ukrainsky Aviazakaz company and a former SBU employee; Yevdokimov was sentenced by the Kiev Appellate Court to six years in prison. The SBU put one more Russian citizen on the wanted list: Igor Shilenko. His case also involved the former head of Ukrainsky Spetsexport, Valery Malev, and an Australian citizen named Haider Sarfraz, both of whom died in automobile accidents—in 2002 and 2004, respectively.

LEONID TYAGACHEV

There's a Russian saying: an old friend is better than two new ones. Sometimes, however, the opposite is true. Putin's new friend Leonid Tyagachev, head of the Russian Olympic Committee, is a vivid example. Tyagachev was born on October 10, 1946, in the Moscow-area town of Dedenevo. For many years, his life was connected with the Turist railroad station, located just outside of Moscow. The landscape around this railroad station is hilly, and these hills have long been used by downhill skiers to practice their skills. One of them was the very young Leonid Tyagachev. After becoming involved in sports, he graduated from the physical education school of the Krupskaya Moscow Regional State Pedagogical Institute in 1973. The institute was not a prestigious one; it prepared gym teachers for Moscow region secondary schools. Tyagachev's education was insubstantial.

However, he possessed other important qualities. He was friendly, particularly with those who occupied high positions in the Soviet party elite and their children. Many people were interested in downhill skiing, but only a very few were able to try it. The necessary equipment was very expensive and nearly impossible to find. By skillfully trading in ski equipment and making the right connections, Tyagachev was gradually able to reach the very top: he became the coach of the USSR's downhill ski team (whose international rating was negligible). Now the necessary people in whom Tyagachev was interested got everything they needed from him, either for a token payment or free of charge. Coach Tyagachev could afford it.

After working as coach for the USSR's downhill ski team for a short time, Tyagachev was able to acquire influential supporters in the USSR's State Sports Committee, in Moscow's municipal CPSU committee, and in the Central Committee of the CPSU. Tyagachev's house near the Turist railroad station became a kind of elite ski base for his sponsors. He also established good working relations with sports administrators around the USSR at those locations where the ski team trained. These local administrators were interested in hosting the team, since the training expenses were all paid by Moscow. In addition, a small amount of hard-to-acquire equipment would be left over for them. One phone call from Tyagachev to Ibragim Timofeyev, director of the Elbrus-area council on tourism and a former air force pilot, was enough to find hotel rooms—otherwise impossible to obtain—for the necessary people. Through Zalikhmanov, who was in charge of ski lifts on Mt. Cheget, Tyagachev's "friends" had free access to the lifts and did not have to wait in line. In short, Tyagachev made skillful use of his "administrative resources" (although the Soviet downhill skiers never achieved any significant success in international competition while he was coach).

While the young Tyagachev was becoming established in his new position, Lieutenant Vladimir Alekseyevich Lavrov—a graduate of the KGB's Higher School—started working in the first division of the First Department of the Fifth Directorate of the KGB. He and his older colleague Major Anatoly Sergeyevich Smaznov, deputy head of the first division, were ordered to supervise the USSR's State Sports Committee. It was Lavrov who, in the mid-1970s, recruited into the Fifth Directorate's agent network an agent with the code name "Elbrus," who was known in ordinary life as the coach of the Soviet downhill ski team, Leonid Tyagachev.

Lavrov's and Smaznov's work at the USSR's State Sports Committee opened up broad opportunities. Through the Directorate for Medical-Biological Provisions for the representative teams of the country, it was possible to obtain expensive and hard-to-acquire foreign medicine for personal use. Through the Main Athletic Provisions Office of the State Sports Committee and through Soyuzsportobespechenie, it was possible to obtain athletic equipment and supplies. When it came to "obtaining" these products, Smaznov and Lavrov took orders from their boss, the deputy head of the Fifth Directorate's First Department, Lieutenant Colonel Viktor Timofeyevich Gostev.

Before being hired by the KGB, Gostev was the head of the Komsomol Central Committee's administrative-economic department. At this post, he had clearly learned that the essential thing in building a career was good relations with one's superiors, whose good will could be procured in return for various kinds of offerings. All three—Gostev, Smaznov, and Lavrov—did everything they could to provide necessary athletic equipment and supplies (such as bicycles) for the Fifth Directorate's deputy heads, V. I. Nikashkin and I. P. Abramov, and the Fifth Directorate's head, Lieutenant General Bobkov. But Smaznov, Lavrov, and Gostev were not liked in the KGB. Smaznov was nicknamed "black." His younger colleague Lavrov was nicknamed "little vermin." Ultimately, Gostev ended up being demoted and sent into honorable exile to the Dinamo Sports Association, becoming the deputy head of its central council.

In February 1979, the USSR's downhill ski team, under the supervision of its senior coach, Leonid Tyagachev, was returning home from a world championship competition in Austria. When the team's luggage was passing through customs at Moscow's Sheremetyevo-2 airport, instead of finding ski boots, customs officers discovered 120 pairs of contraband blue jeans—extremely rare and expensive items of clothing in the USSR. Contraband foreign-made blue jeans, which were almost illegal in the Soviet Union, could create serious difficulties for Tyagachev. In order to determine the circumstances of the case, the State Sports Committee—with the Fifth Directorate's approval—sent its representative Mikhail Volfovich Monastyrsky to Austria. Monastyrsky was the director of a number of international mountain-climbing camps and also a security agent with the code name "Vladimirov." During his short trip, Monastyrsky-"Vladimirov" obtained documentary evidence, including invoices signed by Tyagachev, that showed he had removed twelve pairs of ski boots from their boxes and replaced them with 120 pairs of precious blue jeans.

Tyagachev was facing criminal sanctions. The transport prosecutor's office had brought criminal charges against him for trafficking in contraband on a large scale. Even the KGB was refusing to help. Lavrov, who had recruited Tyagachev, was apprehensive that he himself would be punished for his agent's actions. He avoided meeting Tyagachev and did not respond to his requests for help.

At this time, the KGB was preparing to make security provisions for the Moscow Olympics in 1980. The Fifth Directorate's Eleventh Department was considered the key agency in this important project, and in particular its third division, which was being urgently expanded to include agents from other departments who had been transferred there for the duration of the Olympics. Among the new employees of the Eleventh Department's third division was a graduate of the KGB's Higher School, Captain Fyodor Alekseyevich Volkov, who had previously served in the Fifth Directorate's Ninth Department, monitoring Soviet dissidents. And Lavrov, who had become afraid of possible repercussions arising from the Tyagachev incident, handed the supervision of the State Sports Committee's winter sports directorate over to the newly arrived and unsuspecting Volkov. Volkov had no choice but to deal with the problem that he had inherited from Lavrov, the problem of agent "Elbrus." Volkov arranged for Tyagachev's transfer to a supervisory position in the Russian Sports Committee, and Tyagachev was rescued from being held criminally liable for what he had done. The case was closed.

On April 15, 1980, in connection with the Moscow Olympics, the KGB made a decision to establish new positions for active reserve officers in the USSR's main athletic organizations: the State Sports Committee of the USSR, the State Sports Committee of the RSFSR (Russia), and the Sports Committee of the VTsSPS (the All-Union Central Council of Trade Unions). The decision was ratified by the Secretariat of the CPSU Central Committee and signed by Mikhail Suslov, the leading ideologist of the Soviet Union, and by Mikhail Gorbachev, future general secretary of the CPSU Central Committee and president of the USSR. This was how Emerik Merkurievich Shevelev, a longtime employee of the state security organs and a member of the Fifth Directorate, ended up being appointed deputy head of the international department of the RSFSR State Sports Committee.

Tyagachev rather quickly established good informal relations with the new deputy head of his department, and Shevelev and his two sons soon started walking around in clothes made by Western manufacturers of ski wear and developed a passion for downhill skiing, having received all the necessary equipment as a gracious gift from Tyagachev.

Shevelev did his part for Tyagachev as well. He reported to his supervisors in state security that Tyagachev was in all respects an exceptionally reliable man, a valuable agent, and that in order to secure greater counterintelligence oversight of international sports exchange channels, it was absolutely imperative to send him on foreign work assignments as a downhill skiing coach. Since the head of the Fifth Directorate's Eleventh Department, Colonel N. N. Romanov, and the deputy head of the Fifth Directorate, Major General V. A. Ponomarev, also turned out to be lovers of expensive skiing equipment, and since they also had sons who appreciated the expensive, foreign-made athletic gear, the question of whether or not Tyagachev should be sent on foreign work assignments was decided in the affirmative. Shevelev's recommendations were supported by another person—Tyagachev's boss, the head of the RSFSR State Sports Committee, Leonid Drachevsky.

A former coach for the USSR's rowing team, Drachevsky was also an agent of the Fifth Directorate's Eleventh Department. He had been recruited by Valentin Nefedov, an employee of the Fifth Directorate's Seventh Department who had been temporarily transferred to the Eleventh Department. And if Nefedov's career in "sports" did not work out—he was forced to leave the Fifth Directorate's Eleventh Department after the

Moscow Olympics—then the career of his agent Drachevsky ended up being exemplary in all respects. Thanks to the KGB's support, he first became the head of Russian sports, and then was appointed by President Putin as his plenipotentiary representative in the Siberian Federal District. And to replace KGB-FSB agent Drachevsky as head of Russian sports, the government installed KGB-FSB agent Tyagachev.

In Soviet times, the KGB's Second Main Directorate was the primary counterintelligence organ in the country. In the late 1970s, Arkady Guk—a former Soviet intelligence resident in London whose career had been seriously damaged when one of his London subordinates, Oleg Gordievsky, defected to the United Kingdom—was appointed as head of this directorate's Thirteenth Department, which oversaw the selection and processing of state security officers for trips to foreign countries in various Soviet delegations (including athletic ones). The processing of agents for foreign travel with athletic delegations was handled by Valery Fyodorovich Balyasnikov, the former goalie of the Moscow soccer team Dinamo. Balyasnikov had climbed up through the ranks of this department to become the head of his division, and shortly before the collapse of the Soviet Union, he was sent to one of the Latin American countries as a state security officer with the Soviet embassy.

State security officers accompanied Soviet athletic delegations only during major international sporting events: world championships, Universiades, and Olympics. During competitions at lower levels and periods of training abroad, control and monitoring functions were performed by agents permanently embedded within the sports organizations themselves. Active reserve officers who had no relation to sports never traveled abroad with athletic delegations, since this could compromise their cover at their official places of work.

After the creation of the commercial organization Sovintersport in the late 1980s, Sergei Chemezov was sent there as an officer of the active reserve. Formally, however, he became Sovintersport's deputy general manager. This firm handled all purchases of foreign-made equipment for Russian teams, which is what led Tyagachev to seek out Chemezov. Shevelev was also helpful in this respect; like Chemezov, he was an active reserve officer and the deputy head of the RSFSR State Sports Committee's international department. Chemezov and Shevelev worked in the same division—the third division of the Fifth Directorate's Eleventh Department.

Chemezov and Tyagachev quickly came to see eye to eye with respect to purchasing equipment for skiers. They received kickbacks or commission fees either in cash or in kind (ski equipment produced by top foreign firms). Chemezov knew how to please his friend Putin. For a downhill skier such as Putin, good skiing equipment is a matter of pride. Tyagachev did not disappoint. Putin was given the best of everything. This is how Putin and Tyagachev met and how, over the years, they became friends.

SOCHI 2014

Putin's, Chemezov's, and Tyagachev's career paths are all correlated with one another. In 1996, Putin and Chemezov joined the Presidential Property Management Directorate, while Tyagachev became the head of the Russian State Sports Committee. In 1998, Putin was appointed director of the FSB and then prime minister, while Tyagachev became the vice president of the Russian Olympic Committee. In 2000, Putin was elected president. In July 2001, Tyagachev became the head of the Olympic Committee, replacing KGB-FSB agent Vitaly Smirnov, who had occupied this position for over twenty years.

The 2002 Winter Olympics in Salt Lake City were accompanied by a series of scandals involving members of the Russian team. Tyagachev, who spoke no foreign languages and thus had no ability to communicate directly with members of the International Olympic Committee (IOC) and the Olympic Committees of other countries, did virtually nothing. After the Olympics ended, Putin's deputy chief of staff, Alexei Volin, remarked that "Russian sports officials displayed complete indifference and ineffectiveness at the games in Salt Lake City. We did not see their influence within the IOC, we did not see their presence in the international sports federations, and we did not hear them take an articulate and well-argued position on problems and issues that came up."

Many believed that Tyagachev would resign as head of the Russian Olympic Committee, but the controversy remained confined to criticism in the press. Shortly afterward, a conflict occurred between the two heads of Russian sports—the head of Russia's State Sports Committee, Vyacheslav Fetisov, and the head of the Russian Olympic Committee, Tyagachev. Exploiting the criticism directed against Tyagachev after the Salt Lake City Olympics, Fetisov tried to remove him from his post and replace him with his own person, Irina Rodnina, famous in the world of sports as an Olympic medalist and world champion. Fetisov and Rodnina lost this particular competition, however, since Tyagachev had the support of Chemezov and Putin, and their support had a long-standing commitment behind it.

Back in January 1996, Putin had joined the council of Klub-2004, an association of St. Petersburg industrialists and entrepreneurs established to promote the city as host for the 2004 Olympics. St. Petersburg did not even make it to the final round of the Olympic selection process at the time, but Putin did not abandon the idea of holding the Olympics in Russia. When he moved to Moscow, this idea turned into a project to host the Winter Olympics in Sochi, his favorite skiing destination, where he had often spent time with Chemezov and Tyagachev in a little village called Krasnaya Polyana.

For those who have never been to Russia, we should reveal an important state secret. In the winter, a great part of Russia is covered with snow; its Siberian expanses and numerous mountain peaks form natural sites for Winter Olympics. There are hundreds of such locations. There is probably only one place that is obviously unfit for this purpose: the southern Russian resort city of Sochi, on the Black Sea. Sochi is as hot as Florida. But this is the most expensive and popular destination for all "new Russians," and for all Russians in general, because Sochi in Russia is like Nice in France. Clearly it is profitable to invest money in Sochi, and the Winter Olympics are merely a pretext to pump billions of dollars in foreign investment and Russian government resources into the summer resort.

With the same zeal that he had brought to the idea of holding the 2004 Olympics in St. Petersburg, where he was second in command, Putin now supported hosting the 2014 Olympics in Sochi, where he was first in command. The project promised large profits, since by the time of the International Olympic Committee's deciding vote on the issue, Sochi had been entirely "privatized" by Putin-controlled organizations. In other words, all the most important sites and locations involved in the Sochi 2014 project had been bought up in advance, in accordance with a previously coordinated plan, by private organizations and people controlled by Putin and the FSB.

Thus, when Putin spoke about realizing his dream of holding the Olympic Games on territory under his control, it was not sports that was at stake, but business. In order to realize the project, Putin needed a proven, reliable man, and he selected Tyagachev for the job. Fetisov, despite his fame and connections in the world of sports, lost his struggle with Tyagachev because Tyagachev's team turned out to be stronger: it included both Chemezov and Putin.

The contest in the international arena took place in 2007, when the International Olympic Committee had to decide where the 2014 Winter Olympics would be held. The IOC met to vote in Guatemala City on July 9, 2007, following a serious struggle among the contending countries: Austria, Korea, and Russia.

Victory in any sporting event requires money. As usual, the winner is the one who has invested the greatest amount of money to secure a victory. Russia's rivals, Austria and Korea, had spent $12 million and $21 million, respectively, to promote their cities as hosts for the Winter Olympics. Russia had spared no expense, putting out $50 million to promote Sochi. But this was not all. In order to snatch the victory from Russia's rivals, Putin himself came to Guatemala. On the eve of the IOC's deciding vote, he personally met with the IOC's most influential members and its chairman, Jacques Rogge. Putin also did not neglect the IOC's honorary president, Juan Antonio Samaranch, a highly respected figure in international sports circles and among the members of the International Olympic Committee, all of whom had been elected to what in effect are lifelong positions under Samaranch. What Putin and Samaranch talked about, we obviously do not know. What we do know is that the IOC voted to hold the Winter Olympics in the Russian summer resort of Sochi. Moreover, since this vote took place, many of Putin's subordinates have repeatedly stated that President Putin intends to inaugurate the Sochi Olympics in person. A case can probably be made that Putin has one more secret dream that he will try to realize when he is no longer president: to become the president of the International Olympic Committee.

In achieving this ambition, Putin will probably also be able to rely on the help of Samaranch, who remembers very well to whom he owed his own election as head of the IOC in Moscow in 1980, when he was Spain's ambassador to the Soviet Union. Samaranch was supported as a candidate for the presidency of the IOC not only by the Soviet Union, but also by all the countries of the Eastern Bloc. His election was preceded by something of a detective story. As an ambassador to the USSR, Samaranch developed an interest in Russian history and culture. He grew particularly fond of Russian antiques, which he collected with the love of a genuine connoisseur and shipped to his home in Spain. The USSR prohibited taking objects of cultural and historic value out of the country, but this prohibition could easily be circumvented through diplomatic mail, which was not subject to customs inspection. In Soviet times, all antiques were closely monitored by the KGB; so Ambassador Samaranch, as a frequent buyer of increasingly valuable rarities, was taken note of. After a while, an agent from the KGB's Second Main Directorate, which monitored the Spanish embassy, met with Samaranch and gently explained to him that his actions were subject to prosecution in accordance with the RSFSR's Criminal Code (each republic had its own criminal code; there was no general criminal code for the USSR) and were classified by Soviet law as the smuggling of contraband goods. Samaranch was offered a choice: he could either be compromised through the publication of articles in the Soviet and foreign press detailing his unlawful activities, which would undoubtedly have put an end to his diplomatic career, or he could collaborate with the KGB as a secret agent. Samaranch chose the latter option.

It was precisely for this reason that, before the IOC's Moscow meeting at which the question of Samaranch's election as IOC president would be decided, the leadership of the KGB directed the Fifth Directorate's Eleventh Department to prepare an encrypted telegram for its "friends"—the heads of the state security organs of the other Eastern Bloc countries. The telegram requested that the foreign agents embedded in the various National Olympic Committees and Olympic sports federations be briefed concerning the necessity of showing world-wide support for the candidacy of Juan Antonio Samaranch at the upcoming IOC session in Moscow. The telegram was signed by the KGB's deputy head, V. M. Chebrikov, former head of the whole Fifth Directorate. It did not specify that Samaranch was an agent (which would have gone against state security conventions), but indicated that his candidacy was supported by the USSR and asked that it also be supported by its "friends'" agents among the heads of the National Olympic Committees and Olympic sports federations.

As a result, Samaranch was elected president of the IOC, where for many years he loyally served the country to which he was connected by his work as an agent and by his gratitude for its help in getting him a high international position. The KGB officer who had recruited Samaranch was not forgotten either. By secret decree (without an announcement in the press) of the Presidium of the Supreme Soviet of the USSR, he was awarded the Order of the Red Banner for Military Valor.

Other KGB-FSB agents were also involved in working on IOC members before the vote in Guatemala City. Vitaly Smirnov, the IOC vice president and a Russian sports activist, had been recruited by the KGB during the preparations for the Moscow Olympics in 1980. His immediate supervisor was the head of the Fifth Directorate, Lieutenant General Bobkov, and as Bobkov's protégé, Smirnov even called Bobkov's deputy General Abramov by his first name—Ivan—despite the difference in their ages and in front of Abramov's subordinates.

Shamil Tarpischev, who had been the head of Russia's State Sports Committee during the Yeltsin presidency, also helped as much as he could. He, too, had been recruited by the KGB during the preparations for the 1980 Olympics. The agent who had recruited him was Major Albina Gavrilovna Demidova, a former track-and-field athlete who had served for a number of years as an officer in the KGB's Seventh Directorate—which monitored the activities of persons of interest to the KGB—and had then been appointed senior operative in the third division of the Fifth Directorate's Eleventh Department. Finally, the head of the State Sports Committee's soccer and hockey division (and subsequently president of the Russian Soccer Federation), Vyacheslav Ivanovich Koloskov, also exerted his influence on the members of the IOC. He had been recruited in the late 1970s under the code name "Yantar" by the deputy head of the third division of the Fifth Directorate's Eleventh Department, Lieutenant Colonel Ernest Leonardovich Davnis. In short, Putin had no shortage of assistants. But the most important among them turned out to be Tyagachev. He was ordered to keep silent during all the meetings in Guatemala City. Tyagachev executed this task with consummate skill.

YURI SHUTOV

By way of contrast to our description of President Putin's habit of not forgetting his friends, we should say something about how he deals with his enemies. Once he sets a goal to "finish someone off," he does not rest until he does so.

When Putin started working for Anatoly Sobchak in 1990, Sobchak had people working for him who, according to Putin, "have since then become notorious and who did Sobchak a bad service."[2] Putin was referring first and foremost to Yuri Shutov, a shady businessman and politician who was the unofficial advisor to Lensovet chairman Sobchak during the spring and fall of 1990. (Officially, Shutov served as Sobchak's advisor only for several days, from November 5 to November 12, 1990.)

In Soviet times, Shutov the petty bureaucrat had been charged with attempting to set fire to Leningrad's city hall (Smolny) with the aim of destroying evidence of his financial misdeeds. He was put in prison. During Gorbachev's perestroika, Shutov was pardoned and then exonerated. Obviously, he had had no intentions of setting fire to Smolny. After Sobchak first took him under his wing and then banished him in shame (apparently, not without Putin's advice), Shutov began gathering incriminating evidence against Sobchak and his entourage. The times were difficult, everyone broke the laws, and there was plenty of incriminating evidence to be had. Later, part of the material collected by Shutov went into his book-length pamphlet "Sobchak's Heart" (*Sobchachie serdtse*, a pun on the title of Mikhail Bulgakov's famous novella *Sobachie serdtse*, "The Heart of a Dog") and its sequel, "Sobchak's Mischieviad, or How Everyone Was Robbed" (*Sobchachya prokhindiada*, *ili kak vsekh obokrali*). These books were intended to be the first two parts of a trilogy titled "Thievery."

In working on his books, Shutov was helped by Mark Grigoriev, a professional journalist who had once published an article in the magazine *Ogonyok* about the attempt to "set fire" to Smolny, which had strongly contributed to Shutov's pardon and exoneration. Shutov's office was located in the Leningrad Hotel. He rented a room for his co-author in the same hotel, and the two writers worked on their book in peace—a book that, of course, could bring no great joy to Sobchak.

In February 1991, there was a fire in the Leningrad Hotel that killed Mark Grigoriev. This did not stop Shutov, who stubbornly went on with the work that he had begun. Somehow, he had gotten hold of a tape of a casual conversation between Sobchak and the resident of French intelligence in Russia. Sobchak asked Putin to intervene and prevent the publication of this conversation. And Putin, using the Leningrad Regional Directorate for Combating Organized Crime (RUBOP), launched a raid on Shutov's apartment and confiscated the tape.

The raid and search were conducted unofficially and illegally. On the night of October 6, 1991, Shutov entered his own apartment and discovered robbers there. As they fled from the scene, they broke Shutov's skull with a hammer. Several months later, in March 1992, when Shutov was visited by government authorities with an official search warrant and an order for his arrest (for preparing an assassination attempt against Azerbaijan's President Abulfaz Elchibey, which sounded about as believable as the previous charge of trying to set fire to Smolny), Shutov recognized one of them, Dmitry Milin, as one of the robbers who had cracked his skull. The second "robber" turned out to have been Milin's co-worker Dmitry Shakhanov. Both were top-ranking officials at the Leningrad RUBOP. After spending a year and a half in pretrial detention, Shutov first was released on the condition that he not leave the country, and then, in 1996, was completely acquitted by St. Petersburg's Vyborgsky District Court.

In his first two anti-Sobchak pamphlets (first published in 1992 and 1993, respectively), the vengeful Shutov did not once mention Putin. But in 1998, Shutov became a deputy in the St. Petersburg Legislative Assembly and began to believe that he was now truly protected by parliamentary immunity, which he enjoyed according to his status. Through the *Novy Peterburg* newspaper, which he sponsored and for which he wrote a column titled "All the King's Men," Shutov launched a rumor to the effect that the new director of the FSB, Vladimir Putin, had been recalled from East Germany during his tenure there as a foreign intelligence officer for treasonous offenses against Russia: "During his almost five-year term of service in East Germany, KGB captain Putin achieved no visible results. However, he was observed entering into unsanctioned contact with a member of the enemy's agent network. After which he was immediately sent to the Soviet Union, where he arrived in a used GAZ-24 Volga automobile, purchased in East Germany, with three German-made rugs."[3]

In the same article, Shutov proposed his own interpretation of the relations between Putin and Sobchak when the former was the KGB's overseer of Leningrad State University and the latter a professor at the university's law school. Sobchak, according to Shutov, had been a freelance agent and informer to Putin, who was "required to collect information for the KGB, to work with agents employed by the university, and to recruit new informers." Shutov further explained:

> Professor Sobchak ended up in the net of the KGB's interests [and he] willingly informed the pro-rector's assistant, Putin, about the entire spectrum of issues that interested him. Subsequently, in 1990, a small folder containing this informer's original handwritten reports, which in KGB bureaucratic terminology is called "the agent's working case," became a very weighty argument in support of Putin's appointment as advisor to Leningrad city council head Sobchak.[4]

Novy Peterburg readers never found out whether or not what Shutov had written was true. The response from Putin, who was the director of the FSB, came less than two months after Shutov's controversial article was published. In February 1999, by a decision of the court, Shutov was stripped of his parliamentary immunity and arrested on suspicion of organizing a number of serious crimes, including the murder of a prominent city official, Mikhail Manevich, in St. Petersburg in 1997; and the murder of a prominent democratic activist, Galina Staro-voitova, in 1998. In order to attack Shutov, Putin even made use of the famous official TV reporter Mikhail Leontiev, who appeared on Channel One of Russian television demanding punishment for the "thug and bandit."

In November 1999, however, St. Petersburg's Kuybyshev District Court changed Shutov's pretrial restrictions to a prom-ise not to leave the country and ruled that Shutov be released from jail. Shutov was freed right in the courtroom, but several minutes later, armed and masked men burst into the court. A tussle ensued, in the course of which several people were hurt, including a TV cameraman, whose arm was broken, and Shutov himself, who was hit several times on the head with gun butts and fists, and passed out. According to Shutov, the masked men then took him to the building of the municipal prosecu-tor's office and subjected him to a beating. As a result, Shutov lost half his hearing and one of his eyes. Independent doctors were not allowed into the prosecutor's office, while the gov-ernment's medical experts diagnosed the defendant as being in perfect health. Several days later, however, a court hearing was called at the request of Shutov's lawyers; and the ambulance paramedics who had been summoned to the hearing submitted a medical report calling for Shutov's immediate hospitalization. But instead, Shutov was sent to St. Petersburg's pretrial deten-tion facility, and later transferred to the Vyborg prison.

At first, it was not even clear who had organized Shutov's abduction from the courtroom. Subsequently, the St. Peters-burg municipal prosecutor's office assumed responsibility for the action. The special forces unit (OMON) that had burst into the courtroom had been sent from Moscow for this operation.

Human rights activists and democrats took a weak and indecisive stance in the "Shutov affair," since Shutov's anti-liberal and anti-Western views were undeniable, and since he probably had connections with the criminal world. Despite Shutov's court acquittal and the Russian Supreme Court's sub-sequent ruling about the illegality of keeping him under arrest,[5] despite Shutov re-election to the city's legislative assembly in 2002, Putin's personal enemy spent seven (!) years being shut-tled between different pretrial detention facilities without a conviction, and in February 2006 was finally sentenced to life in prison for organizing a number of contract killings of business-men. (The charges of murdering Manevich and Starovoitova were dropped.)

It was never discovered who killed Manevich and Staro-voitova. The latter was killed in the entrance to her apartment building. Manevich's murder was carried out in a highly profes-sional manner. The killer fired an optical-sight rifle from the roof of a high-rise building at a car that had stopped at a traffic light; the bullets went through the roof of the vehicle. Manev-ich's wife was with him at the time of the murder, but she was not hurt. Criminal investigators developed several possible the-ories regarding this incident. They also discovered how Man-evich first met his future wife. A certain FSB agent had asked a young female courier to take a train to Moscow and hand a sealed bag to a man who would meet her at the Leningradsky Station. In the train, a young man named Mikhail sat down next to the girl. They spent the whole night talking and exchanged phone numbers. In Moscow, the girl was indeed met by a man when she got off the train. He took the bag, moved some dis-tance away, and believing that he was no longer seen, tossed the bag in a garbage can without opening it.

The young man on the train was Mikhail Manevich. The young woman was his future wife. The FSB agent who had asked her to deliver the bag was Vladimir Putin. One can only guess who was whose "agent" in this incident and who was whose "object."

P.S. WHO IS MR. ZUBKOV?

In February 2007, Anatoly Serdyukov became Russia's defense minister. On February 16, in a Radio Liberty interview, Vladimir Pribylovsky commented on Serdyukov's appointment:

> Of course, the most amusing and most surprising innovation here is the appointment of a former major furniture dealer to the post of defense minister. He is, by the way, a classic oligarch, since oligarchy really means political rule by a rich minority. And Mr. Serdyukov is a classic oligarch of this kind: a millionaire, and now a defense minister to boot. One can only guess what motivated this appointment. . . . For example, perhaps Serdyukov himself is not being groomed for the post

of successor. But Serdyukov is married to the daughter of the head of the Federal Financial Monitoring Service, Zubkov. Zubkov is quite close to Putin. Maybe they want to make Zubkov the successor?[6]

Viktor Zubkov, Russia's ninth prime minister, is a friend of Vladimir Putin's, Viktor Ivanov's, Boris Gryzlov's—and the father-in-law of Anatoly Serdyukov.

Zubkov was born on September 15, 1941, in the village of Arbat in the Kuvshinsky district of the Sverdlovsk region. He is a Russian by nationality. In 1965, he graduated from the economics department of the Leningrad Agricultural Institute. Zubkov holds a doctorate in economics, having defended his dissertation in 2000. Its title: "Improving the Tax Structure of the Mineral and Raw Materials Complex: On the Example of the Leningrad Region."

From August 1958 until August 1960, Zubkov worked as a metal worker. After graduating from the Leningrad Agricultural Institute, he served in the army in 1966–1967. He joined the CPSU in August 1967 and remained a party member until August 1991. From 1967 until 1985, he worked at state farms in the Leningrad region. From 1985 until 1991, he worked in Soviet and party organs in the Leningrad region, serving as head of the Priozersky municipal executive committee (1985); first secretary of the Priozersky party municipal committee for the Leningrad region, and head of the department of agriculture and food industry and the agrarian department of the party's regional committee (1986–1989); and first deputy head of the Leningrad region executive committee (1989–1991).

From January 1992 until November 1993, Zubkov worked under Putin at the International Relations Committee (IRC) of the St. Petersburg mayor's office as deputy head in charge of agriculture. In other words, he served as Putin's deputy, since Putin was head of the IRC at the time.

In November 1993, Zubkov was appointed head of the State Tax Inspectorate for St. Petersburg and deputy head of the State Tax Service (GNS). He joined Our Home Is Russia in May 1995. (Putin was the head of the organization's St. Petersburg office at the time.) In November 1998, Zubkov was relieved of his duties as deputy head of the GNS "due to a transfer to a different place of work," according to his resignation papers. He was then appointed head of the Ministry of Taxes and Receipts for St. Petersburg. In July 1999, he was appointed deputy minister of taxes and receipts for the Northwestern District. A few days later, he was also appointed head of the combined Ministry of Taxes and Receipts Directorate for St. Petersburg and the Leningrad region. He occupied these positions until November 2001, supervising the activities of twelve regional tax inspectorates.

Zubkov was registered as a candidate for governor of the Leningrad region on August 12, 1999. His campaign was managed by Boris Gryzlov, the future minister of internal affairs. Zubkov came in fourth out of sixteen candidates in the election on September 19, with 8.64 percent of the vote.

In 2000, Zubkov joined the St. Petersburg initiative group (led by Sergei Mironov and Vladimir Litvinenko) to elect Putin as president. He was "candidate Putin's election agent."

From February 2001 until October 2004, Zubkov was part of an interagency task force (led by Viktor Ivanov) to propose ways of improving the Russian Federation's migration regulations. In November 2001, Zubkov was appointed first deputy minister of finance—head of the Committee on Financial Monitoring, which worked on preventing money-laundering and became unofficially known as "financial foreign intelligence."

In June 2002, Zubkov joined the Central Coordinating Council of the supporters of United Russia. From June 2002 until April 2004, he was a member of the government commission on migration policy. In March 2004, he was appointed head of the Federal Financial Monitoring Service within the Ministry of Finance. Since July 2004, he has been deputy head of an interagency task force to develop national strategies for preventing the legalization of criminal profits. In June 2006, he joined the government commission on preventing substance abuse and illegal drug sales.

Zubkov has received Soviet honors: the Badge of Honor (1975) and the Order of the Red Banner of Labor (1981). He has also received Russian honors: "For Service to the Fatherland" in the fourth degree (2000) and "For Service to the Fatherland" in the third degree (2006).

But why was it specifically Zubkov who was appointed prime minister? Evidently, those who nominated him have faith in his loyalty. Until 1989, Zubkov was the first secretary of the Priozersky municipal committee. The Priozersky district of the Leningrad region is a favorite dacha location for Russia's elite. It was in the Priozersky district that dachas were purchased, through Zubkov's assistance, by Putin and Yakunin and Koval- chuk and the Fursenko brothers, who in 1996 united their newly built estates into the Ozero dacha cooperative, which today, along with the FSB, rules Russia.

9

Managed Democracy

"Managed democracy" is the official term for Russia's nomenklatura oligarchy, in which elections constitute a key aspect of management. Ideally, a managed election is one that creates the illusion of a choice—to keep up appearances for the sake of Western presidents and prime ministers—and at the same time guarantees a victory for the ruling party's candidate.

The "administrative resources" used to arrange a managed election include a variety of different methods. Some of them are extreme, such as starting a war before an election, reaching a peace settlement before an election, campaigning against corrupt law enforcement agents, persecuting an "oil oligarch," physically eliminating a separatist leader. Other methods are more routine: exploiting convenient laws, relying on media monopolies, taking advantage of the military vote, raising retirement pensions before an election, repairing roads and bridges before an election, auditing the tax records of the opposition's backers, recruiting popular singers and entertainers.

An "administrative resource" consists of two parts, one of which may be considered relatively honest, and the other wholly dishonest.

The "honest" component of an administrative resource consists of the natural advantages, as it were, that an administrative oligarch or his handpicked candidate enjoys over an ordinary candidate. A part of the Russian electorate—approximately 10 percent—always votes in favor of those who are in power (in the broadest sense of the word, from the president down to the precinct policeman). Such votes are cast for various reasons: out of respect for the country, which is identified with the government; based on the principle of "better the devil you know than the devil you don't"; out of fear of possible persecution for deviant voting; out of a fundamental lack of faith in the honesty and productivity of the opposition. In addition, government-backed candidates have no problems with financing and invariably have greater opportunities for promoting themselves in the media.

The dishonest component of an administrative resource consists, first of all, in the ability either to prevent the opposition candidate from registering his candidacy or to have his registration disqualified. Second, it consists in the "right" to replace the owner of an opposition media outlet by orchestrating a "property rights conflict." Third, it consists in the "right" to initiate criminal proceedings against opposition candidates, sometimes based entirely on trumped-up charges. Fourth, it consists in the possibility of "correcting" election results through dishonest vote counts, the addition of extra ballots, and the defacement of "undesirable" ballots.

The first four years of Putin's rule saw the dissemination across the entire country of the so-called "Bashkirian election technology," in which potential winners from the opposition either are not permitted to register as candidates or have their registrations revoked in the course of the campaign. This method was used under Yeltsin as well, but principally on the local level and with the permission of the federal government rather than at its direct command. In addition, this method was employed only in a limited number of regions—first and foremost in Murtaza Rakhimov's Bashkortostan, Kirsan Ilyumzhinov's Kalmykia, and Yevgeny Nazdratenko's Primorye.

Even before the new electoral legislation went into effect, the "Bashkirian election technology" was used in the elections for governor of the Saratov region (March 2000), governor of the Khanty-Mansi Autonomous District (March 2000), governor of the Kursk region (October 2000), governor of the Komi-Permyatsk Autonomous District (December 2000), mayor of

Sochi (April–May 2001), governor of Primorye (June 2001), governor of the Nizhny Novgorod region (July 2001), governor of the Rostov region (September 2001), president of Yakutia (December 2001–January 2002), president of North Ossetia (January 2002), president of Ingushetia (April 2002), mayor of Nizhny Novgorod (September 2002), mayor of Kyzyl (October 2002).

After the new legislation went into effect, candidates were not allowed to register or had their registrations disqualified in the elections for the Bashkortostan State Assembly (March 2003), mayor of Novorossiysk (March 2003), the Rostov Region Legislative Assembly (March 2003), mayor of Norilsk (April 2003), the Vladivostok City Duma (June 2003), governor of the Omsk region (August–September 2003), president of Chechnya (September–October 2003), the State Duma of the Russian Federation (December 2003), governor of the Kirov region (December 2003); and also in the runoff election for mayor of Noyabrsk (January 2004), the Krasnodar region gubernatorial race (March 2004), the Vladivostok mayoral race (July 2004), and the Chechnya presidential election (August 2004).

In addition, a "soft" form of the "Bashkirian election technology" was employed in the St. Petersburg gubernatorial race (September–October 2003): the undisputed favorite, Vladimir Yakovlev, acting governor at the time, was effectively bought off in advance by being offered the position of deputy prime minister, in order to eliminate any serious opposition to the government-backed candidate and to secure the transition of power in the second capital into the hands of the president's personal friends. A similar "soft" form of the "Bashkirian technology" was put into use in the runoff election for mayor of Noyabrsk (January–February 2004) and in the gubernatorial race of the Voronezh region (March 2004): in both cases, potential winners were persuaded to withdraw their candidacies "voluntarily."

The "super-Bashkirian" election of Akhmad Kadyrov as president of Chechnya in October 2003 was secured by widespread and undisguised fraud. After Kadyrov's murder in May 2004, the election of the next Chechen president, Alu Alkhanov, was likewise arranged in a "super-Bashkirian" fashion.

The Vladivostok city duma election in June 2003 ended with a victory for the opposition, even though a number of opposition candidates had their registrations disqualified. However, on the initiative of the municipal election commission, the court rejected the election outcomes for two districts carried by candidates unfavored by the local authorities, thus depriving the opposition bloc Freedom and People's Government of the majority that it had won.

The government did not prevent the most significant political forces from taking part in the State Duma race of December 2003, but two opposition parties were barred from the election: Eduard Limonov's left-wing National Bolshevik Party and Boris Berezovsky's and Ivan Rybkin's right-wing Liberal Russia. In addition, dozens of candidates from single-constituent electoral districts were shut out of the race; most of them were opponents of either the federal or the local government, and many of them had serious chances of beating the official candidates.

Finally, it was only through the direct falsification of the voters' will that a pro-Putin constitutional majority was achieved in the State Duma, and it was only through direct falsifications that the liberals lost their representation in the Duma—at least, this is what happened to one of the two liberal parties (Grigory Yavlinsky's Yabloko). The Bashkirian presidential election was falsified in an undisguised and brazen manner (December 2003). Against the background of such "strong-arm" approaches, the traditional television monopoly enjoyed by the nomenklatura's candidates—as well as other, relatively "honest" means of attracting voters to the ruling party—seems almost excusable.

GUBERNATORIAL ELECTIONS IN THE SARATOV REGION AND THE KHANTY-MANSI AUTONOMOUS DISTRICT

On March 26, 2000, gubernatorial races in several regions were held concurrently with Putin's first presidential election. The regime of "managed democracy" and the "vertical of power," with the acting president at the top, were only a few months old, but the development of its techniques was already in full swing. The main objective of the central and local authorities was to avoid a second round in the presidential election. This objective was successfully realized, although this meant that the results had to be "corrected" by about 3 or 4 percent. A number of regional governors also took measures to ensure their own electoral futures. This was done in the most crude and dishonest fashion in two constituent subjects of the Russian Federation: the Saratov region and the Khanty-Mansi Autonomous District.

In the Saratov region, Governor Dmitry Ayatskov was running for another term. Outside the region, Ayatskov is known primarily for his proposal to legalize brothels, as well as for his statement that he is so fond of Bill Clinton that he "sincerely envies" Monica Lewinsky.

The incumbent governor (at that time, a member of the national political council of the pro-Putin Unity bloc) had one significant opponent: the leader of the local Communists, Valery Rashkin. In addition to the left-wing and protest vote, Rashkin stood to win the support of a substantial part of the liberal-minded voters concentrated in the region's capital, who were tired of their governor's authoritarianism and administrative caprices. Local businessmen (with the exception of those who were close to the ruling administration) also dreamed of getting rid of Ayatskov and even made secret financial contributions to the campaign of the Communist Party candidate. The only thing that put the opposition's victory in doubt was the fact that the procedures for "correcting" election results were long established in the Saratov region.

Not wishing to rely on "correction" alone, however, the governor's team preferred to get rid of the dangerous opponent. At the last moment, the regional election commission refused to register Rashkin as a candidate for governor on the pretext that there was "a significant number of infractions in the lists of signatures" gathered in support of his nomination. The regional court and then the Supreme Court in Moscow both rejected the Communists' appeal.

According to the official records, Ayatskov won and approximately 20 percent of the votes were cast for "none of the above." In reality, however, as copies of the voting records indicate, "none of the above" received a considerably greater percentage of the vote.

In the Khanty-Mansi Autonomous District, Governor Alexander Filipenko (from the Fatherland–All Russia bloc) also decided to ensure his victory by eliminating his main opponent, Sergei Atroshenko, a businessman and leader of the Russian Pensioners' Party. Atroshenko's platform centered on an attractive proposal to give local residents certificates—nicknamed "happiness certificates"—that would make them eligible to receive a part of the region's oil and gas profits.

On February 18, 2000, Atroshenko registered as a candidate, but on March 9 he was disqualified for "violating election spending rules" and for buying off voters (by promising them "happiness certificates"). In the absence of any serious opponents, the incumbent was re-elected on March 26.

Since both Filipenko in the Khanty-Mansi district and, especially, Ayatskov in the Saratov region had done everything within their powers to secure Vladimir Putin's victory in the first round of the presidential election, the Kremlin and the Central Election Commission (CEC) turned a blind eye—if not an approving one—on the maneuvers they went through to get themselves re-elected.

ELECTION FOR GOVERNOR OF THE KURSK REGION

Among the regional leaders that Putin inherited from Yeltsin, it was Alexander Rutskoy, the governor of the Kursk region, who became the first victim of "managed elections." In 1996, under Yeltsin, the Kursk regional election commission had also refused to register Rutskoy (at that time, one of the leaders of the Communist-"patriotic" opposition) as a candidate for governor of the region. After unsuccessful appeals to the Kursk Regional Court and the Supreme Court, Rutskoy finally obtained a favorable ruling from the Presidium of the Supreme Court, which forced the Kursk regional election commission to register him as a candidate. In the end, he won 78.9 percent of the vote.

By the election of 2000, Rutskoy had lost a considerable part of his popularity in the region—he had broken with the Communists and with the local business elite—but he nonetheless remained a practically undisputed favorite. Then on October 21, only thirteen and a half hours before the election, the regional court disqualified his registration, ruling in favor of two other candidates who had accused the incumbent governor of illegally using his official position, providing unreliable information about his personal finances, and breaking campaign ethics rules.

This was the first (and thus far the only) time in post-Communist Russia that an incumbent governor was disqualified from taking part in an election. In all previous cases, election commissions and courts had disqualified candidates who presented a threat to the local government. In this instance, however, the local "ruling party" effectively betrayed its own governor and allied itself with a higher figure: the president's plenipotentiary representative in the Central Federal District, FSB Lieutenant General Georgy Poltavchenko. One of the two candidates who had brought charges against Rutskoy was FSB Major General Viktor Surzhikov—the chief federal inspector of the Kursk region, Poltavchenko's protégé and immediate subordinate.

It was precisely to please Moscow's plenipotentiary representative in the region that the regional court made its unexpected ruling. While the president's chief of staff, Alexander Voloshin, and the head of the CEC, Alexander Veshnyakov, feigned neutrality, "Operation Rutskoy" had undoubtedly been coordinated with the president's deputy chief of staff for personnel policy, FSB Lieutenant General Viktor Ivanov.

The first round of the election was held on October 22. Voter turnout was 51.79 percent, barely above the required minimum of 50 percent. One hour before the polls closed, however, voter turnout had barely reached 45 percent, and election commission officials chaotically ran around the streets of Kursk with portable ballot boxes, persuading people to vote wherever they could find them. The day before, special forces units (OMON) had been ordered to surround local television and radio offices due to fears that the incumbent governor might attempt to address voters on regional television or radio with an appeal to boycott the election and thus undermine voter turnout. "Who controls OMON controls the election." This was effectively a military-police coup on a regional scale, organized and successfully carried out by one of the candidates—the Kremlin's overseer for the region—with the support of the Kremlin's representative in the region.

But the coup turned out to be only a partial success: the first round of voting gave the lead not to Surzhikov, but to the first secretary of the CPRF's Kursk regional committee, Alexander

Mikhailov, a Duma deputy who won 39.52 percent of the vote (compared with Surzhikov's 21.58 percent and 12.26 percent for "none of the above").

On October 23, something unusual for Russia happened: Vyacheslav Molokoyedov, a deputy in the city duma of Kurchatov (in the Kursk region), committed harakiri in protest against Rutskoy's exclusion from the election. Molokoyedov's suicide note read: "I am giving my life so that democracy might live and so that an unbeatable man might stand at the head of the region." As it turned out, doctors managed to save the deputy, who had fumbled the complicated Japanese ritual.

On November 2, the Supreme Court of the Russian Federation let stand the Kursk Regional Court ruling that had barred Rutskoy from the gubernatorial election. But in the second round of voting, on November 5, the Communist Party candidate, Alexander Mikhailov, won the governor's seat with 55.54 percent of the vote, leaving nothing to the chekists Surzhikov and Poltavchenko (and Viktor Ivanov along with them). Voter turnout in the second round was below 50 percent, but most regions have no turnout requirements for the second rounds of gubernatorial races.

"Operation Rutskoy" gives rise to a legitimate question: Why? Among regional heads, the governor of Kursk was by no means the most disloyal toward the new government. In the fall of 1999, he threw his official weight behind the pro-Putin Unity bloc (Medved). In December 1999, he served on a committee (headed by Oleg Kutafin) to nominate Vladimir Putin as a candidate for president. In February 2000, he joined Unity's political council (although he failed to get elected to Unity's party leadership in May 2000). The regional office of Unity, incidentally, officially supported Rutskoy's candidacy up to the last minute and was unpleasantly surprised by the court's decision (after which it had time to speak out in favor of the chekist candidate). In March 2000, Rutskoy—openly using his official position—campaigned for Putin and even proposed converting the governorship from an elected position into one appointed by Putin (evidently, in the hope that he would himself be appointed).

In the summer of 2000, however, Rutskoy continued to maintain contacts with Boris Berezovsky—apparently not yet knowing that Putin's and Berezovsky's friendship was moribund. In August, the Kursk governor was too conspicuously active in connection with the *Kursk* submarine disaster, portraying himself—in circumvention of Moscow—as the main benefactor of the widows and children of the deceased sailors.

The case of Rutskoy in effect marked the first time that two competing approaches to regional elections among the president's entourage came into conflict. One approach, represented mainly by Alexander Voloshin's "old Kremlin," "family" faction, was that caution was the best policy and that loyal old personnel should not be squandered. The other approach, represented by the "new Petersburg" chekists headed by Viktor Ivanov, argued in favor of appointing new personnel who belonged entirely to their own camp, even if this meant entering into conflicts and abusing government power.

Several factors converged against Rutskoy. First, the new government—at least, one of its wings—wanted to arrange a "show whipping" (roughly speaking, to oust Rutskoy in order to put the fear of God into Murtaza Rakhimov in Bashkortostan and Eduard Rossel in the Urals). Second, no one in the Kremlin was especially committed to Rutskoy (not even Voloshin), because Rutskoy may have been loyal at the moment but could easily switch sides in the future (as was true of almost all governors). Third, through his headstrong policies, Rutskoy had spoiled relations with the local administrative-economic clans. And fourth, it was precisely in the Kursk region that the chekist faction had an FSB candidate ready to be installed in the governor's seat.

By contrast, the numerous objections and grievances against Governor Rutskoy's attitude toward the law—including his handling of his election campaign—had little if any importance. All regional leaders use their "administrative resource" to get elected. As the Kursk regional election unfolded, opponents raised analogous and no less justified objections against Alexander Volkov, head of the Udmurtia State Council; but Volkov was supported by the plenipotentiary representative for his district (Sergei Kiriyenko) and thus successfully won both his court case and the presidential election.

In 2000, Russia had at least two regional leaders whose very legitimacy was suspect because their elections had taken place with flagrant violations of federal law.

In June 1998, Murtaza Rakhimov was re-elected president of Bashkortostan in an undisguisedly "Bashkirian" election, which left Rakhimov's forestry minister, Rif Kazakkulov—who actually campaigned for Rakhimov—as his only "opponent." The Bashkirian election commission, obedient to Rakhimov, refused to register his rivals Alexander Arinin and Marat Mirgazyamov as candidates in the race. The CEC upheld Mirgazyamov's appeal, and a year later, in March 1999, the Supreme Court of the Russian Federation ruled that the disqualification of the candidates' registrations had been illegal . . . but did not declare the outcome of the election invalid.

In October 1995, Kirsan Ilyumzhinov was "elected" president of Kalmykia for a seven-year term, running unopposed altogether. The federal government, which had proclaimed its intention to make regional czars and khans obey the law, and did indeed wish to teach them a lesson, should have started establishing order by dealing with these two regional autocrats. For example, it could have put the issue of the legitimacy of Rakhimov's and Ilyumzhinov's victories before the Constitutional Court. But neither the government's choice of punishment nor the person it chose to punish indicated any intention to promote the rule of law. The methods used to disqualify Rutskoy drew no criticism from the "Guarantor of the Constitution" (and needless to say, the instigators of the controversy went unpunished), nor did the "ministry of elections"—Alexander Veshnyakov's CEC—make any protest.

ELECTION FOR GOVERNOR OF THE KOMI-PERMYATSK AUTONOMOUS DISTRICT

The end of 2000 saw the election for governor of the Komi-Permyatsk Autonomous District. The incumbent governor, Nikolai Poluyanov, had no solid support. He was officially backed by the president's Unity party (whose district office he himself had established), but the party's district office had no independent significance in Komi-Permyatsk, since it was made up of the same people as the governor's administration and the executive "vertical of power."

Poluyanov's main opponent in the race appeared to be a "Varangian" from Yekaterinburg: Dmitry Anfalov, the deputy speaker of the Sverdlovsk Region Duma. Anfalov had been delegated to conquer the Komi-Permyatsk district by the May movement, a left-populist coalition that was popular in a number of districts in the Ural region, created by local businessmen who had broken with their regional governments and gone over to the opposition. Anfalov's nomination was also supported by the Rossiya movement (led by Gennady Seleznev, speaker of the State Duma). On October 26, 2000, at a joint meeting of the central council and the central executive committee of the Rossiya movement, Anfalov was nominated as a candidate for the position of governor of the Komi-Permyatsk Autonomous District in the December election.

In reality, however, the main threat facing the governor was not the Rossiya movement, which was practically unknown in the district, nor even the May movement, which was somewhat better known, but rather Anfalov's and his sponsors' money, which was capable of bringing the May movement's anti-governor demagoguery into the home of every voter. "Having spent considerable resources on his campaign, Anfalov was the confident frontrunner in the race," wrote the *Nezavisimaya Gazeta* reporter who followed the campaign. "His inevitable victory was blocked by the fact that he was disqualified on the eve of the election for violating electoral laws."[1]

In November, the Komi-Permyatsk District Court ordered the district election commission to disqualify Anfalov's registration as a candidate in the election "for violating campaign rules and for exerting an unauthorized influence on voters."

The outcome of the first round of voting, on December 3, was not encouraging for the incumbent. With Anfalov out of the running, the lead went to a candidate who had not been reckoned with earlier: Gennady Savelyev, deputy head of the Accounts Chamber of the Komi-Permyatsk Autonomous District. Despite the fact that Anfalov had been barred from the election, voter turnout was quite high: 60.15 percent of the eligible voters participated in the election. Savelyev won 27.14

percent of the vote, Poluyanov won 24.23 percent, and 17.81 percent went to "none of the above." In the second round of voting, on December 17, Savelyev was elected governor with 44.25 percent of the vote.

The "Bashkirian election technology" failed in the Komi-Permyatsk Autonomous District. But the district government ended up in the hands of more or less the same regional administrative-economic clique, which had simply exchanged its old chief executive for a new one. The local "vertical of power" and the Unity party (or United Russia since the end of 2001) painlessly realigned themselves under Savelyev.

SOCHI MAYORAL ELECTION

The frontrunner in the Sochi mayoral election of spring 2001, Vadim Boyko—a reporter and former Duma deputy—was disqualified for violating campaign rules. Boyko had already almost won (receiving 48.95 percent in the second round of voting) in December 2000, but did not become mayor due to a quirk in regional law, which required an absolute majority rather than a plurality in the second round of voting.

The "victim" had the backing of one of Moscow's administrative-economic clans (Alexander Voloshin, Vladislav Surkov), the personal support of the press minister, Mikhail Lesin, and the endorsement of a powerful financial-industrial coalition (Mikhail Fridman's Alfa Group). United against him, however, were Sochi's old oligarchy, which had close ties with the mayor of Moscow, Yuri Luzhkov (through Luzhkov's advisor Konstantin Zatulin, originally from Sochi); Moscow's official and unofficial owners of palaces and estates in Sochi's seaside districts; the government of the Krasnodar region, headed by Governor Alexander Tkachev; Alfa Bank's competitors; and all of "the family's" ill-wishers in Moscow and St. Petersburg.

The winner was the local "ruling party" candidate, Leonid Mostovoy, although at Boyko's urging 27 percent of the votes were cast for "none of the above" in the first round on April 22, 2001, and 15.6 percent in the second round on May 13. By contrast with other regions, the voting regulations of the Krasnodar region have a minimum turnout requirement (25 percent) in the second round as well as the first. It was announced that voter turnout in the second round was 30 percent, but there are grounds for questioning the validity of this claim.

Subsequently, Governor Tkachev became disappointed with Mostovoy, who turned out to be more Luzhkov's man than his, and called for his resignation. But Mostovoy managed to resist Tkachev's pressure for two months with the support of the Moscow mayor's office, and resigned in January 2004 only when Tkachev—having reached some kind of agreement with Luzhkov—gave him the post of senator from the Krasnodar region, which had been vacated following Nikolai Kondraten-ko's election to the State Duma.

ELECTION FOR GOVERNOR OF PRIMORYE

In long-suffering Primorye, the disqualification of candidates and the invalidation of election outcomes became the norm back in Yeltsin's time, when the region was ruled by Yevgeny Nazdratenko. The perpetual victim of the election commissions was Viktor Cherepkov, former mayor of Vladivostok and a rather extravagant politician (and psychic), who nonetheless was elected a State Duma deputy on March 26, 2000. Putin, however, managed to lure Nazdratenko away from the gubernatorial seat by offering him a post in Moscow: head of the state committee on fishing.

In the early election for governor of Primorye on May 27, 2001, Cherepkov won second place, receiving 20.02 percent of the vote, and entered the second round of voting together with the businessman and crime boss Sergei Darkin, who was supported by former governor Nazdratenko and had won 23.94 percent. Meanwhile, the president's plenipotentiary representative in the Far Eastern Federal District, Konstantin Pulikovsky, had had his own candidate in the election: his deputy Gennady Apanasenko, who had come in third in the first round of voting.

On June 13, the Primorye Regional Court began looking into a claim brought by three local residents who had accused Cherepkov of violating campaign rules: he had not paid for his TV advertising out of his campaign fund; he had received a transfer of money from an unknown sponsor; and he had incorrectly indicated his place of residence. (He had named Moscow, where he—now a Duma deputy—actually lived, rather than Vladivostok, where he was registered. It is obvious that had he written Vladivostok, he would have been told that his "correct" place of residence was Moscow.) The regional election commission was already reviewing these charges on the eve of the first round of voting, but it confined itself to handing out a warning to Cherepkov at that time.

On June 14, however, the court disqualified Cherepkov from taking part in the election. The frontrunner, Darkin, spoke out in categorical terms against the court's decision, declaring that "this was done precisely by those who are trying to undermine the election, who are trying to push Primorye into another abyss of anarchy."[2] Darkin, naturally, was referring to plenipotentiary representative Pulikovsky and his deputy Apanasenko.

Instead of Cherepkov, it was Apanasenko who became the second contender for the governor's seat. Even so, the outcome was the same as in Kursk: in the second round of voting on June 17, Apanasenko lost to Darkin. Voter turnout in the second round was 35.9 percent, with 40.18 percent of the votes being cast for Darkin, 24.32 percent for Apanasenko, and 33.68 percent going to "none of the above" (including 100,000 of Vladivostok's 180,000).

ELECTION FOR GOVERNOR OF THE NIZHNY NOVGOROD REGION

The gubernatorial election campaign in the Nizhny Novgorod region began in May 2001. One of the serious contenders for the governorship was Nizhny Novgorod's mayor, Yuri Lebedev. But he was on extremely strained terms both with the incumbent governor, Ivan Sklyarov, and especially with the president's plenipotentiary representative in the Volga Federal District, Sergei Kiriyenko. Kiriyenko supported the candidacy of Vadim Bulavinov, a Duma deputy (from the pro-Putin People's Deputy bloc).

On the day following Lebedev's announcement that he was starting to collect signatures, the regional election commission began receiving allegations—predominantly from anonymous sources—that employees at city works projects were being forced to sign for Lebedev at the threat of losing their jobs. As a result, the regional election commission unanimously refused to register Lebedev as a candidate. Lebedev explicitly named the people who had ordered the regional election commission's decision as "a group of businessmen close to Sergei Kiriyenko" and even accused Kiriyenko himself of involvement in "a plot against the president."[3]

The Kiriyenko-backed Bulavinov lost in the first round of voting on July 15 (19.07 percent). In the second round, on July 29, Gennady Khodyrev—a moderate Communist at the time, who had not yet resigned from the CPRF—won with 59.80 percent.

ELECTION FOR GOVERNOR OF THE ROSTOV REGION

Vladimir Chub, the governor of the Rostov region, enjoyed the consolidated support of the regional oligarchy; he was on friendly terms with the plenipotentiary representative of the president in the Southern Federal District, Viktor Kazantsev; and he had no enemies in the Kremlin. At the beginning of 2000, Chub established a regional office of the Unity movement, and when it was transformed into a party in May of that year, he built the party's regional office from his own people.

The only opponent—but a very serious one—that Chub might have faced in the election was the leader of the local Communists, Leonid Ivanchenko, one of Gennady Zyuganov's party deputies at that time. Ivanchenko had already run against Chub in the previous election (September 29, 1996). The incumbent governor had won (62.05 percent for Chub, 31.73 percent for Ivanchenko), but there were serious suspicions of large-scale voter fraud. Ivanchenko tried to contest the regional election commission's vote tallies in court, but the Rostov Regional Court rejected the case, and the Russian Supreme Court's Judicial Chamber for Civil Cases let the lower court's decision stand.

At the beginning of August 2001, Chub and Ivanchenko were both registered as candidates for governor of the Rostov region in the September 23 election. On August 23, the regional election commission received a statement from one of Ivanchenko's former colleagues from the regional office of the Popular-Patriotic Union of Russia (NPSR). The former colleague accused the Communists of falsifying lists of signatures gathered in support of their candidate's nomination by using voter information records that the CPRF had obtained while collecting signatures for the State Duma election; among other things, he alleged that relatives had signed for one another. Meanwhile, the Communists had no need of any falsification: the CPRF's membership in the Rostov region alone far exceeded the minimum number of signatures required for a candidate's nomination.

An investigation determined that over 10 percent of the signatures presented by the Communists had been forged—including signatures that voters themselves, in personal declarations submitted to the court and to the election commission, had confirmed as their own. The regional election commission refused to register Ivanchenko as a candidate, and the findings of the investigation were even sent to the regional prosecutor's office (although the case never went to trial).

Also barred from the election was Vladimir Dek, a local truth-lover known for having bitten a policeman's finger during the previous election (for the regional parliament in 1998) and having been sentenced to six years in prison but released after four months due to public protest.

In order to present voters with a formal choice in the election, the head of one of the rural districts was registered as Chub's only "opponent" (as was always done in Bashkortostan). Just in case, he asked voters to cast their ballots not for him, but for the incumbent governor.

On September 17, 2001, the Rostov Regional Court upheld the election commission's decision not to register Ivanchenko, and on September 23, the election commission achieved its final victory over the voters: Chub was re-elected with 78.19 percent of the vote, with a voter turnout of 48.32 percent (regional law required a minimum of 35 percent) and 12.69 percent going to "none of the above."

Interestingly, Ivanchenko seems to have played no role in the low turnout and the large number of votes cast for "none of the above." A few days before the election, the president's plenipotentiary representative, Viktor Kazantsev, invited the Communist leader for a "preventive chat," in the course of which General Kazantsev—speaking in the name of "Putin himself"—explained to Ivanchenko that a second round of voting would cost the regional budget 70 million rubles, which could be used to build 140 two-bedroom apartments for Rostov residents waiting to get housing.

Moved by this tête-à-tête with the Kremlin's representative, Ivanchenko promised that "the Communists will not undermine the election." The regional CPRF office made no appeal to voters either to boycott the sham election or to cast their votes for "none of the above." A flyer calling for a boycott was distributed by unknown persons in the name of the mayor of Novoshakhtinsk, but the mayor immediately declared it a fake.

ELECTION FOR PRESIDENT OF YAKUTIA

The main participants in the election for president of Yakutia at the end of 2001 were Moscow's administrative-economic clans. The president's chief of staff, Alexander Voloshin, as usual favored stability and was against tinkering with the status quo: he wanted to leave the incumbent president, Mikhail Nikolayev, in place. Voloshin's deputy for personnel policy, Viktor Ivanov (chekist clan), favored nominating Russia's deputy general prosecutor, Vasily Kolmogorov (a Yakut by nationality), for the presidency. Another one of Voloshin's deputies, Vladislav Surkov, from the very beginning favored a "rational compromise," which was in fact the ultimate outcome of the election.

On October 8, CEC head Alexander Veshnyakov declared that Nikolayev had "no legal basis" for seeking a third term in office. (Yakutia's constitution, which the president had neglected to amend in time, was against him.)

Under such circumstances, courts and election commissions at different levels made contradictory decisions about allowing or not allowing Nikolayev to take part in the election. The battle between "the president's side" and "the general prosecutor's side" grew so heated that at the end of November, the Yakutia prosecutor's office even arrested several reporters from Moscow who had been employed by the president's campaign headquarters, and charged them with writing and distributing flyers that were found to contain "incitement to ethnic strife and defamatory remarks about certain presidential candidates."[4] After spending a few days under arrest, the reporters were released only after the opposing sides were able to reach a compromise.

The agreement was that Nikolayev and Kolmogorov would both sit out the election and leave the field open for Vyacheslav Shtyrov, president of the Almazy Rossii–Sakha company. According to *Kommersant*, Nikolayev's "voluntary" withdrawal from the election followed his December 10 conversation with Putin in Moscow.[5]

On December 12, Nikolayev formally withdrew his candidacy, and on December 15, Kolmogorov followed suit. At the beginning of January 2002, Shtyrov was elected president. He immediately appointed Nikolayev his representative in the Federation Council; this was the ex-president's severance pay.

ELECTION FOR PRESIDENT OF NORTH OSSETIA

There were two main contenders in the North Ossetia presidential election, scheduled for January 27, 2002: the incumbent president, Alexander Dzasokhov, and the former head of the republic's Council of Ministers (during the late Soviet and early post-Soviet period), Sergei Khetagurov.

In November 2001, the North Ossetia prosecutor's office initiated criminal proceedings in connection with the illegal sale of nonferrous metals in the early 1990s. Khetagurov was called in as a witness by the General Prosecutor's Office, his subpoena was widely discussed in the press, and the candidate not without reason discerned the incumbent president's scheming hand in the matter. But the criminal case was not pursued any further.

On January 11, 2002, the North Ossetia election commission was supposed to consider the issue of barring Khetagurov from the election. Three reasons for disqualifying his registration had been named: Khetagurov had provided unreliable information about the income of his family members; he had indicated an incorrect place of residence for himself (naming Vladikavkaz as his permanent place of residence, although he had been living in Moscow since 1994); and he had submitted a "false passport" when registering (as the election commission was able to determine with the help of the police, Khetagurov had two passports: a new one, which he had obtained as a replacement for one that he had declared lost, and an old, Soviet passport, which had not been lost at all). The committee's hearing was then indefinitely postponed, however; by all appearances, a decision had been made to consult with Moscow first.

On January 16, mass demonstrations in support of Khetagurov were held in Vladikavkaz. But by that time the Kremlin had already secretly sanctioned Khetagurov's removal from the race. He was considered to have more rigid views than Dzasokhov on the issue of bringing the Ossetia-Ingushetia conflict under control, and the Kremlin feared an escalation of the conflict in case Khetagurov won.

On January 17, the Supreme Court of North Ossetia revoked Khetagurov's registration, citing the inaccurate information that he had provided about his family members' income, his place of residence, and his passports.

On January 19, Khetagurov went on local television and urged his supporters—in the event that the Russian Supreme Court should also find his registration invalid—to vote for Colonel General Stanislav Suanov.

On January 27, Dzasokhov was re-elected president of North Ossetia, winning 57 percent of the vote in the first round. (Stanislav Suanov came in second, with 29 percent.)

ELECTION FOR PRESIDENT OF INGUSHETIA

An early election for president of Ingushetia was scheduled for April 7, 2002, following the resignation of Ruslan Aushev from this post. Aushev intended to stay on after resigning; at any rate, his team—which was closely connected with the Gutseriev brothers' financial-industrial BIN Group, headed by Mikael Gutseriev—intended to stay on. Aushev, who enjoyed great popularity among his countrymen, called on voters to cast their ballots for his minister of internal affairs, Khazat Gutseriev. In case Gutseriev was barred from participating in the election, the Aushev-Gutseriev faction nominated several of his "doubles" as well, the most important one among them being Alikhan Amirkhanov, a State Duma deputy.

Aushev's independent platform—including his views on the Chechen war—had always irritated the Kremlin and provoked undisguised hatred toward him in the leadership of the FSB and the army. His relations with the president's plenipotentiary representative in the Southern Federal District, V. Kazantsev, were openly hostile (which is why Aushev was forced to resign).

Kazantsev decided to eradicate Aushev's group completely and install an absolutely loyal man in Aushev's place. With this aim, he delegated his deputy, FSB Major General Murat Zyazikov, to run in the Ingushetia presidential election.

On March 12, 2002, an open letter to President Putin, signed by forty-three famous Ingushes, including six candidates for the presidency of the republic, was published in *Kommersant* as a paid advertisement. The letter read:

> Ingushetia public television and radio reporters have been subjected to unprecedented and unembarrassed pressure from the representatives of the Southern Federal District, who have demanded greater and better coverage of the activities of one of the deputies of the president's plenipotentiary representative in the Southern Federal District, an FSB general who is registered as a candidate for the presidency of Ingushetia.[6]

On April 5, the Russian Supreme Court's Judicial Chamber for Civil Cases granted a motion, made by a certain reporter, to disqualify Gutseriev's registration because he had not resigned from his post as minister of internal affairs and, consequently, had illegally used his official position.

During the first round of voting, on April 7, no candidate won half of the vote. Amirkhanov came in first (33 percent), Zyazikov second (19 percent). In the second round, on April 28, Zyazikov won (with 53.3 percent).

Amirkhanov claims that the election results were falsified: "60,000 ballots were given out, and 80,000 voters supposedly voted. . . . These [additional] 20,000 ballots were printed by the FSB in Nalchik. They literally added them to the pile, and we couldn't do anything about it."[7] According to the weekly *Kommersant-Vlast*, the number of registered voters who participated in the first round was 120,000, while the number of registered voters in the second round was 146,000.[8]

On October 5, the newly elected chekist president of Ingushetia, Murat Zyazikov, named a street after Putin in the Ingush village of Olghetti.

ELECTION FOR GOVERNOR OF THE SMOLENSK REGION

The election for governor of the Smolensk region on May 19, 2002, was a relatively honest contest between two local administrative-economic clans. The candidates were the incumbent governor, Alexander Prokhorov, and the head of the FSB regional office, Viktor Maslov. Both declared that they had the full support of President Vladimir Putin, and General Maslov in addition underscored his departmental ties to the president.

Maslov, however, was able to employ a distinctly FSB-based administrative resource against Prokhorov: using his Moscow connections, he arranged for a visit to Smolensk by an investigator for the General Prosecutor's Office, Sergei Kochergin, who had been ordered to look into the inappropriate use of funds set aside for the construction of the Staraya–Smolenskaya highway. The former deputy governor Yuri Balbyshkin was formally charged in connection with this matter (later receiving a suspended sentence of two years), while the other deputy governors and Prokhorov himself were dragged in for questioning as witnesses.

During the election campaign, Prokhorov's closest collaborator, Deputy Governor Anatoly Makarenko, became the victim of an assassination attempt. On May 16, three days before the election, he was traveling from his dacha to work. Near the village of Bor, at the entrance to Smolensk, criminals with automatic weapons opened fire on his car. Makarenko, his five-year-old daughter, his bodyguard, and his driver were inside the vehicle. The driver was killed and Makarenko himself was lightly wounded, as was the bodyguard, who had covered the child with his body. On the same day, Makarenko accused General Maslov of trying to assassinate him. "Victor Maslov has explicitly threatened me . . . in front of witnesses," Makarenko said. " . . . I have received no threats from anyone else. The head of the region's FSB office is a criminal." In response, General Maslov expressed the opinion that the assassination attempt had been "a piece of pre-election theater deliberately staged" by Prokhorov's team.[9]

The local law governing elections for governor of the Smolensk region did not provide for a second round of voting at the time, and the winner would be the candidate who won a plurality of the vote in the first round. On May 19, Maslov was elected by a margin of 20,000 votes, winning 40.15 percent compared with Prokhorov's 34.4 percent.

The criminal overtones of the Smolensk election were reinforced two and a half months later: on August 7, unknown persons killed Maslov's own deputy, Vladimir Prokhorov (same last name as the former governor), who had been head of Maslov's campaign headquarters in May.

As for Makarenko—no longer deputy governor but simply an ordinary businessman out of favor with the government—he once again reiterated his conviction that Maslov was involved in the assassination attempt against him when the incident was being investigated. According to Makarenko, Maslov wanted to eliminate him as an undesirable witness: before being appointed deputy governor, Makarenko had repeatedly delivered protection money to General Maslov from the local Petrosyan-Olevsky crime group.

The new governor explained to the investigators that the purpose of those regular meetings with businessman Makarenko was not to receive bribes, but to obtain confidential information related to the work of the regional FSB. The investigators and the court chose to believe Maslov's account of the events. Makarenko was given a suspended sentence of one year for libel against the governor and arrested on charges based on three other articles of the Russian Criminal Code, including the now standard (in cases of conflict with law enforcement officials) charge of "possessing an unregistered weapon"—namely, thirty-seven bullets from an Izh-76 pistol.[10] In 2004, Makarenko was handed a second sentence, and this one was not suspended: five years at a correctional facility for fraud and unlawful possession of ammunition.

ELECTION FOR MAYOR OF NIZHNY NOVGOROD

During the election for mayor of Nizhny Novgorod in September 2002, the plenipotentiary representative for the Volga district, Sergei Kiriyenko, faced a difficult problem.

First of all, under no circumstances could he allow the entrepreneur and irrepressible populist Andrei Klimentyev to get elected. Klimentyev, who had been taken to court many times, had already almost won the mayor's seat once in an honest race, in March 1998; but on the following day he was removed from his post by order of the municipal election commission, arrested, and then convicted of stealing currency credits. (The theft possibly did take place, but the criminal case and conviction happened only because Klimentyev had taken part in the election and won.) Another win for Klimentyev would show that the plenipotentiary representative was not in control of the situation in the region's capital.

Second, for the same reasons, Kiriyenko could not allow Mayor Yuri Lebedev to get re-elected. Back in the spring, unhappy with the experiment of introducing an alternative service program in Nizhny Novgorod, President Putin himself predicted that Lebedev "had no chance of getting re-elected" because "he has a miserable approval rating."[11] After this, there was nothing left for Kiriyenko to do but make sure that the president's scientific prediction came true. In addition, Kiriyenko and Lebedev were "connected" by personal hostility, which had already come out into the open during the gubernatorial election a year earlier.

Meanwhile, the voters themselves favored Klimentyev, while Lebedev competed for second place with Vadim Bulavinov, a State Duma deputy and deputy head of the People's Party of the Russian Federation, who was backed by Kiriyenko (and by Viktor Ivanov in Moscow).

On the evening of September 14, less than twenty-four hours before the polls opened, Klimentyev was disqualified. On that day, his adversaries had managed to find a witness who told the court that she had broken election rules by contributing money to Klimentyev's campaign fund that had been given to her by a third party.

According to the official records for the first round of voting on September 15, Lebedev came in first with 31.4 percent of the vote, Bulavinov was second with 30.85 percent, and 30.35 percent had been cast for "none of the above." Together, the number of ballots for "none of the above" and the number of defaced ballots (on which all the names were crossed out or more than one name was checked off) *exceeded* the number of votes cast for the frontrunner. This raised suspicions that a portion of the ballots for "none of the above" had been defaced deliberately. In addition, according to the exit polls of the Nizhny Novgorod department at the Russian Academy of Sciences' Institute of Sociology, "none of the above" had actually come in first.

Nonetheless, a second round of voting was held on September 29.

While votes were being counted that night, the ballots in all the city's electoral precincts were impounded at the request of Bulavinov and on the orders of a city district judge. Bulavinov suspected that the incumbent mayor's people in some election commissions were falsifying the results in the mayor's favor. But the next day, after all the ballots were examined, it became known that Bulavinov was the winner with 35.57 percent of the vote (34.93 percent for Lebedev, 29.5 percent for "none of the above"). On the same day, Bulavinov dropped his charges and the court released the ballots.

On October 2, defending the actions of his protégé and the court officers, Kiriyenko stated that he had "absolutely certain information that on the night after the mayoral election, after the polls closed, an order came to open up the bags with the ballots and to put a second check on [i.e. to deface] those that had been cast for the winner, Vadim Bulavinov."[12]

According to the exit polls, however, the winner was once again "none of the above."[13]

THE KRASNOYARSK ELECTION AS A BATTLE OF ADMINISTRATIVE RESOURCES

It is widely known and universally recognized that the election for governor of the Krasnoyarsk region in the fall of 2002 (held early due to the death of Alexander Lebed) represented a clash between two powerful financial-economic groups: Vladimir Potanin's Interross–Norilsk Nickel group, whose candidate was the governor of the Taimyr (Dolgan-Nenets) Autonomous District, Alexander Khloponin; and Oleg Deripaska's Bazovy Element–Russian Aluminium group, which backed the speaker of the Krasnoyarsk Region Legislative Assembly, Alexander Uss.

It is less well known and not as universally recognized that an even more important factor in the September 2002 Krasnoyarsk election was the rivalry between Moscow's administrative clans.

The administrative resource of the Krasnoyarsk region itself was also not monolithic. On the contrary, it was divided into three parts: the regional administration (the region's acting governor, Nikolai Ashlapov, supported Uss); the government of the northern part of the region (the governor of the Taimyr district, Khloponin, was running himself); and the administration of the regional center (the mayor of Krasnoyarsk, Pyotr Pimashkov, was also running for governor).

Each of the three federal oligarchic factions also had its preferences. The "old Kremlin" or "family" clan (Alexander Voloshin) favored Uss; the "old Petersburg" group (Anatoly Chubais) supported Pimashkov; and the "new Petersburg" group (the president's deputy chief of staff for personnel, Viktor Ivanov) backed Khloponin. The plenipotentiary representative of the Siberian Federal District, Leonid Drachevsky, remained neutral until President Putin's own preferences became known.

The three main candidates all had some relation to the United Russia party: Pimashkov and Uss were members, while Khloponin, though not formally a member, sat on its supreme council (like United Russia's leader and head of its supreme council, Boris Gryzlov, who is also "not a member" of the party).

The divided "ruling party" had a powerful opponent: Sergei Glazyev, the candidate of the left bloc. Glazyev's role was complicated, however: his participation objectively played into the hands of one of the leading candidates, namely, Khloponin. There were even suspicions that Khloponin's patron Potanin had contributed to the financing of Glazyev's campaign. At the same time, Glazyev's advancement to the second round of voting—which initially had not been expected by anyone, but with every day of the campaign seemed more and more likely—was not desirable for either Khloponin or Uss.

Therefore, in the first round of voting, on September 8, "administrative counting techniques" were applied first and foremost against Glazyev, and this was done by the northerners and the southerners alike. Ballots were defaced and extra ballots were added both in the north (in Norilsk and the Taimyr district in favor of Khloponin, against Glazyev and Uss) and in the south (in favor of Uss, against Glazyev and Khloponin).

The first round of voting was won by Uss, with 27.67 percent of the vote. Khloponin came in second, with 25.16 percent.

As far as is known, ballots in favor of Khloponin were falsified more openly than those in favor of the other candidates, due to the insignificant numbers of Uss's and Glazyev's observers in Taimyr. However, the southerner-controlled regional election commission initially did not react to the way in which the northerners were counting ballots, hoping that in the second round of voting Uss would win the votes of some of Glazyev's and Pimashkov's supporters. This did not happen, which forced the regional election commission—after the second round was over—to take a closer look at the northerners' falsifications in both the first and the second round.

On September 22, it was announced that Khloponin had won with 48.07 percent in the second round. Uss had 41.83 percent. But on September 29, the Krasnoyarsk regional election commission declared the results of the gubernatorial election invalid, in view of the large number of violations. In the opinion of the election commission, voters had been prevented from freely expressing their will by the candidates' use of administrative resources, pressure, bribery, and fraud. The number of voters whose will was impossible to ascertain was named: about 200,000 people. In making these announcements, the election commission was looking only at complaints about Khloponin's violations submitted by Uss's representatives. ("We have detected violations on both sides, but only Uss's representatives filed a complaint," said Alexander Bugrey, deputy head of the commission.)[14]

On September 30, Khloponin contested the election commission's decision. He claimed that the commission first had to announce the official outcome of the election, then to declare the results for specific precincts to be invalid if any violations were found, and only then to declare the outcome of the election for the region as a whole to be invalid. The following day, the Krasnoyarsk Regional Court reversed the regional election commission's decision to declare the election invalid and ruled that it had to determine the outcome of the election.

On October 3, President Putin signed a decree making Khloponin temporary acting governor of the region until the newly elected governor came into office.

In the end, it was precisely the president's decision that determined the outcome of the Krasnoyarsk region gubernatorial race. The actions of the Central Election Commission, which had recognized Khloponin's victory, had already pretty clearly indicated the president's preferences, but this turned out to be not enough for the regional election commission. The president had to become directly involved. Moreover, Khloponin's appointment as acting governor was not carried out correctly from a legal point of view. (By law, the president could have appointed only the first deputy governor—Ashlapov—to the position; alternatively, he could have dismissed Ashlapov first and then appointed Khloponin as first deputy governor.) Only the president's decree could persuade the regional election commission to accept the outcome of the election.

At a session of the regional election commission on October 11, Khloponin was officially recognized as governor of the Krasnoyarsk region. Shortly after the election, CEC head Alexander Veshnyakov dissolved the upstart Krasnoyarsk regional election commission.

ELECTION FOR MAYOR OF KYZYL

Another case in which a leading contender was not permitted to register as a candidate was the election for mayor of Kyzyl (Tuva Republic), scheduled for October 13, 2002. The victim of the "Bashkirian election technology" was the incumbent mayor of the republic's capital, Alexander Kashin, who was in opposition to the president of Tuva, Sherig-ool Oorzhak. Kashin was considered the leader of the Russian-speaking part of Kyzyl's population, unhappy with the ethnocratic policies of the republic's government.

Kashin had first been elected mayor of Kyzyl on April 5, 1998 (when he headed the local branch of Zhirinovsky's LDPR), with the support of a paradoxical alliance between Zhirinovsky supporters and democrats. Genrikh Epp, head of the Tuva branch of Yegor Gaidar's Democratic Choice party, became Kashin's deputy mayor (killed in July 1999).

In 2002, Kashin—who had gone over from the LDPR to the Union of Right Forces (SPS)—ran against Sherig-ool Oorzhak in the Tuva presidential race, but in the election on March 17, he came in third, with only 7.6 percent of the vote. Sherig-ool Oorzhak won with 53 percent, but not without suspicions that the vote tallies had been "corrected."

Kashin announced his intention to run for mayor of Kyzyl in the election on October 13, but was unable to register as a candidate. The municipal election commission's pretext was that Kashin had submitted lists of signatures in support of his nomination without providing passport details for some of the names.

ELECTION FOR PRESIDENT OF KALMYKIA

In the election for president of Kalmykia that took place in October 2002, two Kremlin factions—the "Petersburg chekists" and "the family"—came to blows. Alexander Voloshin and Vladislav Surkov were strongly in support of the incumbent president, Kirsan Ilyumzhinov. Their argument (probably convincing to Putin) for keeping such odious regional "khans" as Ilyumzhinov and Rakhimov in power was that in elections on the federal level, the "khans" provide exactly the percentage of votes that the Kremlin orders. Nonetheless, the "Petersburg chekists," supported by the "Petersburg economists," nominated their own candidate, the Moscow banker Baatr Shondzhiyev, and did not allow Ilyumzhinov's election commission to disqualify his registration.

In order to discredit Ilyumzhinov and to encourage the voters who were afraid to vote against the incumbent president, criminal charges were brought against members of the Kalmyk president's inner circle (including the republic's minister of internal affairs, Timofey Sasykov). Attempts were made to have Ilyumzhinov himself disqualified from taking part in the election for illegally using his official position, but these attempts proved futile: "the Kremlin is far away, but Kirsan is right here."

In Kalmykia itself, both candidates' supporters claimed that their leaders had the backing of President Putin, with the Ilyumzhinov camp pointing to Voloshin and Surkov, and the Shondzhiyev camp citing Viktor Ivanov and Igor Sechin. Although the election went to a second round of voting, Ilyumzhinov remained in power. Shondzhiyev argued that the outcome had been falsified, but his chekist sponsors accepted defeat and did not insist on an investigation.

CHANGES IN ELECTORAL LEGISLATION (2002–2004)

On June 12, 2002, Putin signed a new law: "On the basic guarantees of electoral rights and the right of citizens of the Russian Federation to participate in a referendum" (passed by the State Duma on May 22 and approved by the Federation Council on May 29). On the face of it, the new law—which went into effect in November—had certain advantages over the old one.

For example, the registration of a candidate or list of candidates could now be revoked no later than five days before an election and mainly through the courts. Inaccuracies and omissions in a candidate's declarations of property ceased to be a basis for denying him registration or disqualifying him from a race; election commissions retained the right merely to inform voters about such omissions or distortions. It became possible to nominate party candidates without collecting lists of signatures and making a monetary deposit. Yabloko party deputy Sergei Mitrokhin introduced an amendment that required elections in the constituent subjects of the federation to go to a second round when no candidate was able to win an absolute majority in the first round.

On the other hand, the new regulations greatly enhanced the capacity of the "ministry of elections" and its local subdivisions to "manage democracy." In essence, they legalized the "Bashkirian election technology"—the use of "administrative resources" to bar dangerous candidates from participating in elections.

The new law recognizes thirteen (!) reasons for denying a candidate the right to register, four reasons for which a candidate's registration may be annulled by the election commission, and six reasons for which a candidate's registration may be revoked by a decision of the court on a motion brought by the election commission. In addition, election results can be invalidated either by higher-level election commissions ("if, in the course of an election or while the outcome of an election was being determined, this federal law was violated, or if another law governing the said election was violated . . .") or by a decision of the court. The new law recognizes four different reasons for invalidating election results.

The following three universal pretexts ("grounds") for denying a candidate the right to register or annulling his registration probably have the greatest potential for "managing democracy":

1. A candidate or bloc must not exceed the campaign spending limits established by law by more than 5 percent. This pretext can also be used to declare election results invalid—although in that case, the spending must exceed the legal limits by more than 10 percent.
2. A candidate, coalition, or bloc must not violate Article 56, par. 1 of this federal law—that is, "abusing the right to campaign before an election," which is open to a very broad interpretation.
3. A candidate must indicate his position and place of work correctly. This is also subject to an infinitely broad and selective interpretation, and during the State Duma election campaign in 2003, the government made especially broad use of this pretext.

Moreover, as subsequent experience demonstrated, the new regulations made it possible to block candidates from participating in elections for more exotic reasons as well: for example, due to an "expired passport" (this is what happened in the summer of 2004 to the opposition candidate for the presidency of Chechnya, Malik Saidullaev) or because a candidate had "concealed" the fact that he was a professor (as with the former general prosecutor Yuri Skuratov in the 2003 Duma election). The new regulations preserved and even strengthened the possibility of using the law in an instrumental and selective fashion.

For the duration of an election campaign, the new law prohibited any "actions intended to induce or inducing voters to vote for or against candidates (lists) or for 'none of the above,'" except advertisements paid for with registered campaign funds. In other words, the law substantially restricted the constitutional right of the media—and of citizens who appear in the media—to voice their opinions. In effect, a ban on political analysis was established for the duration of an election campaign, since the law equated political analysis with campaigning, which was legal only when it was paid for with official campaign funds. Violations of this ban by supporters of opposition parties have invariably led to charges of "abusing the right to conduct an election campaign," and the latter could constitute legal grounds for disqualifying a candidate's or a political bloc's registration.

The new law endowed election commissions with a broad measure of authority, including the right to use contradictions in the existing legislation. For example, electoral legislation prohibits financing an election campaign except through a campaign fund, but at the same time media regulations require the media to inform the population about all significant events. Therefore, a TV channel that promotes a president or a minister will be seen by the CEC as lawfully informing the population. But if an opposition candidate appears on a program, then the question arises: did he pay for the program out of his campaign fund, and if not, should he not be disqualified from participating in the election?

In theory, the law declares the right of any citizen to express his opinion. On the other hand, it prohibits government officials from campaigning or making use of their official positions in elections. In practice, this means that if the president campaigns for United Russia or for his own candidate in a gubernatorial race, then he is enjoying his *legal* right as a citizen to express his opinion. But if the assistant of an opposition deputy takes part in the campaign of his boss, then the deputy is using his official position in an *illegal* manner. Meanwhile, if a candidate for the Duma from a pro-presidential party uses his assistant in exactly the same way, the issue of its legality or illegality simply never comes up.

The new law also includes an attempt to make it more difficult to use the only real defense against the "Bashkirian election technology": voting for "none of the above." In effect, only registered candidates are now allowed to campaign or in any other way incite voters to vote for "none of the above," because other supporters of "none of the above" by definition cannot have a campaign fund. No legal mechanism yet exists for punishing private individuals who campaign for "none of the above" without having officially registered campaign funds, but it is already possible to penalize media outlets that express this viewpoint.

In addition to these changes in electoral legislation, the right to a referendum was substantially abridged and revisions were introduced into media regulations in 2002–2004 (in two stages, September 2002 and May–June 2004). Also, the departmental affiliation of the GAS-Vybory electronic voting system was changed.

In September 2002, the president's administration, relying on a right-wing, pro-Putin majority in the Duma, pushed through provisions that imposed time constraints on the right to a referendum: from now on, it was prohibited to hold a referendum during the year preceding and the three months following a federal election—for the Duma and for the presidency. Votes in favor of this amendment were cast not only by the SPS's deputies (apart from the human rights activist Sergei Kovalev, who voted against it), but by Yabloko's deputies as well (apart from the St. Petersburg lawyer Sergei Popov, who refrained from voting). The law "To amend and supplement the Federal Constitutional Law on the Referendum in the Russian Federation" was passed by the Duma on September 20, 2002, approved by the Federation Council on September 25, and signed by Putin on September 27.

In March 2003, as part of a reform of the security services, the FSB was given control over the GAS-Vybory electronic voting system. GAS-Vybory had been controlled by the Federal Agency for Government Communication and Information (FAPSI), which was henceforth eliminated. The FSB had reasonably concluded that it was easier to control one central computer than multiple election commissions at different locations.

In June of that year, new presidential amendments to media regulations introduced a mechanism—previously lacking—for punishing the media for violating election regulations. However, at the height of the Duma election campaign in the fall, in response to a claim brought by a number of reporters and deputies, the Constitutional Court handed down a weaker interpretation of the new law. The court found no grounds to interpret the law as effectively prohibiting, for the duration of the campaign, information and political analysis that was not paid for out of the candidates' campaign funds. But this ruling only provided reporters with a means to fight against the most blatant excesses (which is to say, to file complaints with the appropriate offices by citing the court's decision); election commissions still retained the right to decide which information and political analysis should be considered political advertising.

On May 19, 2004, the president introduced amendments to legislation governing referendums, which were passed by the Duma on June 11. (The Federation Council approved them on June 23, and the president signed them into law on June 28.) The law made it considerably more difficult to initiate a referendum. In particular, instead of a single initiative group, the law now required the existence of a minimum of forty-five initiative groups, in different constituent subjects of the federation, each with at least one hundred members. The deadline for collecting two million signatures in support of the initiative was shortened from three months to two.

In August, the CEC proposed introducing a new amendment packet into the electoral legislation, with the aim of increasing the dependence of voting procedures and results on the "ministry of elections." The most radical reform proposed by Veshnyakov's agency was to increase the "proportional-representation component" in the election of Duma deputies to the point of having all deputies elected on a proportional basis. In order to expand its capacity to disqualify candidates, the CEC proposed reducing the allowed percentage of inauthentic and invalid signatures collected in support of a candidate from 25 percent to 5 percent. On September 13, on the pretext of fighting terrorism, President Putin expressed support for the idea of allowing only party-list candidates to run for the State Duma and announced the upcoming repeal of direct elections for the heads of the constituent subjects of the federation. From now on, governors would be appointed by the president and then confirmed by local legislative assemblies.

Putin's new course, which manifestly went against the Russian constitution, was criticized both in Russia and abroad. A group of over one hundred foreign scientists and politicians sent an open letter to the leaders of the European Union and NATO, accusing the Russian president of rejecting democratic values and harboring dictatorial ambitions. In the West, Putin's political trajectory was seen as a threat to Russian democracy and the country's economy. To foreign analysts, Russia appeared to be shifting toward a social-political model characteristic of Latin American countries.

ELECTION FOR THE KURULTAI OF BASHKORTOSTAN

The election for the Kurultai (state assembly) of Bashkortostan was held on March 16, 2003—in other words, after the new law "On the basic guarantees of electoral rights" had been passed. This law did not make it more difficult to deny opposition candidates the right to register in the election; on the contrary, it became a convenient weapon in the hands of Murtaza Rakhimov's election commissions.

The Bashkirian branch of the SPS—servilely loyal to Rakhimov's regime—managed to register all fifteen of its candidates. The Bashkirian branch of the CPRF—which opposed Rakhimov—registered only about thirty of its candidates, out of forty-four nominated. Bashkortostan's Yabloko, also in the opposition, managed to register six out of its eight nominated candidates. But particular resistance was felt by the candidates from the Tatar Public Center (TOTs). There are more Tatars than Bashkirs in Bashkortostan, but Rakhimov is conducting a policy of Bashkirizng the Tatars, which is opposed by the Tatar nationalists and nationalist-democrats who form the TOTs.

Thus, the election commission denied registrations to TOTs activists Zagir Khakimov and Marat Ramazanov, finding all 100 percent (!) of the signatures gathered in their support to be invalid. After examining Khakimov and Ramazanov's appeals, the court in Ufa made a ruling that was tantamount to mockery: it found most of the signatures to be valid, but ruled that neither of the candidates had enough signatures to register—both were off by a single signature.

Other methods were used as well: one of the opposition candidates was forced to withdraw from the election when his daughter suddenly found herself in danger of losing her job.[15]

In this election, 91 of the Kurultai's 120 seats went to the Bashkirian branch of the United Russia party, firmly controlled by Rakhimov's administration. Not one of the prominent opposition candidates (Tatar, Russian, Communist, Yabloko) was elected.

ELECTION FOR MAYOR OF NOVOROSSIYSK

The Novorossiysk mayoral election on March 23, 2003, also took place after the new law had been passed.

The previous mayor, Valery Prokhorenko, had come into conflict with the governor of the Krasnodar region, Alexander Tkachev, and had been forced to resign. The Novorossiysk Duma appointed Tkachev's nominee, Vladimir Sinyagovsky, as acting mayor on November 27, 2002.

The Novorossiysk election commission reviewed the registration applications of six candidates on February 20, 2003. Only three ended up getting registered: Sinyagovsky and two straw-man candidates by the names of Ivan Nudnoy and Pyotr Kashirin, about whom nothing was known except that they were residents of a Kazan village. The deputy head of the election commission even declared that more detailed facts about these candidates were "confidential information."

Sinyagovsky's main rival, State Duma deputy Sergei Shishkarev—at that time a member of the People's Party, later a member of the Homeland bloc—was denied registration. The applications of Alexander Zhirov, former head of the Chernomortransneft company, and Igor Zinchenko, a retiree, were turned down as well. According to the election commission, the stamps on a number of Shishkarev's lists of signatures were too pale; they had to be verified; and the experts of the regional Directorate of Internal Affairs found them invalid. In addition, Shishkarev's financial forms turned out to have been filled out incorrectly.

"Why would I forget the stamps if the signatures were real?" Shishkarev protested. (Incidentally, like all the members of his Duma faction, Shishkarev had voted in favor of the new electoral legislation.) "As for the missing details in the copies of my financial records . . . we have the original bank statements that show all the necessary information."[16] But the election commission remained unresponsive to these arguments.

All three of the rejected candidates attempted to register by submitting monetary deposits. The election commission, however, found that the "documents pertaining to the transfer of financial resources to the campaign funds of candidates Shishkarev, Zhirov, and Zinchenko had not been filed in accordance with the requirements of the law." As a result, the commission ruled that the deposits had no force.

Paradoxically, not one of the registered candidates—including the acting mayor—even lived in the city, while all of the artificially excluded aspirants were Novorossiysk residents.

In the end, Tkachev's man, Vladimir Sinyagovsky, was elected mayor.

ELECTION FOR THE LEGISLATIVE ASSEMBLY OF THE ROSTOV REGION

On March 30, 2003, there was an election for the Legislative Assembly of the Rostov Region. An official from the office of the plenipotentiary representative in the Southern Federal District told the *Vremya Novostey* newspaper that there was a danger that the Communists were "quite capable" of winning a majority of the seats in the regional parliament, because the population was extremely discontented by the 50 percent rise in energy prices. The regional branch of the CPRF nominated candidates in 33 out of 45 districts.[17] However, the regional election commission refused to register a total of 30 candidates, including

12 official CPRF nominees. According to the regional election commission, over one-fourth of the signatures collected in support of the CPRF candidates were invalid.[18]

In the end, 40 out of 45 seats in the legislative assembly went to avowed supporters of Governor Vladimir Chub (mainly officials and businessmen—members of United Russia and candidates without party affiliation), and four seats went to candidates from parties that were loyal to Governor Chub (one from the Agrarian Party, two from Yabloko, and one from the SPS). Only one more or less oppositional candidate (a Communist) was elected.

ELECTION FOR MAYOR OF NORILSK

The imperfection of the new law—or, on the contrary, its perfection as a government-controlled instrument—was demonstrated with particular clarity by the called-off election for mayor of Norilsk in the spring of 2003. An early election was announced when Mayor Oleg Budargin was elected governor of the Taimyr Autonomous District (replacing Alexander Khloponin, who became the governor of the Krasnoyarsk region) in January. The frontrunners in the first round of the Norilsk election, on April 20, were Valery Melnikov (46.95 percent), an opposition labor-union leader, and Sergei Shmakov (31.7 percent), an employee of Norilsk Nickel who was backed by the administration of the Krasnoyarsk region (i.e. by Khloponin).

On April 23, the municipal election commission brought a motion before the Norilsk Municipal Court to annul Melnikov's registration. Citing the findings of the prosecutor's office, the election commission accused Melnikov of receiving illegal material assistance in the amount of 1.6 million rubles by overstating the prices of 60,000 promotional pamphlets: in the official documents, each pamphlet was listed as having cost 30 rubles, while in reality the cost was only 2.30 rubles. The court upheld the election commission's claim on April 28 and revoked the registration of the winner in the first round. Melnikov argued that the court's ruling "had been made under the influence of Norilsk Nickel and predetermined in advance."[19]

In accordance with the court's ruling, the election commission put Shmakov and Leonid Frayman—the third-place candidate in the first round (2.8 percent)—on the ballot for the second round, scheduled for May 4. Melnikov expressed the hope that the majority would vote for "none of the above."

Since this was indeed the most likely outcome, Shmakov immediately announced his intention to withdraw from the race. He explained his decision by citing noble motives ("I have no right to be simply appointed to a position without taking into account the democratically expressed will of the people of Norilsk"). In this way, the Norilsk Nickel candidate "elegantly withdrew from the battle, without eliminating the option of participating in a new election."[20] The third- and fourth-place candidates—who had won less than 3 percent (Frayman) and about 1 percent (Alexander Glisman) of the vote—followed suit and also withdrew. A new election was scheduled for the fall; in the interim, Khloponin appointed first one acting mayor and then another.

In the fall of 2003, instead of Shmakov, who had disappointed their hopes, the regional administration and the management of Norilsk Nickel (which became practically indistinguishable after Khloponin was elected governor) nominated the popular Dzhonson Khagazheyev, formerly the Soviet general manager of the Norilsk Combine and currently the first deputy general manager of Norilsk Nickel. Nonetheless, Melnikov was elected in the first round of voting on October 26, with 53.3 percent of the vote (Khagazheyev won 32.93 percent).

Melnikov was unable to enter into office until April 2004, however. His official duties continued to be fulfilled by the acting mayor, Lev Kuznetsov, who had been recommended by Khloponin and unanimously approved by the city council. Two outsider candidates, Arsen Borisovets and Valery Glazkov, had lodged a complaint against Melnikov with the Norilsk municipal election commission, accusing him of spending 144,664.47 rubles in excess of his campaign fund. The election commission found that the complaint was justified and, citing the fact that this sum constituted over 10 percent of the maximum permitted size for a campaign fund, brought a motion before the court to invalidate the outcome of the mayoral election of October 26, 2003.

The election commission also argued—correctly, from a formal point of view—that no person could be mayor and a deputy in the regional parliament at the same time. Melnikov had filed for a resignation from the Krasnoyarsk Region Legislative Assembly immediately after being elected mayor; but on November 11, 2003, the motion to relieve him of his position in the assembly had failed to pass by three votes. Wishing to please Governor Khloponin, the assembly had denied Melnikov's resignation request a second time on November 25.

Only in March 2004 was Melnikov able to resign from his ill-starred position in the legislative assembly. On April 7, the Norilsk Municipal Court finally dismissed the election commission's motion to invalidate the outcome of the October election.

ELECTION FOR MAYOR OF NOYABRSK

May 2003 marked the beginning of a long-running controversy surrounding the mayoral election in the city of Noyabrsk in the Khanty-Mansi Autonomous District. The incumbent mayor, Yuri Link, enjoyed the support of the district's governor, Yuri Neyelov (United Russia). In the mayoral election on May 4, Link beat his main rival, Anatoly Kudryashov, chairman of the board of directors of the Noyabrskelectrosetstroy company, by only a couple of hundred votes (0.9 percent). This happened because in several precincts where Kudryashov was winning, the final results were invalidated by the municipal election commission.

Kudryashov's supporters accused the election commission of falsifying the outcomes. The city's radio station, after repeating these accusations, was seized by special forces (OMON) without an order from the prosecutor's office, and tear gas was used to disperse a peaceful demonstration in defense of the station. On May 6, Kudryashov brought charges against the election commission; he was joined by the other losing candidates.

On May 30, the court ruled in favor of the municipal election commission, and this ruling became law on June 9. Yuri Link was inaugurated on June 11, but already in July he received and accepted an offer from Governor Neyelov to become his deputy. Link's deputy, Nikolai Korobkov, became acting mayor, and another election was scheduled for February 1, 2004.

Korobkov became the ruling party's candidate. Kudryashov once again announced his candidacy for the mayor's seat, but he and eight (!) other nominees were denied registration.

The pretext chosen by the election commission to deny Kudryashov registration was the fact that he had not fully declared his yearly income; he had indicated his salary of one million rubles, but had omitted to mention his retirement pension of 23,000 rubles. Even under Veshnyakov's new law, however, the municipal election commission could do no more than censure this "violation" by publicizing it through the media. Therefore, two days before the election, the CEC in Moscow ruled that it had been illegal to deny Kudryashov registration.

And yet, the government still won in the end: Kudryashov himself withdrew from the race "due to illness," and on February 1, with an official voter turnout of 40.99 percent, Korobkov was elected mayor with 67.01 percent of the vote. "None of the above" received 20.04 percent.

ELECTION FOR THE MUNICIPAL DUMA OF VLADIVOSTOK

Although a number of opposition candidates had been denied registration, the election for the municipal duma of Vladivostok on June 8, 2003, produced a win for the opposition. The informal Freedom and People's Government bloc (a coalition of the supporters of Viktor Cherepkov, leader of the Freedom and People's Government party, former mayor, and State Duma deputy) won 14 out of 25 seats, thus forming an absolute majority in the municipal duma.

At the first session of the Vladivostok municipal duma on July 16, however, two deputies left Cherepkov's bloc. Cherepkov declared that his deputies had been bought out by his opponents—Mayor Yuri Kopylov and the businessman-deputy crime boss Vladimir Nikolayev. The resulting breakdown of votes (twelve against twelve, with one seat remaining unfilled) prevented the duma from electing a chairman and a deputy chairman.

The final vote counts for two precincts that had been carried by Cherepkov's supporters (No. 10 and No. 24) were invalidated on July 31 by a decision of the court on a claim brought by the municipal election commission, and Cherepkov's Freedom and People's Government coalition, which was headed by deputy Igor Shpakovsky, ended up with only ten deputies. Later, two more deputies withdrew from the coalition.

In December 2003, despite the absence of a quorum due to a boycott by Cherepkov's supporters, the Vladivostok duma elected a speaker. This was Vitaly Subbotin, a deputy who at that moment more or less satisfied both of the region's two rival administrative-economic factions—the regional administration (Governor Sergei Darkin) and the Vladivostok mayor's office (Mayor Yuri Kopylov, a supporter of the former governor, Yevgeny Nazdratenko).

ELECTION FOR GOVERNOR OF THE OMSK REGION

Leonid Polezhayev, the governor of the Omsk region since 1991, remained the region's most influential politician in 2003 and had an approval rating twice as high as that of any other politician in the region. The problem was that this high approval rating was still below 50 percent, while the new law on gubernatorial elections—the so-called "Mitrokhin amendment"—called for a second round of voting if no candidate won over 50 percent in the first round. There was a danger that the governor, although a frontrunner in the first round of voting, might lose in the second.

The second-place candidate was Leonid Mayevsky, a moderate Communist (later banished from the CPRF), State Duma deputy, and businessman. Mayevsky could not win in the first round, but in the event of a second round he was quite capable of consolidating and winning the support of everyone who was dissatisfied with Polezhayev.

For the governor, it was vitally important not to allow for the possibility of a second round. Mayevsky's voter base was stable but limited; to reduce or increase it in the first round would have been difficult. Alexander Korotkov, formerly a member of Polezhayev's team (as first deputy governor), presented a danger: any votes he won in the first round would all be taken directly from Polezhayev. This created the prospect of a second round—an unpleasant prospect for the governor. At the same time, Korotkov's voters could very well go over to Mayevsky in a second round. Therefore, the governor did everything he could to bar Korotkov from participating in the election, or at least to make his campaign as difficult as possible.

Korotkov's registration was disqualified and reinstated by the CEC only nine days before the election on September 7, 2003. He had no time to conduct a full campaign, and he won only 10 percent of the vote, coming in third after Polezhayev (55.95 percent) and Mayevsky (27.94 percent). The governor had attained his goal—there was no second round—even if he had done so at the price of a low (but adequate) voter turnout and suspicions that six or seven extra percentage points had been added to his total. The opposition, however, was unable to present any convincing evidence of fraud.

ELECTION FOR GOVERNOR OF ST. PETERSBURG

Rumors of Vladimir Yakovlev's impending replacement as governor of St. Petersburg circulated for almost four years. Under Anatoly Sobchak, two discreet deputy mayors, Vladimir Yakovlev and Vladimir Putin, effectively governed the city for the charismatic mayor, who traveled around the world and would be gone from the northern capital for months at a time. No conflicts were observed at the time between Putin, who was involved in the "new economy," and Yakovlev, who was in charge of the "old economy." But in the spring of 1996, when Yakovlev suddenly ran against their common boss (and the title of the executive was changed from mayor to governor), Putin publicly—although behind Yakovlev's back—called him "Judas." After Yakovlev won, he called Putin—also behind his back—an "asshole."[21]

When he became president, Putin was expected to punish Yakovlev. Sobchak's widow, Lyudmila Narusova, was particularly passionate in encouraging him to do so.

Despite Yakovlev's obvious shortcomings as an administrator—the habits and style of a Soviet-era paymaster, the corruption of the governor's and his wife's inner circle—no one doubted that he would win again in the next election. Under Yakovlev, some kind of order had finally been established in St. Petersburg, something that had been absent under Sobchak. A straightforward system for "resolving problems" developed in the city (including a reliable, "single-channel" method for handling bribes), based on the same principles as the system that had been established years earlier in Yuri Luzhkov's Moscow. This bureaucratic, corrupt, but functioning system was more or less acceptable to both large-scale and mid-level businesses and even to a considerable part of the ordinary population. (In fact, it is just this kind of order that Putin's bureaucracy is trying to establish on the scale of Russia as a whole—only with military-police overtones and centered around a somewhat different group of individuals.)

The office of the plenipotentiary representative in the Northwestern Federal District did its best to bring one criminal charge after another against Yakovlev's corrupt deputies, but paradoxically this only increased the governor's electoral potential. In addition, the "anticorruption" campaign against Yakovlev's team was conducted in a highly erratic fashion. As Yulia Latynina rightly noted, "by initiating criminal proceedings in connection with shortfalls in the city budget and then abandoning them halfway, like casual lovers, the government has shown St. Petersburg residents that it does not consider theft to be a wrongdoing. By intending to replace the governor and then dragging it out for four years, the government has discredited its own intention to seek revenge."[22] Latynina proposed a simple and accurate explanation for this erratic approach: "St. Petersburg is a small city. And too many of the president's friends are also friends of Yakovlev's."[23] To this it may be added that too much of the corrupt business of Yakovlev's friends is also the business of certain friends of Putin's.

It seemed that only a direct declaration by the president that Yakovlev was an absolutely unacceptable leader for the second capital could have overthrown the "boss" of St. Petersburg. Putin, however, found another method—the same that he had used to unseat Yevgeny Nazdratenko, the governor of Primorye, three years earlier. On June 16, 2003, Yakovlev was appointed deputy prime minister for social issues in the federal government. An early gubernatorial election was scheduled for September.

It is not known for certain what means (threats or promises) were used to force Yakovlev to accept a position that he could lose at any time at Putin's whim. Nonetheless, he agreed, and the Kremlin inaugurated a meddlesome campaign to promote the bland Valentina Matviyenko—who had shortly before been appointed the president's plenipotentiary representative in the Northwestern Federal District—as a loyal supporter of Putin and therefore the inevitable winner in the gubernatorial race.

All the pro-Putin parties, including the SPS, approved of the president's choice. The Kremlin managed to persuade almost all aspirants for the gubernatorial post from Yakovlev's old team to abandon their ambitions. The only transgressor of nomenklatura discipline turned out to be Anna Markova, who had earlier been one of Yakovlev's deputies.

On September 2, 2003, Putin met with Matviyenko as his plenipotentiary representative, despite the fact that she was on official leave precisely in connection with her participation in the gubernatorial race. After discussing plans for the "revival of St. Petersburg" with her, the president wished Matviyenko success in the election. All state-run television channels aired long stories about this meeting. Such undisguised campaigning by a top government official on behalf of one candidate—which was obviously "not paid for with campaign funds"—was a clear violation of electoral regulations (even though Veshnyakov's law itself, which discriminates against one specific category of citizens, is evidently unreasonable). The Kremlin's political analysts, however, had convinced the president that without him Matviyenko would lose, but with his support she would definitely win, and maybe even in the first round.

Markova, naturally, accused Matviyenko of using illegal campaign methods. "How much does it cost to make a political commercial with the president of the country and to have it shown on federal television? Did the deputy pay for this commercial out of her campaign fund?"[24] Markova dared to charge even Putin himself with violating a number of the law's provisions:

> President Putin has clearly expressed his preference for candidate Matviyenko (art. 48, par. 1, cl. b). . . . The president has disseminated information with a clear predominance of facts about candidate Mat-

viyenko, accompanied by positive comments (art. 48, par. 1, cl. g). . . .
The president has taken steps to foster positive attitudes toward candidate Matviyenko among voters (art. 48, par. 1, cl. e).[25]

But CEC head Alexander Veshnyakov preferred to put the blame for violating electoral law not on Matviyenko or, heaven forfend, the president, but on the media, which in his opinion simply should not have covered the president's meeting with one of the candidates. In Veshnyakov's opinion, if the media had not run stories about the meeting, everything would have been ethical and legal.

From the start, the candidates who had no ties to Yakovlev—including Mikhail Amosov, the leader of the regional branch of Yabloko and in opposition to both Moscow and Matviyenko, and Sergei Beliayev, former minister of federal property management—had no chances of winning.

Matviyenko, however, could lose the election, and there were three different ways this could happen. First, Markova could manage to consolidate all pro-Yakovlev voters behind her (although Yakovlev himself was compelled to call on his supporters to vote for Matviyenko) and the other anti-Kremlin candidates could agree to forget her "Yakovlevian" past and to support her in the second round of voting. Second, a majority could vote for "none of the above," especially in the second round, especially if all prominent candidates (Markova, Beliayev, Amosov) urged voters to do so. This was probably the most likely scenario, taking into account the fact that it was psychologically impossible for democrats to vote for one of Yakovlev's collaborators. Third, the election could simply be called off due to insufficient voter turnout. This was also a realistic scenario—but only in the first round, because the second round had no minimum turnout requirement.

Since Markova, against all expectations, was able to achieve a high approval rating relatively quickly, Matviyenko attempted to use the old Bashkirian methods to get her thrown out of the election. Contrary to law, the St. Petersburg Directorate of Internal Affairs (GUVD) was requested to check the lists of signatures gathered in support of Markova's nomination, and it "identified" over 25 percent of the signatures as questionable—even though the initial check by the municipal election commission had determined only 701 signatures to be invalid, which constituted 9.4 percent of the signatures submitted for verification. Another gubernatorial candidate, the businessman and former Komsomol leader Viktor Yefimov (effectively a stalking horse for Matviyenko in case the other candidates should suddenly collectively withdraw from the election in order to undermine it), brought a claim before the municipal court, requesting that Markova's registration be revoked because of the GUVD report.

Markova was able to prove the authenticity of most of the signatures that the police had declared invalid. But the case closed only a few days before the election: on September 18, the Supreme Court ruled that Markova could remain a candidate. This decision came after Gleb Pavlovsky's Foundation for Effective Politics—a team of political analysts who were working for Matviyenko—had determined that if Markova were barred from the election, either the election would be called off due to low voter turnout (less than 25 percent) in the first round, or "none of the above" would win in the first or second round.

Over the course of the campaign, the police regularly detained supporters of Markova, Amosov, and Beliayev, and also the distributors of the *Peterburgskaya Liniya* newspaper, which advocated voting for "none of the above." On September 4, in the Moskovsky district of St. Petersburg, law enforcement officials confiscated campaign flyers "with a negative content" aimed against Matviyenko. On September 17, the general manager of the typesetting company that had printed the flyers was charged with libel (Article 129, par. 2 of the Russian Criminal Code). Beliayev's campaign flyers were impounded while being transported to St. Petersburg, on the pretext that the shipment might contain materials that discredited . . . Beliayev.

The first round of voting took place on September 21, 2003. Matviyenko, with 48.73 percent of the vote, was unable to win in the first round. Markova won 15.84 percent (while 10.97 percent had voted for "none of the above," 8.8 percent for Beliayev, 7.5 percent for Amosov). The official turnout of 29 percent was incredibly low for the normally politically active city of St.

Petersburg, and it is possible that this figure itself was a deliberate overestimate.

After Yabloko's defeat in the first round (and fourth place was definitely a defeat), the party's St. Petersburg branch gave in to Grigory Yavlinsky, who was being pressured by the Kremlin—which had demanded that Yabloko withdraw Amosov from the running and endorse Matviyenko even before the first round—and called on its supporters to vote for Matviyenko in the second round. On October 5, Matviyenko was elected with 63.16 percent of the vote and an official turnout of 28.25 percent. (Markova won 24.18 percent, and 11.75 percent went to "none of the above.")

ELECTION FOR PRESIDENT OF CHECHNYA

The "democratic" election of the ex-mufti Akhmad Kadyrov as president of Chechnya was, at least in the Kremlin's opinion, supposed to crown the dubious stabilization of the rebellious republic. On January 9, 2003, Chechnya's election commission announced a referendum on a draft of a new constitution, which presevered Chechnya as a part of the Russian Federation. The referendum was held on March 23. According to official records, the constitution was approved by a margin that was absurd even by the standards of Putin's Russia: 96.5 percent in favor of the new constitution, with a voter turnout of approximately 80 percent.

The Kremlin itself, however, understood perfectly well that Kadyrov would have no chance in a fair race against any candidate with the slightest credentials. The greatest danger was presented by the possible candidacies of Ruslan Khasbulatov, former speaker of Russia's Supreme Soviet, and Aslambek Aslakhanov, a State Duma deputy and colonel general of the police. Neither of them concealed his disapproval of Kadyrov's cruelly repressive regime, and although both were federalists, they believed in the possibility of peace negotiations with the separatist leader, Aslan Maskhadov. In the event that Khasbulatov and Aslakhanov did not run, a part of the population could still vote for any other candidate who was not entirely a puppet, or at least did not look like one—for example, the

Moscow-Chechen businessmen Hussein Dzhabrailov and Malik Saidullaev.

Khasbulatov's vacillation resolved itself in August, when he decided not to participate in the election. By all appearances, he had been pressured to make this decision.

On September 2, Dzhabrailov announced that he was withdrawing from the race as well. Several days before the beginning of the campaign, he was invited to the Kremlin and informed that "Moscow will support the acting head of the republic, Akhmad Kadyrov, in the upcoming election."[26] Dzhabrailov enjoyed the support of Chechnya's press minister, Bislan Gantamirov. But on September 3, Gantamirov was dismissed from his post, and on the night of September 4, Grozny television and the editorial offices of all eight of Grozny's newspapers were taken under armed guard by Kadyrov's security service.

The Supreme Court of Chechnya disqualified Saidullaev's registration on September 11 and barred him for taking part in the presidential election. The reason cited was the unreliability of a number of the signatures gathered in support of his nomination. It was on the basis of these signatures that Saidullaev had been registered as a candidate. Saidullaev reminded the court that he had also submitted a monetary deposit, and he demanded that, if the signatures were invalid, he should be registered on the basis of the deposit. His request was denied, however, and in a mocking fashion: "If the lists of signatures and the deposit are submitted on the same day, then in accordance with the law, the election commission has the right to decide which of these two options to use as a basis for registering a candidate."[27] It would have been more accurate to say: "The election commission has the right to decide which of these two options to use as a basis for *not* registering a candidate."

The only rival left was Aslankhanov—possibly the most dangerous of all the opposition candidates. In August 2000, he had won the special election for the State Duma in the Chechen electoral district, despite the obstacles put in his way by Kadyrov.

Aslankhanov received a threat from the Grozny election commission: "He will be disqualified because one of his documents cites a wrong home address. There is also no statement about his income."[28] At the same time, Aslankhanov was called in for a chat with President Putin. According to the deputy, he told Putin about these threats, and Putin offered him the position of his assistant. The grateful Aslankhanov did not try to convince the "Guarantor of the Constitution" to take measures against the threats of the Grozny election commission. Instead, he submitted to the threats (just as if the "Guarantor" had backed them up), withdrew from the Chechen election, and accepted the president's offer—basically, as a kickback. He also lost his place in the Duma as a result of his new appointment.

In January 2004, the Dzhabrailov family also received a kickback, which had most likely been agreed upon in advance: Hussein Dzhabrailov's brother Umar was appointed senator of Chechnya (replacing Akhmar Zavgayev, who became United Russia's Duma deputy from the Chechen district).

After such a wholesale "cleansing" of the candidate list, voter turnout became an issue. The official turnout was patently false. According to one member of a precinct election commission:

> In October, 2,500 voters were registered in our precinct. Only 146 came to vote. The voting took place in a hospital. . . . We had special people sitting at the reception desk and filling in ballots. Then we simply invited all observers to lunch in another building, and we ourselves changed the ballot box, threw all those ballots inside it, added the 146 that had been filled out honestly, and in the evening made a record of the totals. There were no objections from the observers, but I myself now know the ropes too well to go and vote.[29]

On October 5, 2003, Akhmad Kadyrov was "elected"— supposedly winning over 80 percent, with a voter turnout of 86.8 percent—only to be killed by a separatist-planted bomb in Grozny's Dinamo stadium on May 9, 2004.

THE STATE DUMA ELECTIONS

In terms of its tactical-technical characteristics, the election for the fourth convocation of the State Duma on December 7, 2003, occupied a middle ground between the fall elections in St. Petersburg and Chechnya. It was considerably more free than the election in Chechnya and substantially less honest than the election in St. Petersburg.

Two relatively well-known and significant parties were barred from participating in the election: Eduard Limonov's National Bolshevik Party (NBP) and Boris Berezovsky's and Ivan Rybkin's Liberal Russia.

The NBP's attempts to participate in the election were nipped in the bud: the party was unable to obtain a registration from the Ministry of Justice. The formal reasons cited by the ministry for denying the registration were patently hypocritical. The real reason was an unwillingness to let the NBP, which is popular among young people—and has even greater *potential* popularity among young people—to participate in the election. Of course, at this point the NBP does not constitute a serious electoral force; but it is still a more serious force than about 13 of the 23 parties and blocs that did take part in the Duma election of 2003. Under the right conditions, the NBP could even hope to pass the 5 percent threshold.

As a result of being barred from the race, the NBP remained nothing more than a gang of tomato-, egg-, and mayonnaise-throwing hoodlums; and the votes of the teenagers who showed up at the polls, instead of going to the NBP, went to Vladimir Zhirinovsky's LDPR, which with every election loses more and more of its support among older voters. And this was, apparently, just what was wanted inside the Kremlin, where Zhirinovsky's party has been prized and cherished since the time of Yeltsin, while Limonov's party is hated and frankly feared.

Berezovsky's and Rybkin's Liberal Russia party had emerged after the old Liberal Russia (Sergei Yushenkov, Viktor Pokhmelkin, Boris Berezovsky) split into two identically named parties. The Ministry of Justice and the CEC chose to consider Viktor Pokhmelkin's Liberal Russia the only legitimate one of the two, and it was this party that participated in the election under the name "The New Course–Automobile Russia." (It won 0.84 percent of the vote, coming in twelfth.)

Berezovsky's party was considered unelectable, and indeed its rating did not rise above 1 percent. But these estimates were made under conditions in which the party had practically no means (apart from *Nezavisimaya Gazeta* and the Internet) to present itself to the public. Registration and official participation in the election could have given it a forum for self-presentation that was at least comparable to that enjoyed by Pokhmelkin's Liberal Russia. But if the "automobile version" of Liberal Russia was not in any way politically distinct from the general background of other moderately democratic parties, then Berezovsky's Liberal Russia could genuinely claim to be the only systematic democratic opposition to Putinism. This was all the more true because Yabloko, which had occupied this position previously, forfeited it in the fall of 2003 when it voted to curtail the right to a referendum, supported Matviyenko in the second round in St. Petersburg, and stopped criticizing Putin personally. Berezovsky's Liberal Russia could have swallowed up Yabloko's anti-Putin voters and thus passed the 5 percent threshold.

In any case, hypotheses about the NBP's and Liberal Russia's chances could not be experimentally tested because these two parties were prevented from participating in the election on rather dubious formal grounds.

Participants who were not favored by the government were barred from the race in a particularly shameless, frank, and disdainful manner in majoritarian, single-constituency districts. In the Duma election of 2003, dozens of candidates were denied registration or had their registrations revoked. Sometimes this was simply the result of a struggle between rival candidates themselves, who tried to remove each other from the election by using the courts and the election commissions; in such cases, the CEC and the Supreme Court in Moscow sometimes displayed impartiality and reinstated candidates' registrations. Sometimes this was done by local governments intent on eliminating their critics; in such cases, Moscow could either uphold or not uphold a candidate's disqualification, based on its political desirability. But sometimes it was the result of an order that came directly "from behind the wall" (of the Kremlin)—and in such cases, all appeals by the would-be candidate were futile.

Here are some of the most conspicuous examples of the use of this "electoral technology" in the Duma election of 2003.

In Buryatia's district No. 9, in order to secure the victory of the United Russia candidate Anatoly Starikov, registration was denied to Yuri Skuratov, a CPRF candidate and former general prosecutor, about whom Putin himself (as director of the FSB) had once said on TV that the "person resembling the general prosecutor" on the famous videotape in fact *was* the general prosecutor. Shortly before that, a "person resembling the director of the FSB" had given the very same videotape to Mikhail Shvydkov to have it shown on Rossiya TV (Channel Two). Apparently, after this episode Putin began to think of Skuratov as a personal enemy who was dreaming of revenge.

The former general prosecutor was denied registration on the absurd pretext of "providing unreliable and incomplete information about [his] professional position." Specifically, Skuratov had indicated that he was a department chairman at Moscow State Social University, but had "concealed" from the voters the fact that he was also a professor at this university. In addition, Skuratov's party affiliation statement had been signed not by the head of the Central Committee of the CPRF, Gennady Zyuganov, but by his deputy Valentin Kuptsov.

CEC head Alexander Veshnyakov initially tried to keep up appearances: on November 4, the CEC contested the decision to deny Skuratov registration. But on November 11, the regional election commission upheld the denial. When Skuratov filed another complaint and the CEC met for another session, Veshnyakov, who had grasped the Kremlin's wishes, simply called in sick. In the absence of its leader, the CEC let the decision of the regional election commission stand. Skuratov appealed to the Supreme Court, but the court declined to hear the case.

(A couple of months later, presidential candidate Vladimir Putin indicated in his registration documents that he occupied the position of president, "concealing" from the voters the fact that he was also head of the Security Council and commander-in-chief. Vadim Solovyev, the CPRF's representative in the CEC, posed a malicious question to Veshnyakov about this fact, citing the "Skuratov incident." Putin, however, was permitted to register.)

In addition to being barred from the race in a single-constituency district, the former general prosecutor was also denied the right to run on the CPRF ticket. Skuratov once again tried to appeal, but the Supreme Court refused to take his side.

In Kursk's district No. 97 (Kursk region), Alexander Rutskoy—the former vice president of Russia—had his registration revoked. Like Skuratov, he was suspected of harboring vengeful feelings against the president, because in 2000 the Kremlin had blocked his re-election as governor of the Kursk region. The pretext cited was the diametrical opposite of the one used to deny registration to Skuratov: in his registration documents, Rutskoy *had* indicated his position as rector and pro-rector in charge of general questions at Moscow State Social University, which he effectively occupied. As evidence, Rutskoy submitted a copy of his employment record and a copy of his letter of appointment; but as it turned out, his position did not appear in the university's staff listing at the time of the registration. The Kursk Regional Court refused to hear charges against Rutskoy, finding that the documents had been filed correctly, but Rutskoy's case then went to the Supreme Court, which proceeded to revoke his registration.

In Tikhoretsk's district No. 45 (Krasnodar region), CPRF candidate and Duma deputy Nikolai Denisov had his registration revoked, "which enabled the governor's brother Alexei Tkachev to win in this district."[30] In the Duma, Tkachev—a member of the Central Council of the Agrarian Party of Russia—joined the United Russia faction.

In Moscow's district No. 197 (Orekhovo-Borisovo), Konstantin Zatulin—an advisor to Mayor Luzhkov—ran on the United Russia ticket. For most of the candidates from the so-called "Luzhkov team," Duma seats were almost automatically guaranteed. But Zatulin was a figure with a bad "credit history." At the end of the 1980s, he effectively served as head of a surveillance network that monitored the political activities of Moscow State University students. Thirteen years ago, denunciations ("reports") from informers at the university addressed to Zatulin—about who was reading dissident literature, who sympathized with the underground church, who frequented avant-garde art exhibits—were published for the first time.[31] Since then, these denunciations have been republished by Zatulin's opponents during every election in which he has taken part.

Zatulin has also been dogged by the memory of an early 1990s controversy involving an apartment lottery, organized by commercial entities to which he had ties.[32] It turned out that the apartments won by the participants had never been purchased from the mayor's office by the organizers of the lottery.

Nevertheless, Zatulin himself soon became the owner of real estate in the Alicante, on the Mediterranean coast of Spain.

The mayor's office went to unprecedented lengths to secure a seat in the Duma for this somewhat problematic candidate. Luzhkov sent a special order to Yuri Biriukov, the prefect of Moscow's Southern Administrative District (which includes election district No. 197), saying:

> Recently, much has been done in the Southern Administrative District to make every neighborhood, courtyard, and building more comfortable for Muscovites. To improve coordination and communication, I am directing Konstantin Fyodorovich Zatulin, advisor to the mayor of Moscow, to the Southern Administrative District, where he will remain in constant contact with local government offices and their counterparts in Moscow city government, in order to provide aid in resolving problems for the district's residents.

This was a very transparent hint to the prefect that his job depended on Zatulin getting elected.

Finally, to make candidate Zatulin perfectly happy, his rival for the votes of right-wing voters—the human rights activist Lev Ponomarev, nominated by the SPS and supported by Yabloko—was denied registration for not having submitted all the necessary documents to the election commission in time.

In Achinsk's district No. 47 (Krasnoyarsk region), in response to a complaint by the United Russia candidate and Duma deputy Alexander Klyukin, the regional court annulled the registration of the famous businessman and crime boss Anatoly Bykov because his employment record did not indicate the fact that he had spent time at a temporary detention facility. Among the local population, most of which consists of former convicts of Stalin's era and czarist times, Bykov has the reputation of a Robin Hood and a victim of Moscow's corrupt bureaucracy. Klyukin—an inveterate political party-hopper (having switched from Lebed to Bykov, from Bykov to Zhirinovsky, from Zhirinovsky to Unity)—had no hope of beating Bykov in a fair race. However, Klyukin's Moscow image-makers managed to convince first the election commission and then the judges that "Putin himself" would be displeased if the "bandit" Bykov got elected.

But it is not only in the Krasnoyarsk region that voters, in choosing between officially recognized "criminals" and the administrative oligarchy's candidates—suspected of corruption but officially "clean"—tend to favor the "criminals," especially if they run on a populist, anticorruption, and antibureaucracy platform.

When Andrei Klimentyev announced his candidacy in Kanavin's district No. 120 (Nizhny Novgorod), he had already been disqualified from a mayoral election (in September 2002) and had even been stripped of a mayoral post that he had won (in March 1998) and sentenced to a term in prison. United Russia's candidate, Lyubomir Tyan, had no other hope of beating Klimentyev except by having the election commission revoke his registration. This is precisely what was done—in response to a complaint by another candidate, Denis Gorbushkin—by a decision of the regional court. The pretext cited was that over half the signatures collected in support of Klimentyev's nomination were allegedly inauthentic. On November 28, 2003, the Supreme Court declined to hear Klimentyev's appeal and upheld the regional court's decision. In revenge, Klimentyev called on voters to vote for "none of the above." (In the end, Tyan won with 27 percent; 20 percent went to "none of the above.")

In Privolzhsky district No. 27 (Tatarstan), Duma deputy Sergei Shashurin had his registration revoked. Shashurin headed the regional office of the Russian Pensioners' Party (RPP) and had been Mintimer Shaimiev's opponent in the Tatarstan presidential election of March 2001. (Shashurin had taken second place with an official vote count of 5.78 percent; Shaimiev won with 79.39 percent.)

In Soviet times, the young Shashurin had twice been sentenced to short terms in prison for disorderly conduct and resisting arrest, in 1978 and 1979; specifically, he was convicted of beating up several policemen simultaneously. Later, he was arrested for taking part in the events of 1993 in Moscow on the side of Khasbulatov's parliament, and also was accused of attempting to kill an investigating officer during his interrogation.

On March 18, 1995, still awaiting trial in solitary confinement, Shashurin was elected to Tatarstan's State Council as a deputy from Arbuzov territorial election district No. 80. In

July, the court found him guilty only of resisting a representative of the government, and he was released from custody in the courtroom, getting prison credit for the term of one year, nine months, and thirteen days that he had already served. This instance of a candidate being elected to a regional parliament directly from a prison cell was a rare occurrence for Russia, perhaps the only time it has ever happened.

Shashurin's multi-industry Tan Corporation—which, as rumor has it, began as a racketeering outfit—is an active economic force in the region and is involved in a great amount of noisy charity work. Consequently, Shashurin enjoys an even greater reputation as a Robin Hood in Tatarstan than Bykov does in the Krasnoyarsk region.

President Shaimiev once tried to use Shashurin's popularity for his own interests. Thus, Shashurin's registration as a candidate for the Duma, and his subsequent triumphal election directly from a prison cell, would of course have been impossible without Shaimiev's tacit agreement. The same is apparently true of Shashurin's election to the Duma as a deputy from Tatarstan in 1999.

Shashurin, in turn, began to refrain from personal criticism of Shaimiev and came out in support of his policies. In 2001, however, he challenged Shaimiev in the Tatarstan presidential election, aspiring, if not to victory, then to the status of second most important politician in the republic. In addition, he never ceased his attacks on the Ministry of Internal Affairs, the prosecutor's office, and the leaders of the local administrative-economic clans and government factions. In June 2003, Shashurin accused Tatarstan's minister of internal affairs, Asgat Safarov, of arranging murders and facilitating trade in arms and narcotics.

The Kazan government made plans to take the deputy seat of Tatarstan's Privolzhsky district away from Shashurin and give it to United Russia's candidate, Ayrat Khairullin. But Khairullin had no chance of beating Shashurin in an honest race. At the end of November 2003, Shashurin was registered, but on December 1—the last day when this was possible, literally two hours before the deadline—the civil board of the Tatarstan Supreme Court granted a motion brought by the regional election commission of Privolzhsky district No. 27 to revoke his registration. The infraction that Shashurin had been found guilty of was "bribing voters." The courtroom testimony of the witnesses in the case was never published, and a videotape that allegedly demonstrated Shashurin's "acts of bribery," which had been promised by the election commission, was also never shown.[33]

When the votes were counted after the December 7 election, the Privolzhsky district turned out to have a record-high number of "defaced ballots": a grand total of 37 percent according to the official records. Most likely, all the ballots cast for "none of the above" had been deliberately defaced—they had extra check marks added. If the number of ballots cast for "none of the above" had exceeded 31 percent (Khairullin's official total), it would have been necessary to hold a repeat election. But the number of defaced ballots has no influence on the outcome of an election, so Khairullin was recognized as the winner. Meanwhile, in four precinct committees of Privolzhsky district No. 27, observers from the Union of Right Forces (SPS) were able to detect instances in which extra ballots had been added to the ones actually cast and voting records had been altered.[34]

The subsequent fate of Tatarstan's second most important politician unfolded as follows. On March 15, 2004, Shashurin was arrested in Moscow by the Tatarstan Ministry of Internal Affairs' Main Investigations Directorate and Economic Crimes Directorate. On March 18, he was formally charged with embezzling the material assets of the Tatarkhlebprodukt and Suvar companies in 1996–1997. On March 22, Tatarstan's Main Investigations Directorate additionally charged Shashurin with libel against the heads of Tatarstan's Ministry of Internal Affairs, specifically, the minister of internal affairs, Asgat Safarov; his first deputy, Renat Timerzyanov; and the head of the Main Investigations Directorate, Andrei Vyazanov. The Ministry of Internal Affairs made Shashurin an offer: if he apologized, the charges would be withdrawn. But the "godfather" of the Tan corporation declined the proposal.[35]

The regional election commission of the Kurgan region, in November 2003, brought a motion before the court to revoke the registration of Pavel Fedulev, a businessman and a candidate from Kurgan district No. 96. The court proceeded to revoke Fedulev's registration. The official reason was "bribing voters": Fedulev's Novoselskoye company had given 169,450 rubles to a school and a hospital in the Titovsky district for the purchase of copy machines and a car. In addition, the candidate was accused of using non-campaign-fund resources to pay for his campaign advertising. The local authorities in Kurgan wanted to secure deputy Nikolai Bezborodov's re-election to the Duma. (Bezborodov was a nonpartisan candidate who joined the United Russia faction after being elected.)

In Tyumen's district No. 179, in order to secure victory for Gennady Raikov, head of the People's Party of the Russian Federation (NPRF), the registrations of his two main rivals, Alexander Cherepanov (a radical Communist from the Russian Communist Workers' Party, nominated by the CPRF) and Vadim Bondar (SPS), were disqualified. The same reason was cited in both cases: the candidates were charged with illegally using their official positions because their own deputy assistants had taken part in their election campaigns. The CEC upheld the annulment of the registrations. In the words of CEC advisory member Vadim Prokhorov, the committee's decision was influenced by the "powerful lobbying capabilities" of Viktor Ivanov, Putin's deputy chief of staff, who was "taking down candidates right and left to clear the way for Gennady Raikov, who cannot withstand any competition."[36]

After allowing the Ivanovsk regional election commission to bar Bondar and Cherepanov from the race, the CEC at once reinstated the registration of Tatyana Yakovleva (Ivanovsk region district No. 80), a United Russia candidate whose registration had been revoked by the regional election commission to make way for the region's Communist governor, Vladimir Tikhonov, and his protégé and CPRF regional committee secretary, Galina Kusmina.

In Kineshma district No. 81 (also in the Ivanovsk region), despite the intervention of the same Communist governor, the local court revoked the registration of CPRF candidate Valentina Krutova for using her government-issued car to drive around the region. The way was being cleared for United Russia candidate Mikhail Babich, assistant to the minister of economic development. The decision to revoke Krutova's registration was upheld in the Supreme Court of the Russian Federation. In this instance, Moscow's "administrative resource" turned out to be more powerful than that of the Communist governor.

In Vostochny district No. 207 (St. Petersburg), the front-runner, Alexander Morozov—a deputy in the city's legislative assembly—was taken out of the race at the request of the United Russia candidate, Irina Rodnina. Her campaign head-quarters had unearthed a pretext in the documents pertaining to Morozov's educational background: his diplomas from Chu-vash State University and the Tobol Pedagogical Institute had turned out to be false. In response, Morozov's team conducted a successful campaign to encourage voters to vote for "none of the above," and Rodnina failed to win the Duma seat. A repeat election had to be held, and this time Morozov won; the gov-ernment this time supported Morozov in order to forestall a victory by Matviyenko's former rival, Anna Markova.

In Vladivostok's district No. 52, the local initiative to revoke Viktor Cherepkov's registration found no support in Moscow. On October 8, 2003, the local election commission denied Cherepkov registration on the pretext that he had failed to sub-mit a complete set of necessary documents. This was the twen-tieth time that Cherepkov had been barred from participating in an election at one level or another. On October 10, the Primo-rye Regional Court ruled in favor of the election commission. In Cherepkov's own opinion, this was done in order to give an advantage to his rival from the United Russia party, Pavel Patsvald. According to electoral regulations, the documents required for registration could be submitted at any time dur-ing the forty-five days preceding the election; in other words, Cherepkov still had time to register until the end of October.

On October 15, the CEC declined to hear Cherepkov's appeal against the Vladivostok regional election commission, on the pretext that he had already filed an appeal with the regional court. Cherepkov, however, claimed that he had not filed such an appeal; the appeal had been filed, ostensibly on his behalf, by individuals who had actually been hired by his opponents. But on October 23, the Supreme Court overruled the regional court's decision, and on October 27, the CEC reg-istered Cherepkov as a candidate for the Duma, instructing the regional election commission to issue a registration certificate to him. Even after this, the head of Primorye's regional election commission, Sergei Knyazev, continued trying to make things difficult for Cherepkov; he sent a declaration to Moscow stating that his committee stood by its decision.

A second attempt to revoke Cherepkov's registration also failed. Its initiators were another rival, Yevgeny Kolupayev, and his brother, Anatoly Kolupayev, head of Primorye's LDPR office. Yevgeny Kolupayev brought a motion before the Primorye Regional Court to have Cherepkov's registration annulled for infringing electoral regulations: Cherepkov had repeatedly flown to Moscow to file appeals with the CEC and the Supreme Court, using his right as a Duma deputy to obtain a free ticket. On December 1, the Primorye Regional Court rejected Kolupayev's claim.

Cherepkov won 31.69 percent of the vote on December 7 and thus became a deputy in the fourth convocation of the State Duma of the Russian Federation.

In Chertanovo district No. 204 (Moscow), two candidates—including former KGB officer Vladimir Gruzdev (United Russia)—made an attempt to disqualify the joint candidate of the SPS and Yabloko, Vladimir Kara-Murza, on the grounds that Kara-Murza, after being officially nominated by the SPS, had "illegally" informed voters that he was also backed by Yabloko. This absurd claim was rejected by the court, but Kara-Murza was still required to present a declaration signed by Grigory Yavlinsky.

OUTCOME OF THE ELECTION OF DECEMBER 7, 2003

With a voter turnout of 55.75 percent, the United Russia party—whose slogan was "Together with the president!"—won 37.57 percent of the vote on December 7, 2003, according to official records, and 228 of the Duma's 450 seats (120 party-list candidates, 100 candidates from majoritarian districts, and eight more nonpartisan candidates backed by United Russia or candidates from affiliated parties). With the addition of single-constituency deputies from the People's Party (seventeen seats), the Union of Right Forces (three seats), the Agrarian Party of Russia (two seats), as well as the non-party candidates and candidates who had switched parties (two from Homeland, one from Yabloko, one from the CPRF), United Russia's faction in the Duma added up to 306 seats. In other words, United Russia won more than a constitutional majority in the Duma.

The oppositional CPRF won only 12.61 percent of the vote and 51 seats. The LDPR, which sells its votes to the highest bidder in the Duma, won 11.45 percent and 36 seats. The semi-oppositional, left-nationalist Homeland bloc (Sergei Glazyev, Dmitry Rogozin, and Sergei Baburin) won 9.02 percent and 37 seats; 38 deputies entered the Homeland faction; and in February 2004, a pro-Putin subgroup effectively emerged within the faction (at least 17 out of 38 deputies), under the leadership of Dmitry Rogozin.

Yabloko and the SPS failed to pass the 5 percent threshold, winning four and three seats, respectively, in majoritarian districts. (Immediately after the election, all three SPS candidates and one Yabloko candidate joined the United Russia faction.) In addition, about five small-party and non-party democrats were elected to the Duma. Three seats remained empty—for districts in which the greatest number of votes had been cast for "none of the above."

VIOLATIONS OF ELECTION LAW

As international organizations noted, the election campaign and the election itself were completely dominated by the rule of the "administrative resource."[37]

Observers from different parties, reporters, and ordinary citizens who came to vote on December 7, noted an enormous number of violations that paved the way for falsifying outcomes in favor of the "ruling party" and/or constituted such falsifications.

We will describe only a few examples.

In precinct No. 1714 (Orekhovo-Borisovo's district No. 197 in Moscow, election of Konstantin Zatulin), the lights were suddenly turned off while ballots were being counted. The committee sent all the observers out of the room, and for some reason all the windows were opened. In the dark, anything at all could be passed through the open windows—from a stack of filled-out ballots to a whole ballot box. Lights were turned off and observers were expelled at other precincts in this district as well.

Many observers formed the impression that the lights had been turned off on purpose, and that in their absence ballots cast for "none of the above" had been either removed or defaced, and extra ballots had been added for Zatulin.

In precinct No. 2702 (Tushinsky district No. 200 in Moscow, election of Vladimir Vasiliev), an elderly female voter who had a portable ballot box carried out to her noticed that the box was not sealed. Such a ballot box could have any number of "desirable" ballots added to it and any number of "undesirable" ones removed. At the voter's request, attempts were made to reseal the box, but the paper could not be glued onto the plastic box. Other portable ballot boxes had similar properties, convenient for tampering.

In precinct No. 622 (Medvedkovo district No. 196, election of Georgy Boos), voters with absentee ballots were not given ballots for voting in single-constituency districts (which was absolutely correct), but they were nonetheless asked to sign not for two ballots (the party-list Duma election and the mayoral election), but for all three. A voter who noted this fact insisted that his signature be crossed off, but he noticed that *all* voters with absentee ballots had signed their names three times in the ballot record books. This warrants the suspicion that the unused ballots for which voters had signed were added to Boos's total when votes were being counted.

In Babushkinsky district No. 192 in Moscow (election of Sergei Shirokov), observers from the camp of the Yabloko candidate Sergei Mitrokhin were denied copies of the voting records until OSCE representatives intervened at their request. After the polls closed, Yabloko's observers noted that unsealed ballots were being transported from precinct election commissions to the regional election commission.[38]

As a consequence, according to the official data, Mitrokhin lost to Shirokov by 1.5 percent.

During this election, and by contrast with previous years, observers in Moscow frequently received copies of records that were riddled with the same kinds of problems that had always been characteristic of Tatarstan and Bashkortostan: many precinct committees refused to sign the records without first having them approved by the territorial committees. Consequently, observers were given copies of records only after they had been "checked" and approved by the territorial committees.

In precinct No. 1064 of Balashov's district No. 157 (election of Pyotr Kamshilov; Krasnoznamenny village, Samoilov district, Saratov region), the secretary of the precinct committee added a packet of ballots to the ballot box in front of the voters. Observers complained, but the head of the committee refused to listen.[39]

In precinct No. 1546 in the Rostov region, the composite records of the GAS-Vybory electronic voting system showed that zero absentee ballots had been handed out, while the copies of the same committee's records received by the CPRF observer indicate that 406 absentee ballots had been handed out.[40]

In Ingushetia, the election outcomes were completely falsified in favor of United Russia. One of the losing candidates, Musa Ozdoyev—head of the Ingush office of the People's Party and by no means an opposition candidate—checked the records of several precinct commissions with the assistance of his friends and relatives by going around to voters' homes and interviewing them.

In precinct No. 67 (Ingush district No. 13, election of Bashir Kodzoyev), fifty-three people failed to recognize their own signatures, their passport information, or both. Forty-six citizens could not be interviewed because they did not reside at the addresses indicated on the voters' list: some of them had long ago moved to other cities, some to other countries, and some had died.[41] Musa Ozdoyev observed:

> The precinct committees were in a hurry. They simply had no time to find voters' names for the enormous number of ballots that were added to the ballot boxes after the polls had closed. . . . In the already mentioned precinct No. 67, for example, United Russia won 164 votes, and this is what the precinct committee's records indicate. But in the records of the territorial committee, United Russia's total has grown to 1,784 votes. The exorbitant difference of 1,620 votes was only partly offset by lowering the totals of the other parties; for the most part, this hole was patched up by filling in new ballots for about a thousand citizens.[42]

In some of the other national republics—above all, Mago-medali Magomedov's Dagestan, Alexander Dzasokhov's North Ossetia, and Valery Kokov's Kabardino-Balkariya—the Duma election outcomes were falsified on as large a scale as in Murat Zyazikov's Ingushetia.

In April 2004, Ingushetia's Supreme Court ruled against a claim brought by People's Assembly deputy Musa Ozdoyev against Ingushetia's election commission and denied his request to invalidate the commission's final vote count in the December election. The courts declined to review the overwhelming majority of claims brought against the results of the election in various districts.

QUESTIONS ABOUT THE NUMBER OF ELIGIBLE VOTERS

According to the State Committee on Statistics, 2,160,500 people died in Russia in 2003. Taking into account the birth rate and immigration, the population of the country fell by 767,600 during that year.[43] The vast majority of the over two million people who died were voters. Newborn babies and practically all immigrants (with the exception of a few thousand) are not voters. Yet according to official statistics, the number of voters in the country did not fall in 2003, but rose. In the first half of 2003 alone, according to the records of the CEC, the electorate grew by two million.[44]

Similarly, over the course of two weeks between the first and second rounds of voting in the presidential election of summer 1996, the number of voters increased by 100,000. Between the Duma election of December 1999 and the presidential election of March 2000, the number of voters grew by 1,300,000.

Irina Zbarskaya, head of the demography and census department at the State Committee on Statistics, gave the following official response to *Nezavisimaya Gazeta*'s query concerning these figures:

> Despite the fact that Russia's population has been shrinking since 1992, the number of people age eighteen years and over has grown by 3.7 million over the past ten years, which has resulted in a growing number of voters. This increase has been due to the aging of people born at the end of the 1970s and the beginning of the 1980s, and to

immigration. . . . According to estimates, the increase in the number
of people in this age group in 2003 may have amounted to approximately 300,000.[45]

But 300,000 is still not 2,000,000! In the first half of 2003 alone,
the CEC (or its sources of information) counted an increase in
the number of voters that was almost seven times as great as
the State Committee on Statistics' forecast!

It turned out, however, that this was not the limit. "At a CEC
meeting on February 10, 2004, it was revealed that, in the span
of only a few months, the number of voters had unaccountably
risen by 400,000."[46] Thus, in 2003 the number of voters supposedly grew by 2,400,000, when according to population data it
grew by only about 300,000.

The CEC receives its information about citizens who are
eligible to vote from the regional governments. These regional
governments are responsible to the central government for
carrying out its voting plans, and it is precisely they that are
most interested in "dead souls" whose existence is registered
only on paper. In an interview with *Nezavisimaya Gazeta*,
Boris Makarenko, deputy general manager of the Center for
Political Technologies, pointed out that "'dead souls' cannot
vote. And since they won't show up at the polls, their ballots
can be cast for them by someone named 'the administrative
resource.'"[47]

Subtracting the State Committee on Statistics' realistic estimate of 300,000 from the 2,400,000 voters added in 2003, we
get a difference of 2,100,000 votes. This is approximately the
size of the reserve of votes that local governments and election
commissions have at their disposal for "adding" to the totals of
"desired" candidates and parties.

EVIDENCE OF FRAUD

The most obvious fraud, naturally, took place in occupied
Chechnya. In the Grozny district, United Russia won 97.25 percent of the vote—a record for Russia, especially remarkable
because United Russia is the "war party" (although the military also voted in Chechnya, in addition to Chechens). But even
more remarkable are the outcomes for specific precincts:

Precinct No. 66 (Chechen electoral district No. 32): 1,005 voters, 886 ballots handed out, 884 of them (99.77 percent) cast for United Russia and two invalidated.

Precinct No. 90 (the same Chechen district): 666 ballots handed out, all 666 cast for United Russia.[48]

Furthermore, according to Alexander Veshnyakov himself, in Chechnya and Ingushetia the number of ballots cast exceeded the number of voters by 11 percent, which was explained by President Akhmad Kadyrov's press secretary as a result of "very intense immigration."[49] There is a more realistic explanation: clandestine sabotage by certain election commissions, which, by deliberately "over-fulfilling" their assignments, tried to draw attention to the fact that election outcomes were being falsified. At the same time, the number of ballots cast was also found to exceed the number of registered voters in the Moscow region by 4.5 percent, and in the Kaluga region by 5 percent.[50]

Traditionally, election outcomes have been drastically "corrected" in a number of national republics, such as Bashkortostan, Tatarstan, Kalmykia, and Dagestan. As one Tatar official admitted off the record, "in the morning we planned to give them 78 percent, but then we received an order from Moscow not to raise the bar and to stop at 60 percent."[51]

Despite the various obstacles that they encountered in many regions, the Union of Right Forces (SPS), Yabloko, and the Communists were able to collect a rather large number of copies of precinct records. Both Yabloko and the CPRF used their copies to recount the votes, and they immediately discovered significant discrepancies. "We reviewed 12,500 records," said Grigory Yavlinsky, "and found that 16 percent of them did not match the CEC's official data."[52] According to Boris Nemtsov, the SPS obtained similar results: "The party's executive committee labored day and night to review 14,000 copies. A fifth of them turned out to be falsified."[53]

Galina Mikhaleva, head of Yabloko's analytic center at the time, said the most common discrepancies were found in column 10 (number of valid ballots) of the precinct copies and the composite records of the territorial election commissions and the CEC. For example, "the records from Smolensk region precinct No. 389 indicate that the committee counted 964 valid ballots. The CEC lists 1,020 valid ballots for the same precinct. . . . Udmurtia, precinct No. 817: the precinct records show 762 valid ballots; the CEC indicates 1,108."[54]

The Communists noted the same thing. In precinct No. 1574 in the Rostov region, the figures in column 10 did not match up: in the records of the GAS-Vybory electronic voting system, thirteen extra votes were added to United Russia's total.[55]

According to Mikhaleva, "Officially, over half of the registered voters participated in the election. In reality, voter turnout was far lower—certainly below 50 percent."[56]

Yabloko identified a number of discrepancies in the official records themselves. This led to the discovery that election commissions had illegally indicated in their records that at least 250,000 ballots had been handed out for voting in the common federal district. Normally, citizens voting outside their home precincts are given absentee ballots by their election commissions. If they are voting not only outside their home precinct but outside their home district, they are given ballots for voting in the common federal district, but receive no ballots for voting in single-constituency districts. A total of 572,926 people voted by absentee ballot on December 7, 2003, and 424,926 of them voted in their own districts. The difference had to be 147,997. But the official records indicate that the election commissions handed out 403,809 ballots for voting in the federal district. That amounts to more than 250,000 "extra" ballots.[57]

It is not difficult to guess for which party they were cast.

Observers' copies of records also indicate that election commission records were falsified. In this way, votes were stolen outright.

In Privolzhsky district No. 27 (Tatarstan), as already mentioned, the SPS's observers found that records had been falsified by four precinct committees.[58]

In electoral precinct No. 1559 (Samara region), comparison of the record copy handed out to the Communist observer with the official composite record of the GAS-Vybory electronic voting system revealed that 60 votes had been deducted from the CPRF's total, 20 from Yabloko's total, 31 from the total of the "New Course–Automobile Russia" party, 20 votes from the total of the Rus' party, and 50 votes had been added to the SPS's total.[59]

According to Yabloko's analytic center, for "precinct No. 284 in North Ossetia, the record given to our observer proves that Yabloko got sixteen votes. The CEC sharply reduced the number of 'wrong' votes to six. In precinct No. 233, seventeen people voted for our party; we were given only seven votes. . . . Also in precinct No. 233, the records indicate 218 votes for United Russia, but the CEC's records give United Russia 356 votes."

According to the CPRF, records from precinct No. 925 (Orenburg region) indicate that 536 people voted for the CPRF; in other official records, these votes shrank to 136.[60] Ivan Melnikov, deputy head of the CPRF Central Committee and a professor of mathematics at Moscow State University, commented:

> They said we got 12 percent, but I think our actual outcome was more on the order of 18 percent. Two-thirds of the election commission record copies that we possess differ from the records that were used to establish the official vote count. And most importantly, they contain internal contradictions. If you add up the votes that were cast for all of the parties, you find that it is greater than the number of people who voted.[61]

According to FairGame, a parallel system for vote-counting created by the Communists, the figures on 60,000 records (two-thirds of their total number) differ from the official outcomes announced by the CEC. "The number of all ballots that were handed out and the sum of all valid, defaced, annulled, etc., ballots do not coincide. This can mean only one thing: extra ballots were physically added to the original total. FairGame's operators find that 3.5 million extra ballots were added in the country as a whole." The greatest numbers were added in the Kurgan, Rostov, Samara, Orel, Tver, and Stavropol regions, Dagestan, Tatarstan, Bashkortostan, and Moscow. According to the Communists, Yabloko and the SPS had actually passed the 5 percent threshold, while United Russia was given an extra 3 or 4 percent.[62]

In some places, it was not only United Russia's totals that got an artificial boost, but those of the SPS as well. This is what happened in the Samara region, for example.[63]

In its official letter to the CEC, the CPRF gave the following outcomes for its parallel vote count (based on a review of 94 percent of the copies of precinct records): United Russia, 33.1 percent (37.57 percent according to the CEC); CPRF, 12.73 percent (12.61 percent); LDPR, 11.46 percent (11.45 percent); Homeland, 10.69 percent (9.02 percent); Yabloko, 5.98 percent (4.30 percent); SPS, 5.12 percent (3.97 percent).[64]

In addition to the almost complete alternative vote count carried out by the Communists, Yabloko's large-scale recounts, and the SPS's selective recounts, we also have figures from two different exit polls. One of them was conducted by the ROMIR monitoring center in conjunction with the *Moscow Times*, a Moscow-based English-language newspaper, and Renaissance Capital Bank; the other was done by the Public Opinion Foundation (FOM). According to both exit polls, United Russia got less than 37.57 percent of the vote; and according to FOM's exit poll, Yabloko passed the 5 percent threshold.

There is another piece of evidence indicating that Yabloko got more than 5 percent. This is how Viktor Shenderovich puts it in *Novaya Gazeta*:

> Given: when the votes were counted to the east of the Urals, Yabloko ended up with 4.2 percent. Then 10 percent of the voters in Moscow and St. Petersburg voted for this party (which is equal to 1 percent of Russia's population). Question: how many percent did Yabloko get? We look at the answer, and we see basically the same number that Yabloko had to the east of the Urals. . . .[65]

Summing up the findings of the alternative vote counts and exit polls, we can state with a high degree of certainty that for Russia as a whole, at least 3 or 4 percent was added to United Russia's totals. Because official voter turnout went up as a result of these artificially added votes, the shares of the other parties decreased, and in the case of Yabloko, the loss of 1 percent turned out to be fatal. In addition, the Communists, Yabloko, and other parties and blocs, as well as the "none of the above" category, simply had votes taken away from them and transferred to United Russia—particularly in the national republics. In single-constituency districts, too, votes were "redistributed" in favor of the government-backed candidates (United Russia and the NPRF).

If there had been no falsifications, Yabloko—and perhaps the SPS as well—would have had representation in the fourth convocation of the Duma; the Communists would have had a few more seats; and United Russia, together with its allies from the NPRF, would have been able to get about half or even somewhat more than half the seats, an absolute majority or something close to it, but definitely not two-thirds, a constitutional majority. In order to pass many different laws, particularly those requiring a constitutional majority, Putin's regime would have had to take into account either the opinion of the Communists or the opinion of the liberals—as happened in the third convocation of the Duma.

Shortly before the official final results were announced, the Communists submitted to the CEC approximately two hundred copies of precinct records that contained the most conspicuous discrepancies with the records of the territorial committees. As in earlier elections, however, the CEC had no intention of taking the record copies into account.

First of all, the law allows election commissions to rewrite records on the pretext of correcting mistakes. Therefore, higher-level election commissions effectively have the right to declare discrepancies between copies of the original records and later versions to be a completely natural phenomenon, and to disregard those discrepancies.

Second, few observers manage to obtain accurate copies. Although precinct election commissions are required to hand out copies of their records upon request, these copies are often flawed and incomplete, and therefore are unfit to be used in court. As for the Duma election of 2003 and the incriminating copies of precinct committee records, Alexander Veshnyakov has stated that "only about 20 copies of the records are filled out correctly from a legal point of view. The rest have no legal significance."[66]

Mikhail Shneider, coordinator of the election observers' program at SPS headquarters, believes that Veshnyakov's objections about legal niceties are unsubstantiated:

> The law that governs Duma elections states that the precinct election commission must notarize the copies of the records. But it does not prescribe how exactly they must be notarized. All of our observers received their copies directly from the heads of the precinct commissions. And if the copies were filled out incorrectly in some way, then that's not our problem.[67]

Nonetheless, although it was Veshnyakov's department that gave observers copies that were unfit to use in court, this naturally became a problem for the parties that sent the observers. Based on its copies of the records, Yabloko filed about 100 lawsuits in 44 regions to have the election results invalidated. In most instances, the courts simply refused to hear the case. The Novgorod Regional Court refused to hear Yabloko's suit to invalidate the Duma election outcomes in the region by claiming that such cases must be heard by district courts; the Supreme Court upheld the Novgorod Regional Court's decision.[68] About fifteen of Yabloko's claims were granted a hearing. By June 2004, all of them had been thrown out of court because the record copies had "no legal weight."[69]

INTERNATIONAL OBSERVERS' EVALUATIONS

International observers assessed the parliamentary elections of December 7, 2003, in a negative fashion.

David Atkinson, rapporteur on Russia for the Parliamentary Assembly of the Council of Europe (PACE), commented that the elections were "technically free, but not fair":

> In my opinion and the opinion of PACE, the Duma election campaign was intrinsically and fundamentally flawed, so these elections could not be described as fair. The reason for this is the obvious partiality and lack of objectivity in the coverage of the election campaign on state-run or state-controlled television. Preference was crudely given to one or two specific parties at the expense of all the rest.[70]

The OSCE concurred with this assessment. Among its comments were the following:

> Russia has failed to meet many of its obligations before the OSCE and the Council of Europe to conduct a fair and free democratic election. . . . Democracy is regressing in Russia.
>
> The extensive use of the state apparatus and media favoritism to the benefit of United Russia [created] an unfair environment on a countrywide basis for other parties and candidates contesting these elections. This undermines the fundamental principle that parties and candidates should be able to compete with each other on an equal footing.
>
> At the local level, the government often used taxpayers' money for the benefit of a specific party.
>
> This election can no longer be considered either fair or democratic. All of this has led to a distortion of the election outcomes.
>
> It is unfair when laws and regulations are applied not to everyone equally, but selectively. . . .
>
> Russia has become anti-democratic. . . .

"DIRTY ELECTIONS" IN KALMYKIA

Two elections took place in Kalmykia at the same time in December 2003: the election for the State Duma deputy from Kalmykia (in district No. 15), and the election to the People's Khural (Kalmykia's regional parliament).

According to the official records, United Russia's list won 50.63 percent of the vote in Kalmykia, which considerably exceeded the "ruling party's" total for Russia as a whole (37.57 percent). According to the same official records, the United Russia candidate Gennady Kulik carried Kalmykia's single-constituency district No. 15 with 41.10 percent of the vote, beating the non-party candidate Valery Ochirov, who had been Kirsan Ilyumzhinov's rival in Kalmykia's presidential election in 1993. It is precisely for such wonderful results that the heads of the national republics are so well loved in the Kremlin.

But Kalmykia was the only region that failed to submit its election results to the CEC before the appointed deadline. According to the opposition, this happened because precinct committee outcomes kept being revised and "corrected" by the territorial election commissions.

On December 8, Ochirov's supporters announced that they had evidence of falsifications. Specifically, the records of the precinct election commissions were filled in with a pencil and then rewritten with a pen at the territorial level immediately before being sent to the computers of the GAS-Vybory electronic voting system. After this, the corrected results were again returned to the precinct committees for revision.[72] The opposition counted more than 10,000 votes that were stolen from Ochirov and given to Kulik.[73]

Several thousand outraged voters came out to demonstrate in the center of Elista. On December 9, 2003, the opposition's representatives met with President Ilyumzhinov and presented him with an ultimatum: either the votes must be recounted or he must resign. Ilyumzhinov took twenty-four hours to think about it. In the meantime, Sergei Fridinsky, deputy general prosecutor of the Southern Federal District, and Viktor Kazantsev, the president's plenipotentiary representative in the Southern District, arrived in Elista with several special forces units from neighboring regions (Rostov, Astrakhan, Volgograd). These troops blocked the entrances to the city in order to prevent the opposition from receiving support from the rural districts.

The demonstrators were also surrounded by two rings of special forces troops. The opposition was persuaded to call off the demonstration and was promised that a committee would be created to look into the allegations of voter fraud. However, on December 11, 2003, the Southern Federal District's press relations service disavowed the entire agreement and stated that Kazantsev had promised nothing to the demonstrators.[74]

ELECTION CONTROVERSY IN THE KIROV REGION

Elections for a number of regional leaders—mayor of Moscow, president of Bashkortostan, and the governors of the Vologda, Kirov, Moscow, Novosibirsk, Orenburg, Sakhalin, Tambov, Tver, and Yaroslavl regions—took place simultaneously with the Duma elections on December 7, 2003.

The election for governor of the Kirov region was particularly dishonest and controversial. The principal contenders for power in the region were Nikolai Shaklein, a Duma deputy and former deputy prosecutor of the Russian Federation; Alexander Strelnikov, head of the region's legislative assembly; Oleg Valenchuk, a businessman; and Georgy Briling, president of the Azot Agrochemical Corporation. The first three of these candidates were all United Russia members. United Russia's Moscow leadership and Sergei Kiriyenko, the president's plenipotentiary representative in the Volga Federal District, came out in support of Strelnikov, while Valenchuk was expelled from United Russia for taking part in the race. Briling had a high chance of winning, based on his financial capabilities and because United Russia had failed to settle on a single candidate.

On November 27, 2003, at Strelnikov's request, the regional court revoked Briling's registration for spending 500,000 rubles in excess of his campaign fund to promote his candidacy, and for bribing voters through free concerts featuring the popular singers Dmitry Malikov and Valentina Tolkunova. In response, Briling sent a counterclaim to Moscow and in the meantime called on his supporters to vote for "none of the above."

In order to block Briling's attempt to have the case reviewed by the Supreme Court, criminal proceedings that had been initiated against him earlier were once again revived (in connection with the transfer of the Kirovo-Chepetsk Chemical Combine's assets to its daughter companies, and for losses caused by the Azot Corporation to Gazprom's Mazhregiongaz). On November 30, Briling's apartment and office in Kirovo-Chepetsk were raided, and documents, photographs, and computers were confiscated. Since Briling himself was not found at either location, he was put on the wanted list.

In the election on December 7, United Russia's principal candidate, Strelnikov, won only 6 percent of the vote. With a voter turnout of 54.74 percent, Shaklein (33.67 percent) and Valenchuk (14.08 percent) went on to a second round; 10.19 percent had voted for "none of the above."

United Russia came out in support of Shaklein in the second round, while Briling left for Spain and from there continued to encourage voters to choose "none of the above" using his regional election team. His campaign flyers accused Shaklein of having ties with the "economic mafia" of Sergei Kiriyenko, the plenipotentiary representative, and promised that he would pay for all expenses connected with holding a repeat election if "none of the above" received a majority of votes.

On December 18, the police set up a blockade around Briling's regional and district headquarters. They were looking for his flyers. Since they had no warrant to search the premises, they searched people and cars on the pretext of inspecting their documents. One day later, the police finally obtained a search warrant, the doors of Briling's office were forced open, and 20,000 copies of a campaign newspaper were removed from the premises along with Briling's "personal letters" to voters calling on them to vote for "none of the above."

On December 21, Shaklein won in the second round.

ELECTION FOR PRESIDENT OF BASHKORTOSTAN

In Bashkortostan, too, a presidential election took place concurrently with the Duma election.

Murtaza Rakhimov had become president in 1998 by having the registrations of all his serious rivals annulled and leaving as his only "opponent" a candidate who himself encouraged voters to cast their ballots for Rakhimov. In 2003, Rakhimov tried to employ similar tactics again. The role of the straw-man candidate was assigned to Bashkortostan's senator Igor Izmestyev. Rakhimov faced a threat from Ralif Safin, former vice president of Lukoil and a Federation Council member from the Altai Republic (and father of the popular singer Alsu); from Alexander Arinin, the leader of Bashkortostan's Rus' coalition; and especially from Sergei Veremeyenko, co-owner of Mezhprombank, because Veremeyenko was backed by the "*siloviki* oligarchs"—the military-chekist wing of President Putin's entourage (Igor Sechin, Viktor Ivanov). Rakhimov, however, completely controlled the "administrative resource" within the republic, and also had allies in the "family" wing of the administrative oligarchy (Alexander Voloshin, Vladislav Surkov).

Veremeyenko was first denied registration on October 27, after Izmestyev accused Veremeyenko of using non-campaign-fund resources to promote himself in the mainstream press. According to Veremeyenko himself, the articles that were held against him had no connection to his campaign and were ordinary newspaper and magazine materials, for which he bore no responsibility.

The CEC initially misjudged the power dynamic within the Kremlin, took Veremeyenko's side, and on November 3 demanded that the matter be reviewed once more. On November 11, the Bashkortostan election commission denied Veremeyenko registration a second time on the same grounds. At the same time, a motion to disqualify Safin's registration was brought before the Supreme Court of Bashkortostan. Plans to disqualify Arinin's registration were also in the works.

On November 17, the CEC unanimously voted in favor of registering Veremeyenko as a candidate and compelling the head of Bashkortostan's election commission, Boris Kinzyagulov, to give him his registration certification within three days. However, just as Veremeyenko was about to be handed his registration certification on November 20, the election commission received a ruling from the Leninsky District Court in the city of Ufa, prohibiting "Bashkortostan's CEC to carry out in any form the resolution made by the Russian Federation's CEC on November 11, 2003, regarding S. A. Veremeyenko's appeal." The district court's decision came as a result of a motion brought before the court by a certain resident of Ufa who claimed that the Russian Federation's CEC had deprived him of his rights as a citizen by repealing the Bashkortostan election commission's decision.

After the CEC reminded Bashkortostan's election commission about the sad fate of the Krasnoyarsk regional election commission (which had been dissolved in 2002 for disobeying the CEC), Veremeyenko received his registration certification. As a consequence, attempts to disqualify candidates Safin and Arinin ceased in Ufa, since this would have now strengthened Veremeyenko as the leading opposition candidate.

On December 3, a candidate for the State Duma, Airat Dilmukhametov, informed Veremeyenko and Safin that President Rakhimov's printing plant was clandestinely printing fake ballots for the presidential election. Late in the evening, Dilmukhametov, Veremeyenko, and Safin sent statements about this fact to the FSB regional office, the prosecutor's office, and the Ministry of Internal Affairs; and that night Veremeyenko's and Safin's supporters and CPRF activists surrounded the printing plant. By that time, between 500,000 and 800,000 fake ballots had been printed.

At five o'clock in the morning, Bashkirian law enforcement agents reached the printing plant and began to block the building from the protestors. An attempt was made to transport the ballots out of the printing plant inside a police vehicle, but the crowd stopped the car. Then, fifteen minutes later, a fire started inside the facility. The opposition called the fire department, but the police did not allow opposition activists to approach the burning building either before or after the firemen arrived. Most of the fake ballots were burned and did not end up in the hands of the FSB and the prosecutor's office.

Based on the scale of the events, however, the Bashkortostan prosecutor's office decided that Rakhimov's days were numbered and initiated criminal proceedings in accordance with Article 142 (falsification of election documents) and Article 167 (willful destruction of property) of the Russian Criminal Code. On December 4, 2003, Vladimir Korostylev—head of the investigation and Bashkortostan's first deputy general prosecutor—told Interfax that the individual who had placed the order for the fake ballots had been identified; this was the Bashkortostan president's chief of staff, Rady Khabirov. CEC head Alexander Veshnyakov commented: "If the details of this venture—which may have involved government officials—are corroborated, then all guilty parties must be punished to the fullest extent of the law."[75]

Then the tide turned. A prediction made earlier by the political strategist Marat Gelman came true: "Democracy in Bashkiria will be sacrificed to the necessity of collecting the greatest possible number of votes for United Russia."[76]

First, the republic's prosecutor, Florid Baykov, disavowed the statement by his deputy Korostylev concerning Khabirov's involvement in the printing of the fake ballots, calling it "premature." Next, Sergei Veremeyenko's brother Alexander Veremeyenko "voluntarily" resigned from his important post as head of the Bashkortostan tax ministry. The CEC stopped responding to questions about the "Bashkirian affair." On the Chelyabinsk–

Ufa highway, all vehicles carrying opposition literature about "Bashkiria-gate" printed outside Bashkortostan were stopped.

Rakhimov was the frontrunner in the first round of voting, on December 7, 2003, winning 44 percent of the vote according to official records (Veremeyenko, 25.38 percent; Safin, 23.03 percent). United Russia won seats in all six of Bashkortostan's majoritarian, single-constituency districts; its total in Bashkortostan's common federal district was 33.89 percent.

Committees at various levels received a total of 199 complaints about violations committed during the Bashkortostan presidential election; these complaints came mainly from Veremeyenko's lawyers. In six precincts where the violations had been most obvious, the results were invalidated. Twelve of Safin's supporters went on a hunger strike in his headquarters, demanding that the results of the whole election be annulled.

On December 8, President Putin gave Rakhimov a favorable reception in the Kremlin. From this moment, the outcome of the election was no longer open to doubt. On December 12, the president's plenipotentiary representative Kiriyenko and deputy chief of staff Surkov visited Rakhimov in Ufa and praised Bashkortostan for "stability and inter-ethnic unity."[77]

On December 15, Vladimir Korostylev—the deputy prosecutor of Bashkortostan who had been outed as Rakhimov's enemy—was dismissed from his post, while the republic's prosecutor—who had vacillated—resigned voluntarily. Several opposition websites were shut down. Large numbers of Veremeyenko's, Safin's, and Arinin's supporters started losing their jobs, in both the public and the private sector.

Veremeyenko was invited to Moscow to meet with Surkov, after which, on December 18, he announced that he had "made the decision to wind down his election campaign, but he would still take part in the election, as he had promised voters."[78] Surkov also met with Safin, after which Safin's supporters in Ufa ended their hunger strike.

In the second round of voting, on December 21, Rakhimov was elected president, winning 78 percent of the vote, with a voter turnout of 69 percent, according to official records. Veremeyenko, who had "wound down" his campaign, won 15.85 percent.

THE PRESIDENTIAL CAMPAIGN AS AN OPERATION BY POLITICAL STRATEGISTS

The Russian presidential election campaign began at the end of December 2003. By contrast with the Duma election, in which the Kremlin restricted the number of candidates and parties, in the presidential election the Kremlin aimed to expand the list of candidates. This was done, first, in order to present voters with a choice at least on a formal level—even though they lacked any choice in reality—and thus to render the election legitimate in the eyes of the West. And second, it was done in order to prevent an "obscenely low" voter turnout, which was a real possibility.

An "obscenely low" turnout was secretly decided to be a turnout below that of the 2000 election (68.74 percent); the goal was set at 70 to 75 percent. (The turnout in the Duma election in December had been only 55.75 percent, but as the experience of the past fourteen years has shown, voter turnout is always considerably higher in elections for heads of state than in other elections.) The likelihood that voter turnout would be less than 50 percent—which would render the election null and void—was equal to zero, and the deliberately overwrought discussion of this possibility was in reality an instrument for raising turnout.

Sergei Mironov, speaker of the upper house of the Russian parliament and head of the Russian Party of Life, was roped into participating, and efforts were made to persuade Yavlinsky and Zhirinovsky. Yabloko, resenting the way it had been treated in the Duma elections, refused to play the Kremlin's games and even returned to the opposition: it initiated a pact among the democratic parties not to participate in the presidential election if the democrats were unable to agree on a single candidate—and as expected, the democrats could not agree on a single candidate.

Vladimir Zhirinovsky carried out the Kremlin's order with subversive irony: the LDPR did nominate a candidate for president—not Zhirinovsky himself, but his boxer-bodyguard, Oleg Malyshkin. The Communists also played down the significance of this election as far as they dared, nominating as the CPRF candidate not their leader, Gennady Zyuganov, but a left-wing Agrarian, Nikolai Kharitonov. But the democrats' pact was broken with the nomination of Irina Khakamada, who ended up representing the liberal voice in the election—despite the wishes of Yabloko and the SPS.

The CEC effectively ignored numerous violations, first and foremost the purchase of falsified signatures by the headquarters of practically all the candidates nominated by nonparliamentary parties (with the exception of Putin—signatures for his nomination were collected in accordance with bureaucratic standards and were thus genuine).[79]

The Kremlin's attitude toward the candidacies of Sergei Glazyev (Homeland party) and Ivan Rybkin (Liberal Russia) was ambivalent, however. On the one hand, they increased voter turnout. On the other, they were capable of raising unpleasant topics in their election campaigns. (Khakamada turned out to be capable of doing this as well, but she quickly stopped doing so after being called to order.) In addition, if Glazyev won the second-highest number of votes, he would remain a dangerous opponent of the ruling party's candidate in the next presidential election in 2008—by contrast with the invariably defeated Zyuganov. In other words, Glazyev's participation gave the president's campaign team another problem: the runner-up had to be Kharitonov, not Glazyev.

In reality, even if this problem did worry the bureaucrats, it was a source of inspiration for the political strategists: if there's a problem, then there is financing for its solution. The bureaucrats in Putin's election team were in favor of barring Glazyev from the election, but Putin's strategists insisted on— and obtained—more "democratic" methods of eliminating this candidate. Indeed, the strategists took up the project of "destroying Glazyev" with creative zeal and pleasure; they also periodically used Glazyev to frighten their own bureaucratic management and to obtain increases in financing.

The political strategists' attitude toward Rybkin's participation in the election was similar: "Let him be!" But the "Rybkin problem" had certain special aspects in Putin's eyes that ultimately resulted in its being solved completely separately.

As for the key problem of voter turnout, its solution entailed the use of both sophisticated, "technological" means and purely bureaucratic ones. For example, Vsevolod Khmy-rov, the administrative head of St. Petersburg's Frunzensky district, sent the following letter—which smacked of admin-istrative blackmail and political racketeering—to the district's housing cooperatives:

> Please have your housing cooperative's management office submit a work plan to the district administration before 02.01.04 to ensure that residents vote on 03.14.04 in the Russian presidential election. Your work must guarantee a turnout of at least 79 percent of the eligible voters among your residents. The results of your work will be evalu-ated after the results of the election are calculated.[80]

Called to account by St. Petersburg's Yabloko office (the reporter B. Vishnevsky, co-author of the article that described these let-ters, was one of the heads of Yabloko's St. Petersburg office), Khmyrov started claiming that the idea had not come from St. Petersburg city government, but "was my own idea, exclusively my own initiative. I did not do it on anyone's instructions." But he let the truth slip out accidentally: "Our district has two dis-trict election commissions. As district head, I am obliged to assist them. I am in constant communication with them. The committees have not criticized this letter in any way."[81]

In the final analysis, the official voter turnout on March 14, 2004, was purportedly 64.39 percent, out of which 71.31 per-cent voted for Putin.

FALSIFICATIONS IN THE PRESIDENTIAL ELECTION

In 2000, the CEC deliberately increased its list of eligible voters by 1,300,000 compared with the Duma election of December 1999, apparently in order to have a reserve of "dead souls"—who helped Putin get elected president in the first round of voting.

In 2004, the government used a different approach. This time, no one doubted that Putin would win in the first round; what was open to doubt was voter turnout. Therefore, the list of eligible voters was now reduced by 842,000 compared with the Duma election of December 2003. Thus, the main figure that was falsified was voter turnout, and of course the fabricated percentage points were not added to Kharitonov's, Glazyev's, or Khakamada's totals.

It is difficult to estimate the scale of the falsification. Official observers from Yabloko and the SPS were not able to monitor the election. But the CPRF (because Kharitonov was a candidate) had around 200,000 observers. It was the Communists who were able to uncover the most blatant falsifications. By April 2004, Kharitonov's campaign headquarters had analyzed and published the materials they had collected. The Communists' evidence consisted of copies of records from eighteen precinct election commissions in Moscow and composite tables provided by the territorial commissions of the Ramenki, Troparevo-Nikulino, and Vnukovo districts.

For example, the following instance of a falsification in voter turnout was identified:

> In precinct No. 2572 [in Ramenki], on March 14, 1,430 ballots were handed out according to the precinct election commission's records, and 2,214 ballots were handed out according to the territorial election commission's records. The precinct election commission reported that 1,377 ballots had been taken out of stationary ballot boxes, while the territorial election commission corrected this number: 2,214 ballots had been taken out as well.[82]

Tables published in *Nezavisimaya Gazeta* showed the totals for the four candidates in three Moscow precincts. The first column gave the number of votes won by each candidate according to the precinct committee records, the second column indicated the same figure according to the territorial committee records, and the third column showed the difference between the two numbers.

In precinct No. 2565 (Ramenki), 100 votes were stolen from Khakamada, 50 from Glazyev, 50 from Kharitonov, and 46 from "none of the above"; 650 were added to Putin's total.

In precinct No. 2572 (Ramenki), 170 votes were stolen from Khakamada, 50 from Glazyev, 50 from Kharitonov, and 150 from "none of the above"; 1,257 were added to Putin's total.

In precinct No. 2620 (Troparevo-Nikitino), 70 votes were stolen from Khakamada, 20 from Glazyev, 10 from Kharitonov, and 60 from "none of the above"; 170 were added to Putin's total.[83]

After analyzing the information that they received from their Moscow observers, the CPRF's lawyers identified several general patterns:

1. The territorial committees reported a higher voter turnout than was indicated in the records of the precinct election commissions.

2. All of the additional votes that appeared in the territorial election commissions' records were given to one candidate, V. V. Putin. In eighteen electoral precincts, this candidate received a total of 5,479 additional votes. Only in two precincts did several dozen additional votes go to S. M. Mironov and O. A. Malyshkin.

3. The greatest losses from the territorial committees' "corrections" were sustained by candidate I. M. Khakamada. In one precinct, she was given only 35 out of a total of 135 votes that had initially been cast for her; in another, 41 out of 181; and in eighteen precincts overall, this candidate lost a total of 870 votes or 35.4 percent.

4. Almost everywhere, votes were taken away from "none of the above." Evidently, this was done freely, in the belief that this "candidate" would definitely not complain.

5. The difference between the precinct and the territorial committees' figures is usually divisible by 10: for instance, 30, 50, 70, 110. Kharitonov's lawyers explain that this makes counting easier: round numbers are easier to add and subtract than not round ones. It is true that this also makes it easier for investigators to spot falsifications—provided, of course, that they are interested in doing so.[84]

The evidence of fraud in these Moscow districts was so convincing that CEC head Alexander Veshnyakov was forced to agree with them. "A review of the complaint has determined that falsifications have taken place in the Ramenki and Troperevo-Nikulino territorial election commissions," Veshnyakov stated. "The Moscow municipal election commission, which reviewed these matters under the CEC's supervision, has resolved to file a claim with the prosecutor's office to investigate and hold the guilty parties accountable. Evil must be punished, and it must be punished firmly."[85]

The Moscow municipal election commission's resolution was passed on March 30, 2004, and on April 6 it was sent to the Moscow prosecutor's office. After which the file was lost. "In this case, the people who deliberately increased voter turnout and the number of votes cast for candidate Putin will have to go to jail. . . . What we have here are falsifications in favor of the incumbent president. According to the notion of 'managed democracy,' this is more of a good deed than a crime."[86]

If the CEC's accounts are to be believed, Ingushetia turned out to be the frontrunner in terms of voter turnout and votes for Putin on March 14. Voter turnout: 96.23 percent; Putin's total: 98.18 percent. In terms of voter turnout, Ingushetia was surpassed only by Kabardino-Balkaria (97.72 percent), which, however, fell somewhat short in terms of Putin's total (96.49 percent). The other top performers are also familiar: Dagestan (94.59 percent for Putin, voter turnout 94.08 percent); Chechnya (92.35 percent for Putin, voter turnout 94.19 percent); Bashkortostan (91.79 percent for Putin, voter turnout 89.09 percent); Mordovia (91.35 percent for Putin, voter turnout 94.57 percent); North Ossetia (91.25 percent for Putin, voter turnout 89.24 percent).

Musa Ozdoyev, the Ingushetia People's Assembly deputy who uncovered the falsification of the Duma election results in Ingushetia, conducted his own investigation of the presidential election in the republic. Ozdoyev claims that "not even half of Ingushetia's voters participated in the presidential election. The election was basically subverted." Ozdoyev collected copies of all lists of voters from all precinct committees in Nazran and compared the lists used in the Duma election with those used in the presidential election.

A remarkable thing was discovered: on December 7, a voter obtained a ballot by presenting one passport, while on March 14, he obtained a ballot by presenting a different passport. And he signed his name differently in both cases as well. Here, for example, are the lists of Nazran's electoral precinct No. 67. . . . Citizen Magomed Zalikhmanovich Abiyev, born in 1983, voted in December with passport No. 26 01

132102, while in March he presented passport No. 26 01 001477. Among such "two-passport" voters, Ozdoyev found his own brother Mikail and a great number of his friends: "In reality, these people did not vote. Their passport details were supplied by the election commission. And their signatures, too. The election commissions evidently did not expect anyone to check them, so they simply made up the passport numbers . . . as long as they had 10 digits and the same republican series number, 26. Notice that the passport numbers are the same in both lists in about 10% of the cases. This indicates the actual voter turnout in Ingushetia on March 14. The rest was added."[87]

At the end of March 2004, Vadim Solovyev—advisory member of the CEC from the CPRF—sent a claim to the General Prosecutor's Office with a request to "initiate criminal proceedings in connection with signs of voter fraud in the presidential election in the Republic of Adygea." The claim continued:

Such signs have been identified by observers from Kharitonov's campaign headquarters in thirteen of the republic's electoral precincts. The pattern is the same in all cases: candidate Putin has everywhere been given a greater number of votes than is indicated in the precinct election commission records (in large precincts, 300–500 votes have been added to his totals), while his opponents have been given a smaller number. . . . [In Adygea], the greatest number of votes has been taken away from the "red" candidate Kharitonov.[88]

But while the CEC agreed that the election results had been falsified in Putin's favor in two Moscow districts, it refused to acknowledge similar evidence of fraud in other regions—as usual, citing the fact that the record copies had been improperly filled out from the legal point of view.

As Alexander Veshnyakov stated in an interview with *Nezavisimaya Gazeta,* "in terms of handing out the record copies, although there are rules for everything, unfortunately the observers' poor understanding of legal procedure leads to completely unfounded objections. . . ." Veshnyakov explained:

The observer must wait for the vote totals to be counted and for the records to be signed. But if he gets tired of waiting, writes down the preliminary totals that he overheard while the votes were being counted, and then takes this document, which has not been signed by anyone, and goes with it to his party's headquarters—should the committee be blamed? . . .

If there are objections that some committee refused to hand out copies of its records, then there are indeed grounds for a claim against it. But I do not accept such objections against our committee. The first thing that we did in the parliamentary election, and then in the presidential one, was to publish a special reminder for observers (although this is in principle not our responsibility). It says everything: how to conduct observations, how to fill out record copies; if your rights are being violated, then immediately go to the next-highest committee or to the courts. They are obligated to respond. Second, we had all of the precinct election commission records posted on the Internet the day after the election. Please, go ahead, compare them with your copies and verify the vote tallies. But when observers collect materials—including materials that have no legal weight—and send them to their party headquarters and two months later start complaining that they weren't given real copies. . . . Well, how can we establish that two months after the fact? . . .

Moscow is another matter. In Moscow, the precinct committees did hand out copies of the records, and this made it possible to determine that falsifications had taken place on the level of the territorial election commissions. Criminal charges have already been filed, and the guilty parties will answer for what they have done.[89]

The Moscow voter fraud materials were known to have finally reached the Moscow prosecutor's office as of September 2004, but the prosecutor's office was resistant to filing criminal charges against the forgers.

Galina Mikhaleva, head of Yabloko's regional office, estimates that voter turnout in the presidential election was inflated by at least 10 percent. Liliya Shibanova, director of the voters' association Golos and the coalition "For a Fair Election," believes that in the regional centers, where Golos and the coalition had their own (mainly unofficial) observers, the turnout was about 51–53 percent, which is not far from the official numbers. In the small towns and especially in the villages, however, where even the CPRF often did not have its own observers, the local election commission simply made up whatever voter turnout it wished.

On average, voter turnout around the country was inflated by about 10–15 percent. In a number of regions, especially in the national republics and several rural districts, the inflation was even higher. Turnout numbers for the national republics are absurd, inflated by about 30–40 percent. The inflation was lower in regional centers. When the Communists speak of votes being "physically added" to the totals, this does not always mean that extra ballots were literally placed in the ballot boxes. In most cases, the numbers were simply revised by the territorial election commissions when they were entered into the GAS-Vybory electronic voting system.

ELECTION FOR GOVERNOR OF THE VORONEZH REGION

FSB General V. Kulakov first became governor of the Voronezh region following a convincing victory in the election of December 24, 2000. That election had been relatively fair: candidates were not prevented from registering, and the Communist governor Ivan Shabanov's "administrative resource" was balanced by the administrative resource of Georgy Poltavchenko, the president's plenipotentiary representative in the Central Federal District, who backed Kulakov. No one had any doubts that Kulakov had indeed won (with 58.08 percent against Shabanov's 15.21 percent). Kulakov's use of the president's name was possibly in poor taste, but the voters, who had grown tired of Shabanov, really did prefer "Putin's colleague" to the incumbent governor.

By the time a year had elapsed, the new governor began to realize that the heavily subsidized region's deep-rooted problems could not be solved by "personal friendship with Vladimir Vladimirovich Putin" alone. Budget-related conflicts between the Voronezh mayor's office and the regional administration had grown worse: most taxes came from the region's capital (and went into the federal and regional budget), while subsidies from Moscow were received mostly by the rest of the region. In the struggle between the governor and the mayor, Yuri Khoroshiltsev—the region's chief federal inspector, who had once helped Kulakov against Shabanov—ended up on the mayor's side.

In March 2002, the prices of Voronezh's public utility services were raised several times, sparking mass protests by the city's residents. For the first time since the early 1990s, a large regional city saw thousands of people take part in demonstrations, calling for the resignation of both the regional and the municipal administrations.

Belatedly distancing himself from the mayor's unpopular utility price hikes, Kulakov managed to shift the people's discontent onto the mayor of Voronezh, Alexander Kovalev. The Protest Action Headquarters, created by the Communists in the summer of 2002, officially stopped calling for Kulakov's resignation: it now demanded the resignation of Mayor Kovalev alone. (Kovalev had served as governor in 1992–1996, with a reputation as a Yeltsin supporter and even a democrat.) In June 2003, Kulakov was able to get Poltavchenko, the president's plenipotentiary representative, to recall federal inspector Khoroshiltsev from the Voronezh region, and in October, Mayor Kovalev was forced to resign as well.

When they resigned, both Kovalev and Khoroshiltsev announced that they would run against Kulakov in the gubernatorial race in December 2004. In order to shorten the time that they and other potential opponents had for gathering funds and campaigning, Kulakov pushed through the obedient regional parliament a bill to reschedule the gubernatorial election for March 2004, combining it with the presidential election.

An election for mayor of Voronezh, held in January 2004, served as a kind of rehearsal for the gubernatorial election. The governor lost this race: his candidate Ivan Obraztsov came in third. Boris Skrynnikov, the deputy speaker of the regional duma, became the new mayor, with 23.1 percent of the vote. Another candidate not backed by the governor, Viktor Vitinnik, the deputy speaker of the Voronezh duma, came in close behind him with 22.4 percent. Obraztsov got only 17.5 percent.

Kulakov faced a real danger that the gubernatorial election would go to a second round of voting, with an almost certain defeat for him. Kovalev, Khoroshiltsev, and Alexei Nakvasin— speaker of the regional duma, who was considered an ally of the newly elected mayor—all had chances of entering the second round with Kulakov. In the end, Kovalev and Khoroshiltsev decided not to run, while Nakvasin did become a candidate, conducted a successful campaign, and had a chance of getting elected not just in the second round of voting, but already in the first.

But on March 2, less than two weeks before the election, Nakvasin withdrew from the race, explaining that he had already achieved the aims for which he was running: he had focused people's attention on the region's social-economic problems, on the "closed and absolutely obsolete style of government." According to one theory, the frontrunner was threatened with incriminating evidence against him, and he became afraid of a confrontation with the FSB, the plenipotentiary representative's office, and the governor. By another account, it was the Moscow leadership of the United Russia party that had demanded that Nakvasin withdraw. *Kommersant*, citing the views of Voronezh political analysts, speculated about the existence of an agreement between Nakvasin and the regional administration: Nakvasin was given the choice either to remain speaker of the regional duma after the election in March 2005, or else to become the head of the local United Russia office.[90]

If such an agreement existed, however, then Kulakov did not stick to it. On the contrary, on March 30, 2004, the governor's supporters in the Voronezh regional duma removed Nakvasin from the speaker's post, accusing him precisely of not having consulted with his colleagues among the deputies before announcing his candidacy in the gubernatorial race.

On March 14, the incumbent governor had won the early election with 52.5 percent of the vote and a turnout of 62.44 percent, according to the official records. The Communist candidate, Sergei Rudakov, came in second (20.16 percent).

But there was every reason to doubt the authenticity of these results. In the presidential election, which took place on the same day, substantial numbers of ballots were "added" with the aim of inflating turnout in the Voronezh region, as in most other regions. A corresponding number of extra ballots had to be added to the gubernatorial race as well (10 percent on average around the country). Naturally, the "added" ballots were all counted in favor of the incumbent governor. Most likely, Kulakov would have come in first anyway, but without the absolute majority needed for a victory in the first round of voting.

ELECTION FOR GOVERNOR OF THE KRASNODAR REGION

Alexander Tkachev, the governor of the Krasnodar region, was a clear favorite in the gubernatorial race that took place on March 14, 2004, the same day as the presidential election. One of Russia's most nationalistic governors—if not the most nationalistic among them—Tkachev had earlier been considered a left-winger as well: besides belonging to former governor Nikolai Kondratenko's Fatherland movement, he was also a member of the CPRF and the Agrarian Party, at the same time. In 2000, Tkachev was elected not only as heir and successor to "Papa Kondrat," but also as the favorite of all the left-wing forces in the region (although the pro-Putin Unity movement gave him its support).

In 2003, however, Tkachev left the CPRF and declared his complete support for the policies of President Putin. The break with the CPRF reinforced his ties with the president's administration (although they had already been pretty strong, particularly with the chekist faction in Putin's entourage—despite Tkachev's radically xenophobic pronouncements, which were not always convenient for the Kremlin). But in the Krasnodar region, the governor's allegiance to the federal government was a two-edged sword: it could cost him a part of his voters, especially if his opponent was another Kondratenko supporter, but with an anti-Moscow and an openly antiliberal bias, and particularly if his opponent had Kondratenko's own support. Tkachev neutralized one such potential opponent, Nikolai Priz, by promising to help him get re-elected as mayor of Krasnodar in March. But another candidate emerged to challenge Tkachev with a left-nationalist platform: former Duma deputy Oleg Maschenko, once Tkachev's companion in the CPRF and the Homeland movement and now a member of the People's Patriotic Party (NPP) and the Homeland bloc.

Maschenko's chances of winning were slim, especially because "Papa Kondrat" had in the end declined to give him his support. Nonetheless, the governor became scared—if not of a defeat, then of an unconvincing, tainted victory. The regional election commission, which was completely loyal to him, denied registration to Tkachev's only viable opponent. As a result, Tkachev won 83.98 percent of the vote and "none of the above" came in second (7.62 percent), with an official voter turnout of 63.13 percent (practically identical to the region's official voter turnout in the presidential election).

The victory was uncontestable, apart from the fact that voter turnout in the Krasnodar region—in both the gubernatorial and the presidential election—was inflated by about 10 percent.

ELECTION FOR MAYOR OF VLADIVOSTOK

The Vladivostok mayoral race began as partly a farce and partly a crime drama. There were three principal contenders: Vladimir Nikolayev, deputy of the Primorye regional duma, businessman, and crime boss, previously convicted but pardoned; Yuri Kopylov, the incumbent mayor of Vladivostok; and Viktor Cherepkov, State Duma deputy, former mayor of Vladivostok, and psychic. Nikolayev, called "Winnie-the-Pooh," was supported by Governor Sergei Darkin and United Russia. Kopylov, who opposed Darkin, was a creation of former governor Yevgeny Nazdratenko and was backed by the Nazdratenko-supporting businessmen who had fallen out of favor with the government. Cherepkov represented the left-right opposition from outside the establishment.

The ten registered candidates included Viktor *Grigorievich* Cherepkov, head of the limited liability corporation Freedom and People's Government—deputy Viktor *Ivanovich* Cherepkov is head of the tiny Freedom and People's Government party—and Yuri *Ivanovich* Kopylov, administrative head of the noncommercial foundation "City of Vladivostok" and a "double" for Mayor Yuri *Mikhailovich* Kopylov (while two other Kopylovs were denied registration).

During the course of the campaign, many bad things happened to candidate Winnie-the-Pooh's opponents. For example, Cherepkov (the psychic deputy) was beaten up on the street, and Senator Oleg Kozhemyako's assistant received threats in the stairwell of her building and over the telephone.

In the first round of voting, on July 4, 2004, Nikolayev came in first with 26.79 percent, closely followed by Cherepkov with

26.37 percent. The psychic's "double" came in ninth, but managed to reduce the "real" Cherepkov's total by 1.21 percent. Kopylov came in third, with 18.11 percent, while his double came in sixth with 1.95 percent.

Given Nikolayev's reputation, the winner of the second round in a fair election would have been either Cherepkov or "none of the above," in which case Kopylov would have remained acting mayor. In an unfair election, taking into account the Sergei Darkin factor, the winner would have been Winnie-the-Pooh. On July 9, however, the election commission brought a motion before the court to have Cherepkov barred from the election—citing complaints by three citizens who believed that he had violated their electoral rights by using his position as a State Duma deputy to promote his candidacy.

On the night of July 9, a grenade that had been hung up with a pair of suspenders exploded at the entrance to Cherepkov's campaign headquarters; the candidate was wounded and suffered a serious concussion. Nikolayev's supporters immediately declared that the assassination attempt had been staged by Cherepkov himself, while Anatoly Zolotaryev, head of the Main Directorate of Internal Affairs for the Far Eastern Federal District, proposed that the incident be considered an "act of disorderly conduct by unidentified individuals."[91]

On June 12, Vladivostok's Leninsky District Court ruled in favor of the municipal election commission in its suit against Cherepkov—despite the fact that the defendant himself was at the Pacific Fleet Hospital at the time—and disqualified him from participating in the second round of voting. The court found that Cherepkov had violated electoral regulations by using his State Duma reception room, office telephone and fax, and State Duma letterhead for letters and claims sent to government officials.

As a result of this court decision, the second round of voting on July 18 became a race between Nikolayev and Kopylov. But Kopylov withdrew his candidacy and called on voters to cast their ballots for "none of the above" in the second round. Candidate Alexander Perednya—who had come in fourth in the first round of voting (9.07 percent)—followed suit, calling the election a "circus." Nikolai Markovtsev, a regional duma deputy who had come in fifth in the first round (2.35 percent), also called on voters to select "none of the above," but decided to leave his own name on the ballot, "so as to preserve at least some ability to monitor the electoral process: my observers will be working at the voting precincts. But I call on voters to vote for 'none of the above' and will consider myself a winner if I get zero votes, but Nikolayev does not win."[92]

It would seem that the election was bound to fall apart under such conditions. According to Natalya Menshenina, director of the Pacific Institute of World Politics and Law, "I am convinced that, following the wholesale refusal of candidates to participate in the election, up to 75 percent of the voters will vote for "none of the above" in the second round. But in Primorye, there is a difference between how people vote and how their votes will be counted."[93]

This is exactly what happened. On July 18, Nikolayev won with 53 percent, according to the official records, which showed 36 percent for "none of the above" and 9 percent for Markovtsev. But "the population was left with the impression that the number of voters for 'none of the above' had in reality been greater."[94]

Four days after the election, Pyotr Fradkov, son of the prime minister, Mikhail Fradkov, was appointed deputy general manager of the Far Eastern Shipping Company (FESCO) in Vladivostok. This coincidence gave rise to legitimate suspicions that Governor Darkin was not alone in supporting Winnie-the-Pooh's campaign to take over Vladivostok's municipal administration, but that the prime minister himself was supporting Nikolayev. *Novaya Gazeta* even ascribed ownership rights over FESCO to Nikolayev.[95]

Actually, the connection between Winnie-the-Pooh and FESCO is not quite so direct. Like other Primorye-based commercial entities, FESCO had been forced—due to its relative dependence on the governor—to participate in Nikolayev's election campaign in one fashion or another. But Nikolayev's own organizations can own (directly or indirectly) no more than 15 percent of FESCO's shares, which are held by private individuals and small businesses. Another 20 percent of its shares are owned by the regional government (and thus controlled by

Governor Darkin). The remaining 65 percent are controlled·by the Industrial Investors group of Sergei Generalov, former State Duma deputy from the SPS.

Therefore, although the appointment of Pyotr Fradkov to a lucrative position in a major commercial entity might constitute a kickback to the prime minister in return for some favor—possibly even his support in getting Winnie-the-Pooh elected—it cannot have come from Nikolayev himself, but more likely originated with Darkin and Generalov. It is also possible that this is not so much a kickback as an advance to the prime minister in return for his future support. In this case, Vladivostok's new mayor—as an ally and partner of the governor and of the Industrial Investors group—will also be able to rely on this support.

On July 29, the Primorye Regional Court upheld the Leninsky District Court's ruling to disqualify Cherepkov's registration as a candidate in the election.

ELECTION FOR THE NEW PRESIDENT OF CHECHNYA

After the separatists murdered Akhmad Kadyrov, the Kremlin was faced with the necessity of finding a new puppet ruler to install in Grozny. Chechnya's minister of internal affairs, Alu (Ali) Alkhanov, was chosen for this role. As a backup candidate—in case Alkhanov should meet Kadyrov's fate—the Kremlin registered the head of the FSB's Chechnya directorate, Movsur Khamidov. The election for president of Chechnya was scheduled for August 29, 2004. Everything that followed happened exactly as it did in Kadyrov's "election."

On July 22, Malik Saidullaev was denied registration. As a reason for the denial, the head of the Chechen central election commission, Abdul-Kerim Arsakhanov, stated that Saidullaev's passport was "invalid": it indicated his place of birth as "Alkhan-Yurt, Republic of Chechnya," while it should have said "Alkhan-Yurt, Chechen-Ingush ASSR," since on October 5, 1964, when Malik Mingayevich Saidullaev was born, Chechnya was part of the Chechen-Ingush ASSR.

As *Novaya Gazeta* correspondent Orkhan Dzhemal discovered, the ruling party's candidate, Alu Alkhanov, had the same "mistake" in his passport, which had been issued on June 7, 2004: his place of birth was listed as "Kirovsky village, Kirovsky district, Taldy-Kurgan region, Kazakhstan." But only three weeks later, on June 29, Alkhanov was given a new passport in which "Kazakhstan" was corrected to "Kazakh SSR." Evidently, "the Chechen central election commission had already decided in June that it would 'remove' Saidullaev from the election. It then became clear that, in this case, Alkhanov's registration would also have to be disqualified. And so his brand-new passport was promptly changed."[96]

The voters practically ignored this election. An hour after the polls opened, the head of precinct No. 372 in Grozny's Leninsky district, with about 1,100 eligible voters, told a *Vremya Novostey* reporter that three hundred people had already come and voted. But an observer had seen "about seventy people at most." The reporter is inclined to believe the observer:

> In order to let three hundred people vote in one hour, the passports must be checked against the lists of registered votes at a rate of five per minute. Obviously, there had not been any such wave of voters. The *Vremya Novostey* reporter spent about an hour at this voting precinct and saw only two or three people who had come to vote.[97]

This reporter's observations were confirmed by practically all the other reporters who were present at the Chechen "election" on August 29, 2004. A *Kommersant* reporter even conducted an experiment, attempting to vote in five different precincts. He was permitted to vote in four of them.[98]

The official outcome of the event: 73.67 percent of the vote for Alkhanov, with a voter turnout of over 85.25 percent. When the preliminary totals were announced at a press conference given by Abdul-Kerim Arsakhanov, head of the Chechen election commission, the reporters started laughing at the turnout figures.

Putin held a press conference on August 31. Pretending that he did not know how the election had been staged, he stated—in front of his guests, the leaders of France and Germany—that "no one can force people to vote. People cannot be dragged from their homes by their collars or by their hair. Many observers were present at the polls, including observers from Arab countries, and I have not heard a single serious person make a serious declaration about violations in the Chechnya elections."[99]

The FSB's "Operation Chechen Election" cannot be characterized simply as a sham or a falsification. Everyone knew that there was no election, and Putin and Veshnyakov knew that everyone knew it. Nonetheless, with their honest chekist eyes wide open, they proceeded to call this special operation a "democratic election." A state capable of lying with such self-assurance is a state that undermines itself. As Yulia Latynina wrote in *Novaya Gazeta*, "it was precisely Alkhanov's election that triggered the terrorist attack in Beslan."[100]

Putin used the Beslan tragedy as a pretext to introduce still further constraints on the institution of voting. On September 13, 2004, he announced that regional heads would no longer be elected directly; rather, the governors and regional presidents would be "elected" by the regional parliaments as advised by the president. Also, the mixed proportional-majoritarian voting system in the State Duma was going to be replaced by a purely proportional system based on party lists.

10

The Suppression of the Media

People who came to power by relying exclusively on TV are doomed to see TV the way Ivan the Fool saw the magic wand in the fairy tale. If the magic wand is theirs, then everything will be all right; if someone steals it, then everything is over. (Yulia Latynina, *Novaya Gazeta*)

I know what Putin's nightmare is. . . . Obviously, it was the press that made him president. . . . So you can imagine the kinds of nightmares he must have: a nobody named General Shamanov appears out of nowhere, and Channels One and Two make him president. I think that's what torments him. (Alexei Venediktov, *Demokraticheskiy Vybor*)

Assembling the media into a unified front was a top priority of President Putin's policies for the entire duration of his first term in office. It was more important than "establishing a constitutional order in Chechnya," more important than the makeover in federal-regional government relations, more important than all judicial transformations, more important than talk of military reform. In no other sphere was the Putin administration's approach as systematic and methodical as in this one. And in almost no other sphere (except perhaps in the fight against Chechen separatists) did Putin display such an active personal interest.

The most significant and notable episodes in the Putin administration's fight against journalists and freedom of speech were: the Babitsky affair (February–March 2000), the Gusinsky affair (May–December 2000), the confiscation of ORT from Berezovsky (August 2000–January 2001), the dismantling of the "old" NTV (April–May 2001), the "TV-6 affair" (2002), the purge at the "new" NTV (February 2003), the media regulations overhaul (May–June 2003), the shutting down of TVS (June 2003), and the recurring waves of new "anti-extremist" regulations (summer of 2006 and summer of 2007). To the extent that this was possible, each of these operations was portrayed either as a nonpolitical "property rights conflict" or as a fight against economic abuses. Attempts were made to camouflage Putin's personal involvement, but it was practically impossible to conceal his interest in these matters.

There were also less visible actions and episodes, in which Putin apparently had no direct involvement, but which were highly characteristic of the regime of "managed democracy" that took shape under him: the Khinshtein affair (February 2000), the FSB-organized framing and arrest of the writer Eduard Limonov on weapons-buying charges (April 2001), the attempt to shut down *Novaya Gazeta* (May 2002), the shutting down of *Obschaya Gazeta* (June 2002), the raid on the editorial offices of Ad Marginem Press (September 2002), the raid on the editorial offices of *Versiya* (November 2002), the shutting down of the "old" *Novye Izvestiya* (February 2003), the confiscation of the premises of the magazine *Novoye Vremya* (September 2003), repressive press censorship before the 2004 election (September–December 2003), the increase in TV censorship before the 2004 election (September–December 2003), the purges at REN TV and *Izvestiya* (fall of 2005 to spring of 2006).

Concurrently with these developments, government control over regional media outlets also increased, as did the persecution of reporters in the provinces. The most widely publicized instances of such persecution by regional authorities included the Yulia Shelamydova affair (Ulyanovsk, August 2002) and the Galkin affair (Chelyabinsk, August 2003), the case of Bakharev and Sterlyadev (Perm, September 2003), the case of Sergei Savelyev (Kursk, August 2004), the case of Yuri

Bagrov (September–December 2004), the case of Dmitrievsky (Nizhny Novgorod, October 2005–February 2006), the case of the *Gorodskie Vesti* newspaper (Volgograd, February 2006), the case of Anna Smirnova (Vologda, March–May 2006), the case of Viktor Shmakov (Bashkiria, April–May 2006), the case of Igor Rudnikov and Oleg Berezovsky (Kaliningrad, 2007). Dozens of such episodes are mentioned in the reports of Alexei Simonov's Glasnost Defense Foundation and Oleg Panfilov's Center for Journalism in Extreme Situations.

The number of criminal charges filed against reporters and editors during 2001–2003 was several times greater than in the 1990s. "In the 1990s, the initiation of criminal proceedings against a reporter was always a big controversy and a sufficiently rare occurrence," notes Panfilov. "In 2000, the Center for Journalism in Extreme Situations counted 19 cases of reporters being accused of crimes; in 2001, we counted 31; in 2002, 49; and in the first half of 2003, already more than 20."[1]

In addition to a general deterioration in journalists' working conditions, these years saw an increase in purely criminal actions against representatives of the press and media, particularly in the provinces: murders of reporters (up to two or three per month in the fall of 2003), attacks on reporters, attacks on editorial offices, illegal confiscation of premises. All together, several hundred such episodes are noted in the reports of the Glasnost Defense Foundation.

THE ANDREI BABITSKY AFFAIR

Serious problems in relations between the government and the press in the Putin years commenced with the Babitsky affair, while Putin was still only acting president and a candidate for the presidency. At the beginning of January 2000, Andrei Babitsky, a Radio Liberty correspondent known for his reports from Chechnya—which were extremely disagreeable to the government—disappeared in Grozny. Radio Liberty's management supposed that Babitsky had most likely been arrested by Russian security services and interned at the Chenokozovo filtration camp.

The government categorically denied that Babitsky had been arrested, until incontrovertible reports began appearing in the Moscow papers from witnesses who had seen federal officers apprehend Babitsky on his way out of Grozny. At this point, the acting general prosecutor, Vladimir Ustinov, was forced to admit that Babitsky had indeed been arrested on January 27, in accordance with Article 90 of the Russian Criminal Code, on "the rules of conduct for journalists working in a zone of antiterrorist operations."

Attempting to blandish Western public opinion, the acting president's assistant Sergei Yastrzhembsky carelessly let slip that the Babitsky incident was "under the personal control" of Putin. Soon, it was officially announced that Babitsky had been released on February 2, on the condition that he not leave the location. But the "released" Babitsky failed to get in touch with his family or his co-workers. It then became known that on February 3, allegedly with his consent, Babitsky had been handed over to "field commander Sayid Usakhodzhayev" in exchange for a group of Russian prisoners of war who had been captured by Chechen combatants. Anticipating questions about the acting president's "personal control" of the matter, Yastrzhembsky announced that, from the moment of the "exchange," "the federal government [was] no longer responsible for what happens to Babitsky."

Footage of the "exchange," made by the FSB, was shown on television. Babitsky looked nothing like a person acting of his own free will. On the contrary, it was clear from what could be seen and heard on the footage that the video had been made over Babitsky's protests, and that his transfer to unknown people in masks took place under the escort of federal troops with automatic weapons. The government-released document in which Babitsky gave his consent to be handed over to Chechen combatants was dated January 31, *before* the date when it was announced that he had been released after promising not to leave the location.

Both the president of the separatists, Aslan Maskhadov, and their main propagandist informed Radio Liberty that they knew nothing about any exchange, that there is no field commander with the Uzbek last name "Usakhodzhayev," and that they knew nothing of Babitsky's fate following his arrest. All Russian security services and law enforcement agencies denied their involvement in the exchange, including the Ministry of Defense, although the defense minister, Igor Sergeyev, commented on ORT that he "wouldn't be sorry to exchange ten Babitskys" for one of his soldiers.

In the independent media—for example, in the *Segodnya* newspaper—speculations began to appear that there had not been any exchange at all: "Someone was [simply] covering their tracks, and not doing a very good job at it."[2] The Babitsky affair was analyzed most exhaustively and without a shred of patience for the government's lies on NTV, in the newspapers *Obschaya Gazeta* (a special edition was devoted to the incident), *Novaya Gazeta, Segodnya, Novye Izvestiya, Moskovskiye Novosti,* and in the magazines *Itogi* and *Novoye Vremya.*

Commentators expressed fears that Babitsky had already been killed by the security services. The likelihood that Babitsky was indeed no longer alive—or would soon cease to be so—was far from negligible. During the first Chechen war, the reporter Nadezhda Chaykova had been kidnapped, tortured, and shot; Chaykova was hated by the federal authorities for reporting on war crimes in Chechnya and for not even concealing her sympathy toward the idea of an independent Ichkeria. The fact that federal organs were denying their involvement in the "exchange" gave reason to suspect the worst.

An *Izvestiya* reporter, Maksim Sokolov, came to Putin's defense against charges of being responsible for Babitsky's fate. "There are certain 'hot spot' fanatics who can no longer live without these spots and without the adrenalin that is to be had there," he wrote. ". . . Meanwhile, the government-guaranteed right to adrenalin has yet to appear in any constitution. At your own risk, please."[3]

On February 7, 2000, Andrei Babitsky, who had officially been handed over to "combatants," was no less officially "called in for questioning" by the General Prosecutor's Office. The employees of the office announced that if the reporter failed to come of his own free will, he would be placed on a wanted list and arrested when found.[4]

All of February, the most contradictory information circulated concerning Babitsky's location. From time to time, government officials named Chechen villages in which Babitsky was supposed to be hiding and field commanders who were supposedly hosting him, while the separatists denied these reports and continued to insist that Babitsky had not been handed over to them. Finally, on February 25, it was announced that the reporter had been arrested in Dagestan, carrying a false passport with another person's name.

Babitsky was delivered to Makhachkala in the trunk of a car by unknown individuals who had been holding him in some Chechen village after the "exchange." In Makhachkala, Babitsky did not immediately turn himself in to the police, but booked a hotel room and made several phone calls, including calls to his wife in Prague and to Radio Liberty in Moscow. After this, he was soon recognized and arrested for carrying a false passport.

In his opinion, the masked combatants to whom he had been handed over by the federal agents were indeed Chechens; however, they were not separatists and supporters of Maskhadov, but combatants with pro-federal leanings who supported some collaborationist field commander. They had tried to pass themselves off as Maskhadov supporters, and Babitsky had pretended that he believed them. Subsequently, just as he had supposed, they turned out to be not separatists but fighters from the armed wing of the Adamallah party, headed by Adam Deniev. The Adamallah party stood for Chechnya remaining a part of Russia, and Deniev's younger brother, Gazi Deniev, was an active lieutenant colonel in the FSB.

Deniev's fighters had taken away both of Babitsky's passports—domestic and foreign—and instead had given him a passport bearing his photograph but under an Azerbaijani name, Aliyev.

At the Makhachkala temporary detention facility, Babitsky went on a hunger strike.

On February 28, the acting president remarked that he saw no need to keep Babitsky under guard in Makhachkala. The next day, Babitsky was put on the empty plane of the internal affairs minister, Vladimir Rushailo, and flown to Moscow's Chkalovsky airport, where he was set free, with an injunction not to leave the city. In October, Babitsky was sentenced to pay a fine for using a false passport, but was pardoned by the judge.

At approximately the same time, in October 2000, FSB Lieutenant Colonel Gazi Deniev was shot and killed in Moscow by a businessman from whom he was extorting a million dollars. In April 2001, Adam Deniev was blown up by Chechen separatists. Whether there was any connection between the Deniev brothers' deaths and their involvement in the Babitsky affair remains unknown.

Before his "exchange," Babitsky was held at the Chenokozovo filtration camp, where inmates were kept in a way that, according to him, was an exact replica of what he had read about Hitler's death camps. Babitsky had signed his consent to the "exchange" without yet knowing that news of his arrest had already gotten out. It is almost certain that Babitsky would not have been allowed to leave Chechnya alive, with his personal impressions of Chernokozovo, if Putin's reputation in the West had not depended directly on his fate at that moment.

THE ALEXANDER KHINSHTEIN AFFAIR

Simultaneously with the Babitsky affair, which received worldwide press coverage, the less-publicized "Khinshtein affair" also came to an end in Moscow. Alexander Khinshtein was a widely read columnist for *Moskovsky Komsomolets* who published exposés about various figures in the Ministry of Internal Affairs, including the head of the ministry, Vladimir Rushailo. The police had been trying to get Khinshtein put in an insane asylum, or at least to get him convicted for forging his driver's license—although the statute of limitations for this violation had long passed.

During the preceding, pre-election year, Khinshtein had taken an active part in the mud-slinging between the various rival parties, lending his support to the Fatherland–All Russia bloc headed by Yevgeny Primakov and Yuri Luzhkov. He repeatedly wrote extremely unflattering pieces not only about "the family" and its Unity bloc, but also about the director of the FSB (and later prime minister), Vladimir Putin.

Although Khinshtein had already ceased his attacks on Putin, Rushailo proceeded to act without any restraints, assuming that the gadfly editorialist could be dealt with quickly and easily. In the end, however, the minister had to pull back—apparently, due to instructions that came from above.

As a conflict between a bureaucratic power-seeker and a muckraking journalist, the Khinshtein affair was typical of the new regime. Under Yeltsin, it would probably have been impossible to openly persecute such a well-known Moscow journalist as Khinshtein. Yet Khinshtein's exposés also had a natural place within the new political context: they were just another round in the fight between the various oligarchic groups in the Kremlin. In this contest, the Kremlin power-seeker (the minister of internal affairs) turned out to have very influential enemies at the Moscow mayor's office and in the FSB, while the journalist discovered powerful protectors in the FSB.

In fact, already during the perestroika years, Alexander Khinshtein—a very young reporter at the time—had been noted favorably by the employees of the Sixth Department of the KGB's Fifth Directorate. These agents were engaged in preparing analytic overviews of the work of the KGB's divisions around the country. During the perestroika years, the KGB found it useful to leak certain materials to the press; they were written by the employees of the Fifth Directorate's Sixth Department. Later, the KGB came up with the idea of enlisting actual reporters in order to publish such materials under their bylines. It was to this end that Oleg Mikarenko, an agent from the Sixth Department, recruited the young reporter Khinshtein. And it was through Khinshtein that Mikarenko and his colleagues from Directorate K (for the Defense of the Constitutional Order) continued to carry out counterpropaganda in the press, by publishing materials useful to the KGB. Khinshtein's work came to be used especially actively after the creation of the KGB Center for Public Relations, and after Mikarenko—the agent who had recruited Khinshtein—was transferred to work there.

PUTIN'S QUARREL WITH THE TV SHOW "PUPPETS"

The "NTV affair" effectively began on February 8, 2000, when the newspaper *Sankt-Peterburgskie Vedomosti* published a written declaration by St. Petersburg University's Task Force to Nominate Acting President Vladimir Putin for President of Russia. The authors of the declaration—led by the university rector, Lyudmila Verbitskaya, and the dean of the law school, Nikolai Kropachev—expressed grievances against the two latest episodes of the TV show *Puppets* (*Kukly*) on NTV, which had inspired them with "a feeling of profound indignation and revulsion and [constitute] eloquent examples of the abuse of freedom of speech with which Russian citizens are confronted more and more often in anticipation of the election, however deplorable this may be."

In the opinion of the professors of Putin's alma mater, their student had been "the victim of egregiously vicious and furious defamation that displayed no regard for his dignity and honor." Since this defamation occurred while he was serving in an official capacity (as acting president), the actions of the show's creators were "subject to prosecution in accordance with Article 319 of the Russian Criminal Code." And, as the authors of the declaration pointed out, criminal proceedings based on Article 319 could be "initiated regardless of the wishes of the person who has been wronged." In this way, the obliging professors shielded the acting president in advance from the necessity of any personal involvement on his part in the criminal prosecution of NTV and exonerated him of any criticism that such prosecution might draw.

But as Viktor Shenderovich, one of the show's scriptwriters, put it, "there are certain doubts concerning the authorship [of the declaration] (rumor has it that a fax with the text of the letter came from Moscow)."[5]

Verbitskaya and the others were particularly outraged by Shenderovich's clever fairy tale "Little Zaches," based on the story by E. T. A. Hoffmann, whose main character was "Putin-Zinnober"—an acting president whose hair had been combed with a "magic television comb." The St. Petersburg professors' outrage reflected the reaction of their student in the Kremlin to the fairy tale. "After 'Little Zaches,'" wrote Anna Bossart in *Novaya Gazeta*, "it was as if the character's prototype had declared: 'I'll put him in jail.' Not the author, of course—we have freedom of speech, after all. But the man who owns the store."[6] The "man who owns the store" was the owner of Media-Most, Vladimir Gusinsky.

Similar reports reached Shenderovich, who remarked: "*Up there* [upward glance], they are particularly offended by the fact that the show's hero turned out to be a creature of diminutive height."[7]

Apart from *Puppets*, by this time Putin and his entourage had a whole series of grievances against Gusinsky's media outlets, and first and foremost against NTV:

1. Their unapologetic position in covering the "anti-terrorist operation" in Chechnya.
2. Their failure to support Putin and the Medved bloc in the Duma election and the presidential election—and their sympathy for Primakov-Luzhkov's Fatherland–All Russia bloc and Yavlinsky's Yabloko in the Duma election, and their support for Yavlinsky in the presidential election.
3. Their attempts to find out the truth about the apartment-house bombings in Moscow and the FSB-organized stockpiling of explosives in an apartment house in Ryazan—the so-called "learning trials"—in September 1999.
4. Their "rummaging" in corruption scandals surrounding Pavel Borodin, the Kremlin property manager; Vladimir Ustinov, acting general prosecutor; Alexander Voloshin, the president's chief of staff; Yuri Zaostrovtsev, deputy director of the FSB; Prime Minister Mikhail Kasyanov; and other people close to the president.

The law professors' foray, however, had no legal consequences. Their former student took a different path.

THE FIRST ATTACK ON MEDIA-MOST

At the end of April and the beginning of May 2000, the editors of *Segodnya*, a newspaper belonging to Vladimir Gusinsky's Media-Most holdings, wrote and mailed what turned out to be three very dangerous letters. The first (dated April 28) was sent to Sabir Kekhlerov, deputy general prosecutor; the second (dated May 3) to Yuri Zaostrovtsev, deputy director of the FSB; and the third (dated April 27) to Vladimir Putin himself, who had already been elected president, but had not yet been inaugurated.

Each of these government officials was presented by the newspaper with several ticklish questions. For example, the deputy general prosecutor was asked:

- Did the assistant general prosecutor of the Russian Federation, Nikolai Yemelyanov, write a report in 1994 about you using your official position in the interests of the Balkar Trading Corporation?
- Do you or your close relatives have any relation to Mosstroyeconombank?
- With what resources was your son Artur's apartment purchased in 1997, at such-and-such an address?

The deputy director of the FSB was asked:

- For what reason did you resign from the FSB in 1993?
- What instigated your departure from Tveruniversal-bank?
- What happened to the security and sourcing companies that you founded during your years of commercial activity?
- Do you help your father, the founder of the private security company Fort Professional, with his work?

In the letter sent to the acting president, *Segodnya*'s editor-in-chief, Mikhail Berger, complained that after *Segodnya* became interested in General Zaostrovtsev's past history in business and published an article about it, the general began intensively gathering incriminating evidence against the Media-Most group. In doing so, Berger stated, "whenever Zaostrovtsev has tried to exert pressure on the group's subdivisions, he has claimed that with respect to Media-Most, he was acting on your [Putin's] personal instructions."

The response that came back from the deputy general prosecutor, the deputy director of the FSB, and the newly elected president was, to use the language of military strategists, asymmetric. Kekhlerov initiated criminal proceedings against

Media-Most based on three articles of the Russian Criminal Code: Article 137, violation of personal privacy; Article 138, violation of the secrecy of correspondence; Article 183, illegally obtaining and distributing commercial secrets.

The direct attack by the prosecutor's office and law enforcement organizations against "the man who owns the store" began immediately after Putin's inauguration on May 7, 2000. Four days later, on May 11, the Media-Most offices were raided and searched. In the course of the operation, dozens of Media-Most employees were detained for several hours without being charged. Those who demanded either to be presented with a charge or to be released after the three hours permitted by law were threatened with being handcuffed and forced to lie on the ground. This time around, however, the threats remained just that.

At first, the masked agents claimed to be merely the "tax police," although the General Prosecutor's Office later stated that the search had been carried out as part of a two-year-old criminal case involving an unnamed Ministry of Finance official. But one of the officers in charge of the search admitted in front of a TV camera that he was from the FSB. By that evening, the official reason for the search had changed: it was no longer a criminal case involving a Ministry of Finance official, but concerned "illegal invasion into citizens' private lives using special technical means"—a charge formulated by Sergei Debitsky, the investigator on cases of special importance at the General Prosecutor's Office. The "illegal invasion into citizens' private lives" was evidently meant to refer to the journalistic investigation into General Zaostrovtsev's business dealings.

The secretariat of the Russian Reporters' Union stated that it viewed this operation as an "unconstitutional act and an expression of arbitrary rule intended to intimidate the independent media."

As for Putin, whose official term was only four days old when this repression began—against a media holding company that was hostile to him personally—he categorically denied that the operation had any political subtext. He assured the public that he was an adherent of the principle of free speech and let it be known that he had no intention of interfering in the matter, since the law was the same for everybody, including Vladimir Gusinsky.

A joke about the incident quickly surfaced on the Internet, however: "Why did the people who raided Media-Most wear masks? Because the new president likes to do everything himself."

On Yevgeny Kiselev's TV show *Itogi* for the Sunday following the Thursday raid, all of Media-Most's enemies were again given their due: Kekhlerov, and Zaostrovtsev, and the leadership of the FSB in general (for the "instructional" stockpiling of hexogen in a residential building in Ryazan), and Alexander Voloshin (for his involvement in the AVVA company swindle), and Mikhail Kasyanov ("Mr. Two Percent"), and Putin himself (for the Babitsky affair). The program also included an appropriately somber monologue by Alexander Solzhenitsyn, which had been recorded by NTV ten days earlier. And concluding this two-hour-long bout of artillery fire—which delayed all other programming on the network by about forty minutes— was another deadly episode of Viktor Shenderovich's *Puppets*, this one based on Alexander Dumas's *Twenty Years After*.

As one might suppose, there was no unanimous agreement inside the Kremlin on the methods to be used in conducting the "NTV affair." The chekists wanted to rely on coercion and to strangle Gusinsky once and for all with the hands of the prosecutor's office. The more flexible "family" was willing to employ the carrot as well as the stick.

"In May 2000, Media-Most was contacted by a top Kremlin official," writes Shenderovich. "During a personal meeting, he produced a list of conditions and said that if they were fulfilled, the attack against NTV would be called off. There were several conditions—changing news policies with regard to Chechnya, stopping attacks against the so-called 'family'—but the first thing on the list was that the president's puppet had to be removed from *Puppets*."[8]

In the next episode of *Puppets*, with Kiselev's agreement, Shenderovich fulfilled the condition of NTV's persecutors in a subversive manner: in place of the president, the story of the "Ten Commandments" featured a cloud on a mountain and a burning bush, which were interpreted by Moses-Voloshin as "simply *Gospod' Bog* [the Lord God]. Abbreviated as *GB* [Russian slang for KGB]."

Two weeks later, on June 13, Gusinsky was arrested.

A charge was filed against him on June 16. He was no longer accused of "illegal invasion into citizens' private lives using special technical means," but charged with "large-scale embezzlement by a group of individuals by means of fraud and breach of trust, and abuse of an official position" (Russian Criminal Code, Article 159, par. 3). The fact that the charges against Gusinsky had been changed yet again, for the third time in a month, indicated that the security organs had not been sufficiently prepared: the order to attack had come too suddenly.

However, Gusinsky's measure of restraint was changed and he was released on the condition that he not leave the country. Vladimir Kara-Murza relates:

> We got him released after three days. I called Gorbachev, he called Juan Carlos, and Juan Carlos told Putin that if he, Putin, didn't let Gusinsky go, he himself would regret it later. And Putin was forced to send Minister Lesin to jail. But he gave him instructions: "Bargain with him, make sure he gives all those shares away. We'll have to let him go in any case."[9]

SAVONAROLA'S REVENGE

The scale of the pressures leveled against NTV made the channel's reporters feel like they had nothing left to lose. All the critical arrows of "Kiselev's team" were now aimed directly at Putin.

On July 15, 2000, *Puppets* featured another puppet play by Viktor Shenderovich. This episode was about Girolamo Savonarola, who was made to look like President Putin. Shenderovich's funny and inflammatory satire ended with a transparent allusion: The citizens of Florence, made to look like Russians, are disappointed that their preacher's fight against the luxury and decadence of the rich has not had any effect on their own lives, except that their eyes sting from the smoke of the fires on which their barons are being burned—which can hardly be called a change for the better.

"Do something at least!" the Florentines yell at Savonarola. Then one of them flips an hourglass and says: "Time's up." Savonarola, as is well known, was himself burned at the stake in 1498, to the cheers of his recent supporters.

On July 16, as usual, the episode was aired a second time.

On July 19, two investigators from the General Prosecutor's Office, Leonid Chelenko and Zigmund Lozhis, accompanied by a car carrying FSB security agents, paid a visit to the home of NTV's owner Vladmir Gusinsky in the town of Chigasovo outside Moscow. They carried out a search, which was officially called an "inventory of the property," and impounded the objects listed in the inventory—in connection with the criminal case of "large-scale embezzlement by means of fraud and breach of trust." This charge referred to Media-Most's acquisition of the Russkoye Video company. Most of Gusinsky's inventoried property consisted of paintings and other works of art, as well as furniture and silverware, since Gusinsky naturally did not keep his money and shares in a safe at home.

The confiscation of Gusinsky's silverware looked like a direct response from "Savonarola" to the challenge by *Puppets*—and possibly was meant as such.

THE SIXTH PROTOCOL

The operation against Gusinsky also served a pragmatic function. Fearing another stint at a temporary detention facility, Gusinsky signed an agreement the next day (July 20) to hand over to the Gazprom Media Holding Company all media outlets belonging to Media-Most as payment for debts amounting to $300 million. By contrast with the fabricated "invasions into private life" and "embezzlement by means of fraud and breach of trust," Media-Most's debts to Gazprom were real. The press minister, Mikhail Lesin, participated in the negotiations. At Gusinsky's insistence, he signed the agreement's "Appendix 6," which stipulated that, in recognition of Media-Most's agreement to repay its debts, the criminal case against Gusinsky would be dropped.

Gusinsky's property was released from impoundment on July 26, and the criminal charges against him were dropped for lack of evidence that any crime had been committed.

NTV's reporters expected to be fired any day and felt that they had nothing to lose. It is almost incomprehensible how *Izvestiya* dared to publish a short interview with Shenderovich in which the satirist, comparing President Yeltsin with Putin, said: "The old boss was big, bibulous, and blissful; the new one is small, sober, and mean. It would be better if he were a drinker."[10] In similarly fearless fashion, NTV commented on the tragedy of the submarine *Kursk*, which had been abandoned to its fate both by the navy and by the president personally, who did not even cut short his vacation on the Black Sea.

But the Kremlin was somewhat premature in celebrating its victory over Media-Most: after leaving the country, Gusinsky immediately disavowed his agreement with Gazprom Media, since it had been signed under duress from Russian law enforcement and thus had no more juridical weight than promises given to racketeers at the threat of being branded with a hot iron. As proof of this fact, Gusinsky presented the same "Appendix 6"—or the "sixth protocol," as it came to be known—which had been signed by the press minister. Gusinsky did not refuse to pay his debts. But he refused to do so by handing over his media assets.

Shielding Putin from charges of extortion, Lesin stated that he "had not informed" the president about the agreement that he had signed with Gusinsky, although he had informed Prime Minister Kasyanov. On September 26, the president announced through his press secretary, in a politically correct fashion, that he was not interfering and had no intention of interfering with the Media-Most controversy, and that the opposing sides must resolve all conflicts by judicial means.

THE CONFISCATION OF ORT FROM BORIS BEREZOVSKY

In its approach to the *Kursk* submarine disaster, NTV found an unexpected ally: Berezovsky's ORT (Channel One), which had previously lambasted all of Putin's enemies. News anchor Sergei Dorenko's criticism of the government differed from Shenderovich's in style, but was the same in substance. By contrast with NTV, ORT was watched by the whole country. If Shenderovich was loved by the Moscow intelligentsia, Dorenko was popular among the people. For the first time, Putin's popularity rating trembled.

Berezovsky says he first had "serious doubts" about Putin "in December 1999, once the Duma election had already passed." He explains:

> This was when Putin didn't stop in Chechnya, after reaching the Terek River. . . . But these were not yet serious differences. . . . But the disagreements about the seven federal electoral districts, the Federation Council, and the right to remove elected governors—yes, these were already insurmountable differences. . . . The turning point, of course, was the *Kursk* submarine tragedy. Channel One, which I still owned, covered it in a very critical way. It showed the despair of the widows, and the cowardice and hypocrisy of the government officials.[11]

In August 2000, Berezovsky's former protégé Alexander Voloshin, Putin's chief of staff, told Berezovsky that if he did let go of his shares in ORT, he would "follow in Gusinsky's footsteps."[12]

Berezovsky attempted, if not to save ORT from Putin, then at least to drag out the process. To this end, an effort was made to transfer ORT's shares not to the government or its representatives, but to a newly formed, privately owned company named Teletrust, which consisted of members of the creative intelligentsia, including a number of NTV reporters. The Teletrust idea was probably unfeasible—for many reasons, including the fact that without sponsorship and financing, the creative intelligentsia would not be able to maintain the television channel.

Berezovsky, however, did succeed in delaying the transfer of ORT to the president's chekist entourage. And by opening this "second front," he drew the Kremlin's attention away from finishing off NTV, which also was delayed because of this.

But in December, the Kremlin took a "hostage" from Berezovsky: the media magnate's close friend and collaborator Nikolai Glushkov was arrested. Previously, Glushkov had been forbidden to leave the country in connection with his and Berezovsky's financial operations involving the Aeroflot joint-stock company. And so, in January 2001, Berezovsky was finally forced to sell his ORT shares to the person Voloshin had told him to sell them to: the government's loyal man, Roman Abramovich.

THE ATTACK ON NTV CONTINUES

Although Gusinsky had disavowed his agreement to transfer his media assets to Gazprom and the criminal case against him had effectively fallen apart, Media-Most's debt to Gazprom remained outstanding. In addition, any commercial enterprise in Russia could easily be accused of tax violations. Therefore, the Kremlin still had ways to fight for the ownership of NTV within the framework of a so-called "property rights conflict." The task of subjugating NTV, which the FSB and the General Prosecutor's Office had been unable to manage, was assigned to the general manager of Gazprom Media, Alfred Kokh.

But this path was a long one; and so the authorities, aiming to accelerate the process, constantly resorted to breaking legal procedure and threatening Gusinsky to renew the embezzlement case against him. They also got the tax agency involved in the battle.

On December 9, 2000, the Ministry of Taxation initiated court proceedings to liquidate NTV. Tatyana Luzhina, head of the ministry's inspections office for the Moscow Central District, filed a suit with the Moscow Arbitration Court to "liquidate the NTV Television Company, as well as a number of other companies belonging to Media-Most." The suit was based on Article 99, par. 4 of the Russian Civil Code, which states:

> If upon the expiry of the second and of each of the next fiscal years the cost of a company's net assets proves to be less than its authorized capital, the company shall be obliged to declare and to register the reduction in its authorized capital, in conformity with established procedures. If the cost of the said company's assets falls below the minimum size of the authorized capital, fixed by the law, the company shall be subject to liquidation.

Up to that time, the government had never before used Article 99 to liquidate any company; moreover, this article had been slated for deletion from the Civil Code. Normally, if there was a discrepancy between a company's authorized capital and its net assets, the tax inspectorate would either simply ignore it or instruct the company to eliminate this formal difference. Although Luzhina stressed at a press conference that her suit had no political subtext, few believed her.

On December 12, Gusinsky, once again charged with embezzlement, was arrested in Spain in connection with a request by the Russian General Prosecutor's Office that he be extradited. He was soon released, and the request for his extradition was officially denied, because the prosecutor's office was unable to offer convincing proof that Gusinsky was being prosecuted as a criminal and not on political grounds. Trying to turn the public against NTV, the prosecutor's office began disclosing facts to the press about the cost of apartments that NTV reporters had received from Media-Most. (Incidentally, these costs were far below that of General Prosecutor Ustinov's own apartment, which had been given to him in perpetuity by the Presidential Property Management Directorate: over $400,000.)

Since the "hostage experiment" had produced results—Berezovsky sold ORT in return for a promise that Glushkov would be released (a promise that was not fulfilled, however)—the government "took a hostage" from Gusinsky as well. Anton Titov, the former head of Media-Most's financial management department, was arrested on January 16, 2001, on charges of large-scale embezzlement, theft, and money-laundering in collaboration with Gusinsky. Nightly interrogations of Titov began.

At the end of January, "Kiselev's team" made an attempt to bring its conflict with Putin under control. Following a request voiced on the air by Svetlana Sorokina, Putin received a large group of NTV reporters, with Yevgeny Kiselev at their head, in his Kremlin office. The meeting produced no results: the reporters expressed no signs of contrition, while the president assured them that he had no connection to the pressures being exerted on Media-Most by Gazprom, the General Prosecutor's Office, and the FSB. In response to the request that Titov be released, Putin replied that, as a democrat, he did not wish to resort to "law by telephone."

Titov ended up remaining in custody until December 2002, when he was finally tried, sentenced to three years in prison, and then pardoned. During his trial, most of the charges against him were dropped.

THE END OF THE "OLD" NTV

In the spring of 2001, a number of reporters fled from the sinking ship of NTV. As Viktor Shenderovich recalls, "reporters who agreed to leave NTV had their debts cancelled and their salaries increased."[13]

Gazprom Media called a meeting of NTV shareholders on April 3. There, a decision was made to remove Yevgeny Kiselev from the positions of general manager and editor-in-chief, and to appoint new management for the television company under the leadership of Alfred Kokh (general manager of Gazprom Media) and the American businessman Boris Jordan (general manager of NTV). The shareholders' meeting had not been convened in an entirely legal manner, nor were its resolutions wholly sound from a legal standpoint. NTV was simultaneously a media outlet and a joint-stock company; and Kiselev's dismissal went against Russian media law, although it did meet regulations governing joint-stock companies.

Kiselev blamed the president personally for what had happened: "Putin's signature style is to start a war and then step aside" (NTV, April 4, 2001).

NTV's staff reporters became divided. Some prominent journalists—in particular, Leonid Parfenov and Tatyana Mitkova—agreed to accept the new management, while others—Kiselev, Shenderovich, Svetlana Sorokina, Vladimir Kara-Murza, Dmitry Dibrov—refused to recognize the takeover as legal.

On April 7, Anatoly Chubais, responding to reporters' questions about his attitude toward the situation surrounding NTV and its possible occupation by Gazprom, stated that Gazprom "was asserting its ownership rights—rights that are sacred and untouchable." Moreover, he emphasized that Gazprom was acting in accordance with the law and doing so "very carefully," even though, "with a court decision in its hands, it could act in a much more forceful manner." According to Chubais, "Alfred Kokh is proceeding with caution, trying not to hurt the dignity of NTV's people and unique staff." On the night of April 13–14, the occupation of NTV was completed: security workers from the Invest Security agency, brought over by Kokh and Jordan, took over the company along with its "unique staff."

As a side effect of the Kremlin's victory over Media-Most, the publication of the newspaper *Segodnya* was discontinued. In addition, the management of the magazine *Itogi* changed to one that was loyal to the Kremlin. (By the end of the year, the staff of the old *Itogi*, led by Sergei Parkhomenko, created the magazine *Yezhenedelny Zhurnal*.)

In June–July 2001, Gazprom Media also acquired controlling shares in the radio station Ekho Moskvy as part of its debt settlement. But Gazprom did not replace the station's management, headed by Alexei Venediktov, who has seemingly been able to preserve an independent editorial policy at the station.

In 2002, the management of NTV was partly replaced: Kokh was dismissed, and Jordan became the general manager of Gazprom Media, while remaining general manager of NTV. This is how Kokh explained to the reporter Yevgenia Albats why it was precisely Jordan who had been chosen for the job: "Jordan is the ideal choice. He's the great-grandson of a White Army officer who ran away from the Bolsheviks shortly after the Revolution. He's Russian Orthodox, with an American passport in his pocket, and on top of everything not a Jew, an anti-Semite. Only such a person could be accepted by the chekists as head of NTV."[14]

"Gauleiter Kokh," as he was called at pro-NTV meetings, was not being precise: the White Army officer was not Boris Jordan's great-grandfather, but his grandfather.[15] Colonel Boris Jordan the elder and his son Lieutenant Alexei Jordan, the father of Boris Jordan the younger, were officers in Hitler's Wehrmacht who had fought against the Yugoslavian resistance under the command of SS Gruppenführer Neuhausen.[16] The son is, of course, not responsible for the actions of the father and grandfather, but still the apple does not fall all that far from the tree.

THE TV-6 AFFAIR

The core of "Kiselev's team," exiled from NTV, found a refuge in June 2001 on the previously apolitical TV-6 channel, owned by the Moscow Independent Broadcasting Corporation (MNVK), which was still under Boris Berezovsky's control.

Meanwhile, Putin had already begun an operation to take TV-6 away from Berezovsky. In order to push Berezovsky out of the media business, he kept using his "hostage"—Nikolai Glushkov, who had been arrested in connection with the Aeroflot case. Glushkov's term at the temporary detention facility was repeatedly prolonged, even though he had come down with a blood disease in prison and was diagnosed with severe disability. He was partially acquitted and released only in March 2004.

On March 2 and 13, 2001, the secretary of the Security Council (and subsequently minister of defense and deputy prime minister), Sergei Ivanov, twice met with Berezovsky's representative Badri Patarkatsishvili in the government building at 34 Kosygina Street. The object of their negotiations was Glushkov's release.

According to Patarkatsishvili, Ivanov specified—"on Putin's instructions"—that in order to obtain Glushkov's release, Berezovsky had to renounce all political activity and sell all his media holdings: "everything, including the newspapers. *Kommersant*, too. . . . The agreement was that, before March 25, we would be told whom to negotiate with." Ivanov delegated further negotiations about the fate of TV-6, *Nezavisimaya Gazeta*, and *Kommersant* to Vagit Alekperov, head of Lukoil. Patarkatsishvili recalled:

> We were supposed to negotiate the sales of all our media outlets with Alekperov. But Alekperov, apparently, really wanted to please the Kremlin, on the one hand, and not to pay any money, on the other. The negotiations came to nothing. I was pressed for time, because I had to sell part of my TV-6 shares to a foreign investor, with whom I already had an agreement. . . . I started intensively searching for Ivanov, told him that time was of the essence, that a shareholders' meeting had already been scheduled. I was told: we cannot decide these questions; we need time; please reschedule the shareholders' meeting. . . . I don't think that Ivanov was fooling. He simply wanted to carry out Putin's orders—to meet with me and reach a settlement. But at the same time, he wanted to distance himself from this as much as possible and to have no relation to it. Probably, that is why he wasn't able to see this

business through to the end. He lacked the will. Ivanov took one step: he met with me. Then he took a second step: he assigned the case to Alekperov. And then he removed himself.[17]

In April 2001, Lukoil initiated court proceedings through its daughter foundation Lukoil-Garant (a minority shareholder in TV-6) to liquidate TV-6, claiming that TV-6 had violated the rights of minority shareholders.

In June 2001, the court failed to satisfy Lukoil's claims, but in the fall, a court decision was finally made to liquidate TV-6. At the beginning of January 2002, TV-6's appeal contesting the court's decision was rejected by the arbitration court, although the law on which the decision to liquidate TV-6 was based had just then, on January 1, become ineffective.

On January 15, President Putin announced that the government would not interfere in the situation surrounding TV-6: the TV channel was involved in "a conflict between absolutely independent economic entities, to which the government has virtually no relation."

A few days later, on the night of January 21, TV-6's broadcasting was suspended by order of the press minister, Mikhail Lesin, in accordance with the court decision. On January 29, the president ordered the government to come up with a plan for the creation of a national sports channel.

The liquidation of TV-6 was met with approval by the nationalist-patriotic press. Dmitry Dudko, a priest who enjoys popularity among nationalists, welcomed the move:

I am now putting very high hopes on Vladimir Putin. . . . In many ways, he reminds me of Joseph Stalin. . . . Putin, I hope, will take the same path. He is difficult to understand. Many bad things are still done in the country. But Stalin also did not become resolute all at once. We are witnessing a fight over television, a fight with the oligarchs, a fight for the health of the nation, for our children.[18]

In the Kremlin, however, no final decision about the further fate of the "sixth button" had yet been reached. "The family's" members within the Kremlin administration were still hoping to tame NTV's former staff. It was announced that the "sixth button" would be auctioned off to the highest bidder. Kiselev's banished team was able to participate in this auction twice as part of the nonprofit partnership Mediasocium, headed by Yevgeny Primakov and Arkady Volsky. On March 27, 2002, despite the president's order to create a national sports channel, Mediasocium won the auction.

While the former staff of NTV was preparing to resume broadcasting, on May 17, the Khimkinsky Municipal Court of the Moscow region ruled the MNVK's actions to suspend TV-6's broadcasting to be "illegal, infringing on the constitutional right of television viewers to obtain information freely," and ordered the MNVK—which continued to exist as a formal entity—to put TV-6 back on the air. The situation around Channel Six thus became absurd. Two "legal" licenses to one and the same frequency had been issued—Berezovsky's old MNVK license (now without Kiselev) and Primakov-Volsky's new Mediasocium license (with Kiselev). The new TVS television channel, which began broadcasting in June, ended up in legal limbo as a result of the court decision.

The government could always put this decision into effect if it needed to do so. This is precisely what happened a year later.

THE CASE OF EDUARD LIMONOV

On April 7, 2001, Eduard Limonov, a writer and leader of the National Bolshevik Party (NBP), was arrested in an Altay town on charges of illegally buying weapons and escorted to the Lefortovo prison. Half a year later, Limonov was additionally charged with terrorism and the creation of an illegal armed formation—although the NBP's "terrorism" never went beyond the bounds of what is usually classified by Russian criminal law as disorderly conduct. The arrest of the NBP's leader was preceded by a strange episode in which members of his party purchased several automatic weapons from Nazis belonging to the Russian National Unity movement; after the transaction, the buyers were arrested, while the sellers were allowed to remain at liberty as "persons whose identity has not been established."

Limonov was the only notable activist from the nationalist camp who from the very beginning was intent on undermining Putin's credibility among the nationalist-patriotic part of the electorate, particularly among the young. In some sense, Limonov's role was similar to that of Shenderovich, but based on different principles and aimed at a different audience. The Russian PEN Club, while stressing that it did not share Limonov's political views, called for his release at least until his court date; but this call had no effect.

The trial of Limonov and several of his followers began in Saratov on September 9, 2002. The charges of "terrorism," of "creating armed formations," and even of simple involvement in the buying of automatic weapons fell apart before everyone's eyes, and the FSB began actively "working with" witnesses in order to obtain a sentence for the writer at least equal to the amount of time that he had already served. In the end, the court found Limonov guilty on only a few counts and sentenced him to four years in prison, of which he had already served more than two.

THE CASE OF "NOVAYA GAZETA"

In April 2002, Mezhprombank was awarded 15 million rubles (about $500,000) for "lost profits" in its suit against *Novaya Gazeta*. This court decision made it uncertain whether the newspaper would be able to survive. The suit was preceded by a November 2001 article in *Novaya Gazeta* claiming that Mezhprombank's management and its head, Sergei Pugachev (close to Putin and the chekists in his entourage), were involved in laundering money for the Russian mafia at the Bank of New York.

In fact, a suit against *Novaya Gazeta* for the protection of honor and dignity would not have been unfounded: the newspaper had given no evidence of Pugachev's crime. But Pugachev did not defend his personal honor and dignity; instead, Mezhprombank filed suit for the protection of its business reputation and for the material losses it had sustained because of this article. According to Mezhprombank, one of its clients—the joint-stock company Veststroyservis—had become concerned that the possible repercussions of the article might destabilize the bank and on the same day altered the terms of its account with the bank, which allegedly caused the bank to suffer losses—an actual loss in the amount of 15 million rubles and forgone gains in the amount of another 15 million rubles (about one million dollars in total).

The unprecedentedly high sum of the fine revealed a wish on the part of those who had organized the lawsuit not merely to punish the reporters, but to terminate the existence of the newspaper altogether.

Alexei Simonov, president of the Glasnost Defense Foundation, has argued that "*Novaya Gazeta* was attacked on orders from above. . . . When a court starts awarding unimaginably high amounts—a million dollars, then half a million . . . then the lawsuit is not an end, but a means to an end." Simonov has also named the possible agencies that may have "placed the order": the Ministry of Defense (antagonized by Anna Politkovskaya's and Vyacheslav Izmailov's articles), the FSB (because of Georgy Rozhnov's articles), the Security Council, the Moscow Municipal Court.[19]

The only thing that ended up saving *Novaya Gazeta* was the fact that the evidence presented by Mezhprombank about its "losses" had one flaw that had been "overlooked" by the court, but was brilliantly demonstrated by *Novaya Gazeta*'s editor, Yulia Latynina: the joint-stock companies Veststroyservis, Business Master 2000, and UTEK Concern, "due to whose agreements and letters Mezhprombank incurred losses, are controlled either by Mezhprombank itself or by Mezhprombank's managers and founders." Among the managers and founders named by Latynina was Sergei Pugachev himself, his wife, Galina Pugacheva, and other managers of the same Mezhprombank.[20]

"This element in Russian business, this kind of forged bankruptcy, is familiar to the public," commented *Novye Izvestiya*. "Now we can say that the ruling group of oligarchs has invented a new technique for the 'legitimate' liquidation of a politically inconvenient media outlet: through false losses."[21]

At the end of May 2002, Latynina herself and *Novaya Gazeta*'s editorial board filed a request with the Moscow prosecutor's office and municipal law enforcement agencies to "look into instances of swindling (in accordance with Article 159 of the Criminal Code) against *Novaya Gazeta* committed by

Mezhprombank's management and a number of companies affiliated with the bank." In this case, the "property rights conflict" was resolved in favor of the reporters: Mezhprombank became frightened of a loud scandal and declined the money it had won in court.

THE SHUTTING DOWN OF "OBSCHAYA GAZETA"

Novaya Gazeta had avoided bankruptcy and survived. But at approximately the same time, the fate of another independent newspaper, *Obschaya Gazeta*—the last mouthpiece of the "sixties generation"—was permanently decided.

Its founder and editor-in-chief, Yegor Yakovlev, unable to find financing to continue its publication, sold the newspaper to the St. Petersburg businessman Vyacheslav Leibman—better known as the former boyfriend of Ksenia Sobchak, a popular figure in the gossip columns and daughter of St. Petersburg's first mayor. Leibman immediately shut down *Obschaya Gazeta*, and in its place he began to publish *Konservator*, a newspaper with a completely different (pro-Putin) political slant. Up to the very end, Yakovlev seems to have been convinced that *Obschaya Gazeta* would survive after its sale—even if it would assume a different form—and that its staff would not be dismissed, at least not all at once.

It was never revealed why the businessman, before starting to publish his own newspaper, spent a great deal of money to silence another newspaper. A plausible hypothesis is that Leibman did not spend his own money to buy the newspaper, but someone else's, and with only one goal: to prevent some other party from buying the newspaper—for example, Putin's enemy Berezovsky. As for Leibman's *Konservator*, it did not last long: its publisher ran out of money within half a year.

THE CASE OF VLADIMIR SOROKIN AND THE RAID ON AD MARGINEM PRESS

The "Sorokin affair" itself, which was instigated by functionaries from the pro-Putin youth organization Iduschie Vmeste ("Traveling Together"), has no direct relation to the topic of press freedom. The bloodiest episode in Vladimir Sorokin's harassment was the triumphal dunking of his novel *Blue Lard* in a symbolic toilet set up across from the Bolshoi Theater. However, following a denunciation by the forty-nine-year-old Artyom Maguniants—who "traveled together" with the Putin-loving youth—a criminal lawsuit was soon filed against *Blue Lard*'s publisher, Ad Marginem Press, in accordance with Article 242 of the Russian Criminal Code (distributing pornography).

The main subject of Sorokin's "art" is actually not sex, but defecation, as well as necrophiliac fantasies in the spirit of the serial killer Chikatilo. Readers with traditional tastes are more likely to lose their sexual instincts by becoming too closely acquainted with Sorokin's work. (In other words, his books are, if anything, a form of "anti-pornography.")

But that is not the point: TV channels are not persecuted for showing pornography, while Ad Marginem Press had criminal charges brought against it. Moreover, on September 16, 2002, after receiving a positive expert opinion from literary specialists, Moscow municipal law enforcement raided the offices of the publishing house. It is possible that the pornography charge was used as a pretext to punish—or more precisely, "to seriously warn"—the director of Ad Marginem Press, Alexander Ivanov, for publishing a completely different book: Alexander Prokhanov's political thriller *Mr. Hexogen*.[22]

Mr. Hexogen is devoted to a topic that is quite painful for the Putin regime: the Moscow apartment-house bombings as a chekist electoral technique. Even the old NTV went only so far as to raise this question, without ever answering it so unequivocally.

Prokhanov himself is the author of brilliant pamphlets, which he publishes in his newspaper *Zavtra*. As a writer of novels, however, he is only a verbose bore. Without Ad Marginem's cover, *Mr. Hexogen* would have been doomed to languish in the Communist-nationalist ghetto. By publishing the novel, Ivanov took Prokhanov out of the ghetto and turned his book into a national bestseller—thus dealing a serious blow to the government's propaganda.

Therefore, there is every reason to consider the raid on Ivanov's offices a *political* event. At the same time, it undoubtedly constituted an attack on freedom of the press even if the presence of the "pornographic element" was its real cause and not merely a pretext.

THE REPEAL OF THE DECREE CONCERNING RADIO LIBERTY

On October 4, 2003, President Putin repealed Boris Yeltsin's decree of August 27, 1991, "permitting the management of the independent radio station Liberty/Liberty Europe to open a permanent office in Moscow and to station reporters across the territory of the RSFSR." The repeal of Yeltsin's decree had no direct practical significance, since the radio station operated and continues to operate in Russia not on the basis of this decree, but on the basis of Russian media law.

In the opinion of Andrei Sharyi, one of the heads of the station's Moscow bureau, who compares Yeltsin's 1991 decree with a medal "for the defense of the White House," "there are two sides here—a formal and legal side, and, let us say, a symbolic side. As far as the first of these sides is concerned, this event is not a tragedy for us. The station's status remains unchanged. In the summer [of 2003] our broadcasting license is supposed to be renewed, and then we will find out whether Putin's decision was an empty formality or something more."[23]

In 2003, Radio Liberty's broadcasting license was indeed renewed—the Ministry of the Press did not dare to become involved with the United States Congress without direct orders from above. Or else it received direct orders to avoid such involvement.

THE RAID ON "VERSIYA"

After the death of Artyom Borovik in March 2000, the newspapers of his Sovershenno Sekretno publishing enterprise—the monthly *Sovershenno Sekretno* and the weekly *Versiya*—almost immediately halted their attacks on Putin personally and substantially tempered their critical stance toward his entourage.

In addition, after Putin was elected president, Yevgeny Primakov—the political ideal and partial sponsor of Sovershenno Sekretno—ceased to be an active political player and began to emphasize his loyalty to the new regime in all kinds of ways (although he declined to join the pro-Putin United Russia party). Another one of Sovershenno Sekretno's political guiding lights, Yuri Luzhkov, fell even lower and did join United Russia, taking his own Fatherland party with him.

Nonetheless, under Rustam Arifdzhanov as editor-in-chief, *Versiya* and *Sovershenno Sekretno* maintained a sufficiently independent stance. These newspapers could be accused of indulging in a certain amount of "yellow journalism," of taking part in feuds between the oligarchs (publishing compromising stories about members of "the family," apparently at the behest of the Moscow mayor's office), of publishing certain articles in return (presumably) for payment; but they could not be accused of toadyism.

In September 2000, the *Versiya* office was raided and its files were confiscated by the FSB when the newspaper was preparing to publish exclusive materials concerning the sinking of the submarine *Kursk*.

At the end of October 2002, after the tragic mishandling of the hostage-rescue operation at Moscow's Dubrovka theater, no law enforcement officials were punished for allowing the terrorists to penetrate into Moscow. The government's criticism focused mainly on TV reporters, whose mistakes in covering the event were alleged to have possibly helped the terrorists.

Versiya was the first newspaper to be hit with troubles stemming from the hostage crisis after its reporters undertook an independent investigation of the tragedy. FSB operatives showed up at *Versiya*'s offices on November 1 and confiscated the newspaper's computer and server, paralyzing its work for several days. Back in May, *Versiya* had published an article titled "Camouflage," describing illegal construction projects at classified government sites. A criminal suit against the newspaper had been filed on October 18, and this was the reason given for the confiscation of its property.

The real reason, however, as Arifdzhanov immediately surmised, was not the now largely forgotten article, but the FSB's desire to prevent *Versiya* from publishing a detailed report on the elimination of the terrorists along with the hostages at the Dubrovka theater. On October 26, *Versiya*'s deputy editor-in-chief, Andrei Soldatov, had been a witness to the operation to "rescue" the hostages, and his reports about the victims differed significantly from the official accounts: many hostages were already dead when they were carried out of the theater, yet they were immediately taken to the hospital, apparently in order to create the impression that they had died not during the "rescue operation," but at the hospital or on the way there.

There were copies of Soldatov's files on a computer that the FSB had not confiscated, and eventually the article did come out. Those who had ordered the raid on *Versiya* evidently had good reasons to fear the truth, but their apprehensions turned out to have been exaggerated: the published materials revealed no facts that would have put government or law enforcement officials in mortal danger.

After this, the criminal case against "Camouflage" was closed, and *Versiya*'s computers and files about the hostage crisis were returned to its offices. Formally, the incident had no further consequences. "Camouflage" was forgotten by the prosecutor's office, and Soldatov's exposés of the government's lies about the hostage crisis were ignored.

Yet *Versiya*'s conflict with the FSB could not but make relations more difficult between Arifdzhanov and the newspaper's owners. On July 14, 2003, Arifdzhanov was given notice by the president of Sovershenno Sekretno, Veronika Borovik-Khilchevskaya (who was Artyom Borovik's widow). The direct cause of his departure was the fact that the newspaper had lost a case filed against it with the arbitration court by the Alfa Group.[24]

However, Arifdzhanov believes that the "loss in the arbitration court was only a pretext [for the dismissal]. . . . In three years of working together [with Borovik-Khilchevskaya], we were able to do some good work, but we had also become somewhat tired of each other."[25]

THE OVERHAUL OF MEDIA REGULATIONS

Immediately following the hostage crisis, Putin's administration initiated the passage of legislation in the Duma aimed at amending media regulations. The new regulations included numerous restrictions on reporters' activities during a state of emergency, effectively making it illegal even to criticize "antiterrorist operations." Then, at a meeting with the heads of pro-government media outlets on November 25, 2002, Putin announced that he had vetoed the legislation—which had already passed both houses of parliament—after it drew criticism and calls for a presidential veto from the press.

The reporters were too quick with their celebrations, however: two days later, the president sent a letter to the heads of both houses of parliament with the recommendation to continue developing the new media law, proposing the introduction of "additional regulations for media activities during states of emergency, under martial law, and in the coverage of emergency situations of a natural or technological character." Putin's veto did not signify a refusal to "develop and pass into law a set of restrictions on reporters' activities, as it has been portrayed by enthusiastic staff reporters and well-paid optimists, but [was] merely the formal expression of the president's displeasure at the imperfection of the proposed measures."[26]

On December 15, the FSB director, Nikolai Patrushev, opened a meeting with the heads of a number of Russian media outlets—ITAR-TASS, Interfax, RIA Novosti, ORT, and the Rossiya Channel—by noting that he was satisfied with the cooperation between his agency and the Russian media: "We are doing the same thing: working for the society, for the state." If the FSB and the media in Russia are "doing the same thing," then that "thing" can be considered as good as done.

THE FIRST PURGE AT THE "NEW" NTV

The *Nord-Ost* hostage catastrophe had one more direct consequence: it finally brought about a change in the management of NTV. The son and grandson of Hitler's officers, Boris Jordan, appointed "Gauleiter" at the occupied TV territories confiscated from the Jew Gusinsky, turned out to be a relatively liberal superintendent. After an initial scare and a momentary swerve toward servility (the transformation of *Puppets* was particularly striking), the "new" NTV's signature style became that of the show *Namedni*, cultivated by Leonid Parfenov and his school: aestheticism, intellectualism, irony, and apparent political neutrality, but not without concealed derision.

Jordan treated the channel that had been entrusted to him as a business that must sooner or later begin to yield a profit. A TV channel that is burdened with petty censorship is a bad business, as illustrated by the entirely state-run Channels One and Two. Jordan freed the reporters from routine surveillance, allowing them to preserve at least a stylistic independence. For a while, this drew no direct censure from the Kremlin.

After *Nord-Ost*, the situation changed radically. In their coverage of the catastrophe, NTV's reporters fully displayed their natural professionalism, without being especially concerned about the risk of incurring displeasure from above. The manner in which Jordan's employees covered the crisis angered the president personally. Jordan's imminent dismissal was "spoken of as a personal decision by the president, who had been infuriated by the fact that NTV had shown the storming of the theater on the air."[27] Although no important reporters were fired at the time, Jordan himself was dismissed during the latter half of January 2003—first from one general manager's position (Gazprom Media), then from another (NTV).

On January 22, Nikolai Senkevich, a doctor by profession, was appointed acting general manager of NTV, and the TV producer Alexei Zemskov became his deputy. On February 6, two days after a meeting with Alexei Miller, head of Gazprom, Leonid Parfenov stated in an interview with Ekho Moskvy radio that *Namedni* was going to end production and that he would take a three-month vacation. In addition to Parfenov, Tatyana Mitkova and Savik Shuster expressed public displeasure and indignation at the fact that NTV's new manager had no connection to journalism. But the disgruntled parties were forced to come to terms with the situation. On May 18, *Namedni* came back on the air.

Under Senkevich, NTV's political programming began to retreat into the background, yielding the spotlight to entertainment. For example, the weekly program *Faktor Strakha* ("Fear Factor") became typical of the "new new" NTV. Disguised as a fight against phobias and squeamishness, *Faktor Strakha* effectively promotes sadism and necrophilia (the show's participants kill or torture small animals or eat them alive), as well as coprophagia (they also eat their feces).

THE FIRING OF THE EDITORIAL STAFF OF "NOVYE IZVESTIYA"

Novye Izvestiya was one of two newspapers (along with *Novaya Gazeta*) that from the very beginning treated President Putin without any deference. The financial sponsor of *Novye Izvestiya* was Boris Berezovsky, but the formal owner of more than the controlling percentage of shares was the businessman Oleg Mitvol (canning industry, green pea production). Seventy-four percent of the shares of the Novye Izvestiya News Publishing Group were in Mitvol's name, having been transferred to him by Berezovsky when the latter left Russia, and the rest were owned by the newspaper's staff.

When Berezovsky transferred his shares to Mitvol, he did not have time to safeguard himself against possible foul play. In any case, Mitvol did not initially try to cheat Berezovsky out of anything.

Novye Izvestiya's formal owner did not interfere with its editorial policies, nor did he contribute anything to its financing; the newspaper continued to be financed by the London exile. But all payments apparently went through Mitvol's commercial entities—most likely not without some profit to himself (as a payment for risk).

On February 20, 2003, however, Mitvol presented the newspaper's management with a complaint that his financial contributions were being improperly handled, fired the general manager of the Novye Izvestiya News Publishing Group, Igor Golembiovsky, and stopped the newspaper's publication. He also sent the prosecutor's office a declaration that Golembiovsky and his deputy, Sergei Agafonov, had for several years supposedly been engaged in criminally siphoning assets from *Novye Izvestiya*.

"What Oleg Mitvol says about financial schemes is funny," noted *Novye Izvestiya*'s deputy general manager, Valery Yakov, in an interview with *Kommersant*. "It was precisely Mitvol who was in charge of our finances. We believe that the events at the newspaper are connected with the fact that it has recently published critical articles about Putin. For example, the last issue contained a long article titled '. . . Plus Putinization of the Whole Country.'"[28]

Berezovsky expressed a similar view in an interview with the Internet publication Gazeta.ru. "Yesterday, for example, they published an article about the revival of a cult of personality around Putin, and the Kremlin evidently did not like it," said Berezovsky. "I think that Mitvol got a signal from the Kremlin, because he himself is a cowardly person."[29]

Two months later, a group of former *Novye Izvestiya* employees led by Golembiovsky and Agafonov founded the newspaper *Russky Kurier*, while the remaining staff, headed by Valery Yakov, began once more to publish *Novye Izvestiya*. In connection with these events, one of the pro-Putin pundits (a hereditary defender of the government—the son of a high-ranking apologist for Brezhnev's "developed communism") made a sarcastic remark in the English-language *Moscow Times* about how scary Putin's autocratic regime truly was: as soon as one opposition newspaper closed, sponsors were found to replace it with two new ones.[30]

In reality, Valery Yakov's "new" *Novye Izvestiya* has a neutral editorial policy rather than an oppositional one. As for *Russky Kurier*, it lasted as an opposition newspaper—although a notably more cautious one than the "old" *Novye Izvestiya*—for less than two years.

There were no visible repressions against the management of *Russky Kurier* for its political stance and previous ties to Berezovsky; but the criminal case against Golembiovsky and Agafonov continued to unfold. During questioning, the defendants stated that they considered themselves completely innocent, and explained all of their allegedly criminal transactions involving newspaper property as being motivated by financial necessity. The case of Golembiovsky and Agafonov was a classic example of "selective justice": *all* commercial entities, including those involved in publishing, make use of loopholes and contradictions in the law with the aim of minimizing their expenditures; but the only ones punished for doing so are those that have in some way incurred the wrath of the government, one of the government's clans, or some specific government official. (Mikhail Khodorkovsky's case is another example.)

On June 18, 2004, the Ministry of Internal Affairs' Committee of Inquiry completed its investigation of the criminal case against Golembiovsky and Agafonov. The Committee of Inquiry reached the conclusion that Golembiovsky and Agafonov, in managing *Novye Izvestiya*, had deliberately impoverished the newspaper and siphoned its assets. It was announced that, after the accused had a chance to study the twenty-two volumes of the criminal case, the materials would be handed over to the court.[31] On August 16, this indeed happened—the prosecutor's office handed the case over to the court, after which, however, it was returned for further inquiry, and then forgotten.

THE DEATH THROES AND DEMISE OF TVS

The shutting down of the TVS television channel in June 2003 completed the liquidation of all independent television outlets. This process began with the persecution of NTV's owner, Vladimir Gusinsky, in the spring and summer of 2000, and the confiscation of Channel One (ORT) from Boris Berezovsky at the end of 2000. It continued with the April–May 2001 dismantling of the "old" NTV and the shutting down of TV-6 in January 2002.

When in March 2002, based on the outcome of an auction, the "sixth button" (of the former TV-6) was allocated to the non-profit partnership Mediasocium, which had been created by the staff of the former TV-6, this (at first glance, unexpected) decision had one main goal: to soften the displeasure of Western public opinion at the preceding events and to draw criticism away from President Putin. To this end, the president even temporarily abandoned his idea of creating a national sports channel.

The outcome of the auction was meant to demonstrate to the West that there was no government policy to check freedom of speech—that all the transformations in Russia's media stemmed from nothing more than "conflicts over property rights." The government's role was that of a disinterested arbiter. Thus, for example, it had conducted the auction for the "sixth button" fairly and objectively, and the reporters who had just recently been the losers in one case were now the winners in another. The reporters, on the other hand—according to the Kremlin's designs—were given to understand the opposite: the government has its policies, and they had better take them into account.

The new TV channel received sponsorship and investment from the Shestoy Kanal joint-stock company, a consortium of business magnates to whom the Kremlin had effectively assigned the custodianship of TVS. In addition to being financed by businessmen who were dependent on the government, TVS found itself under yet another constraint: it had been placed in "legal limbo" by a court decision. Already on May 17, 2002, the Khimkinsky Municipal Court had ruled that the Moscow Independent Broadcasting Company's (MNVK) actions to suspend TV-6's broadcasts were "illegal, infringing on the constitutional right of television viewers to obtain information freely," and ordered the MNVK to put TV-6 back on the air.

Actually, there was no one to "put the channel back on the air," since the MNVK—after fulfilling earlier court decisions (shutting down TV-6)—had effectively ceased to exist. At the same time, the Ministry of the Press, Television and Radio Broadcasting, and Mass Media (MPTR) had acquired the option of putting the Khimkinsky court decision into effect whenever it pleased and thus depriving TVS of the "sixth button." This is what ultimately happened.

During the whole period of TVS's existence, two competing groups of co-owners in the TV consortium—headed by Anatoly Chubais and Oleg Deripaska, respectively—tried, first, to establish complete control over the channel, and second, to force the reporters to formulate self-censorship guidelines that were acceptable to the president's administration. Their success in achieving the second of these goals was not great (from the Kremlin's point of view, it was poor), while their success in achieving the first was nonexistent. Neither Chubais's nor Deripaska's group was able to derive any kind of commercial or semicommercial benefit from the channel's existence. Meanwhile, the Kremlin constantly expressed displeasure at the continuing opposition of "Kiselev's team," blaming the experiment's failure on the channel's co-owners, who had not solved the problem that had been assigned to them.

TVS—which lasted exactly one year, from June 2002 to June 2003—was significantly different from the "old" NTV and from TV-6. It featured programming that would have been inconceivable on the "old" NTV and TV-6, such as the Islamophobic TV show *Men's Work* (the heroic struggle of FSB agents against Chechen bandits, including a traitor-reporter who was easily recognizable as a stand-in for Radio Liberty's Chechnya correspondent Andrei Babitsky) or the whitewashing "examination" of the case of Colonel Yuri Budanov, who had strangled an eighteen-year-old Chechen girl to death during "questioning." TV-6 had already made an effort to attract a new kind of viewer, and new advertising sponsors, through fundamentally apolitical "reality shows" such as the primitive and ethically suspect *Behind Glass*. This effort continued on TVS: the reality show *Behind Glass: You're in the Army Now* was as lowbrow as its predecessor, but in addition presented itself as promoting military-patriotic values.

Yevgeny Kiselev himself became so cautious on his show *Itogi* that it sometimes seemed as if the calmly ironic Leonid Parfenov on the "new" NTV was allowing himself greater liberties. But Viktor Shenderovich's brilliant *Free Cheese* and Andrei Cherkizov's *Out of Spite!* were fully in keeping with the traditions of the "old" NTV. Alexander Tatarsky and Vladimir Neklyudov's shows *Kremlin Concert* and *Shut the Lights!*, which NTV purchased from the Pilot TV production studio, were also distinguished by their political acumen and talent.

The sad denouement of TVS was also predetermined by the fact that the second half of 2003 and the first half of 2004 was a period of two national election campaigns, for the parliament and for the presidency. It was completely inconceivable that *Free Cheese*, *Out of Spite!*, *Kremlin Concert*, or *Shut the Lights!* would be allowed to survive until the elections.

Already by the spring of 2003, the Kremlin had come to the conclusion that it was necessary to end the experiment, and at the end of April the co-owners of the consortium effectively terminated TVS's financing. In the middle of May, Pilot TV's shows *Shut the Lights!* and *Kremlin Concert* disappeared due to a lack of financing. Mostelecom, a joint-stock company owned by the Moscow government, stopped receiving payments for the TV signal and at the beginning of June it began shutting down TVS's broadcasting in Moscow, district by district. Then the Ministry of the Press took advantage of the Khimkinsky

Municipal Court's decision from the previous year regarding the illegality of shutting down TV-6, and on June 22 announced the termination of TVS's broadcasting.

Naturally, the "sixth button" was not returned to Berezovsky's paralyzed MNVK—although this was precisely what had to be done, from a formal point of view, according to the Khimkinsky Municipal Court's decision. The frequency was taken over by the new Sport TV Channel: President Putin's dream of a national sports channel had come true at last.

Despite the indisputable love of Russians for televised sporting events, the Sport TV Channel turned out to be economically ineffective and was still not making a profit as of the summer of 2004. Contributions for its maintenance add up to millions of dollars. (Formally, the funds are disbursed to the state company VGTRK, which controls Rossiya TV, but in practice they are used for the maintenance of the Sport TV Channel. According to Alexei Samokhvalov, director of the National Research Center for Television and Radio, "VGTRK's international partners do not even suspect that their programs are being illegally used by a different channel.") The transmission of the European soccer championship cost the government $10 million; the American hockey championship cost $4 million; the Winter Olympics cost approximately $7.5 million.[32]

The Brezhnev-era ideologist Mikhail Suslov liked to say: "We don't skimp on ideology." The ideologists of the Putin era never skimp on managed elections.

The shutting down of TVS did not mean that the Kremlin's experiment had failed. The main goal—to deceive Western public opinion, and at least for a time to deflect criticism for persecuting the media away from the Russian president—had been accomplished. But Putin preferred to end the duplicity rather than jeopardize the electoral triumphs planned for December 2003 to March 2004.

THE CASE OF GERMAN GALKIN

In June 2002, Andrei Kosilov, deputy governor of the Chelyabinsk region, filed a formal charge against the reporter German Galkin, claiming that the *Rabochaya Gazeta* newspaper published by Galkin had printed libelous statements against Governor Pyotr Sumin and his two deputies, Konstantin Bochkarev and Andrei Kosilov himself.

Galkin—deputy editor-in-chief of the newspaper *Vecherny Chelyabinsk*, publisher of *Rabochaya Gazeta*, and co-chairman of the regional office of the Liberal Russia party (LR)—was at that time also an assistant to one of LR's leaders, Duma deputy Vladimir Golovlev (killed in Moscow in August 2002). Galkin had published a number of materials in *Rabochaya Gazeta* detailing irregular expenditures of budgetary resources by Chelyabinsk region government officials. One of his articles included incautious words about "young boys from poor families [being] brought to government property managers," which Deputy Governor Bochkarev (also a government property manager) took to be an assertion that he was a pedophile.

The two deputy governors instigated a criminal case against Galkin. The reporter's court summons began with words that revealed the political subtext of the whole affair: "German Galkin, who opposes the social and economic policies of the Chelyabinsk regional government . . ." The hearings were closed, since the two deputy governors did not wish the "facts of their private lives" to be examined in open court.

On August 15, 2003, Galkin was found guilty of libel by Svetlana Ryabkova, justice of the peace at the Kalinin District Court, and sentenced to serve one year at a correctional institution. The sentence was handed out during a closed hearing.

Subsequently, 140 Duma deputies signed a request that the Supreme Court review Galkin's case. On November 13, the Chelyabinsk Regional Court suspended his sentence.

Galkin's sentence became the first case in recent times when a reporter was sentenced to an actual term in prison for his articles. Under Putin, however, the handing out of suspended sentences to reporters has become a fairly widespread phenomenon. According to the Center for Journalism in Extreme Situations, in 2001 there were only two such cases:

The first was the case of Yevgeny Rukin, president of the Perm television company Rifey-TV, who on December 25, 2001, was handed a suspended sentence of four years in prison, with the confiscation of property. The second was the highly publicized trial of the Belgorod reporter Olga Kitova, who in December 2001 was handed a suspended sentence of two and a half years in prison.

In 2002, there were already eight such cases:

Nizhny Novgorod reporter Shodmon Ibragimov (suspended sentence of two years in prison and the deduction of 15 percent of income).

Vyacheslav Semerikov, editor-in-chief of the Nizhnevartov newspaper *Semeyny Byudzhet*, and reporter Sergei Kapralov (suspended sentence of one year in prison for each).

Alexander Kobezsky, reporter for the Nizhny Novgorod newspaper *Leninskaya Smena Plyus* (suspended sentence of two and a half years in prison).

Alexei Andreyev, editor-in-chief of the newspaper *Novy Peterburg* (suspended sentence of two years in prison, pardoned against the defendant's wishes).

Yana Porubova, editor of the newspaper *D.S.P.* (suspended sentence of one and a half years in prison, pardoned).

Ivan Gusev, reporter for the newspaper *Stolitsa* (fined 57,000 rubles).

Viktor Barinov, editor-in-chief of the **Nizhny Novgorod** newspaper *Leninskaya Smena Plyus* (fined one hundred times the minimum wage).

Yulia Shelamydova, acting editor-in-chief of the newspaper *Simbirskie Izvestiya* (suspended sentence of one year of correctional service).[33]

THE CASE OF KONSTANTIN BAKHAREV AND KONSTANTIN STERLYADEV

In 2001, the Perm newspaper *Zvezda* published an article by Konstantin Bakharev and Konstantin Sterlyadev titled "A Super-Agent Named Artyom." The reporters became interested in why a local drug dealer, a certain Dudkin, not only did not go to prison after being discovered, but was continuing to engage in his illicit trade. It turned out that Dudkin was a paid informer for the FSB, as well as a double and even a triple agent, also working for Tajik and Israeli intelligence—apparently, with the FSB's knowledge.

In February 2002, Bakharev and Sterlyadev were charged with divulging a state secret.

The novel aspect of this case consisted in the fact that, according to the law, only those people who publish classified materials to which they have official access may be charged with divulging state secrets (for example, the FSB officer who recruited the drug dealer); by contrast, the publication of the findings of a newspaper investigation cannot in any way be considered to be the disclosure of a state secret, even if from the perspective of the security organs they contain information that is extremely classified. For example, the military reporter and environmentalist Grigory Pasko, no matter how fabricated were the espionage charges against him, was accused of divulging information that was accessible to him precisely because of his prior official position.[34]

Nonetheless, this groundless criminal case, which would never have gotten off the ground in Moscow—not as things stand thus far, at any rate—dragged on for a whole year in Perm, interfering with the normal work of the newspaper. In November 2002, the Perm FSB even raided *Zvezda*'s editorial offices. The reporters were acquitted only in September 2003—in a trial that, by law, was not supposed to take place at all. During the investigation and trial, Bakharev and Sterlyadev were defended by the well-known St. Petersburg lawyer and civil rights defender Yuri Schmidt; and it is quite possible that, if not for him, the timorous provincial court would not have been able to withstand the FSB's pressure.

THE BAN ON THE KREMLIN DIGGER

In the fall of 2003, the reporter Yelena Tregubova published *The Tales of a Kremlin Digger*, a controversial book about the mores and morals of the Kremlin under Boris Yeltsin. One of "Czar Boris's" courtiers in the book was FSB director Vladimir Putin. By Tregubova's account, Putin wanted either to have an affair with her or to recruit her as an agent—she herself could not figure out which.

On November 15, NTV announced that Leonid Parfenov's show *Namedni* would feature a segment about the book. The three-and-a-half-minute segment was to include an interview with Tregubova, as well as with two Kremlin officials who also figured in the book, Mikhail Margelov and Alexei Volin. In addition, one of the scenes from the book was recreated in Parfenov's studio: a dinner at Izumi, a Japanese restaurant where FSB director Putin had invited Tregubova in December 1998.

By order of NTV's general manager, Nikolai Senkevich, the segment was not allowed to air. According to Parfenov, Senkevich called him and positively forbade him to broadcast the segment.

Senkevich himself stated in an interview with Ekho Moskvy radio that the segment had been suppressed out of respect for the viewers:

> NTV is not a garbage dump that has room for insults and vulgarity. I believe that our channel and Leonid Gennadievich's highly respected program are too refined and always too precariously positioned to allow themselves to tumble down to such vulgarity. NTV cannot be accused of being insufficiently critical, and the program *Namedni* especially cannot be accused of this. The removal of this segment in no way reduces the critical thrust of today's edition of *Namedni*. Freedom of speech is one thing, but insults and vulgarity are another. There is a big difference. I will not allow such things to go on the air from now on.[35]

On February 2, 2004, a bomb exploded in the hallway next to the door of Tregubova's rented apartment on Nikitsky Boulevard. The unknown terrorists had tapped her phone and detonated the bomb right when Tregubova—preparing to catch a taxi that she had ordered—said on the phone that she was about to leave her apartment. The reporter was saved only because she stopped in front of a mirror for a few seconds.

"NOVOYE VREMYA" AND THE HOUSING QUESTION

Another "property rights conflict" took place in Moscow on September 17, 2003: the representatives of the little-known company Primex expelled the janitors of the magazine *Novoye Vremya* from the magazine's premises on Maly Putinkovsky Lane, near Pushkinskaya Square, and four days later, on a Sunday evening, tried to evict the magazine's reporters as well. Two

Novoye Vremya employees managed to barricade themselves in the reception office and make calls to Ekho Moskvy radio and to Rossiya TV. Duma deputies Vladimir Lukin and Nikolai Gonchar found out about the incident, and thanks to them the police became involved in the conflict, receiving an order from Boris Gryzlov, the minister of internal affairs, to "settle the argument."[36]

But rather than "settle the argument," the police preferred to remain neutral. On February 19, 2004, Primex sent two dozen strongmen to take over *Novoye Vremya*'s premises on Maly Putinkovsky Lane. The reporters had their arms twisted behind their backs and were thrown out on the street. The intruders tossed computers, books, file cabinets with archives, and desks with personal belongings into one pile, and then they started tearing down the walls.[37]

This takeover had a backstory. On April 1, 2003, *Novoye Vremya*'s financial director, Dmitry Minakov, contracted to sell the building to a certain commercial firm, the joint-stock company Kontsept, after which he resigned from *Novoye Vremya*. According to *Novoye Vremya*'s bylaws, Minakov had not been authorized to do this, and his contract carried no legal weight. But Kontsept sold the building to another company, Primex, which thus became, from the legal standpoint, a "bona fide acquirer"—although Kontsept's and Primex's registration papers listed the same telephone number. Primex, in turn, sold the building to the company Effekt, which would have become an even more "bona fide" acquirer, except that this third transaction was not officially registered and did not become legally effective.

In the opinion of *Novoye Vremya*'s editors, all three companies were run by the businessmen Yevgeny Antimony (who owns the Kruzhka pub franchise) and Vladimir Palikhata (Giprokhim company).[38] The editors explain their defeat in the "property rights conflict" as follows:

> In order to occupy a building, it is not enough to have proof of ownership; one needs to obtain a special court decision. Takeover specialists such as Primex prefer to take the law into their own hands. They brazenly climb through a loophole in the law. The loophole is that those who take over buildings are not sued. It is hard to deny that when grim-faced thugs take over a building by force, the law is broken

in the most crude and obvious manner. But as soon as this is done, the crime vanishes: the intruder proudly displays the papers proving his right of ownership. He can be contested only in a court of law. And a trial in court can drag out for years—including a trial based on illegal actions in the takeover of a building. Without an appropriate court decision, no police officer will come to expel the intruder, and it turns out that justice can be restored only by the same means—by force, which is, first of all, again illegal, and second, usually beyond the means of the lawful owner.[39]

Most likely, Antimony and Palikhata seized the poorly situated piece of real estate not on orders from the president's administration, but purely in their own interests. Had they tried to use similar means to take over the premises of a pro-Putin media outlet, the conflict would certainly have had a completely different outcome. In the case of *Novoye Vremya*, the "lawful owner" understood perfectly well that no law enforcement official would stand up for a magazine that regularly published attacks on the "holy of holies."

A similar incident involving the Open Society Institute (affiliated with the Soros Foundation) took place almost at the same time. The institute's building on Ozerkovskaya Embankment was taken over by Kantemir Karamzin's company, Spektr-1. Interestingly, in January 2004, Karamzin rented the same building to Irina Khakamada's election campaign headquarters.

As for *Novoye Vremya*, its activities were paralyzed for several months.

Yevgeny Antimony apparently plans to turn the occupied building into a hotel.

ALEXANDER PODRABINEK IS QUESTIONED

At the beginning of 2004, the FSB tried to initiate criminal proceedings against Alexander Podrabinek—a legendary dissident, head of the Prima News Agency, and former editor-in-chief of *Express Khronika*, a newspaper devoted to defending human rights. On January 28, 2004, Podrabinek was called in for questioning, as a witness, to the FSB's Investigations Directorate at the Lefortovo prison, where he was asked to answer a series of questions about the publication and shipment to Russia of

Alexander Litvinenko and Yuri Felshtinsky's book, *Blowing Up Russia*. It turned out that the publication of this book had provoked a criminal lawsuit—with the charge being "divulging state secrets" (and not, say, libel).

According to the letter of the law, among those who wrote and published this book, only Litvinenko, a former FSB officer, could have been charged with "divulging state secrets," since his information (or suspicions) about the FSB's involvement in the apartment-house bombings of 1999 was acquired in the line of duty. Neither his co-author, Felshtinsky, nor the book's publisher (Boris Berezovsky was the sponsor or effective publisher of the Russian edition of the book), nor its Russian distributor, Podrabinek, was subject to criminal charges for divulging government secrets.

Despite the fact that no Russian court has ruled Litvinenko and Felshtinsky's book to be libelous or extremist, the FSB has obstructed its distribution in Russia. On December 31, 2003, a shipment of copies of *Blowing Up Russia* was to be delivered from Riga to Moscow. The shipment successfully crossed the Latvian-Russian border, but on the 111th kilometer of the Volokolamskoye highway, the truck with the books was stopped by the highway patrol, who confiscated the shipment.

Since Podrabinek's Prima News Agency was the client (or the representative of the client) that ordered the shipment, intending to sell the book, it was Podrabinek who was called in for questioning by the FSB. Despite his interrogators' threats to turn him from a witness into a defendant—a common tactic of Russian law enforcement—Podrabinek, in keeping with ancient dissident principles, refused to answer any questions.

The incident had no visible consequences. Some copies of the book did penetrate into Russia, although book dealers, fearing trouble from the FSB, are not willing to sell them. But the book is easily accessible on the Internet, for example on the websites Biblioteka Maksima Moshkova (lib.ru) and Kompromat.ru.

REGULATING THE INTERNET

The idea of the government regulating the Internet has always been close to the hearts of Putin's bureaucrats. Pronouncements in its favor became especially common in 2004. In March, information was leaked to the media about proposed legislation to regulate the Internet and Internet media outlets. One bill allegedly proposed that special permission be required to access the Web. Another bill would have required all Internet media outlets to register with the government. (At present, the registration of Internet media outlets is voluntary.)

The president's old collaborator Leonid Reiman, the deputy minister of transportation and communications (previously and subsequently the minister of communications), once again expressed his concern about the rights of information consumers. "It is necessary to regulate the relations between providers and consumers," he opined, "and not allow information that goes over the Internet to be subject to distortions."[40]

Lyudmila Narusova, a Federation Council deputy from Tuva and the widow of Anatoly Sobchak, also repeatedly voiced concern about "simple people" who "suffer" because "no one carries any responsibility for unreliable information published on the Internet."[41] Among the "simple people" who "suffer" from the Internet, a prominent place is occupied by Narusova's daughter Ksenia Sobchak, whose romantic adventures are diligently followed by the yellow press. Nor is the mother—herself a former "lady in a turban" (Alexander Nevzorov's expression)—neglected by the media, including the Internet media.

On April 13, the participants of a Moscow roundtable discussion on "The normative-legal basis for the development of the Internet in Russia: current condition and future prospects" expressed a negative attitude toward such ideas and proposals.

A special meeting of the OSCE devoted to Internet-related issues took place in Paris on June 16–17. The official position of the Russian government was represented at the meeting by FSB General Viktor Ostroukhov, who proposed increasing international cooperation in controlling the content of the Web and holding Internet service providers accountable for websites that promote xenophobia, terrorism, extremism, nontraditional religious sects, and antiglobalization movements. The Russian representative even expressed disapproval of the Yandex search engine, which enables "anyone who wants to do so to become easily acquainted with the teachings of the Aum

Shinrikyo sect, the Jehova's Witnesses . . . to access the web-sites of the Hare Krishna organization . . . to learn about various Satan-worshipping cults."[42]

Bills for new media regulations have periodically appeared in the Duma since 2004. Proposals have included revising the definition of "media" to include all communication and materials that pass over the Internet, as well as permitting Internet media outlets to be run only by legal or physical persons who have registered with the government as private business owners.[43]

In 2006–2007, the government's pressure on the political sector of the Internet increased, although it has not yet given rise to a comprehensive new law. Inconvenient websites are blocked or forced to find foreign hosting when law enforcement organs threaten Russian Internet service providers (the websites of Limonov's party and the Internet outlets of the coalition Another Russia in late 2006 to early 2007; the Antikompromat Internet library in March 2007); or shut down websites accused of making "extremist" and "libelous" pronouncements (the court decision to "confiscate" Mikhail Afanasyev's site "Novy Fokus" in Khakassia at the end of 2006); or, finally, employ hackers' methods to achieve their ends, such as the so-called "ddos-attack" (the "hacker" terrorist campaign against oppositional Internet resources at the end of May 2007 looked like a dress rehearsal for the possibility of a future crisis).

LEONID PARFENOV IS FIRED

Nikolai Senkevich, after replacing Boris Jordan, was unable to provide the degree of loyalty that was expected of him in the Kremlin. In any event, NTV continued to overstep the monolithic norms that had become established on Channel One and Rossiya TV (Channel Two).

The vestiges of its freethinking roots and its enduring professionalism prevented NTV from remaining silent about the grandiose fire in the Manezh, which darkened the evening of Putin's election on March 14, 2004, becoming a terrible omen for the misfortunes and catastrophes of his second term. Something analogous was seen on May 9—Victory Day, a national holiday—when the president of Chechnya and the speaker of

Chechnya's parliament were blown up in a stadium in Grozny, while the prime minister survived only by a miracle, having left for Moscow the previous day. NTV's special editions showing Akhmad Kadyrov's bloody body at 11:40 A.M. and reporting his death at noon made too striking a contrast with the silence of the government channels, which did not wish to "spoil Victory Day." Reporting the death of the Chechen leader, the anchor of the program *Segodnya*, Alexei Sukhanov, was pulled off the air literally in the middle of a word. The three-hour silence of the government channels ended at 2 P.M. when the news show *Vesti* reported that Kadyrov had been *wounded*.[44]

The state-run Rossiya Channel, headed by Oleg Dobrodeyev, has a formal list of "prohibited words." On Dobrodeyev's channel, the following expressions cannot be uttered on the air: "substituting money payments for benefits" (reporters must say "benefit payments"), "banking crisis," "shahid," and even "Chechnya" (reporters must say "the Chechen Republic").[45] A comparable list of forbidden expressions for Channel One has not yet been seen by the public, but it is clear that something like it exists there.

By contrast, even in defeat, NTV never had anything of this sort—at least not until the summer of 2004.

Although NTV had already been purged twice, it was the only nationally televised channel where one could see reports about the death following a hunger strike of a worker involved in liquidating the consequences of the Chernobyl disaster; about demonstrations by Yabloko's youth organization against the cult of Andropov and Putin; about the provocative anti-Putin protests of the National Bolsheviks. When the test-firing of a ballistic missile in the Northern Fleet went awry, it was only NTV's *Strana i Mir* that even alluded to the fact that the missile had failed to come out of its silo—while the government channels droned on at length about the success of the "large-scale" test-firing. The two main havens for freethinking attitudes on NTV were Leonid Parfenov's *Namedni* and Savik Shuster's *Svoboda Slova*. Alexander Gerasimov's news and analysis program *Lichny Vklad* did not broach forbidden subjects—by contrast with Parfenov's show—but it did cultivate an objective, disinterested tone that contrasted strongly with the Putin-mania of *Vesti* (Rossiya) and *Vremya* (Channel One).

(Mention should also be made of REN TV, particularly Olga Romanova's news and analysis program *24* on this channel. Prior to the summer of 2005, REN TV—a channel that broadcasts predominantly in Moscow, and even there is not available in all districts—was controlled by a management led by Irena Lesnevskaya and was under the economic and ideological influence of Anatoly Chubais. Up to November 2005, when Olga Romanova was fired, *24* took a rather critical stance toward the government, both in its choice of news stories and in its approach to presenting them. Even after Romanova's departure, certain vestiges of freedom can still be seen on REN TV—at least in Marianna Maksimovskaya's program *Nedelya.*)

On June 1, 2004, NTV's general manager Nikolai Senkevich announced that the program *Namedni* would be going off the air and that its host, Leonid Parfenov, was fired. *Namedni's* commercial time was the most expensive on NTV: one minute cost $141,600 (including value-added tax).[46] But this did not stop Senkevich.

Shortly before Parfenov's dismissal, NTV's management had cancelled a *Namedni* segment featuring an interview by the reporter Yelena Samoilova with Malika Yandarbiyeva, the widow of the former president of Chechnya-Ichkeria, Zelimkhan Yandarbiyev, who had been killed by Russian GRU agents in Qatar. The segment "To Marry Zelimkhan" was taken off the air in the European part of the country after being shown in the Far East, Siberia, and the Urals. As Parfenov told it, NTV's deputy general manager, Alexander Gerasimov, had "cancelled the segment at the request of the security services."[47] In another account, which became known to the *Kommersant* correspondent Arina Borodina, the order to cancel the interview with Malika Yandarbiyeva had come from the president's press secretary, Alexei Gromov.[48]

After being instructed to cancel the segment, Parfenov requested and obtained an order in writing from Gerasimov. Parfenov then sent a copy of this order to *Kommersant*, where it was published (May 31, 2004). Gerasimov declared that handing over this order to the press was an "unacceptable infringement of corporate ethics," while Senkevich called this act—and not the segment itself—the cause of Parfenov's dismissal.

As for the ill-starred interview, Parfenov himself had shortened the segment and cut out all the parts that might have been unpleasant to the Kremlin. For example, he had deleted a fragment about the fact that Zelimkhan Yandarbiyev (who was killed in February 2004), acting on his own initiative, had telephoned the Chechen terrorists who had hijacked *Nord-Ost* and demanded that they should die themselves rather than allow the death of a single hostage. The revised version of the interview had already been seen by viewers in the Far East—and it had not contained anything particularly revealing. Nor had it contained anything that might have made life worse for the GRU agents who had been caught in Qatar.

The real reason for Parfenov's firing, apparently, was not this interview at all. Parfenov's ironic remarks about the president and his "sovereign style," which in the spring of 2004 had become a constant leitmotif of his programs, had exceeded the patience of Kremlin officials and Putin himself. The last straw was an advertisement for an upcoming episode of *Namedni*— the same episode that was supposed to feature the interview with the widow of the Chechen separatist. "Who is Mr. Putin?" asked Parfenov's voice in the commercial. "Nobody and nothing!" replied the voice of Putin. Then, after a pause, came Putin's words to the effect that "nobody and nothing will be able to do anything bad to Russia." On the Saturday before the final episode of *Namedni*, this mocking advertisement was played every hour on NTV.

The authorities were too embarrassed to ban the commercial. Instead, they instigated a conflict around the Chechen interview that drew attention away from their actual grievance.

In Parfenov's opinion, if his dismissal had been at Senkevich's personal initiative, then "Senkevich would have made this decision a long time ago. He obviously needed someone's approval."[49]

Many people, however, believe that Senkevich might not have needed a direct intervention from the Kremlin. For example, Alexander Ryklin of the magazine *Yezhenedelny Zhurnal* wrote:

When the channel's managers state that they fired Parfenov independently, without any pressure from above, I believe them completely.

Today, the trust and understanding that exist between Kremlin officials and our media generals have reached such high levels that direct
instructions are no longer necessary: everyone already understands
perfectly well what kind of television the country must have today. As
the Kremlin says: "Don't teach Dobrodeyev—you'll only ruin him."[50]

The uncompromising Vladimir Kara-Murza, who never forgave Parfenov his switch to the victors' side in May 2001, commented on the incident in a pitiless manner:

This is a kind of show-whipping for the benefit of NTV's other employ-
ees and reporters, meant to teach Tanya Mitkova, Misha Osokin, and
Savik Shuster not to get out of line. Kick your own to instill fear in
everyone else—that's the principle. Leonid was in the front ranks of
Gazprom's invaders when Gazprom took over the channel in 2001.
Then he resigned at the right moment, and wrote a letter about us in
Kommersant that looked more like a denunciation.[51]

Igor Malashenko, former co-owner of NTV, believes that
"the cancellation of *Namedni* and the firing of Parfenov demonstrate that a new degree of control has been established." As
Malashenko put it,

Parfenov walked a certain fine line and played hide-and-seek with his
bosses and with the ruling party (not United Russia, of course, but
with the party of the security services, let us call it that). . . . Previously,
reporters were controlled by being made to remove certain segments;
then they were allowed to talk about what they liked. But now that is
not enough. Today, reporters must be controlled to the point of not
being allowed to think. . . .
    When a person accepts one compromise after another, people
inevitably begin demanding greater and greater compromises of him.
And at some point he either turns into a rag that they wipe their feet
on, or rebels—and discovers with surprise that more is demanded of
him than three months ago. This is what happened with Parfenov.[52]

The secretary of the Reporters' Union, Igor Yakovenko,
summed up the situation this way:

Before this we all knew that we had censorship and government control over national channels, but at least we got doses of glasnost when the TV maestros were allowed to do something. Now it turns out that even the maestros are not allowed to do anything, and that the TV channel is not even concerned about its ratings.[53]

THE PURGE AT NTV CONTINUES

Parfenov was gone. Next came the turn of Alexander Gerasimov and his news program *Lichny Vklad*, as well as Savik Shuster's program *Svoboda Slova*.

At the beginning of July 2004, Senkevich was promoted to head of Gazprom Media's board of directors, and his place as general manager of NTV was taken by Vladimir Kulistikov, who had come over from the Rossiya Channel but had earlier worked at NTV. On July 7, 2004, at a meeting of the channel's new management, Kulistikov declared his intention to terminate all political programming on the network: Shuster's *Svoboda Slova*, Gerasimov's *Lichny Vklad*, and the Pilot TV production *Krasnaya Strela*, which was a toned-down version of the old TVS show *Shut the Lights!*

The only programs with political content that Kulistikov left untouched were Alexei Pivovarov's news show *Strana i Mir* and Vladimir Solovyev's talk show *K Baryeru!*

Kulistikov explained the liquidation of *Svoboda Slova* as follows:

The show was considered a forum for the exchange of opinions. But not all opinions. People with a certain status, people who made decisions, remained in the minority or did not participate at all, and as a result the show stopped being an objective reflection of the arguments going on in society today. . . . Often, it looked like a club of armchair warriors who were essentially intent on proving one proposition: that Putin doesn't know what he's doing.[54]

NTV's new overseer was not entirely correct: the opinion that "Putin doesn't know what he's doing" was not expressed by most guests on Shuster's program—on the contrary, most argued the opposite. For all of 2004, *Svoboda Slova* was dominated by Dmitry Rogozin (Homeland) and Alexei Mitrofanov (Zhirinovsky's LDPR), who on key issues in Russian politics—Chechnya, "managed democracy," freedom of speech, the redistribution of large-scale property—are more pro-Putin than Putin himself. But *Svoboda Slova* did sometimes offer critics of the regime a chance to express their views, from both left-wing (Communists, Eduard Limonov) and liberal perspectives (Yavlinsky, Nemtsov, Khakamada).

Although Kulistikov has the reputation of a reporter who will do whatever he is told, he himself was placed under a supervisor, "a certain Tamara Gavrilova. Very little is known about her, but the main thing is that Tamara Gavrilova was Vladimir Putin's classmate at the university."[55]

The liquidation of the "old" NTV—and the shutting down of TVS as the last chapter in this history—was the turning point in the story of the Russian media. The government's subsequent policies toward Russian television have not made much of a difference. This is the opinion of Vladimir Neklyudov, the producer of the Pilot TV studio, who was one of the biggest casualties of the July purge on the "new" NTV: "The only real event on television took place in April 2001, when they killed NTV."[56]

And yet, the practically complete elimination of NTV's political broadcasting also marks a certain watershed. If Parfenov was banished for doing what he did—ridicule Putin-mania—then Gerasimov was asked to leave for what he did not do—praise Putin.

THE CASE OF SERGEI SAVELYEV

On August 19, 2004, the Leninsky District Court in Kursk sentenced Sergei Savelyev, editor-in-chief of the newspaper *Svobodny Golos Kurska*, to one and a half years at a correctional facility for libel against the prosecutor of the Kursk region, Alexander Babichev. In his articles in 2002, Savelyev had accused Babichev of falsifying documents concerning construction projects for the regional and district prosecutors' offices.

In addition to "libel" (Article 129 of the Russian Criminal Code), the court found Savelyev guilty of "insult" directed at the same prosecutor (Article 130) and "hooliganism" (Article 213). For "hooliganism," the reporter was sentenced to two more years, but released from serving them because the statute of limitations had passed; and for "insult," he was sentenced to pay a fine of 10,000 rubles.

AGAINST THE BACKGROUND OF THE BESLAN CRISIS

At the beginning of September 2004, Russia was shaken by another crisis produced by the Chechen war and the actions of Northern Caucasian terrorists: in the Ossetian city of Beslan, terrorists occupied a school and took 1,200 people hostage. In the operation to free the hostages, a large number of children were killed.

During the crisis and immediately afterward, it seemed as if the government was worried less about rescuing the children than about preventing the leaking of accurate information (about the number of hostages, the terrorists' demands, the actions of government and law enforcement officials). In order to prevent certain reporters from reaching Beslan, frankly criminal actions were taken against them: Anna Politkovskaya (*Novaya Gazeta*) was poisoned in an airplane and ended up in a hospital in serious condition; Andrei Babitsky (Radio Liberty) was initially not allowed to board an airplane, on alleged suspicions of a bomb having been planted in his luggage, and then accused of disorderly conduct.

On September 6, in Mineralnye Vody, the head of the Al Arabiya news channel's Russian bureau, Amr Abdul Hamid, a Russian citizen, was taken off an airplane and detained. (An AK-47 bullet was "found" in his luggage.) In Beslan itself, two Georgian TV reporters, Nana Lezhava and Levan Tetvadze, were detained for two days on the pretext that they had no entrance visas— although they were legal residents of Georgia's Kazbeg district, which is located on the Russian border and whose residents, according to an agreement between Russia and Georgia, have the right to cross the border without visas and to remain in North Ossetia for up to ten days. In North Ossetia, Anna Gorbatova and Oksana Semyonova (*Novye Izvestiya*), Madina Shavlokhova (*Moskovskiye Novosti*), and Yelena Milashina (*Novaya Gazeta*) were also detained, albeit briefly.[57]

Over a period of several days in late August and early September, Vladimir Pribylovsky—president of the Panorama Information and Research Center, and author of the *Novye Izvestiya* article about the cult of personality surrounding Putin—noticed that he was being openly followed in the metro and on the streets of Moscow. This "external surveillance" had been preceded by assassination threats from an unknown person in an airplane from Rostov to Moscow, and Pribylovsky's subsequent six-hour detention at Vnukovo airport. Pribylovsky was not charged with anything, but was threatened with being jailed for "resisting police."

After the Beslan crisis, Putin stated that "war on Russia has been declared." What this meant was quickly elucidated for the public by Channel One's political commentator Mikhail Leontiev:

> In times of war, one doesn't fight one's own government. That's called a "fifth column" . . . In times of war, the laws of war go into effect and certain public procedures are suspended. . . . The only way to re-establish order quickly (and in times of war, it must be done quickly) is undoubtedly to expand the authoritarian component [of the government].[58]

RAF SHAKIROV IS FIRED

On September 6, 2004, Raf Shakirov resigned as editor-in-chief of *Izvestiya*, which at the time was owned by the billionaire Vladimir Potanin's Prof-Media. *Izvestiya* is in no respect an antigovernment publication. The tone of the newspaper is set by right-liberal and right-conservative (in the Western sense of the word) statists—writers who are not antipathetic to Islamophobia, but are absolutely hostile to all forms of separatism, and loyal to moderate forms of authoritarianism (Alexander Arkhangelsky, Maksim Sokolov, and others). However, Putin's authoritarianism is supported by *Izvestiya* without sycophancy. The newspaper permits itself to criticize the actions of specific agencies and officials. In addition, it also publishes liberal writers, whose attitude toward "managed democracy" is not extreme, but nonetheless critical (for example, Irina Petrovskaya, who writes a weekly television overview).

Shakirov stated in an interview that Prof-Media objected to the way *Izvestiya* had covered the events in Beslan—above all, to the September 4 issue, which focused on the Beslan tragedy. Eight columns of the newspaper had been devoted to the battle for the school. Large photographs of bloody children appeared on the front and back pages, and there were many large photographs inside the paper as well, some showing dead bodies.

According to Prof-Media's general manager, Rafael Akopov, his disagreements with Shakirov were not political but stylistic. "The Saturday issue was excessively naturalistic," he said.[59] It is also possible that Akopov's (or even Potanin's) apprehensions were triggered by Irina Petrovskaya's television overview, which was more emotional than usual: Petrovskaya wrote about the way in which state-run TV channels had lied to the people and pandered to government officials during the Beslan crisis.

Reporters and political pundits interpreted the firing of *Izvestiya*'s editor-in-chief as the sign of a new phase in the Kremlin's policies toward the media: they saw it as a transition toward the establishment of firm control over the print media. In the opinion of *Kommersant*'s general manager, Andrei Vasiliev, "this was a deliberate signal from the Kremlin to the reporters and the elites that it was now turning its attention to the print media."[60]

The following opinions were voiced in a survey of reporters organized by *Nezavisimaya Gazeta*:

Alexei Venediktov, head of Ekho Moskvy radio: "I believe that there were people in the Kremlin who wanted to do the president a service by accusing *Izvestiya* of improperly covering the events."

Irina Petrovskaya, *Izvestiya* columnist: "I think that the order came from the Kremlin. Neither Potanin nor Prof-Media had any reason to fire Raf. This was a show trial, meant to discourage others."

Alexei Simonov, general manager of the Glasnost Defense Foundation: "The security services started working on Raf and he was fired to please them, in order to change the informational climate in the country. . . . I remember how enthusiastically Potanin applauded Putin's speech at the congress of the RSPP (Russian Union of Industrialists and Entrepreneurs)."

Svetlana Sorokina, Channel One news anchor: "This was decided in the Kremlin. I don't think that Potanin would have sacrificed Shakirov. Muscovites believe newspapers more than TV. That's why you couldn't buy any newspapers in those days. They were giving readers what television was not."[61]

Irina Rykovtseva of Radio Liberty: "Potanin is afraid of becoming another Khodorkovsky. Therefore, today, Shakirov was fired."[62]

Despite episodic persecution and the provocation of "economic" conflicts, the press was not subjected to the same kind of systematic control and pressure during Putin's first term as the televised media. The clear-thinking part of Putin's entourage rightly considers rigid control over the press an excessive measure. In addition, Putin—who, as is well known, watches all news programs on all channels daily—stopped reading newspapers and magazines after becoming president; and in the government's daily overviews of the press, he pays special attention only to what is written about him by Western reporters.

The relative freedom of the press is by no means guaranteed to last, however. An article that came out in *Vedomosti* the day after Shakirov was fired had the title "And Now They Are Going after Paper."[63]

REFORM OF RETAIL COMMERCIAL SPACE IN MOSCOW

In the spring of 2004, the Federal Antiterrorist Commission recommended that Moscow's metro and surrounding areas be cleared of retail commercial activity. Although this was a "recommendation" and not an order, Moscow municipal offices stopped renewing licenses for selling newspapers and magazines in the metro and within twenty-five meters of metro stations. By the beginning of October, practically all mobile newspaper kiosks inside metro stations and within twenty-five meters of them had been liquidated.

It is expected that the place of mobile newspaper kiosks in the metro will be taken by special automatic newspaper dispensers—which, however, will not be able to sell more than six different publications at the same time; while outside the stations they will be replaced by pavilions run by large companies that deal in printed matter—whose owners, however, are by no means always willing to sell printed matter that is not wholly enthusiastic about the government, whether of a left or a liberal stripe.

This reform has led to a rise in the prices of practically all newspapers and magazines, but above all it has hit such publications as *Novaya Gazeta, Nezavisimaya Gazeta, Russky Kurier.* The number of places where these newspapers can be bought in Moscow has very visibly shrunk. In addition, the metro has been completely cleared of "unaffiliated" distributors of printed matter, who deal mainly in the marginal and semi-marginal publications of left-wing and right-wing radicals.

THE CHECHEN SOCIETY INCIDENT

At the end of July 2004, an attempt was made to shut down the newspaper *Chechen Society.* It is not a separatist publication, but one that condemns human rights abuses in Kadyrov's Chechnya. The newspaper is actually put together in Moscow, but in 2004 it was printed in Nazrani (Ingushetia) and distributed both in Chechnya and among the Chechen diaspora in Moscow and the North Caucasus. On oral orders from Ingushetia's Ministry of Internal Affairs, the Nazrani printers stopped production of the newspaper.

In Chechnya at that time, preparations were being made for the election of President Alu Alkhanov, and the anti-Kadyrov *Chechen Society* was especially inconvenient.

After the August election, the printers managed to resolve the problem with their press.

"IDUSCHIE VMESTE" INTERVENES

In the summer of 2004, the pro-Putin youth organization "Iduschie Vmeste" sent a request to the Moscow prosecutor's office to look into the activities of *Novaya Gazeta, Yezhene-delny Zhurnal, Nezavisimaya Gazeta,* and the Kommersant Publishing House, in order to ascertain whether everything was being done in accordance with Russian media regulations. As a pretext for its request, Iduschie Vmeste chose to use, first, allegedly libelous articles about their own organization, and second, the publication of texts containing false information that Iduschie Vmeste itself had placed in the newspapers—through middlemen—as paid advertisements. (Unfortunately, in some cases the newspapers carelessly agreed to conceal the fact that the texts were being published as paid advertisements.)

All the newspapers denounced by Iduschie Vmeste are characterized by their lack of piety toward the person of Putin and lack of support for his policies, while *Novaya Gazeta* is distinguished additionally by its special interest in the Chechen war and the corruption of Putin's officials.

The pro-government activities of Iduschie Vmeste, Nashi, Molodaya Gvardiya, Rossiya Molodaya, Mestnye, and other "Putin-Jugend" associations do not always have institutional consequences. More commonly, these "youth" initiatives are employed as trial balloons in order to sound out public opinion. This is what happened in this instance.

THE CASE OF YURI BAGROV

On August 25, 2004, agents from the FSB's North Ossetia regional office raided the premises of a Radio Liberty correspondent, Yuri Bagrov, searching his home, garage, office, and his mother's apartment. In all, about forty regional FSB agents participated in the raids, headed by the director of the counter-intelligence department, Lieutenant Colonel Sergei Leonidov. Criminal charges were filed against the reporter on September 17: he was accused of using a forged court decision to obtain Russian citizenship.

In 1992, Bagrov had moved from Georgia to Vladikavkaz, where his wife, mother, and grandparents lived, all of them Russian citizens. When his Soviet passport expired in 2003, he exchanged it for a Russian passport—which required getting a court decision. In the spring of 2004, Bagrov published material about the FSB's involvement in kidnappings in Ingushetia. After this, he became the object of surveillance, and his place-of-residence registration was removed from the passport office.[64]

Vladikavkaz's Iristonsky Court denied a request from the defendant's lawyers to have experts analyze the handwriting and seal on the court decision to grant Bagrov Russian citizenship. In December 2004, the court found Bagrov guilty of knowingly using a forged document, sentenced him to pay a fine in the amount of 15,000 rubles, and revoked his Russian passport. The Supreme Court of North Ossetia let the lower court's decision stand. Bagrov, who had become a person without citizenship—and from the standpoint of the law enforcement organs, apparently a citizen of the hostile Republic of Georgia—began encountering persistent difficulties in the fulfillment of his professional duties. In September 2005, for instance, he was arrested in Beslan while attempting to attend memorial services at the former School No. 1, because he had no accreditation from the Ministry of Foreign Affairs.[65]

At the beginning of 2007, impossible working conditions and threats from law enforcement organs forced Bagrov to leave his homeland and seek political asylum in the United States. He was granted asylum in June.

THE PIVOVAROV INCIDENT

On December 8, 2004, NTV's general manager, Vladimir Kulistikov, decided to take one of the hosts of *Strana i Mir* off the air for one month. The cause was Alexei Pivovarov's comment about Leonid Parfenov's appointment as editor-in-chief of the magazine *Russky Newsweek*. Pivovarov had made a jibe against Nikolai Senkevich, head of Gazprom Media, reminding viewers that "half a year ago, the general manager of NTV made his personal contribution to the history of Russian television by firing Parfenov as part of a staff reduction."[66]

Kulistikov described Pivovarov's comment as a "settling of personal accounts" and punished him by temporarily taking him off the air.

THE REFORM OF RUSSKY KURIER

The former *Novye Izvestiya* reporters who under Golembiovsky's and Agafonov's leadership had begun publishing their own newspaper, *Russky Kurier*, were fired once again in March 2005.

Russky Kurier had been acquired by Yakov Soskin (Mediapress Corporation). Initially, Soskin—like Oleg Mitvol before him—was interested neither in the content of the newspaper, which sharply criticized "managed democracy" and President Putin personally, nor in the fact that it operated at a loss. But in early 2005, Soskin took it into his head to become a Duma senator from the Koryak autonomous district. To do this, he needed the support of the president's administration.

By contrast with Mitvol, Soskin did not present any complaints to the *Russky Kurier* editorial board, but simply shut the newspaper down and fired the entire staff. (After a while, he started publishing a tabloid weekly under the same name— moderately pro-government in tone and equally unprofitable.) *Russky Kurier*'s staff writers were paid what they were owed when they were fired, but the millionaire publisher held back the payments due to freelancers who wrote for the paper.

Soskin failed to get the reward that he expected from the Kremlin: he did not manage to become a senator. The Kremlin refrained from driving his candidacy through the Federation Council because of a five-year-old scandal that had been dug up by *Kommersant* at the very beginning of Soskin's "Koryak venture": in 2000, when the publisher was going through a divorce and dividing his property, Soskin's wife tried to shoot him but—according to the officially accepted story—accidentally shot herself instead.[67]

In April, the duma of the Koryak district elected a Communist, Alexander Suvorov—whom it had been unable to elect in January—as its representative in the Federation Council.

CHANGES AT "IZVESTIYA"

At the beginning of June 2005, the partly state-owned Gazprom Media Holding Company acquired 50.19 percent of *Izvestiya*'s shares from Vladimir Potanin's Prof-Media publishing house. In November, a new editor-in-chief was appointed at *Izvestiya*. Vladimir Borodin—who had run the newspaper since the firing of Shakirov in September 2004—was replaced by Vladimir Mamontov, who had previously been in charge of Potanin's *Komsomolskaya Pravda.*

Gazprom Media's general manager, Nikolai Senkevich, as usual declared that the replacement of the editor-in-chief had no political subtext and that *Izvestiya*'s editorial policies would remain unchanged. A different point of view was expressed by

Shakirov: "Did Gazprom buy *Izvestiya* in order to deviate from the party line? They want to radically clean up the press. . . . They want to turn *Izvestiya* into *Pravda*."[68]

After settling in, the new editor-in-chief confirmed the former editor-in-chief's fears. He laid out his vision for *Izvestiya*'s future in a special and rather expansive "Memorandum" to the newspaper's employees. After a while, this "Memorandum" showed up on the Internet; its authenticity has not been contested by anyone. From Mamontov's "Memorandum":

> *Izvestiya* is not an opposition newspaper. Our front door says: "national public newspaper." Today, this sign is deceptive. Often, we are very far from the people. . . . It is odd for us, who belong to a practically state-owned corporation, to pretend that we are radically antigovernment. This contradiction is enough to make one lose one's mind.
>
> Those who are not satisfied with such a stance—and that is precisely how things will be from now on—should look for another job.
>
> We must become a genuinely liberal, influential, vital, respectable, interesting Russian newspaper. No one will prevent us from providing a forum for competing opinions, but it will be good always to stay within the bounds of common sense. The limit (and best example) of liberalism for me is A. Chubais. He stands for liberalism, and he is also building the Bureya hydroelectric dam.
>
> I want to assure you: with the arrival of the new editor-in-chief, and those who have already come and are yet to come with him, the period of *Izvestiya*'s strange journalistic life outside the political and social mainstream of the country is over.[69]

In the spring of 2005, the president's administration delegated Ilya Kiselev, the head of United Russia's information directorate, to fill the position of *Izvestiya*'s deputy editor-in-chief. Kiselev replaced Andrei Kolesnikov, a liberal reporter close to Chubais (and not to be confused with the other Andrei Kolesnikov, from *Kommersant*).

CHANGES AT REN TV

At the end of July 2005, Alexei Mordashov's Severstal Group holding company purchased nearly 70 percent of REN TV's shares from RAO UES. Another 30 percent of the shares, which belonged to the family of the channel's founder and general manager, Irena Lesnevskaya, were bought by RTL Group, a German media concern. In October, Severstal sold half its REN TV shares to Surgutneftegaz. The transformation of the channel's financial structure led to administrative changes as well: Lesnevskaya was replaced as general manager by Alexander Ordzhonikidze.

On November 23, Ordzhonikidze ordered that two segments in Olga Romanova's show *24* be deleted from the program: one on the closing of the criminal case against the son of Sergei Ivanov, the minister of defense, who had struck and killed an elderly woman while driving; and another about the building of a new chapel on Manezh Square, at a cost of $15 million. Romanova threw out the segment about the minister's son, but left in place the one about the chapel.

The following day, Romanova was supposed to go on the air with two editions of the evening news, but employees from the Eurasia private security agency, which had been hired by the channel's management, prevented her from entering the TV studio, citing the general manager's orders.

On November 28, Ordzhonikidze announced that Romanova had broken corporate ethics rules and that she would remain off the air for at least three months, duirng which time she could "prepare a concept for a new show." On December 5, Romanova resigned from the channel.

NEW MEDIA ACCREDITATION RULES AT THE MOSCOW MUNICIPAL COURT

The head of the Moscow Municipal Court, Olga Yegorova, signed an order in September 2005 prohibiting reporters from attending court sessions without special permission from the court's press service. In addition, even reporters who possess such accreditation must notify the court at least one day in advance of their wish to be present at a session of the court.[70]

THE CASE OF STANISLAV DMITRIEVSKY

In January 2006, Stanislav Dmitrievsky, the executive director of the Society of Russian-Chechen Friendship (ORChD) and editor-in-chief of the newspaper *Pravo-Zaschita*, appeared in court in Nizhny Novgorod. One year earlier, *Pravo-Zaschita* had published Akhmed Zakayev's appeal to the Russian people—not to vote for Putin in the election—and Aslan Maskhadov's appeal to the European Parliament. The regional prosecutor's office initiated criminal proceedings in accordance with Article 280 of the Russian Criminal Code (public appeals for a forcible change of the constitutional system of the Russian Federation), but the investigation failed to find calls for violence in the publications, and in September 2005, the charge was changed to Article 282 (incitement to national and racial enmity).

The case went to trial in October. The prosecutor's office demanded that Dmitrievsky be sentenced to four years in prison.

On February 3, 2006, Nizhny Novgorod's Sovietsky District Court gave Dmitrievsky a suspended sentence of two years in prison and four years of probation. According to the court's decision, the national and racial groups toward which Dmitrievsky had incited and promoted "hatred or enmity" turned out to be the "leadership of the Russian Empire" and the "mindless, bloody Kremlin regime." The court struck from the record Dmitrievsky's question to Larisa Teslenko—expert witness for the prosecution—whether such a thing as the "leadership of the Russian Empire" was currently in existence.[71]

THE RUSSIAN ECHO OF THE DANISH CARTOON CONTROVERSY

The so-called Danish cartoon controversy—aggressive protests by Muslims around the world against cartoons of the Prophet Mohammed published in Denmark—found a completely unexpected echo in Russia. Caricatures of the leaders of all religions have been published many times in Soviet, pre-Soviet, and post-Soviet Russia; suffice it to recall the multiple reissues of the magazine *Satirikon*, with its irreverent history of the world. Not only has this never provoked mass protests, but most often it has simply been ignored by believers and members of the clergy. This time, however, the functionaries of the ruling party—United Russia—decided to use the cartoons to initiate repressive measures against the media.

On February 9, 2006, the Volgograd newspaper *Gorodskie Vesti*, published by the mayor's office, ran an article titled "Racists Do Not Belong in the Government." The article reported that local public organizations and offices of political parties had signed an agreement to jointly oppose nationalism, xenophobia, and religious strife. The text was illustrated with a caricature depicting the founders of world religions engaged in friendly conversation and lamenting the misdeeds of their followers—"That's not what we taught them."

The leadership of United Russia's Volgograd office, which was at odds with the city's mayor, Yevgeny Ivchenko—who incidentally was also a member of their party at the time—saw the article as a convenient pretext to attack the mayor's office. The controversy was initiated by United Russia's regional Duma deputy, Alexander Scherban. It was then taken up by the secretary of the political council of United Russia's regional office, Oleg Kersanov. Writing in the name of the regional public organizations controlled by United Russia, Kersanov sent a collective denunciation to the regional prosecutor's office. In Moscow, the Scherban-Kersanov initiative was supported by Boris Gryzlov, the party's leader and speaker of the Duma.

The regional prosecutor, Leonid Belyak, announced that "effective preventive measures [had to be] taken." On February 15, the General Prosecutor's Office—in the person of Nikolai Shepel, the deputy general prosecutor for the Southern Federal District—began investigating the facts of the publication. On the same day, without waiting for the outcome of the investigation, the deputy mayor and acting mayor, Andrei Doronin, signed an order to shut down *Gorodskie Vesti*.

Also on the same day, the Vologda newspaper *Nash Region* published an article about the worldwide cartoon controversy. The text of the article cited the opinions of various experts—political pundits, clergymen, and independent reporters—and was accompanied by some of the controversial cartoons, the most "offensive" among them reproduced with cuts.

In Vologda, the attacks against the press were initiated by the head of the Vologda region's Muslim society, Ravil Mustavin. The article was criticized by Governor Vyacheslav Pozgalev, and the regional prosecutor's office filed a criminal suit against the editor-in-chief of *Nash Region*, Anna Smirnova, in accordance with Article 282 of the Russian Criminal Code (incitement to national, racial, or religious enmity). Mikhail Smirnov, the owner of the newspaper, and Anna Smirnova's husband, shut down the newspaper himself—which did not save his wife from the Vologda Municipal Court, where she appeared in April 2006.

The prosecution asked the court to give the defendant a suspended sentence with two years' probation. Speaking for all Muslims, Mustavin demanded that the reporter be prohibited from occupying management positions in the media for a period of five years, and estimated the compensation for emotional distress in the amount of one million rubles.

On April 14, the court found Smirnova guilty of inciting national, racial, and religious strife, sentencing her to pay a fine of 100,000 rubles. Mustavin's request for compensation for emotional distress was denied.

The Vologda Regional Court partly acquitted Smirnova on May 25 and exempted her from paying the fine for publishing the cartoon, but let her guilty verdict stand.

THE CASE OF VIKTOR SHMAKOV

Viktor Shmakov, publisher of the local opposition newspaper *Provintsialnye Vesti* and winner of the national journalism award, was arrested in the city of Ufa on April 26, 2006.

Shmakov had a track record as an antigovernment activist. In 1989, he founded *Vmeste*, the first independent newspaper in Bashkortostan. In 2001–2002, he headed the local office of the Liberal Russia party (and joined the pro-Berezovsky wing after the party split up). In 2006, together with Airat Dilmukhametov, he founded a steering committee for Mikhail Kasyanov's Russian People's Democratic Union in Ufa.

Shmakov was arrested after *Ploschad Vosstania*, a publication affiliated with *Provintsialnye Vesti*, published his articles titled "Instructions for the Conduct of Revolutionaries during Mass Public Protests" and "The Bashkirian Revolutionary Committee's Brief Program of Extraordinary and Priority Measures Following Successful Revolutionary Action." On May 8, he was charged in accordance with two articles of the Russian Criminal Code: Article 280, par. 2 (public appeals to extremism) and

Article 212, par. 1 (organization of mass riots). The Supreme Court of Bashkortostan ruled on May 15 to change the measure of restraint and to release the reporter on the condition that he not leave the city.

In August, Shmakov's charge was changed from Article 212, par. 1 (organization of mass riots) to Article 212, par. 3 (incitement to mass riots), which carried not a ten-year but only a three-year prison term. The Bashkortostan prosecutor's office withdrew the charge of incitement to mass riots in November. Shmakov was acquitted of the remaining charge (Article 280, par. 2) in the spring of 2007, while his accomplice Airat Dilmukhametov—author of "extremist" texts—was given a suspended sentence of one year.

CHANGES IN ANTI-EXTREMIST LEGISLATION

On July 26, 2007, President Vladimir Putin signed into law a bill introducing "Amendments to Articles 1 and 15 of the Federal Law 'On opposing extremist activity,'" which increased liability for extremist activity. The new law defined all acts injurious to the public that carry a criminal liability as forms of "extremist activity."

Commenting on the change in anti-extremist legislation in an interview with the magazine *Vlast*, the president's representative in the Federation Council, Alexander Kotenkov, noted:

> The media cannot make accusations against government officials. A governor by definition cannot engage in extremist activity. He enjoys a presumption of innocence, just like any other citizen. To accuse a government official of extremist activity is not simply to insult him personally, but to undermine people's faith in government. And that is extremism.[72]

LEGISLATION CONCERNING "PERSONAL DATA"

On July 27, 2006, President Putin put his signature on bill No. 152-FZ, "On personal data." This law prohibits government organs from divulging "personal data" about physical persons without their written consent.

The formulation of the law, however, is such that it can easily be given a broad interpretation: for example, it can be read as denying the right to divulge personal data to the media, sociologists, political analysts, historians, and so on. Moreover, according to the letter of the law, "personal data" can include any information about a person—such as name, date of birth, address, or political views. In principle, reporters who quote political activists, businessmen, or other newsmakers must from now on obtain their written consent to mention their names.

Such a requirement obviously cannot be fulfilled in practice, but like all laws that are impossible to carry out, it can be enforced selectively. Thus, it can be used to prohibit the dissemination of uncomplimentary information about politicians without their written consent—for example, how a deputy voted on the issue of substituting money payments for benefits or the issue of ceding islands in the Khabarovsk region to China.

As of the summer of 2007, this law is not enforced, either by reporters or by government organs.

THE CREATION OF "ROSSVYAZOKHRANKULTURA"

If the reader believes that hard-to-pronounce abbreviations are incomprehensible only to foreigners, and that Russians perceive them as something natural, then he is mistaken. There is nothing natural to the Russian ear about the Russian government's countless abbreviations of endlessly long names. The tradition of creating acronyms first appeared in the years after the Russian Revolution, when largely illiterate people—Bolshevik revolutionaries—came to power. Due to their general ignorance, they started inventing long and complicated names, and due to their illiteracy, they were unable to memorize them, much less to write them. It was then that they started making up abbreviations and acronyms that cannot be pronounced in any language, including Russian, and which cannot be memorized by any brain, including a highly developed one.

On March 12, 2007, President Putin signed an order to combine two federal agencies—Rosokhrankultura and Rossvyaznadzor—into a single department, the Federal Service for the Oversight of Mass Communications and the Protection of the Cultural Heritage (Rossvyazokhrankultura). In this way, a new regulatory agency was created: the functions of media licensing and media oversight were taken away from two ministries (the Ministry of Culture and the Ministry of Communications) and combined in a single new service, under the direct control of the prime minister.

Boris Boyarskov—a former KGB employee, an officer of the FSB's active reserve, and the former head of Rosokhrankultura—became the head of Rossvyazokhrankultura on March 27. His first important act in this capacity was to send an inquiry to the General Prosecutor's Office concerning the publication of a transcript of Akhmed Zakayev's interrogation on the *Kommersant* website. Investigators at the General Prosecutor's Office had questioned Zakayev in connection with the Russian investigation into the murder of the former FSB officer Alexander Litvinenko. Boyarskov suspected *Kommersant* of divulging secret information pertaining to the investigation.

In addition to the inquiry to the General Prosecutor's Office, Rossvyazokhrankultura demanded that the website's editor-in-chief, Pavel Chernikov, not allow "the publication of materials that might lead to violations of the law." At the same time, the agency denied that its inquiry represented an official warning to *Kommersant*. Rossvyazokhrankultura stated that the letter had been sent merely as a preventive measure, and that so far the agency had no claims against the Kommersant Publishing House or its publications.[73]

NEW CHANGES IN ANTI-EXTREMIST LEGISLATION

On May 10, 2007, Putin signed legislation (No. 71-FZ, "Amendments to Article 13 of the Federal Law 'On opposing extremist activity'") that increased the penalties for crimes of an extremist nature, effectively equating them to felonies.

On June 27, the president signed into law an amendment packet, approved by the Duma on July 4, concerning "the improvement of government procedures for opposing extremism" (Federal law No. 148-FZ, "Amendments to Articles 1 and

15 of the Federal Law 'On opposing extremist activity'"). The most important changes were the following:

Articles of the Criminal Code pertaining to crimes against individuals, as well as crimes against public safety and public order—murder, willful infliction of damage, disorderly conduct, and so on—had an aggravating circumstance added to them: "for motives of political, ideological, racial, national, or religious hatred or enmity or for motives of hatred or enmity with respect to any social group." As opponents of these amendments have rightly noted, there was already a tendency in the courts to interpret media criticism of certain "social groups," including "Kremlin officials," "the government of Mordovia," and even "bad cops," as incitement to social strife. The new formulation makes it possible to define the criticism of any government official or government organ as an extremist crime, if necessary.

An article added to the Administrative Violations Code established criminal liability for the "mass distribution" of extremist materials. From now on, such materials would also be put on a special watch list.

In accordance with changes introduced into media regulations, whenever the mass media name organizations that have been found by the courts to be extremist, they are required under penalty of law to report this fact.

Yet another offense of an "extremist" nature was defined: "knowingly, falsely, and publicly accusing" a government official "of committing acts, during his term in office, that are named in the present article and constitute extremist crimes."

According to the political commentator Andrei Piontkovsky (two of whose books were investigated in May 2007 to determine whether they were of an extremist nature),

This law—and the latest amendments are merely a continuation of the same logic—has been passed, of course, not in order to fight with people such as Basayev. Because the Criminal Code contains enough instruments for fighting terrorists and murderers. Rather, this is simply a direct replication of Article 58 from Stalin's Criminal Code—about counter-revolutionary agitation; and of Article 190 from Brezhnev's Criminal Code—knowingly distributing false information about the

Soviet social order. This is an instrument for fighting political dissent, any political opposition.[74]

RUSSIA, A COUNTRY WITHOUT FREEDOM; THE PRESIDENT, AN "ENEMY OF THE PRESS"

Since the spring of 2001, Russia has regularly figured in the reports of various human rights organizations as a country with serious problems in the area of press freedom.

On May 3, 2001, on World Press Freedom Day, the international Committee to Protect Journalists (CPJ) named its "Ten Worst Enemies of the Press" for the year. President Putin of Russia came in fifth—after Iran's Ayatollah Ali Khamenei; the president of Liberia, Charles Taylor; the president of China, Jiang Zemin; and the president of Zimbabwe, Robert Mugabe. According to the CPJ,

> Vladimir Putin has presided over an alarming assault on press freedom in Russia. The Kremlin imposed censorship in Chechnya, orchestrated legal harassment against private media outlets, and granted sweeping powers of surveillance to the security services. . . . [T]he Kremlin-controlled Gazprom corporation took over NTV, the country's only independent national television network. Within days, the Gazprom coup had shut down a prominent Moscow daily and ousted the journalists in charge of the country's most prestigious newsweekly. Despite Gazprom's insistence that the changes were strictly business, the main beneficiary was Putin himself, whose primary critics have now been silenced.

Also in May 2001, the international organization Reporters Without Borders, which likewise compiles an annual list of "Enemies of Press Freedom," gave Putin twenty-second place out of thirty in its list for 2000. The four top spots were occupied by Fidel Castro, Saddam Hussein, Kim Chen Ir, and Alexander Lukashenko. The Reporters Without Borders press freedom index for 2002 included President Putin among the forty-two greatest enemies of press freedom. Putin made the list again the following year, along with the presidents of Belarus, Kazakhstan, Turkmenistan, and Uzbekistan.[75]

In October 2004, Reporters Without Borders published an international index of press freedom, in which Russia was number 140 out of 167. (In 2002, it had been number 121; in 2003, number 148.) The two last spots were occupied by Cuba and North Korea.

In April 2004, the international human rights organization Freedom House published an index of press freedom in various countries; out of 193 countries on the list, Russia came in at number 148. In December 2004, Freedom House published its yearly "Freedom in the World" survey, which ranks 192 countries as "free," "partly free," or "not free." For the first time since 1991, Russia was classified as "not free." When the next Freedom House survey came out in December 2005, Russia was still among the 45 "not free" countries, but had moved several places down the list, which ended with Turkmenistan and Uzbekistan.[76]

On May 3, 2006, Reporters Without Borders published its list of 37 "Enemies of Press Freedom" for 2005, which once again included the president of Russia. A report published on the organization's website stated: "Putin is using the techniques he learned as a KGB officer to bring all media outlets in Russia under his control. The government controls the press, radio, and television through the powerful energy conglomerate Gazprom, and Putin appears on television more and more often, usually lecturing his ministers."[77] Along with Vladimir Putin, other enemies of press freedom in the survey included Alexander Lukashenko, president of Belarus; Turkmenbashi Saparmurat Niyazov, president of Turkmenistan; Islam Karimov, president of Uzbekistan; and Nursultan Nazarbayev, president of Kazakhstan; as well as Fidel Castro, Kim Chen Ir, and King Gyanendra of Nepal.[78]

In Freedom House's index of May 2006, Russia was listed as one of 67 "not free" countries. In terms of press freedom, it was ranked 158th out of 194 countries, on the same level as Bahrain and Venezuela. According to the press freedom index published by Freedom House in May 2007, Russia had moved six more places down the list, to share the 164th place with Azerbaijan, coming in below Brunei, Kazakhstan, Tajikistan, and Swaziland. (The last ten spots included three CIS countries: Turkmenistan, Uzbekistan, and Belarus.) The report also noted that Russia continued to oppress the independent media and had plans to regulate use of the Internet.[79]

In June 2007, President Putin was awarded the international Closed Oyster prize by Netzwerk Recherche, a German reporters' association. The award was announced at an annual conference of media representatives in Hamburg. Putin was cited for his "bad attitude toward reporters," for "obstructing the development of the free media," for the absence of results in the investigation of Anna Politkovskaya's murder, and generally for "destroying the free press."[80] Vladimir Putin was the first head of state to receive the Closed Oyster prize.

11

The Age of Assassins

ORIGINS: THE POISONING OF LENIN AND THE MURDER OF TROTSKY

Spiridon Putin—Putin's grandfather on his father's side (according to his official biography) or on his mother's side (according to the unofficial one)—spent his whole life working as a cook, first for Lenin, then for Stalin. This is an established fact. We have the testimony of Lenin's other cook, Gavriill Volkov.

After Lenin died, Volkov was arrested and, like the man in the iron mask, spent the rest of his life in prison. "Not only was I never interrogated, but no one was ever allowed to speak to me about my case," Volkov told Yelizaveta Lermolo, whom he met by accident during a walk in the prison yard. Here is what Lermolo remembered about this encounter:

> One day a man was added to my exercise shift. He was an old-time prisoner, Gavriil Volkov, a Communist. Heretofore he had been allowed to take his walks only in solitude. . . . There were rumors that he was being held in "strictest isolation," accountable directly to the Kremlin. But no one actually knew what case he was involved in or why he had been imprisoned. . . .
>
> We fell into a lengthy conversation. He told me that he was an Old Bolshevik, that he had taken part in the Bolshevik uprising in

Moscow in 1917. Until 1923 he was employed in the Kremlin as the manager of a dining room that was maintained there for the high-up party functionaries. Later he became the chef at the Kremlin sanatorium in Gorki. . . . Volkov had been arrested . . . in 1932. He had just passed his "third anniversary" at the isolator. . . . He didn't know the term of sentence. As to the reason for his imprisonment, he could only guess. He was never tried. No one had ever interrogated him. "Not only was I never interrogated but no official was even permitted to discuss my case with me. . . . For a period of eleven years I have been carrying sealed within my heart a deep secret. I haven't disclosed it to a living soul. . . ."

When Lenin became ill in 1923, Volkov went on to say, it was decided to hospitalize him in the Kremlin sanatorium at Gorki. Volkov was sent there to serve as Lenin's personal chef. . . . On January 21, 1924 . . . at eleven in the morning, as usual, Volkov took Lenin his second breakfast. There was no one else in his room. As soon as Volkov appeared, Lenin made an attempt to rise and extended both his hands, uttering unintelligible sounds. Volkov rushed over to him and Lenin slipped a note into his hand. . . . The note, scratched in a nervous scrawl, read: "Gavrilushka, I've been poisoned. . . . Go fetch Nadya [Krupskaya] at once. . . . Tell Trotsky. . . . Tell everyone you can."[1]

There is also Trotsky's testimony. In 1939, after the leaders of the Communist Party and the government had been convicted in open trials in Moscow, after the top commanders of the Red Army had been executed, after Trotsky's collaborators and friends had been annihilated along with members of his family, and finally after Stalin had made a pact with Hitler, Trotsky published a sensational article in which he revealed that Lenin might have been poisoned by Stalin. It is possible that this was Trotsky's first cautious attempt to tell the truth. If what he had to say—which bordered on divulging a government secret— had met with interest in the West, Trotsky might have become more talkative. But the public and political opinion of the free world remained silent. No one was interested in Trotsky's disclosures. The left, which sympathized with the Soviet Union, did not want to compromise Stalin and the socialist order. The anti-Soviet right suspected Trotsky of lying, just as they did any other Communist. And absolutely no one understood the totality and scale of Stalin's criminal regime.

Trotsky's article, which he first submitted to *Life* magazine on October 13, 1939, was never published there. On August 10, 1940, after losing ten months, Trotsky finally published it in an abridged form in the magazine *Liberty*. Ten days later he was killed by an NKVD agent, Ramon Mercader.

We have gotten used to the fact that the security services are constantly being renamed in Russia. The NKVD was the prototype of the KGB, the same organization that is known today as the FSB. Let us note that Trotsky's murder led to no public discussion between Mexico and the Soviet Union, such as the discussion between the United Kingdom and Russia that followed the murder of Alexander Litvinenko in November 2006. Moscow did not claim that the NKVD agent who had killed Trotsky was in reality a Mexican foreign intelligence officer or a member of a group of former agents who had broken off from the NKVD; the USSR's General Prosecutor's Office did not claim that it would indict Trotsky's murderer if it was proved in a Soviet court that he was indeed guilty. And certainly no one had the idea of nominating Ramon Mercader—who never admitted the fact that he had killed Trotsky on orders from Soviet foreign intelligence—for the Supreme Soviet of the USSR (the equivalent of today's Russian parliament). Everything was done quietly and unofficially, without involvement by the press. But it was fully understood that only Stalin could have given the order to kill Trotsky, and that only the NKVD could have conducted a special operation to assassinate him.

On June 6, 1941, the people's commissar of internal affairs, Lavrenty Beria, submitted a report to Stalin requesting that Trotsky's assassin be decorated with high state honors: "In 1940, a group of NKVD employees successfully completed a special assignment. The NKVD of the USSR requests that the six comrades who carried out the assignment be decorated with the Order of the USSR. I request a resolution from you." Stalin stamped his approval: "In favor (no public announcement)."

By secret order of the Presidium of the Supreme Soviet of the USSR, Ramon Mercader's mother, Caridad Mercader, a Soviet foreign intelligence agent, was decorated with the Order of Lenin. So were the organizers of the operation: NKVD agents L. P. Vasilevsky, P. A. Sudoplatov, I. R. Postelnyak, I. R. Grigulevich, N. I. Eitingon.

Ramon Mercader himself spent twenty years in a Mexican prison. Upon his release on May 6, 1960, he was delivered first to Cuba and then to the USSR. Soon afterward, by a secret decree of the Presidium of the Supreme Soviet of the USSR, Mercader was awarded the title of Hero of the Soviet Union and decorated with the Order of Lenin and a Gold Star medal. He was given an apartment in Moscow, a dacha in Kratovo (a prestigious Moscow suburb), and a pension equivalent to that of a KGB general: 400 rubles per month, a very high pension in the USSR at that time. Mercader and his wife, Raquelia Mendoza—who apparently had also worked for Soviet foreign intelligence—lived in Moscow for a while. Mercader worked at the Institute of Marxism–Leninism, while his wife was a newscaster on Moscow radio's Spanish-language edition. In the mid-1970s, at Castro's invitation, Mercader moved to Cuba, where he served as an advisor in the Ministry of Foreign Affairs. He died in 1978 of lung cancer. Mercader's remains were transferred to Moscow and buried in the Kuntsevo cemetery under the name Ramon Ivanovich Lopez.

Naum (Leonid) Eitingon (or Eitington—there are several variations on the spelling) was a high-ranking Soviet foreign intelligence agent in charge of a group that carried out illegal operations. He worked in China, in Paris, and in Spain during the Spanish Civil War. Eitingon was the lover of Caridad Mercader and the tutor of her son Ramon. It was assumed that Ramon, after killing Trotsky, would be able to leave the mansion where Trotsky lived, and that Caridad and Eitingon would be waiting for him, ready to take him out of Mexico. Ramon was caught, however. Caridad and Eitingon fled to Cuba, then to the United States and to China, returning to Moscow in May 1941. Stalin received Eitingon personally, thanked him for organizing the operation, and promised that as long as he, Stalin, lived, no one would touch a hair on Eitingon's head. Ten years later Eitingon, who by this time had become a major general in the MGB—the Ministry of State Security, the former NKVD and the future KGB—was fired from his job and put under house arrest. But he was not put in prison or executed. After Stalin's death, Eitingon was released from house arrest and, in May 1953, was allowed to return to his place of work as deputy head of the Ninth Department of the Ministry of Internal Affairs (MVD). At the end of 1957, he was again arrested for crimes committed during Stalin's rule and sentenced to twelve years in prison. He was pardoned in 1964, but not allowed to return to his old job. Eitingon went on to work as a senior editor in the Inostrannaya Literatura publishing house and died in 1981.

By the time of Stalin's death, Pavel Sudoplatov had reached the rank of lieutenant general of the MGB and was head of the First Bureau of the MGB. After Stalin's death, he was appointed deputy head of the Second Main Directorate of the Ministry of Internal Affairs, counterintelligence. In May 1953, on Beria's orders, he was appointed head of the MVD's newly formed Ninth Department—the foreign intelligence and sabotage department, which was involved in individual terrorism and sabotage. On July 31, shortly after Beria's arrest, the department was eliminated, and Sudoplatov himself was arrested on August 21.

Sudoplatov feigned insanity and remained in a psychiatric hospital until 1958. He was then sentenced to fifteen years in prison for conducting experiments on people, kidnappings, and numerous murders. He was released in 1968 and died in 1996. His memoirs, published posthumously, became required reading for many FSB officials.

Iosif Grigulevich was a Lithuanian Karaite Jew. As a gymnasium student in the early 1930s, he became involved with the Komsomol underground, served a short sentence in a Polish prison, and then left for Spain as a volunteer. There he was recruited by Soviet counterintelligence. From Spain, Grigulevich made his way to Latin America, where he continued working as a Soviet agent. Recalled to Moscow after Stalin's death, he earned a doctorate in history and became a member of the Russian Academy of Sciences, a specialist on Latin America, and the author of many books.

This is the group of people that was given the assignment to assassinate Trotsky at the end of the 1930s. But what was the last straw that made Stalin decide to go ahead with the assassination? Why was Mercader, who had been close to Trotsky since March 1940, given the assignment to kill him immediately after the appearance of Trotsky's article on August 10, 1940?

"I am going to talk about a particularly crucial topic," Trotsky wrote.

Did [Lenin's] student [Stalin] take any measures to accelerate his teacher's death? I, more than anyone, understand the monstrosity of such an allegation. But what can one do if it is suggested by the situation, by the facts, and particularly by the personality of Stalin? Lenin warned us urgently in 1921: "This cook will prepare only spicy dishes." It turned out that the dishes were not just spicy, but poisoned, and not just figuratively, but literally.

Two years ago, I first wrote down facts that were once (1923–1924) known to not more than seven or eight persons, and only in part. The only ones among them who are still alive, apart from myself, are Stalin and [Vyacheslav] Molotov [people's commissar of foreign affairs]. . . .

During Lenin's second illness, probably in February 1923, at a meeting of the Politburo, after the secretary left, Stalin informed the members of the Politburo (Grigory Zinoviev, Lev Kamenev, and myself) that Lenin had summoned him unexpectedly and had asked for poison to be brought to him. . . . I remember how unusual, mysterious, and strange Stalin's face looked. The request that he had told us about was a tragic one; but his face was frozen in a half-smile, like a mask. I had observed a similar incongruity between his words and his facial expression on earlier occasions. This time, it was completely unbearable. The horror was further augmented by the fact that Stalin did not express any opinion about Lenin's request, apparently waiting to see what the others would say. . . .

"Obviously, fulfilling this request is out of the question!" I exclaimed. ". . . Lenin might get better."

"I told him all that," Stalin objected, not without disappointment, "but he just waves it off. The old man is in pain. He says he wants to have poison near him. . . . He will resort to it if he becomes convinced that his situation is hopeless. . . . The old man is in pain," Stalin kept repeating, looking absently past us and still not taking either one side or the other. . . .

I now ask myself another, more far-reaching question: Did Lenin really ask Stalin for poison? What if Stalin made up this whole story in order to prepare his own alibi? He didn't have the slightest reason to fear that we would check up on him: none of us would have asked the ailing Lenin if he had really asked Stalin for poison. . . .

[Stalin] was surrounded by collaborators whose fate was completely tied to his own. The pharmacist Genrikh Yagoda was near at hand. Whether Stalin handed poison to Lenin as a hint that the doctors had given up all hope of recovery, or whether he resorted to more direct measures, I don't know. But I do know . . . that when I questioned doctors in Moscow about the immediate cause of Lenin's death, which had come unexpectedly for them, they were at a loss for an answer. The autopsy, naturally, was performed with every formality: as general secretary, Stalin had seen to this before anything else. But the doctors did not look for poison, even if the more penetrating among them admitted the possibility of a suicide. They probably did not suspect anything else. In any case, they couldn't have had any inclination to go into the matter too deeply. They understood that politics was above medicine.[2]

There is also the testimony of Boris Nicolaevsky, a well-known and respected historian, who collected a vast archive on the Russian Revolution, which is now stored at the Hoover Institute at Stanford University:

Trotsky . . . told about one extremely important episode which will possibly force historians to recognize Stalin as Lenin's killer . . . in the literal meaning of this word, a poisoner. . . . That Lenin made such a request of Stalin is open to serious doubt: by this time, Lenin regarded Stalin without any trust, and it is not clear how he could have turned to him, of all people, with such an intimate request.

This fact acquires particular significance in light of another story. The author of this article was acquainted with an émigré of the war years. . . . In the Chelyabinsk pretrial detention facility, she had met an old convict who in 1922–1924 had worked as a cook in Gorki, where the ailing Lenin was living at the time. This old man confessed to my acquaintance that he had added drugs to Lenin's food that made his condition worse. He did this on the instructions of people whom he considered to be Stalin's representatives. . . . If we consider this story to be true, then Stalin's announcement to the Politburo—the one related by Trotsky—has a definite meaning: Stalin was creating an alibi for himself in case people should find out about the work of the poisoner-cook.[3]

There is also a story that Stalin himself once told when he was drunk, which is known to us from indirect sources. Lidiya Shatunovskaya was sentenced to twenty years in prison "for the intention to emigrate to Israel" and spent seven years in solitary confinement in the Vladimir prison. She was released shortly after Stalin's death (March 5, 1953), and soon after that she met an old acquaintance, Ivan Gronsky (1894–1985). Gronsky was a party critic, reporter, editor, and party functionary. In 1932–1933, Gronsky was the head of the Soviet Writers' Union steering committee; in 1928–1934, he served as managing editor of the newspaper *Izvestiya*, and during the years 1932–1937, he was the editor-in-chief of the magazine *Novy Mir*. In addition, Gronsky was something like a commissar of literature under Stalin. "Through him, Stalin obtained information about everything that went on in literature, and through him, Stalin stayed in contact with writers' circles. . . . Gronsky was one of the very few people who had the right to enter Stalin's office without being announced."[4]

In 1937, Gronsky was arrested and convicted, and spent sixteen years in prisons and labor camps. After being released in 1953, he met his fellow ex-prisoner, Lidiya Shatunovskaya, who recalled:

> After we renewed our acquaintance, Ivan Gronsky and I often took walks together and told one another about many things. . . . During one of our walks, Gronsky, a very smart man and a very careful man, shared with me, a woman and not a party member, his suspicions about Lenin's death and about the mysterious role played by Stalin in the acceleration of this death. . . . He candidly told me of his conviction that Stalin had actively and deliberately accelerated Lenin's death, since no matter how sick Lenin was, as long as he lived the road to absolute dictatorship was closed to Stalin.[5]

What did Gronsky say, then? At the beginning of the 1930s, during a meeting with writers at which Stalin, along with everyone else, had had a fair amount to drink, Stalin "to Gronsky's horror began to talk to those present about Lenin and about the circumstances of his death," wrote Shatunovskaya.

> He muttered something to the effect that there he was the only person who knew how and why Lenin died. . . . Gronsky carried out the drunken Stalin into a neighboring office and laid him down on a couch, where he immediately fell asleep. . . . After he woke up, he [Stalin] for a long time strained to remember what had happened the night

before. Once he did, he jumped up in horror and rage and pounced on Gronsky. He shook him by the shoulders and shouted deliriously: "Ivan! Tell me the truth. What did I say yesterday about Lenin's death? Tell me the truth, Ivan!" Gronsky tried to calm him down, saying: "Iosif Vissarionovich! You did not say anything yesterday. I just saw that you were not feeling well, brought you to this office, and put you to sleep. Anyway, all the writers were so drunk that no one could hear or understand anything."

Gradually, Stalin began to calm down, but then another thought occurred to him. "Ivan!" he shouted. "But you yourself were not drunk. What did you hear?" . . . Gronsky, of course, tried to convince Stalin that nothing had been said about Lenin's death, that he had not heard anything, and that he took Stalin away simply because everyone present had already had too much to drink. . . . From that day on, Stalin's relation to Gronsky changed completely, and in 1937, Gronsky was arrested.[6]

The person in charge of the operation to poison Lenin was probably Genrikh Yagoda, the future head of the NKVD. One of Stalin's former secretaries who fled to the West related the following episode, which took place on January 20–21, 1924: Stalin called Yagoda and the two doctors who were treating Lenin into his office and ordered one of the doctors, Fyodor Getye, and Yagoda to go to Gorki and see Lenin at once. Shortly after Getye's and Yagoda's visit, on January 21, Lenin suffered another heart attack and died. When his wife, Nadezhda Krupskaya, entered his room, she saw several empty vials on a table beside his bed. At 7:15 P.M., the telephone rang in Stalin's office: it was Yagoda informing him that Lenin had died.[7]

At eleven o'clock in the morning on January 22—sixteen hours after Lenin's death—an autopsy was performed, with nine doctors present. It was completed at four in the afternoon. The medical report stated that Lenin had died of "disseminated sclerosis." A week later, Doctor Vaysbrod, who was present during the autopsy, wrote in *Pravda* that doctors were not yet able to assemble all the details of Lenin's illness into a single clinical picture. Evidently, Vaysbrod was implying that he was not satisfied by the medical report that had come out after the autopsy. Indeed, the report did not include a toxicological analysis and did not describe the contents of Lenin's stomach; it indicated only that his stomach had been empty and that the walls of the stomach had contracted, although it was known that Lenin had eaten two meals on the day of his death. The report referred to irregularities in the spleen and liver, but did not go into details. On the whole, the doctors had avoided discussing those organs in which traces of poisoning might have been detected. Nor had they done a blood analysis.

A MURDER EPIDEMIC

In January 1924, Stalin tried to get rid of Trotsky as well. Trotsky's description of the assassination attempt against him is exceedingly modest, consisting only of a single phrase: "In the second half of January 1924, I left for the Sukhumi in the Caucasus to try to recover from a mysterious infection that I was unable to get rid of, whose character doctors have not been able to determine to this day. News of Lenin's death reached me while I was traveling."[8]

This is all that Trotsky tells us about the government coup that Stalin organized and carried out in January 1924—the elimination of Lenin and the attempt to eliminate Trotsky.

Right before he left Moscow, on January 18, Trotsky was twice visited by Doctor Getye. Three days later, Lenin died. Trotsky recovered from his illness, though he was unable to recover all his former political weight. But since the mysterious cause of the illness that doctors could not explain was so obvious to Trotsky himself, from that moment on he stopped buying medicines prescribed to him at the Kremlin pharmacy.[9] These precautions saved him only up to a point: three years later, Trotsky was sent into internal exile; a year later, he was sent out of the country; and after that, he was killed. Ultimately, he was unable to avoid Lenin's fate.

On March 25, 1924, Trotsky's deputy Ephraim Sklyansky, the country's third most important military commander (after Lenin and Trotsky), was unexpectedly removed from his post and appointed head of the Moscow Textile Trust (Mossukno). Trotsky was still the people's commissar of war and chairman of the Revolutionary Military Council of the Republic. All the same, this was a bad sign for Trotsky. He had worked with Sklyansky during the entire Russian Civil War (1918–1922), knew him well, and valued him. It was obvious that Sklyansky's removal was a prelude to the removal of Trotsky himself. And indeed, in April 1925, Trotsky was dismissed from his post as head of the military branch of the government by order of the Central Committee. He was replaced by Mikhail Frunze, whose star, it seemed, was only beginning to rise.

By way of compensation, Sklyansky was allowed to take a vacation in the United States. He never came back to Russia: on August 27, 1925, he drowned in a lake. At the same time, rumors began circulating in Moscow that Sklyansky had been killed by GPU agents on Stalin's orders.

Frunze also did not last long. In November 1925, he died under the surgeon's knife. His position was filled by Stalin's appointee Klement Voroshilov. Immediately after Frunze's death, rumors spread that he had been killed on the operating table on Stalin's orders. The famous American anarchist Alexander Berkman, who was well informed and acquainted with many Soviet leaders, wrote about this to the American Sovietologist Isaac Don Levine in 1927.[10] Thirty years later, Boris Nicolaevsky wrote the same thing to the head of the French Communist Party, Boris Suvarin: "By the way, I met a man—a professor at the Frunze Military Academy—who told me that Tukhachevsky (they were friends at the Mikhailovskoye Artillery School) had told him in 1925 that Frunze's 'operation' was a murder."[11]

But there's an even better-informed contemporary who has left us his view of this episode: Trotsky. There are drafts for an unfinished biography of Stalin in his archives, which contain the following note about Frunze:

> He was not destined to remain long at his post as head of the armed forces: in November 1925, he died under the surgeon's knife. But during these few months, Frunze showed too much independence by protecting the army from the GPU. . . . Based on the facts of the case, the following course of events may be deduced. Frunze had a stomach ulcer, but believed—following the opinion of doctors who were close to him—that his heart would not be able to handle chloroform and was decidedly set against having an operation. Stalin ordered the Central Committee's doctor—in other words, his own trusted agent—to convene a specially selected consultation board. This board recommended

a surgical intervention. The Politburo ratified the recommendation. Frunze had to submit, in other words, to face death from an anesthetic. . . . At the end of 1925, Stalin's power was already so great that his administrative plans could easily include an obedient medical consultation board, and chloroform, and the surgeon's knife.

The first operations to poison Soviet deserters abroad took place in 1925. On August 6, 1925, the Golke brothers—members of the military wing of the German Communist Party—poisoned V. L. Nesterovich-Yaroslavsky in a cafe in Mainz, on orders from Moscow. Nesterovich-Yaroslavsky was a Soviet foreign intelligence agent. During the Russian Civil War, he had served as a cavalry brigade commander and was decorated with the Order of the Red Banner and awarded an honorary weapon for courage. Later, he organized an operation to eliminate the king and prime minister of Bulgaria in Sofia. A bomb was blown up inside a cathedral where the king and the prime minister were attending a mass. The explosion was very powerful and claimed many lives, but the king and the prime minister were not harmed. The failure of the operation made a heavy impression on Nesterovich-Yaroslavsky; he fell into depression, made his way to Germany, refused to return to Moscow, and announced that he was cutting ties with Soviet intelligence. At this point, it was decided that he should be eliminated.

Also in 1925, Ignatiy Dzevaltovsky, the USSR's illegal resident in the Baltics, broke with Soviet intelligence for similar reasons. He was poisoned in December.

Immediately after Lenin's death, in 1924–1926, a struggle for power began between Stalin and Dzerzhinsky—the general secretary of the Communist Party and the head of the Joint State Political Directorate (OGPU), which was another name of the future KGB. We know about this struggle from photographs. In January 1924, an important Soviet tradition began: from then on, the commission that arranged the funeral of a deceased leader would always be headed by the main claimant to the position of the deceased. The commission that arranged Lenin's funeral was headed by Dzerzhinsky, who, along with Stalin, had taken part in the conspiracy to eliminate Lenin. Dzerzhinsky was the immediate superior of Yagoda, who had visited Lenin on January 21, the day of his death. And Dzerzhinsky was the first in a row of government officials who carried Lenin's coffin.[12]

Stalin could not tolerate such rivalry. On July 20, 1926, Dzerzhinsky suddenly died—according to the official story, of a heart attack.

Rumors that Dzerzhinsky did not die of natural causes have circulated for a long time. Here is what Nicolaevsky wrote on September 1, 1954, in a letter to N. V. Valentinov-Volsky, the well-known Russian social democrat, writer, émigré social activist, and author of several books about Lenin:

"Stalin's favorite technique for a long time was to use doctors to poison people. . . . I myself first refused to believe that Dzerzhinsky had been poisoned . . . but later I heard the same story . . . from a man who was the head of one of the groups that worked for" Georgy Malenkov, the secretary of the party's Central Committee. "Now, reading Reiss's notes"—Reiss was a Soviet intelligence agent who had fled to the West and was killed on Stalin's orders in Switzerland in September 1937—"I came across [NKVD head Nikolai Yezhov's words to the effect that] Dzerzhinsky was unreliable. Under such circumstances, I am no longer as categorical in my rejection of any possibility of poisoning." "I know that Dzerzhinsky opposed putting the GPU under Stalin's control. . . . I know, furthermore, that Stalin's apparatus began to carry out major operations in the fall of 1926," i.e. after Dzerzhinsky's death; "that Stalin brought the apparatus in other countries under his control in 1927–1928. And that Stalin undoubtedly made use of Dzerzhinsky's death, because Dzerzhinsky's death was useful to him."[13]

Nicolaevsky's epistolary evidence should be supplemented with documentary evidence. On June 2, 1937, Stalin delivered a long speech about the discovery of a military-political conspiracy at an extended session of the Military Council of the People's Commissariat of Defense. Concerning Dzerzhinsky, Stalin said the following:

It is often said that in 1922 . . . Dzerzhinsky voted for Trotsky, and not just voted for him, but openly supported Trotsky, under Lenin and against Lenin. Did you know this? He was not a man who could remain passive in anything. He was a very active Trotskyite and he wanted to bring the entire GPU to Trotsky's defense. He was unable to do this.[14]

"Unable to do this" in Stalin's language meant that Dzerzhinsky had been eliminated.

Stalin's wife and Lenin's secretary, Nadezhda Alliluyeva, died tragically either at Stalin's own hands or by suicide. On April 10, 1956, the Parisian émigré newspaper *Russkaya Mysl* published a short article on this topic under the undiplomatic heading "Stalin—Alliluyeva's Murderer." Here the newspaper reported:

In Moscow, Stalin is being openly accused of killing his second wife, Nadezhda Alliluyeva. This information first appeared in London newspapers on April 3. They referred to the Moscow periodical *Sovietsky Kommunist*, which reported that Stalin had "personally shot his second wife."

Vyacheslav Menzhinsky, who replaced Dzerzhinsky as head of the OGPU, died in 1934. At Genrikh Yagoda's public trial in Moscow in 1938, Yagoda—who by that time had reached the rank of people's commissar of internal affairs (head of the secret police)—admitted that he had organized Menzhinsky's murder with the assistance of doctors. In his unfinished draft for a biography of Stalin, Trotsky wrote:

Doctor I. N. Kazakov has given his testimony: "As a result of my conversation with Yagoda, L. G. Levin and I developed a method for curing Menzhinsky that in reality destroyed his last strength and accelerated his death. In this way, Levin and I practically killed Menzhinsky. I gave Levin a mixture of lysates, which, in combination with alkoloids, produced the desired result, i.e. Menzhinsky's death."

Kazakov's colleague Levin—the attending physician of the Soviet Union's top government officials—also testified that he had accelerated Menzhinsky's death on Yagoda's orders.

Of course, the arrested men were tortured and their testimony may have been beaten out of them by their executioners. But we know from numerous sources that the NKVD did in fact have a poison laboratory, known as Laboratory No. 12, and that it had been established by Yagoda—who had medical training—in 1921. The first head of this "special office" was Ignaty Kazakov, professor of medicine.

Konstantin Petrov, a prominent Communist, recalled Yagoda's toxicological laboratory in 1987. Once, he was invited to Yagoda's office and saw "a large cabinet along the office wall. The door was slightly open. The cabinet was filled with vials, jars with medicines of some kind. There were too many medicines for personal use. Their location and use could not but give rise to certain thoughts."[15]

Kazakov, who was arrested and executed in 1938, was replaced by Professor Grigory Mayranovsky, who had worked at the NKVD's "Twelfth Department" since March 1937. He studied "the influence of lethal gases and poisons on malignant tumors." There was a building on Varsonofyevsky Lane that was adjacent to the NKVD's jail on Bolshaya Lubyanka Street. Inside this building was a special cell where poisons were tested out on people who had been sentenced to death. The main purpose of the tests was to develop poisons that would leave no traces in the victim's body. This is how the poison known as K-2 was created. An injection of it caused death in fifteen minutes. In 1943, NKGB head Vsevolod Merkulov ordered that Mayranovsky be given a doctoral degree in medicine and the title of professor "for all of his work, without defending a dissertation." In his request, Merkulov indicated that, "while working at the NKVD, comrade Mayranovsky has completed ten classified projects of operational importance."

Menzhinsky died (or was killed) on May 10, 1934. Maxim Peshkov, son of the famous Soviet writer Gorky, died on the following day. "Yagoda did not like Gorky's son's way of life," Trotsky wrote.

> He felt that he was a harmful influence on his father and surrounded his father with "undesirable people." This made him decide to eliminate the son and he invited Doctor Levin to assist him in liquidating Gorky's son. . . . Yagoda had a special cabinet with poisons. When he needed to, he took out precious vials from this cabinet and gave them to his agents along with corresponding instructions. The head of the GPU—a former pharmacist, by the way—always displayed an exceptional interest in poisons. He had several toxicologists at his command, for whom he had created a special laboratory, funding for which was supplied in unlimited amounts and without monitoring.

With the assistance of doctors who worked at the Kremlin, Genrikh Yagoda—the deputy head and then the head of the NKVD—poisoned two other well-known figures in the USSR: Valerian Kuibyshev, a member of the party's Central Committee and the head of the Gosplan of the USSR, who died on January 25, 1935; and Maxim Gorky, who died on June 18, 1936.

The official story is that Kuibyshev died of a heart attack. However, Kuibyshev's son Vladimir claimed that his father was absolutely healthy: "A medical consultation was held by a board of specifically selected doctors and an autopsy was performed. They concluded that the cause of death was a heart attack. This conclusion leaves room for doubt, and even perplexity, since father had a healthy heart. Two days before he died, on January 23, father, laughing, told his sister Yelena as he saw her out the door: 'The healthiest part of my body is my heart!'" Vladimir Kuibyshev believed that Kuibyshev's attending physician, Doctor Levin, had killed his father by administering "carefully calculated doses of specially selected 'medicines'-poisons."[16]

The theory that Kuibyshev was murdered gains further credibility from the fact that three years later, in 1938, Valerian Kuibyshev's brother Nikolai was executed. Nikolai Kuibyshev was a military leader, corps commander, and Russian Civil War hero, who had been decorated with four Orders of the Red Banner and thrice wounded in battle. At the time of his arrest, he was the commander of the Transcaucasus Military District. He was summoned from Tbilisi to Moscow and arrested on the train back, at night. On August 1, 1938, while he was being interrogated inside Butyrka prison, Nikolai Kuibyshev was shot personally by Lavrenty Beria, the new head of the NKVD.

On February 16, 1938, Trotsky's son Lev Sedov suddenly died in Paris. The cause of death was never determined. Much later, it became known that Sedov had been poisoned by a Soviet agent. Also in 1938, Stalin publicly accused Yagoda and the Kremlin's attending physicians of killing Menzhinsky, Peshkov, Kuibyshev, and Gorky. Trotsky wrote:

> Next to Yagoda on the defendants' bench sat four Kremlin doctors who were accused of killing Maxim Gorky and two Soviet ministers: "I plead guilty," testified the venerable Doctor Levin, who was once

my own doctor, "to applying medical treatments that were counter-indicated for the illness." In this way, "I caused the premature deaths of Maxim Gorky and Kuibyshev." Kazakov was particularly useful in this respect, since, according to Doctor Levin, he had operated on his patients using medications that he prepared himself without any monitoring in his own laboratory, so that he alone knew the secret of his injections. . . .

The testimony of Doctor Levin, an old man of sixty-eight years, made the most shocking impression. According to him, he had deliberately helped accelerate the deaths of Menzhinsky, Kuibyshev, and Maxim Gorky himself. He had acted on Yagoda's instructions, since he feared that "his family would be destroyed." Gorky presented a serious danger. He corresponded with European writers, he was visited by foreigners, people who had been wronged complained to him, he shaped public opinion. There was no way to force him to remain silent. To arrest him, to send him into exile, or to execute him was even less feasible. The thought of accelerating the liquidation of the ailing Gorky "without bloodshed," through Yagoda, must have appeared to the boss of the Kremlin as the only solution.

This is how Stalin's mind works: such solutions occur to him instinctively. . . . After the writer's death, suspicions arose at once that Stalin had slightly helped the destructive power of nature. Another purpose of Yagoda's trial was to clear Stalin of this suspicion.[17]

Lenin's widow, Nadezhda Krupskaya, died on February 27, 1939. In 1957, at a session of the Politburo, Nikita Khrushchev—citing materials from the Lubyanka archives—announced that Krupskaya had been poisoned by Stalin, who had sent her favorite cake to her on the occasion of her seventieth birthday.

The Second World War for a long time distracted the Soviet security services from poisoning operations against individual political enemies, mainly because enemies were usually transported from territories occupied by the Soviet army directly to the USSR during the war. After the war, kidnapping was a common technique, and not in the occupied territories alone. Thus, in August 1947, Mikhail Korostovtsev, the former head of the Egyptian bureau of the Telegraph Agency of the Soviet Union (TASS), was kidnapped in Egypt. In September, Yuri Tregubov, an activist from the anti-Soviet organization National Alliance of Russian Solidarists (NTS), was kidnapped in West Berlin. Also in 1947, the NKGB kidnapped the American general Stanley Dubik in Vienna; during the war, Dubik had been in charge of U.S. foreign intelligence in Poland, first under occupation by the Germans and then by the Soviet army. In 1948, the director of German counterintelligence in Paris, General Sartorius, was kidnapped in West Berlin.

In the 1950s, the kidnappings suddenly stopped and the murders and poisonings began anew. In February 1951, the well-known anti-Communist journalist Nikolai Fevr was poisoned in Argentina. In 1953, plans were made to poison the Yugoslavian leader Josip Broz Tito, who had entered into an ideological conflict with Stalin. The assassination was called off only at the very last moment due to Stalin's illness.

It is very likely that Stalin's final illness was also the result of poisoning, and that it was precisely by poisoning that Stalin met his death on March 5, 1953. The conspiracy against him had four organizers: Lavrenty Beria and three party leaders—Georgy Malenkov, Nikolai Bulganin, and Nikita Khrushchev. Beria led the plot. He also aspired to replace Stalin as head of the party and the government. But Beria—who had been head of the NKVD since December 1938 and was a murderer and a rapist who kept kidnapped girls in his private prison—was too much hated by the entire party elite. In June 1953, he was arrested by his own co-conspirators, and subsequently he was shot right in prison by Pavel Batitsky, Marshal of the Soviet Union, some time around December 22, 1953.

Thus, all the early heads of Soviet state security died under unusual circumstances: Dzerzhinsky died suddenly in 1926; Menzhinsky, who replaced him, was medically treated to death or poisoned by doctors and died in 1934; Yagoda, who replaced him, was shot in 1938; Nikolai Yezhov, who replaced Yagoda, was discharged in December 1938 and shot in 1939; Beria, who replaced Yezhov, was shot in 1953. And Vsevolod Merkulov, who replaced Beria, was also shot in 1953. Viktor Abakumov, who replaced Merkulov, was shot in 1954. This pattern was broken only by Semyon Ignatyev, who followed Merkulov to lead the Ministry of State Security (MGB) in 1951–1952. After his dismissal, he occupied various party posts, and then was sent into retirement in 1960.

In December 1951, Professor Mayranovsky was arrested. He was charged with spying for Japan, kidnapping, illegal possession of poisons, and abusing his official position. In prison, Mayranovsky fought desperately to be rehabilitated, wrote several letters to Ignatyev, the minister of state security, and later to Beria. Even so, the MGB's Special Council sentenced Mayranovsky to ten years in prison. After being released at the beginning of 1961, he was forbidden to live in Moscow, Leningrad, or the capitals of the Soviet Union's republics. Mayranovsky spent the last years of his life working at a scientific research institute in Makhachkala, and died in 1971.

The USSR's general prosecutor Andrei Vyshinsky—who had coordinated the trials of the Stalin years, personally signed death warrants, and was responsible for Stalin's purges of the party, state, and military apparatus in the 1930s—was by this time the Soviet Union's UN representative in New York. At the end of October 1954, he was summoned to Moscow to deliver a report. Realizing what was waiting for him in Moscow—inevitable arrest and execution for the crimes that he had committed during the years of Stalin's rule—Vyshinsky delayed his return and refused to budge. Consequently, a special MGB agent with a diplomatic passport arrived in New York from Moscow on November 19 and poisoned Vyshinsky. At 9:15 A.M. on November 22, the Soviet delegation officially announced that Vyshinsky had suddenly died of a heart attack during breakfast at the USSR's UN mission at 680 Park Avenue. No outsiders—diplomats, reporters, policemen—were allowed to enter the building. Vyshinsky's death certificate was signed by "Doctor Alexei Kassov," the official doctor of the Soviet embassy in Washington and the Soviet UN delegation in New York.

A conflict immediately arose between the Soviet delegation and American law enforcement, which did not want to recognize "Doctor Kassov's" death certificate since the doctor had no license to practice medicine in the state of New York. Nonetheless, on the morning of November 23, Vyshinsky's body was placed on a special flight and transported to Moscow. It was accompanied by the agent with the diplomatic passport who had come from Moscow four days earlier, and by the embassy's "Doctor Kassov," who did not return to the United States again.

THE KGB'S BASIC INSTINCT

With Stalin's death, assassination techniques improved. In 1954–1955, A. Trushnovich, a representative of the National Alliance of Russian Solidarists (NTS), was killed in Berlin, and NTS members V. Tremmel and S. Popov were kidnapped in Linz and Thuringia. KGB Captain Nikolai Khokhlov traveled to Germany to assassinate the NTS leaders Georgy Okolovich and Vladimir Poremsky; he was assisted by the German KGB agent Wildprett.

Khokhlov deserves separate mention. He was born in 1922 in Nizhny Novgorod and worked in Soviet foreign intelligence. In 1943, in German-occupied Minsk, he took part in an operation to eliminate Wilhelm Kube, the German Gauleiter of Belorussia. Later he was stationed as an illegal resident in Romania and Austria. In March 1952, Khokhlov was preparing for his next assignment: the elimination of Alexander Kerensky, the former head of Russia's Provisional Government, now living abroad. After Beria was arrested, however, Khokhlov was recalled to Moscow and told that the operation to assassinate Kerensky was being called off. Instead, he was ordered to organize the assassinations of Okolovich and Poremsky in Frankfurt. But Khokhlov did not carry out this assignment. He arrived at Okolovich's apartment and told him that he had been sent to organize the assassination of the NTS's leaders in Frankfurt. A lengthy conversation ensued. Finally, they decided that Khokhlov would become a deserter and that Okolovich would put him in touch with the CIA. Khokhlov's German collaborator Wildprett—whose identity Khokhlov revealed in talking to the Americans—immediately turned himself in to the German government. The operation to eliminate Okolovich and Poremsky ended in failure, and Khokhlov was sentenced to death in Moscow for treason.

On September 15, 1957, shortly after publishing his memoirs, Nikolai Khokhlov fainted in the Palmengarten in Frankfurt while attending an annual political conference organized by the NTS's émigré weekly *Posev*. One of the NTS's Belgian activists who had been present at the conference, Yevgeny Drevinsky, later recalled that Khokhlov had taken a sip from a cup of coffee brought to him at his request by an attendant, but had then heard that an interesting speech was about to begin and ran to hear it without finishing the coffee. It is possible that Khokhlov survived only because he did not consume a sufficient dose of poison.

The doctor at the university hospital where Khokhlov was taken suspected poisoning. Khokhlov was vomiting, his head was spinning, he was running a high temperature and was in pain. He was put in the gastroenterological ward and diagnosed with food poisoning.

Five days later, red and brown stripes, dark spots, and black and blue marks appeared on Khokhlov's face and body. A sticky liquid started to ooze from his eyes. Big clumps of hair fell out at the slightest touch. Blood appeared in his pores, and his skin became dry and tight, cracking when it was stretched. In places where the skin is particularly thin, such as behind the ears and under the eyes, Khokhlov had to be constantly wiping blood off. He could not be bandaged because the bandages rubbed his scabs off and reopened his wounds. His blood was undergoing a rapid process of decomposition that the doctors were unable to understand. Tests conducted on September 22 revealed that his white blood cells were being quickly and irreversibly destroyed, having fallen to a count of 700 from a normal level of 7000. Khokhlov's salivary glands atrophied. Then a bone marrow sample was taken. It turned out that a large portion of his blood-forming cells were dead. Necrosis of the mucous membranes of the mouth, throat, and esophagus set in. It became difficult for him to eat, drink, and even speak.

Khokhlov was transferred from the German hospital to an American military hospital in Frankfurt, where six American doctors began to treat him. They gave Khokhlov continuous injections of cortisone, vitamins, steroids, and other experimental medications, while keeping him alive through intravenous feeding and almost continuous blood transfusions. An anesthesiologist was always at hand to relieve his suffering. Solutions were prepared for his mouth, which had absolutely no saliva. Various specialists were called in for consultation. New medicines were quickly sent to Frankfurt. After three weeks, Khokhlov's condition began to improve. Soon he left the hospital, although for many months he remained completely bald and covered with scars.

The diagnosis had been thallium poisoning. Somewhat later, a famous American toxicologist in New York studied the history of Khokhlov's illness and concluded that Khokhlov had been poisoned with radioactive thallium. This was the first mention of a radioactive poison being used by Soviet intelligence.

Khokhlov's defection in 1954 and the unsuccessful attempt to kill him were not the KGB's only failures abroad. The work of the KGB's foreign groups was always a combination of successes and failures. In Munich on October 9, 1957, the KGB agent Bogdan Stashinsky shot a capsule of hydrocyanic acid through a specially designed tube into the face of Lev Rebet, a leader of the Ukrainian émigré community. Rebet died on the spot. The autopsy revealed that he had died of a heart attack. Two years later, again in Munich, Stashinsky repeated the operation, shooting a cyanide-filled capsule into the face of the Ukrainian nationalist leader Stepan Bandera, who also died on the spot. Both operations should be characterized as successes. But in another two years, Stashinsky fell in love with a West German woman, deserted, turned himself in to West German counterintelligence, and confessed everything.

In the 1960s, the KGB started poisoning writers. In November 1961, the émigré journalist and writer Mikhail Baykov was poisoned in Buenos Aires. Soon, attempts were made to poison dissident writers in the USSR as well: Alexander Solzhenitsyn and Vladimir Voinovich. Both attempts failed. In line with the medieval tradition of not hanging a person who has already slipped from the noose, the KGB decided to let both writers live. Solzhenitsyn was sent out of the country, while Voinovich was asked to emigrate.

In 1978, the forty-nine-year-old Bulgarian dissident Georgi Markov was killed in London. He was poisoned with ricin, which had been manufactured in Laboratory No. 12 in the USSR. Along with poison, Soviet agents had given their Bulgarian colleagues a specially designed umbrella that fired poison capsules. Markov had been returning to work after lunch on September 7. Near a bus stop by Waterloo Bridge, he felt a sharp pain in his right leg. Turning around, he saw a man of about forty years of age who was bending over an umbrella that had fallen down. After picking up the umbrella, the man departed in a waiting taxi. Markov started choking, his head began to spin, and on his leg he discovered a bleeding wound. After making his way to the BBC's Bulgarian studio where he worked, Markov told his colleagues about the incident with the umbrella. Soon he became completely ill and was taken home. Four days later, he died. The diagnosis at the time was heart disease.

A couple of weeks before Markov's murder, Bulgarian security agents tried to eliminate another Bulgarian dissident, Vladimir Kostov, who had been granted political asylum in Paris. While going down the escalator in the metro, Kostov felt a sharp, light pain in his buttock. That evening, he suddenly developed a high temperature. On the following day, constant fevers began. Kostov saw a doctor, but the doctor could not give him a diagnosis. It was August, and all serious doctors in Paris were on vacation; the doctor who examined Kostov turned out to be an intern. Only when news of Markov's sudden death reached Paris was Kostov examined again. This time, doctors discovered and removed from Kostov's soft tissue a microscopic capsule similar to the one that had been found in Markov's leg. The casing of the capsule was made of 90 percent platinum and 10 percent iridium, and it contained ricin.

In 1980, Boris Korzhak, a Soviet citizen and a CIA double agent, felt a pinprick like a mosquito bite while he was in a store in Virginia, in a suburb of Washington, D.C. He developed a temperature. Several days later, he had internal bleeding and arrhythmia. A doctor extracted a capsule from the "mosquito bite." Just as in Paris and London, the capsule had two small holes, which had been sealed with wax. Inside the body, the wax melted and the poison penetrated into the tissues. Neither Kostov nor Korzhak understood how the capsules had managed to enter their bodies. Years passed. The Soviet Union collapsed.

The participants of those long-gone operations began to talk. And today we know all the details about Markov's murder and the assassination attempts against Kostov and Korzhak.

THE FSB'S BASIC INSTINCT

The 1990s brought new trends into the work of Russia's state security organs. The FSB uses poison—an ancient murder weapon—not for fighting ideological enemies, as in Soviet times, but against critics of the KGB-FSB. This category of victims includes Yuri Shchekochikhin, a State Duma deputy and the deputy editor-in-chief of *Novaya Gazeta*; Anna Politkovskaya, a reporter for that newspaper; and Alexander Litvinenko, a former FSB lieutenant colonel. The next class of victims consists of enemies of the Russian state with claims on government power in territories that the Russian government views as its own fiefdoms. This group includes the current president of Ukraine, Viktor Yushchenko; the Chechen field commander Amir Khattab; and the former and acting presidents of the insurgent Republic of Chechnya—Dzhokhar Dudayev, Zelimkhan Yandarbiyev, and Aslan Maskhadov (all of them killed). Finally, the FSB also counts among its deadly foes all those who have ascended the hierarchical ladder too rapidly and, passing to a different orbit, have laid claims to a redistribution of government power in Russia. These people include the businessmen-politicians Ivan Kivilidi and Boris Berezovsky, as well as those who knew too much and could compromise the Kremlin and the upper leadership: Roman Tsepov, former head of Putin's security in St. Petersburg; Anatoly Sobchak, former mayor of St. Petersburg; and Vladimir Barsukov-Kumarin, former godfather of St. Petersburg, arrested in September 2007.

The only thing that all the people who were killed, poisoned, arrested, or pushed out of Russia had in common was that they presented a threat to the government. Therefore, it stands to reason that it was precisely the government that made the decision to eliminate these people by using, among other means, powerful poisons developed in FSB laboratories, stored in FSB safes, and applied by professionally trained FSB agents who specialize in poisoning people.

If we also take into account the fact that the law enforcement organs—especially the General Prosecutor's Office, the investigative agencies, the FSB itself, and the courts—protect the professional killers and the super-professional poisoners by all manner of means as if they were the country's greatest treasure, it becomes clear why not one of these murders or poisonings has been or will be solved. The immunity of the killer-agents (and poisoner-superagents) is assured by the same people who give out the orders to eliminate the victims.

THE POISONING OF IVAN KIVILIDI

Ivan Kivilidi—president of the Russian Business Round Table, head of the Russian government's Entrepreneurship Council, president of Rosbiznesbank, head of the Free Labor Party (PST)—died at Moscow's Central Clinical Hospital on August 1, 1995. He succumbed to a very rare poison, which had been slipped into the receiver of his mobile phone. This murder deserves a closer look, since it became one of the first in a series of poisonings organized by Russia's security services in recent years.

As the list of positions held by Kivilidi makes clear, he was not simply a businessman. He was one of the businessmen who tried simultaneously to become a politician capable of influencing the Russian government. Thus, Kivilidi took an active part in the 1995 Duma election campaign. His views should be characterized as liberal. Here are a few of his pronouncements:

> Most entrepreneurs have a perfectly clear grasp and understanding of the liberal values that the PST stands for and that the party's members are persistently trying to introduce into the constitution. . . . The members of the PST also wish to take part in the constitutional process and to have an influence on the creation of a code of federal laws. . . . We have formed a bloc with the Russian Democratic Reform Movement (Gavriil Popov, Anatoly Sobchak) because our programs are completely identical except for our conceptions of the country's military doctrine.

The democratic parties decided to unite in a bloc for the parliamentary election, calling themselves the Russian Democratic

Reform Movement. At a press conference in St. Petersburg on October 27, 1994, Sobchak announced the bloc's candidates. The third name on that list, after Sobchak and Professor Svyatoslav Fyodorov, was Ivan Kivilidi.

As a representative of Russia's entrepreneurs, Kivilidi was thus able to speak to the government from a position of power. At a Russian Business Round Table (RBRT) meeting on October 29, he declared that entrepreneurs "have the possibility and, most importantly, the necessity to pound their fists on the table and demand something from the government." He remarked that "all of the apparatchiks are making nefarious attempts to climb on the backs of entrepreneurs" and to implement reforms in a top-down fashion, as it has always been done. But the times have changed. Now "they will have to reckon with the entrepreneurs for real."

In September 1994, the RBRT obtained the release of Lev Vainberg, a businessman who had been arrested on bribe-taking charges. Kivilidi characterized this arrest as "the heartburn of certain circles that have long been irritated by the entrepreneurs' immunity," and he called Vainberg's release a victory "by the entrepreneurs, who have been able to unite in the face of approaching danger." As *Kommersant* reported later, the meeting organized in support of Vainberg "turned into a discussion about protecting entrepreneurs from the tyranny of the government." At Kivilidi's suggestion, the RBRT decided to hold a nationwide congress of representatives from commercial enterprises in November, and to "obtain a mandate to represent the interests of all of Russia's entrepreneurs."

In 1995, Kivilidi acquired another title in addition to all those that he already had: he became a State Duma deputy. For his ill-wishers, it seemed, he had become unapproachable and untouchable. But it was precisely because the Russian business world had turned to politics that 1995 saw a wave of murders of entrepreneurs. On April 10, Vadim Yafyasov, the thirty-three-year-old vice president of Yugorsky Bank, was killed in Moscow. He became the forty-third banker to be killed in recent years. On the night of July 20, the forty-fourth banker—Oleg Kantor, president of Yugorsky Bank and a member of the supreme council of the Russian United Industrial Party (ROPP)—was brutally murdered together with his bodyguard. It happened at the dacha that Kantor rented on the grounds of the Snegiri government sanatorium in the Instrinsky district of the Moscow region. Kantor had been stabbed and shot; his eyes had been gouged out. When the leaders of the RBRT convened for a press conference several days after the murder, the ROPP chairman Vladimir Scherbakov sadly remarked that the Round Table had begun to resemble a funeral parlor: "We meet on a regular basis to take note of the fact that another entrepreneur has been murdered and to call on the government to put an end to this lawlessness. . . . It is becoming impossible to live in a country in which the entrepreneurial class is being systematically exterminated."

Indeed, of the thirty members of the Round Table's board, eight had already been killed.

Kivilidi described what was happening as a "genocide of the brains of the nation." He elaborated:

Not one murder of a factory director or bank director has been solved. Entrepreneurship is today the most dangerous profession, and one has the impression that all of this lawlessness, this complete inaction, is useful to the government. There used to be an Entrepreneurship Council in the government. It has been done away with. Private security agencies in banks have their weapons taken away from them. And soon, it will not be just the entrepreneurs who will be caught in the crosshairs, but anyone who has any kind of property.

Kivilidi grimly prognosticated that "Oleg Kantor will not be the last victim."

And he was not mistaken. The next victim was Kivilidi himself: the forty-fifth banker to be murdered, the ninth member of the board of the RBRT to be killed, the fifty-second major Russian entrepreneur to be eliminated in 1995. On August 1, Kivilidi was brought to Moscow's Central Clinical Hospital in a coma. He died on August 4, without coming out of his coma. On August 2, Kivilidi's secretary, Zara Ismalova—who had spent the whole previous day answering calls on Kivilidi's mobile phone—had a seizure and was taken to the First Municipal Hospital. She died the next day.

For ten days, Kivilidi's and Ismalova's bodies were examined in the morgues of the Central Clinical Hospital and the

Burdenko Military Hospital. Their death certificates cited acute heart failure as the cause of death. But at least one person already suspected poisoning at the time. Iosif Laskavy, an anatomic pathologist, refused to perform an autopsy on Ismalova's corpse, and in the history of her illness he wrote: "There are indications of poisoning with an unknown poison."[18]

On August 18, it was reported in the press that Kivilidi and his secretary had been poisoned with a radioactive agent. The newspaper *Tverskaya Zhizn* reported that the poison was a heavy metal of the cobalt group, while ITAR-TASS claimed that "a military employee [had] been arrested" and that "containers with radioactive materials" that had likely been used in the poisoning of Kivilidi and Ismalova "had been confiscated from him. . . . Law enforcement organs are investigating the incident."

This was the first and last time that the Russian media mentioned radioactive poison in connection with Kivilidi's murder. Nor were there any further comments from law enforcement concerning the arrest of the officer in possession of radioactive poison. It was as if no officer, no arrest, and no radioactive poison had ever existed.

Experts did, however, establish the formula of the poison. It had been produced at the state chemical defense center in Shikhany, in the Saratov region. The media had obtained this information from Dmitry Ayatskov, the governor of the Saratov region. Ayatskov was indignant that military chemists were not paid their salaries for months at a time, which forced them to take jobs on the side.

In 1997, Russia's Ministry of Internal Affairs also reported that analysis had revealed that the substance used to poison Kivilidi and his secretary was a phosphorous-based military-grade nerve agent, and that it was produced at the Shikhany secret chemical laboratory. The chemical agent that was the basis of this poison had been discovered in Sweden in 1957. It penetrates the body through pores in the skin or respiratory pathways. The person dies several hours later. Without extremely sophisticated analysis, the cause of death is impossible to determine.

Stanislav Nesterov, the administrative head of Shikhany, was puzzled by the Ministry of Internal Affairs' announcement:

This is a super-modern poisonous substance whose formula is strictly classified. Neither I nor the local FSB know of a single case of such poisons being sold illegally. If this were the case, there would be an enormous international scandal. Can you imagine: in Shikhany, at the state institute of organic synthesis, anyone who wants to can buy poison, and even poison that's used by professional spies![19]

Of course, to imagine that "anyone who wanted to" could "buy" such a poison was indeed impossible. Who, then, had access to such poisons and was at the same time interested in killing Kivilidi? Who, in 1995, was the second man in the country, after the president? Who was using every possible means to acquire money and trying to put the banks under his control before the 1996 presidential election? The man in question was the head of the Presidential Security Service, General Alexander Korzhakov.

The Russian press must be given its due. It named the people who were interested in Kivilidi's death. The best and most serious Russian newspaper, *Kommersant-Daily*, reported on April 19, 1997:

During the final years of his life, Ivan Kivilidi was involved not so much in entrepreneurship as in public service. As the head of the Russian Business Round Table, he could sharply criticize the Presidential Security Service's attack on Most Bank or deposit auctions aimed at transferring state-owned share packets to major financial organizations. "Ivan Kivilidi supported competitive auctions and was against backroom decisions and deals between government officials and business fat cats. We have concrete information that one of these people threatened him with physical retribution if Kivilidi did not shut his mouth," one of the investigators admitted to *Kommersant-Daily*'s correspondent.[20]

On July 22, 1999, the newspaper *Moskovskaya Pravda* named another person who had an interest in Kivilidi's death: Oleg Soskovets. The newspaper also reported that Rosbiznesbank's surveillance cameras, which monitored the bank's surroundings, had been turned off by someone on the day that Kivilidi was poisoned.[21]

For some reason, however, no one was interested in these hints by Moscow's two most important newspapers. In 1999, Russia's law enforcement organs officially announced that "the case had reached a dead end." The statement was made by Svetlana Petrenko, the press secretary of the Moscow municipal prosecutor's office, which was investigating the crime. "At the present time, the investigation has been halted," she said. "Investigators have thus far been unable to obtain any evidence that might indicate who could have been interested in committing this crime."[22] The million-dollar reward that Kivilidi's colleagues had offered in 1995 for information leading to the arrest of the perpetrators was left unclaimed.

On January 17, 2001, Russia's Ministry of Justice triumphantly announced that it, too, had conducted a forensic analysis of the causes of Kivilidi's death. True, Alexander Kaledin, the head of the Federal Center of Forensic Inquiry at the Ministry of Justice, refused to specify the concrete cause of the banker's death, saying that it was up to the investigative authorities to decide whether this information should be made public. Kaledin did make it known that the substance with which Kivilidi had been poisoned had "a rare formula and a name that is highly classified."

On October 9, 2006, Moscow prosecutor Yuri Semin stated in an interview that investigators had fully established the mechanism of Kivilidi's murder. "He was poisoned with a substance that simply has no analogues. And we know how it is made."

But the man who had been arrested on suspicion of organizing the murder had no connection to poisons. On June 30, the police arrested Kivilidi's former deputy, Vladimir Khutsishvili, an entrepreneur and banker. Khutsishvili denied any wrongdoing.

Khutsishvili—Kivilidi's partner and a member of Rosbiznesbank's board of directors—was first arrested on October 31, 1995. But he denied guilt, and in the absence of any incriminating evidence against him, he was released in thirty days, in accordance with the law. In December 1999, Moscow criminal investigators arrested a man (whose name was not made public) who had testified that he had personally sold poison to Khutsishvili. For unexplainable reasons, Khutsishvili was not arrested, and he left the country. The Moscow municipal prosecutor's office put him on the wanted list. Alexei Kondratov, investigator in charge of cases of special importance, announced that Khutsishvili was liable to criminal prosecution for the murder of Kivilidi and his secretary, Ismalova, although no attempts were made by the Russian side to secure an international arrest warrant for Khutsishvili.

In 2006, Khutsishvili returned to Moscow, believing that the ten-year-old case had been closed. But at 8:30 in the morning, outside building No. 7 on Yefremov Street, where he was staying with a friend, Khutsishvili was arrested. Just how he had obtained poison and how he had gotten it into the receiver of Kivilidi's mobile phone were details that the Russian General Prosecutor's Office was unable to explain.

According to experts, Kivilidi could have been poisoned only by a professional, and his deputy could certainly not be characterized as such. Here is what Yefim Brodsky, the head of a laboratory at the Institute of Evolutionary Morphology and Ecology of Animals, told a *Moskovskiye Novosti* reporter:

"Using special equipment, we were able to determine the formula of the toxic substance relatively quickly. It is a nerve agent like zarin."

"Is it known where such toxic substances are produced?"

"I know several such laboratories."

"Could you name them?"

"No."

"Who, in your opinion, could have placed the toxic substance inside the receiver?"

"Only someone who knows how to handle it."

"Let's suppose that the killer who bought the toxic substance had received detailed instructions."

"It's impossible to teach an outsider how to conduct such a difficult operation without putting him at risk of poisoning himself."

This led the reporter to a conclusion that was all but self-evident:

> If the poison could have been put in place only by a specialist who worked in a laboratory with toxic substances, then what motive could have impelled a scientist to take such a risky step? . . . The

sophistication of the operation indicates that it could have been performed only by well-prepared people for whom security was not an obstacle and who were in a position to recruit an employee of a secret laboratory for the operation. Only the security services have such capabilities. This conclusion is also indirectly supported by the fact that it has already been almost ten years and the investigators still cannot solve the crime. But the poison used to kill Kivilidi was one of a kind. The laboratories where it is produced and the people who had access to it can be traced without much difficulty.

POLONIUM AND THALLIUM

Polonium was discovered by Marie Curie. The Russian subject Marie Sklodowska (Curie) was born in 1867 in Poland, which was a part of the Russian Empire at the time, and became the only woman to win the Nobel Prize twice, for her research on radioactivity. She received the first of these prizes with her husband, Pierre Curie, who died in a carriage accident. Marie survived her husband by twenty-eight years and died of exposure to radiation. One of Marie and Pierre Curie's two daughters, Irène, followed in her mother's footsteps and, together with her husband, Frédéric Joliot, also received the Nobel Prize for research on radioactivity. Irène and Frédéric died of the effects of prolonged exposure to radiation, Irène at age fifty-nine, Frédéric at fifty-eight.

Marie and Pierre Curie discovered radium as well as polonium, the latter named after the Latin term for Poland in honor of Marie's homeland.

Thallium is a silver-white metal with a grayish tinge, soft and malleable. It was discovered in 1861 by Sir William Crookes in England. This extremely toxic chemical element is mentioned as a "murder weapon" both in detective novels and in contemporary history. Thallium has no taste or smell, which makes it useful to criminals—it is a poison that cannot be recognized. Thallium poisoning is all the more dangerous because the symptoms of poisoning that appear in the victim resemble inflammations that doctors have learned to deal with. The poison's effects are diagnosed as a flu or pneumonia. The antibiotics usually prescribed in such cases have no therapeutic effect and the illness continues to develop. Thallium is a slow-acting poison. It kills from within, slowly and irreversibly. Everything depends entirely on the dosage. The only known antidote against thallium is the so-called "Prussian blue."

In order to understand how poison is used as a murder weapon by the FSB, it is important to note that radioactive poisons such as polonium-210—which was used to poison Alexander Litvinenko in London in November 2006—produce thallium as a byproduct as they decay. It is thallium that experts often detect when they encounter poisonings today. And it is usually not asked whether the victim has indeed been poisoned with thallium or whether a more sophisticated poison has been used, such as polonium-210. In Russia, such a question could be answered only by the FSB, which controls the secret laboratories that produce these poisons and which has no interest in making information about them public. Outside Russia, suspicions regarding the use of radioactive poisons did not arise before November 2006, nor was there mobile equipment that could detect the presence of such poisons in the victim's body on location.

THE DEATH OF ANATOLY SOBCHAK

Anatoly Sobchak, acting as an authorized representative of presidential candidate Vladimir Putin, arrived in the Kaliningrad region on February 17, 2000, for a meeting with the region's governor, Leonid Gorbenko. All criminal charges against Sobchak had been dropped; all the prosecutors and investigators who initiated proceedings against him had been dismissed from their posts; and Sobchak's heart disease, exacerbated by his troubles, had long made itself known. There was a reception for Sobchak in Kaliningrad, during which he consumed only a small amount of alcohol. Then he returned to his hotel room and died. This occurred on the night of February 19 in Svetlogorsk.

The cause of death was determined to be heart failure. But already there were rumors—which came from unknown sources—that two other people had been present in Sobchak's hotel room at the time of his death, and that he had died because the medicine he was taking was incompatible with the alcohol that he had consumed. Between the lines, the perceptive reader was supposed to recognize a coded message: Sobchak had been taking Viagra and died in the company of two call girls.

With a cynicism typical of Russian journalism, one newspaper described the tragedy that had befallen Sobchak as follows:

> Sobchak arrived in Kaliningrad not as an out-of-favor and persecuted criminal and one of the godfathers of the Russian mafia, but as the mentor, teacher, and authorized representative of the country's acting president. Sobchak entered Kaliningrad as a winner on a "white horse," as a man whose political career was once again on the rise. By this time, all the criminal charges against Sobchak had been dropped, not without Putin's help, and his "persecutors" themselves had been dismissed from their posts—all of them, to a man, from the general prosecutor of Russia down to the run-of-the-mill criminal investigator. Thanks to his favorite student and president, Sobchak had won all his suits against the media, which had at various times "dared" to publish unflattering information about him. During the whole time of his visit to the Kaliningrad region, Sobchak radiated well-being and a smile never left his face. Under such circumstances, one can get a heart attack only from too much happiness.

In other words, neither Sobchak's supporters nor his opponents believed that he had died of natural causes.

The medical conclusion reached by the press was unanimous—Sobchak had been murdered:

> Today, the security services mainly use products whose effects can be disguised to resemble nonviolent causes of death: heart attack, stroke, etc. Many of these poisons kill their victim only after several days, when the actual chemical substance that is the cause of death has already left the body. It is extremely difficult or impossible to discover such a poison through chemical analysis. The most popular of such "masked" poisons in the Russian security services are "fluoroacetates," which are derived from fluoroacetic acid. These are hard, water-soluble substances or volatile liquids that have no taste, color, or smell. Sixty to eighty milligrams constitute a lethal dose. A person who has

been poisoned with fluoroacetates cannot be treated and after several days dies of heart failure.

"The only person with a vital interest in Sobchak's death is Vladimir Putin," another newspaper said.

Too much is at stake, too much in Putin's plans could be disturbed by Sobchak's simple physical existence. It is no secret to anyone that it was precisely Putin who did everything he could to make it possible for Sobchak to return to Russia after he fled abroad in a panic when his criminal activities as mayor of St. Petersburg started being investigated. . . . It is important to understand that, during this whole time and up to Sobchak's death, the threat that the investigation of Sobchak's criminal activities would be renewed hung like a sword of Damocles over Putin's head . . . which would inevitably have led to charges against Putin himself. Sobchak's death naturally changes the situation in a radical fashion.

But the most important thing is that, by having all charges against Sobchak dropped, and by making it possible for him to return to Russia and to high-level politics, Putin had pushed himself into a corner. On the one hand, he could not refuse to help his favorite teacher to realize his political ambitions. On the other hand, in terms of Putin's campaign, receiving explicit endorsement from Sobchak is equivalent to, say, appointing Berezovsky as prime minister. . . .

Sobchak was a healthy man. His death is an act of political murder aimed at preventing Sobchak's image from negatively influencing the election campaign of his student Vladimir Putin. There can be no doubt that Sobchak's killer is his student and poisoner, Vladimir Putin.

Putin himself did a great deal to cement Russian public opinion in the belief that Sobchak had indeed been poisoned. Thus, at the beginning of 2000, shortly before Sobchak's death, Putin said in an interview that the persecution of Sobchak had been initiated by Alexander Korzhakov and Oleg Soskovets, and that "a very dirty game was played" against the former mayor. On the day when he arrived in St. Petersburg for Sobchak's funeral, Putin remarked in a Radio Baltika interview that "Sobchak's departure is not simply a death, but a murder and the result of an attack against him [*travlya*]." In Russian, the word *travlya* has two meanings: persecution or poisoning. One can only guess which of them Putin had in mind.

Sobchak's autopsy in Kaliningrad was accompanied by unprecedented security measures on direct orders from Putin. A special police unit blocked all access to the forensic analysis department of the traumatological hospital where, under conditions of extreme secrecy, the autopsy took place. Policemen, traffic police officers, and personnel from the Kaliningradavia security agency were likewise stationed at the Khrabrovo airport, from which a special "funeral" flight left for St. Petersburg on the same day. Sobchak's body was transported to St. Petersburg and hastily buried on February 24, without a second examination of the body by the country's leading specialists, which might have been expected in a case of such political importance. Against this background, an announcement by the head of the press service of the Federal Protection Service (FSO), Sergei Devyaty, that an assassination attempt against President Putin had been averted during Sobchak's funeral in St. Petersburg went unheard and unnoticed.

THE POISONING OF YURI SHCHEKOCHIKHIN

On July 3, 2003, Yuri Shchekochikhin died after several days of torment. He was a State Duma deputy from the Yabloko party, the deputy head of the Duma Committee on Security, a member of the Duma anticorruption commission, a reporter, and the deputy editor-in-chief of *Novaya Gazeta*. In July 2001, in Zagreb, Yuri Felshtinsky had given Shchekochikhin the manuscript of the book *Blowing Up Russia* for publication in *Novaya Gazeta*. In August, several chapters from the book were published in a special edition of the newspaper. It was Shchekochikhin who initiated an attempt to organize a Duma investigation of the FSB's crimes as described in that book.

Shchekochikhin felt ill on June 16, 2003. He was in Ryazan for the opening of an anticorruption commission and took part in a press conference that day. On June 18, his condition grew worse. On June 19 and 20, his skin started to peel off, as after a severe burn. On June 21, he was delivered to Moscow's Central Clinical Hospital in grave condition, with a high temperature, loss of mucous membranes and epidermis, impaired kidney function, and increasing respiratory failure. Eventually he was put on a respirator.

According to forensic analysis, the immediate cause of Shchekochikhin's death was severe toxic epidermal necrolysis, or Lyell's syndrome, an acute allergic reaction that usually develops in response to medications. Lyell's syndrome occurs relatively rarely: one case in a million. Signs of a systemic toxico-allergic reaction were evident in Shchekochikhin. It was not ruled out that such a "rare allergic reaction" could have been provoked by an "unknown agent"—that is, by a poison of unknown nature. It was never determined how this "unknown agent" could have penetrated into the victim's body, since no analysis was conducted and the forensic documents were not made public. On the contrary, the results of Shchekochikhin's autopsy and the history of his illness were classified as a "medical secret." They were even kept secret from his family. Shchekochikhin's relatives never received an autopsy report. When they tried to initiate criminal proceedings in connection with Shchekochikhin's probable murder, their request was denied, although already on July 3, Alexander Gurov, the head of the Duma's Committee on Security, filed a request with the General Prosecutor's Office to initiate criminal proceedings in connection with Shchekochikhin's death.

Shchekochikhin died shortly before a planned trip to the United States, where he was intending to tell the American public and legislators about the major corruption cases that he was investigating. One of the most important among them was the case of the company Tri Kita, which was under the protection of high-ranking officials in the General Prosecutor's Office and the FSB. In what way, then, was Shchekochikhin dangerous to the FSB? Here is an excerpt from an interview that he gave before he died:

> I'm forced to work on two fronts—as a deputy in the State Duma and deputy head of the Committee on Security, whose aim is to fight terrorism and cross-border crime, and also in the Duma's anticorruption commission and in *Novaya Gazeta*, which also occupies an important place in the fight against corruption. I don't like the word "fight," however. This is more of an analysis of the situation, of what is happening

today. Many years ago we . . . summed up the mafia in the following phrase: "The lion has jumped." This year, in January, we gave the mafia a new characterization: "The lion has jumped and is already wearing epaulets."

By comparison with what is going on today in our security services, in our prosecutor's office, all bandits are simply boy scouts. Today, it is precisely the people who are needed to fight crime and corruption that have raised the flag of corruption and crime. This has not bypassed the FSB; what has never happened before happens constantly now—the protection that they provide, the enormous amounts of money that they receive, and the control over ports and banks that they exercise.

I'm not even talking about the police. . . . The whole system and its foundations must be changed. I'm not even talking about the fact that there are too many policemen. For example, there are about 110,000 policemen in Moscow alone. In London, there are about 40,000, although you feel safer in London.

Shchekochikhin fought above all against corruption on the level of the national government, and he was most hated by national government officials. Among those who had grounds for viewing him as a personal enemy were the deputy general prosecutor, Yuri Biriukov, and the deputy director of the FSB, Yuri Zaostrovtsev. The general prosecutor (Vladimir Ustinov) and the director of the FSB (Nikolai Patrushev) themselves could hardly have been pleased by Shchekochikhin's investigative reporting. Sergei Sokolov, the deputy editor-in-chief of *Novaya Gazeta*, described Shchekochikhin's activities during the last weeks and months of his life as follows:

In recent days, Yuri Shchekochikhin was intensively working on the Tri Kita case. In addition, he was actively preparing materials connected with the Chechen problem, with the search for peace, and with this whole topic in general. He traveled to Chechnya as part of a Duma commission. This was immediately before his trip to Ryazan. And naturally, he was working on new materials for another session of the Duma's anticorruption commission. This was again connected with Tri Kita and facts related to it that concerned the General Prosecutor's Office.[23]

But because it was precisely the General Prosecutor's Office and the FSB that decided whether or not to initiate criminal proceedings in connection with Shchekochikhin's death, the investigation was never even begun. It was not in the interests of the General Prosecutor's Office and the FSB, which were most likely responsible for organizing Shchekochikhin's poisoning.

THE ATTEMPTS TO POISON ANNA POLITKOVSKAYA AND NANA LEZHAVA

Anna Politkovskaya almost died several times. The first known attempt to poison her occurred in early September 2004, aboard a plane to North Ossetia. Politkovskaya was intending to cover the hostage crisis in Beslan, which began on September 1. It was believed that Politkovskaya, who enjoyed great respect among the Chechens, could take part in negotiations with the terrorists and obtain the release of the hostages. Politkovskaya was also intending to try to get in touch with Aslan Maskhadov, the president of the self-proclaimed Chechen Republic, and to ask him to risk his life by coming to Beslan to negotiate with the terrorists, which might have induced them to end their takeover of the school.

For this reason, it was vitally important for Russia's security services to prevent Politkovskaya from arriving in North Ossetia, since in such an event the credit for putting an end to the crisis and for rescuing the children would go not to Russia's security services, but to Politkovskaya and Maskhadov— a reporter and a president unrecognized by Moscow. Aboard the airplane, Politkovskaya, who had prudently refused to eat any food, asked the flight attendant for a cup of tea. Then she fainted, fell into a coma, and woke up in a hospital. She survived, but was too late for the negotiations with the terrorists in Beslan since she had spent those tragic days in intensive care.

By contrast, Nana Lezhava, a reporter for Georgia's independent TV channel Rustavi-2, managed to arrive in Beslan and to send back several riveting reports about the terrorists' takeover of the school there. On September 3, she was arrested along with her cameraman, Levan Tetvadze, after reporting that the first explosion in the school had actually occurred outside the wall of the gym. From this it followed that it was not the terrorists who had opened fire first, as the Russian authorities claimed, but the Russian security services, who had blown up the wall in order to penetrate into the school building. During her five-day stay at the FSB's detention facility, Lezhava was repeatedly interrogated. At some point, she was offered coffee. She drank it and fainted. Subsequently, a life-threatening toxin was identified in her body. The poisonous drug belonged to the class of strong psychotropic substances that cause diffuse changes in the brain and lead to permanent brain damage.

THE POISONING OF ROMAN TSEPOV AND THE ARREST OF VLADIMIR BARSUKOV–KUMARIN

Not everything in Roman Tsepov's business career went smoothly. In 1994, his rivals and opponents initiated criminal proceedings against him for illegally possessing and carrying firearms—although it is hard to believe that the head of a security agency did not have the right to bear firearms. Tsepov did manage to profit from his arrest, however. "When I was in jail at the pretrial detention facility," he said, "the St. Petersburg crime boss Malyshev was in the next cell. He told me: 'When you come out, protect my family.' And I protected them, because they paid me for it. And many crime bosses—I won't mention any names—are today also protected by my people." In this way, business relations were formed between Tsepov's private security agency and St. Petersburg's largest crime organizations.

Criminal charges were again brought against Tsepov in March 1998. During the investigation, it came out that Tsepov was simultaneously an agent or employee of several different law enforcement agencies: the FSB, the Ministry of Internal Affairs, and the Foreign Intelligence Service (SVR); and that he had five different documents to conceal his identity.

In 1999, without waiting for the outcome of the investigation, Tsepov used his foreign passport and driver's license (both of them issued under a different name) to leave for the Czech Republic. He soon returned, however, and continued to run his operations, controlling—though rarely formally heading—a number of legal commercial enterprises and extralegal "businesses," collecting protection money and distributing and redistributing these resources.

Tsepov's sphere of activity gradually expanded. It came to include the security and pharmaceutical businesses, ports, tourism, shipping operations, insurance, and even the mass media. After Putin moved to Moscow and became president, Tsepov maintained close contacts with many of the *siloviki*—from the minister of internal affairs, Rashid Nurgaliyev, to the head of the president's security, Vladimir Zolotov. In addition, Tsepov lobbied for the appointment of various Ministry of Internal Affairs and FSB officers. He was on close terms with Igor Sechin, the deputy head of the presidential administration, and even with Vladimir Putin himself.

Tsepov began to feel ill on September 11, 2004. In the morning, he ate breakfast at his dacha and then went to the St. Petersburg FSB office at 4 Liteiny Prospect. There he drank some tea. Next he went to the St. Petersburg Directorate of Internal Affairs, where he met with a department head and ate ice cream. At around four in the afternoon, he started feeling sick. His symptoms resembled severe food poisoning, but the doctors could not establish an exact diagnosis. Tsepov was delivered to one of St. Petersburg's private clinics in critical condition. On September 22, he was transferred to the Center for Leading Medical Technologies (formerly Sverdlov Hospital). Plans were made to fly him to Germany for emergency treatment, but the illness advanced too quickly and he died on September 24.

Preliminary forensic analysis revealed that Tsepov's blood contained a large amount of a medicine used to treat leukemia. But the deceased did not have cancer. According to doctors, a lethal dose of the medicine—in the form of a solution or crushed pills—could have been added to Tsepov's food. Experts had different opinions: radioactive isotopes, an unknown poison, heavy-metal salts.

For many years, Tsepov had been seen by his personal physician, Pyotr Perumov, the head of a department at hospital No. 32. We will let Perumov speak for himself, since this was the first time that a victim's own doctor described the poisoning of his patient:

Everything began on a Saturday in September. His wife called me: "Pyotr Ashotovich, Roman is feeling sick. He has some kind of poisoning." What are the symptoms? "Vomit and diarrhea." Although I was 300 kilometers away from the city, I called my hospital and sent a team of people to his home. I know from my work in Afghanistan that this combination of symptoms is very dangerous: if it's not stopped, the organism becomes dehydrated and desalinated, the person quickly loses his strength. . . . The problem is to fill him up. To give him fluids and to detoxify him. The only thing that immediately gave me pause was that there was no temperature. Usually, toxicoinfection is accompanied by a sharp rise in body temperature.

All night long, from Saturday to Sunday, he was treated by a team of emergency physicians. He started feeling a little better, but his symptoms did not go away. I arrived on Sunday and persuaded him to check into a hospital. His condition was bad. He wasn't vomiting any more and had less diarrhea. But most importantly, there were no signs of infection. This was a poisoning without a poisoning.

I invited a major specialist in this field from the Botkin Hospital. We did bacteriological analysis and continued treating him at the same time. The thing that we didn't like right from the start was that there was no leukocytosis. Usually, the organism fights the illness, and the number of leukocytes rises sharply. In his case, the organism wasn't reacting. The defense wasn't working.

I should say that Roman had spent almost the entire previous week in Moscow and had only arrived in St. Petersburg on Friday. We asked him what he ate on that day. "Nothing," he said, only drank. Everything indicated that he had gotten poisoned already in Moscow.

You had to know Roman—he was very careful about his food. In recent days, he had become a vegetarian. I don't know what the reason for this was—health or something else—but he did not eat in random places.

I spent the whole first night in his hospital room. We gave him all the necessary medicines intravenously, protected all of his organs, worked very hard. He started feeling better. But we still had no clinical picture of the poisoning. And this very much alarmed me. Moreover, his leukocyte count started going down gradually. At first it was something like 7000. Then it fell to 4000. I already suspected that something was going on. And Roman—he became more and more silent and didn't really respond to my questions about what he had eaten and where.

Just in case, I decided to check him more thoroughly. I went through all the labs in St. Petersburg, looking for those that could identify heavy-metal salts. I found only one. With difficulty, I persuaded them to make an urgent analysis. Three days later, we got the answer: everything is normal, but there's mercury in his urine. This was also within normal limits, but still no one expected to find such a quantity.

Meanwhile, with all the treatment that he was receiving, he gradually started to feel better. I sent him to get a light massage and little by little he started to come back to life. And on the following Friday, Roman decided to check out of the hospital. Moreover, he got behind the wheel himself and said that everything was coming back to normal. But his leukocyte count continued to drop, and on the day that he checked out it was already 2500. I told him: it's very dangerous to go around like this, your body can't resist anything, it's open to any infection. If this is the lowest it's going to get, good. But if it isn't? Still, Roman insisted on checking out of the hospital, saying that he would be careful.

On the day before he checked out, we arranged a consultation with St. Petersburg's leading doctors . . . discussed all of the analyses, and I calmed down somewhat—no one made any especially bad prognoses. We thought that it might be . . . radiation poisoning—the clinical picture was the same as with radiation sickness. But we used a dosimeter and found everything within normal limits.

Nonetheless, on Saturday I sent a nurse to his home to set up an IV and take his blood. She called me on Sunday and said: "Pyotr Ashotovich, I don't like his condition."

I dropped everything and went to see him. He had developed stomatitis. It was as if someone had torn off the skin from his tongue and lips. His symptoms were the same as if he had just gone through chemotherapy. We thought this was some kind of allergic reaction to medicine. But there's no medicine that will produce such a reaction. Everything looked as if he had been given chemotherapy for leukemia. Because the point of chemotherapy is to kill the tumor, to kill the fast-growing cells. At first, the person doesn't notice anything; then his leukocyte count starts dropping and he develops stomatitis. After that, his bone marrow cells start feeling the damage and his platelet count drops. And then the third stage begins, which in medicine is called cytopenia. This is when you can't even come close to the patient; he picks up any infection at a distance of five to seven meters. In Roman's case, everything resembled the symptoms people have when they're treated for leukemia with chemotherapy. By this time, the second stage had just begun—a pronounced reaction that led to the depletion of the spinal marrow. The leukocyte count was down to 1000.

We arranged another consultation and said that he needed to be put in a general hospital where he could receive blood transfusions and be monitored by infectious disease doctors. Prof. Golofinsky offered to take him to the Medical Academy's hospital. They had everything he needed there, all kinds of specialists. But Roman categorically refused. . . .

Finally, his family made the decision to put him in hospital No. 31. I immediately called up an acquaintance of mine at that hospital, a very capable person—Prof. Belogorova. I asked her to return from her dacha, because it was the weekend. She called me three hours later. "You know," she said, "everything is very bad here. He's literally disintegrating in front of our eyes. This looks a lot like . . . there's a kind of hemotoxic poison that's used to treat leukemia."

The next day, I sent the results of all the tests to the hospital. But it was already too late—Roman died shortly afterward.

The examination was very unprofessional. Infinitely less serious cases have been examined far more thoroughly. I wasn't even asked for a history of the illness. And then there was a strange phone call. "Hello, Pyotr Ashotovich," they said. "We are forensic specialists from such-and-such a place. We would very much like to hear your opinion about what happened." I told them that I could come to see them. "No," they said, "let's have a conference call." Fine. I described the whole clinical picture. I told them my theories about hemotoxic poison. They listened to everything carefully, and then they said to me: "Pyotr Ashotovich, we've already determined what he died of. Roman Igorevich had prostate cancer and he medicated himself to death." I told them: "You should be ashamed of yourselves. What did you do? Talk to the nurse? I didn't just give him all kinds of ultrasound tests—we examined him from top to bottom twenty times over, and believe me, we would have found this cancer, we would have found it a hundred times over. And what kind of cancer is going to give you a complete depletion of the spinal marrow?! This is what you're telling me?" In short, I told them: "I don't like talking to you. I don't respect you." And I hung up. This phone call convinced me that there was more to this whole story than met the eye.

The church service at Tsepov's funeral was attended by Viktor Zolotov, head of the president's security service; Konstantin Romodanovsky, head of the FSB's Departmental Security Directorate; Andrei Novikov, head of the Main Directorate of Internal Affairs for the Northwestern Federal District (currently a deputy minister); Mikhail Vanichkin, head of the St. Petersburg Directorate of Internal Affairs; Alexander Sabadash, a "liquor-and-vodka oligarch" and Federation Council member from the Nenetsk District; State Duma deputy Alexander Nevzorov; lawyer and FSB general Dmitry Yakubovsky; and Tsepov's longtime business partner and collaborator in many clandestine operations, Vladimir Barsukov-Kumarin.

Only close friends and relatives went to the cemetery—Barsukov-Kumarin among them. A troop of policemen honored Tsepov's memory by firing into the air. (According to military rules, such honors can be bestowed only on officers with a colonel's rank or higher.) Tsepov was buried in St. Petersburg's famous Serafimovskoye cemetery.

Criminal proceedings were initiated in connection with Tsepov's death based on Article 105 of the Russian Criminal Code (murder). The results of the investigation were not made public. But at least one newspaper, *Moskovskiye Novosti*, accused Putin of murdering Tsepov, though without naming the Russian president by name. The author of the article wrote:

Tsepov's name is well known in St. Petersburg. But few people are aware of this person's real status. Seven years ago, I obtained a document that by all appearances had been put together by one of Russia's security services. The document stated that Tsepov collected protection money from a number of St. Petersburg's casinos for one of the FSB's top-ranking officials. I tried to get Yuri Vanyushin, the General Prosecutor's Office investigator for cases of special importance, to corroborate this information about Tsepov. The team that Vanyushin supervised was looking into a criminal case connected with deliveries of imports into St. Petersburg that avoided customs by passing through a military port. Vanyushin (who has since died) confirmed this information: according to facts possessed by his team of investigators, Tsepov indeed collected money from commercial enterprises and personally handed it over to a "top-ranking official in Moscow." So the rumors about Tsepov's special role that have circulated both in

Moscow and in St. Petersburg are not groundless. For example, rumors that the scale of the commercial projects in which he participated corresponded to the expanding possibilities of the same Moscow official to whom he had once delivered off-the-books cash.

The "Moscow official" was, of course, Putin.

The arrest of Vladimir Barsukov-Kumarin, the leader of the Tambov crime group and former vice president of the Petersburg Fuel Company, in St. Petersburg in August 2007 may be seen as a kind of postscript to Tsepov's poisoning. After Putin moved to Moscow, Barsukov-Kumarin stayed on in St. Petersburg and was literally forgotten by the reporters and the law enforcement agencies. Unexpectedly for everyone—most of all for himself—he was arrested on August 22 in an unprecedented operation involving a thirty-man special forces unit that had been dispatched from Moscow.

At the request of the General Prosecutor's Office, the St. Petersburg District Court had issued a warrant for Barsukov-Kumarin's arrest for "crimes committed, including murder and the attempt to organize a contract killing with the aim of subsequently acquiring possession of the St. Petersburg oil terminal . . . complicity in raids and takeovers of large pieces of real estate, a number of contract killings, and other felonies." For example, Barsukov-Kumarin was suspected of organizing an assassination attempt against Sergei Vasiliev, co-owner of the St. Petersburg oil terminal, in the fall of 2006.

Barsukov-Kumarin could have been arrested long before; the evidence against him was substantial. But he was arrested only in August 2007, not because of a decision by the St. Petersburg prosecutor's office, but on orders from Moscow. He could have been killed, as many of the godfathers of the Russian mafia have been killed in recent years. Such a murder would not have surprised anyone; there had been repeated assassination attempts against Barsukov-Kumarin by his fellow criminals. But he was left alive, as a hostage, as a carrier of compromising information against those who ruled St. Petersburg in the 1990s. Under arrest, Barsukov-Kumarin was a trump card in the deck of the FSB corporation as it prepared for the 2008 presidential election, safeguarding itself against unforeseen steps by the current president of the corporation and the country, Vladimir Putin. Barsukov-Kumarin could have met Tsepov's fate. But he was preserved, in order to become an ace in the hand that would be played against the "Moscow official."

THE ATTEMPT TO POISON VIKTOR YUSHCHENKO

September 2004 turned out to be a busy month. It was the month when the Ukrainian presidential candidate Viktor Yushchenko was poisoned.

On September 5, at the height of his election campaign, Yushchenko was eating dinner and conducting negotiations at the dacha of the former deputy head of the Ukrainian Security Service (SBU), Vladimir Satsyuk. Another deputy head of the SBU, Taras Zalessky, was also present at this dinner and brought dishes of plov to Yushchenko's table. After dinner, the future president felt ill. He was hospitalized on September 10 at the Rudolfinerhaus clinic in Austria, where he was diagnosed with acute pancreatitis with complications arising from toxic poisoning. The time of the poisoning: about five days earlier.

Chemicals were identified in Yushchenko's body that are usually not found in food. Specifically, a group of American doctors found toxic levels of dioxin in his blood. It was known that one of Russia's secret laboratories had already successfully worked with dioxin several years before.

On September 21, Ukraine's General Prosecutor's Office initiated criminal proceedings in connection with Yushchenko's poisoning. Vladimir Satsyuk, Taras Zalessky, and Alexei Poletukha were considered suspects. The last of these was Satsyuk's old acquaintance, having worked with him in a number of commercial organizations before Satsyuk was appointed deputy director of the SBU. In 2001, Poletukha was put on the wanted list in connection with financial crimes that he had committed as deputy director of Ukraina Bank, and he left the country. According to the head of Interpol's Ukrainian bureau, he remains on the wanted list to this day and is possibly hiding out in Russia. He was named as a suspect in Yushchenko's poisoning because he was believed to have delivered the dioxin from Russia to Ukraine.

President Yushchenko himself has repeatedly stated that he knows who poisoned him, that the dioxin used to poison him had been made in Russia, that he knows who transported it to Ukraine and how this was done, and that the persons responsible for his poisoning are currently in hiding on Russian territory. "You would be astonished by roles played by many politicians in my poisoning, including Ukrainian politicians," Yushchenko once said. But he went no further. Officially, this information was never corroborated, just as the list of suspects was never officially announced.

After September 2004, Yushchenko was examined several more times. An analysis conducted at the end of May 2006 again revealed the presence of dioxin in his body. This analysis was carried out by a commission of Ukrainian specialists as well as representatives from the United States, Germany, and Japan. They confirmed prior results obtained by Dutch, German, British, and Belgian laboratories, attesting to the presence of toxic levels of dioxin in Yushchenko's body.

Three years after the incident, the investigation has formally made little progress. Yushchenko has in the meantime made a few outspoken pronouncements. For example, on September 10 and 11, 2007, on the anniversary of his poisoning, he declared that the Russian government was refusing to hand over the key suspects and to provide the evidence needed to solve the case, and was thus slowing down the investigation. He noted that the substance used to poison him was produced only in the United States, the United Kingdom, and Russia. The U.S. and the U.K. had already submitted their samples long ago. Russia, on the other hand, was refusing to submit its samples. Yushchenko once more indicated that the people suspected of organizing his poisoning were hiding out on Russian territory.

On September 21, Ukraine's General Prosecutor's Office announced that Russian law enforcement agencies had agreed to investigate Russia's dioxin. Alexander Chaly, the deputy head of the Ukrainian president's secretariat, noted that Russia's General Prosecutor's Office had responded to requests to conduct an analysis of Russian-made dioxin only after six such requests had been made. The first five had gotten no response. It was evident that Russia had become frightened of Yushchenko's candid and outspoken pronouncements, which accused Russian law enforcement of complicity in the crime.

THE POISONINGS OF CHECHEN SEPARATIST LEADERS

On March 19, 2002, field commander Amir Khattab—a Saudi-born international terrorist and a leader of the Chechen insurgency—was poisoned. This was done in the Nozhay-Yurt district of Chechnya by means of a letter. The FSB managed to intercept a letter from Saudi Arabia addressed to Khattab and treat it with a poisonous substance that caused the heart to stop functioning. On April 11, the FSB announced that the operation had been carried out successfully. According to the FSB's Center for Public Relations, Khattab was liquidated in "a meticulously planned special operation whose details will remain classified for at least ten years."

According to one account, an agent from the FSB's Dagestan office—officer M.—had used a certain Ibragim Magomedov for the operation. Magomedov was a young man, an Avar by nationality, born in the village of Gimry in the Untsukulsky district of Dagestan. He was a trusted agent of Khattab's and acted as a courier for him, constantly going out of the country through Azerbaijan and Turkey to receive money and then bringing it back to Chechnya. Magomedov was assisted in this by officer M. In fact, Magomedov's trust in M. was so great that the latter succeeded in treating an envelope addressed to Khattab with a special solution and Magomedov unwittingly gave it to Khattab. Two or three days after reading the letter, Khattab died. Soon it was reported that Chechen fighters had executed a Dagestani resident named Ibragim Alauri (Magomedov).

On June 1, 2004, Aslan Maskhadov's Georgian representative Khizri Aldamov, his son, and his nephew were brought to a hospital in Tbilisi and diagnosed with poisoning. The Georgian Ministry of Internal Affairs determined that the Aldamovs' car had been treated with a toxic substance that contained phosphorus. Khizri Aldamov claimed that he was the victim of an assassination attempt ordered by the FSB.

In the fall of 2004, Leche Islamov, a Chechen fighter sentenced to nine years in prison, was poisoned in jail with an unknown substance. After he was sentenced but before he was sent to prison, Islamov was seen in jail by three FSB agents. They proposed that he collaborate with them and gave him tea and sandwiches. Islamov refused to collaborate with the FSB. Shortly after this conversation, Islamov's health suddenly and sharply deteriorated. His body turned red, his skin began to flake and peel, he developed a high temperature, his hair started to fall out. Islamov soon died.

THE ATTEMPT TO POISON PAVEL BASANETS

At the beginning of August 2007, Pavel Basanets, the fifty-year-old first secretary of the CPRF's Western district committee, a father of four, was poisoned with an unknown substance in Moscow.

Basanets had graduated from the Dzerzhinsky KGB Higher School. He had served for ten years in foreign intelligence and was a resident in Dresden when Putin was stationed there. Basanets is fluent in Chinese, English, Indonesian, and Malay. For fifteen years, he practiced various forms of single combat and had a brown belt in karate. In 1991, he did not leave the Communist Party but remained involved in party work and public service. In particular, he was the co-chairman of the Committee for the Defense of Citizens' Rights and a member of the Council of the Veterans of Labor, War, and Law Enforcement. In terms of his political views, he may be considered a Stalinist.

On December 7, 2006, at a meeting of the FSB in the Lubyanka building celebrating the eighty-sixth anniversary of the founding of Soviet foreign intelligence, Basanets spoke out in criticism of Putin, calling him a traitor to Russia, to his own people, and to officers' honor.

The response was immediate. Basanets started receiving threats directed at him and his children. The Communists tried to expel him from their ranks, six times; but certain influential Communists stood up for him, including some members of the State Duma.

Basanets's former colleagues warned him that very serious people were angry at him, that he would not be forgiven for his Lubyanka speech, and that there would most likely be an attempt to eliminate him. In July, Basanets was contacted by his former foreign intelligence colleagues from one of the former republics of the USSR and warned that an assassination attempt was being prepared against him. They suggested that Basanets leave Russia and move to one of the Soviet Union's former republics. But Basanets refused, understanding that he would not be able to escape from the FSB in a new location.

At the beginning of August, Basanets suddenly felt ill. A rash appeared on his body, and he became extremely weak. The symptoms did not abate, as would be normal for ordinary food poisoning; on the contrary, his condition got worse. Serious medical experts became involved in his treatment. By the end of August, in addition to the symptoms associated with poisoning, Basanets was diagnosed with unstable angina and stable hypertension. (Previously, his blood pressure had been completely normal; Basanets was always distinguished by good health and a sound constitution.) His doctor's main diagnosis was poisoning with an unknown agent.

Basanets did not go to the hospital, understanding that it would be easier to kill him off there. He commented on his condition as follows:

> I refused to go to the hospital and am now at home with an IV. I think that I'm safer here. What is most interesting is that the doctors who examined me did not find an allergen in my body. My echocardiogram shows a serious blow to the heart. But, to be honest, I now feel a little better than I did three weeks ago. Only the sores on my body won't heal.

THE MURDER OF ANNA POLITKOVSKAYA

On October 7, 2006, Vladimir Putin's birthday, Anna Politkovskaya was murdered in Moscow. Rejecting the possibility of any involvement by the Russian government in the murder, President Putin said: "This murder has done more harm to Russia than Politkovskaya's articles."

During a Russian-German meeting in Berlin in January 2007 attended by Gerhard Schröder, former chancellor of Germany, President Putin's advisor Igor Shuvalov had this to say to reporters concerning the murder:

We see Politkovskaya's murder as a provocation. The president has given orders to solve this crime. It is silly to connect the murder with the leadership of the country. Polonium, Litvinenko, Politkovskaya—all of these are connected. There are powerful groups that have joined together in order constantly to attack the president's program and the president personally. We have nothing to gain from any of these murders. From a political point of view, they only cause harm, while in human terms, of course, one is sorry for the victims.

On August 28 of that year, Russia's General Prosecutor's Office announced the arrest of several individuals on suspicion of organizing and carrying out the murder of Anna Politkovskaya. Among the people arrested was Lieutenant Colonel Pavel Ryaguzov, an employee of the FSB's Moscow office. According to the general prosecutor, Yuri Chaika, this same group of hired killers may have been involved in the murder of Paul Klebnikov, an American journalist and editor-in-chief of the Russian edition of *Forbes*, in July 2004.

Since the General Prosecutor's Office has plainly been indecisive in identifying those responsible for the contract killings of Anna Politkovskaya and Paul Klebnikov, let us try to determine for ourselves who may have ordered the murders.

First, there are many theories regarding Paul Klebnikov's death. Only one of them is correct. He may have been killed by the hero of his book *Conversation with a Barbarian*, published in July 2003: Khozh-Ahmed Tembakirovich Nukhaev, also known as "Khozha." In an organized crime database compiled some time ago by Russian law enforcement, this man was given the following brief description: "Date of birth, 1954; place of birth, the Kyrgyz SSR; resident of Chechnya. Has prior convictions; is capable of murder. Lives in Moscow without a resident permit in apartments belonging to criminals."

Klebnikov knew that Nukhaev was dangerous. In September 2001, in New York, Yuri Felshtinsky had given him a printout of the organized crime database.

Nukhaev was repeatedly arrested but always released. For some reason, whenever criminal charges were brought against him, Russia's Supreme Court would always close the case. Nukhaev fought in Chechnya; it was believed that he was on the side of the separatists. He was wounded, received medical treatment in Austria, and returned to Moscow, where he lived in one of the city's best hotels and gave interviews at Ostankino TV studios. Although Nukhaev was on the federal wanted list at this time, no one pursued or arrested him. His instructions were carried out by the FSB agent Max Lazovsky and his supervisor, Pyotr Suslov, an SVR staff employee. So who could this man have been? The answer is obvious. This man could only have been a high-ranking official from the central apparatus of the FSB. And that is the only explanation for the fact that he remained uncatchable and untouchable.

Among Russian journalists, Yulia Latynina went the furthest and came the closest to the truth in explaining the causes of Klebnikov's murder. On a show on Ekho Moskvy radio, she said: "Klebnikov was sent to Nukhaev by Korzhakov, the former head of the Presidential Security Service. They had a rather complicated relationship. . . . This relationship has been best described by Korzhakov himself in his memoirs. Being a fairly simple-minded man, he wrote with transparent resentment" that "two-thirds" of Klebnikov's book on Berezovsky, *The Godfather of the Kremlin*, was based on Korzhakov's own account. "It was Korzhakov that sent Klebnikov to Nukhaev," according to Latynina. It was the publishing house of Korzhakov and his former subordinate Valery Streletsky, head of the Department P of the Presidential Security Service, that published Klebnikov's book. "It is obvious that Korzhakov understood Chechen psychology and everything that it might entail better than Klebnikov. But what is interesting is that neither Korzhakov nor Streletsky told Klebnikov anything about a possible danger to himself."

Korzhakov and Streletsky didn't tell Klebnikov anything about a possible danger because the whole project had been coordinated at the top levels of the FSB. Except for one aspect: the financial component. Nukhaev agreed to help Klebnikov write a book that would discredit the Chechen people in return for the money that Klebnikov promised to pay Nukhaev out of his royalties. Just how much money Klebnikov had promised to Nukhaev is probably something that we will never know. But somehow one suspects that the figure must have been a round one and not less than one million dollars. Nukhaev gave Kleb-nikov a year to pay the money. And when he did not receive it by the appointed time, he killed Klebnikov—exactly one year after the publication of the book—on July 9, 2004.

By stating that Klebnikov's and Politkovskaya's murders were organized by the same people, the General Prosecutor's Office has helped us a great deal. It is highly likely that Polit-kovskaya's murder was also organized by Nukhaev. But Nukhaev could not have put out the contract on her. Politkovskaya was never involved in investigating his activities, and Nukhaev had no personal motives to kill her.

Nukhaev could have been asked to kill Politkovskaya by several possible contractors. Possible contractor number one: the central leadership of the FSB—as a birthday present for Putin. Possible contractor number two: Ramzan Kadyrov—also as a birthday present for Putin, in the hopes of receiving a pres-ent in return: the presidency of Chechnya (a hope that was real-ized). Possible contractor number three: Chechnya's current representative in the Federation Council, Umar Dzhabrailov, a well-known Moscow-based Chechen businessman and owner of the Radisson Slavyanskaya Hotel—as a favor to Kadyrov, and again as a birthday present for the president. Dzhabrailov is suspected of organizing at least two other crimes: the murder of the American businessman Paul Tatum, former co-owner of the Radisson Slavyanskaya Hotel, on November 3, 1996; and the assassination attempt against Moscow's deputy mayor, Iosif Ordzhonikidze, on June 20, 2002.

Apart from these three possible contractors, no one else could have ordered a hit on Politkovskaya.

THE ATTEMPT TO POISON YEGOR GAIDAR

Yegor Gaidar, the former prime minister of Russia's first demo-cratic government and currently the director of the Institute for the Economy in Transition, spoke at a conference at the National University of Ireland, November 24, 2006. The con-ference was on "Ireland and Russia: History, the Rule of Law, and the Changing International System." Gaidar started to feel unwell after breakfast. According to his daughter Maria, the breakfast had been simple—a fruit salad and a cup of tea. Eka-terina Genieva, the organizer of the conference, recalled that Gaidar had eaten breakfast in the cafeteria of Maynooth College, where the delegation from Moscow was staying. Of the ten people who had eaten in the cafetaria at the same time as Gaidar, he alone became ill.

During his presentation at the conference, Gaidar felt sick, left the lecture hall, and fainted. He lay unconscious on the floor, with blood gushing out of his nose and mouth. Gaidar remained in this condition for over half an hour. Then he was taken to the intensive care unit of the James Connolly Memorial Hospital in Blanchardstown. The former prime minister was unconscious for about three hours in intensive care. After he came to, he was still unable to move, and for another day his life hung by a thread.

Gaidar was given a full preliminary detoxification—the standard complex treatment for patients showing signs of food poisoning. The symptoms of the poisoning were so ambiguous that doctors hesitated to give a diagnosis. Gaidar checked out of the hospital on November 26. His condition was no longer life-threatening in the doctors' opinion, and he felt somewhat better. After leaving the hospital, he telephoned the Russian embassy and asked for permission to spend the night there. "It would be safer," he said. The request was granted. He was still pale the next day, and complained of nausea and weakness. Nonetheless, he left for Moscow, where he was immediately hospitalized. On his way there, trying to make sense of what had happened, Gaidar remembered: "That tea didn't taste very good. . . ."

The doctors who examined Gaidar in Moscow reached the unanimous conclusion that he had been poisoned in Ireland. And although the nature of the poison was not determined, it was clear that the poisoning had been deliberate. In other words, there had been an attempt on his life. Evidently, this was the reason why Gaidar's location in the hospital in Moscow was initially kept secret. His relatives did not rule out the possibility that the attempt to poison him might be repeated.

Who provided security for Gaidar at that time, we do not know. What we do know is who his chief of security was when

Gaidar was the prime minister of Russia. That was Andrei Lugovoi.

THE POISONING OF ALEXANDER LITVINENKO

Yegor Gaidar was poisoned on November 24. Alexander Litvinenko died on the evening of November 23. This is one angle of a polygon.

Andrei Lugovoi was in charge of Gaidar's security, he was in charge of Boris Berezovsky's security, and he took part in the poisoning of Litvinenko. This is the second angle of the polygon.

There is some kind of connection between the murder of Anna Politkovskaya in October and the murder of Alexander Litvinenko in November. This is the third angle of the polygon.

Alexander Litvinenko and Roman Tsepov were poisoned by the same people. By finding Tsepov's killers, one can also track down Litvinenko's killers. And conversely, by determining who killed Litvinenko, one can solve Tsepov's murder. This is the fourth and probably the most important angle of the polygon.

And there are many other angles that are not immediately apparent or not so obvious: the poisoning of Yuri Shchekochikhin, the attempt to poison Viktor Yushchenko, the sudden death of Anatoly Sobchak. . . .

There are also some very small and almost undescribed angles. But it would be wrong to leave them out of this chapter simply because they contain no direct proof of murder. For example, the death from leukemia on July 20, 2005, at the age of fifty-seven, of Nikolai Aksenenko, former railways minister, former deputy prime minister, and then first deputy prime minister. After the resignation of Yevgeny Primakov in May 1999, it was Aksenenko who was supposed to become prime minister and then Yeltsin's successor as president of Russia. His candidacy was supported by Boris Berezovsky, among others. In fact, Aksenenko's candidacy for the post of prime minister had already been signed by Yeltsin and submitted to the Duma for a vote. But at the last moment, the all-powerful hands of the FSB replaced Aksenenko with the former director of the FSK-FSB, Sergei Stepashin, and then gradually squeezed Aksenenko out of the government altogether. On January 10, 2000, Aksenenko was relieved of his duties as first deputy prime minister; in 2001, criminal proceedings were initiated against him; in 2002, he was dismissed from the post of railways minister. In 2003, Aksenenko developed leukemia, traveled to Germany for treatment, and died there.

In October 2006, the polygon of murders was known only to those who had planned them.

"Congratulate me. I just became a British citizen. Now they won't dare to touch me. No one would try to kill a British citizen."

These were the words with which Alexander Litvinenko greeted Yuri Felshtinsky in London on October 13, 2006, at a memorial service for Anna Politkovskaya, who had just been killed. Nineteen days later, on November 1, Litvinenko was poisoned.

On that day, he met with several people who had come to London from other countries: FSB agent Andrei Lugovoi, FSB agent Dmitry Kovtun, FSB agent Vyacheslav Sokolenko, and apparently one more—unknown and unidentified—agent of the FSB. (Or maybe Litvinenko did not meet this fourth agent on this day, although the agent, apparently, was also in London and took part in their meeting without being noticed by Litvinenko.) With his former colleagues from the FSB, Litvinenko drank green tea. Finally, he also met with Mario Scaramella, an Italian citizen, in Picadilly at three in the afternoon. He ate sushi and drank mineral water at a Japanese restaurant. Scaramella did not eat; he only drank.

In the evening, Litvinenko felt ill and began to vomit. Realizing that he had been poisoned, he dissolved some potassium permanganate in water—a common Russian treatment, which he learned in the army—and started drinking it and throwing up intermittently. He had stomach spasms and difficulty breathing, his temperature dropped, his pulse became irregular. This is how Litvinenko spent the first day after his poisoning.

On November 2, Litvinenko got a call from Andrei Lugovoi. They had agreed earlier to meet on that day, but Litvinenko told Lugovoi that he was sick and would not be able to keep the appointment. An ambulance was called. The doctor said that it was a seasonal infection. Litvinenko was told to drink water. He continued vomiting, but some kind of foamy liquid started coming out of his mouth approximately every twenty minutes. He had stomach cramps and developed severe diarrhea with blood.

Lugovoi and company flew back to Russia on November 3, when it became clear that their mission had been accomplished. Meanwhile, former FSB Lieutenant Colonel Alexander Litvinenko—who had spent his whole life working in the Russian military and the KGB, who had entered into conflict with the KGB-FSB in 1998, who had spent nine months in prison in 1999, who had fled from Russia in October 2000, who had written (as a co-author) the book *Blowing Up Russia* in 2001, and who had since then published dozens of articles against the FSB and Putin—had no idea on November 2, 2006, that his three former colleagues from the FSB had added a slow-acting poison to his green tea. Had such an idea occurred to him on November 2, though, Scotland Yard would not have had to request Lugovoi's extradition from Russia.

Another doctor was called on November 3. He said that Litvinenko was suffering from an infection, but did not rule out the possibility of poisoning. (No one suspected deliberate poisoning yet.) An ambulance was called again and Litvinenko was taken to the hospital, where he was put on an IV and his blood was taken. The results of the blood analysis were not bad, but the doctors said he should remain at the hospital. Alexander was promised that he would be able to leave in three or four days. His wife, Marina, said they would keep him at the hospital for the time being, since they had found some kind of bacteria. Litvinenko kept his condition secret; neither his friends nor the police were told anything about it. He did not want people to find out that he had gotten food poisoning from sushi. Who knows—later on he might be poisoned for real but everyone would think it was just food poisoning again, as on November 1, 2006.

By the time a week had passed, Alexander could not eat or drink, and he had lost thirty-three pounds. He realized that he had been poisoned, but thought he had saved himself by washing out his stomach with potassium permanganate.

"You know, if I were given a choice: either to go through all this a second time or to spend a year in a Russian prison, I would choose a year in prison, honestly. You can't imagine how bad I feel," he told Yuri Felshtinsky.

But Alexander no longer had the option of spending a year in prison. He had only fifteen days of suffering left.

Rows of abscesses appeared in his throat. Doctors thought this was a reaction to the antibiotics—the flora had been killed and an irritation had appeared. After another couple of days, the patient could no longer open his mouth. All the mucous membranes were inflamed. Litvinenko's hair started to fall out. At this point, doctors thought his spinal marrow had been harmed. He was transferred to the cancer ward. The initial theory of thallium poisoning appeared, and the police became involved in the investigation. Litvinenko was prescribed a thallium antidote ("Prussian blue"). But the antidote was useless, since it could have worked only during the first forty-eight hours after the poisoning, and a week had already passed. Moreover, the antidote was effective against thallium, but Alexander had been poisoned with polonium-210. This became known only on November 23, a couple of hours before his death, when Litvinenko's urine was sent for analysis to the Atomic Weapons Establishment at Aldermaston—the only laboratory in the U.K. that could detect radiation poisoning by an agent that emitted alpha radiation.

If Litvinenko had not managed to hang on until November 23, for reasons that were not clear to anyone, then we would never have known that he had been poisoned with polonium; that a group of FSB agents had taken part in the poisoning; that the poison had come from Moscow; and that the participants of the operation had flown back to Moscow. We would still have thought that Litvinenko's death raised more questions than it answered, and that there was a chance he had died of food poisoning or an allergic reaction to sushi.

From a ticket for city bus No. 134 that was found in his pocket, British investigators established that Litvinenko had not yet been contaminated with polonium-210 when he went to meet with Lugovoi and his colleagues, and that the exact scene of Alexander's poisoning was the Millennium Hotel. The bus ticket had been purchased near Litvinenko's home in North London. From there, Litvinenko had gone to meet with the men from the FSB at the Millennium Hotel. It was the first location that Litvinenko visited after he got off the bus. Traces of polonium-210 were found on the cup and saucer from which Litvinenko had drunk green tea with the Soviet agents. It followed from all this that it was not Litvinenko who had brought polonium to his meeting with Lugovoi and company, but the group of FSB operatives from Moscow who had brought polonium with them for their meeting with Litvinenko.

We will undoubtedly find out every detail about all the angles in this mysterious polygon of murders. We will find out how Litvinenko's poisoning was prepared and who signed the order to kill him. But this will happen later, not today. We learned the details of the operation to kill Trotsky fifty years after the event. From the perspective of history, this isn't a long time to wait.

CONCLUSION

On May 7, 2000, Russia became a new kind of republic: a corporate republic. A corporation took over the government of the country and put its own president in charge. But by contrast with the classic model, the banana republic, this corporation did not deal in fruit. It was called the Federal Security Service of Russia (FSB). Vladimir Putin—who until August 1999 had been the president of the FSB and who on March 26, 2000, was elected president of the country—began to rule Russia in the corporation's name.

Today, the proportion between the two corporations' shares in the government—the FSB's and the oligarchs'—is no longer what it was in 2000. Those who in 2000 had only political power (the clan of the state security men, who had come to power with Putin at their head), had by 2008 acquired economic power as well—control over the entire economy of Russia. This economic power is reflected in concrete numbers. The individuals who sit on the board of directors of the "Russian Corporation" own the actual shares of Russia's largest corporations and receive actual dividends from these corporations, worth millions of dollars. Numerous Russian oligarchs who in 2000 believed that they possessed not only billions of dollars but also political power have learned from the examples of Gusinsky and Berezovsky that they have no political power whatsoever. And from the example of Khodorkovsky they understand that the money in their pockets is real only as long as the Kremlin allows them to remain oligarchs. Indeed, the example of Khodorkovsky turned out to be eloquent enough to eliminate any traces of opposition to the government among the oligarchs.

The situation in Russia is so firmly controlled by the security services that President Putin could not allow himself to take any chances with his successor. Instead of appointing FSB General Sergei Ivanov, as everyone had expected, Putin named Dmitry Medvedev, his old partner in the corporate business, with whom he had undoubtedly come to see eye to eye after working with him for the past eighteen years. With Ivanov, Putin would have been taking a risk: the FSB general might have become a dictator, refusing to resign after his allotted four to eight years in office, and taking away from the denizens of the Kremlin—first and foremost from Putin himself—all the wealth that they had amassed between 2000 and 2008. With Medvedev, the only risk that Putin is taking is that Medvedev, not being an officer of the FSB, will be less ardent in promoting the interests of Russia's security services. But whether Medvedev will have the desire and opportunity to liberalize the state and to change the corporate structure that has developed, only time will tell.

By once again becoming prime minister, Putin certainly assured a smooth transition of power from one president to another. Russia managed to steer clear of a power vacuum, which is always dangerous for those who rule the country. General Patrushev has been removed as head of the FSB, leaving behind him a bloody trail of wars and murders stretching back to August 1999—including the murder of Litvinenko, which could not have been organized without Patrushev's direct involvement.

At the same time, Putin's departure from the presidential post represents the first legal retirement of a Russian head of state since 1917. Every Russian leader before Putin either was forced to resign or died in office: not a single one retired from his post at the end of a constitutionally prescribed term. Nicholas II and Alexander Kerensky were overthrown. Lenin was distanced from power and possibly murdered. Stalin died, most likely the victim of a conspiracy. Nikita Khrushchev was forced to resign. Leonid Brezhnev, Yuri Andropov, and Konstantin Chernenko ruled until their deaths. Mikhail Gorbachev resigned after the KGB's first, unsuccessful attempt to take over the government in Russia. Yeltsin resigned before the end of his term in order to facilitate the transition of power to Putin. (After Yeltsin's departure, Putin became the acting president, and to defeat Putin the acting president in the election was considerably more difficult than to defeat Putin the prime minister.)

In 2008, Putin had a choice. Since he controlled the necessary two-thirds of the votes in the Russian parliament, he could have changed the Russian constitution and stayed on as president of Russia for a third term. This would have been a controversial and risky move. And it would probably have made absolutely everyone, including the authors of this book, regard Putin as a usurper who had violated the country's constitution. Let us give Putin his due: he either did not want to become a dictator or was unable to become one because the other members of his corporation's board of directors would not have allowed such an infringement of the law. He chose for himself the post of prime minister—traditionally dependent on the president—as a subordinate to the new president of Russia, Dmitry Medvedev. No one today would venture to predict what will happen next—not even Putin or Medvedev. Along with our readers, all we can do is wait and see how events unfold in eternally unpredictable Russia.

NOTES

CHAPTER TWO: WHO IS MR. PUTIN?

1. Vakha Ibragimov has researched the Georgian period of Putin's life. In 2000, Vagrius Press published in Russian a small number of copies of Ibragimov's book, *Tainaya biografiya presidenta Rossii* (The Secret Biography of the President of Russia). He has also videotaped numerous interviews with V. V. Putina and the residents of the village of Metekhi, which he has kindly placed at our disposal.

2. M. Vignansky, "U i.o. presidenta Rossii v Tbilisi est i.o. sestry," *Segodnya*, March 1, 2000.

3. O. Larionova, "Skolko materei u Putina?" *Sobesednik*, March 2, 2000.

4. V. Ibragimov, *Tainaya biografiya presidenta Rossii*, p. 69.

5. N. Gevorkyan, A. Kolesnikov, N. Timakova, *Ot pervogo litsa: Razgovory s Vladimirom Putinym* (First Person: Conversations with Vladimir Putin) (Moscow: Vagrius, 2000), p. 7.

6. See *Moskovsky komsomolets*, June 2, 2000.

7. See *Komsomolskaya pravda*, July 18, 2002.

8. *Sobesednik*, March 2, 2000.

9. Ibid.

10. *Ot pervogo litsa*, p. 43.

11. *Kommersant*, March 10, 2000; *Ot pervogo litsa*, p. 47.

12. *Versiya*, no. 3 (77), January 25–31, 2000.

13. *Moskovsky komsomolets*, August 18, 1999.

14. D. Filimonov, "Genatsvale Putin: V gorah Gruzii obnaruzhena mama prezidenta Rossii?" *Versiya*, April 25, 2000.

15. *Moskovskie novosti*, no. 2 (1021), January 25–31, 2000.

16. V. Usoltsev, *Sosluzhivets* (Moscow: EKSMO, 2004), p. 287.

CHAPTER THREE: PUTIN IN ST. PETERSBURG

1. N. Gevorkyan, A. Kolesnikov, N. Timakova, *Ot pervogo litsa: Razgovory s Putinym* (Moscow: Vagrius, 2000), p. 76.

2. O. Blotsky, *Vladimir Putin*, vol. 2, *Doroga k vlasti* (Moscow: Osmos-Press, 2002), p. 271.

3. V. Usoltsev, *Sosluzhivets*, (Moscow: EKSMO, 2004), pp. 241–42. V. Usoltsev (real name: Vladimir Gortanov) served with Putin in Dresden during the years 1985–1988, and retired, like Putin, with the rank of lieutenant colonel. A year before the publication of these memoirs, an interview with the author and excerpts from his book were published in *Izvestiya* on March 4 and 5, 2003, under the pseudonym Vladimir Artomonov.

4. O. Blotsky, *Doroga k vlasti*, pp. 307–8. Blotsky refers to this colleague as Gleb Novoselov, and adds that "his name has been changed." Presumably, this is Boris Miroshnikov—since 2001, the head of the Ministry of Internal Affairs' Main Directorate for Special Operational Arrangements.

5. Ibid., pp. 271–73.

6. Ibid., p. 283. According to Putin himself, his position at the university was called not "assistant to the rector on international *issues*," but "assistant to the rector on international *relations*." *Ot pervogo litsa*, p. 77.

7. B. Vishnevsky, "Prikomandirovannyi k vlasti: Vladimir Putin mezhdu Lubyankoi i Kremlem," *Nezavisimaya gazeta*, July 31, 1998; *Rossiyskaya elita: Psihologicheskie portrety* (Moscow: Ladomir, 2000), p. 178; B. Vishnevsky, "Gospodin Nikto," in *K demokratii i obratno* (Moscow: Integral-Inform, 2004).

8. L. Brichkina, "Vladimir Putin: Poslednyi patron," *Profil*, no. 32 (154), August 30, 1999.

9. *Literaturnaya gazeta*, no. 8 (5778), February 23–29, 2000.

10. M. Tokareva, "Zdes kazhdyi kamen' Putina znaet," *Obschaya gazeta*, no. 2 (336), January 13–19, 2000.

11. *Ot pervogo litsa*, pp. 78–79.

12. Ibid., p. 79.

13. O. Blotsky, *Doroga k vlasti*, p. 287.

14. B. Vishnevsky, "Smertel'naya oshibka Lensoveta," *Politichesky zhurnal*, May 23, 2005.

15. I. Arkhipov, "Hozhdenie v razvedku i v politiku," *Kommersant*, September 14, 1996; B. Vishnevsky, "Prikomandirovannyi k vlasti: Vladimir Putin mezhdu Lubyankoi i Kremlem," *Nezavisimaya gazeta*, July 31, 1998; B. Vishnevsky, "O biografii V. Putina," *Izvestiya*, August 12, 1999.

16. L. Bobrova, M. Markina, C. Bychkob, M. Rostovsky, A. Khinshtein, E. Deev, "Sem' mgnoveny iz zhizni preemnika," *Moskovsky komsomolets*, August 18, 1999.

17. V. Usoltsev, *Sosluzhivets*, pp. 7–8.

18. O. Blotsky, *Doroga k vlasti*, p. 154.

19. *Ot pervogo litsa*, p. 41.

20. O. Blotsky, *Doroga k vlasti*, p. 309.

21. *Ot pervogo litsa*, pp. 104–5.

22. O. Blotsky, *Doroga k vlasti*, p. 331.

23. *Novye Izvestiya*, December 26, 2002.

24. *Ot pervogo litsa*, pp. 81–82.

25. *Izvestiya*, August 12, 1999.

26. *Ot pervogo litsa*, p. 107.

27. "Prezident tebe tovarisch" (Ekho-TV's reporters have once again tried to answer the question: 'Who is Mr. Putin?' But Russians won't see their answer on the air), *Moskovskie novosti*, no. 25, July 9, 2004; http://www.mn.ru/issue.php?2004-25-51

28. O. Blotsky, *Doroga k vlasti*, p. 327.

29. *Ot pervogo litsa*, pp. 89–90.

30. K. Bonimi, D. D'Avanto, "Gody Putina mezhdu mafiei I KGB," *La Repubblica*, July 13, 2001.

31. The original copies of the documents have disappeared, however. By all appearances, they vanished sometime between 1997 and 1999, when Putin was the head of the president's Main Control Directorate and director of the FSB, while the St. Petersburg Legislative Assembly (which acquired the Petrosovet's archives in 1994) was headed by people close to Putin—Yuri Kravtsov, Viktor Novoselov, Sergei Mironov. But copies of the materials of the Salye-Gladkov commission have survived in part.

In March 2000, Marina Salye published an article titled "V. Putin—the 'President' of a Corrupt Oligarchy!" (Putin—"prezident" korrumpirovannoi oligarhii!) on the website of Sergei Grigoryants's Glasnost Foundation. See also: V. Ivanidze, "Nerazborchivye svyazi severnoi stolitsy," *Sovershenno sekretno*, August 2000; O. Lur'e, "Kolbasa dlya Pitera," *Novaya gazeta*, no. 10 (581), March 13–19, 2000.

32. *Ot pervogo litsa*, p. 91.

33. M. Salye, "Putin—'prezident' korrumpirovannoi oligarhii!"

34. Ibid.; O. Lur'e, "Kolbasa dlya Pitera."

35. M. Salye, "Putin—'prezident' korrumpirovannoi oligarhii!"; K. Bonimi, D. D'Avanto, "Gody Putina mezhdu mafiei I KGB."

36. I. Pitch, *Pikantnaya druzhba* (Moscow: Zakharov, 2002), p. 171.

37. M. Salye, "Putin—'prezident' korrumpirovannoi oligarhii!"

38. Ibid. Here is one such agreement:

> Agreement No. 11/92. On Organizing Barter Operations in Order to Provide St. Petersburg with Food. January 13, 1992. St. Petersburg.
>
> The International Relations Committee at the St. Petersburg mayor's office, represented by the deputy head of the committee, A. G. Anikin, referred to below as "the Committee," and the Dzhikop Corporation, represented by deputy general manager S. V. Ivanov, referred to below as "the Provider," have entered into the present agreement about the following:
>
> *The Object of the Agreement.* The Committee will issue to the Provider licenses to export rare-earth materials, eight positions, in

accordance with the appended list and certificates. The total amount available in stock is 13,997 kilograms. The Provider will carry out barter transactions by exchanging the indicated materials for food products.

The agreement's Supplement no. 1 listed these "eight positions": anodized niobium, niobium pentoxide, tantalic pentoxide, terbium, cerium dioxide, yttrium, scandium, zirconium—indicating the amounts, in kilograms, and the prices per kilogram in German marks (niobium pentoxide: 3000 kg at 711 DM; scandium: 7 kg at 72.6 DM; and so on). O. Lur'e, "Kolbasa dlya Pitera," *Novaya gazeta*, no. 10 (581), March 13–19, 2000.

The joint venture Dzhikop had two other co-owners, Dzhangir Ragimov and Sergei Viktorovich Ivanov—apparently, the same Ivanov who, as deputy general manager of the Dzhikop Corporation, signed a contract with the IRC, "represented by the deputy head of the Committee, Anikin." Beginning in September 1992, Anikin became the general manager of the Lenfintorg Foreign Trade Financing Association, which in December 1994 became a co-founder of the Kontrast-Tur company. Ragimov became the head of Kontrast-Tur. In another of Ragimov's companies, the Russian Trade Chamber, Sergei Mironov made his start as a builder of capitalism in Russia when he served as its executive director in 1991–1993. Somewhat later, Mironov became a manager for the Molchanovs, father and son; then, under Putin's patronage, a deputy in the St. Petersburg Legislative Assembly; and then the speaker of the upper house of the Russian parliament. Dzhangir's brother was Ilgam Ragimov—Putin's university classmate, the leader of his student cohort, and one of his four closest friends from his student days. The three others were Vladimir Cheremushkin, who died during judo practice, Nikolai Yegorov, and Viktor Khmarin.

39. M. Salye, "Putin—'prezident' korrumpirovannoi oligarhii!"

40. D. Ezhkov, "Problema 2000–2008," *Novaya gazeta* (*Svobodnoe prostranstvo*), no. 9 (19), March 16, 2007.

41. O. Lur'e, "Kolbasa dlya Pitera."

42. M. Salye, "Putin—'prezident' korrumpirovannoi oligarhii!"

43. K. Bonimi, D. D'Avanto, "Gody Putina mezhdu mafiei I KGB."

44. D. Ezhkov, "Problema 2000–2008."

45. *Ot pervogo litsa*, p. 90.

46. K. Bonimi, D. D'Avanto, "Gody Putina mezhdu mafiei I KGB," *La Repubblica*, July 13, 2001; "Kakie dokumenty est' za razoblacheniyami I. Rybkina i M. Salye," *Novaya gazeta*, no. 9, February 9–11, 2004.

47. *Ot pervogo litsa*, pp. 93–94.

48. *Kommersant*, September 4, 1993.

49. Ibid.

50. A significant detail: Dmitry Rozhdestvensky was the head of the Russian Grand Priory of the "Maltese Order," based in Cannes—one of the numerous self-proclaimed, illegitimate "Maltese Orders." But even here, in the "Maltese Order" in Cannes, Rozhdestvensky's deputy at the Russian Grand Priory was the former head of the Leningrad KGB's T ("terrorism") service, Colonel Vladimir Grunin.

51. A. Tsyganov, "U Putina takih firm shtuk 800 ili 1800," *Kommersant*, no. 60 (2899), April 5, 2004.

52. R. Shleinov, "Rossiei vladeet odin chelovek—ee upravlyauschiy," *Novaya gazeta*, no. 9, February 7, 2005.

53. I. Sedykh, "V Lihtenshteine obvinyaut rabotodatelya Vladimira Putina i Germana Grefa," *Kommersant*, July 23, 2001.

54. Y. Borisova, "My v 'chernom spiske' iz-za Putina," *Moscow Times*, August 29, 2001.

55. R. Shleinov, "Rossiei vladeet odin chelovek—ee upravlyauschiy."

56. "Otvet kompanii 'SPAG St. Petersburg Immobilien und Beteiligungen Aktiengesellschaft' na publikatsiu: Est' voprosy k svidetelu: Prezidentu Rossii (*Novaya gazeta*, no. 18 (1043), March 14, 2005)," *Novaya gazeta*, no. 79, October 24, 2005.

57. *Obschaya gazeta*, no. 2, 2000; *Ot pervogo litsa*, pp. 114–17.

CHAPTER SIX: "OPERATION SUCCESSOR"

1. *Kommersant*, September 15, 1999.

2. *Express-khronika*, no. 46 (601), December 1999.

3. *Literaturnaya gazeta*, no. 51/52, December 1999.

4. *Moskovsky komsomolets*, February 1, 2000.

5. "An Election Is the Only Race in Which the Majority Wins," interview with Igor Borisov, vice-president of the ROIIP Council, www.roiip.ru/press

6. *Duel*, no. 4 (184), October 10, 2000.

7. Y. Borisova, "And the Winner Is?" *Moscow Times*, September 9, 2000.

8. A. Saliy, "Dagestanskaya tekhnologiya falsifikatsii," *Sovetskaya Rossiya*, April 27, 2000.

9. *Sovetskaya Rossiya*, April 6, 2000.

10. Zh. Kasyanenko, "Saratovskaya nepreryvka," *Sovetskaya Rossiya*, March 18, 2000.

11. Y. Borisova, "And the Winner Is?"

12. "An Election Is the Only Race in Which the Majority Wins."

13. The full text of A. Zh. Makasheva's answer is published in *Duel*, no. 4 (184), October 10, 2000.

14. A. Germanovich, "Korrektirovka? Klub edinodushnogo golosovaniya," *Vedomosti*, March 28, 2000.

CHAPTER SEVEN: THE FSB, THE OLIGARCHS, AND THE CLANS

1. A. Solzhenitsyn, "K nyneshnemu sostoyaniu Rossii," *Obschaya gazeta*, no. 47 (175), November 28–December 4, 1996.

2. *Dal' V. Tolkovyi slovar zhivogo russkogo iazyka'* (Dictionary of the Living Russian Language), vol. 2 (Moscow, 1979), p. 671.

3. *Izvestiya*, August 2, 2000.

4. "AntiPutin. Neobhodimost otstraneniya presidenta ot vlasti ochevidna," *Stringer*, no. 6, October 2000.

5. A. Borodai, A. Rudakov, " 'Priglashenie' v prem'ery. Zamenit li Kasyanova Sergei Ivanov?" *Zavtra*, no. 47 (364), November 2000.

6. *Komsomolskaya pravda*, July 8, 1999.

CHAPTER EIGHT: THE PRESIDENT'S FRIENDS OR "AGENTS AND OBJECTS"

1. "Gospodin Okhrannik," interview with R. Tsepov, *Versiya*, November 2, 1999.

2. N. Gevorkyan, A. Kolesnikov, N. Timakova, *Ot pervogo litsa: Rasgovory s Vladimirom Putinym* (Moscow: Vagrius, 2000), p. 79.

3. "Neuzheli eto Pravda?" *Novyi Peterburg*, December 24, 1998.

4. Ibid.

5. *ITAR-TASS*, September 30, 2002.

6. Pribylovsky told the magazine *Russky Zhurnal* (February 16, 2007) more or less the same thing: "The appointment of Serdyukov as defense minister is the strangest part of the whole operation. It is unlikely that the president wanted deliberately to spit in the face of his generals (this happened by itself, as a side effect). There are two possible explanations. First, that he wanted to surprise everyone and make everyone think that 'our president is anything but simple.' Second, perhaps the hoped-for successor and heir to the throne is Mr. Serdyukov's son-in-law, Putin's old friend Viktor Zubkov?"

CHAPTER NINE: MANAGED DEMOCRACY

1. N. Ivanov, "Chto dlya Permi blago, dlya Ekaterinburga—smert," *Nezavisimaya gazeta*, April 2, 2003.

2. Gazeta.ru, June 14, 2001.

3. Strana.ru, May 31, 2001.

4. *Kommersant*, November 28, 2001.

5. *Kommersant*, December 17, 2001.

6. *Kommersant*, March 12, 2002.

7. *Kommersant*, April 30, 2002.

8. *Kommersant-Vlast*, May 14, 2002.

9. *Kommersant*, May 17, 2002.

10. D. Pushkar, "Konets agenta," *Moskovskie novosti*, April 23, 2003.

11. *Nezavisimaya gazeta*, September 17, 2002.

12. Lenta.ru, October 2, 2002.

13. Gazeta.ru, October 1, 2002.

14. Polit.ru, September 29, 2002.

15. A. Vedernikov, "Imidzh Rossii stradaet ot narusheniy na regional'nyh vyborah," *Nezavisimaya gazeta*, February 21, 2003.

16. M.-L. Tirmaste, "Vse proishodyashchee—absolutnyi bespredel!" *Kommersant*, February 22, 2003.

17. I. Burakov, "Ozhestochennye i bespartiynye," *Vremya novostey*, February 28, 2004.

18. A. Shapovalov, "Donskie kommunisty soshli s distantsii," *Nezavisimaya gazeta*, March 13, 2003.

19. V. Ivanov, "Horilsk bez golovy," *Vedomosti*, April 29, 2003.

20. Ibid.

21. *Moskovskie novosti*, July 9, 2004.

22. Y. Latynina, "Kluchevye vybory," *Yezhenedelny zhurnal*, no. 35 (86), August 25–31, 2003.

23. Ibid.

24. *Kommersant*, September 3, 2003.

25. "Zayavlenie o narushenii federalnogo zakona 'Ob osnovnyh garantiyah izbiratelnyh prav i prava na uchastie v referendume grazhdan Rossyiskoi Federatsii,' June 12, 2002, no. 67; FZ prezidentom RF Putinym V. V.," *Yezhenedelny zhurnal*, no. 35 (86), September 8–14, 2003.

26. *Izvestiya*, September 3, 2003.

27. *Vedomosti*, September 26, 2003.

28. A. Mitrofanov, "Aslakhanova ubrali s pomoshch'u knuta i pryanika," *Novye izvestiya*, September 12, 2003.

29. I. Sekhov, "Luchshe by presidenta naznachili," *Vremya novostey*, August 30, 2004.

30. *Nezavisimaya gazeta*, February 2, 2004.

31. V. Poegli, " '1984' i drugie, ili polemicheskie zametki o dobrovol'nom syske," *Moskovsky komsomolets*, January 23, 1990.

32. A. Efimova, "Lotto 'Million voprosov' i 'Moskva i moskvichi'—avanturnyi roman s prodolzheniem," *Stolitsa*, no. 2 and no. 42, 1993.

33. I. Simonova, "Tatariya izbavilas ot neugodnogo deputata," *Kommersant*, December 3, 2003.

34. *Nezavisimaya gazeta*, December 9, 2003.

35. *Kommersant*, March 22, 2004.

36. *Kommersant*, November 10, 2003.

37. See for example: M. Melnikov, B. Panteleev, "Press-vybory," *Novaya gazeta*, no. 94 (926), December 11–14, 2003.

38. I. Stadnik, "Obratnyi podschet," *Yezhenedelny zhurnal*, no. 49 (100), December 15–21, 2003.

39. "Soobshchenie IA 'VolgaInform,'" *Agentstvo politicheskih novostei (APN)*, December 9, 2003; www.apn.ru/elections/2003/12/9/41296.html

40. N. Vorobyeva, "Bessmyslennoe vorovstvo," *Politichesky zhurnal*, no. 1 (4), January 19, 2004.

41. A. Kostukov, "Po dva pasporta v odni ruki," *Nezavisimaya gazeta*, April 27, 2004.

42. Ibid.

43. *Izvestiya*, January 31, 2004.

44. O. Tropkina, A. Skrobot, "Mertvye dushi rossyiskogo elektorata," *Nezavisimaya gazeta*, December 3, 2003.

45. Ibid.

46. A. Kornya, "Uchetnyi material bolshoi mobilnosti," *Nezavisimaya gazeta*, February 11, 2004.

47. *Nezavisimaya gazeta*, December 2, 2003.

48. D. Oreshkin, "Iz getto v Kreml," *Novaya gazeta*, no. 5, February 13–19, 2004.

49. http://www.polit.ru/event/2003/12/26/veshnyakov.html

50. Ibid.

51. A. Dyemin, "Koney podkuut do perepravy," *Yezhenedelny zhurnal*, no. 50 (101), December 22–28, 2003.

52. N. Gromova, "Grigory Yavlinsky: 'Strana uhodit, i nichego nelzya podelat,'" *Moskovsky komsomolets*, January 30, 2004.

53. Gazeta.ru, January 22, 2004.

54. O. Kitova, "Raznye arifmetiki 'Yabloka' i Tsenrizbirkoma," *Russky kur'er*, December 19, 2003.

55. N. Vorobyeva, "Bessmyslennoe vorovstvo," *Politichesky zhurnal*, no. 1 (4), January 19, 2004.

56. O. Kitova, "Raznye arifmetiki 'Yabloka' i Tsenrizbirkoma."

57. A. Kornya, "'Yabloko' i KPRF ob'edinilis," *Nezavisimaya gazeta*, June 24, 2004.

58. *Nezavisimaya gazeta*, December, 9, 2003.

59. N. Vorobyeva, "Bessmyslennoe vorovstvo."

60. O. Kitova, "Raznye arifmetiki 'Yabloka' i Tsenrizbirkoma."

61. A. Mitrofanov, "Razdvoenie linii," *Russky kur'er*, April 13, 2004.

62. Dzh. Orkhan, "Vybory 2003: Mertvye dushi proshli 5-protsentnyi bar'er," *Novaya gazeta*, no. 6 (936), January 29–February 1, 2004.

63. N. Vorobyeva, "Bessmyslennoe vorovstvo."

64. *Vremya novostey*, December 17, 2003.

65. V. Shenderovich, "Tsentrizbirkom chuvstvuet rezultaty vyborov dushoi," *Novaya gazeta*, no. 97 (929), December 22–24, 2003.

66. N. Galimova, "Listogonnoe sredstvo," interview with CEC chairman A. Veshnyakov, *Moskovsky komsomolets*, February 7, 2004.

67. Ibid.

68. A. Kornya, "'Yabloko' i KPRF ob'edinilis."

69. Ibid.

70. D. Suslov, "Vybory v Gosdumu byli porochnymi" (David Atkinson, PACE rapporteur on Russia, says that "voters were blatantly and straightforwardly lied to" on December 7; interview with David Atkinson), *Nezavisimaya gazeta*, January 26, 2004.

71. D. Suslov, "OBSE: vybory iskazheny" (The main international observer tells *Nezavisimaya gazeta* about the reasons for his dissatisfaction with the Russian election; interview with OSCE Parliamentary Assembly president Bruce George), *Nezavisimaya gazeta*, December 9, 2003.

72. A. Terekhov, "Hanskyi gambit: Kirsan Ilyumzhinov obygral kalmytskuu oppozitsiu," *Novye izvestiya*, December 11, 2003.

73. V. Ulyadurov, "Kirsan Ilyumzhinov—stepnoi Shevardnadze," *Novaya gazeta*, no. 94 (926), December 11–14, 2003.

74. V. Ulyadurov, "Prishel, uvidel, obmanul...," *Novaya gazeta*, no. 94 (927), December 15–17, 2003.

75. V. Ivanov, A. Nilolsky, A. Voronina, "Palenye bulleteni obnaruzhila FSB v bashkirskoi tipografii," *Vedomosti*, December 5, 2003.

76. N. Gulko, "Ralif Safin ne pozvolit oporochit' Alsu...," *Kommersant*, November 20, 2003.

77. I. Sukhov, "Golosovanie zheludkom," *Vremya novostey*, December 15, 2003.

78. I. Sukhov, "Tretiy srok Murtazy Rakhimova," *Vremya novostey*, December 19, 2003.

79. At the beginning of January 2004, Saratov's colleges received an order: to submit signatures in support of the nomination of Putin for president of Russia. Students who did not give their signatures would not be allowed to take their exams. V. Soborov, "Putin v zachetke," *Moskovsky komsomolets*, January 10, 2004.

80. B. Vishnevsky, N. Donskov, "Sankt-Petersburg: kolybel rezolutsii," *Novaya gazeta*, no. 12 (942), February 19–25, 2004.

81. Ibid.

82. A. Kostukov, "Rezultaty ne shodyatsya s itogami," *Nezavisimaya gazeta*, March 29, 2004.

83. Ibid.

84. Ibid.

85. A. Egorov, "Tsennoe pismo Mosgorizbirkoma popalo v rozysk," *Nezavisimaya gazeta*, April 19, 2004.

86. Ibid.

87. A. Kostukov, "Po dva pasporta v odni ruki," *Nezavisimaya gazeta*, April 27, 2004.

88. A. Kostukov, "TsIK i Mosgorizbirkom usomnilic v chistote vyborov," *Nezavisimaya gazeta*, April 2, 2004.

89. A. Kornya, "Urodov nado lechit," *Nezavisimaya gazeta*, April 28, 2004.

90. *Kommersant*, March 3, 2004.

91. I. Verba, "Tak, pohuliganili nemnozhko," *Nezavisimaya gazeta*, July 12, 2004.

92. A. Chernyshov, "Svoei pobedoi budu schitat, esli naberu nol golosov," *Kommersant*, July 15, 2004.

93. Ibid.

94. D. Oreshkin, "Prezrenie sozrevaet gnevom," *Rossiya*, July 22–28, 2004.

95. A. Shamburova, "Novyi mer Vladivostoka prigrel syna prem'er-ministra Rossii," *Novaya gazeta*, no. 53 (983), July 26, 2004.

96. Dzh. Orkhan, "Pasportgeit. Domashnyaya zagotovka chechenskogo izbirkoma," *Novaya gazeta*, no. 56 (986), August 5–8, 2004.

97. I. Sukhov, "Luchshe by prezidenta naznachili," *Vremya novostey*, August 30, 2004.

98. M. Muradov, "Lovkost nog—i nikakogo moshennichestva," *Kommersant*, August 30, 2004.

99. A. Barakhova, "Drus'ya poznautsya v Chechne," *Kommersant*, September 1, 2004.

100. Yu. Latynina, "Poslanie polkovnika," *Novaya gazeta*, no. 68 (998), September 16–19, 2004.

CHAPTER TEN: THE SUPPRESSION OF THE MEDIA

1. O. Panfilov, "Svyashchennye korovy" rossiiskoi verticali," *Nezavisimaya gazeta*, September 22, 2003.

2. *Segodnya*, February 5, 2000.

3. *Izvestiya*, February 5, 2000.

4. *Nezavisimaya gazeta*, February 8, 2000.

5. V. Shenderovich, *"Zdes bylo NTV" i drugie istorii* (Moscow: Zakharov, 2004), p. 14.

6. A. Bossart, "Zashchita Buratino," *Novaya gazeta*, no. 26 (669), April 12–15, 2001.

7. V. Shenderovich, *"Zdes bylo NTV" i drugie istorii*, p. 16.

8. Ibid., p. 26.

9. *Stringer*, no. 7, May 2003.

10. *Izvestiya*, August 2, 2000.

11. Ryklin A., "Beseda s Borisom Berezovskim," *Yezhenedelny zhurnal*, no. 48 (99), December 8–14, 2003.

12. Ibid.

13. V. Shenderovich, *"Zdes bylo NTV" i drugie istorii*, p. 51.

14. Y. Albats, "Komu prodali NTV: Chekisty podminaut pod sebya SMI," *Novaya gazeta*, no. 72 (810), September 30–October 2, 2002.

15. *Materialy po istorii russkogo osvoboditel'nogo dvizheniya*, vol. 2 (Moscow: Isdatelstvo imeni Ignatiya Stavropolskogo, 1998), pp. 456–57.

16. Y. Tsurganov, *Neudavshiysya revansh: Belaya emigratsiya vo Vtoroi mirovoi voine* (Moscow: Intrada, 2001), pp. 116–18.

17. *Kommersant*, July 4, 2001; *RIA Novosti*, January 15, 2002.

18. *Zavtra*, no. 8 (431), February 2002.

19. A. Simonov, "Brakonerskiy udar kartech'u," *Nezavisimaya gazeta*, June 26, 2002.

20. Y. Latynina, "Mozhno li sdelat iz stiralnoi mashiny avtomat Kalashnikova?" *Novaya gazeta*, May 27–30, 2002.

21. Y. Komarov, "Ushcherb radi 'svobody slova,'" *Novye izvestiya*, no. 95 (1101), June 7, 2002.

22. A. Tarasov, "Gospoda Geksogen, Ivanov, Sorokin, na vyhod! Pochemu 'Idushchie vmeste' 'naehali' na Sorokina," *Novaya gazeta*, no. 47, 2002.

23. S. Shargunov, "U nas otobrali medal," interview with Andrei Sharyi, *Novaya gazeta*, no. 74 (812), October 7–9, 2002.

24. Back in May 2002, *Versiya* had published Oleg Lurye's article "A Russian Crime Novel"—purportedly an interview with an FBI agent who accused the Alfa Group heads Pyotr Aven and Mikhail Fridman of dealing in narcotics and having ties to criminal organizations. Alfa Group's management brought a suit before the arbitration court to protect its business reputation. At the beginning of 2003, the court ruled that the plaintiffs had to be compensated: three million rubles to Aven, three million rubles to Fridman, and £172,000 to the Kroll Detective Agency, which had been hired by Alfa Group to conduct an investigation.

At the beginning of 2001, a similar article about Mezhprombank in *Novaya gazeta* by the same Oleg Lurye had almost bankrupted and shut down the paper.

At the end of 2003, Oleg Lurye, who had avoided taking part in the trial between *Versiya* and Alfa Group, obtained financing for the publication of his own glossy magazine, which he named *VVP* (for *Valovoy Vnutrenny Produkt*,

"Gross Domestic Product"). The "goal of the magazine," as announced on its title page, was "to facilitate businesses and organizations in promoting their ideas and possibilities . . . in light of President V. V. Putin's demands concerning the doubling of the VVP."

25. Strana.ru, July 15, 2003.

26. S. Agafonov, "Kremlyevsky napyerstok," *Novye izvestiya*, October 27, 2002.

27. Y. Latynina, "Ya sam budu vashim tsenzorom: Televidenie—edinstvennaya otrasl economiki, kotoruiu kontroliruet lichno president Rossii," *Novaya gazeta*, no. 4 (837), January 20–22, 2003.

28. *Kommersant*, February 21, 2003. The author of this article in *Novye izvestiya* is Vladimir Pribylovsky.

29. Gazeta.ru, February 20, 2003.

30. *Moscow Times*, April 8, 2003.

31. *Vremya novostey*, June 21, 2004.

32. K. Latukhina, "'Shestaya knopka" vzbuntovalas" (*Nezavisimya gazeta*'s Interview with the Director of the National Research Center for Television and Radio Angers Sports Channel Supporters), *Nezavisimaya gazeta*, August 4, 2004.

33. O. Panfilov, "'Svyashchennye korovy' rossiyskoi verticali," *Nezavisimaya gazeta*, September 22, 2003.

34. G. Pasko, "Yury Shmidt: Stukachei nado berech: I dannye o nih hranit v taine," *Novaya gazeta*, September 29–Ocotber 1, 2003.

35. News.ru, November 17, 2003.

36. "Sred bela dnya; Zloklucheniya redaktsii; Ograblenie kak biznes-proekt; Anatomiya banditskogo kapitalizma," *Novoye vremya*, no. 24, June 13, 2004.

37. Ibid.

38. Ibid.

39. Ibid.

40. I. Korolyev, "Zakon zhizni: Popytki otregulirovat Internet ne prekrashchautsya," *Vremya novostey*, April 14, 2004.

41. Ibid.

42. "Rossiya v 'setyah obshchego polzovaniya': O tolerantnosti i probleme borby s propagandoi terrorizma i ksenofobii v Internete na vstreche v OBSE dokladyval general FSB," *Novaya gazeta*, June 28–30, 2004.

43. V. Plakhova, "Novosti uhodyat v podpol'ye: Duma reshila izbavit telezritelei ot stressa," *Novaya gazeta*, no. 69, September 20–22, 2004.

44. E. Afanasyeva, "'Ekho Moskvy' v 'Izvestiyah,'" *Izvestiya*, no. 99 (26656), June 5, 2004.

45. S. Varshavchik, "Na televidenii zachishchaut terminologiu," *Nezavisimaya gazeta*, August 2, 2004.

46. *Izvestiya*, June 5, 2004, p. 9.

47. A. Borodina, "Parfenonsens," *Kommersant*, June 3, 2004.

48. Ibid.

49. Ibid.

50. A. Ryklin, "Ah, Parfyenova uvolili! Da kak zhe oni posmeli?! . . ." *Yezhenedelny zhurnal*, no. 22 (123), June 7–13, 2004, p. 7.

51. A. Rebel, "Namedni ne stalo 'Namedni,'" *Russky kur'er*, June 3, 2004.

52. I. Malashenko, "Konets puti," *Yezhenedelny zhurnal*, no. 22 (123), June 7–13, 2004, p. 8.

53. A. Rebel, "Namedni ne stalo 'Namedni.'"

54. A. Borodina, "NTV Must Rediscover Its Aura of Objectivity and Impartiality: The First Interview with the Television Company's General Manager, Vladimir Kulistikov," *Kommersant*, July 19, 2004.

55. V. Shenderovich, "Venerolog Basaev, odnokursnitsa presidenta, a takzhe—pochemu Zuganov pozhalovalsya Putinu na nego samogo," *Novaya gazeta*, no. 51 (981), July 19–21, 2004.

56. V. Plakhova, "Gosteleradio zakazalo Hruna i Stepana," *Novaya gazeta*, no. 51 (981), July 19–21, 2004.

57. Y. Serova, "Spetsoperatsiya v Beslane proshla uspeshno: Protiv zhurnalistov," *Novaya gazeta*, no. 69, September 20–22, 2004.

58. M. Leontyev, "Po zakonam voennogo vremeni," *Nezavisimaya gazeta*, September 9, 2004.

59. A. Voronina, "Dobralis do bumagi," *Vedomosti*, September 7, 2004.

60. Ibid.

61. "Kto uvolil Rafa Shakirova?" *Nezavisimaya gazeta*, September 7, 2004.

62. "Pochemy uvolen glavnyi redaktor gazety 'Izvestiya'?" Radio Liberty, September 7, 2004.

63. *Vedomosti*, September 7, 2004.

64. E. Milashina, "'Svoboda' ne imeet grazhdanstva: Radiozhurnalista Bagrova lishili konstitutsyonnyh prav," *Novaya gazeta*, no. 4 (102), December 23–26, 2004.

65. *Vremya novostey*, September 9, 2005.

66. A. Borodina, "Na NTV proveli profilakticheskuiu rabotu," *Kommersant*, December 9, 2005.

67. *Kommersant*, January 28, 2005.

68. N. Rostova, "V 'Izvestiyah' ne pomenyaetsya nichego, krome glavnogo," interview with Raf Shakirov, Vladimir Borodin, Nikolai Senkevich, *Novaya gazeta*, no. 84 (1109), November 10–13, 2005.

69. www.anticompromat.ru/ 06.01.html

70. G. Petrov, "'Da' protiv Mosgorsuda: Doch Egora Gaidara 'povyazali' za svobodu slova," *Moskovsky komsomolets*, September 19, 2005.

71. E. Sannikova, "Khronika suda: Prava cheloveka v Rossii," www.hro.org/ngo/about/2006/02/02

72. "Rossiya: vlast protiv pressy," *Ezhenedelny bulleten tsentra exstremalnoi zhurnalistiki*, vol. 30 (185), July 25–31, 2006.

73. www.lenta.ru/articles/2007/07

74. *Politichesky barometr*, no. 102, July 2–8, 2007; www.demos-center.ru/reviews/19030

75. *Yezhenedelny zhurnal*, no. 18 (119), May 10–16, 2004.

76. S. Strokan, "Rossiya poluchila nezachet po demokratii: Freedom House vkluchil eye v spisok 'nesvobodnyh stran,'" *Kommersant*, December 21, 2004.

77. *Kommersant*, May 4, 2006.

78. "10 stran s samoi zhestokoi tsenzuroi," *Komitet po zashchite zhurnalistov*, May 2, 2006, www.cpj.org/censored/censored_ru.pdf

79. Grani.ru, May 2, 2007; *see* www.freedomhouseuse.org/template.cfm

80. www.svobodamews.ru/Transcript/2007/06/19

CHAPTER ELEVEN: THE AGE OF ASSASSINS

1. Elizabeth Lermolo, *Face of a Victim* (New York: Harper & Brothers, 1955), pp. 132–37.

2. L. D. Trotsky, *Portrety revolutsionerov: Sverh-Bordgia v Kremle* (Moscow, 1991).

3. B. Nicolaevsky, *Tainye stranitsy istorii* (Moscow: Izd-vo Gumanitamoi lit-ry, 1995), pp. 228–29.

4. L. Shatunovskaya, *Zhizn' v Kremle* (New York: Chalidze Publishing, 1982), pp. 227, 229, 230.

5. Ibid., pp. 232–33.

6. Ibid., pp. 234–35.

7. Yves Delbars, *The Real Stalin* (London: George Allen & Unwin Ltd., 1951), pp. 129–30.

8. L. D. Trotsky, *Portrety revolutsionerov*, p. 77.

9. See: N. V. Valentinov, *Nasledniki Lenina* (Moscow: Terra, 1991), app. 8, p. 214.

10. Letter from A. Berkman to Don Levine, August 4, 1927, in Archive of the International Institute of Social History (Amsterdam), A. Berkman collection, folder III (10).

11. Letter from Boris Nicolaevsky to Boris Suvarin, April 11, 1957, sheet 1, in Archive of the International Institute of Social History (Amsterdam), B. K. Suvarin collection.

12. *The Unknown Lenin: From the Secret Archive*, ed. R. Pipes (New Haven: Yale University Press, 1996), p. 77.

13. N. V. Valentinov, *Nasledniki Lenina*, pp. 214, 216–17.

14. See: I. V. Rech', *Stalina v Narkomate oborony*, published by Y. Murin, *Istochnik*, no. 3, 1994, pp. 72–88.

15. F. D. Volkov, *Vzlyet i padenie Stalina* (Moscow: Izd-vo Spektr, 1992), p. 66.

16. Vospominaniya Vladimira Kuibysheva, *Moskovskie novosti*, March 2, 1995.

17. L. D. Trotsky, *Portrety revolutsionerov*, pp. 75–76.

18. Y. Svetlova, "Kogda vrachi bessil'ny," *Sovershenno sekretno*, October 30, 2001.

19. L. Berres, "Saratovskie himiki zarabotali na smerti izvestnogo bankira," *Kommersant,* April 19, 1997.

20. Ibid.

21. E. Kotlyar, "Echshe o gromkih ubiystvah," *Moskovskaya pravda,* July 22, 1999.

22. "V dele Kivilidi—nikakih podvizhek," *Argumenty i fakty,* June 9, 1999.

23. S. Sokolov, "Vrachebnaya taina: Obstoyatel'stva, kotorye ne mogut ne vyzvat' voprosov," *Novaya gazeta,* July 1–4, 2004.

INDEX

Shchekochikhin, 466; and theater hostage crisis, 405; on TVS, 392

Chelenko, Leonid, 369

Chemezov, Sergei Viktorovich, 40, 112, 113, 221–26; and arms sales, 221; and Putin, 221; and Rosboronexport, 236–38; and Sovintersport, 244–45; and Tsepvo, 227; and Tyagachev, 245–46, 247

Chentsov, Vyacheslav, 37

Cheremushkin, Vladimir, 496

Cherepanov, Alexander, 316

Cherepkov, Viktor, 271–72, 298–99; and Vladivostok mayoral race, 349–50

Cherkesov, Viktor, 66–67, 119, 205; as Putin friend, 49; as Putin's representative, 108, 172; and Sobchak, 54

Chernenko, Konstantin, 490–91

Chernikov, Pavel, 424

Chernobyl, 403

Chernomyrdin, Viktor: and Berezovsky, 24; and Gazprom, 70, 192; and NDR, 57, 59, 154, 168; as oligarch, 183, 184; and Security Council, 128

Cherny, Ernst, 214

China: arms sales to, 224–25, 239; and scientific research, 210–11, 215–17

China Precision Machinery Import-Export Corporation, 216

Chub, Vladimir, 273–74, 295

Chubais, Anatoly, xi, 23, 24, 145, 417; and Krasnoyarsk election, 283; on NTV, 374–75; as oligarch, 184; and Putin, 118; and REN TV, 404; and Sobchak, 51–52; and TVS, 391; as Yeltsin chief of staff, 28, 111

CIA, 207–8, 451

CIS (Commonwealth of Independent States), 126, 177

Clinton, Bill, 263

Coca-Cola, 62

cocaine, 67–68

Colombia, 96, 101–2

Committee for External Economic Relations (CEER), 72, 76, 80

Committee for State Security. *See* KGB

Committee of Soldiers' Mothers, 139

Committee to Protect Journalists, 426

Communist Party of the Russian Federation (CPRF), 59, 150, 151–52, 154, 191, 316; and Basanets, 478; in Bashkortostan, 292–93; in Duma elections (2003), 319, 321, 325–28; Khodyrev, 273; opposition to Yeltsin, 129–30; and presidential election (2004), 337–38, 340–41, 343, 344–45; and Putin, 132, 151, 160; Putin election challenge, 163–64, 167; in Rostov region, 273–75, 294–95; in Saratov region, 263; and Tkachev, 348

Communist Party of the Soviet Union (CPSU): and Chechnya, 25; Department of Agitation and Propaganda, 3; and KGB, 8, 9; property of, 113; Putin's membership in, 37, 41, 54.; and Tyagachev), 240; Zyuganov, 27, 28

Congress of People's Deputies of the USSR, 50, 198

Congress of Russian Communities, 157

Constitutional Court of the Russian Federation, xxv, 172, 291

Conti casino, 65, 87

Conti Group, 89

Council of Europe, 214; Parliamentary Assembly, 329–30

Council of Ministers (Russia), 88

Criminal Code of the RSFSR, 233–34, 248

Criminal Code of the Russian Federation: and Dmitrievsky case, 419; and elections, 166, 335; on espionage & treason,

election fraud: in Bashkortostan,
165–66; in Chechnya, 168; in
Dagestan, 160–63, 169; in Duma
elections (2003), 319–33; in
Ingushetia, 168, 170; investigation
of, 160–65; in Kalinngrad region,
167; in Kalmykia, 170; in Kursk
region, 167; methods, 155–58; in
Mordovia, 165; and observers,
158–60, 165–66, 167; in Saratov
region, 163–65, 169–70; in
Tatarstan, 166–67
Entrepreneurship Council, 453, 455
Epp, Genrikh, 123, 286
Eritrea, 238
Eural TG, 192
European Court for Human Rights,
209
European Space Agency, 217
European Union, 143, 194, 292; as
model, 179
Express Khronika, 399

FairGame, 326
"family, the," 124, 145, 184, 185, 270,
283; vs. checkists, 194, 197, 286;
and Customs Committee, 192;
Khinshtein's criticism of, 361; and
NTV (Gusinksy), 367, 377; and
Rutskoy, 267; and Ustinov, 190;
and Veremeyenko, 333
Far Eastern Shipping Company
(FESCO), 351–52
Fatherland party, 146, 263; and
Luzhkov, 184, 195; and Putin, 154;
and Tkachev, 348; Unity merger,
178, 384
Fatherland–All Russia bloc (OVR),
150–51, 195, 263; and Khinshtein,
361; NTV support for, 364
Federal Agency for Government
Communication and Information
(FAPSI), 70, 120, 291
Federal Antiterrorist Commission,
141, 412
Federal Counterintelligence Service
(FSK), xxv, 130, 133, 484

Federal Protection Service (FSO),
190, 226–27, 464
Federal Security Agency (AFB), 83,
84
Federal Security Service of Russia
(FSB), viii–xiii, xxv, 5, 84,
200, 489; active reserve, 8–9,
85, 113, 114, 117, 189–90, 220,
226, 424; and Aksenenko, 484;
assassinations, 452–53, 461; and
Babitsky affair, 358, 360–61;
and Barsukov-Kumarin arrest,
474–75; and Basanets poisoning,
478–79; and Baskhortostan
election, 334–35; and Chechen
assassinations, 477–78; and
Chechen elections, 352, 354; and
Chechnya (terrorist attacks),
25–26, 171; Collegium, 119;
counterintelligence, 66; "Day of
the Chekist," 149; Department of
Counterintelligence for Strategic
Objects, 118, 120; Department of
Economic Counterintelligence,
118, 120; Directorate for the
Defense of the Constitutional
Order, 28; and electronic voting
system, 290–91; and entrance
visas, 234; and federal structure,
172; headquarters bombed, 120,
123; and Khinshtein, 361–62;
and Klebnikov murder, 480–82;
and Lezhava poisoning, 467–68;
and Limonov case, 379; and
Litvinenko poisoning, 485,
487–88; and Media-Most raid,
366–67, 372, 373; and media
regulations, 386; Moscow
office, 5, 26, 119; and *Novaya
Gazeta* suit, 380; and oligarchs,
489–90; and Ostankino, 22; and
plenipotentiary representatives,
172; and Podrabinek, 399–400;
and Politkovskaya murder, 482;
Putin as director, 63–64, 117–28;
Putin's reorganization, 118–20;
Radio Liberty raid, 414; regional

159, 162, 164–65, 343–44; and
GKU, 115; and *Gorodskie
Vesti* case, 420; Khapsirokov
& Yeghiazarian cases, 233–35;
on Kivilidi poisoning, 459; and
Kommersant, 424
and Media-Most, 366, 369, 372,
373; and Miroshnik, 81; and
North Ossetia election, 276; on
Politkovskaya murder, 480, 482;
and Russkoye Video, 64–65; and
Shchekochikhin's death, 465–67;
and Skuratov case, 126; and
Sobchak investigation, 229–32;
on SPAG, 96; and Yeltsin, 130;
and Yushchenko poisoning, 476
Generalov, Sergei, 352
Genieva, Ekaterina, 483
Georgia, Republic of, xiv–xv, 409,
414–15, 477; Chechen refugees
in, ix; Putin's childhood in, 30–35,
37–38
Gerasimov, Alexander, 403, 404, 407,
408
Germany, 67, 225, 353, 446, 448,
450, 479; Chemezov in, 221;
Communist Party, 440; Putin in,
38–41, 43–44, 75, 118–19, 252; and
SPAG, 90–102
Getye, Fyodor, 437, 438
Ginzburg, Alexander, 50
Ginzburg, Vitaly, 214
GKU. *See* Main Control Directorate
Gladkov, Yuri, 73
Glasnost Defense Foundation, 214,
357, 380, 411
Glazkov, Vadim, 200
Glazkov, Valery, 296
Glazyev, Sergei, 27, 283–84; and
Homeland bloc, 191, 319; and
presidential election (2004), 338,
340
Glisman, Alexander, 296
Glushkov, Nilolai, 371, 373, 376
Gochiyaev, Achemez, 135
Gogolashvili, Nora, 33
Golembiovsky, Igor, 388–90, 415

Golos, 344
Golov, Anatoly, 59
Golovin, Alexander, 222
Golovlev, Vladimir, 152, 394
Golubev, Valery, 66, 202
Golushko, Andrey, 122
Golushko, Nikolai, 222
Gonchar, Nikolai, 398
Gontov, Alexander, 122
Gorbachev, Mikhail, xxiv, 243, 250,
368, 491
Gorbachevsky, N. M., 83
Gorbatova, Anna, 409
Gorbenko, Igor, 87, 88, 89–90
Gorbenko, Leonid, 461
Gorbushkin, Denis, 313
Gordievsky, Oleg, 244
Gorky, Maxim, 443–45
Gorodskie Vesti, 420
Gortanov, Vladimir. *See* Usoltsev,
Vladimir
Goskontsert, 10
Gosplan, 444
Gostev, Viktor Timofeyevich, 241
Govorit Moskva radio, 196
GPU (State Political Directorate),
xxiii, 439, 441
Gref, German, 92–93
Grigoriev, Alexander, 66, 119, 232
Grigoriev, Mark, 251
Grigoryeva, Klavdiya, 165
Grigulevich, I. R., 431
Gromov, Alexei, 404
Gronsky, Ivan, 436–37
GRU. *See* Main Intelligence
Directorate of the Russian
Federation
Grunin, Vladimir, 87, 496
Gruzdev, Vladimir, 318
Gryzlov, Boris: Duma speaker, 420;
minister of internal affairs, 138,
141, 200; on *Novoye Vremya*,
398; as oligarch, 182, 190; prime
minister candidate, 194; and
Unity party, 151, 154, 191, 283;
and Zubkov, 255, 256
Gudkov, Gennady, 191

election, 275; and Zubkov, 255, 256
Ivanov, Yevgeny Fyodorovich, 9
Iyadze, Oleg, 33–34
Izmailov, Vyacheslav, 380
Izmestyev, Igor, 333
Izvestiya, 359, 370, 410–12, 416–17, 436

Jackpot Moscow Gambling System, 90
Joint State Political Directorate (OGPU), xxiv, 440, 442
Joliot, Frédéric, 460
Joliot, Irène, 460
Jordan, Boris, 374–75, 386–87, 402
JT Communications Services, 68

Kadyrov, Akhmad-Hadji:
   assassination attempt on, 121, 123; and human rights abuses, 413; murder of, 142, 352, 403; "super-Bashkirian" election of, 261, 305–7, 324
Kadyrov, Ramzan, i, ix, 143, 482
Kaledin, Alexander, 458
Kalmykia, 170, 184, 192; and "Bashkirian election technology," 260, 268; Duma election in, 324, 330–31; People's Khural election, 330–31; presidential election, 286–87
Kaluga Regional Court, 213
Kalugin, Oleg, 44, 47–48
Kalyadin, Viktor, 217
Kamshilov, Pyotr, 321
Kantor, Oleg, 454–55
Kapralov, Sergei, 395
Kapysh, Pavel, 66
Karachay-Cherkess Republic, 123, 233
Kara-Murza, Vladimir, 318, 368, 374; on Parfenov, 406
Karamzin, Kantemir, 399
Karbainov, Alexander Nikolayevich, 9
Karimov, Islam, 427

Karmatsky, A. I., 83
Karmishin, Alexander, 135
Kashin, Alexander, 286
Kashirin, Pyotr, 293
Kassov, Alexei, 447–49
Kasyanenko, Zhanna, 164
Kasyanov, Mikhail, 193, 194, 370; NTV criticism of, 364, 367; and Russian People's Democratic Union, 421
Katyshev, Mikhail, 65, 66, 205
Kazakhstan, 426, 427
Kazakkulov, Rif, 268
Kazakov, Ignaty (I. N.), 442–43, 445
Kazan crime group, 225
Kazantsev, Viktor, 148, 273–75, 331
Kekhlerov, Sabir, 364–67
Kerensky, Alexander, 448, 490
Keres, Yuri, 121
Kersanov, Oleg, 420
KGB (Committee for State Security), xxiv; active reserve, 7–9, 50, 53–54, 78, 220, 242; alternative names, 84; Andropov era, 20; Andropov Red Banner Institute, 37, 38–39, 44, 52, 202, 240, 242; assassinations, 448–52; Center for Public Relations, 9, 362; and democratic organizations, 50; Directorate for the Defense of the Constitutional Order, 9, 12, 221, 362; Directorate for Government Communications, 224; dismantling of, 1–2; Dresden office, 39–41, 43–44, 52, 221; Dzerzhinsky Higher School, 478; and entrance visas, 234; Fifteenth Directorate, 1; First Main Directorate (PGU), 10, 38, 199, 221; Group A (Alfa), 9; Higher School, 37, 201, 202, 240, 242; Inspections Directorate, 222; Leningrad (St. Petersburg) office, 38, 54, 66, 119; Moscow region office, 16–17; Ninth Directorate, 1, 6, 11–12; and Olympics, 245–50; and perestroika, 362;

Kodzoyev, Bashir, 321
Kokh, Alfred, 372, 374–75
Kokov, Valery, 322
Kolesnikov, Andrei, 417
Kolmogorov, Vasily, 275–76
Koloskov, Vyacheslav Ivanovich, 249–50
Kolovay, Vladimir, 58, 78
Kolupayev, Anatoly, 318
Kolupayev, Yevgeny, 318
Komelkov, Alexander Petrovich, 9–14, 28; and Listyev, 15, 17; and ORT ad revenue, 20–24; and Ostankino, 10, 12, 13, 20
Komi-Permyatsk Autonomous District, 268–70
Komkon security agency, 95
Kommersant, 43, 100, 276, 376, 404; on arms trade, 238; and Berezovsky, 126; on Chechen election, 353; on Ingushetia election, 278; on *Novye Izvenstiya*, 388; on RBRT, 454; on Shakirov firing, 411; Soskin story, 416; on Voronezh election, 347; Zakayev interrogation, 424
Kommersant Publishing House, 413, 424
Kommersant-Vlast, 278–79
Kompromat.ru, 400
Komsomol, 9, 13, 35, 51, 223, 233, 304, 433; Central Committee, 25, 241
Komsomolskaya Pravda, 416
Kondaurov, Alexei (Gen.), xii, 9
Kondratenko, Nikolai, 271, 348
Kondratov, Alexei, 459
Konservator, 381
Konstantinov, Anatoly, 224
Konstantinov, Arkady, 224–25
Konstantinovsky Palace, 108–9
Kontsept, 398
Koppel, Ted, 155
Kopylov, Yuri, 298–99, 349–50
Koreshkov, Igor, 226
Korobeinichev, Oleg, 218
Korobkov, Nikolai, 297–98

Korolyova, Tatyana, 135
Korostovtsev, Mikhail, 445
Korostylev, Vladimir, 335, 336
Korotkov, Alexander, 299–300
Korzhak, Boris, 451
Korzhakov, Alexander, x–xi, 117, 118; and Ananiev, 236; arms trade revenue, 26–27; assassinations by, 23; and Bobkov, 2, 4–6, 11–14; creates SBP,1–2, 4–5; extortion, 19; firing of, 28; and Gusinsky attack, 6; and Kivilidi poisoning, 457; and Klebnikov, 481; and Komelkov, 11–14; Kremlin eavesdropping, 19–20; and Most Bank, 194–95; as oligarch, 183, 184; and ORT, 20–24; and Skuratov, 124; and Sobchak, 60, 228–29, 463; and Yeltsin, 1–2, 6, 18–19, 20, 23, 50
Kosilov, Andrei, 393–94
Kosmonaut Vladimir Komarov, 78
Kosovo, 131
Kostechko, Lt. Gen., 134
Kostov, Vladimir, 451
Kotelkin, Alexander, 27
Kotenkov, Alexander, 177, 422
Kovalchuk, Yuri Valentinovich, 78, 108, 257
Kovalev, Alexander, 346
Kovalev, Nikolai, 118, 127
Kovalev, Sergei, 152, 214, 290
Kovtun, Dmitry, 485
Kozak, Dmitry, 185, 196–97
Kozhemyako, Oleg, 349
Kozhin, Vladimir, 190
KPMG, 62
Krasnodar region, 270–71, 293, 311; governor's election, 348–49
Krasnoyarsk region, 116; Duma election, 312; governor's election, 192, 282–85; scientist suppression in, 216
Krasnoyarsk State Technical University, 215–16
Kravtsov, Yuri, 57, 196, 495
Kropachev, Nikolai, 363

Olympic Games: Barcelona (1992), 11, 12; Moscow (1980), 3, 223, 242–45; Salt Lake City (2002), 245–46; Sochi (2014), 246–48

OMON (special forces), 265, 297

Omsk region, 199; governor's election, 299–300

Oorzhak, Sherig-ool, 286

Open Society Institute, 399

Ordzhonikidze, Alexander, 418

Ordzhonikidze, Iosif, 194, 482

Orekhovo crime gang, 23

ORT (Channel One), 6, 19, 20–24, 253; and Babitsky affair, 359; censorship of, 387; and FSB, 386; on *Kursk*, 186–87, 370–71; privatization of, 20, 21; as pro-Putin, 150, 151, 154, 403; takeover of, 390, 402

OSCE (Organization for Security and Cooperation in Europe), 320, 330; on Internet issues, 401

Osepashvili, Sofia Georgievna, 34

Osherov, Mikhail, 121

Osokin, Misha, 406

Ostankino (television center), 7–8, 9–14; and Korzhakov, 20–24

Ostroukhov, Viktor, 401

Ostrovsky, Vladimir, 201–2

Our Home Is Russia party (NDR), 57–60, 154, 168; and oligarchic clans, 184; and Putin, 255; and Sobchak investigation, 230; as United Russia, 184

OVR. *See* Fatherland–All Russia bloc

Ozdoyev, Musa, 321–22, 342–43

Ozero cooperative, 105–8, 257

Pacific Fleet, 206, 209

Pacific Military Court, 207

Palikhata, Vladimir, 398–99

Panfilov, Oleg, 357

Parfenov, Leonid, 374, 386–87, 392, 396–97; firing of, 403–7, 408; and *Russky Newsweek*, 415

Parkhomenko, Sergei, 375

Parliamentary Assembly of the Council of Europe (PACE), 329–30

Pasko, Grigory, 206–7, 214, 396

Patarkatsishvili, Badri, 188, 376

Patrushev, Nikolai, 98–100, 190, 200; and Antiterrorist Commission, 141; as FSB director, 108, 132, 134; and Litvinenko, 490; on media regulation, 386; and Peace Corps visas, 218; and Rosneft, viii; and Rosvooruzhenie, 236; and Shchekochikhin, 466; and terrorism, 135, 137, 138, 148

Patsvald, Pavel, 317

Pavlovsky, Gleb, 166, 198, 304

Peace Corps, 218

Pelshe, Arvid, 115

PEN Club, 379

People's Deputy bloc, 154, 272

People's Party of the Russian Federation (NPRF), 281, 293; and chekists, 191; in Duma elections, 316, 318, 321, 328

People's Patriotic Party (NPP), 348

Perednya, Alexander, 350

perestroika, 6–9, 10; and nationalist movements, 13; Shutov pardon, 250

Perm organized crime group, 228

Peru, 236

Perumov, Pyotr, 469–72

Peshkov, Maxim, 443

Peterburgskaya Liniya, 304

Petersburg Fuel Company (PTK), 58, 94, 121, 200, 202, 474

Petersburg Oil Terminal, 202

Petrenko, Svetlana, 458

Petrosyan-Olevsky crime group, 280

Petrov, Boris, 58

Petrov, Konstantin, 443

Petrovskaya, Irina, 410–11

Pietsch, Irene, 41, 75

Pilot TV, 392, 407, 408

Pimashkov, Pyotr, 283–84

Pinochet, Augusto, 146

Piquant Friendship (Pietsch), 41

Pugacheva, Galina, 380
Pulikovsky, Konstantin, 271–72
Putin, Mikhail Illarionovich, 34
Putin, Spiridon Ivanovich, 35, 429
Putin, Vladimir (Volodya, Vova), vii–
ix, xi, xii, xxvii, 489–91; as acting
president, 150–52, 491; appoints
governors, 292; and Babitsky,
357–59, 361, 367; and Berezovsky,
126–28; and Beslan crisis, 142–43,
354, 410; biographical secrets,
30–38; and Borodin, 113–15;
business privatization, 56, 64–65;
cabinet changes, 200; campaign
funds, 58–59, 102–5; casino
licenses, 65; and Chechnya, vii,
xiv, 134, 135–43, 145–50, 175,
307, 353–54; and chekists, 82,
148, 149, 177, 185, 189–94; and
Chemezov, 221–26; childhood
sadness, 31–33; citizenship laws,
178–79; on "comrade wolf,"
218; contradictory promises,
154; and CPRF, 132, 151, 160;
and CPSU, 37, 41, 54; crime list
(St. Petersburg), 63–67; dacha,
105–8, 257; and Drachevsky,
244; in Dresden, 39–41, 43–44,
75, 118, 221, 252; and Dubrovka
theater crisis, 140, 141; and
Duma control, 151–52; economy
under, 188–89; education, 36–37,
38–39; and election law, 290,
302–3; export licenses, 71–82; on
"extremist activity," 422; family
resemblance, 33, 34; and federal
districts, 171–73; "friends" of,
220–57; and FSB active reserve,
114; as FSB director, 63–64,
117–28, 146; FSB reorganization,
118–20; and gambling business,
82–90; and Georgia, xiv–xv;
and Gusinsky, 186, 368; on
Kaspiysk bombing, 136–38; in
KGB, 30–31, 38–41, 53–54, 109,
219; and Khinshtein, 361; and
Krasnoyarsk election, 285; and
Kuchma Tapes, 98–100; and
Kursk submarine, 186–87, 191;
at Lenfintorg, 109; at Leningrad
State University, 44–45, 49, 252;
lieutenant colonel rank, 118–19;
and Main Control Directorate
(GKU), 115–17; and media,
201, 355–428; and Media-Most
(NTV), 364–70, 373; and media
regulations, 385–86; in Metekhi
(Georgia), 30–35, 37–38, 39; and
military counterintelligence, 149;
Moscow apartment, 105–6, 114;
and national sports channel,
377–78, 390, 393; and NDR, 58–60;
news consumption by, 412; and
Novye Izvestiya criticism, 388–
89; and "NTV affair," 362–64; and
oil prices, 188; and "Operation
Rutskoy," 266–67; Order of
Honor (& immunity), 71; and
Our Home Is Russia, 255; and
Ozero cooperative, 105–8, 257;
and Patrushev, 134; and people
skills, 41, 52–53; and perks of
power, 185; on Politkovskaya
murder, 479, 482; populism,
153; presidential campaign,
133, 149–50, 152–55, 219, 310;
presidential election (2004),
338–42; and Presidential Property
Management Directorate, 92, 107–
9, 111–15; presidential residences,
108–9; as press enemy, 426–28; as
prime minister, 131–32, 145–47,
490–91; private security for, 65,
75, 226–27; pro-Russian laws, 179;
and *Puppets*, 362–64, 367–69; and
Radio Liberty, 383; and Rakhimov,
336; and regional governors,
116–17; and Rostov election, 274;
on Security Council, 128–31; and
Shutov, 250–54; and *siloviki*,
189–94; and skiing, 245; and
Skuratov, 124–26, 235; as Sobchak

Rozhvestdensky, Dmitry, 58, 61, 64, 87; conviction & death, 90; and "Maltese Order," 496
Rudakov, Sergei, 347
Rukin, Yevgeny, 394
Rumyantsev, Alexander, 200
Rus' Insurance Company, 198
Rus' party, 326, 333
Rushailo, Vladimir, 200, 360, 361–62
Russian Academy of Sciences, 204, 209, 214, 433; Siberian branch, 218; Institute of Sociology, 282
Russian Business Round Table (RBRT), 453–55, 457
Russian Civil Code, 372–73
Russian Civil War, 438, 440, 444
Russian Communist Workers' Party, 316
Russian Criminal Code. *See* Criminal Code of the Russian Federation
Russian Democratic Reform Movement, 453–54
Russian National Unity movement, 378
Russian Olympic Committee, 239, 245–46
Russian Party for Life, 337
Russian People's Democratic Union, 421
Russian Public Institute of Electoral Law (ROIPP), 159, 164
Russian Railways Company, 108
Russian Reporters' Union, 366
Russian State Sports Committee, 245–46
Russian Technologies, 236, 238
Russian United Industrial Party (ROPP), 454–55
Russkaya Mysl, 442
Russkoye Video, 58, 61, 64–66, 87, 90, 369
Russky Kurier, 389, 413, 415–16
Russky Newsweek, 415
Rutskoy, Alexander, 81, 191, 264–68
Ryabkova, Svetlana, 394
Ryaguzov, Pavel, 480
Rybakov, Yuli, 152

Rybkin, Ivan, 262, 308, 338
Ryklin, Alexander, 405–6
Rykovtseva, Irina, 412
Ryzhkov, Vladimir, 152
Ryzhkov, Yuri, 214

Saavedra, Juan Carlos, 101–2
Sabadash, Alexander, 473
Sabadazh, A. V., 64
Safarov, Asgat, 314, 315
Safin, Ralif, 333–34, 336
Safronov, Ivan, 238
Saidov, Akmad, 121
Saidullaev, Malik, 289, 306, 352–53
Sakharov, Andrei, 41
Saliy, Alexander, 160–63, 169
Salye, Marina, 48, 73, 79
Samaranch, Juan Antonio, 247–49
Samara region: election in, 325–36, 327
Samoilova, Yelena, 404
Samokhvalov, Alexei, 393
Samtrest Liquor Factory, 64
Sankt-Peterburgskie Vedomosti, 362
Sansud Company, 78
Saratov region: governor's election, 262–64; and Putin's election, 155, 159, 160, 163–65, 169–70
Sarfraz, Haider, 239
Sartorius, General, 446
Sasykov, Timofey, 287
Satirikon, 419
Satsyuk, Vladimir, 475
Sauer, Klaus-Peter, 95
Saushkin, Yevgeny, 50
Savelyev, Gennady, 269–70
Savelyev, Sergei, 408–9
Savostyanov, Yevgeny, 5–6
SBR. *See* Security Service of Russia
SBP. *See* Presidential Security Service
Scaramella, Mario, 485
Schelenkov, Andrei, 26
Scherbakov, Vladimir, 455
Scherbakov, Vyacheslav, 57
Scherban, Alexander, 420
Schmidt, Yuri, 396